African Yearbook of International Law
Annuaire Africain de Droit International

A C.I.P. Catalogue record for this book is available from the Library of Congress.

ISBN 90-411-1530-7
ISSN 1380-7412

Published by Kluwer Law International,
P.O. Box 85889, 2508 CN The Hague, The Netherlands.

Sold and distributed in North, Central and South America
by Kluwer Law International,
675 Massachusetts Avenue, Cambridge, MA 02139, U.S.A.

In all other countries, sold and distributed
by Kluwer Law International, Distribution Centre,
P.O. Box 322, 3300 AH Dordrecht, The Netherlands.

Printed on acid-free paper

All Rights Reserved
© 2001 African Association of International Law
Kluwer Law International incorporates the publishing programmes of
Graham & Trotman Ltd, Kluwer Law and Taxation Publishers,
and Martinus Nijhoff Publishers.

No part of the material protected by this copyright notice may be reproduced or
utilized in any form or by any means, electronic or mechanical,
including photocopying, recording, or by any information storage and
retrieval system, without written permission from the copyright owner.

Printed in the Netherlands

AFRICAN YEARBOOK OF INTERNATIONAL LAW ANNUAIRE AFRICAIN DE DROIT INTERNATIONAL

Volume 7
1999

Published under the auspices of
the African Association of International Law

Publié sous les auspices de
l'Association Africaine de Droit International

Edited by/Dirigé par

ABDULQAWI A. YUSUF

KLUWER LAW INTERNATIONAL
THE HAGUE / LONDON / BOSTON

AFRICAN ASSOCIATION OF INTERNATIONAL LAW
ASSOCIATION AFRICAINE DE DROIT INTERNATIONAL

FIRST VICE-PRESIDENT AND ACTING PRESIDENT:	Mr Kéba Mbaye	(Senegal)
VICE-PRESIDENTS:	Mr Kader Asmal	(South Africa)
	Prof. Mikuin Leliel Balanda	(Zaire)
	Prof. Majid Benchikh	(Algeria)
	Prof. Blondin Beye	(Mali)
	Mr Teshome G.M. Bokan	(Ethiopia)
	Mr M.D. Bomani	(Tanzania)
	Judge A.G. Koroma	(Sierra Leone)
	Mr Muna Ndulo	(Zambia)
SECRETARY-GENERAL:	Dr. Tunguru Huaraka	(Namibia)
ASSISTANT SECRETARY-GENERAL:	Dr. B.A. Godana	(Kenya)
PATRON:	His Excellency Dr K.D. Kaunda, former President of the Republic of Zambia	
HONORARY LIFE MEMBER:	His Excellency Mr Nelson Mandela President of the Republic of South Africa	

GENERAL EDITOR	DIRECTEUR DE L'ANNUAIRE

DR. ABDULQAWI A. YUSUF (Somalia)

Associate Editors	Directeurs Adjoints
Dr. Mpazi Sinjela (Zambia)	Dr. Fatsah Ouguergouz (Algeria)

EDITORIAL ADVISORY BOARD – COMITÉ CONSULTATIF DE RÉDACTION

Prof. Georges Abi-Saab (Egypt)	Dr. Yilma Makonnen (Ethiopia)
Dr. A.O. Adede (Kenya)	Prof. N. Makoundzi-Wolo (Congo)
Prof. G.K.A. Afosu-Amaah (Ghana)	Prof. E.I. Nwogugu (Nigeria)
Prof. R.H.F. Austin (Zimbabwe)	Prof. Ebere Osieke (Nigeria)
Judge Mohammed Bedjaoui (Algeria)	Prof. Nasila Rembe (Tanzania)
Prof. J-M. Bipoun Woum (Cameroon)	Prof. Albie Sachs (South Africa)
Mr R.M.A. Chongwe (Zambia)	Prof. Akolda Man Tier (Sudan)
Prof. Robert Dossou (Benin)	Prof. Francis V. Wodie (Ivory Coast)
Prof. Aziz Hasbi (Morocco)	

The Editor and the African Association of International Law are not in any way responsible for the views expressed by contributors, wether the contributions are signed or unsigned.

Les opinions émises par les auteurs ayant contribué au présent annuaire, qu'il s'agisse d'articles signés ou non signés, ne sauraient en aucune façon engager la responsabilité du rédacteur ou de l'Association Africaine de Droit International.

All communications and contributions to the Yearbook should be addressed to:

Prière d'adresser toute communication ou contribution destinée à l'Annuaire à:

The Editor, African Yearbook of International Law
c/o Kluwer Law International
P.O. Box 85889, 2508 CN The Hague
The Netherlands

TABLE OF CONTENTS

Special Theme: REGIONAL ECONOMIC INTEGRATION IN AFRICA: Part II
Thème spécial: L' INTÉGRATION RÉGIONALE ÉCONOMIQUE EN AFRIQUE, 2ème Partie

African Integration Schemes: A case Study of the SADC-
  M. Ndulo — 3

Trade Liberalization Under ECOWAS-
  E. K. Kessie — 31

The Treaty For the Establishment of the New East African Community: An Overview
  W. Kaahwa — 61

GENERAL ARTICLES/ARTICLES GÉNÉRAUX

The Role of International Law in the Colonization of Africa: A Review in Light of Recent Calls for Re-colonization
  D.C.J. Dakas — 85

La protection constitutionelle des minorités en Afrique
  V. Zakane — 119

La clause des droits de l'homme dans un Accord de Coopération économique étude contextuelle de l'article 5 de la convention de e lomé
  P.C. Ulimubenshi — 167

The Realisation of Human Rights Through Sub-regional Institutions
  F. Viljoen — 185

NOTES AND COMMENTS/NOTES ET COMMENTAIRES

The 51st Session of the UN International Law Commission
  J. Kateka — 217

Constitutionalism, Culture and Tradition: African Experiences in
the incorporation of Treaties into Domestic Law
A.O. Adede   239

The Trial of the Lockerbie Suspects in the Netherlands
C. Morgan   255

Le Mécanisme de Règlement des différends dans le Cadre de
l'Organisation pour l'Interdiction des Armes Chimiques
S. Pounjine   265

The United Nations and Internal/International Conflicts in Africa:
A Documentary survey
M. Sinjela   283

BASIC DOCUMENTS/DOCUMENTS

OAU: Declarations and Decisions adopted by the Thirty-Fifth
Assembly of Heads of State and Government (Algiers, July 1999)   375

OUA: Déclarations et decisions adoptées par la trente-cinquieme
session ordinaire de la conference des Chefs d'Etat et de
Gouvernement (Alger, Juillet, 1999)   393

OAU: Sirte Declaration adopted at the Fourth Extraordinary Session
of the Assembly of Heads of State and Government (Sirte, Libya
September 1999)   411

OUA: Déclaration de Syrte adoptée par la quatrième session extraordinaire de la conference des Chefs d'Etat et de Gouverment
(Sirte, Libye, Septembre, 1999)   415

TREATY FOR THE ESTABLISHMENT OF THE EAST AFRICAN COMMUNITY/TRAITE INSTITUANT LA COMMUNAUTE DE L'AFRIQUE ORIENTALEA

Treaty for the Establishment of the East African Community, Signed
in Arusha,Tanzania, 30 November 1999   421

ANALYTICAL INDEX   511

INDEX ANALYTIQUE   537

SPECIAL THEME:

REGIONAL ECONOMIC INTEGRATION IN AFRICA:

PART II

THÈME SPÉCIAL: L'INTÉGRATION RÉGIONALE ECONOMIQUE EN AFRIQUE

2ème PARTIE

AFRICAN INTEGRATION SCHEMES: A CASE STUDY OF THE SOUTHERN AFRICAN DEVELOPMENT COMMUNITY (SADC)

Muna Ndulo*

I. INTRODUCTION

Regional economic integration as a strategy for achieving greater economic development and growth is currently being implemented in many parts of the world. There has been increased debate as to its relevance and efficacy in the efforts to attain meaningful development in Africa, particularly, in the wake of the phenomenon of globalization and the increased marginalization of Africa in world trade.

We will therefore analyze regional integration in the context of a case study of one of Africa's more promising integration schemes- the Southern African Development Community (SADC). We will look at the benefits of and obstacles to integration in Africa before examining the SADC approach to Southern African economic integration. Countries in Southern Africa, comprising: Angola, Botswana, Congo (Kinshasa), Lesotho, Malawi, Mauritius, Mozambique, Namibia, Seychelles, South Africa, Swaziland, Tanzania, Zambia and Zimbabwe are grouped together in the Southern African Development Community (SADC) with the objective of developing closer economic, political and social ties among themselves and eventually establishing an economic community. The Community was established by the 1992 Treaty of the Southern African Development Community.[1]. The Treaty after citing the objectives in the "Southern African Toward Economic Liberation" – a Declaration by the Governments of Independent States of Southern Africa

---

* LL.B., Zambia, LL.M. (Harvard), D.PHIL... (Oxon), Advocate of the Supreme Court of Zambia, Visiting Professor of Law, Cornell Law School.
[1] *Treaty of Southern African Development Community, Windhoek, August, 1992.* The Treaty was established following "Southern African Toward Economic Liberation" – a Declaration by the Governments of Independent States of Southern Africa made at Lusaka, 1 April, 1980, established SADC.

made at Lusaka, 1 April, 1980, established SADC. The Treaty sets out the Organization's objectives, including areas of cooperation, the Organization's institutions and the modalities for the achievement of its goals.

II. INTEGRATION SCHEMES AND ECONOMIC DEVELOPMENT

(a) Background to African Integration Efforts

The concept of African economic cooperation has a long history beginning with the African and Malagasy Organization of Economic Cooperation (OAMCE) established in September 1961 and the CASABLANCA Group established in January 1961 and later the formation of the Organization of African Unity (OAU) in 1963.[2] Regional economic integration is generally seen by many African development economists as a vehicle for enhancing the economic and social development of African countries.[3] The 1980 Lagos Plan of Action underlined Africa's objective of attaining a more self-sufficient and more economically integrated continent by the year 2000 through, inter-alia, the accelerated process of regional economic integration.[4] Two stages mark the historic development of the definition and preparation of the Lagos Plan of Action: 1963 to 1973 and 1973 to 1980. The first was characterized by the search for legitimacy in the economic competence of the OAU. The second, on the contrary, was marked by an awareness of the inadequacy

---

[2] AMR Ramolefe and AJGM Sanders, "The Structural Pattern of African Regionalism", *Comparative and International Law Journal for Southern Africa*, 1971, p. 155.

[3] See, generally, *Sub-Saharan Africa: From Crisis to Sustainable Growth*, World Bank Report (1989); "African Alternative Framework to Structural Adjustment Programs for Social-Economic Recovery and Transformation (AAF-SAF)", *United Nations Economic Commission for Africa* (E/ECA/CM.15/6/Rev.3); Pierre-Clasver, "Development Strategies-Lessons from Experience", African Leadership Forum,(Ota, Nigeria) 1988 and Olayiwola Abegunrin, *Economic Dependence and Regional Cooperation in Southern Africa: SADC and South Africa in Confrontation, 1989.*

[4] The Lagos Plan of Action was adopted in 1980 and its central theme was regional integration. It called for the establishment of the African Economic Community by the year 2000. See, Organization of African Unity Lagos Plan of Action for the Implementation of the Monrovia Strategy for the Economic Development of Africa (Lagos, April 1981). The SADC Treaty in its preamble states that, the Southern States, in establishing SADC took into account the Lagos Plan of Action and the Final Act of Lagos of April 1980, and the Treaty establishing the African Economic Community at Abuja, concluded on 3 June, 1991.

of aid, technical assistance and international strategies for development and worse still "ineffectiveness of the measures adopted during the past decade to combat underdevelopment and the inability of the international community to create conditions favorable for the development of Africa."[5]

(b) Arguments for Economic Integration

The idea of regional integration is reinforced by the relatively successful experience of integration among European states in the European Union and other promising integration schemes such as the North American Free Trade Agreement (NAFTA). Development experiences and achievements in these integrated schemes have demonstrated that economic cooperation can be an important and potentially effective means for facilitating social and economic development.[6] In a common market, the concept of a "domestic market" is redefined to imply the integrated individual member state's national markets. This larger "domestic market" greatly enhances the growth of small scale and medium scale enterprises.[7] The growing need for economic cooperation in Africa arises from both external and internal circumstances. Internally, there is increased realization of the Unvaibility of many African economies due to the smallness, uneven and untapped resources, the small size nature of African markets, and distortions in the pattern of economic activity which impede development based purely on a national scale approach. Only two Sub-Saharan African countries-South Africa and Nigeria- can be said to be sufficiently large markets to make multinationals feel they must be represented there. For the rest of the region, market size is a crucial constraint. Study after study of motives underlying foot loose foreign investment projects (projects not tied to specific locations as the case of energy, mining, and tourism) emphasize market size and growth rates along with the availability of skills and infrastructure as major factors in investment decisions. Externally, the increasing and irreversible movement towards the globalization of the world economy creates the necessary impetus for economic integration in that it raises the question of how does Africa effectively participate and protect its interests in the global economy.[8]

---

[5] Organization of African Unity, *The African Economic Community: Destiny of a Continent*, OAU, Addis Ababa, (undated).
[6] "Cooperation verses Integration: The Prospects of the Southern African Development Coordinating Conference (SADC)" – Occasional Papers of the German Development Institute (GN) No. 77.
[7] R. Bhala and K. Kennedy, *World Trade*, 1998, p.159.
[8] See, *Summary Report of the Secretary-General on Economic Cooperation and Integration in Africa*: "Towards the Establishment of the African Economic Community": OAU Document AHG/162 (XXV).

Clearly this can only be done by creating competitive African economies through economic growth and development.[9]

Development economists argue that regional cooperation can help to promote, on a more complementary and sustained basis, the development of the economies of the member countries of an economic community.[10] This may emerge as a result of the reinforcement of the existing regional infrastructure, the development of a more efficient system of payments, greater access to credit, a greater awareness of each others' products and economic agents operating in the different countries that comprise the community. Above all, member economies may be developed through growing technical cooperation and a greater development and integration of the productive sectors of the countries involved. Market integration will also hasten the creation of a common market. This will also result in forward and backward linkages in major sectors such as agriculture, industry, energy, environment, transport and communications and human resources development, thereby enabling the attainment of economies of scale. The SADC experiment is important for Africa, for if it succeeds it may raise hopes for Africa and lessen the perception that Africa is an economic basket case.

(c) SADC's Approach to Integration

In recognition of the lack of production in Africa, SADC's approach to integration is not based on the orthodox trade liberalization strategies alone. Rather, its strategy is based and places the development of infrastructure and production on a level as important as the elimination of tariffs. SADC, from its inception, has maintained that the reduction or even the elimination of tariffs to trade does not always yield increased trade, in the absence of tradable goods. In its view, the greatest single barrier to trade in Africa is lack of production and infrastructure; hence the focus on cooperation in several areas of production and investment in its programmes.[11] In pursuit of this

---

9 Susan Rice, "US and Africa", speech to the African Studies Association, Columbus, Ohio, November, 14, 1997. See also Jozef M. Van Brabant, *Economic Integration Among Developing Countries: Towards a New Paradigm, in Economic Cooperation and Regional Integration in Africa*, ed. By Naceur Bourename, 1996, p.31.

10 Rose Mtengeti-Migiro, *Institutional Arrangements for Economic Integration in Eastern and Southern Africa: a Study of SADCC and the PTA with Experiences from the EEC*, 1992; See also Lagos Plan of Action, (1980) and Olayiwola Abegunrin, *Economic Dependence and Regional Cooperation in Southern Africa: SADCC and South Africa in Confrontation*, supra, Chapters 1 and 2.

11 The Economist Intelligence Unit, "SADCC in the 1990s: Development on the Front Line", Special Report, No. 1158, (1989).

strategy, SADC has embarked on a number of projects which are designed to increase production and improve the region's infrastructure. For example, the first phase of SADC's program to rehabilitate the Beira corridor-the railway, road, and pipeline from Mutare, Zimbabwe, to the port of Beira in Mozambique is nearing completion. The Beira corridor group, based in Harare, Zimbabwe, comprises private companies formed to facilitate investment and development along the Beira corridor and in the surrounding regions. Other transportation corridors being built or rehabilitated are the Nacala line from Malawi to Nacala, Mozambique; the Limpopo line from Zimbabwe to Maputo, Mozambique; the Northern corridor from Zambia to Dar es Salaam, Tanzania; the Caprive Strip Corridor from Windhoek, Namibia to Ndola, Zambia; and the Maputo corridor from Mpumalanga, South Africa to Maputo, Mozambique. Furthermore, in the area of tourism, a regional body to oversee the development of tourism has been established. An example of such cooperation is the Okavango Upper Zambezi International Tourism Spatial Development Initiative (OUZITSD). This project seeks to establish a Southern African wildlife sanctuary in the wetlands of the Zambezi and Okavango deltas involving Namibia, Zambia, Zimbabwe, and Botswana. The initiative seeks to jointly develop game parks in Angola, Namibia, Botswana, Zambia and Zimbabwe.[12]

SADC has been active in other areas of cooperation as well. It has concluded protocols on water and education, training and the promotion of culture. The protocol provides a policy framework that allows the SADC region to progressively move towards equivalence, harmonization and standardization of member states' educational and training systems.[13] It has also agreed in principle to a scheme to speed up the extradition of fugitives and offenders within the region. Currently, SADC countries are discussing a prisoners exchange scheme which would allow convicts to serve sentences in their own countries.[14] SADC has created a SADC security organization known as the SADC Security Organ which encompasses a regional mechanism for the settlement of regional conflicts.[15] The principal task of the agency is to prevent, manage and resolve political conflicts within the fourteen member countries by peaceful settlement of disputes through negotiation, mediation and arbitration.

---

[12] "Cooperation in Southern Africa Enters New Era", *Xinhua General Overseas News Agency*, December 18, 1997.
[13] The Educational Protocol was adopted at the 1997 SADC Annual Summit, held in Blantyre, Malawi.
[14] Xinhuna General News Agency, April 29, 1998.
[15] The Security Agency was established at the 1997 SADC Annual Summit, Ibid.

III. THE HISTORY AND BACKGROUND OF SADC

(a) The Formation of SADC

As discussed earlier, the Southern African Development Community was established in pursuant to a declaration made by Heads of State or Governments of Southern Africa at Windhoek, in August 1992.[16] The declaration was entitled "Towards a Southern African Community".[17] In it, the signatories, affirmed their countries' commitment to establish a development community in Southern Africa. The idea developed out of an earlier Southern African organization created by the Front Line States – Southern African Development Coordinating Conference (SADCC).[18] This earlier organization grew out of a response to South Africa's proposal for the formation of a Constellation of Southern African States (CONSAS) in 1979. As part of what was termed the policy of total onslaught designed to deal with the threat posed by liberation forces to apartheid South Africa's survival, South Africa proposed the formation in Southern Africa of an economic forum which would spearhead economic development in the region. The idea was, without doubt, an attempt by South Africa to contain the rising opposition to the repugnant system of apartheid by seeking the cooperation of Southern African states in ensuring South Africa's military and economic domination of the region. The proposal, however, was rejected by South Africa's black-ruled neighbors.[19] Instead, South Africa's efforts inspired the surrounding black ruled states to seek ways and means to counter South Africa's efforts and its domination of the region.

---

[16] *Treaty of the Southern African Development Community (Windhoek)* August, 1992.

[17] "Towards a Southern African Development Community" – Declaration made by Heads of State or Government of Southern Africa, Windhoek, August, 1992.

[18] SADCC's formation had been a subject of serious discussion since 1978, and was promoted particularly by the late Botswana President, Sir Seretse Khama. It grew as an economic extension of the Front line States (Angola, Botswana, Mozambique, Tanzania, Zambia and Zimbabwe). See, Economist Intelligence Unit, SADCC in the 1990s, supra; see also, Rose Mtengeti-Migiro, *Institutional Arrangements for Economic Integration in Eastern and Southern Africa: A Study of SADCC and PTA with Experiences from the EEC*, supra, Chapter 2; and also Margaret Lee, *SADCC the Political Economy of Development in Southern Africa*, 1989, Chapter, 1.

[19] Margaret Lee, ibid, p. 3 and See also Douglas Anglin, "Economic Liberation and Regional Cooperation in Southern Africa: SADCC and PTA", *International Organizations*, vol.37 no. 4, 1983 and R. Davis and D. O'Meara, "Total Strategy in Southern Africa: An Analysis of South African Regional Policy Since 1978", *Journal of Southern African Studies*, Vol. 11, No.2, 1985.

In July 1979, Southern African states agreed on a policy of regional cooperation to counter South Africa's machinations. This agreement, led to the signing of the Lusaka Declaration on Economic Liberation on 1 April, 1980.[20] At the same meeting, the states also agreed to form SADCC.[21] The objectives of SADCC were to break South Africa's economic domination of its neighbors and to simultaneously create conditions for sustainable economic development within Southern Africa. It must be remembered that during this period, South Africa used its economic and military muscle to destabilize those countries in the region that were playing host to, and supporting, liberation movements. At a summit meeting in Arusha, Tanzania, in 1991, the Member states of SADCC stated the principal objectives of the organization in the following terms:

The gradual reduction of economic dependence particularly, but not only, on the Republic of South Africa; forging of links to create genuine and equitable regional integration; the mobilization of resources to promote the implementation of national interstate and regional policies; and concerted action to secure international cooperation within the framework of their strategy for economic liberation.[22]

(b) Legal Status of SADC

SADC is established as an international organization with legal personality with the capacity and power to enter into contracts, acquire, own or dispose of movable or immovable property and to sue and be sued.[23] In the territory of each member state, SADC has such legal capacity as is necessary for the proper exercise of its functions.[24] The Community may also hire staff, run offices, maintain relations with member states and third states, as well as enter into agreements with such states. SADC's legal personality, however, is

---

20 See, Economist Intelligence Unit "SADCC in the 1990s: Development on the Front Line", supra; see also, "Southern Africa: Towards Economic Liberation": A Declaration by the Governments of Independent States of Southern Africa Made at Lusaka on the 1st of April, 1980 and Memorandum of Understanding of the Institutions of the Southern African Development Coordination Conference, Harare, 20 July, 1981 as amended (in Article 111, para. 2) in Gaborone on 22 July, 1982.
21 Ibid. The founding members of SADCC were: Angola; Botswana; Lesotho; Malawi; Mozambique; Swaziland; Zambia and Zimbabwe. Namibia joined at independence in 1989.
22 SADCC Annual Meeting, Arusha, Tanzania, 1991.
23 SADC Treaty, Article 3 (1)
24 SADC Treaty, Article 3 (2)

limited by the SADC treaty in that it must act within the purposes and functions of SADC as specified or implied in the documents constituting SADC.[25] Initially, SADCC operated with a small secretariat and for most of its early existence was run on an informal basis. It did not have a large staff. It remained this way and operated without a formal treaty until its transformation into SADC in 1992.

(c) Early Successes of SADCC

Within the context of its objectives – to counter South African influence – SADCC had major successes such as the rehabilitation of the railway line from Zimbabwe to Beira in Mozambique; the upgrading of the port of Beira for handling and ferrying cargo and merchandise to and from Zimbabwe and Malawi; the improvement of telecommunications in the region,[26] and cooperation in power generation and distribution.[27] SADCC also improved air and satellite links amongst its members.[28] It further established a number of regional research institutes in the fields of agriculture and transport. For example, in 1992-1993, it successfully coordinated the importation and procurement of grain into the region during a period of severe drought.[29] The structure established in this process has now developed into an early warning system on the food situation in the region thereby enabling governments to plan ahead for forecast food shortages.

---

[25] For a discussion of this see, M.A. Ajomo, "International Legal Status of the African Economic Community (AEC)", International Conference on the African Economic Community (AEC) Treaty, Abuja, Nigeria, 27-30 January, 1992.

[26] See, Implementing the SADCC Program of Action: A Joint Study by the SADCC Secretariat and OECD Development Center of Structures and Procedures in Development Cooperation, Gaborone/Paris, 1988; Cooperation Between Electricity Utilities in the SADCC Region; Proceedings of the Seminar, Harare, 12-16, December 1984, SADCC Energy Sector.

[27] See, "Electricity in the SADCC Region, Status and Future Projects on Regional Cooperation", *Proceedings of a Workshop held in Mbabane, 6-9, March, 1988.*

[28] Telecommunications: 10 Year Development Plan, summary SADCC, Maputo, 1987. See, "Transport and Communications, Rehabilitation, Harmonization and Modernization in The SADCC African States", Working Paper presented to a Joint Conference Sponsored by the International Transport Federation, the Friedreich Egbert Foundation and SADCC Transport Trade Unions, Harare, 23-27, September, 1985.

[29] Regional Seed Production and Supply Project, Record of the Meetings of the SADCC Technical Experts to Review the Draft Report, Julias Dakle, Zimbabwe, 11-15, April 1988; Country Profiles SADCC Food Security Sector, Harare, 1988; SATUCC, Gaborone, 1985 Regional Cooperation in Shipping, Phase A, Final Report, Project 301, by ISTEE, University of Trieste, Italy, SADCC, Maputo, 1986.

(d) The Transformation of SADCC to SADC

By 1992, however, it had become apparent that apartheid would soon end in South Africa. Members of SADCC reviewed the future of the organization in order to position it for a new role in a Southern Africa with a non-racial democratic South Africa. As earlier pointed out, in, August 1992, the SADCC states adopted a declaration entitled "Towards a Southern African Development Community" in which they agreed to form an economic community of Southern African States.[30] At the same meeting, the SADCC Member states, adopted a treaty establishing the Southern African Development Community (SADC). The treaty changed the name of the organization from Southern African Development Coordinating Conference to Southern African Development Community and its mission also changed from that of reducing dependence on South Africa to one of creating an economic community in Southern Africa.[31] South Africa joined SADC in August 1994. Mauritius became its 12th member in August 1995. In 1997 Congo (Kishasha) and Seychelles were admitted as the 13th and 14th members respectively. The admission of any state to the membership of SADC is effected by a unanimous decision of all SADC member states at a SADC summit. There is some reference to the requirement that aspiring member states should be democratic. The admission, however, of the Democratic Republic of the Congo into SADC in 1997 suggests that this policy is not uniformly applied.

The SADC region contains a population of about 170 million with a combined gross national product of $170 billion. It is rich in agriculture, mineral and energy resources. Rivers such as the Zambezi, Linyanti, Okavango, Kwando and Orange, across which numerous dams including the Kariba, Kunene and Cabora Bassa were built and have enormous potential for hydro-electric power generation. In addition there are numerous natural lakes such as Malawi and Mweru. These largely untapped water supplies could also be used for irrigation and agricultural production to meet the demands of regional and export markets. In order to create viable agro-industries, for which enormous potential exists, advanced technology and better agricultural and water resource management are necessary. Abundant reserves of diamonds, gold, coal, iron ore, copper, lead, bauxite, nickel, and many other minerals

---

[30] The Treaty of the Southern African Development Community, August, 1992, Article 1. Article 3, states that SADC shall be an international organization, and shall have legal personality with capacity and power to enter into contract, acquire, own or dispose of movable or immovable property and to sue and be sued.

[31] Ibid, Article 5.

are a source of much of the region's employment and generate considerable foreign currency earnings.[32] Finally, the region is well connected by rail and road networks, an important asset in economic development.

While SADC has tremendous potential for economic development, because of a lack of requisite technology, coupled with under capitalization in the region, its resources remain largely untapped. As a result, Southern Africa remains beset by a range of critical problems. There is chronic underdevelopment with the attendant poverty, illiteracy, malnutrition and inadequate provision of social services for the people of the region. Efforts to address these problems are inhibited by balance of payments deficits, an acute debt crisis affecting most of its members except for Botswana; Mauritius; and South Africa, and by an unfavorable international economic climate.[33] There is also a great need for coordination in the attraction of foreign investment and technology to harness the resources of the region. Moreover, there is need for regional coordination on matters of development to maximize economic benefits to SADC member countries. The SADC framework of cooperation must make concerted efforts to exploit its natural resources for self- reliance and sustained economic development. Successful regional integration will engender a major re-orientation of economic activities and the establishment of institutions to promote regional trade and investment.

Initially, SADC was composed of countries with different economic orientations and political ideologies which would have made cooperation much more difficult. A number of countries in the region followed the socialist model while others adopted the capitalist model.[34] With the heralded demise of the Cold War, the situation has drastically changed. All SADC Member states embrace the free market system and welcome the role of private investment in the development of their economies, and all but two have held democratic elections or are committed to democratic governance.

---

[32] See, Margaret Lee, "SADCC The Political Economy of Development in Southern Africa", supra. See also Haarlov, J., "Regional Cooperation in Southern Africa, Central Elements of the SADCC Venture", *CDR Research Report No. 14, Copenhagen 1988* and UNIDO, *Investors Guide to SADCC Countries*, Vienna, 1986.

[33] Minnie Venter (ed.), *Prospects for Progress: Critical Choices for Southern Africa*, 1994, p.1.

[34] Margaret Lee, supra, Chapter 3. The East African Community is said to have collapsed in part because of differing economic policies, Rose Mtengeti-Migiro, supra, p. 31.

IV. GOALS AND OBJECTIVES OF SADC

(a) Creation of a Free Trade Area

The objectives of SADC, as stated in Article 5 (1) of the SADC treaty, are to: (a) achieve development and economic growth, alleviate poverty, enhance the standard and quality of life of the peoples of Southern Africa and support the socially disadvantaged through regional integration; (b) evolve common political values, systems and institutions; c) promote and defend peace and security; (d) promote self-sustaining development on the basis of collective self-reliance, and the interdependence of member states; (e) achieve complementarity between national and regional strategies and programs; (f) promote and maximize productive employment and utilization of resources of the region; (g) achieve sustainable utilization of natural resources and effective protection of the environment; and (h) strengthen and consolidate the long standing historical, social and cultural affinities and links among the peoples of the region.[35]

The strategies for achieving these goals are set out in Article 5 (2). SADC is to: (a) harmonize political and socio-economic policies and plans of member states; (b) encourage the people of the region and their institutions to take initiatives to develop economic, social and cultural ties across the region, and to participate fully in the implementation of the programs and objectives of SADC; c) create appropriate institutions and mechanisms for the mobilization of requisite resources for the implementation of programs and operations of SADC and its institutions; (d) develop policies aimed at the progressive elimination of obstacles to the free movement of capital and labor, goods and services and of peoples of the region generally among member states; (e) promote the development of human resources; (f) promote the development, transfer and mastery of technology; (g) improve economic management and performance through regional cooperation; (h) promote the coordination and harmonization of international relations of member states; and secure international understanding, cooperation and support, and mobilize the inflow of public and private resources into the region.[36]

To give the treaty practical effect, provision is made for states to negotiate a series of protocols which spell out the objectives and scope of, and institutional mechanisms, for cooperation and integration in designated areas. On approval, the protocols become an integral part of the SADC

---

[35] Treaty of the Southern African Development Community, supra.
[36] Ibid.

treaty.[37] Member states undertake to adopt adequate measures to promote the achievement of the objectives of SADC, and agree to refrain from taking any measures likely to jeopardize the substance of its principles, the achievement of its objectives and the implementation of the provisions of the SADC treaty. Member states are also required to accord the treaty the force of national law. This provision, in itself, however, is not sufficient to make the Treaty applicable in a domestic jurisdiction. Member states would have to pass implementing legislation to achieve this result. The situation in states where national constitutions make treaties, once entered into by the state, applicable in the domestic jurisdiction, might be different. Among SADC states that situation prevails only in South Africa under its new constitution.[38]

(b) Political, Social, and Cultural Cooperation

As can be seen from its objectives, SADC is to be a customs union seeking to establish free trade within its internal market and is intended to develop into an economically and politically integrated community. Central to this objective is the lifting of internal tariffs and non-tariff barriers, free movement of persons and capital, establishment of common transport and communications policies, and standardization of trade practices in order to enhance a faster rate of economic development. In the European Union, for example, there were two characteristics of the common market program which were instrumental in ensuring that the objective of a common market was reached and which should be of relevance to the SADC case. The first characteristic was the reduction of tariffs on an "across the board" basis. This principle meant that tariffs were to be reduced, not through a commodity by commodity, approach but on of one of all goods at once approach. This approach ensured that the elimination of internal barriers was taken out of the hands of the negotiators. Also by being formulated in an ex parte fashion the program came into effect automatically. The second characteristic was that there was a time table according to which customs duties and quota restrictions or measures of equivalent effect were to be eliminated. It was perceived that a timetable, laid in advance and agreed to by all parties, would be necessary to guarantee that the economic integration process was not unduly disrupted.[39] This strategy indeed paid off when the Community managed to remove tariff and quota restrictions ahead of the originally envisaged schedule.

The freedom of establishment and the freedom to supply services are an important aspect of economic integration. They cover the right of non-wage

---

[37] Ibid, article 22.
[38] Ibid, article 6. See, the South African Constitution, adopted in May 1996.
[39] Rose Mtengeti-Migiro, supra, p. 21.

earners (the self employed) to establish companies or firms and the freedom to offer services. For individuals, the right of establishment implies the right to take up and pursue activities as a self-employed person in another country. The right to provide services extends to citizens of member countries who are established in a country other than that of the individual for whom the services are intended. The SADC treaty recognizes the importance of this right to economic integration by categorically prohibiting discrimination between nationals of member states and asking member states to take measures that abolish all restrictions on the freedom of establishment.[40] The freedom of movement of capital is complementary to that of movement of goods, persons and services, but it has a special connection with the right of establishment. It would be useless if a person should only have the right to set up an economic activity in a member country but were denied the right to transfer capital to that country to enable that person to acquire the necessary premises and operational facilities required for the activity.

It can be seen, from the areas of cooperation outlined in the Treaty, that SADC is not simply a trading organization or a mechanism restricted to the promotion of cooperation in trade and production based on the creation of a common market. In addition to the integration of national markets and cooperation in production, states joining the Community undertake to cooperate with each other in certain functional areas as well e.g. social, political, diplomatic, sports and regional security.[41] The Member states intend to strengthen and consolidate the long standing historical, social and cultural affinities and links among the peoples of the region and to harmonize political and social policies among member states. The SADC states have many traditional links: the countries in the region all recently emerged from colonial oppression, most of them after bitter and protracted liberation wars; they assisted each other in the liberation wars; and the indigenous ethnic groups in many of the SADC states overlap or have common historical origins.[42] The SADC strategy of encompassing non economic matters among its areas of cooperation is a realization that successful integration invariably has to be anchored on the twin foundations of economic and political integration.

---

[40] Treaty of the Southern African Development Community, supra, Article 6, and 5 (2) (d).
[41] Ibid, article, 5 (1) (a), (b), (h) and (5) (2) (b).
[42] See, R. Hall, *Zambia*, 1965, p.5.

V. SADC INSTITUTIONS AND STRUCTURES

(a) Policy Making Organs

The treaty establishes six institutions for the implementation of community goals. These are: the Summit of the Heads of State or Government; the Council of Ministers; Commissions; the Standing Committee of Officials; the Secretariat and the Tribunal.[43] The Summit is the supreme policy making body and is responsible for the overall policy direction and control of the functions of SADC. It adopts the legal instruments for the implementation of the provisions of the treaty.[44] The decisions of the Summit are by consensus. The Council of Ministers oversees the function and development of SADC and the implementation of the SADC policies and programs. It advises the Summit on matters of overall policy and the development of SADC, approves policies, strategies and work programs of SADC.[45] The Commissions provided for in the treaty, when constituted, are to guide and coordinate cooperation and integration policies and programs in designated areas.[46] The Commissions are composed of experts responsible for planning and developing strategies within each of the SADC sectors. Commissions are created by the Council of Ministers. They are responsible for running each sector or sub-sector. The real functioning units of SADC are the Standing Committees of Officials.[47] They consist of one permanent secretary or an official of equivalent rank from each member state, preferably from a ministry responsible for economic planning or finance. The Standing Committees make recommendations to the Council of Ministers, and the Council in turn makes recommendations to the Summit. They function more or less as a technical advisory committee to the Council of Ministers.

The last major institution of SADC is the Tribunal. It is established by Article 16 of the treaty. Among its tasks, is to ensure adherence to and the proper interpretation of the provisions of the treaty and to hear disputes in relation to it. Its composition, powers, functions, and procedures are to be prescribed by a protocol. For an article governing an institution of such great significance, this article is unsatisfactory and needs to be clarified. Article 16 (5), for instance, states that the Tribunal's decisions are binding on member states. This is somewhat confusing as article 16(4), on the other hand,

---

[43] Treaty of The Southern African Development Community, supra, article, 9.
[44] Ibid, Article 10.
[45] Ibid, Article 11.
[46] Ibid, Article 12.
[47] Ibid, Article 13.

states that "the tribunal shall give advisory opinions on such matters as the Summit or the Council may refer to it." The relationship between these two articles is not clarified. It is not clear which decisions are binding and who can bring actions before the Tribunal. Such an important matter as who has standing before the Tribunal should not have been left to inference or to a subsequent protocol. It might therefore be wise to amend the treaty to clarify this matter.

SADC operates on the basis of a highly decentralized structure. Sectoral programs, based on areas of cooperation, are coordinated by a specific member state as may be decided by the Summit. The current allocation of responsibilities to individual countries are as follows: Angola-energy; Botswana-livestock production and disease control; Lesotho-soil and water conservation and land utilization; Malawi-fisheries, forestry and wild life; Mauritius-tourism; Mozambique-transport and communications; Swaziland-manpower development; Tanzania -industry; Zambia-mining; Zimbabwe-food security and overall coordination; and South Africa-trade and investment.[48] Once SADC has assigned the coordination of a particular sector to a country, the sector-coordinating country designates a relevant ministry in its government to undertake the work. The ministry sets up a sector coordinating unit for that purpose. Each host country is required to service its unit in terms of competent manpower, provision of office space and meeting running costs. In this way, the administrative burden of coordination, is shared without the creation of large formal institutions. SADC operates largely through committee meetings comprising officials of member states' relevant ministries and technical experts, all of whom may take part in the sector task force. Policies, programs, possible regional projects are all discussed in these meetings and information shared. Thereafter, representations are made to the Council of Ministers, which finally decides which projects should be included in the SADC regional pool. On the other hand, the sector-based commissions act as technical advisors to member states and on the other they act as links between member states and cooperating partners. This structure and the method of operation seems to have thus far worked well. Nevertheless,

---

48 See, Haalov, "Regional Co-operation in Southern Africa, Central Elements of SADCC Venture", supra. And also Wolfgang Zehender, "Cooperation Versus Integration: The Prospects of the Southern African Development Coordinating Conference (SADCC)", Occasional Papers of the German Institute, (GN) No. 77. There have been additions since the admission of South Africa and Mauritius. Others argue that this approach to organization weakens SADC as it relegates the running of SADC affairs to increasingly fragile state structures.

this seemingly organizational strength of SADC at this stage of its development, might have to be adjusted in the future as the work load of the organization increases. Clearly, there will be need to establish institutions that can administer the burden of work that is bound to be generated by the process of integration as SADC makes headway in its goals.

(b) A Comparison of SADC and EU Approaches

The approach in SADC can be contrasted with that of the European Union. The European Union countries did not sign the EU treaty simply to create mutual obligations governed by the law of nations. Rather, they limited their sovereign rights by transferring them to institutions over which they had no direct control.[49] Furthermore, it was not only member governments which were bound by the new rights and obligations, but also their citizens who became subjects of the Community. They thus created a "supranational" body as opposed to an international body of law and institutions which stood above individual member states. In contrast, the SADC treaty does not create supranational organs. For instance, SADC organs do not have power to legislate or issue directives binding on member states. As such, implementation of the relevant objectives, depends entirely on individual member states.[50] It is arguable that SADC is being conscious in this area as it does not believe it can get agreement to such delegation of power just yet. In many ways, SADC's approach is appropriate to the circumstances of Southern Africa. At SADC's level of development, it is more productive to focus on somewhat narrower targets than on attempting to integrate entire economies in a declaratory manner. The ambitious nature of many integration schemes in the past has been the precise reason for their failure. The EU could afford to take the approach they did as the EU member countries had already attained extremely high levels of trade integration before the formal start of the European Economic Community in 1958. Furthermore, the disparity in per capita incomes and levels of development and industrialization was not too huge. This provided considerable room for the emergence of intra-industry specialization, which has been the most dynamic force in the expansion of global commerce since the 1950s. Nevertheless, if SADC institutions are to be effective and the community goals achieved, SADC will have to gradually move towards supranational institutions.

---

[49] Rose Mtengeti-Migiro, supra, p. 20.
[50] Treaty of the Southern African Development Community, supra, Article 6.

VI. SADC'S STRATEGIES FOR ACHIEVING A COMMON MARKET

(a) Elimination of Tariff Barriers with in SADC

As observed earlier, SADC proposes to achieve a free trade area by the elimination of tariffs between member countries.[51] To this end, at its annual meeting in 1996, SADC adopted a protocol on trade.[52] The objectives of the trade protocol are to liberalize intra-regional trade in goods and services; ensure efficient production within SADC which reflects the current and dynamic comparative advantages of its members; contribute towards the improvement of the climate for domestic, cross border and foreign investment; and enhance the economic development, diversification and industrialization of the region.[53] The protocol envisages the elimination of tariffs within eight years of its entry into force.[54] The processes and modalities for the elimination of the tariffs are to be determined by a committee of ministers responsible for trade.[55] Member states which consider that they may be or have been adversely affected by the removal of tariff and non tariff barriers to trade may, upon application to a Committee of Ministers of Trade, be granted a grace period to afford them additional time for the elimination of tariffs. The protocol envisages the existence of different common tariffs for different products. The actual method of eliminating barriers to intra-SADC trade, and the criteria of listing products for special consideration, is yet to be negotiated in the context of the SADC's Negotiating Forum(TNF). However, once adopted, the process and modalities for eliminating barriers to intra-SADC trade will be deemed to form an integral part of the trade protocol.[56]

The Trade Protocol in Article 4 provides for the phased reduction and eventual elimination of import duties on goods originating from member states. The key to qualifying for preferential treatment under the Trade Protocol are the rules of origin. These are yet to be adopted. They are currently under negotiation within SADC. Rules of origin are designed to ensure that preferential trade benefits accrue directly to a regional scheme's member states and not to non-member states. Usually, such rules insist that only goods originating from member countries qualify for preferential treatment.

---

51 Article 2, Protocol on Trade in the Southern African Development Community (SADC).
52 Ibid, article 2.
53 Ibid, article 3 (1) (b).
54 Ibid.
55 Ibid., article 3 (1).
56 Ibid., Article 3 (1) (c).

For example, NAFTA's rules of origin provide that goods originate in the territory of NAFTA under the following circumstances: (1) the good is wholly obtained or produced in North America. Article 415 defines such goods as products of farm, forest, or fisheries within the territory of one of more of the parties. In the case of fish on the high seas, it covers fish caught by vessels carrying a flag of one of the NAFTA parties.[57] This approach is preferable to that of looking at the ownership of the corporation providing the goods. That kind of approach would defeat policies aimed at attracting foreign investment to a region.

In SADC the process of eliminating tariffs is to be accompanied by an industrialization strategy to improve the competitiveness of member states products. Pursuant to the objective of eliminating import duties, member states may not raise import duties beyond those in existence at the time of entry into force of the Trade Protocol. This provision does not affect the charging of fees for services rendered by member states to traders. Article 5 provides that member states shall not apply any export duties on goods for export to member states. This does not prevent member states from applying export duties necessary to prevent erosion of any prohibitions or restrictions which apply to exports outside the community, provided that no less favorable treatment is granted to member states than to third countries. In Article 6 member states commit themselves to the elimination of non tariff barriers. Except where this is provided for under the protocol, member states are prohibited from applying any new quantitative restrictions on imports and exports, and are required to phase out existing restrictions on goods originating in other member states. They may apply for a quota system only where such a quota system is more favorable than that applied under the protocol.[58]

There are a number of exceptions to the application of these prohibitions. The exceptions are similar to the ones usually found in most free trade agreements including measures necessary to: (1) protect public morals or to maintain public order; (2) protect human, animal or plant life or health; (3) secure compliance with laws and regulations which are consistent with the provisions of the WTO; (4) protect intellectual property rights, or prevent deceptive trade practices; (5) the transfer of gold, silver, precious and semi-precious stones, including precious and strategic metals; (6) imposed for the

---

[57] See, NAFTA Treaty, Article 401. For an overview of NAFTA's legal obligations, operations, and impact, see, generally North American Free Trade Agreement, Statement of Administrative Action, H.R.Doc.No. 159, 103d cong., 1st sess. (1993).

[58] Ibid., Article 7.

protection of national treasures of artistic, historic or archaeological value; (7) prevent or relieve critical shortages of foodstuffs in any exporting member state; (8) the conservation of exhaustible natural resources and the environment; and (8) ensure compliance with existing obligations under international agreements.[59] Security measures are also excepted provided that the member state instituting such measures notifies the trade committee of any such measures. The protocol provides for national treatment.[60] Member states are required to accord immediately and unconditionally, to goods traded within the community the same treatment to goods produced nationally and to those produced in other member states in respect of all laws, regulations and requirements, affecting their internal sales, offering for sale, purchase, transportation, distribution or use. In addition to removing the tariff based obstacles to free trade, the protocol in Article 6 requires member states to take measures to eliminate non tariff barriers to trade. Member states also promise cooperation in a number of areas including: (1) customs matters; (2) simplification and harmonization of trade documentation and procedures; (3) freedom of transit within the community. Member states promise to base their sanitary and phytosanitary measures on international standards, guidelines and recommendations, so as to harmonize such measures for agricultural and livestock production in the region. These measures are to be harmonized in accordance with WTO Agreement on Application of Sanitary and Phytosanitary Measures.[61]

(b) Technical Barriers to Trade

With respect to standards and technical regulations on trade, member states are required to use relevant international standards as the basis for their measures. If an international standard is used, then it presumably does not constitute an unnecessary obstacle to trade. The problem is that there are already national standards in existence in these countries, and it is necessary to ensure that these are not an obstacle to trade. SADC member states are prohibited from granting subsidies which have the effect of distorting or threatening to distort competition in the region. Member states are, however, allowed to take countervailing measures on a product of another member state to offset the effect of subsidies imposed by the other member state. Market safeguarding measures are allowed provided that a member state has determined that the product attracting such measures is being imported to its

---

[59] Ibid., Article 9.
[60] Ibid., Article 11.
[61] Ibid., Article 16.

territory in such increased quantities, absolute or relative to domestic productions, and under such conditions as to cause or threaten to cause serious injury to the domestic industry that produces like or directly competitive products. These measures, however, have to be in accordance with WTO rules.[62]

The provisions relating to standards and technical regulations could have been more strictly structured. They should clearly discourage the use of standards and technical specifications as such measures can be major obstacles to trade. For example the provisions relating to standards in NAFTA are couched in language which is easier to litigate and thereby discourages abuse. Article 904 of NAFTA establishes four basic rights and obligations of each NAFTA party: (1) the right to adopt standards-related measures; (2) the right to establish a level of protection that the party deems appropriate; (3) the obligation to refrain from discriminatory treatment with respect to standards; and (4) the obligation to refrain from creating or using standards-related measures as an unnecessary obstacle to trade. In addition, parties to NAFTA are required to demonstrate that the purpose of their standards is to achieve a legitimate objective, defined to include safety, the protection of human, animal, and plant life and health, and environmental protection. NAFTA does not harmonize the parties product standards. Instead, NAFTA member states are directed to make their standards-related measures and conformity assessment procedures compatible to the greatest extent.[63]

Subject to WTO provisions, SADC member states are allowed to take temporary measures to protect infant industries in their jurisdictions. The Community realizes the need to encourage foreign investment to the community as a whole. Under Article 22 of the protocol member states are required to adopt policies and measures to promote an open cross -border investment regime within the Community as a way of enhancing economic development, diversification and industrialization. Member states are also required to implement WTO regulations with respect to trade in services and intellectual property rights. They are to accord one another the most favored national treatment and must not enter into agreements with third parties that conflict with the SADC protocol.[64] It is important that SADC recognizes the importance of joint efforts to attract investment to the region. Individually, many of the SADC countries do not have the necessary conditions to attract substantial inflows of foreign investment. In many of the countries, markets are simply too small, skills too scarce, infrastructure inadequate and investment

---

[62] Ibid., Article, 17.
[63] R. Bhala and K. Kennedy, supra. P. 175.
[64] Ibid., Article 24.

opportunities too limited. The picture changes dramatically when an investor is assured access to the regional market.

(c) Difficulties within a program of the Elimination of Tariffs

The reduction of tariffs in any free trade arrangement is not an easy task. In the case of SADC, a number of problems have to be confronted. First, there is the fact that five members of SADC belong to the Southern African Customs Union (SACU). SACU members belong to a free trade area with common external tariffs. There will have to be an agreed formula on how SADC and SACU tariffs are to be harmonized with the view to have one level of tariffs for the whole community. In the long term the existence of SACU is inconsistent with that of SADC. Some countries would be applying tariff reduction rates to already low national tariff rates, leading to inequitable revenue losses and making exports to countries with higher national rates less competitive. The application of tariff reduction programs at different stages by different countries can create complex arrangements and undermine the overall integrative effect of the elimination of tariffs. There are also some tricky areas, for example, sugar is produced by a number of SADC countries. International trade in sugar is not free but regulated by protocols and market access arrangements. Further individual countries may be tempted to raise rather than lower tariffs for domestic reasons. In addition to all this is the fact that trade taxes still amount to some 40% of fiscal revenue in an average African country.[65] This fact makes countries reluctant to reduce tariffs, as in the short term, it represents revenue loss without an immediate alternative to turn to. SADC countries must realize that economic integration, by its very definition, is a process designed to completely abolish discrimination between local and partner goods, services and sectors over an agreed period of time. In other words, economic integration expands the effective market horizon within which economic agents can move the resources they hope to utilize productively. In the short term such movement can translate into unequal benefits among countries participating in the integration scheme. What is important is to maintain a long term perspective of the process as the benefits for a participating region are bound to come in the long run.

(d) The Harmonization of Fiscal Policies

For trade and liberalization measures to be successful they must be accompanied by efforts to harmonize fiscal policies in order to promote

---

65 Lecture by Dr. Chris Stals, Governor of the South African Reserve Bank, Harvard Institute for International Development, May 1, 1997.

economic cooperation and integration. This process should involve harmonization of financial laws, regulations, trade documents and procedures with respect to banking, finance and the movement of capital and goods. It is necessary to ensure continued reforms in the financial sector for the achievement of effective economic integration such as reforms to improve the monetary control mechanisms; institutional and regulatory reforms to improve efficiency and soundness of financial systems; and the adequacy of the interest rate structure. SADC has made good progress in establishing institutions to carry out work in this area. Under the Finance and Investment Protocol, SADC has established an Independent Committee of Governors of Central Banks. The Committee has established a small specialized secretariat and research facility within the South African Reserve Bank to serve the Committee of Governors. As Mr. Stalls, Governor of the Reserve Bank of South Africa, has noted, before the Governors' Committee was established SADC approached financial cooperation in the region on the basis of proposals made by European advisers and was based mainly on the model of financial integration in the European Community.[66] He argues such reliance was a mistake. The current divergences in the stage of economic development of the members of SADC are so vast that there cannot be talk at this juncture of a European type economic integration scheme in Southern Africa.

SADC has adopted a bottom-up approach with respect to the question of financial integration. This approach is based on building financial cooperation by laying an appropriate foundation in the form of effective institutional framework for the financial system in each country. This strategy involves establishing well run banks; securities firms, insurance companies, and pension funds. A successful financial sector also requires a critical mass of loan officers and bank auditors with the requisite skills to carry out the types of financial transactions demanded in a market-based economy and a strong credit culture. More grandiose schemes for the harmonization or integration of macro-economic monetary policies, such as a unitary currency, can be considered later once central banks, private banking sectors and financial markets have been established and are functioning effectively in the participating countries. Central banks must work together in joint efforts to develop compatible and inter-linkable national payments, as well as in clearing and settlement systems for financial transactions. Eventually, the national financial systems must be linked to each other to provide for more effective cross-border settlements for inter-regional financial transactions. This requires a high level of cooperation in the development of compatible

---

[66] Ibid.

electronic data processing and in technology systems in the twelve participating central banks. Attention should also be paid to the development of financial markets in the region. This will involve the introduction of appropriate legal institutional frameworks and of financial instruments, and the improvement of technological systems and expertise in foreign exchange management, money and capital markets. Some rationalization in financial systems to the advantage of the whole region will be necessary.

Recently, SADC central banks agreed on the repatriation of notes within the community.[67] The work by the SADC Central Bank Committee has enabled South Africa to ease exchange controls for companies wanting to invest in the SADC region. Further, dual listings on the Johannesburg stock exchange and other SADC stock exchanges are now permissible. When sufficient work has been done, the community can move into greater harmonization and even integration of macro-economic financial policies such as interest and exchange rate policies, the management of bank liquidity, credit extension on a regional basis and operations by central banks in a more integrated financial market environment. The danger, however, of moving too fast in this area was illustrated by the introduction of travelers cheques and currency units in COMESA in the late 1980s before the regional grouping had dealt with the more fundamental fiscal policies. The result was the collapse and subsequent withdrawal of the COMESA travelers cheques and the currency units after a few years of operation.

(e) Dispute Settlement Under the Trade Protocol

The SADC Trade Protocol provides a dispute settlement mechanism to resolve trade disputes that will inevitably arise in the interpretation of the protocol.[68] The first avenue for any dispute is through negotiations between the member states involved in the dispute. If this effort fails, member states may take recourse to a panel of trade experts. As a last resort disputes will be settled in accordance with Article 32 of the SADC treaty. As it stands, the dispute settlement mechanism is too rudimentary. There is urgent need to work out a dispute settlement mechanism which is endowed with powers to give directives and to make binding decisions. Characteristics of such a mechanism should be speedy resolution of disputes; binding nature of decisions; and a party to a dispute should not have the ability to unilaterally block the implementation of a tribunal's decision. This is the only way

---

[67] Mail Guardian, April 13, 1998.
[68] Protocol on Trade in the Southern African Development Community (SADC) Region, Article, 32.

SADC will ensure the effectiveness and viability of its protocols. This can be done by the establishment of a SADC court. Recently, SADC ministers of justice agreed to establish a SADC tribunal to deal with disputes arising from the interpretation of the SADC treaty. In the case of the European Union, member states have to submit to the jurisdiction of their respective courts of justice which protect community institutions. The absence of institutional mechanisms to enforce treaties and the ability of states to block decisions arrived at by dispute settlement tribunals are some of the major weaknesses of most regional organizations in developing countries.

VII. CONCLUSION

Integration is a laborious and time consuming process with a gradual evolution pattern. It can only be achieved through a well balanced recognition of mutual interests. Agreements on the process can only be concluded with excellent preparatory work by the community institutions and by putting practical goals on the negotiating table. The European experience shows quite clearly that, at the institutional level, a movement towards regional cooperation and integration must give regional institutions real power. Southern Africa has a great opportunity to build a viable economic community, and this opportunity should not be missed. Most of the major historical political conflicts of the region have been resolved or are in the process of being resolved. Namibia attained independence in 1989; in Mozambique the conflict between FRELIMO and RENAMO has been resolved; white minority rule has ended in South Africa thereby removing the dominant source of instability in the region. There are, however, two intractable conflicts-Angola and Congo. Unless resolved, these two conflicts have the potential to seriously undermine SADC integration efforts. The prospects for an enduring settlement in both conflicts do not look good, and efforts to resolve the conflicts are painfully slow.[69] Except for Swaziland and the newly joined Congo (Kishasha), democratic elections have been held in all the SADC Member states. This means that there is a commonality in political systems and out-

---

[69] The Angola Peace Agreement, Lusaka, 19995 that was being implemented has for all intents and purposes collapsed. The United Nations Secretary-General has recommended the termination of the UN Mission in Angola, see, Africa News Agency, " Annan Recommends End of Angola Mission." January 18, 1999. See also "Angola's Claims Affect Congo Talks, " Post News Paper, January 18, 1999, Lusaka, Zambia and " I will Never Talk to Rebels-Kabila,: Post News Paper, January 15, 1999, Lusaka, Zambia.

look. In addition, as we earlier noted, all the countries embrace the free market system and welcome private investment. To maintain the momentum, the countries in the region must ensure that they pursue economic and political policies which promote growth. This means that there must be: (1) political and social stability in the region; (2) macro-economic stability; (3) sound legal and administrative framework; (4) openness to intra-regional trade and investment; and a (5) well supervised, regulated, and competitive financial system and investment in people.

The question that is often raised is the likelihood of any economic community in the Southern African region being dominated by South Africa, the economic and pre-eminent military power in the region. This concern needs to be addressed. It arises from the fact that South Africa's economy is far larger than the combined economies of the rest of the eleven members of SADC. There are already complaints, especially by Zimbabwe and Zambia, that South Africa is destabilizing their economies. These countries accuse South Africa of flooding the region with its goods while preventing reciprocal trade through its high tariffs. This arises because South Africa still has in place a generous system of incentives for its exports put in place in the apartheid era. Zimbabwe and Zambia cannot take similar action as they are both under IMF-sponsored structural adjustment programs. In 1995, South Africa's exports to the rest of the African continent jumped to $3 billion compared to $2 billion the previous year. At the same time, the country's imports from other African countries rose by only 19%. In contrast the other members of SADC (Angola, Botswana, Lesotho, Malawi, Mauritius, Mozambique, Namibia, Swaziland, Tanzania, Zambia and Zimbabwe) depend up to 70% on South Africa for their imports. In the case of Zimbabwe, for example, the country's exports to South Africa increased by 1% in 1995 while its imports from it surged by 54%. Above all, the textile industry, which represented 20% of its total exports at the start of the decade, is being asphyxiated by South Africa's tariffs imposed after the expiration of a bilateral trade agreement in 1992.[70] The South African economy is by far the most advanced in the region. With only forty two million of the people, it accounts for 31% of the total output of all SADC countries together; the South African economy accounts for about 80% of the total gross domestic product of about $170 billion produced in SADC; South Africa equally accounts for almost 70% of the combined exports of $34 billion of the SADC region. Moreover, it has well developed financial markets.[71] To dispel the perception that South Africa is being

---

[70] See, research by African Institute of South Africa, as reported by Agence France Presse, June 12, 1996.
[71] Lecture by Dr. Chris Stals, Governor of the Bank of South Africa, supra.

protectionist and trying to dominate the region by placing high tariffs on its imports, making other SADC countries' exports uncompetitive, South Africa's Department of Trade and Industry (DTI) undertook an extensive review of the region's tariffs. It found that Zimbabwe and Mauritius, and not South Africa, are the most highly protected economies in Southern Africa.[72] South Africa has also shown a commitment and a willingness to participate in regional projects of which the Maputo Corridor project is a good example.[73]

There is no doubt that these difficulties can undermine regional integration and make harmonious regional integration more complex. But as the South African government has aptly observed, " South Africa cannot be an island in an ocean of poverty. Its destiny is linked to the region."[74] For one thing, South Africa will, in the long, run have to abide by the World Trade Organization trading regime. In addition, South Africa has huge domestic problems created by the legacy of apartheid which it needs to address. It requires a high economic growth rate to have sufficient resources to achieve this. This can only be guaranteed if the economies of the other Southern African states are vibrant. South Africa can ill afford unstable and poor neighbors, with the implication such poverty has for migration from those countries to South Africa. Immigration to South Africa from the rest of Africa is already a serious problem and one which, without cooperation by all countries in the region, can only worsen. The only economic community that can work is one where all member states perceive membership as beneficial to their economies. Experience has shown, especially that of failed integration schemes, that economic integration, unless checks are put in place, tends to concentrate benefits in those countries which are relatively more developed. It is understood that all member states in an economic community cannot gain equally at any given time. In fact in the short term gains are sometimes difficult to assess and some members might lose. The long term view is, however, the critical factor. The spirit of give and take which should be the guiding principle in regional integration has to be paramount for a successful community to emerge. Particular measures should be instituted to accommodate the less developed countries of the membership of the community.

South Africa's economic power can be a positive factor for the region. South Africa has the political and economic authority to assume a regulatory role, and the leadership capacity to consolidate and promote the integration

---

[72] See, "Trading Carefully Around SADC", Ministry of Trade, Pretoria, South Africa, August 29, 1997.
[73] This is a project to construct a major highway and other infrastructure to link Maputo to the Mpumalanga Province in central South Africa.
[74] "Trading Carefully Around SADC", op. cit. supra note 72

process. Its expertise and advanced technology is needed and can play a vital part in the development of the region. South Africa's economic dominance places on it an obligation to act as the integration leader in the region and a responsibility to act maturely in its dealings with its partners in SADC. As Professor Davis has observed, for integration to succeed in Southern Africa, it will have to be based on five principles: (a) a regional economic program has to be viewed as an essential component of any strategy to promote growth and development in Southern Africa; (b) inequalities in present relations need to be taken into account in developing closer regional economic ties after apartheid. If this is not done, present inequalities will be reproduced and there will not be a sustainable basis for strengthening ties. It is likely that the socio-political consequences of such polarization will be large-scale migration across the sub-continent's borders; (c) a regional program cannot be based on the unrealistic expectations of weaker partners. Unless all partners can reasonably expect concrete benefits, the political will to sustain a regional program will be lacking; (d) the need to find a combination of cooperation and integration that will help to realize the benefits of closer relations; and (e) the promotion of cooperation in regional security.[75]

Socio-economic problems are the main threats to regional security and a new cooperative approach to security is essential to encourage disarmament and release resources for development. SADC leaders have already shown that they can act together in crisis that reared during the elections in Mozambique and in the resolution of a coup-induced crisis in Lesotho 1993 and more recently the crisis following the May 1998 disputed election results.[76] They are also working together, albeit with great difficulty, to resolve the war in the Congo between the Kabila Government and rebels seeking to remove it from power.[77] Water and Energy protocols have also been concluded. Work on defense, security, police and drugs cooperation is continuing. The Economist Intelligence Unit commenting on the progress thus far made by the earlier organization SADCC, notes that, "nearly a decade later, most of the doubters were convinced. The region's peasant farmers are beginning to plant new crops, strains from a SADC research

---

75 Minnie Venter, supra, chapter 2, pp. 4-71, See also Laurie Nathan, *A Framework and Strategy for Building Peace and Security in Southern Africa*, Center for Intergroup Studies, October, 1992.
76 The Xinhua News Agency, May 31, 1996. Also, Mail Guardian, October 12, Johannesburg, South Africa.
77 Mail Guardian, October 22, 1998, Johannesburg, South Africa. The Congo crisis has severely tested the unity of SADC. Some states, Zimbabwe, Angola and Namibia have deployed troops while others have misgiving about such a move.

center, while business people in different countries can telephone each other over SADC links and ship their goods through ports and railways improved under SADC auspices. Equally important, but less visible because it does not carry the SADC label, is the growing regional cooperation in a wide range of economic, business, political and military matters as officials and politicians and business people get to know each other better and to think in regional terms."[78]

It should also be noted that SADC was developed within the region, and not presented to the member countries by outsiders as was the case with many regional integration schemes in Africa, for example, COMESA, which was established in conjunction with the Economic Commission for Africa. SADC is an appropriate institution to serve as a vehicle for the economic integration of Southern Africa. Integration in this region is not, however, going to be easy. Countries in the area will have to recognize that the only way to create an economic community is to harmonize economic policies and tariffs, and to remove bureaucratic obstacles to the movement of capital, labor and goods within the SADC countries. These are necessary conditions for a fully integrated market and for the establishment of a free trade area. Such actions will certainly involve the surrender of some aspects of sovereignty rights by individual states, but not much more than already relinquished by member states of the European Union or those of the North American Free Trade Association Treaty.

If Southern Africa states fail to bring about genuine economic integration, their economies will stagnate and will be unable to meet the challenges of the region. The ultimate result is that the region's, people will remain poor. SADC countries must put aside narrow nationalistic tendencies in favor of cooperation, coordination and collaboration. Successful economic integration in Southern Africa is bound to have far-reaching political, economic, social, cultural and scientific implications not only for the Southern African region but for the rest of the Africa. SADC could serve as the much needed catalyst that finally launches Africa on the road to development and reverse the decades of increasing poverty in Africa, and the marginalization of the continent in the world.

---

[78] Economist Intelligence Unit, "SADCC in the 1990s", supra, p.1.

TRADE LIBERALISATION UNDER ECOWAS: PROSPECTS, CHALLENGES AND WTO COMPATIBILITY

Edwini Kessie*

I. INTRODUCTION

In recent times, the Economic Community of West African States (ECOWAS) has been getting attention in the world media for its role in bringing peace to Liberia and Sierra Leone through its military intervention force called ECOWAS Monitoring Group (ECOMOG). This has led to the widespread belief that ECOWAS is a regional security body. While ECOWAS has assumed this new role with a high degree of professionalism, it was principally created in May 1975 by the political leaders of West Africa as a regional economic grouping to foster economic development of the sub-region.

Notwithstanding its existence for nearly a quarter of a century, ECOWAS has not achieved much in the field of trade and investment liberalization, hence the dearth of information on the organisation until its recent involvement in the political conflicts in Liberia and Sierra Leone. A number of reasons account for the failure of ECOWAS to achieve its objectives. These range from the very small sizes of the economies of the member states to the lack of political commitment on the part of the region's political leaders who are adamant about losing their sovereignty.

The objectives of this paper are to review the trade provisions of the ECOWAS treaty and examine the problems which have prevented the organisation from achieving its objectives. An analysis is carried out to determine if the trade provisions are consistent with the rules of the World Trade Organisation (WTO). It is assumed that if the constituent members of a regional economic grouping adhere to the rules of the WTO, their organisation would have, in principle, created the conditions which could facilitate

---

* The author is a counsellor in the Technical Cooperation Division of the World Trade Organisation. The views expressed in this Article are those of the author and do not represent the views of the organisation he works for. Helpful comments were provided by Mark Koulen, Reto Malacrida and Maarten Smeets.

trade between themselves and also with the outside world. Although the majority of ECOWAS member states were members of the General Agreement on Tariffs and Trade (GATT), the predecessor institution of the WTO, they neglected to notify their agreement to the GATT Secretariat as required, for an examination to be carried out to determine the consistency of their agreement with GATT rules. As at the time of writing, the ECOWAS treaty had still not been notified to the WTO. It is argued that it would be in the interests of the member states to notify their agreement to the WTO as soon as possible for an examination to be carried out to guarantee certainty and predictability. The costs could be burdensome, should aspects of the ECOWAS treaty be challenged by a Member of the WTO and found not to be in conformity with the WTO rules.

Section II of this paper traces the origins of ECOWAS and examines the factors which influenced the region's political leaders to establish the organisation. It also examines the key objectives of the ECOWAS Treaty and analyses some of the factors which have frustrated the effective functioning of the organisation. The innovative features of the revised ECOWAS treaty are also discussed in this section. Section III reviews the rules of the WTO pertaining to regional trade agreements. Section IV reviews and analyses the main trade provisions of the ECOWAS treaty in the light of WTO rules to determine their consistency. Section V, which is the concluding section, summarises the salient points made in this paper.

II. THE ESTABLISHMENT OF ECOWAS

The sixteen member countries of ECOWAS were all former colonies of either France, the United Kingdom or Portugal. After the attainment of political independence by a majority of them in the 1950's and 1960's, their attention turned to achieving economic self-sufficiency. According to the political leaders, this was necessary to consolidate the political gains that had been achieved. They harboured the feeling that if they did not diversify their trade and markets, they could come under a new form of colonialism (neo-colonialism).

Immediately after achieving independence, a number of West African countries instituted import substitution policies thinking that these would assist them to industrialise and thereby achieve economic development. To nurture domestic industries, most governments erected high tariff walls and resorted to a myriad of non-tariff barriers to effectively discourage imports. Export taxes were imposed on raw materials, so as to discourage their export thereby allowing domestic firms relatively easy access to them. The effects of these policies became apparent in the late 1970s, when the economies of a majority of West African states began to stagnate and contract.[1] To counteract the emerging balance of payments problems, the leaders of West African countries sought to expand trade, *albeit*, on a regional basis. They realised that trade was an engine of economic growth which could facilitate their integration into the world economy. They were, however, reluctant to open up immediately to the rest of the world. They argued that it was necessary to groom their industries to achieve competitiveness at the regional level before exposing them to international companies at the international level. In other words, they wanted to extend the failed import substitution policies from the national to the regional level thinking that would enable them to achieve economies of scale and thereby improve the competitiveness of their firms.

In devising this strategy for economic development, the leaders were conscious of the very small sizes of their economies. Out of the sixteen member countries, twelve are classified as least-developed by the United Nations meaning that the GDP per capita of these countries is less than US$300.[2] Even the GDP per capita of the non least-developed countries is not much different. The GDP per capita of Nigeria, which is the economic powerhouse of the region, is estimated to be around US$400. With the exception of a few countries such as Ghana and Cote d'Ivoire, the rate of economic growth of most of these countries has mostly in the last decade been negative. Their infrastructure is weak and hampers economic development. Foreign investors are deterred by the poor road and rail networks and the inefficient state of the telecommunications sector. The population of most these countries is so small as to support economic development. With the notable exception of Nigeria, Ghana and Cote d'Ivoire, the population of most of these countries is below 10 million. The institutional and human capacities are weak; the labour force is usually not as literate as their counterparts in other parts of the developing world, especially South-East Asia.

With these considerations in mind and also influenced by developments in Europe, the leaders were convinced about the need to pool their resources together and establish an economic grouping which would strengthen their economies and improve the living standards of their people. They reasoned that if the economically advanced countries of Western Europe had deemed it necessary to establish the European Economic Community, then

---

[1] Bundu Abass, "ECOWAS and the Future of Regional Integration in West Africa" in Lavergne Réalet al., *Regional Integration and Cooperation in West Africa: A Multidimensional Perspective* (Trenton: Africa World Press; 1997)p30.

[2] Benin, Burkina Faso, Gambia, Guinea, Guinea-Bissau, Liberia, Mali, Mauritania, Niger, Sierra Leone and Togo.

they had no alternative but to establish a similar economic arrangement. They were also influenced by the relative success, at that time, of the East African Community whose members were Kenya, Tanzania and Uganda, which was later dissolved.

Convinced about the potential of regional trade agreements to facilitate economic development, a conference of West African countries was convened in 1967 at Accra, Ghana. The leaders agreed to establish the West African economic community, although no formal agreement was signed by them. It was not until the following year in Monrovia, Liberia that the Heads of State and Government signed a formal agreement committing themselves to establish the West African Regional Group. The leaders, however, failed to establish an institutional framework for the grouping. Thus, the organisation only existed in name with no machinery to adopt and implement decisions and strategies.

It was not until 1972 that the leaders of Nigeria and Togo attempted to revive the idea of establishing a regional economic grouping which would facilitate the integration of the countries in the sub-region into the global economy. After intensive consultations and deliberations among the leaders, the representatives of fifteen states signed the Treaty of the Economic Community of West African States in Lagos, Nigeria on 28 May 1975.[3] Cape Verde acceded to the Treaty shortly afterwards and became the sixteenth member of the organisation. The organisation did not, however, become operational immediately after the signing of the Treaty by the sixteen countries. The five trade protocols attached to the treaty were not ratified by the necessary number of states until 1977.[4] In a way, the creation of ECOWAS was a significant step, as it was the first time that an organisation had been set up which cut across divisions of language, history and existing affiliations and institutions. Of its member states, eight are officially French-speaking (francophone), five are English-speaking (anglophone), two are Portuguese-speaking (lusophone) and one Arabic-speaking.

---

[3] The signatory states were Benin, Burkina Faso, Cote d'Ivoire, Gambia, Ghana, Guinea, Guinea-Bissau, Liberia, Mali, Mauritania, Niger, Nigeria, Senegal, Sierra Leone and Togo.

[4] The protocols dealt with the following subjects: rules of origin(determining which products originated within the ECOWAS region); re-exportation of goods imported from third countries; assessment of loss of revenue arising out of the implementation of the treaty by a member state; the Fund for Co-operation, Compensation and Development; and contributions by member states to the budget of the Community. Notwithstanding the over-aching principle of equality of member states, the contributions of member states are not the same. Nigeria pays more than all the member on account of its size and resources at its disposal.

1 Objectives of the ECOWAS Treaty

The key objectives of ECOWAS are to "promote co-operation and integration, leading to the establishment of an economic union...in order *to raise the living standards of its peoples, and to maintain and enhance economic stability, foster relations among Member States and contribute to the progress and development of the African continent*" (italics added).[5]

As can be seen from this Article, the focus of ECOWAS extends far beyond trade to cooperation in almost all the key sectors of the respective economies of the member states.[6] The treaty prescribes a number of measures and modalities to ensure the realisation of the stated objectives. These include the establishment of a common market through the abolition of substantially all barriers to internal trade, the adoption of a common external tariff, a uniform commercial policy towards third countries, the harmonisation and co-ordination of national policies and the promotion of integration programmes, projects and activities in a number of sectors including food, agriculture and natural resources, industry, transport and communications, energy, trade, money and finance, taxation, economic reform policies, human resources, education, information, culture, science, technology, services, health, tourism and legislation. The harmonisation and coordination of policies for the protection of the environment, as well as the promotion of the establishment of joint production enterprises are also envisaged.

If the member states were to implement the various plans and programmes outlined above, ECOWAS would easily be one of the most successful regional arrangements in the world. Unfortunately, ECOWAS has not had any appreciable impact in the West African sub-region. Trade creation in the sub-region as a result of the trade liberalising initiatives has been very minimal due to the failure of the member states to fulfil their obligations under the treaty or as a result of external pressures which have made the realisation of the organisation's objectives unattainable.

One of the major problems which has frustrated attempts at integration is what is described by one analyst as "the absence of a development and integration culture."[7] For regional integration to succeed, the constituent parties must themselves have clearly-defined national plans and strategies to achieve economic development. Unfortunately, a significant number of West African countries did not implement coherent economic policies after the

---

5 See Article 3.1 of the revised ECOWAS treaty.
6 Asante, S.K.B., *Regionalism and Africa's Development: Expectations, Reality and Challenges* (London: Macmillan; 1997) pp45-46.
7 *supra* note 1 at p38.

attainment of independence. Too often, economic plans and strategies were discarded immediately after there was a change of government. Policies adopted by some countries were incompatible with the ideals of regionalism. In other words, instead of advancing the cause of regionalism, they rather undermined it creating a sense of apathy among the general public and strengthening nationalist sentiments. This question by Abass Bundu is indicative of the extent of the problem:

> "Since 1975, when the countries of West Africa committed themselves to forming an economic community, how many member states have drawn up national development plans or programs with regional considerations or the regional market as their point of reference? What measures have been introduced by governments as incentives for their business communities to venture into cross-border investments and transactions, and what encouragement are ordinary people offered to think in West African terms?"[8]

He responds by noting that "an integration culture is not yet conspicuous in the region nor is integration accorded the high priority it deserves on national economic agendas."[9] The problem is not only confined to West Africa, but the whole of Africa. As a continent, Africa boasts of many regional integration agreements, but only few are in force or functioning.[10] The results achieved under integration schemes have generally been negligible. As noted by the UNCTAD Secretariat, "the accumulated experience, however, shows that intra-African cooperation has generally proved to be very difficult and that performance has more often than not fallen well short of expectations and declared goals. Despite many cooperative arrangements, intra-African trade flows as well as investment and financial flows continue to be dismal, and joint undertakings for the collective building of infrastructure, and of institutional, human and productive capacities, are too few to contribute meaningfully to strengthening and expanding trade and economic integration."[11]

Another major issue is the political differences between leaders of the sub-region. Until recently, a number of West African countries were either under military rule or one-party dictatorships. Given the fact that most of

---

8   *Ibid.*
9   *Ibid.*
10 *supra* note 6 at p46.
11 UNCTAD, *Regional Experiences in the Economic Integration Process of Developing Countries*, (UNCTAD/ITCD/TSB/1; 25 June 1997)para.7 at p7.

these governments lacked legitimacy, they were very reluctant to cede powers to any *supra*-national body which could rival their authority. They jealously guarded their sovereignty and saw the ECOWAS Treaty, which some of them did not sign, as interfering with the exercise of their governmental powers. Another factor which has impeded the effective functioning of the organisation is the underlying differences in political and economic philosophies. While some countries preferred a nationalist approach to economic matters and favoured a big role for government, others wanted a lesser role for government and preferred adopting measures which would facilitate the greater participation of the private sector in business activity. Abass Bundu gives the example that during the negotiation of ECOWAS rules of origin and the Protocol on Community Enterprises, governments with a socialist inclination argued for "greater state or indigenous participation", while those with liberal convictions pushed for lowering the barriers for third country participation in community projects.[12]

Another factor which has not helped the realisation of the objectives enshrined in the ECOWAS treaty is the mistrust between the anglophone and francophone countries. The knowledge of this rift has been exploited by France to maintain its influence over its former colonies.[13] The francophone countries are suspicious of Nigeria which, they believe, because of its size and relative prosperity, wants to dominate their economies. Nigeria has been extremely cautious in exercising its natural leadership role to the fullest for fear of provoking crisis in the organisation. This mutual distrust is clearly not justified, as in every regional grouping in the world, there appears to be always a dominant or influential partner. In the case of NAFTA, it is the United States. Nevertheless, the other two participating countries, namely Canada and Mexico, have benefitted tremendously from entering into the free trade agreement with the United States. In the case of MERCOSUR, the dominant country is Brazil, while in the European Union, the most influential countries appear to be Germany and France. The concerns of small countries could be overcome by having an elaborate rules-based system, where the rights and interests of all the participating countries will be guaranteed. There could be an effective revenue-sharing scheme, where countries disadvantaged by the integration process could be compensated. Although ECOWAS has set up a compensation fund,[14] it has largely been under-funded, as it relies on

---

[12] *supra* note 1 at p38.
[13] *supra* note 1 at p39.
[14] Article 21 of the revised ECOWAS treaty.

contributions from the member states to compensate countries which may have sustained some financial losses.[15]

The rivalry between the francophone countries and the anglophone countries has led to the establishment of competing regional blocs by the former. This trend has not been helpful for the attainment of the objectives of the ECOWAS treaty. The overlapping membership of the francophone countries in competing bodies such as the West African Monetary and Economic Union (UMEOA) has meant that they have not taken their obligations under the ECOWAS treaty very seriously. More importantly, there are situations where potential conflicts may arise regarding which organisation's obligations should take precedence.

Another impediment to the successful realisation of the objectives of ECOWAS is the state of the individual economies of the constituent countries. As previously noted, the sub-region has the highest concentration of least-developed countries in the world. Most of the countries do not have the necessary institutional and human resources to facilitate economic development. While most of them are signatories to the Lomé Convention, they have not been able to take advantage of the preferences to increase and diversify their exports. In fact, their exports to the European market have been decreasing in recent years as a result of supply-side constraints. As noted by Hazlewood, "integration is not simply a matter of lowering tariffs. The existence of tariffs is not the sole, or even the primary impediment to trade between the countries of Africa. The main reason for the low level of trade is to be found in the economic structure of the countries [and in]...the fact that the 'infrastructure' for intra-African trade is generally lacking."[16]

The collapse of commodity prices and the increase in oil prices have also had a negative impact on the economies of almost all the participating countries. Most of them are highly indebted and spend a significant proportion of their export revenue on servicing their debts. The harsh economic conditions have forced many of the countries to adopt short-term solutions to problems, instead of adopting long-terms solutions which would ensure sustainable development and contribute to the expansion of the regional economy. To quote Abass Bundu:

---

[15] Asante, *supra* note 6 at p63.
[16] Cited in Asante, *ibid* at p66.

"[t]he poor economic health of member states since the early 1980's has been a major impediment to integration efforts. Severe economic recession has obliged member states to abandon all plans for long term economic development, including regional integration, in the pursuit of short-term stabilization. The economic crisis has also emptied government coffers. *The limited revenue that has been available to the public sector has thus had to be rationed in accordance with short-term priorities that excluded regional integration or gave it only token recognition*(italics added)."[17]

Given the fact that customs revenue constitute a high proportion of the GDP of a significant number of the participating countries, there has been the reluctance to reduce tariffs. The situation would have been different, if there were no supply-side constraints hampering the efforts of the countries to increase and diversify their exports. As noted by Asante,:

"the lack of progress of ECOWAS...is also the reflection of the discontent of participating governments with the design and results of the subregional market integration schemes...While they impose maximum constraints on decision-making autonomy, they offer minimal prospects for the realization of immediate benefits. A case in point is the loss of revenue derived from indirect taxes – mainly import and export duties as a consequence of the removal of barriers and tariff harmonization. And while the impact of tariff harmonization on revenue would be felt immediately, the expected benefits might be of a long-term nature and less certain."[18]

The political situation in West Africa has also constrained the ability of ECOWAS to achieve its objectives. Given the scarcity of capital and the low level of domestic savings in the sub-region, it is imperative for the countries to be able to attract foreign direct investment. The civil wars in Sierra Leone and Liberia have damaged investor confidence in the region. It was perhaps this realisation which made the other members of ECOWAS to intervene in the wars. As we will see below, the revised ECOWAS treaty attempts to address most of the issues discussed above.

2   The Revised ECOWAS Treaty

Frustrated by the slow progress that had been made in the implementation of the relevant provisions of the ECOWAS treaty in the individual mem-

---

[17]   Bundu Abass, *supra* note 1 at p40.
[18]   Asante, *supra* note 6 at pp66-67.

ber states, a summit of the Heads of State and Government in 1989 made a declaration to the effect that a new impetus was needed to put the process of regional integration in West Africa back on track. They followed up on this at their 1990 summit by mandating the ECOWAS Secretariat to comprehensively review the original ECOWAS treaty with the view of identifying any deficiencies in the legal bases which have hampered the process of regional integration in the West African sub-region. The Secretariat was also mandated to come up with recommendations which would strengthen the Community and ensure that it realises its objectives. In that context, they were expected to propose specific amendments to the original ECOWAS treaty which, to some extent, had failed to keep pace with global developments. A committee of eminent persons was appointed to revise the ECOWAS treaty under the supervision of the ECOWAS Council of Ministers, which is one of the bodies set up under the original treaty. The committee did its work over a period of two years (1991-1992) and submitted a draft revised ECOWAS treaty to the Council of Ministers for their consideration at their July 1993 meeting.[19] The Ministers adopted the draft revised treaty and presented it to the Heads of State and Government at their Cotonou summit, which took place from 22-24 July 1993, for acceptance.

The revised treaty is much more focussed and action-oriented. It contains 91 articles in 22 chapters instead of the previous 65 articles in 16 chapters. The articles deal with disparate issues including institutional matters, financing of integration efforts, economic cooperation and integration options, political cooperation, regional peace and stability.

The revised treaty contains a number of innovative provisions designed to strengthen the Community and transform it into an engine of economic growth in the West African sub-region. The revised treaty, for example, confers full power on the supreme decision-making body of the organisation, the Authority of Heads of State and Government, to take decisions which will be binding on all the community institutions as well as the member states.[20] For some member states, this was revolutionary given the way West African governments had traditionally carefully guarded their sovereignty. Ceding

---

[19] The Council of Ministers, which is the second highest decision-making body of ECOWAS, is composed of two representatives from each member state. Usually, they are of ministerial rank. Typically, meetings are attended by a member state's Minister responsible for ECOWAS affairs and another minister in charge of a subject which may be on the agenda of the Council. The Council usually meets at least twice a year. It has the basic responsibility for overseeing the proper functioning and development of the Community.

[20] Article 9.4 of the revised ECOWAS treaty.

powers to a supra-national body was as such a big step. As to whether or not the Authority will exercise the powers conferred on it in economic matters remains to be seen.

The revised treaty also establishes a Community Court of Justice whose judgments "shall be binding on the member states, the institutions of the community and on individual and corporate bodies."[21] To increase accountability and the participation of the general public in the integration process, the treaty provides for the establishment of a Community Parliament and an Economic and Social Council. It also establishes eight specialised technical commissions to deal with the issues covered by the treaty and endows them with sufficient powers. Conscious of the political instability in the West-African sub-region and the effect that this was having on the integration process, the treaty has a new chapter on political cooperation and regional security.

To overcome the chronic problem of funding of the Community, the treaty calls for the imposition of a community levy, which will be a percentage of the total value of import duties imposed on goods originating in third countries. There is also a provision stating that ECOWAS "shall ultimately be the sole economic community in the region for the purpose of economic integration."[22] This addresses the problem of overlapping membership of different regional economic groupings.

In many respects, the revised treaty addresses most of the problems which have hampered the process of regional integration in the West-African sub-region. However, whether or not it will galvanise the member states to take up their obligations seriously remains to be seen. As cautioned by Abass Bundu, while the revision of the ECOWAS treaty has enacted "the institutional framework necessary to move forward on regional integration,...[t]he future course and success of that process cannot, of course, be taken for granted, if experience to date is any guide."[23]

III. RELEVANT WTO RULES ON REGIONAL INTEGRATION AGREEMENTS

The non-discrimination principle is the bedrock of the multilateral trading system. The first limb of this principle is the "most-favoured nation" (MFN) clause, which is articulated in Article I of GATT 1994. This clause

---

[21] Article 15.4 of the revised ECOWAS treaty.
[22] Article 2.1 of the revised ECOWAS treaty.
[23] Bundu Abass, supra note 1 at p45.

basically provides that any advantage or benefit granted to a Member of the WTO (or a non-Member) should unconditionally be extended to other Members of the WTO. If carried to its logical conclusion, it would disallow the conclusion and implementation of regional trade agreements, as the guiding principle in such agreements is discrimination vis-à-vis third parties. Whereas parties to the trade agreement are permitted to exchange tariff and other preferences between themselves, they are under no legal obligation to extend the benefits to other Members of the WTO.[24]

Notwithstanding the potential of regional trade agreements to fragment the multilateral trading system, the WTO Agreement contains a number of provisions which permit Members to form regional economic groupings. These are Article XXIV of GATT 1994, the Decision of the CONTRACTING PARTIES on Differential and More Favourable Treatment, Reciprocity and Fuller Participation of Developing Countries, otherwise known as the "Enabling Clause", Article XXV of GATT 1994 and Article V of the General Agreement on Trade in Services. These provisions are discussed below.

1   Article XXIV of GATT 1994

Article XXIV is the main GATT provision which provides legal cover for Members of the WTO to form or join customs unions or free trade areas. Given the fact that regional trade agreements are an exception to the MFN principle, the Article imposes a number of conditions which must be satisfied by Members forming regional trading arrangements. The guiding principle is spelled out in Article XXIV:4 of GATT 1994, which provides that "the purpose of a customs union or a free trade area should be to facilitate trade between the constituent territories and not to raise barriers to the trade of other contracting parties with such territories". Thus, from the view point of the WTO, regional trading arrangements are acceptable, so far as the intention of the parties is to increase trade between themselves, and not to restrict the trade of third countries through the pursuit of discriminatory trade policies. Article XXIV imposes three main conditions which have to be satisfied by parties wishing to form customs unions. All the conditions apply to free-trade areas with the exception of the first one.

---

[24]   The second limb of the non-discrimination principle is the national treatment principle, which provides that Members of the WTO should not discriminate against imported goods, once they have cleared customs procedures, and the duties on them have been paid. In other words, Members are prevented from subjecting imported products to domestic rules or regulations which do not apply to like domestic products.

1.1 Adoption of "Substantially the same Duties and Other Regulations of Commerce"

The requirement that parties to a customs union should adopt "substantially the same duties and other regulations of commerce" marks the distinction between customs unions and free trade areas; in a free trade area, the constituent territories are obliged to eliminate duties and other restrictive regulations of commerce only on trade among themselves. In other words, each constituent member of a free trade area has the right to retain its external tariffs on the trade on third countries. This requirement has not proved controversial in practice, as parties to customs unions have, for practical reasons, adopted a common external tariff in their trade with third countries. Should they not maintain uniform rates, third countries would access the customs union through the member with the lowest tariff rates. While this could be combatted by the other participating countries, it would be costly and time-consuming.

1.2 General Incidence of Duties and Other Regulations of Commerce Should not be More Restrictive

Consistent with its objective to ensure that third countries do not incur any significant losses as a result of the formation of a customs union, Article XXIV:5(a) relevantly provides that, "the duties and other regulations of commerce imposed at the institution of any such union...shall not on the whole be higher or more restrictive than the general incidence of the duties and regulations of commerce applicable in the constituent territories prior to the formation of such a union". This provision generated a lot of debate before the Uruguay Round as to its proper scope. At the heart of the dispute surrounding the interpretation of this requirement is how to calculate the general incidence of duties and other regulations of commerce and make the determination whether they are on the whole higher or more restrictive.

According to the Understanding on the Interpretation of Article XXIV, which was adopted during the Uruguay Round, the assessment shall be based upon an overall assessment of weighted average tariff rates and of *customs duties* collected. It further provides that the assessment shall be based on import statistics for a previous period to be supplied by the customs union, on a tariff line basis and in values and quantities, broken down by WTO country of origin.[25] Before the Understanding went into force, it had been suggested that a simple average of pre-customs union tariffs was sufficient

---

25 See paragraph 2 of the Understanding on the Interpretation of Article XXIV.

for purposes of the Article, and that the benchmark tariff rate to be taken into account was the bound rate as opposed to the duty actually applied.[26]

If in the process of adjusting its tariff schedule to conform to the common external tariff, a participating country increases the level of its former tariffs on some products, the customs union would be liable to provide compensation to the country whose trading interests have been affected by such a measure, unless the increases are offset by decreases in duties previously imposed on the same product by the other parties to the trading arrangement. Although parties to a free-trade area are not obliged to have a CET, there is a similar requirement against increasing tariffs and making other regulations of commerce more restrictive.[27]

1.3 The Substantially All Trade Requirement

Parties to a customs union or a free-trade area are obliged to eliminate "duties and other restrictive regulations...with respect to substantially all the trade between the constituent territories of the union or at least with respect to substantially all trade in products originating in such territories".[28] The purpose of this requirement is said to be a "public choice one": it is an attempt to ensure that participants in regional liberalisation efforts go all the way.[29] It is as such designed to constrain the ability of participating countries to violate their MFN obligations selectively. Generally, customs unions and free trade areas are thought to be welfare-enhancing, while preferential trading arrangements, in which only a few sectors are liberalized, are generally perceived to be protectionist and not in the interest of the multilateral trading system. In his seminal work on customs unions, Jacob Viner introduced the terms "trade-creation" and "trade-diversion". Trade creation, according to his theory, was likely to occur if members of a regional trading arrangement substantially liberalised their economies by lowering all barriers to trade. On the contrary, if there was liberalisation in a few sectors only, there was the likelihood of trade diversion resulting from the trading arrangement.[30]

---

[26] Dam Kenneth, *The GATT: Law and International Economic Organization* (Chicago: University of Chicago Press; 1970) p277.
[27] See Article XXIV:6 of GATT 1994, and paragraphs 5 and 6 of the Understanding on the Interpretation of Article XXIV.
[28] See Article XXIV:8 of GATT 1994.
[29] Hoekman Bernard,"Trade Laws and Institutions: Good Practices and the World Trade Organisation" (Washington: World Bank Discussion Paper No. 282; 1995) p51.
[30] Viner Jacob, *The Customs Union Issue*, (New York: Carnegie Endowment for International Peace; 1950) pp41-56.

The question which has sharply divided trade ambassadors, lawyers and economists is how much liberalisation should occur before the constituent territories could be considered to have satisfied the test in Article XXIV:8. Two distinct schools of thought have emerged in relation to the proper interpretation of the Article. According to one school of thought, the test requires a quantitative analysis to be undertaken to assess the degree of liberalisation. In other words, if the volume of trade between the constituent territories is substantial, then the arrangement would be consistent with the terms of the Article.

Disagreement, however, exists as to which percentage of trade should be liberalised. In the examination of the Treaty Establishing the European Economic Community, some members of the Working Party expressed the view that the test would be satisfied, if the volume of liberalised trade reached 80% of total trade. The majority dissented from that view. The other school of thought is of the view that the Article also requires a qualitative analysis to be undertaken to assess the degree of liberalisation.[31] Put simply, no major sector of economic activity was to be excluded from the coverage of the agreement establishing the customs union or the free-trade area. On this view, it would mean that most regional integration arrangements that are currently in force would be inconsistent with Article XXIV, as the agricultural sector is usually exempted from the ambit of the agreements. The Working Party established to examine the Agreement establishing the European Free Trade Area (EFTA) made it quite clear that the "substantiality" test requires both quantitative and qualitative analyses to be undertaken.[32]

This view that no major sector of economic activity should be excluded seems to have been implicitly endorsed by the Understanding on the Interpretation of Article XXIV, which provides in its preamble that "Recognizing also that such contribution is increased if the elimination between the constituent territories of duties and other restrictive regulations extends to all trade, and diminished if any major sector of trade is excluded".

1.4 Interim Agreements for the formation of Customs Unions and Free Trade Areas

Parties to interim agreements for customs unions or free-trade areas are obliged to phase out barriers to trade among themselves within a reasonable

---

[31] See GATT, *Basic Instruments and Selected Documents* (BISD)1958 Sixth Supplement, para 34 at p.100.
[32] See GATT, *Basic Instruments and Selected Documents* (BISD)1961 Ninth Supplement, para 49 at p84.

period of time. To ensure that Members do not renege on their commitments, Article XXIV:5(c) of GATT 1994 obliges them to annex a "plan and schedule" to their interim agreement for the creation of a customs union or a free trade area indicating when the barriers to their trade will be removed.

In the past, the word "reasonable" provoked a lot of controversy. The Understanding resolves this issue by providing that the "reasonable length of time...should exceed ten years only in exceptional cases."

1.5 Procedural-Notification Requirement

A reading of paragraph 7(a) of Article XXIV would seem to indicate that the parties to the agreements should notify their agreements before implementing them. If the Members are not given the opportunity to examine the agreements before they are implemented, it is hard to imagine how they can fulfil their mandate of making "such reports and recommendations to the...parties as they deem appropriate". Of what use will the reports and recommendations of Members be if the parties to the regional integration agreement have already implemented their agreement?

Notwithstanding the logic underlying the requirement in paragraph 7(a), most agreements are still implemented before they are notified to the WTO. Several reasons have been proffered as to why it is impractical to meet this condition. It has been suggested that because agreements signed by governments often require legislative or popular approval (for example, by a referendum), if notification occurred at a point prior to entry into force, the contracting parties would, in some cases, review agreements which were eventually rejected by one or more of the countries involved. Alternatively, if agreements are examined only after a protracted and perhaps difficult process of domestic legislative approval, the prospect of amending an agreement to reflect the concerns of WTO Members presents its own difficulties.

The Understanding did not tackle this issue, but it is one of the systemic issues being considered by the Committee on Regional Trade Agreements.

2 Agreements Notified Under the Enabling Clause

The Decision of the CONTRACTING PARTIES on *Differential and More Favourable Treatment, Reciprocity and Fuller Participation of Developing Countries*, otherwise known as the Enabling Clause, emerged from the Tokyo Round of Multilateral Trade Negotiations. This clause basically permits developed countries to accord differential and more favourable treatment to developing countries, without according such treatment to other contracting parties. In other words, it provides legal cover for, most notably, trade concessions granted to developing countries under the Generalised System of Preferences (GAP) of 25 June 1971, by waiving the provisions of

Article I in its application to developing countries. Paragraph 2(c) of the clause extends such treatment to regional or global arrangements entered into by developing countries for the mutual reduction or elimination of tariffs and non-tariff measures.

Before the enactment of the "Enabling Clause", developing countries used to invoke Part IV of the General Agreement to enter into such preferential trading arrangements. The enactment of the Enabling Clause in November 1979, however, provided developing countries with a permanent legal basis for forming preferential trading arrangements. The members of ASEAN, which had, for example, notified their preferential trading arrangement under Part IV in 1978, re-notified their agreement under the "Enabling Clause".

2.1 Requirements under the Enabling Clause

Developing countries wishing to invoke the "Enabling Clause" to form preferential trading arrangements are required to comply with a limited number of conditions. The first is that the arrangement should be designed to facilitate and promote the trade of developing countries and not to raise barriers to or create undue difficulties for the trade of any other contracting parties. This requirement parallels that spelt out in paragraph 4 of Article XXIV of the General Agreement. Thus, from the view-point of the WTO, regional trading arrangements entered into by developing countries are acceptable, so far as the intention of the parties is to increase trade between themselves, and not to restrict the trade of third countries through the pursuit of discriminatory trade policies. If trade is not created but diverted from countries which are much more competitive, then regional trading blocs would cease to be welfare-enhancing and become tools for discriminating against other Members of WTO.

The Enabling Clause obliges developing countries entering into preferential trading arrangements to reduce both tariffs and non-tariff barriers to the trade of partner countries. Whereas it provides guidance on how non-tariff barriers may be reduced or eliminated, it does not do the same for tariffs.[33] Unlike Article XXIV, developing countries are not expected to eliminate duties and other regulations of commerce on substantially all their trade. In other words, the provisions of the Enabling Clause would appear to allow the exchange of a few tariff preferences.

This provision has raised a broader issue in the WTO and that is if developing countries such as ECOWAS member states can rely on the provisions

---

[33] WTO Secretariat, *Regionalism and the World Trading System*, (Geneva: WTO; April 1995) p18.

of the Enabling Clause to form a customs union or a free trade area. The view of some developed Members of the WTO is that where the arrangement is quite significant such as in the case of a customs union or a free trade area, then the appropriate legal basis is Article XXIV. Developing countries disagree and have insisted on their right to rely on the provisions of the Enabling Clause to form any conceivable regional trading arrangement. COMESA, which intends to establish a common market among the countries of Eastern and Southern African states was, for example, notified pursuant to the Enabling Clause.

3 Agreements Notified Under Article XXV (Waivers)

Article XXV allowed contracting parties to the GATT (i.e., WTO Members) to obtain a waiver from the CONTRACTING PARTIES (i.e., the WTO General Council), if they were incapable of discharging their obligations under the General Agreement.[34] It could, therefore, be invoked by Members who, in breach of Article I of the General Agreement, wanted to enter into preferential trading arrangements. A waiver to enter into a regional trading arrangement would typically be requested if the parties to the arrangement could not comply with the terms of Article XXIV or the Enabling Clause. In the first two decades of GATT, a number of developed countries invoked it to form preferential trading arrangements. In 1948, France requested and obtained a waiver for a proposed customs union with Italy, which was not at that time a member of the GATT. The founding members of the European Coal and Steel Community (Belgium, Netherlands, Luxembourg, Germany, France and Italy) obtained a waiver for their agreement on free-trade in coal and steel. The limited product coverage of the agreement meant that they could not invoke Article XXIV of the General Agreement. Similarly, the United States and Canada had to obtain a waiver for their agreement on free-trade in automobiles in 1965.

However, out of the thirty or so waivers which have been granted for the formation of regional trading arrangements, a majority have involved preferences granted by developed countries to developing countries on a non-reciprocal basis. Most of such agreements drew inspiration from Part IV of the General Agreement which is intended to aid the development of the

---

[34] Article IX:3 of the WTO Agreement which has superseded Article XXV, provides that "in exceptional circumstances, the Ministerial Conference may decide to waive an obligation imposed on a member by this Agreement or any of the Multilateral Trade Agreements, provided that any such decision shall be taken by three fourths of the Members unless otherwise provided for in this paragraph....".

poorer countries of the GATT. Examples of non-reciprocal agreements are the Australian preferences to products originating in Papua New Guinea (1953), Canada's preferences to imports from the Caribbean Basin (1968) and the United States preferences granted to Caribbean countries under the Caribbean Basin Economic Recovery Act (1985). Recent waivers granted by the CONTRACTING PARTIES include the preferences granted by the United States under the Andean Trade Preference Act in 1992 and those granted by the European Union under the Lomé Convention to countries belonging to the African-Caribbean and Pacific group (ACP) in 1994.[35]

With the entry into force of the Understanding in Respect of Waivers of Obligations under the General Agreement on Tariffs and Trade, it is quite doubtful if Members of the WTO will be able to obtain a waiver to enter into a preferential arrangement very easily. Paragraph 1 of the Understanding provides that "a request for a waiver or for an extension of an existing waiver shall describe the measures which the Member proposes to take, the specific policy objectives which the Member seeks to pursue and the reasons which prevent the Member from achieving its policy objectives by measures consistent with its obligations under GATT 1994". Paragraph 2 of the Understanding tightens the restrictions by providing that all waivers existing as at the time the WTO Agreement went into force (I January 1995) shall lapse on that day or not later than two years, unless extended by the CONTRACTING PARTIES in accordance with the provisions of Article IX of the WTO Agreement.

4. Agreements Notified Under Article V of GATS

The counterpart of Article XXIV of GATT 1994 is Article V under the GATS. Before the entry into force of the WTO Agreement, the services component of regional trading arrangements were not examined, as Article XXIV deals exclusively with trade in goods. Given the increasing share of services in world trade, it was thought this was a serious defect of the GATT system, as it virtually gave parties to a regional trade arrangement a *carte blanche* to pursue discriminatory policies in the field of services.

The provisions of Article V of the GATS mirror those of Article XXIV, although they do not utilise the expressions customs unions or free trade areas. It uses the term economic integration instead, reflecting the fact that the

---

[35] The European Union did not obtain a waiver for the first three Lomé Conventions. It was not until the legal basis of the Convention was challenged and found to be inconsistent with Article I of the GATT that the signatory states decided to obtain a waiver for the fourth Lomé Convention.

GATS covers all four modes of delivery. The guiding principle is set out in Article V:4 which provides that any economic integration agreement "shall be designed to facilitate trade between the parties to the agreement and shall not in respect of any Member outside the agreement raise the overall level of barriers to trade in services within the respective sectors or subsectors compared to the level applicable prior to such an arrangement". Thus, from the view point of the WTO, economic integration agreements entered into by Members are, in principle, acceptable if the intention of the parties to the agreement is to liberalise at a pace faster than they would do in the multilateral context, and not as a medium to pursue discriminatory policies.

With its emphasis on "respective sectors or subsectors", it is generally thought that Article V offers more protection for non-participating countries than in Article XXIV. It has been suggested that as a result of the more desegregated (i.e. sub-sectoral) focus taken in Article V, a WTO Member cannot argue – in contrast to GATT 1994 – that the average level or "general incidence" of protection has not changed, regardless of what might occur at the level of individual products (sub-sectors).[36]

Like Article XXIV, Article V of the GATS makes provision for non-participating members to be compensated, if the participants of an economic integration withdraw or modify specific market access and/or national treatment commitments. Before amending their previously negotiated concessions, the parties to the agreement are required to notify the Council for Trade in Services of their intention at least three months before implementing the proposed amendments. They will then be obliged to hold consultations with the view of compensating *any* Member whose interests would be negatively affected by proposed amendments to the concessions. This provision is broader than its equivalent under the GATT, where compensation negotiations under Article XXVIII are required to be held with countries with initial negotiating rights and those with a principal supplying interest. The effect of such a rule is to deny compensation to smaller countries whose market shares are usually minuscule. Another difference between the provisions of Article V and Article XXIV is that, under the former, it is explicitly provided in Article XXI:2(b) that "compensatory adjustments shall be made on an MFN basis". Furthermore, under Article V, there is no provision which entitles the parties to claim credit for relaxing conditions governing a particular sector or sub-sector. It should be added that the GATS allows questions relating to compensation to be submitted to binding arbitration. The other conditions are as follows:

---

[36] Hoekman, *supra* note 29 at p54.

4.1. Substantial Sectoral Coverage

Like Article XXIV:8, Article V:1(a) of the GATS requires economic integration agreements to have "substantial sectoral coverage", which should be understood in terms of the "number of sectors, volume of trade and modes of supply". An agreement would not be consistent with the terms of Article V, if it provides for the *a priori* exclusion of one of the modes of supply. The reason behind this rule is to prevent Members from entering into narrow discriminatory agreements, which are generally thought not to be welfare-enhancing from the view point of the multilateral trading system. Members wishing to form an economic integration must be prepared to go beyond the liberalization commitments under the GATS, if their agreement is to conform to the provisions of Article V.

Article V:1(b) underscores this point by providing that the agreement should "provide for the absence or elimination of substantially all discrimination...between or among the parties, in the sectors covered under subparagraph(a) through [the] elimination of existing discriminatory measures, *and/or* prohibition of new or more discriminatory measures". It would, however, appear that Article V:1 is limited in its terms, when a comparison is made with the provisions of Article XXIV:8 of GATT 1994, which obliges Members to eliminate duties and other regulations on substantially all trade, which on one view means that no major sector of economic activity should be excluded from the coverage of the agreement. Under the GATS, there is no such requirement, as the parties are only required to eliminate existing restrictions, or in the alternative they can maintain the existing restrictions, provided they do not introduce new ones or make the existing ones more restrictive.[37]

4.2. Interim Agreements for the formation of Economic Integration Agreements

Parties to interim agreements are obliged under Article V:7(b) to submit periodic reports on the state of implementation of their agreements to the Council of Trade in Services (CTS). Unlike Article XXIV, there is no requirement that the parties should annex a plan and schedule nor an indicative time-frame, at the end of which the parties should have eliminated substantially all the restrictions they were maintaining.

---

[37] *Ibid.*

4.3. Procedural-Notification Requirement

A reading of paragraph 7(a) of Article V requires parties to economic integration agreements to promptly notify such agreements, any enlargement or modification to the CTS. It is not clear whether the Article expects Members to notify the Agreement or proposed changes before implementation.

It should be noted that following a decision of the General Council of the WTO in February 1996, all regional trading arrangements, whether notified to the CTG, CTS or the CTD, are to be examined by the Committee on Regional Trading Arrangements (CRTA) with a view to evaluating their consistency with the relevant multilateral rules. The decision whether an agreement has to be examined by the CRTA still rests with the three principal bodies, namely the CTG, CTS and the CTD.

IV. ANALYSIS OF THE RELEVANT TRADE PROVISIONS IN THE ECOWAS TREATY

One of the fundamental objectives of the ECOWAS treaty is the establishment of an economic union among countries in the West African sub-region. To that end, Article 3.2 of the revised treaty provides for the establishment of a common market through: "(i) the liberalisation of trade by the abolition, among Member States, of customs duties levied on imports and exports, and the abolition, among Member States, of non-tariff barriers in order to establish a free-trade area at the Community level; (ii) the adoption of a common external tariff and a common trade policy vis-à-vis third countries; (iii) the removal, between Member States, of obstacles to the free movement of persons, goods, services and capital, and to the right of residence and establishment; ...[and] the establishment of an economic union through the adoption of common policies in the economic, financial, social and cultural sectors, and the creation of a monetary union."

The original ECOWAS treaty envisaged the creation of a customs union within fifteen years from the date of the definitive entry into force of the treaty. As far as the elimination of tariff barriers were concerned, this objective was to be achieved in three stages: (i) the first two years were to be devoted to consolidating import duties applicable within the region; (ii) the following eight years were to be used to progressively reduce and eliminate import duties; and (iii) the last five years were to be devoted to establishing the common external tariff in respect of imported products from non-participating countries. Although the ECOWAS treaty was signed in May 1975, the trade provisions did not formally go into effect until 1977 when the attached trade protocols were implemented following their ratification by the necessary number of member states in November 1976.

1 Implementation of the Provisions of the Treaty

Following the ratification of the trade protocols, the ECOWAS Authority at its May 1979 meeting adopted decision A/DEC.8/5/79 consolidating over a two-year period all tariff and non-tariff barriers facing products produced and traded in the Community. During this period, member states were obliged not to increase existing tariff and non-tariff barriers or introduce new barriers to tradeable goods of Community origin. The same prohibition applied to intra-ECOWAS payment transactions. The next trade liberalising initiative of importance went into force in 1981 and related to the exemption of unprocessed goods and traditional handicrafts from all tariff and non-tariff barriers (quantitative restrictions).[38] While these initiatives were quite important, they did not have any significant impact on intra-Community trade.

The next important trade liberalising initiative with potential impact on intra-Community trade was adopted by the ECOWAS Authority in May 1980. Decision A/DEC.18/5/80 laid down a scheme for the gradual liberalisation of trade in industrial products of community origin within four years. The programme was supposed to have taken effect on 28 May 1981, but was postponed several times and amended. A revised programme was adopted by the Authority in May 1983 but did not go into effect until 1 January 1990. A notable feature of the revised programme was its flexibility; it initially provided for the liberalisation of trade in respect of twenty-five products from eight member states. The list of products is to be expanded to cover most industrial products with the passage of time.

Taking into account the level of development of each of the constituent members, the programme divided the member states into three groups. Total liberalisation in respect of industrial products was to be achieved by the year 2000, thus 10 years from the date of launching the scheme. The programme was subsequently amended in 1992 to quicken the pace of liberalisation. Countries falling within Group III, namely Côte d'Ivoire, Ghana, Nigeria and Senegal are expected to eliminate tariffs on all industrial products within six years; those falling under Group II (Benin, Guinea, Liberia, Sierra Leone and Togo) are expected to phase out tariffs within eight years, while countries falling under Group I (Burkina Faso, Cape Verde, Gambia, Guinea-Bissau, Mali, Mauritania and Niger) are expected to eliminate all tariffs within ten years. Regarding the establishment of a common external tariff, preparatory work began in 1993, with the objective of having it in place within five years of the elimination of all barriers to internal trade.

---

[38] see ECOWAS Council of Ministers Decision C/DEC.8/11/79 adopted in November 1979 and ECOWAS Authority Decision A/DEC.1/5/81 adopted in May 1981.

2 Consistency of the ECOWAS Trade Provisions with WTO rules

Before examining the consistency of the relevant trade provisions of the revised ECOWAS treaty with WTO rules, a preliminary decision should be made and that is whether the examination should be carried out under the provisions of the Enabling Clause or under Article XXIV of GATT 1994. A persuasive argument could be made that since all the constituent members of ECOWAS are developing countries, then the benchmark against which the agreement should be examined for its consistency is the Enabling Clause. On the other hand, since it is the objective of the member states to establish an economic union, it is possible that some members of the WTO would insist on the agreement being examined under other relevant provisions of the WTO, in particular Article XXIV of GATT 1994. As it is difficult to predict the reaction of Members of the WTO, it might be safer for the analysis to be carried out under Article XXIV, as an agreement which complies with the provisions of Article XXIV would, in almost all cases, also be consistent with the provisions of the Enabling Clause. The reverse is, however, not always true. Moreover, should ECOWAS meet the test laid down in Article XXIV, it would have created the conditions which should, in principle, create trade for the benefit of the signatory states and also for third countries. If Article XXIV is chosen as the most appropriate yardstick, then the following considerations are relevant.

2.1 Does the ECOWAS treaty meet the substantially all trade requirement

As previously noted, one of the most important requirements of Article XXIV of GATT 1994 is that customs union and free trade agreements should cover substantially all the trade between the constituent parties. In other words, the agreement should cover as many economic sectors as possible, and also abolish almost all tariff and non tariff barriers to intra-Community trade. It would appear that the ECOWAS treaty meets these requirements, as it is provided in Article 35 that "[c]ustoms duties or other charges with equivalent effect on Community originating imports shall be eliminated. Quota, quantitative restrictions or prohibitions and administrative obstacles to trade...shall also be removed."

The language used is much clearer than the one used in Article XXIV:8 and is not likely to generate any conflicts as the latter has done. Under the terms of Article XXIV:8, parties to a free-trade area or a customs union are expected to "eliminate duties and other restrictive regulations of commerce (except, where necessary, those permitted under Articles XI, XII, XIII...with respect to substantially all the trade between the constituent territories of the union." The proper interpretation of the phrase "substantially all the trade" and whether or not there is an obligation on parties to eliminate quotas and quantitative restrictions on the products of partner countries have generated a lot of discussion among WTO Members and legal scholars. The ECOWAS treaty avoids these loopholes by specifying clearly that quotas, quantitative restrictions and administrative obstacles are to be eliminated by the parties. Instead of using the phrase "substantially all the trade" the ECOWAS treaty provides in Article 36 that all duties and other charges of equivalent effect to be eliminated except those being applied by a member state consistently with the terms of Article 40 of the treaty.[39]

It is thus correct to assert that the obligations under the ECOWAS treaty are much broader than those under the WTO, as it is recognised that WTO Members entering into customs unions or free trade agreements are not obliged to eliminate all barriers to intra-Community trade. In *Turkey – Restrictions on Imports of Textile and Clothing Products*, the Appellate Body held that "substantially all the trade" is something considerably more than merely *some* of the trade" and that parties to a customs union had "some flexibility" when liberalising their internal trade.[40]

2.2 Adoption of "Substantially the same Duties and Other Regulations of Commerce"

While the member states of ECOWAS have yet to apply a common external tariff in their trade with third countries, it is clear that the treaty mandates its adoption within five years after the removal of internal barriers to trade. As provided in Article 37 of the treaty, the member states "agree to the gradual establishment of a common external tariff in respect of all goods imported into the member states from third countries in accordance with a schedule to be recommended by the Trade, Customs, Taxation, Statistics, Money and Payments Commission." To facilitate the achievement of this objective, Article 37.3 provides that member states "undertake to apply the common Customs nomenclature and Customs statistical nomenclature adopted by Council."

While there is no obligation on WTO Members entering into customs unions to immediately apply "substantially the same duties and other regulations of commerce... to the trade of [third countries], there is the obligation that the transitional period for complying with the relevant WTO rules should not usually exceed ten years. Thus, given the possibility that the com-

---

39 Article 40 of the ECOWAS treaty allows member states which have a contractual obligation to maintain otherwise inconsistent internal taxes or charges of equivalent effect on condition that they "shall not extend or renew" it after the expiration of the contract."

40 WT/DS34/AB/R; adopted by the DSB on 19 November 1999, para 48 at p12.

mon external tariff will be operational after fifteen years from the date the trade liberalisation scheme went into force, the ECOWAS treaty could theoretically be said to be in breach of paragraph 3 of the Understanding on the Interpretation of Article XXIV of GATT 1994. However, as foreseen in this paragraph, it is possible for Members to seek an extension of the 10-year period.

2.3 General Incidence of Duties and Other Regulations of Commerce Should not be More Restrictive

As previously mentioned, this is one of the most important obligations imposed on WTO Members entering into customs union or free trade agreements. As noted in a communication from Australia:

> "GATT Article XXIV:5 is concerned with the relationship of the parties to customs unions and free-trade areas with non-members. It is based on four assumptions. The first, an obvious one, is that there is a difference between free-trade areas and customs unions. Second, it assumes that each constituting party maintained a set of duties and other regulations of commerce before the customs union or free-trade area entered into force. Third, it accepts that the details of their incidence on third countries may be varied in the negotiations leading to the formation of the new arrangement. Fourth, it insists that on the whole, the duties and other regulations applied against non-parties must be no higher or more restrictive than they were before the arrangement was put in place".[41]

The ECOWAS treaty does not give any indication as to how this obligation would be met. It should become clearer after the implementation of the common external tariff within five years after the dismantling of barriers to internal trade. Under WTO rules, compensation has to be provided to third parties if the general incidence of duties and other regulations of commerce is higher than its pre-union level. Given the important role which could be played by the common external tariff in shaping the regional economy, it is advised that ECOWAS member states adopt a flexible approach bearing in mind that empirical studies have proved that the adoption of low tariffs on products originating in third countries can provide an important boost to the regional economy and make it more dynamic. Competition from third countries will encourage regional firms to streamline their operations and

---

[41] See WTO Document WT/REG/W/25; 1 April 1998

become more efficient. This could lead to high quality goods being produced and sold at competitive prices. Consumers will also have a broad range of goods to choose from and manufacturers could also have access to cheaper raw materials and other inputs.

2.4 Procedural-Notification Requirement

As of the time of writing, the ECOWAS treaty had not been notified to the WTO. This is clearly a breach of Article XXIV:7(a) of GATT 1994 and should be rectified as soon as possible. The fact that two of the member states are not signatories to the WTO Agreement is no reason for delaying notification of the agreement. Under normal circumstances, the agreement should have been notified to the GATT before its implementation. Trade agreements entered into between WTO members and non-members are considered under the provisions of Article XXIV:10 of GATT 1994. Transparency is one of the most important principles underpinning the multilateral trading system and should be adhered to by all Members of the WTO.

The lack of notification of the agreement has deprived the ECOWAS member states of the opportunity of knowing which provisions should be reinforced so as to facilitate the achievement of their objectives. Notification of an agreement to the WTO for examination brings with it some distinct advantages. First, to avoid trenchant criticism from Members of the WTO, parties to regional trading agreements are more likely to ensure that their agreement does not contain provisions which flagrantly contradict WTO rules. Secondly, during examinations of agreements, Members of the WTO which are parties to such agreements could share their experiences and provide useful advice which could guide countries with no previous or little experience with regional integration. Thirdly, notifying a regional trade agreement to the WTO serves the useful purpose of advertising to the world at large the existence of the agreement, which could facilitate trade with the outside world and encourage investment flows to the region.

The omission to notify the ECOWAS treaty to the WTO will not insulate the member states from legal action under the WTO Agreement, as it is now firmly established that any member of the WTO could invoke the Dispute Settlement Understanding "with respect to any matters arising from the application of those provisions of Article XXIV relating to customs unions, free trade areas or interim agreements leading to the formation of a customs union or free-trade area."[42]

---

42 Paragraph 12 of the Understanding on the Interpretation of Article XXIV of GATT 1994.

V. CONCLUSION

The ECOWAS treaty is primarily a regional economic agreement which seeks to facilitate the integration of the economies in the West African sub-region. The treaty was signed by West African leaders in May 1975 to overcome the disadvantages which are faced by small economies. It was hoped that the agreement would enable them to achieve economies of scale and eventually economic development. However, ECOWAS has not achieved much in the field of trade and investment liberalisation. A number of reasons account for the dismal performance of the organisation. These include the lack of an integration culture in the sub-region, the lack of political commitment on the part of the region's political leaders, linguistic and cultural barriers and the very fragile state of the economies in the sub-region. The political leaders of the sub-region have renewed their commitment to the organisation by adopting the revised ECOWAS treaty in 1993. While this treaty is a vast improvement on the original one, much more needs to be done to ensure that the organisation plays its crucial role in facilitating the integration of the economies of the sub-region.

Although thirteen out of the fifteen member states of ECOWAS are WTO members, the agreement has not been notified to the WTO for examination of its consistency with the multilateral trade rules. While it could be argued that the ECOWAS treaty should be examined under the provisions of the Enabling Clause because of the fact that all the signatory states are developing countries, it is suggested that the assessment should be made under the provisions of Article XXIV, which is much broader in scope. Examining the consistency of the agreement under the provisions of Article XXIV has two distinct advantages. First, it would obviate the discussion as to whether or not developing country Members could rely on the Enabling Clause to conclude far-reaching agreements such as customs unions or free trade agreements. Second, and most importantly, an agreement which complies with the conditions specified in Article XXIV, would have, in principle, created the conditions which would facilitate trade among the constituent territories as well as with third countries.

While the ECOWAS treaty conforms to the WTO requirements in many respects, its implementation could reveal some shortcomings. It is suggested that the member states should implement the common external tariff as soon as possible and also notify the agreement to the WTO for examination. Member states of ECOWAS should resist the temptation of adopting protectionist policies, as such policies constrain their abilities to derive significant benefits from international trade, especially after the implementation of the Uruguay Round Agreements. Empirical studies indicate that the more open a regional trade arrangement is, the more benefits that would accrue to its member states. The adoption of outward-oriented policies by ECOWAS members would not only improve their competitiveness in terms of effective domestic resource allocation, but also would enhance their abilities to attract foreign direct investment into the sectors in which they have a comparative advantage.

In summary, ECOWAS could play a critical role in reversing the marginalisation of the West African sub-region in the multilateral trading system and the global economy, if the appropriate policies are pursued by the member states. Sacrifices should be made by all the member states, which seem to be pre-occupied with short-term goals. All ECOWAS protocols and decisions should be faithfully implemented on time by the member states and revised as and when necessary to take into account relevant trends and experiences.

THE TREATY FOR THE ESTABLISHMENT OF THE NEW EAST AFRICAN COMMUNITY: AN OVERVIEW

Wilbert T.K. Kaahwa*

I. INTRODUCTION

The signing of the Treaty for the Establishment of the East African Community in Arusha, Tanzania on November 30th, 1999 was a culmination of six years of committed efforts by the East African Co-operation Member States of Kenya, Uganda and the United Republic of Tanzania in re-kindling their longtested co-operation.[1]

Upon its establishment in 1993, a Permanent Tripartite Commission for East African Co-operation was mandated to inter alia, identify areas of co-operation and to propose the most appropriate regional arrangement for these states. The process of identifying areas of co-operation got impetus with the launching, in 1997, of the East African Co-operation Development Strategy (1997-2000). The Agreement Establishing the Permanent Tripartite Commission together with the Development Strategy have hitherto been the key blueprints of the region's integration process.

In April 1997, the East African Co-operation Summit of Heads of State directed that in order to give more substance to, and widen the scope of co-operation, that Agreement should be upgraded into a Treaty for Co-operation. Consequently, a Treaty-making process, involving experts from the three Member States' governments, the Secretariat of the Commission for East African Co-operation and the general public, was embarked upon. The process was based on negotiation, pre-negotiation drafting and the tapping of views from the peoples of East Africa through the mass media and other communicative methods. It was, for purposes of treaty-making, quite a unique process. It started with an outline of the proposed content prepared

---

*   Legal Counsel, Secretariat of the Commission for East African Cooperation.
1   East African Co-operation is an inter-governmental arrangement established in 1993 to steer the newly rekindled spirit of co-operation between the Republic of Kenya, the Republic of Uganda and the United Republic of Tanzania

by the Secretariat. The outline, after having been considered by the Member States, gave rise to an initial draft prepared by the Secretariat and a Consultant. It is this draft that was used as a working text for negotiations by the governments and in respect of which, through seminars, workshops and expression of views in writing, contribution by the public was catered for. The process ended with the signing of the Treaty.

The Treaty seeks to strengthen the Member States' economic, social, cultural, political and other ties for their fast balanced and sustainable development by the establishment of an East African Community.[2] It is, to that extent, designed to achieve clear economic and geo-political objectives principally through the enhancement of co-operation in identified key areas.

Kenya, Tanzania and Uganda have a lot of experience in matters of integration having been partners in the defunct East African Community. The three states are members of the Common Market for Eastern and Southern Africa (COMESA), Kenya and Uganda are members of the Inter-Governmental Authority on Development (IGAD) while Tanzania is a member of the Southern Africa Development Community (SADC).

Against that background, this overview addresses the following four basic attributes of the Treaty:
– Integration factors underlying the Treaty;
– The Legal and Organisational framework created by the Treaty;
– Areas of Co-operation provided for in the Treaty;
– Organs and Institutions of the Community; and
– Operationalisation of the Treaty.

II. INTEGRATION FACTORS UNDERLYING THE TREATY

Within East African Co-operation it has been realised that the following broadly categorised basic factors must obtain in order for the Member States to effectively integrate:

1. Formative Factors

Successful integration requires a positive environment characterised by among other factors, a strong political will and commitment and the existence of viable regional structures. The Treaty is anchored on the existence of these factors which find expression in its several provisions.

---

[2] Preamble.

Among the three states such basic factors do obtain. Close social, cultural, economic and formal constitutional integration in East Africa is not a new phenomenon. Twenty years after the dissolution of the last scheme of East African integration, a scheme which had spanned over fifty years, it is not at all surprising, that the three states which are geographically contiguous, whose populations have from time immemorial been socially and culturally inter-related, and which had enjoyed economic integration and uniquely, joint common services such as railways, harbours, post and telecommunication services common customs exercise and income tax services, and a common legislative arrangement, should now after reflection, seek a revival of the past, but one which takes into account present realities.

2. Implementation Principles and Strategies

Given the nature of the three states' levels of economic development implementation of co-operation projects and programmes has to be based on such principles as the Principle of Asymmetry, the Principle of Complementarity, the Principle of Variable Geometry and the Principle of Subsidiarity.[3]

3. Consolidation and Development Factors

It is the general projection of the Treaty that as the integration process takes root, the following key consolidation factors, among others, have to be concurrently addressed.

(a) Decision-making/considerations

In order to obviate problems in decision-making at various levels, the Treaty provides for such time frames as would accommodate East African Community Partner States in the accomplishment of certain targets e.g. the progressive establishment of a Customs Union and the establishment of a Common Market.[4] From a general point of view, a mechanism for decision-

---

[3] The Treaty in its Article 1 defines these principles as follows:

"principle of asymmetry" is the principle which addresses variances in the implementation of measures in an economic integration process for purposes of achieving a common objective;

"principle of complementarity" is the principle which defines the extent to which economic variables support each other in economic activity;

"principle of subsidiarity" is a principle which emphasises multi-level participation of a wide range of participants in the process of economic integration;

"principle of variable geometry" is a principle of flexibility which allows for progression in co-operation among a sub-group of members in a larger integration scheme in a variety of areas and at different speeds.

[4] Articles 75, 76

making at regional level that emphasises consensus is also provided for in the Treaty.

b) Common Market Issues

In order to address initial matters relating to balanced/unbalanced development, trade balance/imbalance and the sharing of benefits and to avoid a "Stag Bull" syndrome, the Treaty provides that the establishment of the Common Market shall be progressive. This would allow for sufficient initial preparation.

Besides, provisions have been made for safeguard measures to assist any state that may be disadvantaged through the application of provisions relating to Co-operation in Trade Liberalisation and Development and Monetary and Financial Co-operation.[5]

c) Funding

The Treaty provides for the Partner States' joint funding of the budget of the Community. This will be through equal contributions.[6] Other sources of funding include receipts from regional and international donations and any other sources as may be determined by the Council of Ministers.[7]

Other resources of the Community shall include such extra budgetary resources as:

– grants, donations, funds for projects and programmes and technical assistance; and
– income earned from activities undertaken by the Community.[8]

As a legal entity, the Community should also be able to borrow externally in its own name.

4. Political and socio-economic convergence factors

Adequate provisions have been inserted in the Treaty to ensure that some kind of regional structural adjustment is undertaken in order to harmonise various economic structures with the ultimate objective of having political and socio-economic convergence.

Likewise provisions that promote the convergence of social policies regarding employment, social welfare, schemes, health, education, environment, women-in-development, human rights etc. have been incorporated.

---

[5] Articles 78, 88
[6] Article 132(4)
[7] *Ibid*
[8] Article 133

5. Private Sector Participation and Involvement

Throughout the Treaty-making process it was realised that on the basis of the need for people-driven and people-centred development, the peoples of East Africa should play an active role in determining the progress of the new Community.

This is pivoted on the premise that the role of Government in modern market-oriented economic integration processes should be that of a facilitator while the actors are the private sector and the civil society. To this extent the Treaty is designed to enable the private sector to fully participate and shape the processes of economic integration. It has, for example, provisions aimed at removing policies and regulations that impede cross-border investments and those which inhibit the free movement of the factors of production. It also seeks to enhance capacity building in the private sector in order to ensure that the building of the Community is, in the main, a process driven by the people and not restricted to governments.

III. THE LEGAL AND ORGANISATIONAL FRAMEWORK CREATED BY THE TREATY

The most significant attribute of the Treaty is the establishment of the East African Community. The Community is established in a manner reflective of intended systematic development of a Customs Union and a Common Market as transitional stages to and integral parts thereof, subsequently leading to a Monetary Union and to a Political Federation.[9]

The key features of the new international organisation are the following:

1. Membership

Initial membership comprises Kenya, Tanzania and Uganda.[10] It is, however, envisaged that any other country may apply to join, to participate in or to be associated with the Community.[11] In considering an application by a non-member country to become a member of, be associated with, or participate in any of the activities of the Community, the following factors shall be taken into account:[12]

---

[9] Preamble, Article 2(2)
[10] Article 3(1)
[11] Article 3(2)
[12] Article 3(3)

- acceptance of the Community as set out in the Treaty;
- adherence to universally acceptable principles of good governance, democracy, the rule of law, observance of human rights and social justice;
- potential contribution to the strengthening of integration within the East African region;
- geographical proximity to and inter-dependence between it and the Partner States;
- establishment and maintenance of a market driven economy; and
- social and economic policies being compatible with those of the Community.

These entry requirements are deliberately necessary to ensure that the long-range economic and geo-political interests of the founding members is not compromised by any new entrants.

The Treaty also envisages participation in the activities of the Community at Observer level by any non-member country, inter-governmental organisation or civil society organisation.[13]

2. Legal Capacity of the Community

The Treaty provides that the Community shall be a body corporate with perpetual succession. The Community, as a body corporate, shall have power to perform any of the functions conferred upon it by the Treaty and to do all things, including acquiring and managing property and borrowing, that are necessary or desirable for the performance of those functions.[14]

3. Objectives of the Community

The Community aims at widening and deepening co-operation among the three states through the development of policies and programmes in various fields for their mutual benefit with a view to achieving economic, social and political integration. The main aspiration is the creation of a bigger market in the region whose purposes will include attraction of investments, expansion of business, encouragement of competition and innovation and creation of employment.

In the fulfilment of these objectives, the Community shall ensure:
(a) the attainment of sustainable growth and development of the Partner States by the promotion of a more balanced and harmonious development of the Partner States;

---

[13] Article 3(5)
[14] Article 4

(b) the strengthening and consolidation of co-operation in agreed fields that would lead to equitable economic development within the Partner States and which would in turn, raise the standard of living and improve the quality of life of their populations;

(c) the promotion of sustainable utilisation of the natural resources of the Partner States and the taking of measures that would effectively protect the natural environment of the Partner States;

(d) the strengthening and consolidation of the long standing economic, social, cultural and traditional ties and associations between the peoples of the Partner States so as to promote a people-centred mutual development of these ties and associations;

(e) the mainstreaming of gender in all its endeavours and the enhancement of the role of women in cultural, social, political, economic and technological development;

(f) the promotion of peace, security and stability within, and good neighbourliness among the Partner States;

(g) the enhancement and strengthening of partnerships with the private sector and civil society in order to achieve sustainable socio-economic and political development; and

(h) the undertaking of such other activities calculated to further the aims and objectives of the Community, as the Partner States may from time to time decide to undertake in common.[15]

In short, the three Partner States agree to give up part of their sovereign rights in several spheres of activity including the political, economic, legal and socio-economic ones, in order to promote integration and economic development.

4. Principles of the Community

The fundamental principles that shall govern the achievement of the objectives of the Community shall include:

(a) mutual trust, political will and sovereign equality;

(b) peaceful co-existence and good neighbourliness;

(c) peaceful settlement of disputes;

(d) good governance including adherence to the principles of democracy, the rule of law, accountability, transparency, social justice, equal opportunities, gender equality, as well as the recognition, promotion and protection of human and peoples rights in accordance with the provisions of the African Charter on Human and Peoples' Rights;

---

[15] Article 5

(e) equitable distribution of benefits; and
(f) co-operation for mutual benefit.[16]

There is another set of principles that shall govern the practical achievement of the objectives of the Community. These, meant, to be operational, include:
(a) people-centred and market-driven co-operation;
(b) the provision by the Partner States of an adequate and appropriate enabling environment, such as conducive policies and basic infrastructure;
(c) the establishment of an export oriented economy for the Partner States in which there shall be free movement of goods, persons, labour, services, capital, information and technology;
(d) the principle of subsidiarity with emphasis on multi-level participation and the involvement of a wide range of stake- holders in the process of integration;
(e) the principle of variable geometry which allows for progression in co-operation among groups within the Community for wider integration schemes in various fields and at different speeds;
(f) the equitable distribution of benefits accruing or to be derived from the operations of the Community and measures to address economic imbalances that may arise from such operations;
(g) the principle of complementarity; and
(h) the principle of asymmetry.[17]

The Partner States further undertake to abide by the principles of good governance, including adherence to the principles of democracy, the rule of law, social justice and the maintenance of universally accepted standards of human rights.

5. Domestication of the Treaty by the Partner States

The Partner States shall:
(a) plan and direct their policies and resources with a view to creating conditions favourable for the development and achievement of the objectives of the Community;
(b) co-ordinate their economic and other policies to the extent necessary to achieve the objectives of the Community; and
(c) abstain from any measures likely to jeopardise the achievement of those objectives or the implementation of the provisions of the Treaty.[18]

---

[16] Article 6
[17] Article 7
[18] Article 8(1)

In this regard the Partner States will secure the enactment and effective implementation of such legislation as will domesticate the Treaty within their respective national jurisdictions. Accordingly Community organs, institutions and laws shall take precedence over similar national ones on matters pertaining to the implementation of the Treaty.[19]

6. Duration of the Treaty
The Treaty shall have perpetual duration.[20]

7. General provisions
The Treaty, like similar instruments has general, transitional and final provisions which address diverse matters including the following:
(a) Official language of the Community;[21]
(b) Status, Privileges and Immunities;[22]
(c) Transition and Transfer of Assets from the East African Co-operation to the East African Community;[23]
(d) Saving provisions;[24]
(e) Sanctions;[25]
(f) Cessation of Membership;[26] and
(g) Amendment of the Treaty.[27]

IV. AREAS OF CO-OPERATION PROVIDED FOR IN THE TREATY

The Treaty in an effort to avail a *modus operandi* for the achievement of the objectives of the Community provides for the establishment or enhancement of co-operation in the following broad areas:
– Trade Liberalisation and Development;
– Co-operation in Investment and Industrial Development;
– Co-operation in Monetary and Financial matters;
– The development of the Infrastructure and Services;

---

[19] Article 8(2), (3), (4), (5)
[20] Article 144
[21] Article 137
[22] Article 138
[23] Article 140, 141
[24] Article 162
[25] Article 143
[26] Articles 145, 146, 147, 148, 149
[27] Article 150

- The development of Human Resources;
- The development of Agriculture and Natural Resources; and
- Provision of a Conducive Environment for Development.

1. Trade Liberalisation and Development

This is mainly addressed through the provisions on:
- the development and adoption of an East African Trade regime;[28]
- the establishment of a Customs Union;[29] and
- the establishment of a Common Market.[30]

The Treaty is not oblivious of the fact that, given the different levels of development in the Partner States' respective economies, imbalances may arise with the application of measures towards co-operation in trade liberalisation. It, therefore, provides for:

(a) A progressive development process towards the conclusion within four years after the coming into force of the Treaty of a Protocol establishing a Customs Union, which will include the following:
  - The application of the principle of asymmetry;
  - The elimination of internal tariff and other charges of equivalent effect;
  - The elimination of non-tariff barriers;
  - Establishment of a common external tariff;
  - Rules of origin;
  - Dumping;
  - Subsidies and Countervailing duties;
  - Security and other restrictions to trade Competition;
  - Duty drawback, refund and remission of duties and taxes;
  - Customs Co-operation;
  - Re-exportation of goods; and
  - Simplification and harmonisation of trade documentation and procedures;[31]

(b) A progressive establishment of the Customs Union over a transitional period and subject to such requirements as the Council of Ministers may determine;[32]

(c) A progressive establishment of a Common Market;[33]

---

[28] Article 74
[29] Article 75
[30] Article 76
[31] Article 75(1)
[32] Article 75(2)
[33] Article 76(2)

(d) The taking of such measures as may be necessary to address imbalances arising from the application of the provisions for the establishment of a Customs Union and a Common Market;[34] and

(e) The possibility of any of the Partner States to take necessary safeguard measures to cater for events of serious injury occurring to its economy following the application of the provisions on co-operation in trade liberalisation and development.[35]

For transitional purposes the need for such cushioning is bound to be inevitable. It is instructive to note that with the aspiration of working towards the establishment of the Customs Union, the Partner States commit themselves to certain measures that support the spirit of convergence. This is borne out by treaty provisions such as those relating to the following:

- With effect from a date to be determined by the Council, the Partner States shall not impose any new duties and taxes or increase existing ones in respect of products traded within the Community and shall transmit to the Secretariat all information on any tariffs for study by the relevant institutions of the Community;[36]
- Except as may be provided for or permitted under this Treaty, the Partner States agree to remove all the existing non-tariff barriers on the importation into their territory of goods originating from the other Partner States and thereafter to refrain from imposing any further non-tariff barriers;[37] and that
- The Partner States shall refrain from enacting legislation or applying administrative measures which directly or indirectly discriminate against the same or like products of other Partner States.[38]

Behind these provisions one notices that the Treaty recognises the need to make the region a competitive single market for local and foreign investment, business and trade. Developments in this regard will provide opportunities for increased exports and investments to the wider East African market as well as jobs for the East African labour force. Cross border investment opportunities are targeted not only on the East African Market but also on the markets of the neighbouring countries and beyond.

---

[34] Article 77
[35] Article 78
[36] Article 75(4)
[37] Article 75(5)
[38] Article 75(6)

2. Co-operation in Investment and Industrial Development

Future East African economies will depend on the development and adaptation of technologies to boost production and diversification. It is acknowledged that competitiveness can only be sustained on the basis of constant improvement and innovation of existing industries and establishment of new ones. The development of technological capacity in the region is a prerequisite for sustained economic growth and development and an incentive to increased foreign as well as local investment. This remains a challenge as far as the creation of a single market and investment area is concerned.

The Treaty, taking cognisance, of such foresightedness, therefore, provides for co-operation in investment and industrial development that would, *inter alia,* promote self sustaining and balanced industrial growth, and encourage the development of indigenous entrepreneurs.[39]

In order to avail impetus to that general provision it lays down as strategic and priority areas such matters as:
- the development of an East African Industrial Development Strategy;
- the promotion of linkages among industries within the Community;
- the facilitation of the development of small scale and food and agro-industries;
- the rationalisation of investments and investment incentives;
- the promotion of industrial research and development; and
- the avoidance of double taxation.[40]

The Treaty further provides for the development of a common policy in standardisation, quality assurance, metrology and testing that would enhance the standard of living of the peoples of the Community, promote trade and improve productivity.[41]

3. Monetary and Financial Co-operation

In addition to the provision on Trade Liberalisation and Industrial Development, there are also those provisions whereby the Partner States will undertake to co-operate in Monetary and Financial matters in order to establish monetary stability within the Community.[42] The fundamental aspects of co-operation in this regard will be based on:

---

[39] Article 79
[40] Article 80
[41] Chapter Thirteen
[42] Chapter Fourteen, Articles 82 - 88

- co-operation in monetary and financial matters and maintenance of the convertibility of the Partner States' currencies as a basis for the establishment of a Monetary Union;[43]
- the harmonisation of Partner States' macro-economic policies especially in exchange rate policy, interest rate policy, fiscal and monetary policies together with macro-economic co-ordination within the Community;[44]
- Banking and Capital Market Development;[45] and
- the removal of obstacles to the free movement of capital within the Community.[46]

As is the case with Trade Liberalisation and Development, the Treaty provides for the approval of any safeguard measures which a Partner State may take to remedy any adverse effects arising out of the application of provisions on Monetary and Financial Co-operation.[47]

4. Co-operation in the Development of Infrastructure and Services

The Treaty obliges the Partner States to ensure co-ordinated and complementary transport and communications policies and to improve and expand the existing transport and communication links and establish new ones as a means of furthering the physical cohesion of the Partner States. This is with a view to facilitating movement of traffic and to promote greater movement of persons, goods and services within the Community.[48]

It, therefore, provides for aspects of integration in roads and road transport, railways and rail transport, civil aviation and civil air transport, maritime transport and ports, inland waterways transport, multimodal transport, freight, booking centres, cargo handling, postal services, telecommunications, meteorological services and energy.[49]

5. Co-operation in the Development of Human Resources

The Treaty seeks to develop human resources in the region. Provisions geared towards human resource development include those on:

(a) the fostering of co-operation in education and training and the development of science and technology;[50]

---

[43] Article 82
[44] Article 83, 84
[45] Article 85
[46] Article 86
[47] Article 88
[48] Article 89
[49] Chapter Fifteen
[50] Articles 102, 103

(b) the free movement of persons, labour, services, right of establishment and residence;[51]
(c) co-operation in health, culture and sports and social welfare;[52] and
(d) enhancement of the role of women in socio-economic development.[53]

Under this broad area, the Treaty once again, realising the Partner States' different levels of socio-economic development, provides for the conclusion of a Protocol on the Free Movement of Persons, Labour, Services and Right of Establishment and Residence at a time to be determined by the Council.[54] It is under this Protocol that the Community will determine appropriate measures for the realisation of free movement of the said factors.

Provisions in this area also vindicate the involvement of the human factor, as a cornerstone of progress, in the building and development of the Community. These provisions, through the creation of an enabling environment for such participation, the strengthening of the private sector and engendering of co-operation among civil organisations in the region, anchor the Treaty's foundation on the participation of all stake holders and sections of the East African peoples in the activities of the Community.[55]

In catering for the enhancement of the role of women, the Treaty has re-affirmed that women in East Africa play an important role in the economic, social and political development of the region, mainly through their activities as producers of goods and services, keepers of family health, first teachers of the children and guardians of morals.

6. Co-operation in the Development of Agriculture and Natural Resources

The Treaty upholds the important roles Agriculture and Food Security, Environmental Management, Natural Resources, Tourism and Wildlife management play in the socio-economic development of the Partner States. In order to determine the scope of co-operation in these vital areas it:
(a) obliges the Partner States to undertake schemes and measures for the achievement of food security and rational agricultural promotion that would promote complementarity and specialisation for sustainable agricultural programmes;[56] and provides for co-operation and development in such areas as Seed Multiplication and Distribution, Livestock

---

[51] Chapter Sixteen
[52] Chapter Twenty One
[53] Chapter Twenty Two
[54] Article 104(2)
[55] Chapter Twenty Five
[56] Chapter Eighteen

Multiplication and Distribution, Plant and Animal Diseases Control, Irrigation and Water Catchment Management and Food Security;[57]

(b) enjoins the Partner States to co-operate for the efficient management and utilisation of natural resources within the Community and for the preservation, protection and enhancement of the environment;[58] including the prevention of illegal trade and movement in toxic chemicals, substances and hazardous wastes;[59] and

(c) provides for an undertaking by the Partner States to develop a collective and co-ordinated approach to the promotion of quality tourism and wildlife management within the Community.[60]

7. Provision of a Conducive Environment for Development

The establishment and development of the East African Community calls for the provision of a conducive environment to spur on the intended development. Accordingly, the Treaty:

(a) incorporates the firm legal cornerstones discussed in section III. above;
(b) provides for co-operation in political matters;[61]
(c) provides for co-operation in Legal and Judicial Affairs;[62] and
(d) provides for the establishment and enhancement of relations with other regional and international organisations and development partners.[63]

7.1. Co-operation in Political Matters

For purposes of enhancing the Community's role and laying a foundation for the eventual establishment of a Political Federation, the Treaty obliges the Partner States to:

(a) define and implement common foreign and security policies;
(b) foster and maintain an atmosphere that is conducive to peace and security through co-operation and consultations with a view to preventing, better managing and resolving disputes and conflicts between them; and
(c) establishment of a framework for co-operation in defense.[64]

---

[57] *Ibid*
[58] Chapter Nineteen
[59] *Ibid*
[60] Chapter Twenty
[61] Chapter Twenty Three
[62] Chapter Twenty Four
[63] Chapter Twenty Six
[64] Articles 123, 124, 125

7.2. Co-operation in Legal and Judicial Affairs

In order to promote the achievement of the objectives of the Community, the Treaty obliges the Partner States to undertake appropriate steps towards:

(a) the revival of the publication of the East African Law Reports,[65] law journals and such other publications as will promote the exchange of legal and judicial knowledge;

(b) the harmonisation of municipal laws in the regional context; and

(c) the establishment of common syllabi for the training of lawyers and judicial officers.[66]

This would be in tandem with the Partner States' general undertaking to ensure the implementation of the Treaty.[67]

7.3. Relations with other regional and international organisations and development partners

Under the present Co-operation Arrangements cognisance is taken of existing regional co-operation agreements and arrangements jointly and severally binding the Member States. In order to underscore the role of development partnership, the draft Treaty obliges the Partner States to, among other things;

(a) honour their commitments in respect of multinational and international organisations; and

(b) foster, as a Community, co-operative arrangements with other organisations whose activities have a bearing on its objectives.[68]

V. THE ORGANS AND INSTITUTIONS OF THE COMMUNITY

The East African Community, not unlike other similar regional organisations, has various organs and institutions charged with the implementation of the provisions of the Treaty and the achievement of the objectives of the Community.[69] These organs and institutions will, largely on the basis of the principle of separation of powers, exercise executive, judicial and legislative powers.

---

[65] Law Reports of the decisions of the erstwhile Court of Appeal for East Africa and the High Courts of Kenya, Uganda and Tanzania published between 1957 and 1977.
[66] Article 126
[67] See part III.5 of this Article
[68] Article 130(2), (4)
[69] The organs and institutions are established by Article 9

1. Organs of the Community

Besides such other organs of the Community as the Summit may establish, the following seven basic organs are established by the Treaty:

(a) The Summit

The Summit will consist of the Heads of State of the Partner States. Its role will be to give general directions and impetus as to the development and achievement of the objectives of the Community. Unlike the Authority under the defunct East African Community, the Summit will have its functions limited to overall policy direction. Implementation and operational policy decisions are to be made by organs subordinate to the Summit.[70]

(b) The Council

The Council of the Ministers, consisting of the Ministers responsible for Regional Co-operation and such other Ministers as each Partner State may determine, will be the major policy organ in as far as implementation of the Treaty provisions and programmes is concerned.

Apart from assisting the Summit in the performance of its functions, the Council is expected to direct, promote, monitor and keep under constant review the efficient functioning and development of the Community. The Council, will among other things initiate and submit Bills to the Legislative Assembly, consider the Budget of the Community, make staff and financial rules and regulations and submit annual reports to the Summit. The Council has powers to make legally binding regulations, issue directives, take decisions and make recommendations. These powers are for crucial purposes of ensuring that decisions are taken on time and that implementation is effectively monitored.[71]

(c) The Co-ordination Committee

The Co-ordination Committee, will comprise Permanent Secretaries responsible for Regional Co-operation and such other Permanent Secretaries as each Partner State may determine. It will be responsible for ensuring consistency and complementarity of projects and programmes as agreed by the Council. It will also facilitate the speedy implementation of the decisions of the Council. The Co-ordination Committee may also on its own initiative submit to the Council reports and recommendations on the implementation of the Treaty.[72]

---

[70] Chapter Four
[71] Chapter Five
[72] Chapter Six

(d) *The Sectoral Committees*

The Sectoral Committees will be established by the Council on the recommendation of the Co-ordination Committee. They will primarily be responsible for the preparation of comprehensive implementation programmes and setting out priorities for different sectors of co-operation. They are also charged with monitoring and keeping under constant review the implementation of the Community's sectoral programmes.[73]

(e) *The East African Court of Justice*

The role of the East African Court of Justice will be to ensure the adherence to law in the interpretation and application of the Treaty. The Court shall be competent to accept and adjudicate upon all matters pursuant to the Treaty. The Court may also be called upon to give advisory opinions regarding questions of law arising from the provisions of the Treaty. The Court is empowered to determine the legality of any act, regulation, directive, decision, action or matter as shall have been referred to it by any Partner State, the Secretary General of the Community or by any legal and natural persons.

Initially the Court's jurisdiction will be limited to this aspect. However, it is envisaged that the Court shall have such other original, appellate, human rights and other jurisdiction as will be determined by the Council at a suitable subsequent date.

Notwithstanding its broad jurisdictional base, the regional Court is not designed to deny national courts their respective jurisdictions in accordance with the respective municipal laws.

This important Court is intended among other things, to create public confidence. It is important for the public to know that the Partner States and the organs and institutions of the Community cannot get away with any wrongdoing under the Treaty. Its Judges will therefore be appointed by the Summit from among persons recommended by the Partner States who are of proven integrity, impartiality and independence and who fulfil the conditions required in their own countries for the holding of such high judicial office, or who are jurists of recognised competence in their respective Partner States.[74]

(f) *The East African Legislative Assembly*

It is proposed that the East African Legislative Assembly shall have twenty-seven elected members elected by the National Assemblies of the

---

[73] Chapter Seven

[74] Elaborate provisions on the creation, jurisdiction and conduct of work of the Court are contained in Chapter Eight

Partner States, and five ex-officio members consisting of the Minister responsible for regional co-operation from each Partner State, the Secretary-General and the Counsel to the Community. The Assembly will be the Community's legislative organ. It will also be charged with among other functions, liaising with the National Assemblies of the Partner States on matters relating to the Community, debating and approving the Budget of the Community, considering annual reports of the Community and discussing all matters pertaining to the Community. It will, to this extent, be the people's mouthpiece on matters relevant to the efficient functioning of the institutions and of the Community as a whole.

In order to fulfil or comply with the operational principle of popular participation and to reflect the people-centred approach of the Community, the views expressed in the debates of the National Assemblies shall be taken into account in the Community Assembly. Reports on debates of the Community Assembly will also have to be passed to the National Assemblies for their consideration.[75]

(g) *The Secretariat*

The Secretariat, headed by the Secretary General of the Community, will be the principal executive organ of the Community. It will, as such, be charged with the strategic planning, management and monitoring of the Community's programmes and implementation of the Council's decisions. It is expected to be an institution of high efficiency and technical competence. It is expected to be kept small and efficient. The appointments to key positions at the Secretariat are expected to be on merit in order to ensure that a functional and effective key organ is in place.[76]

2. Institutions of the Community

The institutions of the Community shall be such bodies, departments and services as may be established by the Summit.[77] The Treaty also provides that upon its entry into force the East African Development Bank and the Lake Victoria Fisheries Organisation and the surviving institutions of the former East African Community shall be deemed to be institutions of the new Community.[78]

---

[75] Chapter Nine spells out the mechanism for the creation and *modus operandi* of the Legislative Assembly
[76] Chapter Ten
[77] Article 9(2)
[78] Article 9(3)

VI. OPERATIONALISATION OF THE TREATY

The basic challenges to the Community will include the incorporation of the Treaty in the Partner States' Municipal Law, the constitution and operationalisation of the new organs, the sustainance of political will and the effective and purposeful involvement of the peoples of East Africa as a driving force of the Community.

It is worth noting however that following the signing of the Treaty, the three governments have addressed the critical issue of its implementation. Accordingly, the Permanent Tripartite Co-operation has formulated a programme, containing key landmarks, for the operationalisation of the Treaty.

Implementation will be based on decisions pertaining to various aspects of co-operation by the Council of Ministers. Some of the decisions may result in the conclusion of annexes and protocols which shall spell out the objectives and scope of the institutional mechanisms for co-operation and integration. Each annex and protocol shall form an integral part of the Treaty.[79]

VII. CONCLUSION

On the whole, the Treaty represents the broad consensus of the Member States and peoples of East Africa. It is an enabling document, which provides the basis for development of dynamic co-operation in the social, economic and political fields as well as boosting the region's capacity as a solid bloc in its trade and other relations with the rest of the world.

Its provisions are a pointer towards the attainment of such pre-requisites of development in today's world as the promotion of peace and security in the region; the enhancement of good governance, democracy, the rule of law, social justice and observance of human rights; the creation of a regional market which will optimize economies of scale; the facilitation of the movement of persons, capital, goods and services; the attraction of international and cross-border investments; the promotion of the role of the

---

[79] The Treaty currently provides for the conclusion of Protocols on:
- decision-making by the Council (Article 15(4);
- the establishment of a Customs Union (Article 75(1)
- the establishment of a Common Market (Article 76(4);
- Standardisation, Quality Assurance, Metrology and Testing (Article 81(4);
- The Free Movement of Persons, Labour, Services and Right of Establishment and Residence (Article 104(2); and
- Combating Illicit Drug Trafficking (Article 124(5)(e)

private sector and civil society; the promotion of sustainable environmental management of shared resources; the development of human resources, science and technology etc..

The Treaty, therefore, constitutes a major step forward in the economic and political integration of East African countries and is capable of contributing to and providing a solid basis for a wider integration scheme in the interest of African states, in general.

GENERAL ARTICLES

ARTICLES GÉNÉRAUX

THE ROLE OF INTERNATIONAL LAW IN THE COLONIZATION OF AFRICA: A REVIEW IN LIGHT OF RECENT CALLS FOR RE-COLONIZATION

Dakas C. J. Dakas*

1. INTRODUCTION: AFRICA AND THE SPECTER OF RE-COLONIZATION

A very alarming trend has been developing lately in certain circles. A case for the re-colonization of Africa is being advanced by some political analysts and academics. For instance, Robert Kaplan[1] paints an apocalyptic portrait of the continent, while William Pfaff refers to the "destitution of Africa" and submits that "the time has arrived ... for honest and dispassionate discussion of this immense human tragedy".[2] He then makes a case for what he labels a "disinterested[!] neo-colonialism" in Africa.

Pfaff acknowledges the fact that when the Europeans first came to Africa, "there were coherent, functioning societies of varying degrees of sophistication" in Africa but these were, as he further concedes, "destroyed by colonialism". However, he contends that "[c]olonialism lasted long enough to destroy the preexisting social and political institutions, but not long enough to put anything solid and lasting in their place".

Additionally, Pfaff challenges the competence of the United Nations or the United States in the reconstruction of Africa. Instead, he thrusts the primary responsibility for this mission on Europe (on account, *inter alia*, of its prior colonial exploits in Africa and its "most urgent material interest in its condition") and advocates the establishment of a cooperative Euro-African trust organization to which the majority of African governments

---

* Lecturer, Faculty of Law, University of Jos, Nigeria.
[1] Robert D. Kaplan, "The Coming Anarchy", ATLANTIC MONTHLY, Feb. 1994, pp. 44-76.
[2] William Pfaff, "A New Colonialism?: Europe Must Go Back into Africa", 74 FOREIGN AFF. 2-6 (1995).

would assign a "defined (and irrevocable) authority", even though he foresees that "this would be the project of a half-century, perhaps a century"!³

Pfaff's claim that colonialism did not last long enough to engender anything "solid and lasting" (presumably positive) in Africa is obviously a crude reinvention of the discredited civilizing-mission rhetoric of colonialism. Yet, Pfaff is not a lone advocate. Paul Johnson also opines that some States "are not yet fit to govern themselves" and so the "civilized world has a mission to go out to these desperate places and govern".⁴ Individual "civilized countries" would, under his proposal, serve as "trustees". Remarkably, Ali Mazrui, a distinguished Kenyan scholar, has also made a case for what he labels "benign" colonialism in Africa – a kind of indigenous colonialism.⁵

It is interesting how Pfaff's view strikingly resembles the much earlier view of George Louis Beer,⁶ Chief of the Colonial Division of the American Delegation to Negotiate Peace, and Alternate Member of the Commission on Mandates. Beer describes German colonial policy in Africa as one of "open contempt" for the "aborigines", as the "native was regarded as an inferior being, whose purpose was to serve the ends of the white man". Consequently, he asserts that "[t]he preëminent consideration in colonial administration must be the welfare of the native", as "[t]he outside world can in the long run gain no benefit from Africa unless its evolution is on a firm and sound economic basis". Additionally, Beer submits that "[i]t is not only abominably selfish, but it is stupidly suicidal" to view Africa "merely as a huge plantation on which the negro toils as a helot for the advantage of Europe".

In spite of the explicit reference to "the welfare of the native", it is evident that Beer is not denouncing colonialism *per se* but "colonial

---

3   *Id.*
4   Paul Johnson, "The Case for a Return to Colonialism", SACRAMENTO BEE, April 25, 1993, Forums 1 & 2.
5   *See*, Ali Mazrui, "Decaying Parts of Africa Need Benign Colonization", INT'L HERALD TRIBUNE, August 4, 1994. Needless to say, invoking colonialism – however polished – as a prescription for Africa does great disservice to the continent. *See* also, Ali Mazrui, "The Message of Rwanda: Recolonize Africa?", NEW PERS. QTY. 18 (1994); Ali Mazrui, "May be the Time Has Come to Recolonize Africa", HOUSTON CHRON, August 3, 1994, at A27; Ali Mazrui, "The Bondage of Boundaries", ECONOMIST, Sept. 11, 1993, S2, 28. But note: Ruth Gordon, "Saving Failed States: Sometimes a Neo-Colonialist Notion", 12 AM. U. J. INT'L L. & POL'Y, 903 (1997).
6   George Louis Beer, *African Questions at the Paris Peace Conference*, 179-180 (Louis Herbert Gray, ed., 1923).

administration". Indeed, Beer leaves no one in doubt about this fact and his perception of Africans: "The negro race", Beer claims, "has hitherto shown no capacity for progressive development except under the tutelage of other peoples". As if in amelioration of this harsh assertion, he submits that "the African's existing stage of civilization is far below his real potentialities for progress". However, having made the extraordinary claim that "the negro" is incapable of "progressive development except under the tutelage of other peoples", he thrusts on the "colonizing powers" the "prime function" of developing and establishing favorable conditions for "the negro" to realize his "real potentialities for progress". In Beer's conception, it was, so to say, "the white man's burden" to show Africans the way forward or, better put, to save them from themselves. Accordingly, although Beer, like Pfaff, appears to have been concerned about the plight of Africans, a careful reflection shows that his position cannot extricate itself from the overall framework of the colonial project.

By its very nature, colonialism is undoubtedly antithetical to the human face that Pfaff and others similarly situated seek to ascribe to it. Indeed, with the possible exception of the loathsome slave trade, Tunkin's description of colonialism as "the most detestable manifestation" of the "exploitation of man by man"[7] is unassailable and calls into question the sincerity of the apostles of re-colonization.

In light of the foregoing, it is essential to revisit the scramble for and partition of Africa by the colonial powers and underscore the perils of complacency. However, unlike most scholarly works on colonialism, our focal point is the role of 19th century international law in the colonial project. Though not quite apparent, the present case for the re-colonization of Africa is embroidered in legal accouterments.

It is important to point out that writing about the scramble for and partition of Africa is both depressing and liberating. One is confronted with, and appalled at, the magnitude of the exploitation and anguish that colonialism unleashed on its victims. Observing this sad reality through the prism of international law – albeit that of the 19th century – is all the more traumatic for an international lawyer as one undertakes a critical examination of a discipline that one cherishes and strives to defend from skeptics who call into question its very existence or, when they choose to be charitable, question its efficacy.

In the circumstance, one could be tempted to focus on the profound transformation that the discipline has undergone over the years and, basking

---

[7] G. I. Tunkin, *Theory of International Law*, 315 (William E. Butler, trans., 1974).

in the euphoria that it has purged itself of its colonial vestiges, be complacent about its past role. However, exposing the ignominious role of international law in the colonial project is an imperative exercise that brings with it the liberating realization that to speak of colonialism and its crippling effects in the past tense is to wallow in idle fantasy; thus underscoring the imperative of vigilance. It is against this background that the following analysis is undertaken:

2. 19TH CENTURY INTERNATIONAL LAW AND THE COLONIAL QUESTION

The 19th century is, from a legal perspective, remarkable in several respects:[8] the decline of natural law and the concomitant triumph of legal positivism, as well as the construction and consolidation of sovereignty and Statehood as the exclusive preserve of the "civilized". Additionally, and as a corollary of the foregoing, the 19th century has the dubious distinction of notoriety for its colonial legacy. As the case for the re-colonization of Africa is raised in certain quarters, it would be tantamount to laboring under a delusion to ignore the question as to whether, notwithstanding the profound transformation that international law has undergone over the years, the ghost of the 19th century still hovers over us.

Africa's contact with the West, the motivation behind colonialism, and the rapacious plunder thereby occasioned on the continent, are the subject of extensive research by historians, political scientists, geographers, sociologists, etc.[9] However, sufficient attention has not been directed at the striking manner in which 19th century international law justified the colonial project. What is even more spectacular is the stupendous manner in which international legal scholars, with few exceptions, availed the colonial project

---

[8] On the legacy of the 19th century, *see* generally, David Kennedy, "International Law and the Nineteenth Century: History of an Illusion", 17 QUINNIPIAC. L. REV. 99 (1997) & Antony Anghie, "Finding the Peripheries: Sovereignty and Colonialism in Nineteenth-Century International Law", 40 HARV. INT'L L. J. 1 (1999).

[9] *See* for instance, Walter Rodney, *How Europe Underdeveloped Africa* (1981); Daniel Offiong, *Imperialism and Dependency* (1980); *General History of Africa: Africa Under Colonial Domination, 1880-1935*, Vol. VII (Adu A. Boahen, ed., 1985); Basil Davidson, *Africa in History* (1991); Basil Davidson, *The Black Man's Burden: Africa and the Curse of the Nation-State* (1992); Mahmood Mamdani, *Citizen and Subject: Contemporary Africa and the Legacy of Late Colonialism* (1996); & Crawford Young, "The Heritage of Colonialism", in *Africa in World Politics*, 19 (John W. Harbeson & Donald Rothchild, eds., 1991).

of their intellectual armory.[10] A notable case in point is John Westlake who, at the material time, was, *inter alia*, the Whewell Professor of International Law in the University of Cambridge, and reputed to be "a jurist of worldwide reputation".[11] Accordingly, the following section essentially examines and critiques Westlake's views, which – with varying degrees of emphasis – are largely representative of the perspectives of his Western contemporaries,[12] on the questions of sovereignty and civilization and, invariably, the colonial question. This is followed by an examination of the colonial question at the Berlin Conference of 1884-85, the partition of Africa, the regime of "colonial protectorates", and the rhetoric of colonialism.

---

[10] The extent, if any, to which the works of these publicists influenced or reflected the norms of international law (such as customary international law and treaties) at the material time will become evident in the course of the analysis undertaken in this article.

[11] J. Fischer Williams, "Introduction", in *Memories of John Westlake*, 1, 7 (J. Fischer Williams, ed., 1914).

[12] Shaw singles out Westlake as the "foremost among... theorists" who took the view that "the organized tribes of peoples of non-European lands had no sovereign rights over their territories and thus no sovereign title by means of effective occupation". Accordingly, the inhabitants were "factually and not legally in occupation of the territory, which could be treated as *terra nullius* and acquired by any State in accordance with the requirements of international law". Shaw further points out that the views of such theorists "appeared to dominate throughout the nineteenth century when Africa was being divided amongst the competing European powers": Malcolm Shaw, *Title to Territory in Africa: International Legal Issues*, 32 (1986). Additionally, a survey of the views of "the leading writers" of the 19th century and the early years of the 20th century – Kent, Wheaton, Phillimore, Hall, Westlake, Oppenheim, Anzilloti, Fauchille, Holtzendorf, Nys, Bello, Rivier and F. de Martens – on international law and western civilization is provided in C. Wilfred Jenks, *The Common Law of Mankind*, 69-74 (1958). Jenks describes these publicists as "so outstanding a company from nine different nations that no one can dismiss their views as unrepresentative or unimportant". He further submits that "their views differ only in degrees of emphasis". Wheaton, for instance, remarks: "Is there a uniform law of nations? There certainly is not the same one for all the nations and states of the world. The public law, with slight exceptions, has always been, and still is, limited to the civilised and Christian people of Europe or to those of European origin": Henry Wheaton, *Elements of International Law*, 16 (6th edn., William Beach Lawrence, ed., 1855). Furthermore, Oppenheim notes that "only such territory can be the object of occupation as belongs to no State, whether it is entirely uninhabited, for instance an island, or inhabited by natives whose community is not to be considered a State": L. Oppenheim, *International Law: A Treatise*, Vol. I, 555 (8th edn., H. Lauterpacht, ed., 1955).

(a) Pre-Colonial Africa as "Uncivilised" and "Devoid of Sovereignty"

John Westlake, proceeding from the premise that reflection on the principles of international law "helps to determine the action of [one's] country by swelling the volume of its opinion",[13] sets up a pyramidal legal edifice in furtherance of the colonial project. He does this principally through his conception of the nature and acquisition of territorial sovereignty. Chapter IX of his text is strikingly captioned "Territorial Sovereignty, Especially with Relation to Uncivilised Regions".

In a sub-chapter titled "The Title to Territorial Sovereignty", Westlake evades the question as to how "the old civilized world" acquired the title to territorial sovereignty, as, according to him, the issue is not "capable of discussion apart from the several dealings, as cession or conquest, which transfer it".[14] However, he unhesitatingly delves into a consideration of the status of "uncivilised natives" in international law.

Westlake submits that "[w]hen people of the European race come into contact with American or African tribes, the prime necessity is a government". Such a government has to be capable of protecting the former in a manner that enables them to "carry on the complex life to which they have been accustomed in their homes" and "protect the natives in the enjoyment of a security and well-being at least not less than they enjoyed before the arrival of the strangers". Questioning whether "the natives [could] furnish such a government" or look up to the Europeans, he submits that "in the answer to that question lies, for international law, the difference between civilisation and the want of it". In his view, most of the populations with whom Europeans came into contact in America and Africa could not furnish the kind of government in question. Accordingly, international law "has to treat such natives as uncivilised" and "regulates, for the mutual benefit of civilised states, the claims which they make to sovereignty over the region, and leaves the treatment of the natives to the conscience of the state to which sovereignty is awarded". In effect, the regions inhabited by such "uncivilised natives" were not, on their own, sovereign. In the circumstance, he challenges the competence of the "uncivilised natives" to effect a transfer of territory by cession: "What is the authority – chief, elders, body of fighting men – if there is one ... empowered to make the cession?".[15]

If, as Westlake claims, "uncivilised natives" were incapable of effecting a transfer of territory through cession, what is the legal status of treaties that,

---

[13] John Westlake, *Chapters on the Principles of International Law*, V (1894).
[14] *Id.*, p. 134.
[15] *Id*, pp. 139-143.

to his knowledge, were entered into between various African chiefs and respective European Powers?

(b) The Legal Status of Treaties with "Uncivilised Natives/Tribes"

According to Westlake "In Africa ... an importance has sometimes been attached to treaties with uncivilised tribes, and a development has sometimes been given to them, which are more calculated to excite laughter than argument.".[16]

Westlake, in grappling with the dilemma occasioned by his condescending treatment of the status of the "uncivilised natives" and its implications for their treaty-making competence, in effect, patronizes them: "[N]o men are so savage as to be incapable of coming to some understanding with other men, and wherever contact has been established between men, some understanding, however incomplete it may be, is a better basis for their mutual relations than force".[17] On the specific status of treaties between European Powers and "uncivilised natives", he contends that the latter "take no rights under international law", with the result that "no document in which such natives are made to cede the sovereignty over any territory can be exhibited as an international title". However, "[t]o whatever point natives may have advanced", cession by them in accordance with their customs "may confer a moral title", and even then only with reference to "property or power as they understand while they cede it". Therefore, "no form of cession by them can confer any title to what they do not understand". Yet, "while the sovereignty of a European state over an uncivilised region must find its justification, as it easily will, not in treaties with natives but in the manner of the case and compliance with conditions recognised by the civilised world", Westlake further submits, "it is possible that a right of property may be derived from treaties with natives, and this even before any European sovereignty has begun to exist over the spot".[18]

This argument is fundamentally flawed. The distinction that Westlake makes between sovereignty and "a right of property" may well be tenable, but that does not explain how the "natives", whose sovereignty he disputes, acquired the competence to alienate property *through treaties* with European

---

[16] *Id.*, p. 149.
[17] *Id.*, p. 143.
[18] *Id.*, pp. 144-5.

States.[19] Additionally, the assertion that "no form of cession by [uncivilised natives] can confer any title to what they do not understand", on the face of it, gives the impression that Westlake's position is informed by concern for the interests of the "uncivilised natives". However, this must be appreciated within the broader context of Westlake's conception and, in particular, his assertion denying the rights of the "uncivilised natives". This is further borne out by the manner in which he selects and contrasts two treaties with "uncivilised" chiefs.[20]

The first, exemplifying, according to Westlake, what a "treaty ... with natives ought not to be", is that concluded between the British South Africa Company and King Umtasa in 1890. Westlake decries the fact that the treaty, to use his own words, "dignifies" the latter as "king or chief of Manika"; preferring, instead, to describe him as a "savage" and "such a drunkard as to be subject to *delirium tremens*". The treaty grants to the company the "sole absolute and entire perpetual right and power" to do the acts specified therein "over the whole or any portion of the territory" of the king. The company, in turn, agrees "under the King's supervision and authority" to perform certain functions, including assisting "in the establishment and propagation of the Christian religion and the education and civilisation of the native subjects of the King" as well as "the extension and equipment of telegraphs and of regular services of postal and transport communications".[21]

Westlake finds fault with this treaty not because, as he claims, the king in question was a drunkard and could not possibly comprehend what he was doing, leaving one to wonder why this issue finds expression in the text in the first place. Instead, he contends that, taken alone, the stipulations in the treaty might not have been beyond the understanding of the king, "but when they were mixed with a farrago which must have been mere jargon to him, the whole must be dismissed as something which could not have received his intelligent consent".[22] It is apparently of no concern to Westlake that the treaty speaks of the "territory" of the king and of his "supervision and

---

[19] Cf. M. F. Lindley, *The Acquisition and Government of Backward Territory in International Law: Being a Treatise on the Law and Practice Relating to Colonial Expansion*, 21 (1926): "[I]t is difficult to see why, if the natives are to be regarded as capable of possessing and transferring property, they should not also be considered competent to hold and transfer the sovereignty which they actually exercise".

[20] J. Westlake, *supra*, note 11, pp. 151-4.

[21] Quoted in Westlake, *id.*, p. 152.

[22] Westlake, *id.*, pp. 152-3.

authority", thus suggesting that the company was conscious of the existence of a government in the territory in question, one capable of providing the "supervision and authority" that the treaty envisages.

In contrast, Westlake "pleasant[ly]" offers as "an example to be followed" an 1889 treaty between "Her Majesty's acting Consul for Nyassa" and, according to him, "the chiefs of a nation [Makololo] which for intelligence and character ranks very high among those which must still be called uncivilized".[23] The treaty, *inter alia*, makes a distinction, which is important, between the "subjects of the queen of England" and "our subjects" (the subjects of the chiefs), grants the former certain rights, which are exercisable "according to the laws in force" in the territory of the chiefs, provides for the payment of "duties or customs" to the chiefs and sets out a framework for dispute resolution. Additionally, there is a stipulation to the effect that the chiefs "will at no time whatever cede any of [their] territory to any other power, or enter into any agreement treaty or arrangement with any foreign government except through and with the consent of the government of Her Majesty the queen of England, &c."[24]

This treaty, according to Westlake, "contains nothing beyond the comprehension of the Makololo chiefs". However, he maintains that "there is no cession of territorial integrity by them". Be that as it may, there is no doubt that the treaty contains an undertaking by the chiefs not to cede any part of their territory to any "other power". Indeed, it is revealing that Westlake glosses over the obvious fact that the treaty reckons with the fact that, but for its provisions, the Makololo Chiefs would have been competent to effect a cession of their territory to a power of their choice. If, contrary to the treaty provisions, the chiefs had ceded their territory or part of it to another power, one wonders whether the British would not have invoked the terms of the treaty and alleged that the chiefs were in breach of their treaty obligations. If, but for the terms of the treaty, the chiefs had ceded their territory or part of it to a power of their choice, one also wonders whether the British would have challenged the title of that other power on the ground

---

[23] Westlake, *id.*, p. 153.
[24] Quoted in Westlake, *id.*

of an alleged absence of sovereignty on the part of the chiefs.[25] Furthermore, it is poignant that the treaty evidences the existence of a government in Makololo, with laws to which the British, by the terms of the treaty, were subject.

Our point is not that the colonizing powers acquired valid title over African lands through cession on the strength of the various treaties that were entered into with African chiefs. Instead, it must be borne in mind that the determination of the validity or otherwise of such treaties depends on several factors. For instance, given the languages in which the treaties were couched, did the African chiefs really appreciate their import? Obviously, this has nothing to do with illiteracy. It is one thing to be literate, while it is quite another thing to comprehend the medium through which treaty stipulations are expressed. In such situations, the role of interpreters could be most invaluable. However, there has to be evidence to the effect that such interpreters are indeed knowledgeable and faithfully carry out their task. Additionally, the existence or otherwise of fraud, coercion, corruption and other vitiating or invalidating elements are relevant considerations. As a matter of fact, some of the terms of the treaties make a caricature of treaty practice by their very absurdity and call into question any claims to the effect that the African chiefs were willing parties. The 1861 treaty between King Docemo and the British concerning the Port and Island of Lagos is instructive:

> "I, Docemo, do, with the consent and advice of my council, give, transfer, and by these presents grant and confirm unto the Queen of Great Britain, her heirs and successors forever ... full and absolute dominion and sovereignty of the said port, island, and premises ... freely, fully, entirely, and absolutely".[26]

---

[25] If they did, that would have put their own title – to the extent that it was claimed to be predicated on the treaty – in jeopardy. Accordingly, it would not have been in the interest of the British, even if they would have ordinarily preferred otherwise, to challenge the sovereignty of the African States. It is against the backdrop of this reality that Shaw's example of how Britain deferred to Germany on the strength of an 1883 treaty between the latter and a "local chief" in respect of the "Cameroons territory" should be appreciated; also, his assertion that "[h]ad the area been regarded as *terra nullius*, the mere signing of a document would not have been sufficient and there would therefore have been scope for Britain to recoup the situation". *See*, Shaw, *supra*, note 12, p. 39.

[26] Quoted in U. O. Umozurike, *International Law and Colonialism in Africa*, 40 (1979).

Beyond the question of free choice and informed consent, it is significant – given Westlake's claims – that the treaty speaks of "sovereignty", which King Docemo, in the exercise thereof, "grant[s]" to the British. In this connection, one readily recalls the maxim *nemo dat quod non habet*. None the less, it is questionable whether the British, in spite of the explicit reference to sovereignty in the treaty, actually recognized the sovereignty of the African States. To the extent that they did, it was merely a self-serving strategy to ward off rival European claimants. If they actually did, one would have expected them to accord the African States a treatment commensurate with this recognition in the process of treaty-making and other relations.

In effect, such treaties had less to do with legal relations between the European Powers and the African States than among the European Powers themselves. Put another way, the European Powers, spurred by their imperial ambitions, were constrained to accord the African States some semblance of sovereignty, so that – as amongst themselves – they could anchor their titles to territories in Africa on the so-called treaties of cession with African States. This is undoubtedly a manifest exhibition of the contradictions and fraudulent character of the colonial project.

In any event, even if the European Powers intended (and this is questionable) that the African States could in fact invoke the treaties against them, the chances were slim because the treaty provisions were often heavily weighed against the latter. Besides, where would the African States have sought redress against the European Powers? An international judicial or arbitral body was obviously out of the question. So were domestic African dispute resolution institutions, where they existed. Apart from the question of sovereign immunity, it is clear that the European Powers would have never submitted themselves to the jurisdiction of such institutions. Indeed, in the few instances where the treaties made provision for dispute resolution, the European Powers were not even ready to allow differences between their "subjects" and the African States to be adjudicated upon by African dispute resolution institutions. They did not also create joint institutions with the African States. Instead, the treaty between the British and the Makololo Chiefs, for instance, provided that should "any difference" arise between "British subjects" and the chiefs, as to the duties or customs payable to the latter, or as to any other matter, "the dispute shall be referred to a duly authorised representative of Her Majesty, whose decision in the matter shall be binding and final".[27]

---

[27] Quoted in Westlake, *supra*, note 13, p. 153.

Furthermore, the reality is that in concluding or, rather, purporting to conclude treaties with African States, the primary concern of the colonizing powers was not compliance with the rules of the game. This is borne out, for instance, by the revelations of a former British infantry commander, A. B. Thruston, who, recounting his personal experience, aptly describes the process of treaty-making with Africans as "an amiable farce" and a "little comedy".[28]

It is clear, from the discussions thus far, that Westlake's conception of the nature and acquisition of territories in the context of colonialism is fraught with contradictions. His spirited attempts to get out of the quagmire only throws him from the frying pan into the fire. In the course of one such attempt, he resorts to "constructing the Makololo chiefs and divining their consciousness" in a vain effort to "give his scheme some semblance of coherence",[29] without articulating a credible basis for such recourse. Eventually, Westlake discloses his true colours: "The inflow of the white

---

[28] In his own words, quoted, on account of its significance, *in extenso*: "I had been instructed ... to make a treaty with Kivalli by which he should place himself under British protection; in fact, I had a bundle of printed treaties which I was to make as many people sign as possible. This signing is an *amiable farce*, ... *the equivalent of an occupation*. The *modus operandi* is somewhat as follows: A ragged untidy European, who in any civilised country would be in danger of being taken up by the police as a vagrant, lands at a native village ... [T]he chief comes and receives his presents, *the so-called interpreter pretends to explain the treaty to the chief. The chief does not understand a word of it* but he looks pleased as he receives another present of beads; a mark is made on a printed treaty by the chief and another by the interpreter, the vagrant, who professes to be the representative of a great empire, signs his name. The chief takes the paper but with some hesitation, as he regards the whole performance as a new and therefore dangerous piece of witchcraft. The boat sails away and the new ally and protégé of England or France immediately throws the treaty into the fire. Kavalli was an important personage and it was desirable that he should perform this *little comedy* with us before he should do so with the Belgians." A. B. Thruston, *African Incidents: Personal Experiences in Egypt and Unyoro*, 170-1 (1900), quoted in Yilma Makonnen, *International Law and the New States of Africa: A Study of the International Legal Problems of State Succession in the Newly Independent States of Eastern Africa*, 14-5 (1983). Emphasis ours.

[29] Anghie, *supra*, note 8, p. 48.

race cannot be stopped where there is land to cultivate, ore to be mined, commerce to be developed, sport to enjoy, curiosity to be satisfied".[30]

(c) Terra Nullius and the Acquisition of Territory By Europeans in Africa

The denial of the sovereignty of pre-colonial African States and their competence to effect transfers by cession is far from academic. The inescapable conclusion – and this suited the colonial project – is that even where lands in Africa were factually inhabited by Africans, such lands were, from the point of view of law, treated as *terra nullius*. It was immaterial, insofar as colonialism was concerned, that Africans inhabited such lands for centuries before the Europeans set foot on African soil. Accordingly, they could be treated as having been newly discovered and liable to acquisition by occupation. Indeed, this is precisely the subtle import of Westlake's statement to the effect that his examination of the "position of the uncivilised natives ... clears the way for a discussion of the titles to territorial sovereignty in uncivilised regions which States belonging to the society of international law invoke against one another",[31] followed by a discourse on discovery and occupation as international titles.

---

[30] Westlake, *supra*, note 13, pp. 142-3. In the circumstance, Westlake submits that if a "fanatical admirer of savage life argued that the whites ought to be kept out, he would only be driven to the same conclusion by another route, for a government on the spot would be necessary to keep them out". Interestingly, in a tribute to Westlake, Symonds has this to say: "He hated injustice and oppression from his very soul, and none who ever heard him speak against them could forget the burning and impassioned words in which he arraigned the tyrant and pleaded for the victims of tyranny": Arthur G. Symonds, "The Balkan Committee", in J. Fischer Williams, *supra*, note 11, p. 115. Apparently, Westlake's crusade, as so described, did not encompass the plight of the "uncivilized".

[31] Westlake, *id.*, p. 155. Similarly, Hyde points out that by deeming the "uncivilized or extremely backward" inhabitants of a territory "to be incapable of possessing a right to sovereignty", a conqueror could "ignore their title and proceed to occupy [their] land as though it were vacant". In such cases, he further notes, "conquest refers merely to the military or physical effort by means of which occupation becomes possible": Charles Cheney Hyde, *International Law Chiefly as Interpreted and Applied by the United States*, Vol. I, 357 (2nd rev. edn., 1947). Reliance on conquest, in the sense in which it is traditionally understood, would have entailed the establishment by the European Powers – at least in their relations with one another – of unprovoked aggression which is a key ingredient of conquest as a mode of territorial acquisition. Thus, the invocation of *terra nullius* had the dubious advantage of dispensing with this requirement. Besides, resort to war against African States would have invariably pitched rival European Powers against one another.

This point is further made explicit by Thomas J. Lawrence.[32] Lawrence submits, evidently in agreement with John Austin,[33] that a sovereign State must have two characteristics: a government that receives habitual obedience from the bulk of the people, and does not render habitual obedience to any earthly superior. For such a State to become a subject of international law, however, it must attain "a certain, or rather an uncertain, amount of civilization" and possess a "fixed territory". Accordingly, a territory is *terra nullius* if it does not meet these criteria and is, therefore, an object (and not subject) of international law, with no standing in the exclusive club of the "family of nations". Lawrence cites, as an example of the affected populations, a "wandering tribe without a fixed territory" which might "obey implicitly a chief who took no commands from other rulers", yet "the necessary degree of civilization would be lacking". Additionally, "even if we could suppose a nomadic tribe to have attained the requisite degree of civilization, its lack of territorial organization would be amply sufficient to exclude it from the pale of international law".[34]

It suffices to point out, at this juncture, that this position is at variance with the Advisory Opinion of the International Court of Justice in the *Western Sahara Case*.[35] The court points out that "Western Sahara was inhabited by peoples which, if nomadic, were socially and politically organized in tribes and under chiefs competent to represent them". Determining that Western Sahara was not *terra nullius*, the court observes that a contrary determination "would be possible only if it were established that [at the time of its colonization by Spain] the territory belonged to no-one in the sense that it was then open to acquisition through the legal process of 'occupation' ".

In further elaboration of his point, however, Lawrence contends that occupation "applies only to such territories as are no part of the possessions of any civilized state". Accordingly, "[i]t is not necessary", he submits, "that [such territories] should be uninhabited" because "[t]racts roamed over by savage tribes have been again and again appropriated, and even the attainment by the original inhabitants of some slight degree of civilization and political coherence has not sufficed to bar the acquisition of their territory by occupancy". Therefore, he concludes that "international morality",

---

[32] T. J. Lawrence, *The Principles of International Law*, 50-1 (7th edn., Percy H. Winfield, ed., 1923). The first edition of the book appeared in 1895.
[33] John Austin, *The Province of Jurisprudence Determined*, 101 (David Campbell & Philip Thomas, eds., 1998). The first edition of the book appeared in 1832.
[34] T. J. Lawrence, *supra*, note 25, p. 51.
[35] I. C. J. REPORTS, 12, 39 (1975).

and not international law, demands that the "natives" be treated with consideration.[36]

It is striking that while Lawrence has no hesitation in treating the "uncivilised regions" as objects of international law, he is willing to treat chartered companies, such as the British South Africa Company (which, as he points out, "ha[d] been called into existence by some of the colonizing powers ... to open up enormous territories when first brought within the sphere of their influence") as "international persons ... though of a very imperfect and subordinate kind".[37] He views such companies as "sovereign in relation to the barbarous or semi-barbarous inhabitants of the districts in which they bear sway", even though they are not so treated by their own States. To reach the conclusion that the companies in question are sovereign in relation to the "barbarous or semi-barbarous", he relies, without credibly indicating how he deciphers the workings of the inner minds of such people, on their perceptions of the authority of the companies.

Lawrence further states that "[t]he subjects of international law are sovereign states and those other political bodies which, though lacking many of the attributes of sovereign states, possess some to such an extent as to make them real, but imperfect, international persons". Such "other political bodies" or "part-sovereign states" he lists as "client states", "confederations, together with the member-states that compose them", "civilized belligerent communities whose belligerency, but not whose independence, has been recognized", as well as "chartered companies" to whom vast governmental powers had been delegated.[38] Accordingly, entities or districts inhabited by "the barbarous or semi-barbarous" could not even be elevated to the status of "real, but imperfect, international persons".

The implication of the denial of the sovereignty of African States, insofar as the mode of their acquisition by the colonizing powers is concerned, offers an interesting contrast with the pre-19th century state of international law. As Lindley's succinct survey of the works of publicists in the pre-19th century era (such as Vitoria, Soto, La Casas, Ayala, Gentilis, Selden, Grotius, etc.) indicates, although they expressed their positions "in different ways, they [did] not differ materially among themselves" to the effect that "wherever a country [was] inhabited by people who [were] connected by some political organization, however primitive and crude, such a country [was] not to be regarded as *territorium nullius* and open to

---

36 Lawrence, *supra*, note 32., p.148.
37 *Id.*, p. 69.
38 *Id.*, pp. 66, 68-9.

acquisition by Occupation".[39] This conclusion, he further attests, is also borne out by the state practice at the material time.[40]

This is not to say, however, that such territories were beyond the reach of the European Powers. As a general rule, the international law of the time excluded non-Christians from its fold, even though in the so-called Christian States the basic tenets of Christianity were not necessarily being faithfully observed. Accordingly, non-Christians States were at the mercy of the "Christian Club" and could lose their territories through conquest or cession.[41] However, although Lindley painstakingly sets out the basic distinctions and premises for the acquisition of "backward territory" through cession, conquest or occupation, at various historical epochs, he fails to state the obvious: Irrespective of the mode of acquisition (including even the so-called cession), Africa – described in different texts as "barbaric", "savage", "uncivilised", "backward", etc. – bore, and continues to bear, the brunt of the onslaught of the European Powers.

(d) Colonialism and the Balkanization of Africa

(i) The Berlin Conference of 1884-85 and the Question of the Sovereignty of Pre-Colonial African States

As recently asserted by an African author, "...[T]he Berlin conference, despite its significance for the subsequent history of Africa, was essentially a European affair: there was no African representation and African concerns were, if they mattered at all, completely marginal to the basic economic, strategic and political interests of the negotiating European powers."[42]

The scramble for Africa and the intense rivalry[43] it occasioned, particularly among the European Powers, led to the convening of the Berlin Conference of 1884-85. If any one was in doubt as to whether or not the European Powers

---

[39] M. F. Lindley, *supra*, note 19, p. 17.

[40] *Id.*, pp. 24 & 43.

[41] *Id.*, p. 26. As Shaw further points out, the essence of the pre-19th century attitude was that the acquisition of sovereignty over the lands of the peoples of such entities "depended upon the concept of conquest not occupation, and accordingly discussion centred around the notion of just war and the legality of hostilities against non-Christians": Shaw, *supra*, note 12, p. 31.

[42] A. I. Asiwaju, "The Conceptual Framework", in *Partitioned Africans: Ethnic Relations across Africa's International Boundaries*, 1884-1984, 1(A. I. Asiwaju, ed., 1985).

[43] Young describes the nature of the scramble thus: "Africa, in the rhetorical metaphor of imperial jingoism, was a ripe melon awaiting carving in the late nineteenth century. Those who scrambled fastest won the largest slices and the right to consume at their leisure the sweet, succulent flesh. Stragglers snatched only small servings or tasteless portions; Italians, for example, found only desserts on their plates": Crawford Young, *supra*, note 9, p. 19.

really reckoned with the sovereignty of African States – as a reality in its own right – the Berlin Conference put the issue beyond dispute. The fact that African States were not represented at the conference is pregnant with meaning. If the European Powers considered the African States at the material time as sovereign entities, why were they not represented at the conference,[44] even in the face of the obvious fact that Africa was the focal point of the conference? How could a conference whose "chief purpose", in the words of Beer,[45] "was to establish freedom of commerce" exclude Africans whose territory was the target? Is this not a reflection of the very nature of the colonial project and its perception of the status of entities and peoples earmarked for colonization? How is it that Africans were not consulted prior to the convening of the conference? If African States were appreciated as sovereign entities in their own right, why were they not invited to the conference, at the end of which any treaty concluded, with their input and consistent with their interests, would constitute the basic legal framework for the "freedom of commerce" envisaged?

What this demonstrates is the fact that the denial of the sovereignty of African States – as a reality independent of the vagaries of the colonial enterprise – and the treatment of their territory as *terra nullius*, was not simply academic theorizing which could be dismissed as the palaver of academics like Westlake who, in the comfort of their ivory towers, were oblivious of State practice and the underpinning intentions of the colonizing powers. To that extent, this bears testimony, in effect, to a concurrence – at least in 19th century Europe[46] – of

---

44 The Final Act of the conference was signed by the plenipotentiaries of Austria-Hungary, Belgium, Denmark, France, Great Britain, Germany, Italy, Netherlands, Portugal, Russia, Spain, Sweden and Norway, Turkey, and United States. On the Berlin Conference generally, *see* S. E. Crowe, *The Berlin West Africa Conference* (1970).
45 George Louis Beer, *supra*, note 6, p. 195.
46 Cf. The Separate Opinion of Judge Ammoun in the *Western Sahara Case*, *supra*, note 35, pp. 85-7. Judge Ammoun refers to the "penetrating views" of Bayona-Ba-Meya (for Zaire, now Democratic Republic of Congo) and Mohammed Bedjaoui (for Algeria), on the issue of *terra nullius*, which he commends as: "the reply which may be given to the participants in the Berlin Conference of 1885, who, during the fierce blaze of nineteenth-century colonialism, the success of which they sought to ensure by eliminating competition, regarded sub-Saharan Africa as an immense *terra nullius* available for the first occupier, whereas that continent had been inhabited since pre-historic times, and flourishing kingdoms had there been established – Ghana, Mali, Bornu – whose civilization survived until the colonial period, and only succumbed to the wounds inflicted by colonization and the slave trade…It was in the southern part of this continent and in Kenya that…ethnologists discovered the remains of the first hominoids." Both Bayona-Ba-Meya and Bedjaoui, had challenged the use of *terra nullius* by the European Powers to deprive Africans of their lands. In essence, they (Bedjaoui in particular) questioned the universal application of a law, purporting to be international, in which Africans had no input.

academic opinion and state practice, on account of either the influence of the former on the latter or the former as a restatement of the latter. Therefore, the pronouncement of the International Court of Justice in the *Western Sahara Case* to the effect that "the State practice of the relevant period[47] indicates that territories inhabited by tribes or peoples having a social and political organization were not regarded as *terrae nullius*",[48] is, with due respect, an uncritical endorsement of appearance over reality if, as it appears,[49] the court had in mind the 19th century practice of European States. As we shall demonstrate later, it was possible, and would have indeed been illuminating, for the court to have reached the same conclusion through a better route. Therefore, the pronouncement must not be construed in isolation of the fact that, insofar as the European Powers were concerned, this was a self-serving strategy and not an indication that the European Powers indeed acknowledged the sovereignty of the African States as a fact in its own right.[50]

Indeed, when Mr. Kasson, the plenipotentiary of the United States at the Berlin Conference, expressed the view that "[m]odern international law follows closely a line which leads to the recognition of the right of native tribes to dispose freely of themselves and of their hereditary territory" and that the acquisition of territories in Africa should be premised on "the voluntary con-

---

[47] In this case 1884, treated by the court as the starting date of the Spanish colonization of the Western Sahara.

[48] *Western Sahara Case, supra*, note 35, p. 39.

[49] The court points out, for instance, that "Spain did not proceed on the basis that it was establishing sovereignty over *terrae nullius*": *Western Sahara Case, id.*, p. 39. Shaw shares the view that the court had in mind the practice of 19th century European States: "...[T]he Court was prepared to move some way towards the acceptance of legal pluralism, but not with regard to the question of *terra nullius*, which was treated purely in the light of the (European) State practice of the period". However, as Shaw further points out, Spain had declared before the UN General Assembly that it had never regarded the territory in question as *terra nullius*. In its written statement, it noted that an area was *terra nullius* if not under the sovereignty of a State authority, but the issue was not discussed in the Spanish submission in the oral pleadings. Having regard to the fact that Spain denied that either Morocco or the Mauritanian entity possessed sovereign rights over the Saharan territory at the material time, or that the tribes of the area constituted a State, it should have accepted the logical conclusion arising therefrom. i.e. that it considered the territory to be *terra nullius*. Having failed to do so, "its position remained to that extent confused and ambiguous": Shaw, *supra*, note 12, pp. 34-5, 56.

[50] Needless to say, the court's determination that Western Sahara was not a *terra nullius* is tenable, but not because the "State practice of the relevant period" bears this out, if by that phrase the court meant to refer to the true position of the European Powers.

sent of the natives whose country is taken possession of, in all cases where they had not provoked ... aggression",[51] he was a lone voice in the wilderness. Herr Busch, German Under-Secretary of State for Foreign Affairs, who was presiding the conference, remarked that Mr. Kasson's views "touched on delicate questions, upon which the conference hesitated to express an opinion".[52] Thus, Westlake proclaims that "it would be going much further, and to a length to which the conference declined to go, if we were to say that, except in the case of unprovoked aggression justifying conquest, an uncivilised population has rights which make its free consent necessary to the establishment over it of a government possessing international validity".[53]

It is, therefore, no surprise that the conference proceedings and the Berlin Act are replete with references to occupation, a mode of acquisition of territory which is traditionally invoked in relation to *terra nullius*. These developments are suggestive of the confluence (at least in 19th century Europe) of academic opinion, State practice and treaty law. Whatever differences existed were, from a practical point of view, inconsequential. Clearly, Westlake, and others similarly situated, considered so-called treaties of cession between European Powers and the "uncivilised" African States to be devoid of legal, as opposed to moral, significance. Accordingly, they preferred to anchor European titles to territories in Africa on modes of territorial acquisition other than cession (especially occupation). On the other hand, although the European Powers accorded legal significance to such treaties, this was primarily insofar as their relations with one another were in issue. One recalls, in this respect, Thruston's account to the effect that it was desirable to perform a "little comedy" (i.e. sign a treaty) with Chief Kivalli "before he [Chief Kivalli] should do so with the Belgians". As against the "uncivilised" African States, however, the reality was that cession (based on such treaties) differed from occupation in name only. Again, one cannot but recall Thruston's revelation that the treaty-making process was "an amiable farce ... the equivalent of an occupation".

Lindley is, however, of the view that it is legitimate to say that although the method of acquiring territory in Africa was generally referred to as occupation at the Berlin Conference, the term was used with a broad meaning equivalent to acquisition or appropriation and was not confined to occupation in the

---

[51] Quoted in Westlake, *supra,* note 13, p. 138.
[52] Quoted in Westlake, *id.*, p. 138.
[53] Westlake, *id.*, p. 139.

strict sense of the word.[54] Lindley's view is informed by his attempt to show that the European Powers recognized the sovereignty of African States and could only acquire territories in inhabited parts of Africa through means other than occupation. However, the fact that the European Powers, at best, had mere pretensions to the sovereignty of African States – and disingenuously so – undermines his position.[55] Lindley himself acknowledges this fact but, for him, it suffices that although "in many cases...treaties [with Africans] were obtained under compulsion ... forced treaties are not unrecognized in international affairs".[56]

It, therefore, follows that the participants at the Berlin Conference could not have come to the conclusion that Africa was to be partitioned as though it was, so to say, a booty of war, without a prior acceptance, even if tacit, of the view that Africans, who had long inhabited their lands, were "uncivilized" and devoid of sovereignty. Accordingly, as Anghie points out, "[c]onventional histories of the Conference make the powerful point that Africans were

---

[54] Lindley, *supra*, note 19, p. 34. Shaw shares this view: Shaw, *supra*, note 12, pp. 34-5. In the *Western Sahara Case*, the court observed that "[o]n occasion ... the word 'occupation' was used in a non-technical sense denoting simply acquisition of sovereignty; but that did not signify that the acquisition of sovereignty through such agreements with authorities of the country was regarded as an 'occupation' of a 'terra nullius' in the proper sense of these terms. On the contrary, such agreements with local rulers, whether or not considered as an actual 'cession' of the territory, were regarded as derivative roots of title, and not original titles obtained by occupation of *terrae nullius*". There is no specific indication, however, that the court had in mind the Berlin Conference and the Berlin Act. The court further points out that it was not called upon to "pronounce upon the legal character or the legality of the titles which led to Spain becoming the administering Power of Western Sahara": *Western Sahara Case, supra*, note 35, pp. 39-40.

[55] Cf. Diane F. Orentlicher, "Separation Anxiety: International Responses to Ethno-Separatist Claims", 23 YALE J. INT'L L., 1, 28-9 (1998). Orentlicher points out that European States acquired sovereignty over some colonial territories through occupation of what was characterized as *terra nullius* and over other areas through conquest. However, in most cases, transfers of sovereignty from African to European governments were formally effected by bilateral treaties, including treaties of cession and treaties establishing protectorates. Such treaties implicitly recognized the African rulers who signed them as possessing "the attributes of sovereignty", while the treaty form "implied a legal equality" between the signatories. Orentlicher, however, makes it clear that, in practice, during the 19th century, "African rulers often executed these treaties under considerable duress". Additionally, the treaties were legally relevant less as a mode of transferring rights between the two parties than as a means by which European Powers could, as against one another, demonstrate their title to a particular territory in Africa: *Id*.

[56] Lindley, *supra*, note 19, p. 44.

excluded from its deliberations. The story of the Conference may also be written, however, from another perspective that focuses on the complex way in which the identity of the African was an enduring problem that haunted the proceedings of the Conference".[57]

What then is the import of our analysis for the validity of the so-called treaties of cession that were signed between European States and African States? Were such treaties invalid on account of the alleged absence of sovereignty on the part of the latter? Quite the contrary. The parties were sovereign and seised of treaty-making competence but not because, as is clear by now, the European Powers – in substance and not merely in form – treated African States as such. However, as earlier pointed out, the validity of such treaties is a matter for determination with reference to the existence or otherwise of vitiating or invalidating elements.

(ii) The Balkanization of Africa

In the words of Wole Soyinka: "…[A]t the Berlin Conference the colonial powers …met to divvy up their interests into states, lumping various peoples and tribes together in some places, or slicing them apart in others like some demented tailor who paid no attention to the fabric, color or pattern of the quilt he was patching together."[58]

Having laid down the basic framework for the partition of those parts of Africa that were yet to come under European subjugation or, euphemistically put, spheres of influence,[59] the European Powers set out to accomplish their mission. In furtherance thereof, Africa was partitioned in a manner that makes a mockery of the entire exercise. A senior British official's description of how the border between Nigeria and Cameroon was created speaks volumes: "In

---

57 Anghie, *supra*, note 8, p. 61. Further criticisms of the Berlin Conference in particular and the colonial project in general, are provided in Makau Wa Mutua, "Why Redraw the Map of Africa: A Legal and Moral Inquiry", 16 MICH. J. INT'L L., 1113 (1995); Makau Wa Mutua, "Putting Humpty Dumpty Back Together Again: The Dilemmas of the Post-Colonial African State", 21 BROOK. J. INT'L L., 505 (1995).

58 THE SACRAMENTO BEE, Sunday, May 15, 1994, Forum 1.

59 The participants at the Berlin Conference essentially laid down a procedural framework under which, as Article 34 of the Berlin Act provides: "[a]ny Power which henceforth takes possession of a tract of land on the coasts of the African Continent outside of its present possessions, or which, being hitherto without such possessions, shall acquire them, as well as the Power which assumes a Protectorate there, shall accompany the respective act with a notification thereof, addressed to the other Signatory Powers … in order to enable them, if need be, to make good any claims of their own."

those days we just took a blue pencil and a rule, and we put it down at Calabar, and drew [a] line to Yola...I recollect thinking when I was sitting having an audience with the Emir [of Yola], surrounded by his tribe, that it was a very good thing that he did not know that I, with a blue pencil, had drawn a line through his territory."[60]

As a former British Prime Minister, Lord Salisbury, further acknowledged at a dinner in 1890, following the conclusion of an Anglo-French convention establishing British and French spheres of influence in West Africa, "[w]e have been engaged in drawing lines upon maps where no man's foot ever trod; we have been giving away mountains and rivers and lakes to each other, only hindered by the small impediment that we never knew exactly where the mountains and rivers and lakes were".[61]

(iii) Consequences of the Balkanization

What are the consequences of the arbitrary partition of Africa? The balkanization of Africa by the colonial powers split persons belonging to the same ethnic group (and hitherto configured in various empires or kingdoms) into different colonial spheres of influence and, in most cases, later constituted the territorial basis for the grant of political independence to present-day African States. Several examples of the arbitrary manner in which ethnic groups were split or amalgamated with other ethnic groups, thus occasioning ethnic heterogeneity, abound: the Somalis severed, at various times, into British Somaliland, French Somaliland, Italian Somaliland, the Northern Frontier District of Kenya and the Ogaden (Ogaadeen) region of Ethiopia; the Maasai, bifurcated by the Kenya-Tanzania border; the Bakongo across the Gabon-Congo, Congo-Democratic Republic of Congo(DRC), formerly Zaire, and DRC-Angola boundaries; the Lunda separated by the DRC-Angola and DRC-Zambia boundaries; the Yoruba split into Nigeria, Benin(formerly Dahomey) and Togo; the Gourma, truncated into Burkina Faso (formerly Upper Volta), Togo and Benin; the Tibu, mutilated by the Libya-Chad and Chad-Niger boundaries, as well as the Ewe, dissected into British Togoland, French Togoland and Ghana (formerly Gold Coast).[62]

In the *Case Concerning the Territorial Dispute (Libyan Arab Jamahiriya/Chad)*[63] Judge Bola Ajibola decries this state of affairs and observes that

---

60 Quoted in J. C. Anene, *The International Boundaries of Nigeria*, 1885-1960, 2-3 (1970).
61 Quoted in Anene, *id.*, p. 3.
62 Asiwaju, *supra*, note 42, p. 2. For an elaborate list, see Asiwaju, "Partitioned Culture Areas: A Checklist", in Asiwaju, *supra*, note 42, pp. 256-8.
63 I. C. J. REPORTS, 6, 52-4 (1994) (Separate Opinion of Judge Ajibola).

"since 1885 when it was partitioned, Africa has been ruefully nursing the wounds inflicted on it by its colonial past. Remnants of this unenviable colonial heritage intermittently erupt into discordant social, political and even economic upheavals". Aspects of this heritage, he further observes, "continue, like apparitions, to rear their heads, and haunt the entire continent in various jarring and sterile manifestations". Questioning how one can "forget unhealed wounds", he states that "[o]ne aspect of this unfortunate legacy is to be seen in the incessant boundary disputes between African States", as exemplified by the dispute in question.

The arbitrary partition of Africa also led to the "systematic application of different cover-names for the same peoples to distinguish between those on different sides of particular inter-state boundaries", especially where they fell "under the control of different colonial powers",[64] as is the case, for instance, with the Yoruba (referred to as such in British Nigeria but called "Nago" in French Benin, sometimes assuming the masculine and feminine forms of "Nagots" and "Nagottes", respectively).[65] This is obviously capable of occasioning a crisis of identity.

Furthermore, in some cases, as exemplified by the plight of nomadic Somalis, the fragmentation cut off entire clans from the traditional sources of water and pasture for their herds. In one instance, the Mareehaan clan was sliced into three different parts: one part under the British in the Northern Frontier District of Kenya, another under the Italians in the South, and a third in the South-West under Ethiopia. The tragedy is that while those nomads in Italian Somaliland had access to water resources from the Shabeelle River, they lost valuable grazing land on the Ethiopian side. In similar fashion, their kinsmen on the Ethiopian side retained the pastures but were cut off the indispensable water resources on the coast.[66] In the *Western Sahara Case*, Mauritania describes a similar scenario: On account of the artificial frontiers created by the European Powers, the same families and their properties could be found on either side of arbitrarily bisected frontiers; the same was true of wells, lands, burial grounds, watering places and palm oases.[67]

Additionally, the fact that the various colonial powers operated different colonial policies (for instance the resort of the British to the so-called indirect rule system and the emphasis of the French on assimilation) meant that

---

64 Asiwaju, "The Conceptual Framework", in Asiwaju, *supra*, note 42, p. 3.
65 Asiwaju, *id*.
66 Said S. Samatar, "The Somali Dilemma: Nation in Search of a State", in Asiwaju, *supra*, note 42, 155, p. 176.
67 *Western Sahara Case, supra*, note 35, pp. 59-60.

persons of the same ethnic group, split into different colonial spheres of influence, had different experiences that impacted on any attempts at re-integration.

(iv) The Arbitrariness of the Partition: In Search of Justifications/ Explanations

Why was Africa partitioned in a manner suggestive that the whims and caprices of the colonizing powers were the driving forces? Brownlie opines that although "in the majority of instances African frontiers divide tribes or ethnic groups ... boundary making in the period of European expansion in Africa took place in circumstances which generally militated against reference to tribal or ethnological considerations" or "tended to be incompatible with tribal distribution".[68] He attributes this to several factors: recourse to geographical features such as rivers and watersheds, and astronomical or geometrical lines; the role of prior exploration and military penetration within the framework of political bargaining; difficulty in the determination of the principles of association by which a group was to be designated as a tribe, people or nation, etc. Brownlie further points out that "in a significant minority of cases substantial (though not necessarily exclusive) reference was made to tribal distribution in delimitation of frontiers";[69] the basic assumption in some of these cases being that "such reference would ease problems of administration". However, he concludes that "whilst colonial policy to some extent equated administrative convenience and avoidance of division of groups, the general principles of colonial thinking were divorced from ethnological considerations".[70]

Similarly, Hargreaves ascribes the arbitrariness of the partition of Africa to several factors, including the fact that "European knowledge of the physical, let alone the human geography of Africa was still rudimentary".[71] Additionally, where the determination of a boundary entailed protracted

---

[68] Ian Brownlie, *African Boundaries: A Legal and Diplomatic Encyclopaedia*, 6 (1979).

[69] Brownlie lists the alignments concerned as follows: Algeria-Morocco (the coast-Teniet-el-Sassi-Figuig); Algeria-Tunisia (the coast-Bir Romane); Ethiopia-Kenya; Egypt-Sudan (the administrative lines); Chad-Sudan (in part); Botswana-Rhodesia (in part); the boundaries of Swaziland; Kenya-Uganda; Kenya-Sudan (with reference to the Red Line Boundary); Sudan-Uganda; Benin-Upper Volta; Niger-Nigeria (in part) and Cameroun-Nigeria (in part): *Id.*

[70] Brownlie, *id.*, pp. 6-7.

[71] J. D. Hargreaves, "The Making of the Boundaries: Focus on West Africa", in Asiwaju, *supra*, note 42, p. 22.

negotiations, the plight of Africans took backstage. Thus, an 1894 proposal by the Governor of Sierra Leone, Col. Cardew, for a revised boundary with Guinea with a view to paying "greater attention to African political alignments and trade routes and respect[ing] the integrity of Samu and Luawa chiefdoms" was aborted because "officials recoiled from the thought of further protracted negotiations":[72] "I sympathize strongly", wrote Secretary Ripon, "with Col. Cardew's desire not to divide the territories of Native Chiefs. *It is a wretched system, unjust to the chiefs and their people, and a fruitful source of disputes and trouble* to the dividing Powers. But of course we cannot now deal with these matters as if the negotiations were to be entered upon for the first time".[73]

However, Hargreaves concludes that the arbitrary partition of Africa was neither determinist nor conspiratorial, but accidental. Whatever may be said of this conclusion, on balance, the colonial powers demonstrated a brazen show of nonchalance, even contempt, for the interests of the Africans, given their failure to engage the latter in any meaningful dialogue or consultation.

(e) The Phenomena of Colonies and Protectorates: Distinction in Form or Substance?

Once an African entity became a colony, any lingering controversy over its international status was considerably whittled down, if not completely resolved, insofar as the colonial powers were concerned. This was not because the fact of colonization transformed an otherwise "uncivilised" entity (and its "uncivilised natives") into the realm of "civilization" and membership of the "family of nations". Instead, the transformation that colonization effected was the establishment of relations among European Powers since, given the sweeping tentacles of colonialism, the colonial power became the reference point. Thus, relations between one European Power and the colony of another European Power were, in effect, relations between two European Powers.

Towards the later part of the 19th century, however, European States resorted to the use of protectorates. How, if any, did these differ from colonies? Westlake acknowledges the existence of the phenomenon of protectorates but only in the "civilised world" as "a relation existing between two states". In such a scheme, "the protected one is controlled or even wholly represented in its foreign affairs by the protecting one, while the latter has such authority in the internal affairs of the former, if any, as the arrangements between them provide for". Additionally, although the protected State

---

[72] Hargreaves, *id.*, p. 24.
[73] Quoted in Hargreaves, *id.*, pp. 24-5. (Emphasis ours).

is not independent, it does not "altogether lose an international existence, for its foreign affairs are distinctly its own, even when wholly managed for it by the protecting state".

However, Westlake faults the use of protectorates with reference to "uncivilised" regions whose sovereignty he disputes. Accordingly, "[w]here there is no state...there can be no protected state".[74] Instead, he considers that "the institution of protectorates over uncivilized regions [gives] greater freedom to the initial steps towards their acquisition", and he would have preferred that a new term be used to depict the extension of the regime of protectorates to entities that, in his conception of statehood, do not qualify as States. [75]

Lawrence shares Westlake's conception of protectorates as between States and strives to avoid the terminological problematique by distinguishing between "old-fashioned protectorates" and "colonial protectorates".[76] He describes the latter as "modern expedients" which differ from the former "in that, instead of being a relation between two states, both known to International Law, each of them may be described as an attitude on the part of a civilized power towards a district and population too uncivilized to be regarded as a state in International Law". Such protectorates, he further argues, "cannot be client states" since they are "not states at all in the sense of being members of the family of nations and subjects of International Law". Like Westlake, he also considers that it is "beyond doubt" that the assumption of a colonial protectorate is a prelude ("a sort of halfway house") to complete annexation.[77]

---

[74] In the *Western Sahara Case*, Judge Dillard observes that "[a]s was cryptically put in the proceedings: you do not *protect* a *terra nullius*": *Supra*, note 35, p. 124 (Separate Opinion of Judge Dillard). (Emphasis in original). However, unlike Westlake, Judge Dillard's pronouncement is intended to show that Western Sahara was not, at the time of Spanish colonization of the African territory, a *terra nullius*.

[75] Westlake, *supra*, note 13, pp. 177-84.

[76] Lawrence also refers to a "third class" of protectorates which he describes as "comparatively modern in their origin and somewhat anomalous in their nature". This arises where a State "belonging to the family of nations, and generally an important member thereof", establishes what it terms a protectorate over "a political community to which it is impossible to deny the name of state, but which is not sufficiently civilized after the European fashion to be regarded as a full member of international society". He cites as illustrations the British protectorate over Zanzibar (established in 1890) and the French protectorate over Annam (dating back to 1886). He distinguishes these two entities from "a tribe of half-naked savages hunting game for subsistence over African plains". However, he submits that their "political destiny is...usually the same" since protectorates are "often instituted over the first, as well as the second, with a view to eventual annexation": Lawrence, *supra*, note 32, pp. 163-4.

[77] Lawrence, *id.*, pp. 69-70.

The regime of protectorates, as invoked with reference to "uncivilised regions", was a convenient mechanism employed by the colonizing powers to exploit Africa's resources without being bogged down by the burdens (cost, manpower, etc.) of local administration. As Lindley points out, this feature of protectorates endeared itself to the European Powers and accounts for the "extensive adoption" of the use of protectorates by them "in the spread of their dominion".[78] To that extent, the regime of protectorates was more insidious than the regime of colonies. On the other hand, the local inhabitants of a protectorate could have a say over their internal affairs. However, this was so only insofar as the interests of the European Powers were not in jeopardy. As Orentlicher observes, "in practice, the internal sovereignty of African protectorates was flagrantly transgressed";[79] thus undermining any argument to the effect that the recourse to the phenomenon of protectorates is evidence that the European Powers actually treated African States as sovereign entities. This is the more so that the regime of "colonial protectorates" was a prelude to outright colonization. Therefore, the reality is that both colonies and protectorates furthered the colonial objective[80] and wrecked havoc on the colonized peoples.

(f) "The White Man's Burden": The Rhetoric of Colonialism

The colonizing powers had no illusions about the nature of their mission: the exploitation of Africa's resources. As Beer acknowledges, "[e]ach of the Powers was interested in preventing its fellows, either singly or in combination, from securing special commercial privileges in a region whose riches loomed unwarrantingly large, not only in the popular imagination but also in the minds of explorers and statesmen".[81] However, they also attempted to give the colonial project a human face. To realize this objective, the

---

[78] Lindley, *supra*, note 19, p. 182.
[79] Orentlicher, *supra*, note 55, p. 29.
[80] Alexandrowicz notes, for instance, that there was a "tendency to deform the original classic concept of the protectorate and to convert it into an instrument of colonialism": C. H. Alexandrowicz, "The Role of Treaties in the European-African Confrontation in the Nineteenth Century", in *African International Legal History*, 55 (A. K. Mensah-Brown, ed., 1975). Shaw also states that "little practical distinction was made between ordinary colonies and protectorates and it marked the development of the colonial protectorate with its substantial differences from the traditional protectorate": Shaw, *supra*, note 12, p. 48.
[81] Beer, *supra*, note 6, p. 195.

wolf had to parade itself in sheep's clothing.[82] The Berlin Conference, though convened primarily for the purpose of engendering a framework for the regulation of the imperial ambitions of the colonizing powers in Africa, was also used to articulate a philosophy of colonialism predicated on a civilizing mission. For instance, the British plenipotentiary enjoined his colleagues not to lose sight of the fact that in the opinion of his government, "commercial interests should not be looked upon as the exclusive subject of the deliberations of the Conference". Therefore, "the welfare of the natives should not be neglected" given that "freedom of commerce, unchecked by reasonable control, [could] degenerate into licence". Reminding his colleagues that "the natives are not represented amongst us", yet the decisions of the conference would have "an extreme importance for them", he made a case for "the advancement of legitimate commerce, with security for the equality of treatment of all nations, and for the well-being of the native races" and thereby "confer the advantages of civilization on the natives".[83] Whatever the sense in which the term "civilization" was employed, this further underscores our point that the European Powers' condescending perception of Africans remained ingrained even though, as a strategic tool of their imperial ambitions, they were prepared to acknowledge the treaty-making competence of African States and yet, without a wink, proceed to bastardize the treaty-making process.

Although the civilizing mission platform was not entirely a new strategy in the armory of the colonial project, it was not only articulated at the conference, but also found expression in the General Act of the conference. By Article 6 thereof, the colonizing powers undertook to watch over the conservation or preservation of the indigenous populations, improve their moral and material conditions, and strive to suppress the slave trade. All religious, scientific, or charitable institutions and undertakings created and organized in furtherance of the above ends, or which aimed at "instructing the natives and bringing home to them the blessings of civilization", were to be protected without distinction of nation or creed. In a further show of collaboration with, or approval of the activities of, missionaries, scientists and explorers, their followers, properties, and collections were to be accorded special

---

[82] In the era of the slave trade, a similar strategy was employed: Some of the slave merchants claimed that they were spurred by humanitarian considerations because, in their view, "by purchasing, or rather ransoming, the Negroes from their national tyrants, and transplanting them under the benign influence of the law and the gospel, they are advanced to much greater degrees of felicity": Quoted in Robert O. Collins, *History: Text and Readings*, 194 (1971).

[83] Quoted in Lindley, *supra*, note 19, p. 332.

protection. Additionally, provision was made for human rights but these were strikingly, though not surprisingly, restricted to freedom of conscience and religious toleration, free and public exercise of all forms of divine worship, right to build edifices for religious purposes, and the organization, irrespective of creed, of religious missions.[84]

What, one might ask, was the motivation behind the so-called civilizing mission of the colonizing powers? The opening speech of Prince Bismarck at the Berlin Conference lends credence to the view that the civilizing mission was not spurred by entirely altruistic motives: "In convoking the Conference", remarked Prince Bismarck, "the Imperial Government was guided by the conviction that all the Governments invited share the wish to bring the natives of Africa within that the pale of civilization by *opening up the interior of the continent to commerce...*"[85] Thus, the civilizing mission was inextricably intertwined with the primary goal of the colonial project. In any event, as borne out, for instance, by the outrageous manner in which King Leopold II of Belgium "turned the Congo into his personal empire and the scene of the worst form of colonial exploitation",[86] the credibility of the civilizing mission is readily called into question.

Hyde further observes that "contacts with backward peoples" were "oftentimes ...marred by harsh and ruthless practices", as "the Nineteenth Century revealed contempt for the culture, aspirations, and equities of peoples regarded as uncivilized when they lacked the power by their own strong arm to resist the demands of an invading or annexing State".[87] Gye-Wado writes in the same vein, submitting that "[o]ne of the glaring index of the colonial period was the denial of the fundamental rights of the colonized people. It is within this context that the argument of civilizing mission can be floored". "While the colonizers pretended notions of human rights, or at least natural rights", he further contends, "they paradoxically never saw the necessity for the enjoyment of these rights by the colonized peoples. Of course the logic of colonialism would have ceased to be relevant".[88] Additionally, Eze opines that the colonial powers contributed to the progressive development of human rights by abolishing certain objectionable practices prevalent at the time in Africa, but emphasizes that, on balance,

---

84   The General Act of the Berlin Conference on West Africa, Feb. 26, 1885, is reproduced in 3 AM. J. INT'L L. 7 (1909) (Supp.).
85   Quoted in Lindley, *supra*, note 19, p. 332. Emphasis ours.
86   U. O. Umozurike, Self-Determination in International Law, 28 (1972).
87   Hyde, *supra*, note 31, p. 127.
88   Onje Gye-Wado, "Africa, Reparations and International Law", 19 NIG. J. INT'L AFF., 115 (1993).

there is no argument as to the fundamental negative effects of colonialism on colonial and independent Africa, since colonialism is essentially antithetical to human rights promotion".[89] While it is true that some individuals and institutions were genuinely interested in the development of Africa, "their saving labours were palliative and peripheral".[90] In any event, any positive development effected by the colonial powers in Africa occurred within a framework that viewed the interests of the metropolis as overriding.[91] Thus, the purported civilizing mission was honored more in the breach than in the observance.

3. REVISITING THE SOVEREIGNTY AND CIVILIZATION QUESTIONS: THE RECONSTRUCTION OF THE LEGACY OF AFRICA'S PRE-COLONIAL HISTORY

(a) The Legacy of History and the Reality of the Sovereignty of Pre-Colonial African States

As so eloquently observed by Paul Bohannan: "Africa has, for generations now, been viewed through a web of myth so pervasive and so glib that understanding it becomes a two-fold task: the task of clarifying the myth and the separate task of examining whatever reality has been hidden behind it…Only if the myth is stripped away can the reality of Africa emerge."[92]

African history has been so distorted, especially by Eurocentric scholars, that for a long time the conventional "wisdom" was that Africa had no history prior to its contact with the West. As Samora Machel, a former president of Mozambique, puts it: "[Africa was] excluded from history, forgotten in geography [and] only existed with reference to a colonial point of reference".[93] Thus, Hegel, a German philosopher, went so far as to proclaim

---

[89] Osita Eze, *Human Rights in Africa: Some Selected Problems*, 18-22 (1984).
[90] Offiong, *supra*, note 9, p. 100.
[91] Reginald Green & Ann Seidman, *Unity or Poverty?: The Economics of Pan Africanism*, 31-2 (1968).
[92] Paul Bohannan, *Africa and the Africans*, 1 (1964). Questioning the myths surrounding the history of Africa, Okoye asserts: Africa has a long and enduring history behind it, longer than any historian has described it. Africa has had its own rich sweep of events which European conquest and settlement have failed to reckon with. Yet, no civilization of the world can be divorced from the continent. The depth of its antiquity, the immensity of its treasure and the resilience of its people form a fascinating study which no single intellect can comprehend, no single volume describe. Mokwogo Okoye, *African Responses*, 389 (1964).
[93] Samora Machel, quoted in Patrick Wilmot, *Ideology and National Consciousness*, 189 (1980).

that Africa is "no historical part of the world; it has no movement or development to exhibit".[94] Indeed, the task of reconstructing Africa's authentic history is so monumental that it continues to engage the attention of African and non-African scholars who have undertaken the historic mission of setting the records straight. While this task continues, numerous studies so far abound that counter the stereotypic labeling of pre-colonial Africa as "uncivilised", "savage", "barbaric", etc. Walter Rodney's How Europe Underdeveloped Africa[95] and the works of a host of other scholars[96] are replete with evidence – including the testimonies of some of the early European explorers[97] – to the effect that the popular portrayals of Africa in Europe were clearly misconceived, and that, far from enabling or facilitating the development of Africa, Europe's contact with Africa – since the days of the infamous slave trade – ushered in the underdevelopment of the continent.

Furthermore, Elias, a former Chief Justice of Nigeria and former President of the International Court of Justice, in his Africa and the

---

[94] Georg Hegel, *The Philosophy of History*, quoted in Joseph E. Harris, *Africans and Their History*, 9 (2nd rev. edn., 1998). Harris' text addresses critical issues such as "A tradition of Myths and Stereotypes [about Africa]" (Chapter 1), "The Evolution of Early African Societies" (Chapter 2), "Early Kingdoms and City-States" (Chapter 3), "The Scramble and Partition" (Chapter 11), "African Diplomacy, Resistance and Rebellion" (Chapter 12), and "The European Colonizers: Policies and Practices" (Chapter 13). Unfortunately, as Harris observes, "[r]ace in general, and myths and stereotypes surrounding physical features and skin color in particular, have been so pervasive and basic in black-white relations and in accounts of those interactions that in spite of a stream of scientific evidence to the contrary, the concept of black inferiority continues to thrive in many minds": *Id*. On the question of race in the United States, for instance, *see* Andrew Hacker, *Two Nations: Black and White, Separate, Hostile, Unequal* (rev. edn., 1995).

[95] Walter Rodney, *supra*, note 9.

[96] *See* generally, Basil Davidson, *Black Mother: Africa – The Years of Trial* (1970); W. N. Huggins & J. G. Jackson, *An Introduction to African Civilizations* (1973); *The African Past Speaks* (Joseph C. Miller, ed., 1980); *Africa in Classical Antiquity* (L. A. Thompson & J Ferguson, eds., 1969); Okoye, *supra*, note 92; *The People of Africa* (H. M. Schieffelin, ed., 1974).

[97] For instance, Blyden is reported to have remarked that an exhibition by Africans opened his eyes to "capacities and susceptibilities altogether inconsistent with the theory that dooms such a people to a state of perpetual barbarism or of essential inferiority to the more favoured races": E. W. Blyden, Report on the Falaba Expedition, 1872, quoted in Schieffelin, ed., *id*., at XI. After witnessing the wonders of Egypt, Volney, a French Oriental traveler, exclaimed: "To think that this black race, today enslaved by us and the object of our disdain, is the same to which we owe our arts and sciences and even our speech": Quoted in Okoye, *supra*, note 92, p. 92.

Development of International Law, provides an insightful summary, predicated on historical facts – which need no repetition here – on the organization and international relations, *with obvious legal connotations*, of "indigenous African States" such as ancient Ghana (reputed to have lasted from 300-1087 A. D.), Mali Kingdom, Songhai Kingdom, Yoruba Kingdom, etc.[98]

The fact is that the Europeans who characterized pre-colonial Africa as "uncivilised" and devoid of sovereignty either exhibited their ignorance of African history or conveniently chose to see Africa and its people through a distinctly European prism. That explains Westlake's earlier conception of a government (his test of civilization) as one that must be capable of protecting "people of the European race" in a manner that enables them to "carry on the complex life to which they have been accustomed in their homes". Such construction is clearly myopic and, concomitantly, flawed.

One must, of course, avoid the risk of reveling in idle fantasy by painting a romantic portrait of Africa that is at variance with the material evidence. Nonetheless, it is undoubtedly the case that Westlake and others similarly situated are either not students of African history or have approached Africa and its peoples from a skewed perspective, which has little to do with objective legal scholarship.

(b) The Locus of the Sovereignty of Pre-Colonial African States in the Colonial Era

Having regard to the reality of Africa's pre-colonial history, the fact that colonialism, in collusion with international law, denied the sovereignty of African States or, at best, paid lip service to it, is a sad commentary on the legacy of 19th century international law. The capacity of law, international or otherwise, to develop in advance of dominant social relations is obviously limited. However, law can, in however limited a sphere, play a liberating role.

The conception of Statehood in the African pre-colonial context does not necessarily accord with modern-day formulations[99] which, in any event,

---

[98] T. O. Elias, *Africa and the Development of International Law*, 6-17 (2nd rev. edn., Richard Akinjide, ed., 1988). See also, U. O. Umozurike, *Introduction to International Law*, 7-8 (1993); Basil Davidson, *African Civilization Revisited* (1991); A. K. Mensah-Brown, "Notes on International Law and Pre-Colonial Legal History of Modern Ghana", in Mensah-Brown, ed., *supra*, note 80, p. 107; T. O. Elias, "International Relations in Africa: A Historical Survey", in Mensah-Brown, *supra*, note 80, p. 87; Godwin-Collins K. N. Onyeledo, " 'International Law' Among the Yoruba-Benin and the Hausa-Fulani", in Mensah-Brown, *supra*, note 80, p. 153; Basil Davidson, *Africa in History* (1991); *Africa in the Nineteenth Century Until the 1880s* (J. F. Ade Ajayi, ed., 1989).

[99] J. C. Anene, *supra*, note 60, pp. 5-6; Brownlie, *supra*, note 68, p. 8; Shaw, *supra*, note 12, pp. 27-8.

have been largely influenced by developments in Europe. Nonetheless, the fact that 19th century international law failed to reckon with, and instead denigrated, the experiences of Africa and its peoples, calls into question its claim to the "international" that precedes "law".[100] Thus, it is not a "heresy" to assert, as we presently do, that international law properly so-called is a 20th century development. Anything prior to that was only a masquerade putting on the garb of international law.

Given that, as we have maintained, pre-colonial African States were sovereign, what became of such sovereignties while colonialism held sway in Africa? Were such sovereignties extinguished? Elias is of the view that "[o]nce the various [European] Powers had parcelled out the continent and consolidated their boundaries by international treaties, the existing sovereignties of the old kingdoms and city states became submerged under the new sovereignties of the 'metropolitan' Powers".[101] Such sovereignties were certainly not extinguished. It is submitted, although the colonial powers in their relations with one another were not so disposed, that while colonialism lasted, the colonial powers were *de facto* sovereigns while *de jure* sovereignty continued to repose in the respective African States. Thus, the sovereignty of African States was, at the very least, in abeyance during the reign of colonialism in Africa. Consequently, on the assumption that the European Powers obtained valid titles to territories in Africa on the strength of the so-called treaties of cession, such titles were, as the International Court of Justice observed in the *Western Sahara Case*, "derivative roots of title, and not original titles obtained by occupation of *terrae nullius*".

As should be obvious by now, we have reached the same conclusion with the court but through different routes. On the one hand, the court's conclusion is based on what it considers to be the State practice (presumably the dominant practice of European States) at the relevant time; an approach that we have dismissed as an endorsement of appearance over reality, to the extent that the court failed to lift the veil that, as we have clearly shown, camouflaged the practice of nineteenth century European States on the question of *terra nullius*. Our conclusion, on the other hand, is informed by our reconstruction of the legacy of Africa's authentic history and its significance for an alternative account of the legacy of 19th century international law; a legacy that bristles with contradictions and tantalizing mirages. To the extent that nineteenth century international law, given its Eurocentricity,

---

[100] The question of legal pluralism was raised, particularly by Algeria, but it was not given adequate consideration by the court in the *Western Sahara Case, supra*, note 35.
[101] Elias, *Africa and the Development of International Law, supra*, note 98, p. 19.

4. CONCLUSION: THE IMPERATIVE OF VIGILANCE

At a time when the issue of reparations to Africa and Africans in the Diaspora, to atone for the havoc that the monstrous slave trade, colonialism and neo-colonialism have wrecked on Africans, deserves to be firmly inscribed on the global agenda, and accorded treatment commensurate with its urgency, it is tragic that a case is being made for the re-colonization of the continent.[102] It is poignant, but not surprising, that the rhetoric of colonialism is being readily resorted to.

International law has undoubtedly undergone a remarkable transformation over the years and no longer portrays itself, at least not explicitly, as the exclusive preserve of the "civilized".[103] Nonetheless, there is often a penchant for recourse to international law in a desperate bid for validation even where the reality is that the discipline is being resorted to or manipulated in furtherance of an otherwise illegal or unlawful scheme. Given this reality, there is no room for complacency. As the saying goes, the price of liberty is eternal vigilance.

---

[102] Our point is not that Africa has a clean bill of health. Africa obviously has an obligation to put its house in order. The role of the international community must, however, proceed from a premise that views, and treats, Africa's interests as overriding.

[103] However, Article 38(1)(c) of the Statute of the International Court of Justice still speaks of "the general principles of law recognized by civilized nations", without enunciating what the test of civilization is: June 26, 1945, 59 Stat. 1055, T. S. No. 993, 3 Bevans 1179.

(Note: the passage begins with "failed to reckon with this reality, its claim to universality is undoubtedly suspect." before the section heading.)

LA PROTECTION CONSTITUTIONNELLE DES MINORITÉS DANS LES ÉTATS AFRICAINS AU SUD DU SAHARA

Vincent Zakane*

INTRODUCTION

Depuis l'éclatement de l'empire soviétique, les minorités sont redevenues, dans les pays de l'Europe de l'Est, l'enjeu de tensions et d'affrontements sanglants dont la crise yougoslave – et la tragédie bosniaque, en particulier – est l'illustration suprême.[1] Cependant, la question des minorités n'est pas propre à l'Europe de l'Est, elle concerne presque tous les pays. Certes, le problème ne revêt pas partout la même intensité, mais il est aujourd'hui général et ne se limite plus à une région donnée.[2] Bien que moins connu cependant, le problème des minorités en Afrique sub-saharienne n'en est pas moins un problème essentiel revêtant parfois un caractère tragique.

En effet, l'évolution politique de plusieurs pays africains s'est caractérisée, au cours des années qui ont suivi leur indépendance, par des tensions internes allant jusqu'à la confrontation inter-ethnique, voire à de véritables guerres civiles dont l'origine réside parfois dans la diversité ethnique des sociétés africaines. On peut citer, comme tristes exemples de tels événements, la guerre civile entre le gouvernement fédéral du Nigeria et la province dissidente du Biafra de 1967 à 1970. Un passé plus récent nous met face aux immenses tragédies humaines et matérielles engendrées par la guerre civile incessante qui sévit entre minorités et majorités ethniques, raciales ou

---

* Enseignant, Faculté de Droit et de Science politique Université de Ouagadougou, Burkina Faso.
[1] Voir, parmi une littérature abondante sur la question des minorités: Bokatola, I.O., *L'Organisation des Nations Unies et la protection des minorités*, Bruxelles, Bruylant, 1992; Chaliand, G., *Les minorités dans le monde à l'âge de l'Etat-nation*, Paris, Fayard, 1985; Djidara, M., "Cadres juridiques et règles applicables aux problèmes européens de minorités", **Annuaire Français de Droit International**, 1991, pp. 349-386; Sanguin, A.L., (sous la direction de), *Les minorités ethniques en Europe*, Paris, l'Harmattan, 1993; Rousso-Lenoir, F., *Minorités et droits de l'homme: l'Europe et son double*, Bruxelles, Bruylant, 1994; Fenet, A., (sous la direction de), *Le droit et les minorités. Analyse et textes*, Bruylant, Bruxelles, 1995.
[2] Cf. Chaliand, G., *op. cit.*; Bokatola, I.O., *op. cit.*

religieuses au Soudan, au Mozambique, en Angola, au Burundi et surtout au Rwanda. Minés par des conflits internes, plusieurs pays du continent sont menacés de désintégration.

Bien souvent qualifiés de conflits inter-ethniques, ces événements cachent en réalité un problème fondamental de minorités dont il convient d'abord de cerner la signification exacte, avant d'analyser les difficultés juridiques qu'il soulève en Afrique.

Toutefois, pour comprendre la situation des minorités en Afrique, il faut d'abord s'entendre sur la notion même de minorité. Mais le phénomène minoritaire est bien plus complexe, car il recouvre des réalités fort hétérogènes.[3] La plupart des définitions actuelles généralement retenues s'inspirent de la notion de minorité telle qu'elle est appréhendée par le droit international.

Cependant, bien que la notion de minorité soit l'une des plus anciennes préoccupations du droit international,[4] elle reste encore largement controversée et est loin de faire l'unanimité. Aucun texte international de portée générale ne définit la notion. La Charte des Nations Unies, tout comme la Déclaration universelle des droits de l'homme, ne fait aucune référence aux minorités. Le Pacte international des Nations Unies sur les droits civils et politiques de 1966 proclame, dans son article 27, des libertés culturelles, religieuses et linguistiques pour les minorités nationales, mais s'abstient de donner une définition au terme de minorité. La Déclaration de l'Assemblée générale des Nations Unies sur les droits des personnes appartenant à des minorités nationales ou ethniques, religieuses et linguistiques s'abstient

---

[3] Le terme de minorité a fait l'objet d'une extension croissante au cours du XXè siècle, en incluant les situations les plus diverses: minorités nationales, minorités ethniques, minorités raciales, minorités politiques, religieuses ou tribales, etc. Ainsi, les minorités sont innombrables et variées, ce qui ne permet pas de dégager une notion unique et générale de la minorité, mais seulement de hasarder un interminable inventaire sans principe. Dans son avis consultatif du 31 juillet 1930 relatif à la question des "Communautés" gréco-bulgares, la C.P.J.I. avait défini la notion de minorité comme une "collectivité de personnes vivant dans un pays ou une localité donnée, ayant une race, une religion, une langue et des traditions qui leur sont propres, et unies par l'identité de cette race, de cette religion, de cette langue et de ces traditions dans un sentiment de solidarité, à l'effet de conserver leurs traditions, de maintenir leur culte, d'assurer l'instruction et l'éducation de leurs enfants conformément au génie de leur race et de s'assister mutuellement" (Question des "Communautés" gréco-bulgares, Série B, n° 17, p. 21).

[4] On sait en effet que la question des minorités nationales était déjà au coeur de la première guerre mondiale. Les Traités de Versailles, qui donnèrent naissance à la Société des Nations, avaient tenté de trouver une solution au sort des minorités nationales dans les Balkans, en leur conférant un certain nombre de droits. Cette tentative fut cependant un échec, en raison de la complexité de la question.

également de donner une définition de la notion de minorité. Toutefois, différentes tentatives ont été faites au sein des Nations Unies pour donner une définition à la notion.[5] Il faut souligner qu'il n'existe aujourd'hui, sur le plan international, aucune définition qui soit généralement acceptée par la communauté internationale.

Cependant l'on accepte aujourd'hui que la définition la plus complète est celle contenue dans le rapport de Francesco CAPOTORTI au Sous-Comité des Nations Unies pour la prévention de la discrimination et la protection des minorités. Selon cette définition, la minorité est *"un groupe de personnes se trouvant dans une situation non-dominante et dont les membres, en tant que ressortissants de l'Etat, possèdent certaines caractéristiques – ethniques, linguistiques et religieuses – différentes du reste de la population, et montrent, même implicitement, un sentiment de solidarité dans le but de préserver leur culture, leurs traditions, leur religion ou leur langue"*.[6] La notion de minorité suppose donc, de ce point de vue, l'existence au sein d'un Etat, d'une communauté humaine distincte du reste de la population, en situation d'infériorité numérique, sociale et économique, et ayant conscience de sa situation de minorité.[7] Cette dernière définition

---

[5] La première tentative fut celle du Secrétaire général des Nations Unies dans son mémorandum du 27 décembre 1949 intitulé "Définition et Classification des minorités"; voir Nations Unies, doc. E/CN, 4/Sub. 2/85, pp. 9 et 10. Dès 1950, une sous-commission des Nations Unies fut chargée du problème de la protection des minorités. Après cependant de nombreuses années, les travaux de la Sous-Commission n'ont pu aboutir à une définition générale largement acceptable de la notion de minorité, en raison notamment de l'impossibilité de parvenir à un consensus sur les expressions à utiliser et les catégories de groupes à inclure dans la notion. La Sous-Commission a fait des propositions de définition en 1950, 1951 et 1952; voir Nations Unies, doc. E/CN, 4/358, pp. 17-19. Plus récemment, les rapports de Francesco Capotorti (Nations Unies, doc. E/CN 4/ Sub. 2/384/Rev. 1, p. 102), de Jules Deschênes (Nations Unies, doc. E/CN 4/Sub. 2/1985/31, p. 29) et de Asbjorn Eide (Nations Unies, doc. E/CN 4/1992/37, pp. 11-18) ont tenté également de donner une définition de la notion de minorité.

[6] Francesco Capotorti, *Etude des droits des personnes appartenant aux minorités ethniques*, religieuses et linguistiques, Nations Unies, New York, 1979.

[7] Cette même définition, à quelques nuances près, est adoptée par Jules Deschenes dans son rapport à la Sous-Commission des Nations Unies pour la lutte contre les mesures discriminatoires et la protection des minorités. Jules Deschenes estime en effet que la minorité est un *"groupe de citoyens d'un Etat, formant une minorité numérique et se trouvant dans une position non dominante au sein de cet Etat, doté de caractéristiques ethniques, religieuses ou linguistiques qui diffèrent de celle de la majorité de la population, éprouvant un sens de solidarité mutuelle, motivé, fût-ce implicitement, par une volonté collective de survie et dont le but est d'obtenir l'égalité de fait et de droit avec la majorité"*. Jules Deschenes, *Proposal concerning a definition of the term "minority"*, U.N. Doc. E/CN.4/Sub. 2/1985/31.

reste utile dans la mesure où elle contient les éléments de définition du statut minoritaire que chacun serait disposé à reconnaître et à accepter. Elle correspond, dans une large mesure, au phénomène minoritaire tel qu'il s'est développé dans les Etats européens.

Toutefois, appliquée à la réalité sociale des Etats africains au Sud du Sahara, la notion de minorité ainsi définie, sans y être étrangère, connaît quelques entorses. En effet, la plupart des Etats africains au Sud du Sahara sont des Etats multi-ethniques dont les populations pratiquent plusieurs religions et connaissent une diversité linguistique prodigieuse. Certains d'entre eux – Afrique du Sud, Madagascar, Mauritanie, Namibie, Soudan, Zimbabwe – connaissent en outre une pluralité de races – Noirs, Blancs, Arabes, Métisses. Une telle situation est de nature à engendrer divers phénomènes minoritaires. Ainsi, en Afrique, l'on a affaire aussi bien à des minorités ethniques qu'à des minorités religieuses, linguistiques, voire raciales. Bien évidemment, la question des minorités ethniques est, de loin, la plus complexe et la plus frappante, en raison de la gravité des conflits inter-ethniques qui ont jalonné l'histoire des jeunes Etats africains.

Toutefois, deux situations paradoxales peuvent se présenter:[8] d'une part, on peut avoir à faire à une situation où une majorité dominante exerce le pouvoir au détriment d'une ou de plusieurs minorités – ethniques, religieuses ou linguistiques – qui se trouvent ainsi marginalisées. D'autre part, il peut s'agir, au contraire, d'une situation où une minorité – ethnique, religieuse ou linguistique – exerce sa domination sur la majorité. La première situation est, de loin, la plus fréquente. La seconde est, en revanche, plus rare. On ne peut guère évoquer que des exemples historiques, tels que la domination de la minorité Blanche en Afrique du Sud (jusqu'en 1993) et au Zimbabwe (jusqu'en 1980); mais le seul exemple actuel le plus frappant reste sans doute celui de la domination de la minorité *Tutsi* sur la majorité *Hutu* au Burundi.[9] Il s'ensuit donc que la situation des minorités revêt en Afrique une réalité fort diverse et complexe et ne saurait s'assimiler simplement à celle des minorités européennes.

---

8   On pourrait également mentionner une troisième situation où les minorités, sans être opprimées, cohabitent harmonieusement avec la majorité, ou s'intègrent sans difficulté à celle-ci. Une telle situation est d'autant plus fréquente que de nombreux Etats africains connaissent aujourd'hui un processus d'intégration nationale relativement avancé.

9   Sur la carte géopolitique des minorités ethniques en Afrique, par exemple, on peut lire, avec profit, Mutoy Mubiala, "La protection des minorités ethniques en Afrique", in *Revue de la Commission Africaine des Droits de l'Homme et des peuples*, Tome 3, 1993, n° 1 et 2, pp. 28-38.

Quoi qu'il en soit, les diverses situations ainsi décrites soulèvent en Afrique des questions politiques et juridiques complexes, voire redoutables, au point que la plupart des Etats africains préfèrent les ignorer pour ne pas devoir les affronter ou affectent de les réduire à des questions ponctuelles. Ces problèmes n'en continuent pas moins de se poser d'une manière sans doute plus actuelle que jamais. De nombreux conflits internes en Afrique ont, en effet, une origine ethnique, religieuse ou linguistique. Dans le contexte actuel de transition démocratique que connaissent la plupart des Etats africains, l'on peut craindre que de nombreuses minorités, ethniques, religieuses ou linguistiques, ne tentent d'en découdre avec des systèmes politiques considérés comme injustes et discriminatoires.[10]

D'une manière générale, le problème des minorités nationales soulève le sentiment d'une contradiction fondamentale entre la logique unitaire de l'Etat national et la logique identitaire de différentes composantes de l'Etat. En effet, les Etats modernes, européens ou africains, aspirent tous à la formation d'une nation unique ayant une culture commune, une langue unique et une destinée commune se traduisant par les principes de l'intégrité territoriale et de l'unité nationale de l'Etat. Mais, cet idéal de l'Etat national homogène se heurte à la réalité de l'hétérogénéité ethnique, linguistique, religieuse ou raciale de la société, engendrant ainsi le problème des minorités. Cette contradiction est d'autant plus insurmontable dans les Etats africains que les sociétés africaines sont d'une grande diversité ethnique, tandis que les Etats eux-mêmes sont fragiles et ont plutôt tendance à recourir à la force pour régler les conflits ethniques, religieux ou linguistiques.

Le problème des minorités, variable selon la réalité de chaque Etat, se présente donc sous la forme des aspirations ou revendications des minorités qui se heurtent aux objections ou à la résistance de l'Etat désireux de conserver son unité nationale et son intégrité territoriale. De ce point de vue, l'Etat africain, jaloux de sa souveraineté, est plus radical que l'Etat européen et tend à rejeter systématiquement ces revendications minoritaires qu'il considère toujours comme autant de facteurs de désagrégation de l'Etat et d'atteinte aux intérêts de la majorité. D'où certaines répressions à l'encontre des minorités accusées de vouloir constituer un "Etat dans l'Etat" ou de vouloir faire sécession. La guerre menée au Nigeria entre 1967 et 1970 par le pouvoir fédéral contre les sécessionnistes du Biafra, ainsi que les répressions organisées pendant près de trente ans par le pouvoir central éthiopien

---

10 Voir notamment Martin, G., "La crise de l'Etat-nation en Afrique: du régionalisme au fédéralisme", in *Afrique 2000, Revue africaine de politique internationale*, n° 21, avril-mai-juin 1995, pp. 51-62.

contre les indépendantistes érythréens constituent des exemples historiques de cette résistance de l'Etat.

Dès lors, il se pose, en fait comme en droit, la question de savoir comment concevoir, sur le plan du droit constitutionnel, la reconnaissance et la protection des minorités dans les pays africains. Il s'agit, en d'autres termes, de s'interroger sur l'état de la protection qu'offrent les constitutions africaines aux minorités nationales. Cette question est fort délicate, dans la mesure où toute protection constitutionnelle suppose non seulement une reconnaissance juridique formelle des minorités en tant que telles, mais en outre l'érection de cette reconnaissance au plan constitutionnel, c'est-à-dire au plus haut niveau de la hiérarchie des normes au sein de l'Etat.

Or, sur cette question, la plupart des Constitutions africaines sont muettes, les Etats africains ne reconnaissant pas constitutionnellement les minorités. Toutefois, il convient de noter que l'attitude des Etats africains à l'égard des minorités n'est ni uniforme ni intangible. En effet, si dans le passé les Etats africains se sont montrés particulièrement réticents à toute expression particulariste au sein de l'Etat, l'on assiste, depuis quelques années, à un infléchissement plus ou moins important de cette position, sous l'influence des idées libérales. Ainsi, alors que certains Etats en sont encore à une négation systématique d'une existence juridique quelconque des minorités, d'autres Etats, sans les nier, préfèrent organiser leur protection sur le plan infra-constitutionnel (législatif ou réglementaire) et d'autres enfin n'hésitent pas à consacrer textuellement l'existence constitutionnelle des minorités. C'est dire donc que la protection constitutionnelle des minorités n'est pas organisée dans tous les Etats. Ceux qui offrent aux minorités une protection juridique ne le font pas nécessairement au même degré ni avec la même ampleur. Mais ils sont tous animés des mêmes craintes: que toute reconnaissance formelle des minorités n'aboutissent à l'éclatement de l'Etat ou, à tout le moins, à un éparpillement de son système juridico-politique.

Toutefois, la tendance de l'Etat africain à maintenir son unité politique et celle de la minorité à conserver son individualité ne sont pas inconciliables. Résoudre le problème des minorités en Afrique revient, pour ainsi dire, à concilier l'Etat, en tant qu'organisation politico-juridique moderne et la diversité sociale qui se traduit par la multiplicité ethnique, religieuse ou linguistique. Cela consiste à trouver, selon la formule de Charles de Visscher, un équilibre fondamental entre *"la tendance de l'Etat à poursuivre son perfectionnement dans une unité politique et morale croissante, et la propension inverse des minorités à développer une culture propre qui, dans une mesure plus ou moins grande, tend à les soustraire à l'emprise de l'Etat"*.[11]

Cet équilibre fondamental peut être recherché à deux niveaux: d'une part, sur le plan strictement juridique, par une reconnaissance d'un statut juridique des minorités garantissant à celles-ci un certain nombre de droits spécifiques et, d'autre part, sur le plan politique, par l'instauration d'un certain pluralisme politique et social. La protection juridique et la protection politique, envisagées séparément ici n'en demeurent pas moins intimement liées et inséparables dans les faits, car la protection constitutionnelle des minorités soulève non pas seulement des questions de droits des minorités, mais également des enjeux de gestion du pouvoir politique, les uns n'allant pas sans les autres. Il faut simplement considérer que la protection politique constitue le complément logique et nécessaire de la protection juridique dans un domaine où se mêlent aisément pouvoir et droit. A cet égard, l'analyse des récentes constitutions africaines et l'observation de la pratique constitutionnelle de nombreux Etats africains montrent que la protection juridique offerte aux minorités en Afrique est encore embryonnaire (I), tandis que la protection politique demeure précaire (II).

I. UNE PROTECTION JURIDIQUE EMBRYONNAIRE

L'organisation de toute protection constitutionnelle des minorités en Afrique, comme ailleurs, suppose d'abord que celles-ci soient reconnues sur le plan juridique, notamment par la définition d'un statut juridique leur reconnaissant des droits spécifiques. Or, rares sont les constitutions africaines qui reconnaissent explicitement les minorités. Bien au contraire, de nombreux Etats, soucieux de conserver leur unité et leur intégrité, refusent clairement toute manifestation identitaire. En fait, les Etats africains hésitent à consacrer un statut juridique spécifique des minorités (A). Ils voient dans une telle reconnaissance officielle une menace pour la stabilité et la sécurité de l'Etat. C'est pourquoi toute forme de reconnaissance juridique fait l'objet d'un encadrement juridique strict (B).

A. La reconnaissance d'un statut juridique des minorités

D'une manière générale, la situation des minorités dans un Etat pose toujours la question de leur statut juridique, c'est-à-dire l'attribution aux

---

11 Cf. de Visscher, Ch., "Unité d'Etat et revendications minoritaires", in *Revue de droit international et de législation comparée*, 1930, p. 330.

minorités de la qualité de sujet de droit, avec, au besoin, l'octroi de droits spécifiques. Toutefois, la reconnaissance juridique du fait minoritaire varie profondément en intensité selon les objectifs poursuivis par les autorités nationales: soit que l'on vise à maintenir et à préserver leurs caractéristiques propres, soit que l'on cherche à assurer l'uniformité juridique au sein de l'Etat. Dans un cas, il leur sera reconnu des droits propres, dans l'autre, il n'en sera pas nécessairement ainsi. De ce point de vue, la grande majorité des Etats africains ne reconnaissent pas officiellement l'existence juridique de minorités sur leur territoire et semblent en conséquence leur dénier tout droit propre. Toutefois, cette position, naguère rigide, n'est plus, aujourd'hui, ni absolue ni générale, dans la mesure où certains Etats n'hésitent plus à s'engager à protéger constitutionnellement leurs minorités.

1. La reconnaissance juridique variable des minorités

L'action propre de reconnaissance des minorités est fondamentalement source d'ambiguïté, dans la mesure où l'expression recouvre elle-même plusieurs hypothèses, allant de la reconnaissance expresse à l'absence de reconnaissance en passant par la reconnaissance implicite.[12] L'absence de reconnaissance officielle équivaut, en principe, à la négation juridique de l'existence des minorités. Mais cela n'implique pas forcément une attitude négative de la part de l'Etat, puisqu'il n'empêche pas, par ailleurs, de garantir les droits et libertés des citoyens ou d'organiser un statut législatif ou réglementaire propre des minorités. La reconnaissance expresse des minorités, quant à elle, suppose une consécration juridique officielle de leur existence, impliquant l'aménagement d'un pluralisme juridique dans l'ordonnancement juridique de l'Etat, notamment sur le plan constitutionnel. Mais lorsque les minorités, sans bénéficier d'une reconnaissance expresse au niveau constitutionnel, font l'objet de textes divers et circonstanciés, de niveau législatif ou administratif, concernant, par exemple, l'usage de la langue minoritaire, il est permis de parler de reconnaissance implicite.

De ce point de vue, l'attitude des Etats africains à l'égard des minorités n'est ni univoque, ni clairement tranchée. Elle a considérablement évolué depuis l'époque des indépendances et varie aujourd'hui encore d'un Etat à un autre.

---

12 Voir Capotorti, F., *Etude des droits des personnes appartenant aux minorités ethniques, religieuses et linguistiques*, Chapitre 1: "La notion de minorité", Nations Unies, Conseil économique et social, Commission des droits de l'homme, Sous-Commission de la lutte contre les mesures discriminatoires et de la protection des minorités, 30è session, 1977, E/CN4/Sub. 2/384/Qdd. 1 (24 juin), p. 34.

En effet, pendant longtemps, les Etats africains se sont montrés particulièrement réticents à toute reconnaissance des minorités sur leur territoire, en dépit de leurs réalités sociologiques caractérisées par la diversité ethnique, religieuse ou linguistique.[13] Dès leur accession à l'indépendance, la plupart des Etats africains ont été en effet confrontés à un cruel dilemme: comment construire une véritable nation dans un Etat aux frontières artificielles et arbitrairement définies par l'ancien colonisateur, composé d'une mosaïque d'ethnies ou de peuples qui, souvent, ne se comprenaient pas entre eux? D'abord soucieux de s'affirmer comme de véritables Etats-nations, à l'instar des Etats européens, ils se sont avant tout attachés à rechercher l'unité nationale et à préserver l'intégrité territoriale de l'Etat. Ce faisant, ils ont refusé tout droit à la différence et l'expression de tout particularisme local, ethnique, religieux ou linguistique. Cette attitude était confortée par l'affirmation, au sein de l'O.U.A., du principe de l'intangibilité des frontières.

Dans ces conditions, il était évident qu'aucune place ne pouvait être laissée à des entités infra-étatiques, telles que les minorités, soupçonnées sinon de vouloir constituer un Etat dans l'Etat, du moins de chercher à déstabiliser l'Etat ou à briser son unité nationale. Tout au plus acceptait-on de maintenir, à titre provisoire, les statuts particuliers des citoyens hérités de la colonisation qui permettaient d'être régi par le droit coutumier, ce qui constituait une certaine forme de respect de la diversité ethnique.

Ce refus de reconnaissance du phénomène minoritaire se traduisait notamment par l'affirmation, tant au niveau constitutionnel, législatif que politique, des principes de l'indivisibilité de la République, de l'égalité et de la non-discrimination entre les citoyens, de l'unité nationale et de l'intégrité territoriale, ainsi que par la condamnation de toute expression ethnique, régionaliste ou raciste.[14] La mise en place, au courant des années 1960,

---

13   L'Afrique est un continent particulièrement hétérogène. Ainsi l'Afrique du Nord, blanche, diffère-t-elle beaucoup de l'Afrique noire en matière de forme de peuplement. La carte ethnolinguistique de l'Afrique noire révèle une grande diversité ethnique, religieuse et linguistique qui n'avait pas été prise en compte par les puissances européennes au moment du partage du continent pendant la conquête coloniale. De sorte qu'au lendemain des indépendances la plupart des Etats se sont retrouvés avec des populations hétérogènes, certaines ethnies se trouvant partagées entre plusieurs Etats.

14   Les premières constitutions prohibaient, soit dans leur préambule, soit dans leur dispositif, toute discrimination basée sur la race, sur l'origine ethnique, religieuse ou régionale ou sur le sexe et affirmaient l'égalité des droits des citoyens devant la loi. La Constitution camerounaise du 4 mars 1960 affirmait déjà l'indivisibilité et l'unité de la République. De même, la Constitution ivoirienne du 3 novembre 1960 proclamait, dans son article 2, que «la République de Côte d'Ivoire est une et indivisible, laïque, démocratique et sociale».

1970, de systèmes politiques à parti unique exprimait également la volonté ferme de refuser toute expression minoritaire.

Cette attitude générale se comprenait d'autant plus que les peuples africains avaient, dans le passé, souffert des effets néfastes de la traite des noirs, de la domination coloniale et de la discrimination raciale et que les jeunes Etats étaient exposés à des risques d'éclatement liés à leur hétérogénéité démographique. Les tentatives de sécession du Katanga en 1960, du Biafra en 1967 et de l'Ogaden en 1978, ainsi que les impératifs du développement économique incompatibles avec l'existence de forces centrifuges ont conforté les Etats africains dans leur attitude négative à l'égard des minorités. D'aucuns en avaient déduit que "Les Etats africains sont fermement déterminés à éviter toute consécration juridique de revendications qu'ils jugent dangereuses pour leur unité territoriale, et répriment avec rigueur les activités des groupes qui pourraient les exprimer".[15]

Mais si le refus systématique de la reconnaissance juridique des minorités ethniques, religieuses et linguistiques a parfois réussi à masquer le problème des minorités, il n'en demeure pas moins qu'une telle attitude a parfois conduit à des conflits ethniques violents. Avec le récent processus de transition démocratique amorcé au début des années 1990 un peu partout sur le continent, il n'est pas impossible que le problème éclate au grand jour, ainsi qu'en témoignent les récents événements au Burundi, en Somalie, au Liberia et au Congo (Brazzaville).

Face à ce facteur belligène qui couve dans de nombreux Etats africains, il est impératif que les Etats intéressés comblent le vide juridique en prenant en compte, au moins sur le plan juridique et institutionnel le phénomène minoritaire.

De fait, la faillite de l'Etat africain dans ses ambitions de construction de l'unité nationale et de développement économique et l'échec des systèmes politiques et économiques centralisateurs au cours des années 1980 ont conduit peu à peu à un assouplissement de l'attitude des Etats africains à l'égard des minorités nationales, notamment à la faveur du processus de démocratisation engagé depuis le début des années 1990.[16] En effet,

---

15   Rouland, N., et al., *Droit des minorités et des peuples autochtones*, Paris, P.U.F, 1994, p. 14.
16   Pour un aperçu sur le processus de démocratisation en Afrique, voir notamment: Baechler, J., "Des institutions démocratiques pour l'Afrique," *Revue juridique et politique – Indépendance et coopération*, n° 2, avril-juin 1992, pp. 163-181; Conac, G., (sous la dir.), *L'Afrique en transition vers le pluralisme politique*, Paris, Université de Paris I – Economica (La vie du droit en Afrique), 1993; Daloz, J.-P. et Quantin, P., (sous la direction de), *Transitions démocratiques en Afrique: dynamiques et contraintes (1990-1994)*, Paris, Karthala, 1997.

depuis quelques années, de nombreux Etats africains se sont dotés de nouvelles constitutions fondées sur la démocratie et l'Etat de droit et proclamant généreusement les droits fondamentaux des citoyens, ou ont modifié leur constitution pour tenir compte des exigences de la démocratie libérale et du pluralisme politique.[17] La lecture des nouvelles Constitutions ou des Constitutions révisées montre leur tendance à se référer au modèle du droit constitutionnel des démocraties libérales. Elles proclament, soit dans leur préambule, soit dans leur dispositif, des valeurs de la démocratie libérale: droits fondamentaux de la personne humaine, Etat de droit, démocratie pluraliste, indépendance de la justice, contrôle juridictionnel de constitutionnalité des lois, etc. Dès lors, leur réticence à l'égard des minorités s'est quelque peu atténuée.

Certes, de nombreuses constitutions nouvelles ou révisées ne consacrent pas un statut juridique spécifique des minorités et condamnent toute expression particulariste de celles-ci. Ainsi, l'article 1er de la Constitution burkinabè du 11 juin 1991 prohibe "les discriminations de toutes sortes, notamment celles fondées sur la race, la région, la couleur, le sexe, la langue, la religion, la caste, les opinions politiques, la fortune et la naissance", ce qui exclut toute reconnaissance de minorités. De même, la Constitution ivoirienne du 3 novembre 1960, révisée le 26 juin 1995, réaffirme, à son article 6, que "La République assure à tous l'égalité devant la loi sans distinction d'origine, de race, de sexe ou de religion (...). Toute propagande particulariste de caractère racial ou ethnique, toute manifestation de discrimination raciale sont punies par la loi". La Constitution de la République gabonaise du 26 mars 1991, pour sa part, dispose, à son article 2, § 2, que "La République gabonaise assure l'égalité de tous les citoyens devant la loi, sans distinction d'origine, de race, de sexe, d'opinion ou de religion".[18] Ces différentes dispositions traduisent sans doute l'hésitation des Etats africains à consacrer juridiquement un phénomène qu'ils estiment menaçant pour leur propre unité nationale.

---

[17] La plupart des Constitutions nouvelles et des Constitutions anciennes révisées des pays francophones d'Afrique font l'objet d'un recueil que l'on pourra consulter avec profit: Du Bois de Gaudusson, J., Conac, G., et Desouches, C., *Les Constitutions africaines publiées en langue française*, 2 tomes, Paris, La Documentation française, Coll. Retour aux textes, respectivement 1997 et 1998.

[18] On retrouve des dispositions analogues dans la Constitution sénégalaise du 7 mars 1963 telle que révisée le 2 mars 1998 (art. 1er), dans la Constitution tchadienne du 14 avril 1996 (art. 14), dans la constitution congolaise du 15 mars 1992 (art. 11 et art. 2), dans la Constitution de la République du Cap-Vert du 14 février 1991 révisée le 4 septembre 1992 (art. 1er, al. 2 et art. 22) et dans a Constitution nigérienne du 12 mai 1996 (art. 8).

Cependant, non seulement ce refus de reconnaissance des minorités n'est plus aussi absolu que dans le passé, mais en outre, il laisse la porte ouverte à une reconnaissance au moins partielle et plus ou moins directe des minorités. Ainsi, l'article 11 de la Constitution béninoise du 11 décembre 1990 reconnaît expressément les communautés linguistiques et culturelles. De la même manière, la Constitution sénégalaise du 7 mars 1963, révisée le 2 mars 1998, tout en assignant à l'Etat le soin d'assurer "l'égalité devant la loi de tous les citoyens, sans distinction d'origine, de race, de sexe ou de religion" (art. 1er), reconnaît expressément les institutions et communautés religieuses (art. 19). Le préambule de la Constitution tchadienne du 14 avril 1996 affirme la volonté du peuple tchadien de "vivre ensemble dans le respect des diversités ethniques, religieuses, régionales et culturelles". La Constitution de la République du Congo du 15 mars 1992 va beaucoup plus loin en affirmant le souci du peuple congolais de préserver son "unité dans la diversité culturelle" et en disposant que "L'Etat garantit le droit des minorités" (art. 50).[19] De même, le préambule de la Constitution camerounaise du 2 juin 1992, telle que profondément révisée par la loi constitutionnelle du 18 janvier 1996, proclame que le peuple camerounais est *"fier de sa diversité linguistique et culturelle, élément de sa personnalité nationale qu'elle contribue à enrichir"* et affirme que *"l'Etat assure la protection des minorités et préserve les droits des populations autochtones conformément à la loi"*.[20]

Mais c'est surtout la Constitution éthiopienne du 8 décembre 1994 qui reconnaît de la manière la plus explicite les minorités nationales. Créant une République fédérale fondée sur la reconnaissance de la diversité ethnique du pays, le constituant éthiopien de 1994 reconnaît explicitement les peuples, nations et nationalités éthiopiennes, ce qui représente une rupture majeure dans l'histoire politique et juridique éthiopienne et une innovation sans précédent sur le continent africain.[21]

---

[19] A noter que cette Constitution a été abrogée et remplacée par l'Acte fondamental du 24 octobre 1997, à la suite du renversement du régime du Président Pascal Lissouba en 1997. Considérée comme la constitution transitoire, l'Acte fondamental ne reprend pas cette disposition protectrice des minorités. Néanmoins, il affirme dans son préambule le souci du peuple congolais de préserver "l'unité nationale dans la diversité culturelle", ce qui constitue une reconnaissance on ne peut plus claire de minorités au Congo.

[20] Sur le cas particulier du Cameroun, lire notamment Olinga, A.D., "La protection des minorités et des populations autochtones en droit public camerounais", in *Revue Africaine de Droit International et Comparé (R.A.D.I.C.)*, juin 1998, tome 10, n° 2, pp. 271-291.

[21] Sur la nouvelle République éthiopienne, voir: Vircoulon, Th., " Ethiopie: les risques du fédéralisme", in *Afrique contemporaine*, n° 174, 2ème trimestre 1995, pp. 35-50.

En tout état de cause, dans la mesure où des instruments internationaux intéressant la protection des minorités trouvent à s'appliquer en droit interne et compte tenu de la place qu'ils occupent dans la hiérarchie des normes juridiques, la reconnaissance juridique des minorités par les Etats africains peut être déduite de ces textes internationaux. En effet, la plupart des Etats africains reconnaissent dans leur constitution la valeur obligatoire des traités internationaux auxquels ils sont parties et affirment leur attachement aux principaux instruments internationaux de protection des droits de l'homme[22] considérés par ailleurs comme partie intégrante aux textes constitutionnels.[23] Or, non seulement certains de ces instruments internationaux relatifs aux droits de l'homme contiennent des dispositions spécifiques concernant les minorités,[24] mais en outre les Etats africains participent largement aux traités internationaux condamnant la discrimination raciale et l'apartheid.[25] Au surplus, ils se sont montrés particulièrement actifs dans l'élaboration d'instruments internationaux non obligatoires relatifs à la discrimination raciale ou à la protection des minorités.[26]

Dans ces conditions, il est permis de considérer que si les Etats africains, dans leur généralité, ne reconnaissent pas les minorités, certains d'entre eux les reconnaissent directement ou indirectement, tandis que d'autres, sans les reconnaître, les prennent un tant soit peu en compte dans leur législation nationale. Reste à savoir si cette reconnaissance juridique hésitante emporte des droits spécifiques au profit des minoritaires.

---

[22] Il s'agit essentiellement de la Déclaration universelle des droits de l'homme de 1948, des Pactes internationaux relatifs aux droits civils et politiques et aux droits sociaux, économiques et culturels de 1966, ainsi que de la Charte africaine des droits de l'homme et des peuples de 1981.

[23] Cf. Gonidec, P.-F., "Droit international et droit interne en Afrique", R.A.D.I.C., décembre 1996, tome 8, n° 4, pp. 789-807.

[24] L'article 27 du Pacte international sur les droits civils et politiques de 1966 vise expressément les personnes appartenant aux minorités ethniques, religieuses et linguistiques. La Déclaration adoptée le 18 décembre 1992 par l'Assemblée générale des Nations Unies est consacrée aux droits des personnes appartenant aux minorités nationales, ou ethniques, religieuses et linguistiques.

[25] Convention des Nations Unies sur la prévention et la répression du crime de génocide (1948), Convention internationale sur l'élimination de toutes les formes de discrimination raciale (1965), Convention sur l'élimination et la répression du crime d'apartheid (1973), Convention sur l'élimination de toutes les formes de discrimination à l'égard des femmes (1979).

[26] Résolution 31/6 de l'Assemblée générale des Nations Unies du 26 octobre 1976 et Résolution 47/135 de l'Assemblée générale des Nations Unies du 18 décembre 1992 relative à la Déclaration sur les droits des personnes appartenant à des minorités nationales, ou ethniques, religieuses et linguistiques.

2 Les droits reconnus aux personnes appartenant aux minorités

La reconnaissance ou la non reconnaissance juridique d'une situation minoritaire détermine le degré de protection dont le groupe concerné pourra bénéficier, c'est-à-dire les droits dont il sera titulaire, soit directement, soit indirectement à travers le système des droits de l'homme mis en place par la Constitution. En effet, reconnaître les minorités, c'est leur conférer un statut de sujet de droit au sein de l'Etat, ce qui implique l'aménagement de droits et d'obligations spécifiques s'attachant à ce statut. Toutefois, dans la mesure où la plupart des Etats africains ne reconnaissent pas constitutionnellement les minorités, celles-ci ne sauraient, en principe, bénéficier de droits spécifiques, constitutionnellement garantis. Même les rares Etats qui les reconnaissent, n'en tirent pas toutes les conséquences juridiques notamment en leur conférant des droits spécifiques. Sur le plan régional, aucun texte conventionnel ne consacre de droits spécifiques pour les minorités. La Charte africaine des droits de l'homme et des peuples est silencieuse sur la question des minorités. En conséquence, il n'est guère possible de dresser un catalogue des droits reconnus aux minorités en Afrique. Pour autant, les Etats africains ne nient pas totalement tout droit aux minorités.

En fait, la principale difficulté soulevée lorsqu'on parle de la nécessité d'octroyer des droits aux minorités est celle de la détermination des sujets bénéficiaires du régime de protection. En d'autres termes, il s'agit de savoir s'il faut reconnaître des droits aux seules personnes appartenant aux minorités nationales ou si, au contraire, ces droits doivent être attribués aux minorités en tant qu'entités collectives. Les minorités peuvent-elles être justiciables de droits collectifs aussi bien qu'individuels? Il s'agit là d'une question de principe, qui renvoie elle-même à celle du rapport de la nation et de l'Etat: reconnaître des droits individuels aux minorités nationales, c'est faire le choix de l'Etat-nation qui ne reconnaît pas de sujets intermédiaires entre la nation et le citoyen, mais accepte tout au plus d'aménager dans ce cadre un certain pluralisme national. Dans ce cas de figure, la protection des droits des minorités ne serait qu'une forme particulière de la protection des droits de l'homme, adaptée à une catégorie sociale déterminée, à l'instar de la protection organisée au profit des femmes ou des enfants. Dans une telle hypothèse, évidemment, il serait erroné de considérer que les Etats africains n'accordent aucun droit aux minorités. En effet, dans la mesure où la plupart des Constitutions africaines proclament des droits inhérents à la personne humaine, affirment avec force leur attachement aux instruments internationaux de protection des droits de l'homme et au principe d'égalité et condamnent toutes formes de discrimination fondée sur l'origine ethnique, religieuse, régionale etc., l'on pourrait en déduire qu'elles garantissent aux minoritaires au moins les mêmes droits qu'aux autres citoyens.

En revanche, reconnaître des droits collectifs aux minorités nationales, c'est considérer ces dernières comme des entités distinctes de leurs éléments constitutifs, c'est leur attribuer une personnalité morale de droit public c'est-à-dire un statut d'entités infra-étatiques, ce qui revient à faire en quelque sorte le choix de l'Etat multinational. Contrairement à l'Etat-nation, dans lequel l'Etat se confond à la nation, l'Etat multinational est composé de deux ou plusieurs nations distinctes de l'Etat lui-même.[27] Dans l'Etat multinational, la nation est nécessairement distincte de l'Etat, puisque celui-ci est formé de deux ou plusieurs nations existant en tant que communautés différentes, chacune ayant conscience de sa spécificité et étant désireuse de la conserver.[28] En tant qu'entités infra-étatiques, ces communautés peuvent se voir reconnaître des droits s'analysant comme des droits collectifs spécifiques. Dès lors, les minorités pourraient être considérées comme des peuples et, à ce titre, pourraient se voir reconnaître certains droits essentiels ayant pour finalité de préserver leur existence et leur identité (libre usage de la langue, droits spéciaux en matière culturelle et scolaire) et accorder le bénéfice du droit des peuples à disposer d'eux-mêmes. En principe, la question de la nature collective des droits minoritaires ne se pose que dans les Etats multinationaux.

Cependant, dans la pratique, de nombreux Etats comportant une pluralité de communautés, s'affirment comme de véritables Etats-nations. C'est le cas, en particulier de certains Etats d'Europe occidentale qui, comme la France, sont composés d'une diversité de communauté, mais affirment leur caractère d'Etats-nations et refusent en conséquence de reconnaître quelque droit collectif que ce soit aux minorités.[29]

---

[27] M. Stéphane Pierre-Caps définit l'Etat multinational comme celui "figurant une société politique composée de plusieurs communautés nationales, mais unies par la volonté de partager un destin commun". Cf. *L'avenir des minorités de l'Europe centrale et orientale,* éd. Odile Jacob, Paris, 1995, p. 9. Voir aussi *l'Etat multinational et l'Europe,* Centre d'étude et de recherche sur le droit international et la paix, Université de Nancy 2, 1997.

[28] Définition and Classification of Minorities, Memorandum submitted by the Secretary-General, United Nations, Commission on Human Rights, Sub-Commission on Prevention of Discrimination and Protection of Minorities, Lake Success, New York, 1950, p. 7.

[29] Ce type de comportement est bien mis en évidence par le Conseil constitutionnel français dans sa décision du 9 mai 1991 relative au statut de la Corse: "Considérant que la France est, ainsi que le proclame l'article 2 de la Constitution de 1958, une République indivisible, laïque, démocratique et sociale qui assure l'égalité devant la loi de tous les citoyens quelle que soit leur origine; que dès lors, la mention faite par le législateur du "peuple corse, composante du peuple français" est contraire à la Constitution, laquelle ne connaît que le peuple français, composé de tous les citoyens français sans distinction d'origine, de race ou de religion". C.C., décision 290 DC du 9 mai 1991, Statut de la Corse, *J.O.-R.F.* 14 mai 1991, p. 6350.

Une telle attitude, qui traduit, en réalité, la méfiance des Etats unitaires à l'égard des minorités se retrouve également dans la plupart des Etats africains qui se montrent plutôt favorables à cette vision individualiste des droits des minorités, alors qu'ils sont les premiers et les plus fervents défenseurs de la théorie des droits des peuples. En effet, la plupart des récentes Constitutions africaines, tout en affirmant leur attachement à la Charte africaine des droits de l'homme et des peuples, ne consacrent que des droits et libertés individuels, refusant ainsi de consacrer des droits collectifs pour d'autres entités que l'Etat. Ainsi, les Constitutions burkinabè (Titre Ier), Djiboutienne (Titre II), gabonaise (Titre préliminaire), malgache (Titre II), malienne (Titre Ier), mauricienne (Chapitre II), mauritanienne (Titre Ier) et centrafricaine (Titre Ier), entre autres, ne reconnaissent que des droits et libertés individuels. Même la Constitution camerounaise de 1972, telle que révisée en 1996, qui proclame que le peuple camerounais est "fier de sa diversité linguistique et culturelle" (préambule), ne consacre aucun droit collectif spécifique. Tout au plus l'Etat camerounais s'engage-t-il à assurer la protection des minorités et à préserver les droits des peuples autochtones.

Toutefois, certaines Constitutions récentes consacrent de façon extrêmement laconique des droits collectifs spécifiques pouvant profiter aux minorités. Ainsi, la Constitution béninoise de 1990 affirme, à son article 11, que "Toutes les communautés composant la nation béninoise jouissent de la liberté d'utiliser leurs langues parlées et écrites et de développer leur propre culture tout en respectant celles des autres".[30] De même, la Constitution sénégalaise reconnaît aux communautés religieuses "le droit de se développer sans entrave" et l'autonomie d'administration de leurs affaires (art. 19). Toutefois, en pareille situation, certains auteurs parlent plutôt de ''droits individuels dont l'exercice est collectif".[31]

Seule la Constitution Ethiopienne de 1994 consacre des droits dont le caractère collectif ne souffre d'aucune ambiguïté. En effet, l'article 39 de la Constitution reconnaît aux nations, nationalités ou peuples éthiopiens un "droit inconditionnel à l'autodétermination", le "droit à une représentation équitable" au sein des gouvernements régionaux et du gouvernement fédéral

---

[30] On trouve une disposition analogue dans la Constitution congolaise de 1992 qui disposait, à son article 35, al. 1, que "Toutes les communautés composant la nation congolaise jouissent de la liberté d'utiliser leurs langues et leur propre culture sans préjudice à celle d'autrui", et se contentait d'affirmer, dans son article 50, que "L'Etat garantit le droit des minorités".
[31] Cf. Sudre, F., *Droit international et européen des droits de l'homme*, Paris, P.U.F., 1989, p. 122.

et, surtout, le "droit à l'indépendance".[32] Cependant, il ne s'agit là que d'un cas isolé davantage dicté par les circonstances historiques et des tactiques politiques qu'imposé par une volonté politique claire de consacrer des droits collectifs en tant que tels au profit des minorités.[33] Certes, la Constitution définitive sud-africaine de 1997 consacre également, à son article 235, le "droit à l'autodétermination" au profit des communautés partageant une culture et un héritage linguistique communs à l'intérieur d'une entité territoriale de la République.[34] Toutefois, ce droit est largement rendu théorique par le principe de l'unité nationale et de l'indivisibilité de la République affirmé par l'article 41.

Toujours est-il que les Etats africains, dans leur grande majorité ne reconnaissent pas des droits collectifs d'une telle ampleur et se limitent généralement à reconnaître des droits individuels. Cette option individualiste est d'ailleurs confirmée par les principaux instruments internationaux auxquels ils sont partis et qui prévoient une certaine protection au profit des minorités. Ainsi, le Pacte international des Nations Unies relatif aux droits civils et politiques, adopté le 16 décembre 1966, dispose, à son article 27, que: "Dans les Etats où il existe des minorités ethniques, religieuses ou linguistiques, les personnes appartenant à ces minorités ne peuvent être privées du droit d'avoir, en commun avec les autres membres de leur groupe, leur propre vie culturelle, de professer et de pratiquer leur propre religion ou d'utiliser leur propre langue". Cette disposition, issue d'un instrument juridique à application générale liant la plupart des Etat africains, consacre, à n'en pas douter, de véritables droits des minorités et impose leur respect. Si ces droits ont un caractère collectif évident, en ce qu'ils peuvent être

---

32 Sur les droits collectifs spécifiques consacrés par la Constitution éthiopienne, voir Gonidec, P.-F., "Les principes fondamentaux du régime politique éthiopien", *Afrique 2000, Revue africaine de politique internationale*, 1996; Vircoulon, Th., "Ethiopie: les risques du fédéralisme", *op. cit.*, pp. 35-50.

33 Selon Thierry Vircoulon, le fédéralisme ethnique officialisé par la Constitution éthiopienne de 1994 vise plutôt à "lâcher du lest puis reprendre en main", *op. cit.*, p. 48.

34 Aux termes de cette disposition: "Le droit du peuple sud-africain dans son ensemble à l'autodétermination tel qu'exprimé dans la présente Constitution n'exclut pas, dans le cadre de ce droit, la reconnaissance du droit à l'autodétermination de toute communauté partageant une culture et un héritage linguistique communs à l'intérieur d'une entité territoriale de la République ou de toute autre manière déterminée par la législation".

exercés en groupe,[35] il n'en demeure pas moins qu'ils sont principalement reconnus aux personnes appartenant aux minorités nationales et non à celles-ci en tant que telles.[36]

La vision individualiste des droits des minorités résulte également de la Déclaration relative aux droits des personnes appartenant aux minorités nationales, ou ethniques, religieuses et linguistiques, adoptée par l'Assemblée générale des Nations Unies en décembre 1992.[37]

La Charte africaine des droits de l'homme et des peuples, qui est l'expression collective des Etats africains en matière des droits de l'homme,

---

[35] Telle est l'idée développée par Marc Djidara, selon lequel le droit des minorités peut apparaître avec la double spécificité d'un droit catégoriel mixte: il appartient aux droits de l'homme en ce qu'il définit les conditions de garantie des droits universels pour les personnes appartenant à des communautés culturelles menacées; il appartient au droit des peuples, en ce qu'il définit la forme politique collective de ces mêmes garanties. En tant que droits de l'homme, ces droits visent à protéger l'individu minoritaire et, en tant que droits des peuples, ils sont destinés à protéger tout le groupe minoritaire. Voir Marc Djidara, "Cadres juridiques et règles applicables aux problèmes européens de minorités", *op. cit.*, pp. 362-363.

[36] Telle est d'ailleurs l'interprétation donnée par le Comité des Droits de l'Homme de l'O.N.U., organe de contrôle du Pacte, le 6 avril 1994 dans son Commentaire général relatif à l'article 27, adopté sur la base de l'article 40, alinéa 4 du Pacte. Selon ce Commentaire, les droits garantis par l'article 27 sont des droits individuels distincts du droit des peuples à disposer d'eux-mêmes, bénéficiant aux personnes qui appartiennent à un groupe et ont en commun une culture, une religion et/ou une langue. Sur le caractère individualiste du Pacte international sur les droits civils et politiques, voir Sudre, F., *Droit international et européen des droits de l'homme*, Paris, P.U.F., Coll. Droit fondamental, 3ème éd., 1997, p. 160 et ss.

[37] Cette Déclaration prévoit, en effet, au profit des personnes appartenant aux minorités nationales, entre autres: le droit à l'existence nationale ou ethnique, culturelle, religieuse ou linguistique (art. 1er, § 1er); le droit de jouir de leur propre culture, de professer et de pratiquer leur propre religion et d'utiliser leur propre langue en privé et en public (art. 2, § 1er); le droit de participation effective à la vie culturelle, religieuse, sociale, économique et publique (art. 2, § 2); le droit de participation effective aux décisions qui sont prises au niveau national et, selon le cas, régional, quand celles-ci regardent la minorité en cause (art. 2, § 3); le droit d'établir et d'entretenir des relations sans discrimination, libres et pacifiques, avec d'autres membres de leur groupe ou des autres groupes, etc. Ces différents droits spécifiques, qui constituent ce qu'il est convenu d'appeler le standard minimum international relatif à la protection des personnes appartenant aux minorités nationales, demeurent des droits fondamentalement individualistes. Voir Zlatescu, I., "Standards internationaux relatifs à la protection des droits des personnes appartenant aux minorités nationales et leur mise en oeuvre", in *L'Etat multinational et l'Europe, op. cit.*, pp. 165-220; Bokatola, I.O., *L'Organisation des Nations Unies et la protection des minorités, op. cit.*

consacre sans doute des droits collectifs pour les peuples: droit à l'existence, droit à l'autodétermination, droit à la liberté, libre disposition des richesses et des ressources naturelles, droit au développement économique, social et culturel, droit à la paix et droit à un environnement satisfaisant et global. Toutefois, ces droits sont explicitement et volontiers présentés comme des droits reconnus aux peuples africains en lutte contre la domination étrangère et qui ne peuvent être revendiqués, en pratique, que par les Etats africains eux-mêmes, à l'exclusion des différents peuples eu sein d'un Etat déjà indépendant.[38] Ce faisant, la Charte ne reconnaît des droits qu'aux individus et aux Etats, à l'exclusion des entités infra-étatiques, telles que les minorités nationales. Si l'on peut en effet considérer les droit reconnus aux peuples dans la Charte comme des droits reconnus également aux minorités, il n'en demeure pas moins que la Charte ne parle pas expressément des minorités. D'aucuns ont pu en déduire qu'il s'agit là d'une lacune de la Charte.[39]

Force est donc de constater que les droits reconnus aux minorités sont essentiellement des droits individuels, même s'ils s'exercent dans un environnement collectif. Cette façon de voir représente, en l'état actuel du droit positif interne, ce que les Etats africains sont disposés à concéder au phénomène minoritaire. Il s'ensuit que le phénomène minoritaire n'est pas totalement ignoré par les Etats africains. Seulement, ces Etats ne reconnaissent que les personnes appartenant aux minorités et non celles-ci en tant que telles.

Ces droits font, en outre, l'objet d'un encadrement juridique destiné à sauvegarder les droits de l'Etat et des autres citoyens.

B. L'encadrement juridique du statut des minorités

La protection effective des minorités nationales et des droits et libertés des personnes appartenant à ces minorités, telle qu'elle est organisée par les textes internationaux et constitutionnels actuels, n'est pas une protection absolue et sans limite. Les droits reconnus aux minoritaires peuvent difficilement

---

[38] Lire, à ce sujet, M'Baye, K., *Les droits de l'homme en Afrique*, Paris, Pedone, 1990; Ouguergouz, F., *La Charte africaine des droits de l'homme et des peuples. Une approche juridique des droits de l'homme entre tradition et modernité*, Paris, P.U.F., 1993; Glele Ahanhanzo, M., "Introduction à la Charte africaine des droits de l'homme et des peuples (Organisation de l'Unité Africaine)", in *Etudes offertes à Claude-Albert Colliard*, Paris, Pedone, 1994, pp. 518 et ss.; Institut international d'études des droits de l'homme, *La Charte africaine des droits de l'homme et des peuples*, Actes du Colloque de Trieste, 30-31 octobre 1997.

[39] Cf. Valère Eteka Yemet, *La Charte africaine des droits de l'homme et des peuples*, Paris, l'Harmattan, 1996, pp. 142-143.

s'exercer en méconnaissance de ceux de l'Etat et des autres citoyens. Dans l'exercice de leurs droits, les minorités ont aussi des obligations. C'est la contrepartie des droits que l'Etat s'engage à protéger. En d'autres termes, les droits fondamentaux de l'Etat limitent ceux accordés aux minorités. Cet encadrement juridique des droits des minorités s'opère généralement, au plan national, à travers deux standards constitutionnels: les principes d'égalité et de non-discrimination, d'une part, et le principe de l'unité politique et juridique de l'Etat, d'autre part.

1   Les principes d'égalité et de non-discrimination

Reconnaître un statut juridique à une minorité nationale, linguistique, ethnique ou religieuse, c'est permettre non seulement l'expression de particularismes locaux dérogatoires au droit commun, mais aussi autoriser des discriminations et favoriser la dispersion des forces vives indispensables pour le développement et le progrès national. Ce risque est d'autant plus réel que tous les Etats africains sont des Etats multi-ethniques composés souvent d'une ethnie majoritaire et d'un nombre plus ou moins important d'ethnies minoritaires. Au lendemain des indépendances, notamment, les formations politiques qui concourraient à la naissance d'une démocratie moderne étaient le plus souvent constituées sur une base ethnique, ce qui devait favoriser le développement de ce que l'on a souvent voulu dénoncer sous le vocable de "tribalisme", terme générique désignant le népotisme basé sur des considérations ethniques.[40]

La reconnaissance étatique du droit à la différence des minorités pose donc un problème de fond, en ce qu'elle heurte apparemment le principe d'égalité entre tous les citoyens de l'Etat sur lequel se fonde le modèle politique de l'Etat-nation. C'est pourquoi la jouissance et l'exercice pacifique des droits des minorités imposent à celles-ci des devoirs envers l'Etat, envers leurs membres, envers les autres minorités et envers les autres citoyens. Il est généralement admis que les personnes appartenant aux minorités nationales doivent notamment respecter les législations nationales et les droits d'autrui, en particulier ceux des personnes appartenant à la majorité ou aux autres minorités nationales, en vertu du principe d'égalité entre les citoyens.

Formulé dès l'article 1er de la Charte des Nations Unies et de la Déclaration universelle des droits de l'homme du 10 décembre 1948[41] et

---

[40]   Cette situation malheureuse se perpétue encore dans de nombreux pays. Lire, par exemple, Ole Balogun, "La société tribale est-elle un atout ou un handicap pour l'Afrique?", in *Le Courrier ACP/CE* n° 140, juillet-août 1993, pp. 60 ss.

[41]   Aux termes de l'article 1er de la Déclaration, "Tous les êtres humains naissent libres et égaux en dignité et en droits... ".

constamment repris par les textes constitutionnels et internationaux,[42] le principe d'égalité participe de la condition même de l'homme. Dans son expression politique, il se rattache directement aux théories de la souveraineté nationale et de la populaire et à la qualité même de citoyen, être abstrait et interchangeable, composante indivise de la nation, jouissant des mêmes droits et des mêmes devoirs sur l'ensemble du territoire de l'Etat.[43] Elle repose sur l'idée de l'exclusivité de la nation étatique, composée de l'ensemble des citoyens – l'universalité des citoyens -, ce qui exclut la prise en compte de tout corps intermédiaire. Autrement dit, le principe de l'égalité n'exclut pas le fait minoritaire en lui-même, dès lors que l'Etat doit veiller à garantir les droits individuels. Ce qu'il tend à exclure, c'est la dimension collective, identitaire, inhérente à l'expression juridique des minorités, notamment par un traitement inégalitaire. Dans ce sens, toutes les Constitutions africaines affirment l'égalité entre tous les citoyens devant la loi, sans distinction de race, d'origine ethnique, de région, de sexe, de religion, d'appartenance politique ou de position sociale.

Ce principe est indissociable du principe de non-discrimination qui en est le corollaire direct et la condition de réalisation et qui tend à le renforcer. Une telle conception, qui participe du credo individualiste du libéralisme politique, ne tolère, par conséquent, le fait minoritaire qu'au titre de l'exercice privé des libertés publiques, les personnes appartenant aux minorités se voyant garantir un droit individuel, comme tout citoyen de l'Etat. Elle exclut la dimension collective, identitaire, inhérente à l'expression minoritaire.

Dans les Etats africains où la nation est particulièrement hétérogène, le principe de non-discrimination revêt une importance déterminante et se trouve, de ce fait, renforcé par l'interdiction de tout particularisme. En ce sens, les Constitutions africaines s'attachent à prévenir le danger particulariste sous la forme du "tribalisme", du "racisme" ou du "régionalisme".

---

42   L'article 26 du Pacte international sur les droits civils et politiques précise que: *"Toutes les personnes sont égales devant la loi et ont droit sans discrimination à une égale protection de la loi. A cet égard, la loi doit interdire toute discrimination et garantir à toutes les personnes une protection égale et effective contre toute discrimination, notamment de race, de couleur, de sexe, de langue, de religion, d'opinion politique et de toute autre opinion, d'origine nationale ou sociale, de fortune, de naissance ou de toute autre situation"*. Le principe de l'égalité est également affirmé avec force par l'article 3 de la Charte africaine des droits de l'homme des peuples, ainsi que par l'article 4 de la Déclaration de l'Assemblée générale des Nations Unies relative aux droits des personnes appartenant aux minorités nationales, ou ethniques, religieuses et linguistiques.

43   Voir Rouland, N. et al., *op. cit.*, pp. 284-285.

Ainsi, la Constitution de la République de Guinée du 23 décembre 1990 précise, à son article 4, que *"La loi punit quiconque par un acte de discrimination raciale, ethnique ou religieuse, ou par un acte de propagande régionaliste, porte une atteinte grave à l'unité nationale, à la sécurité de l'Etat, à l'intégrité du territoire de la République ou au fonctionnement démocratique des institutions"*. De même, l'article 1er, alinéa 13, de la Constitution gabonaise du 16 mars 1991 précise que *"Tout acte de discrimination raciale, ethnique ou religieuse, de même que toute propagande régionaliste pouvant porter atteinte à la sécurité intérieure ou extérieure de l'Etat ou à l'intégrité de la République sont punis par la loi"*. La Constitution ivoirienne de 1960, pour sa part, interdit *"Toute propagande particulariste de caractère racial ou ethnique, toute manifestation de discrimination raciale"*.

En outre, les hommes politiques dénoncent régulièrement le ''tribalisme'', ''l'ethnisme'' ou le ''régionalisme'' comme des facteurs de division sociale portant atteinte à l'unité nationale et susceptibles de mettre en danger l'intégrité territoriale de l'Etat. Le principe de la non-discrimination peut d'ailleurs être considéré comme le droit le plus fondamental reconnu par les Etats parties à la Charte africaine des droits de l'homme et des peuples qui lui confère une place de choix. Cette prévalence donnée au principe de la non-discrimination se comprend d'autant plus que les peuples africains ont, dans le passé, souffert de la discrimination raciale et de l'apartheid.

Evidemment, une telle condamnation générale du particularisme social interdit, en principe, l'aménagement de droits spécifiques plus favorables au profit des minoritaires par rapport aux autres citoyens, c'est-à-dire le traitement différencié des minoritaires. Il s'ensuit que les principes d'égalité et de non-discrimination constituent, de prime abord, des limites objectives à l'organisation de tout statut juridique spécial au profit des minorités. A partir du moment où les citoyens sont tous égaux devant la loi et ne peuvent souffrir d'aucune discrimination, il n'y a pas de raison de privilégier une catégorie de citoyens au motif qu'ils appartiennent à une minorité.

Mais, en sens inverse, le principe de non-discrimination, tout comme celui d'égalité, permet en même temps de protéger aussi les minorités contre les discriminations et les mesures inégalitaires qui pourraient être prises à leur encontre par la majorité.

En fait, les principes d'égalité et de non-discrimination accomplissent une double fonction: ils interdisent l'expression particulariste collective des minorités, tout en protégeant celles-ci contre tout traitement inégalitaire ou discriminatoire défavorable aux minorités. Il n'en va pas de même du principe de l'unité politique et juridique de l'Etat qui tend surtout à contenir les revendications des minorités.

2   Le principe de l'unité politique et juridique de l'Etat

La protection constitutionnelle des minorités se heurte toujours à la conception monolithique, voire mystique de l'unité nationale de l'Etat. Le principe de l'unité politique de l'Etat est une préoccupation constante des Etats unitaires mais qui n'est pas absente dans les Etats fédéraux qui prétendent aussi réaliser l'unité mais dans la diversité. Il constitue, de ce fait, un principe majeur régulièrement affirmé par les constitutions des Etats africains et reconnu par le droit international.

Intimement lié au principe de l'intégrité territoriale de l'Etat, le principe de l'unité politique de l'Etat traduit la nécessité du maintien de la souveraineté de celui-ci.[44] La souveraineté de l'Etat constitue ainsi l'expression de l'unité de l'Etat.

Appliqué à la question minoritaire, le principe de l'unité politique et juridique de l'Etat vise à éviter que la reconnaissance et l'affirmation du droit à la différence des minorités n'aboutissent à encourager les tendances centrifuges au sein de l'Etat. Autrement dit, le droit à la différence ne doit pas occulter la nécessaire intégration des minorités au sein de la nation étatique.

Issu d'une élaboration théorique longue et complexe, le principe de l'unité nationale est au coeur du processus de formation du concept moderne d'Etat.[45] Elle confère à l'Etat non seulement le monopole de l'administration, mais aussi le monopole de l'utilisation légitime de la force et le monopole de la justice civile, pénale et politique. Elle est une puissance unificatrice qui unit tous les membres de la société. Comme le disait Jean Bodin, "La République se reconnaît à l'unité de la souveraineté".[46]

Sur le plan du droit, l'unité de la souveraineté doit déboucher sur l'unité du système juridique et de ses succédanés: administration, justice, armée, police, etc. La souveraineté implique, en principe, sinon l'unité de la loi, du moins l'unité du système juridique. Elle implique également l'unité nationale, l'unité territoriale et de la puissance étatique. C'est pourquoi le rêve de tout Etat nouveau est de reproduire ce modèle.

La résolution 1514 (XV) du 14 décembre 1960 de l'Assemblée générale des Nations Unies précitée stipule que *"toute tentative visant à détruire partiellement ou totalement l'unité nationale (...) d'un pays est incompatible*

---

44   Voir Yadh Ben Achour, "Souveraineté étatique et protection internationale des minorités", in *R.C.A.D.I.* 1994/I, Vol. 245, pp. 321-461.

45   Cf. Affaire des Activités militaires et paramilitaire au Nicaragua et contre celui-ci: Nicaragua c. Etats-Unis d'Amérique, *C.I.J., Rec. 1986*, p. 133, § 263.

46   Cité par Simone Goyard-Fabre, *Jean Bodin et le droit de la République*, P.U.F., Léviathan, p. 86.

avec les buts et la Charte des Nations Unies". En clair, l'Assemblée générale rejette toute utilisation des droits reconnus à une entité infra-étatique qui aboutirait au démembrement d'un Etat par une sécession. Cette idée ressort également de la Déclaration de l'Assemblée générale sur les relations amicales entre les Etats, adoptée le 24 octobre 1970, qui, tout en réaffirmant le principe d'autodétermination des peuples, précise que celle-ci n'autorise et n'encourage aucune action, "quelle qu'elle soit, qui démembrerait ou menacerait totalement ou partiellement (...) l'unité politique de tout Etat souverain et indépendant".

Dès le lendemain de leur accession à l'indépendance, les Etats africains, craignant que la trop grande hétérogénéité de leurs populations ne mette en péril l'oeuvre de construction nationale et l'impératif du développement économique, se sont montrés particulièrement attachés au principe de l'unité nationale qu'il sont érigé en une règle impérative devant laquelle devait céder toute velléité particulariste. Proclamé dans de nombreuses Constitutions d'alors, le principe de l'unité nationale a été compris comme le symbole de la souveraineté, sans lequel l'existence même de l'Etat était menacée. De nombreux dirigeants politiques n'hésitèrent pas, au nom de l'unité nationale, à instaurer des régimes politiques à parti unique et à réprimer toute expression particulariste. Ainsi, en 1970, Julius Nyerere, père de la nation tanzanienne, écrivait: "Maintenant que les colonialistes sont partis, il n'y a plus de division entre dominants d'une part et dominés d'autre part (...). Le multipartisme est un luxe que nous autres, en Afrique, ne pouvons nous offrir. Nous avons trop peu de temps et il y a trop de réalisations sérieuses à faire pour nous laisser aller à ce passe-temps oiseux".[47] Une telle affirmation vigoureuse tendant à sublimer le principe de l'unité nationale condamnait sans appel toute tentative d'expression particulariste minoritaire et justifiait juridiquement, dans de nombreux Etats, l'instauration de partis uniques et le recours à la violence pour réprimer toute expression ethnique, religieuse ou linguistique, jugée attentatoire à l'unité nationale.

Dans certains pays, l'impératif d'unité nationale est doublé d'une exigence d'uniformité religieuse. La religion ayant été érigée en religion d'Etat, elle ne tolère pas la coexistence de religions parallèles de nature à briser l'unité du pays. C'est le cas, notamment, d'Etats qui se sont officiellement proclamés Républiques islamiques, tels que le Soudan ou la Mauritanie, où les structures de l'Etat s'inspirent des lois islamiques.

---

47 Julius Nyerere, *Socialisme, démocratie et unité africaine*, Présence africaine, 1970, p. 48.

Toutefois, comme on le sait, ces politiques d'unité nationale par la force n'ont pas toujours abouti aux résultats escomptés et ont parfois davantage favorisé les tensions ethniques en exacerbant les réflexes identitaires plus qu'elles n'ont consolidé l'unité nationale. L'adoption, au courant des années 1990, de systèmes politiques fondés sur le pluralisme politique n'a pas mis fin, *ipso facto*, au *credo* de l'unité nationale qui reste affirmée, en plus des principes de l'indivisibilité de la République, dans la plupart des Constitutions africaines. Ainsi, la Constitution de la République du Burundi du 13 mars 1992, tout en proclamant des droits au profit de la personne humaine (article 11-39), dispose que "Nul ne peut abuser des droits reconnus par la Constitution ou par la loi pour compromettre l'unité nationale (...)" (article 40). Une ''Charte de l'Unité nationale, adoptée par référendum le 5 février 1991 et intégrée à la Constitution (article 10), vise à éviter la partition du pays entre Hutu et Tutsi. L'article 3 de la Constitution camerounaise de 1972 oblige les partis politiques, qui peuvent se créer librement, à respecter "l'unité nationale".[48] L'article 7 de la Constitution gabonaise de 1991 condamne "tout acte portant atteinte à la forme républicaine, à l'unité, à la laïcité de l'Etat, à la souveraineté et à l'indépendance" considéré comme "un crime de haute trahison puni par la loi". Ces exemples témoignent bien de l'attachement toujours actuel des Etats africains au principe de l'unité nationale.

Toutefois, l'on conçoit désormais que l'unité nationale peut être mieux réalisée dans la diversité que par la force. C'est pourquoi de nombreuses Constitutions reconnaissent désormais les valeurs traditionnelles et confient à l'Etat le soin de promouvoir les langues et les cultures nationales.[49] Comme le souligne, à juste titre, Alain Didier OLINGA, "L'unité nationale, un but légitime pour n'importe quel gouvernement, peut être achevée plus pleinement et plus profondément à travers une authentique diversité, plutôt que par une uniformité artificielle et imposée, sans aucune consistance à côté des véritables sentiments et aspirations de la population".[50] C'est dire

---

[48] Voir aussi article 7 de la Constitution de la République de Côte d'Ivoire de 1960.

[49] Constitution béninoise du 11 décembre 1990 (art. 11, al. 2); Constitution burkinabè du 11 juin 1991 (art. 35, al. 2); Constitution de la République du Cameroun du 2 juin 1972, révisée le 18 janvier 1996 (art. 1er, al. 3); Constitution gabonaise du 26 mars 1991 (art. 3); Constitution guinéenne du 23 décembre 1990 (art. 1er); Constitution de la République du Mali du 25 février 1992 (art. 25); Constitution mauritanienne du 12 juillet 1991 (art. 6); Constitution nigérienne du 12 mai 1996 (art. 3); Constitution sénégalaise du 7 mars 1963, révisée le 2 mars 1998 (art. 1er, al. 2); Constitution tchadienne du 14 avril 1996 (art. 9); Constitution togolaise du 14 octobre 1992 (art. 40).

[50] Olinga, A.D., "La protection des minorités en droit public camerounais", *art. cit.*, p. 284.

donc que la reconnaissance juridique des minorités n'est pas nécessairement incompatible avec les exigences de la préservation de l'unité politique et juridique de l'Etat.

Ainsi, de nombreux Etats africains, tirant les leçons du passé, sont désormais moins réticents à l'expression d'un certain pluralisme juridique, comme le montrent les exemples camerounais, béninois, sud-africain et éthiopien, ce qui marque un début de changement dans la politique juridique des Etats africains à l'égard des minorités. Il y a donc une certaine protection juridique offerte aux minorités dans certains Etats africains. Toutefois, une telle protection demeure encore embryonnaire. Il en va de même de la protection politique qui est marquée par sa précarité.

II. UNE PROTECTION POLITIQUE PRECAIRE

Au-delà de ses aspects juridiques, la question de la protection constitutionnelle des minorités soulève des enjeux politiques et, de façon plus générale, des enjeux de pouvoir. La protection constitutionnelle des minorités ne se limite pas à la seule reconnaissance d'un statut juridique au profit des minoritaires, lesquels se verraient ainsi reconnaître des droits spécifiques différents des droits des autres citoyens. Ces droits seraient vains si les minorités n'avaient pas la possibilité de participer aux décisions politiques qui les concernent. Une véritable protection constitutionnelle des minorités implique en effet que les intérêts de celles-ci soient pris en compte dans l'organisation et l'aménagement du pouvoir politique au sein de l'Etat par une véritable reconnaissance politique des minorités (A). Toutefois, une telle reconnaissance n'est pas sans danger pour la stabilité et l'existence même de l'Etat. Aussi les Etats qui le font s'efforcent-ils d'en réduire la portée dans des limites strictes (B). Il en découle une protection politique précaire des minorités.

A. Le statut politique des minorités

Reconnaître politiquement les minorités, c'est leur conférer un statut politique, c'est-à-dire une existence dans l'ordre politique au sein de l'Etat leur permettant, en tant que groupes, de défendre leurs intérêts légitimes. En d'autres termes, il s'agit de leur permettre de participer à la prise des décisions qui les concernent, c'est-à-dire à la gestion des affaires nationales et de leurs propres affaires. Prolongement logique de la reconnaissance juridique, la reconnaissance politique des minorités peut être assurée soit par le biais de l'organisation politique de l'Etat, c'est-à-dire la forme même de celui-ci, soit à travers leur association à la vie politique nationale.

1 La prise en compte des minorités dans la forme de l'Etat

Outre l'octroi de droits spécifiques aux minorités, leur prise en compte au sein de l'Etat pourrait également se faire sur le plan institutionnel à travers la forme ou les structures de l'Etat. C'est ainsi que la forme fédérale de l'Etat pourrait finalement s'avérer salutaire pour le maintien ou la consolidation de l'unité nationale, dans la mesure où elle tend à respecter les différences culturelles, ethniques ou religieuses, tout en cultivant un sentiment d'appartenance nationale commune. Mais l'Etat unitaire peut aussi prendre en considération la question minoritaire, en permettant une libre expression des identités communautaires à travers des collectivités décentralisées. La prise en compte des minorités dans la forme de l'Etat est la forme la plus radicale de la protection des minorités au plan politique. Elle consiste à prendre en compte les minorités dans les structures politiques mêmes de l'Etat. De ce point de vue, l'on postule qu'il y a généralement un lien direct entre la forme de l'Etat et la composition sociologique de la société sur laquelle il se fonde.[51] Cela revient à dire qu'un Etat unitaire, tel un Etat-nation, se justifierait essentiellement par l'existence d'une nation homogène sur laquelle il se construit et qu'*a contrario* un Etat composé serait le résultat d'une diversité sociale institutionnalisée au plan politique. Dans le premier cas, l'homogénéité de la société supposerait l'inexistence de minorités, ce qui rend toute politique minoritaire inutile. Dans le second cas, en revanche, la diversité sociale dicterait en quelque sorte à l'Etat sa structure, pour tenir compte notamment des minorités qui ne doivent pas être lésées par rapport à la majorité de la population. Dans la mesure où une telle liaison entre la forme de l'Etat et le pluralisme national est établie au niveau constitutionnel, il s'agit d'un indice significatif de la reconnaissance politique et juridique des minorités. Ainsi, les Etats de l'Europe occidentale dans leur grande majorité seraient des Etats-nations constitués autour de nations homogènes unies par une même langue, une même culture et parfois une même religion.[52]

---

[51] Il en irait ainsi, par exemple, de l'évolution constitutionnelle de la Belgique devenue un Etat fédéral depuis la révision constitutionnelle du 5 mai 1993, ce qui traduit le caractère binational de la société belge; de la situation constitutionnelle du Canada dont le fédéralisme remonte à la Constitution de 1867 et reflète la diversité nationale de la société canadienne. Voir Rouland, N. et al., *op. cit.*, pp. 278 et ss.

[52] Sur la notion d'Etat-nation, voir notamment Tran Van Minh, *Théorie générale de l'Etat, Recherche sur la notion juridique d'Etat-nation*, Paris, Les Cours du Droit, 1979-1980, 384 p.; Chaliand, G., *Les minorités dans le monde à l'âge de l'Etat-nation*, *op. cit.*

Cependant, non seulement ce lien logique entre la structure de l'Etat et celle de la société n'est pas toujours vérifié en pratique, mais encore il demeure difficilement vérifiable dans les Etats africains. En effet, bien que caractérisés par leur diversité sociale, la plupart des Etats africains s'affirment comme des Etats-nations et refusent en conséquence de reconnaître politiquement les minorités ethniques, religieuses ou linguistiques.

Les premiers dirigeants, soucieux de construire des Etats-nations plus ou moins centralisés à l'instar des Etats européens, avaient en outre montré une préférence marquée pour un pouvoir centralisé, tendant à renforcer l'emprise du centre sur la périphérie.[53]

La plupart des Etats africains affirment, en effet, leur attachement à la forme unitaire de l'Etat et n'entendent nullement la réorganiser pour tenir compte de la diversité ethnique, religieuse, raciale ou linguistique. D'où une préoccupation constante pour l'unité nationale. Ainsi, la récente Constitution sud-africaine du 1er janvier 1997 refuse de consacrer le caractère multiracial et multiethnique de la société sud-africaine et proclame le caractère unitaire de l'Etat.[54] La Constitution gabonaise du 26 mars 1991 déclare, à son article 2, que *"Le Gabon est une République indivisible, laïque, démocratique et sociale"* et son article 7 affirme que *"Tout acte portant atteinte à la forme républicaine, à l'unité, à la laïcité de l'Etat, à la souveraineté et à l'indépendance, constitue un crime de haute trahison puni par la loi"*. La Constitution de la République de Guinée du 23 décembre 1990 affirme également, dès son article 1er, que *"La Guinée est une République unitaire, indivisible, laïque, démocratique et sociale"*. La Constitution camerounaise du 2 juin 1972, révisée le 18 janvier 1996, tout en proclamant, dans son préambule, que le peuple camerounais est *"fier de sa diversité*

---

[53] La littérature sur la forme unitaire de l'Etat africain et le caractère centralisateur du pouvoir en Afrique est très abondante. A titre indicatif, on pourrait lire: Tchivounda, P., *Essai sur l'Etat africain post-colonial*, BAM, 1982; Gonidec, P.-F., *L'Etat africain*, Paris, L.G.D.J., 2è éd., 1985; Michalon, Th., "Légitimité de l'Etat et solidarités ethniques", *Le Monde diplomatique*, Novembre 1993, p. 26.

[54] A noter que lors des négociations qui avaient précédé l'adoption de la Constitution définitive, l'idée d'un Etat fédéral ou, à tout le moins celle d'un Etat multiracial et multinational, avait été proposée par le Parti national. Toutefois, elle fut rejetée par l'A.N.C. qui craignait qu'un régime fédéral ne pérennise les tendances centrifuges des Zoulous et d'une partie des Blancs et qu'il ne freine les réformes socio-économiques indispensables. Voir Bullier, A.J., "Afrique du Sud: présentation de la Constitution définitive", in *Afrique contemporaine*, n° 179, 3ème trimestre 1996, p. 45-62.

linguistique et culturelle, élément de sa personnalité nationale qu'elle contribue à enrichir", reconnaît néanmoins *"la nécessité impérieuse de parfaire son unité"* et *"proclame solennellement qu'il constitue une seule et même nation"*. Cette volonté unitaire est confirmée par l'article 1er qui proclame une "République unie du Cameroun", "Etat unitaire", "une et indivisible". Même la Constitution burundaise du 13 mars 1992, en dépit des divisions ethniques marquées entre Hutu et Tutsi, réaffirme la foi du peuple burundais *"dans l'idéal d'unité nationale conformément à la Charte de l'unité nationale du 5 février 1991"* et proclame, à son article 1er, *"une République unitaire, indépendante et souveraine"*.[55]

Il résulte de ses dispositions constitutionnelles concordantes un refus explicite de reconnaître le phénomène minoritaire sur le plan politique. Ce faisant, les Etats africains rejettent le fédéralisme qui, pourtant, semble mieux adapté à leur situation marquée par la diversité sociale. Bien entendu, cette préférence marquée pour l'Etat unitaire correspondait à une volonté avouée des Etats africains de ne pas consacrer, sur le plan institutionnel, le phénomène ethnique, une telle reconnaissance étant réputée fatale pour l'unité nationale et l'intégrité territoriale de l'Etat, en raison de ses effets centrifuges.

Toutefois, ce refus de principe n'est ni absolu ni général, dans la mesure où le caractère unitaire de l'Etat est le plus souvent assoupli par le recours à la technique de la décentralisation, parfois consacrée par la Constitution, et offrant ainsi un cadre d'expression politique des minorités. Face à la multiplication des conflits internes due aux effets pervers du centralisme politique,[56] les Etats africains prennent de plus en plus conscience de la nécessité de régler la question nationale à travers l'organisation de la forme de l'Etat. Si, en effet, tous les Etats africains ne sont pas avancés sur la voie de l'adaptation des formes de l'Etat à la résolution de la question nationale, on peut néanmoins observer de nos jours une tendance très nette à la prise en compte de ce problème, dans la mesure où, comme le reconnaît le Professeur GONIDEC, "de plus en plus, l'Etat unitaire, naguère très centralisé, adopte une politique de décentralisation, ce qui le contraint à créer à l'échelon immédiatement inférieur à celui de l'Etat de grands ensembles (régions,

---

[55] De telles dispositions se retrouvent également, en des termes différents, dans la Constitution malgache du 18 septembre 1992 (art. 1er), dans la Constitution malienne du 25 février 1992 (art. 25 et 28), dans la Constitution nigérienne du 12 mai 1996 (art. 4), ainsi que dans la Constitution togolaise du 14 octobre 1992 (art. 1er).

[56] Voir Gonidec, P.-F., "Conflits internes et question nationale en Afrique", *R.A.D.I.C.*, Septembre 1997, tome 9, n° 3, pp. 560 et ss.

provinces, etc.) permettant aux populations de gérer leurs propres affaires".⁵⁷

Ainsi, la Constitution malgache précitée, tout en affirmant le caractère unitaire et indivisible de l'Etat, n'en pose pas moins le principe d'une décentralisation avec la création de collectivités territoriales autonomes distinctes de l'Etat central (art. 2). De même, la Constitution ivoirienne du 3 novembre 1960, telle que révisée le 26 juin 1995 confie à la loi le soin de fixer les conditions de création des collectivités territoriales et les principes fondamentaux de leur libre administration (article 68).⁵⁸ Il est évident qu'une telle décentralisation, même si elle a un objectif d'abord économique, constitue une certaine reconnaissance politique des minorités, dès lors que le découpage territorial tient compte de la diversité ethnique, religieuse ou linguistique.

A cet égard, la Constitution de la République du Cameroun du 2 juin 1972, révisée le 18 janvier 1996, est particulièrement éloquente. Après avoir affirmé, à son article 1er, § 2, que la République du Cameroun est un Etat unitaire décentralisé, elle aménage, dans ses articles 55 à 62, l'organisation et le fonctionnement des collectivités territoriales décentralisées et consacre l'existence politique des minorités à travers le système de la décentralisation. Son article 57 dispose en effet que *"le Conseil régional doit refléter les différentes composantes sociologiques de la circonscription"* et que le bureau du conseil régional *"doit refléter la composition sociologique de la région"*.⁵⁹ La Constitution définitive de l'Afrique du Sud aménage également un Etat unitaire mais largement décentralisé comprenant neuf provinces, lesquelles disposent de pouvoirs étendus et ressemblent fortement à des Etats fédérés.

Certaines constitutions vont même plus loin et reconnaissent directement la diversité sociale et donc l'existence politique des minorités. Il en va ainsi, de la Constitution éthiopienne précitée du 8 décembre 1994 qui consacre on ne peut plus clairement l'existence politique des minorités en reconnaissant aux Etats fédérés créés sur la base ethnique un droit à l'autodétermination.

---

57   Ibid., p. 560.
58   On trouve des dispositions analogues dans la plupart des autres constitutions récentes telles que la Constitution du Burkina Faso du 11 juin 1991 (art. 143-145), la Constitution du Burundi du 13 mars 1992 (art. 4, 177-179), la Constitution de la République du Bénin du 11 décembre 1990 (art. 150-153).
59   Sur l'importance de la reconnaissance politique des minorités au Cameroun, voir Olinga, A.D., *art. cit.*

Somme toute, la reconnaissance politique ainsi naissante des minorités dans des Etats africains trouve une confirmation dans l'organisation de la participation de celles-ci à la vie politique nationale.

2   La participation des minorités à la vie politique nationale

En Afrique, comme dans bien d'autres régions du monde, les particularismes ethniques, religieux ou linguistiques sont des réalités sociologiques incontournables. Les ignorer dans l'exercice du pouvoir politique, c'est fermer les yeux sur une réalité qui pourrait, à tout moment, resurgir sur la scène politique et mettre en péril l'unité, voire la stabilité de l'Etat, comme en témoigne l'histoire récente de l'Ethiopie, du Rwanda, du Liberia ou du Congo démocratique.

Outre l'organisation politique de l'Etat, la reconnaissance politique des minorités peut également se faire à travers l'association de ces minorités à la vie politique nationale. L'expression politique des minorités est en effet une condition essentielle de la démocratie. Quelle que soit la forme de l'Etat, celle-ci peut être inopérante pour régler la question nationale si les minorités ne sont pas associées à la gestion des affaires qui les concernent. Autrement dit, la forme de l'Etat n'est pas une fin en soi, elle est indissociable de la question de la démocratisation des Etats africains et en particulier de la participation des minorités à la gestion des affaires nationales. Il n'y a pas de démocratie là où ne se manifeste aucune minorité, et la réalité d'une démocratie s'évalue au rôle qu'y jouent les minorités. Le système démocratique va de pair avec le pluralisme politique qui implique la possibilité, pour chaque groupe social, de défendre ses intérêts collectifs.

Mais la démocratie libérale, telle qu'elle a été conçue, élaborée et mise au point dans les Etats occidentaux et transposée dans les Etats africains à partir des années 1990, ne permet pas toujours de faire face à la question minoritaire. En effet, la notion de démocratie, qui s'entend non seulement d'un idéal type de gouvernement, mais aussi comme "un mode empirique et rationnel de prise de décision politique",[60] repose sur l'idée de majorité, ce qui lui a valu l'expression de démocratie majoritaire. Or, la démocratie majoritaire, même si elle favorise l'accès de tous les citoyens aux droits politiques, tend à gommer la diversité sociale et les clivages ethniques, culturels, linguistiques ou religieux, lesquels sont constitutifs de l'existence de minorités nationales. La démocratie majoritaire ne connaît, par définition, que les citoyens pris individuellement dans leur rapport avec l'Etat. Aussi s'accommode-t-elle difficilement d'une société hétérogène ou d'un Etat multinational

---

60   Cf. Emeri C., *Droit constitutionnel et institutions politiques*, Paris, Les Cours du Droit, 1990-1991, p. 117.

comme les sociétés africaines. De plus, les instruments de la démocratie majoritaire peuvent être utilisés comme autant de techniques d'assimilation forcées des minorités nationales.

C'est pourquoi, le recours à la "démocratie associative" peut permettre d'adapter les éléments de la démocratie majoritaire au pluralisme national. Le rapport numérique qui sous-tend la démocratie majoritaire peut être en effet corrigé lorsque celle-ci évolue dans une société nationale hétérogène. Déjà largement pratiquée dans la Confédération Helvétique qui en constitue la terre d'élection,[61] l'idée d'une "démocratie associative" a été forgée par des politologues américains qui y voient un correctif de la démocratie majoritaire à l'usage des sociétés plurales.[62] Elle repose sur un "ensemble de mécanismes et d'arrangements institutionnels permettant d'établir un *modus vivendi* dans des sociétés divisées par des clivages profonds".[63] En d'autres termes, il s'agit de rechercher un équilibre entre les éléments constitutifs de la société nationale, notamment par un partage équilibré du pouvoir politique, en permettant à chaque élément de participer à la gestion de ses propres affaires et des affaires nationales.

Ainsi présentée, la notion de démocratie associative n'est pas totalement inconnue dans les Etats africains. Bien au contraire, elle a maintes fois été pratiquée à des degrés divers sous la forme de ce qu'il a été convenu d'appeler la "démocratie consensuelle". Celle-ci, inspirée des valeurs traditionnelles africaines de la "palabre", du "consensus" et de la "solidarité africaine", vise à instaurer un climat pacifique et consensuel dans la société en associant toutes ses composantes sociologiques dans la gestion des affaires de la cité. Il s'agit, en quelque sorte, d'éviter les effets politiques et psychologiques pervers d'une application aveugle du principe majoritaire en veillant à ce que nul ne soit exclu ou marginalisé des affaires de l'Etat. Le

---

61 Il faut, en effet, noter que la Suisse utilise depuis longtemps la démocratie associative par un perfectionnement du fédéralisme, ce qui a conduit Jacques Cadart à la considérer comme une "démocratie des minorités, démocratie équilibrée par les minorités", dans la mesure où "chaque citoyen est membre de plusieurs groupes presque tous minoritaires, mais il n'est jamais majoritaire dans plus d'un groupe et en ce cas seulement dans un groupe religieux ou linguistique". Voir Cadart, J., *Institutions politiques et droit constitutionnel*, Paris, Economica, t. 1, 3è éd., 1990, pp. 607 et 609.

62 Voir notamment A. Lijphart, *Democracy in plural societies. A comparative exploration*. New Haven, Yale University Press, 1977; *Democraties. Patterns of majoritarian an consensus Government in Twenty One Countries*, New Haven, Yale University Press, 1984.

63 De Witte, B., "Minorités nationales: reconnaissance et protection", in *Pouvoirs*, n° 57/1991, pp. 126-127.

sentiment d'être exclu est, en effet, de nature à générer des frustrations nocives qui pourraient engendrer des tensions sociales ou politiques diverses.[64] Au regard de la question minoritaire, la démocratie associative peut s'apprécier à travers une représentation politique des minorités, soit au niveau des assemblées parlementaires, soit au niveau du gouvernement.

La participation des minorités nationales à l'exercice du pouvoir législatif permet à celles-ci d'être associées à l'élaboration des lois qui les gouvernent. Elle peut être assurée soit par le biais des élections nationales, à l'instar de ce que prévoit la Loi constitutionnelle croate de 1992 sur les droits et les libertés de l'homme et les droits des communautés et minorités nationales et ethniques,[65] soit à travers la structure bicamérale du parlement. Toutefois, sur ce plan, les constitutions africaines, dans leur ensemble, se montrent plutôt réticentes à des élections organisées sur une base ethnique, raciale, religieuse ou régionaliste. La plupart d'entre elles interdisent, en effet, le mandat impératif,[66] ce qui suppose que les parlementaires, une fois élus, ne sauraient représenter un groupe social donné mais la nation entière. De plus, il est interdit souvent aux partis politiques de s'identifier à une race, à une ethnie, à un sexe, à une religion ou à une région.[67] Mais de nombreuses constitutions sont plutôt silencieuses sur la question. Il s'ensuit que la démocratie associative est rarement organisée par les textes constitutionnels. Mais il n'est pas rare que la participation des minorités aux élections nationales soit aménagée par les lois électorales, dans la mesure où la plupart des

---

[64] Voir Michalon, Th., " Légitimité de l'Etat et solidarités ethniques", *art. cit.*, p. 26.

[65] La Loi constitutionnelle croate prévoit en effet un droit de représentation proportionnelle au Parlement et au gouvernement croate ainsi qu'au sein des juridictions suprêmes des minorités nationales et ethniques représentant plus de 8 % de la population totale de la Croatie. Pour les minorités n'atteignant pas ce seuil, la Loi constitutionnelle leur donne le droit d'élire au maximum cinq députés à la Chambre des Représentants du Parlement national (art. 18). Pour une vue générale sur la pratique de la représentation parlementaire des minorités en Europe centrale et orientale, voir Benoit-Rohmer, F., "La représentation des minorités dans les Parlements d'Europe centrale et orientale", *Revue française de droit constitutionnel*, 1993, pp. 499-516.

[66] Voir, à titre d'exemple, article 80 de la Constitution béninoise de 1990; article 15 de la Constitution de la République du Cameroun du 2 juin 1972 révisée en 1996; article 35 de la Constitution de la République de Côte d'Ivoire du 3 novembre 1960; article 67 de la Constitution de la République de Madagascar de 1992; article 64 de la Constitution malienne de 1992.

[67] Article 3 de la Constitution sénégalaise de 1963 révisée en 1998; article 7 de la Constitution togolaise de 1992; article 3 de la Constitution guinéenne de 1991.

textes constitutionnels renvoient à la loi le soin d'organiser le processus électoral.[68]

Certaines constitutions se sont néanmoins engagées dans cette voie, notamment en prévoyant un parlement bicaméral dont l'une des chambres représente l'ensemble des citoyens pris individuellement et l'autre les entités infra-étatiques, y compris les minorités. C'est le cas de la Constitution éthiopienne précitée qui prévoit deux assemblées parlementaires représentant, respectivement, la population éthiopienne dans son ensemble et les peuples qui la composent. Le Conseil des représentants du peuple est élu au suffrage universel direct, avec une représentation spéciale pour les minorités (article 54), tandis que le Conseil fédéral est *"composé de représentants des nations, nationalités et peuples"* qui sont élus par les assemblées des Etats fédérés (Conseils d' Etat). De même, en Afrique Sud, l'Assemblée nationale "représente le peuple"(art. 42 de la Constitution de 1997), tandis que le Conseil national des provinces *"représente les provinces pour assurer que les intérêts provinciaux sont pris en compte dans la sphère nationale du gouvernement "* (art. 42-4°). La Loi constitutionnelle camerounaise du 18 janvier 1996, portant révision de la Constitution du 2 juin 1972 et qui apporte des modifications importantes à la Constitution du Cameroun uni dans le sens d'une plus grande adaptation aux réalités socio-politiques, aménage un parlement bicaméral composé d'une Assemblée nationale et d'un Sénat, ce dernier représentant les collectivités territoriales décentralisées (art. 20).[69]

Quant à la participation des minorités à l'exercice du pouvoir exécutif, elle va dans le même sens, mais revêt davantage d'importance en Afrique en raison de la prééminence de ce pouvoir dans les Etats africains.[70] En effet, comme le note, à juste titre, le Professeur GONIDEC, "la vie politique des Etats africain, ponctuée de violence, de coups d'Etat, de guerres civiles, de sécessions, d'émeutes, de rébellions, d'instabilités constitutionnelles, (...)

---

68 Par exemple, la Loi camerounaise n° 97/013 du 13 mars 1997, modifiant et complétant la Loi n° 91/020 du 16 décembre 1991 fixant les conditions d'élection des députés à l'Assemblée nationale, vise non seulement le maintien des grands équilibres sociologiques de certaines circonscriptions, mais aussi la représentation des minorités dans la vie et les institutions nationales du pays conformément à la Constitution.

69 On rappellera que la Constitution camerounaise de 1972, telle qu'elle a été révisée en 1996, établit un Etat unitaire décentralisé comportant deux catégories de collectivités décentralisées: les régions et les communes. Les régions sont administrées par des conseils régionaux dirigés par des présidents, assistés dans leur tâche par un bureau.

70 Voir Kamto, M., *Pouvoir et droit en Afrique noire*, BAM, 1987.

[est] caractérisée par la monopolisation du pouvoir politique par un petit groupe d'individus, voire un homme, mué en chef de clan et soutenu par une clientèle avide de pouvoir et d'avoir".[71] L'essentiel du pouvoir de l'Etat se trouve donc entre les mains de l'équipe gouvernementale et est, en particulier, concentré entre les mains du Chef de l'Etat. Si celui-ci et son équipe sont hostiles à une minorité, celle-ci ne pourra que subir leur domination et, le cas échéant, leurs oppressions sans pouvoir défendre ses intérêts. L'expérience de nombreux Etats africains montre une méfiance permanente des minorités ethniques à l'égard du pouvoir central lorsque celui-ci est concentré entre les mains d'une seule ethnie et tend à marginaliser les autres, ce qui est de nature à engendrer ou à encourager les tensions inter-ethniques. Aussi peut-il être efficace d'aménager la participation des minorités dans l'exercice du pouvoir exécutif. La présence d'un représentant d'une minorité au sein du pouvoir exécutif peut être pour celle-ci une garantie de la prise en compte de ses intérêts et, partant, un facteur d'apaisement des tensions identitaires. Il s'agit, en réalité, d'un partage plus ou moins équilibré du pouvoir exécutif entre les différentes communautés en présence. De fait, une telle solution a déjà été mise en oeuvre avec succès dans certains pays africains.[72]

Ainsi, si la plupart des Etats africains se sont longtemps montrés "fermement déterminés à éviter toute consécration juridique [et politique] de revendications qu'ils jugent dangereuses pour leur unité territoriale, et répriment avec rigueur les activités des groupes qui pourraient les exprimer",[73] force est cependant de constater que depuis quelques années on observe un certain

---

71   Gonidec, P.-F., *Relations internationales africaines*, Paris, L.G.D.J., 1996, p. 20.
72   Un des exemples frappants de partage du pouvoir est le Protocole d'accord entre le Gouvernement de la République rwandaise et le Front patriotique rwandais sur le partage du pouvoir dans le cadre d'un gouvernement de transition à base élargie du 30 octobre 1992, qui aménage, en quelque sorte, un partage du pouvoir entre les Hutu et les Tutsi. Mais, comme on le sait, ce partage du pouvoir n'a pu empêcher le génocide de 1994. Toutefois, on sait également que c'est ce mécanisme de partage du pouvoir qui a permis, en 1995, de ramener la paix après la guerre civile de 1994. Le principe de partage du pouvoir dans le cadre d'un gouvernement de transition à base élargie a été réaffirmé par la Loi fondamentale de la République rwandaise (Préambule) du 26 mai 1995 qui intègre la Constitution du 10 juin 1991, l'Accord de paix d'Arusha du 15 mai 1993, la Déclaration du F.P.R. du 17 juillet 1994 relative à la mise en place des institutions. On trouvera le texte du Protocole et celui de l'Accord de paix d'Arusha du 15 août 1993 qui l'accompagnait dans le recueil de Du Bois De Gaudusson, J., Conac, G., et Desouches, C., *op. cit.*, tome 2, pp. 245-310.
73   Rouland, N., et al., *Droits des minorités et droits des peuples autochtones*, op. cit., p. 300.

infléchissement de cette politique de rigueur. De plus en plus d'Etats, soucieux d'adapter la vie constitutionnelle à la réalité sociologique s'efforcent de reconnaître un statut politique à leurs minorités nationales. Reste cependant à savoir quelle est la portée pratique d'une telle reconnaissance.

B. Les limites au statut politique des minorités

Reconnaître politiquement les minorités c'est, en réalité, consacrer au sein de l'Etat un droit à la différence, c'est-à-dire un droit de ne pas être comme les autres et d'exprimer son identité propre. De ce point de vue, la prise en compte politique des minorités nationales dans certaines Constitutions africaines marque, à n'en pas douter, un début de changement d'orientation dans la politique des Etats africains à l'égard des minorités. De l'approche uniformiste et intégrationniste adoptée au lendemain des indépendances au nom des exigences de l'unité nationale et de l'intégrité territoriale, on s'achemine vers une approche pluraliste, plus respectueuse de la diversité sociale, qui s'efforce d'admettre et de préserver les différences culturelles, ethniques et religieuses existantes. Toutefois, on peut s'interroger sur la signification réelle d'une telle reconnaissance. S'agit-il là de l'établissement d'un véritable statut politique des minorités, comportant notamment pour ces dernières un droit à disposer d'elles-mêmes? A vrai dire, la reconnaissance politique des minorités en Afrique subsaharienne reste encore embryonnaire et précaire et comporte deux limites majeures: d'une part, elle ne saurait s'assimiler à un droit des minorités à disposer d'elles-mêmes au sens du droit à l'indépendance et, d'autre part, elle reste, en tout état de cause, subordonnée au respect de l'intégrité territoriale de l'Etat.

1 L'exclusion du droit des peuples à disposer d'eux-mêmes

Les Constitutions africaines qui reconnaissent sur le plan politique les minorités nationales restent néanmoins extrêmement prudentes, et s'abstiennent généralement d'en préciser le contenu et la portée réelle. C'est qu'en réalité la reconnaissance politique des minorités met en jeu avant tout un principe fondamental du droit international contemporain: celui du droit des peuples à disposer d'eux-mêmes.

Principe essentiellement politique, le droit des peuples à disposer d'eux-mêmes, parfois assimilé au droit à l'autodétermination, n'est pas "une simple règle d'art politique ou diplomatique" mais une règle de droit international coutumier.[74] Consacré par la Charte des Nations Unies qui, à deux

---

[74] Nguyen Quoc Dinh, Alain Pellet et Patrick Daillier, *Droit international public*, Paris, L.G.D.J., 6è éd., 1999, p. 515.

reprises, mentionne le principe de "l'égalité de droits des peuples et de leur droit à disposer d'eux-mêmes" (articles 1er, § 2, et 55), le droit des peuples à disposer d'eux-mêmes est confirmé par de nombreuses résolutions concordantes des Nations Unies.[75] Il s'appuie sur une *opinio juris* indiscutable confortée par la pratique de la décolonisation et renforcée par l'autorité des avis consultatifs de la C.I.J. du 21 juin 1971 et du 16 octobre 1975, dans les affaires de la Namibie[76] et du Sahara occidental.[77] Le droit des peuples à disposer d'eux-mêmes est même parfois présenté comme une règle impérative du droit international général.[78] Comme l'a indiqué la Cour internationale de Justice dans l'affaire du Timor Oriental, il s'agit "d'un des principes essentiels du droit international contemporain", "opposable *erga omnes*".[79] Il est repris par l'article 1er commun aux Pactes internationaux de 1966 relatifs aux droits de l'homme[80] et par la Charte africaine des droits de l'homme et des peuples.

Toutefois, le concept du droit des peuples à disposer d'eux-mêmes s'est révélé progressivement contradictoire[81] et a été délibérément interprété d'une manière extrêmement restrictive de sorte à en exclure le bénéfice aux entités infra-étatiques.

On sait en effet que ce principe a été présenté comme un droit à l'indépendance, en vue de permettre aux pays et peuples sous domination coloniale d'accéder à la souveraineté internationale. Cette vision découlait

---

75 Parmi les résolutions les plus pertinentes de l'Assemblée générale des Nations Unies, on peut citer: la résolution 1514 (XV) du 14 décembre 1960 relative à la Déclaration sur l'octroi de l'indépendance aux pays et peuples coloniaux; la résolution 2625 (XXV) du 24 octobre 1970 sur la Déclaration relative aux principes du droit international touchant les relations amicales et la coopération entre Etats, conformément à la Charte des Nations Unies; et résolution 3314 du 14 décembre 1974 relative à la définition de l'agression.

76 Voir C.I.J., Rec., 1971, p. 31.

77 Voir C.I.J., Rec., 1975, p. 68.

78 Le droit des peuples à disposer d'eux-mêmes figure dans la liste d'exemples de règles ''impératives" fournies par la C.D.I. dans son rapport sur le droit des traités. La Commission d'arbitrage de la conférence pour la paix en Yougoslavie a également qualifié de normes impératives du droit international général les "droits des peuples et des minorités" (Avis n° 1, du 29 novembre 1991, R.G.D.I.P. 1992, p. 265 et avis n° 9, 4 juillet 1992).

79 C.I.J., arrêt du 30 juin 1995, Timor Oriental, Rec., p. 102.

80 Aux termes de l'alinéa 1er de cette disposition, "Tous les peuples ont le droit de disposer d'eux-mêmes. En vertu de ce droit, ils déterminent librement leur statut politique et assurent librement leur développement économique, social et culturel".

81 Voir Charpentier, J., "Autodétermination et décolonisation", *Mélanges offerts à Charles Chaumont*, Paris, Pedone, 1984, pp. 118-133.

notamment de la résolution 1514 (XV) de l'Assemblée générale des Nations Unies du 14 décembre 1960 portant déclaration sur l'octroi de l'indépendance aux pays et peuples coloniaux. C'est, du reste, la mise en oeuvre de ce droit qui a favorisé l'accession à l'indépendance, au cours des années 1950-1960, des anciennes colonies européennes en Afrique et en Asie. D'où l'assimilation abusive du droit des peuples à disposer d'eux-mêmes au droit à la décolonisation.

Or, pris au pied de la lettre, ce principe devrait pouvoir, en toute logique juridique, bénéficier également aux minorités et leur permettre de se constituer en Etat, dès lors qu'elles peuvent être considérées comme formant un peuple.

Toutefois, dans la pratique, il a été interprété comme ne pouvant être invoqué que dans les seules hypothèses de la décolonisation, c'est-à-dire dans la situation des peuples sous domination coloniale afin de leur permettre d'accéder à l'indépendance. Au plan international, craignant que le principe du droit des peuples à disposer d'eux-mêmes ne soit utilisé par des communautés infra-étatiques contre des Etats nouvellement établis pour accéder à leur tour à l'indépendance, créant ainsi un risque d'instabilité des Etats, l'on a cru bon de verrouiller le principe. Considérant que le droit des peuples à disposer d'eux-mêmes constitue "un principe destructeur de l'ordre international"[82] en ce qu'il met en cause l'unité nationale et l'intégrité territoriale des Etats, on a soumis son exercice à deux restrictions essentielles: l'unité politique de l'Etat et son intégrité territoriale. Autrement dit, on a considéré que le droit des peuples à disposer d'eux-mêmes ne peut être exercé lorsqu'il aboutit à la sécession au sein d'un Etat déjà constitué. Le droit international n'admet donc pas le droit à la sécession. L'objectif visé est simple: il s'agit d'éviter que l'exercice de ce droit n'aboutisse, au plan national, à une déstabilisation de l'Etat et, au plan international, à une multiplication indéfinie du nombre des Etats.

Dès lors, il a été dénaturé dans le but de servir une seule cause: la décolonisation. Les nécessités de la décolonisation imposaient que des droits soient reconnus directement aux peuples pour faciliter leur accession à l'indépendance. Mais, une fois l'Etat constitué, le droit des peuples à disposer d'eux-mêmes devient un droit de l'Etat et non du peuple, dans la mesure où les droits formellement reconnus aux peuples sont, en fait et en droit, exercés par l'Etat. A partir du moment où l'Etat décolonisé s'identifie au peuple

---

[82] Combacau, J. et al., *Droit international public*, Paris, Montchrestien, 1975, p. 499.

colonisé, le peuple ne peut plus concurrencer l'Etat comme un sujet du droit international et redevient un simple élément de l'Etat.[83]

Le droit des peuples à disposer d'eux-mêmes se trouve finalement confisqué par l'Etat au nom du ''droit'' à sa propre conservation.[84] Il découle de ces considérations que la réduction du droit des peuples à disposer d'eux-mêmes à un "droit à la décolonisation" et le droit de l'Etat établi à sa propre conservation tendent à ramener celui du peuple au seul droit à devenir un Etat, c'est-à-dire, comme le note le professeur COMBACAU, à un "droit à réalisation instantanée et s'épuisant dans un usage unique".[85] Dans ces conditions, le droit international semble bien ne laisser aux minorités nationales aucune voie d'accès au droit des peuples à disposer d'eux-mêmes,[86] car l'exercice du droit à l'autodétermination des peuples par les minorités signifie généralement le droit de sécession au profit d'entités infra-étatiques à l'intérieur d'un Etat déjà constitué et autonome. C'est ce que Jean CHARPENTIER appelle un "droit des peuples contre l'Etat".[87]

Au plan régional, la Charte africaine des droits de l'homme et des peuples, adoptée par la Conférence des Chefs d'Etats et de gouvernements de l'O.U.A. le 28 juin 1981, est suffisamment explicite à cet égard. Elle fait une place importante aux droits des peuples sans dissiper les incertitudes relatives à la notion de ''peuple'', qui apparaît comme une "entité sociale à géométrie variable".[88] Après avoir reconnu à tout peuple le droit de déterminer

---

83   Le juge Kéba M'Baye en convient aussi lorsqu'il affirme, à propos de la Charte africaine des droits de l'homme et des peuples que "Les peuples sont les titulaires des droits. Mais ce sont les Etats qui les exercent en leur nom par l'intermédiaire des gouvernements". Voir *Les droits de l'homme en Afrique*, Paris, Pedone, 1992, p. 173.
84   Pierre-Caps, S., "Peut-on parler actuellement d'un droit européen des minorités?", *A.F.D.I.*, XL – 1994, p. 81.
85   Cf. Combacau, J., et Sur, S., *Droit international public*, Paris, Montchrestien, 1993, p. 263.
86   Pour une vue générale de la question, voir notamment: Scelle, G., "Quelques réflexions sur le droit des peuples à disposer d'eux-mêmes", *Mélanges Spiropoulos*, Bonn, 1975, pp. 388 et ss.; Batailler-Demichel, F., "Droits de l'homme et droits des peuples dans l'ordre international", *Mélanges offerts à Chartes Chaumont*, op. cit., pp. 23-34; Charpentier, J., "Autodétermination et décolonisation", *ibid.*, pp. 117-133; Carpentier, C., "Le principe mythique des nationalités", *Revue Belge de Droit International*, 1986, n° 2; Pellet, A., "Quel avenir pour le droit des peuples à disposer d'eux-mêmes?", *Mélanges Jimenez*, pp. 255-276; Jouve, E., *Le droit des peuples*, Paris, P.U.F., Que sais-je?, mise à jour, 1992; S.F.D.I., Colloque de Nancy, *L'Etat souverain à l'aube du XXIè siècle*, Paris, Pedone, 1994.
87   Art. cit., p. 118.
88   F. Ouguergouz distingue quatre acceptions du mot peuple dans la Charte: le "peuple-Etat", la population de l'Etat, l'ethnie, le peuple sous domination coloniale ou raciale. Voir *La Charte africaine des droits de l'homme et des peuples*, op. cit., p. 138.

librement son statut politique (art. 20, § 1), elle reconnaît aux peuples colonisés ou opprimés – et à eux seuls – le droit de se libérer de leur état de domination (art. 20, § 2). Dans les faits, l'application du droit d'autodétermination aux minorités nationales s'est heurtée, jusqu'ici à de nombreuses réticences de la part des Etats.

Les Etats africains considèrent, dans leur généralité, le droit à l'autodétermination des peuples comme un droit à l'indépendance reconnu aux peuples colonisés et qui s'épuise avec l'accession à l'indépendance. Une fois celle-ci acquise, il ne saurait être revendiqué au sein du nouvel Etat. En adoptant, en 1964, le principe de l'intangibilité des frontières héritées de la colonisation et en l'érigeant en une règle impérative du droit régional africain, ils ont confondu pratiquement le droit des peuples à disposer d'eux-mêmes avec le droit à la décolonisation. En fait, ils ont voulu éviter de voir s'en nourrir les mouvements subversifs à but sécessionniste.

Le droit des peuples à disposer d'eux-mêmes n'a été reconnu qu'aux peuples sous domination coloniale et a été toujours dénié aux autres peuples dominés, comme en témoigne, dans le passé, l'opposition déterminée de la communauté internationale et de la communauté africaine face aux tentatives de sécession du Katanga, du Biafra et de l'Erythrée.[89] Aujourd'hui encore, la réticence de l'O.U.A. à la tentative de séparation de l'Ile d'Anjouan de l'Etat comorien témoigne de l'attachement profond des Etats africains à cette interprétation restrictive du droit des peuples à disposer d'eux-mêmes.

Pourtant, le droit des peuples à disposer d'eux-mêmes a un contenu à la fois plus large et plus souple. En effet, certains auteurs ont pu démontrer que ce principe peut être entendu aussi bien dans un sens externe que dans un sens interne. Dans sa dimension externe, le droit des peuples à disposer d'eux-mêmes aboutirait à l'indépendance, tandis qu'il n'aboutit pas nécessairement à une telle solution dans sa dimension interne.[90] Cette interprétation était

---

[89] On notera que lors de la tentative de sécession du Katanga, province minière du Congo, entre 1960 et 1961, les résolutions du Conseil de sécurité des Nations Unies ont dénoncé les "activités sécessionnistes illégalement menées par l'administration provinciale du Katanga". De même, à l'occasion de l'affaire du Biafra, qui a menacé d'éclatement le Nigéria entre 1967 et 1970, le Secrétaire général des Nations Unies a déclaré que "L'O.N.U. n'a jamais accepté et n'acceptera jamais, je pense, le principe de sécession d'une partie d'un Etat" (1970). V. Berny, "La sécession du Katanga", *Revue Juridique et Politique Indépendance et Coopération* 1965, pp. 563-573; F. Wodie, "La sécession du Biafra et le droit international public", *R.G.D.I.P.* 1969, pp. 1018-1060.

[90] Voir notamment Olinga, A.D., "Désuétude programmée ou pérennité assurée? Enquête brève sur les mutations conceptuelles du principe d'autodétermination en droit international contemporain", *R.A.D.I.C.*, Décembre 1994, Tome 6, n° 4, pp. 571-593

déjà contenue dans la résolution 2625 (XXV) de l'Assemblée générale des Nations Unies du 24 octobre 1970.[91] D'ailleurs, l'avis consultatif rendu par la Cour internationale de Justice le 16 octobre 1975, à l'occasion de l'affaire du Sahara occidental va dans le même sens.[92]

Le principe de l'intégrité territoriale de l'Etat ne fait que renforcer cet obstacle infranchissable pour l'épanouissement politique des minorités.

2 La subordination au respect de l'intégrité territoriale de l'Etat

Principe fondamental du droit international contemporain, le respect de l'intégrité territoriale a pour objet d'empêcher qu'un Etat puisse être dépouillé de tout ou partie de son territoire ou que celui-ci ne fasse l'objet d'une simple violation. Trouvant son fondement dans l'article 2, § 4 de la Charte des Nations Unies,[93] il est consacré par de nombreux autres textes internationaux[94] et apparaît comme une règle coutumière bien établie en droit international. Dans les relations interafricaines, il est solennellement affirmé par la Charte de l'O.U.A. du 23 mai 1963, dans son article 3, § 3, selon lequel *"Les Etats membres, pour atteindre les objectifs énoncés à l'article 2, affirment solennellement les principes suivants: (...) respect de la souveraineté et de l'intégrité territoriale de chaque Etat et son droit inaliénable à une existence indépendante (...)"*.

De même, les textes internationaux sur les minorités, en même temps qu'ils posent les principes d'une protection, les assortissent toujours d'une

---

91   La résolution 2625 (XXV), tout en affirmant le principe du droit des peuples à disposer d'eux-mêmes, précise cependant que " *Rien dans les paragraphes précédents ne sera interprété comme autorisant ou encourageant une action quelle qu'elle soit qui démembrerait ou menacerait totalement ou partiellement l'intégrité territoriale ou l'unité politique de l'Etat souverain et indépendant se conduisant conformément au principe de l'égalité des droits et du droit des peuples à disposer d'eux-mêmes* (...)".

92   Selon la Cour internationale, "La création d'un Etat souverain et indépendant, la libre association ou l'intégration avec un Etat indépendant ou l'acquisition de tout autre statut politique *librement décidé par un peuple* constituent pour ce peuple des moyens d'exercer son droit à disposer de lui-même", Cf. C.I.J., avis consultatif, affaire du Sahara occidental, 16 octobre 1975, Rec. 1975, § 58, p. 33.

93   Selon cette disposition, *"Les Membres de l'Organisation s'abstiennent, dans leurs relations internationales, de recourir à la menace ou à l'emploi de la force, (...) contre l'intégrité territoriale (...) de tout Etat (...)"*.

94   Cf. Résolution 1514 (XV) du 14 décembre 1960 relative à la Déclaration sur l'octroi de l'indépendance aux pays et peuples coloniaux; Résolution 2625 (XXV) du 24 octobre 1970 relative aux principes du droit international touchant les relations amicales et la coopération entre les Etats conformément à la Charte des Nations Unies; Acte final d'Helsinki de 1975; déclaration de Vienne du 25 juin 1995 de la Conférence mondiale sur les droits de l'homme.

réserve liée à la souveraineté, à l'intégrité territoriale et à l'indépendance de l'Etat. Ainsi, la Déclaration de l'Assemblée générale des Nations Unies sur les droits des personnes appartenant aux minorités nationales ou ethniques, religieuses et linguistiques du 18 décembre 1992, après avoir posé les règles de protection, souligne, à son article 8, § 4, que: "*Aucune des dispositions de la présente déclaration ne peut être interprétée comme autorisant une quelconque activité contraire aux buts et principes des Nations Unies, y compris à l'égalité souveraine, à l'intégrité territoriale et à l'indépendance politique des Etats*".

Il résulte de ces dispositions diverses que la reconnaissance politique des minorités s'arrête là où commence la souveraineté étatique et ses nécessaires implications, notamment l'intégrité territoriale. Les minorités ne peuvent donc remettre en cause l'indivisibilité de l'Etat et de son territoire. En particulier, l'intégrité territoriale interdit le droit à la sécession des minorités.

Cette exigence fondamentale du droit international est également reprise et réaffirmée par la plupart des Constitutions africaines. Ainsi, la Constitution camerounaise précitée dispose, à son article 1er, que la République du Cameroun est "une et indivisible" et interdit toute révision constitutionnelle portant atteinte "à l'intégrité territoriale de l'Etat" (art. 64). Des dispositions analogues se retrouvent dans la Constitution béninoise (art. 156), dans la Constitution du Burkina Faso (art. 165), dans la Constitution ivoirienne (art. 73), dans la Constitution de la République du Mali (art. 118), ainsi que dans la Constitution de la République Centrafricaine (art. 101, al. 2). La Constitution béninoise, tout en proclamant une République "*une et indivisible*" (art. 2), oblige les partis politiques à "respecter le principe de la souveraineté, de la démocratie, de l'intégrité territoriale..." (art. 5); en outre, son article 32 précise que "*La défense de la nation et de l'intégrité du territoire de la République est un devoir sacré pour tout citoyen béninois*". La Constitution sénégalaise, pour sa part, précise que "*Tout acte de discrimination raciale, ethnique ou religieuse de même que toute propagande régionaliste pouvant porter atteinte à la sécurité intérieure de l'Etat ou à l'intégrité du territoire de la République, sont punis par la loi*". Mais la Constitution togolaise est encore plus formelle, puisqu'elle précise, à son article 43, que "*la défense de la patrie et de l'intégrité du territoire national est un devoir sacré de tout citoyen*".[95]

---

95 On trouve une disposition analogue dans la Constitution nigérienne du 12 mai 1996 (art. 28).

Le moins que l'on puisse dire, c'est que les Etats africains sont particulièrement attachés à leur indépendance, à l'unité politique et à l'intégrité de leur territoire. Or, les revendications des minorités, surtout si elles s'expriment sur le plan politique, peuvent menacer l'unité politique ou l'intégrité territoriale de l'Etat, en ce que les minorités peuvent être amenées à réclamer un droit à disposer d'elles-mêmes, notamment en se séparant de l'Etat par la sécession. L'affirmation du principe de l'intégrité territoriale permet ainsi d'empêcher, au moins sur le plan du droit, tout démembrement de l'Etat en contenant les revendications des minorités. La reconnaissance politique des minorités pourrait donc s'avérer fatale pour l'intégrité territoriale de l'Etat, notamment si la minorité considérée est regroupée sur un territoire donné et constitue une entité culturelle ou économique assez homogène. La tentative de sécession du Biafra contre l'Etat fédéral du Nigéria entre 1967 et 1970 en est une illustration historique suffisamment éloquente. La guerre déclenchée par le mouvement indépendantiste érythréen contre le pouvoir central éthiopien, qui a abouti récemment à l'indépendance de l'Erythrée, témoigne encore de nos jours de l'actualité d'une telle menace. La reconnaissance d'un statut politique aux différentes minorités ethniques pourrait ainsi, estime-t-on, aboutir à l'éclatement de l'Etat. Le meilleur moyen d'éviter une telle désagrégation de l'Etat est la conservation de l'intégrité territoriale de l'Etat. Comme l'écrit André N'KOLOMBUA, "La stabilité de l'Etat postule le respect de son intégrité territoriale".[96] En ce sens, les Constitutions africaines s'attachent à prévenir le danger de l'éclatement de l'Etat.

Dans la pratique cependant, ce principe a le plus souvent été utilisé par les Etats contre les minorités auxquelles ils ont dénié tout droit à l'existence politique, considérée, parfois à tort, comme une menace contre l'unité politique et l'intégrité de l'Etat. Toutefois, l'expérience de nombreux Etats africains démontre que le principe de l'intégrité territoriale, poussé à l'extrême, pourrait produire des effets pervers tendant à encourager plutôt les minorités à rechercher à tout prix leur autonomie. La séparation de la minorité érythréenne de l'Ethiopie en 1993 et l'admission de l'Erythrée en 1996 comme membre de l'O.U.A. en dépit du principe de l'intégrité territoriale affirmé par la Charte panafricaine montre clairement les limites pratiques de ce principe.[97]

---

[96] "L'ambivalence des relations entre le droit des peuples à disposer d'eux-mêmes et l'intégrité territoriale des Etats en droit international contemporain", *Mélanges offerts à Charles Chaumont*, op. cit., p. 435.

[97] Pour un aperçu général sur les difficultés soulevées par ce principe, voir notamment: Gonidec, P.-F., *L'O.U.A., trente ans après*, Paris, Karthala, 1993, pp. 109 et ss.

Pourtant, dans la mesure où l'expression politique des minorités ne se traduit pas nécessairement par la sécession, elle peut parfaitement être conciliée avec l'intégrité territoriale de l'Etat, tout comme avec le droit des peuples à disposer d'eux-mêmes, notamment par l'instauration d'un système de pluralisme politique permettant de concilier les intérêts des minorités avec ceux de l'Etat.[98] De fait, la protection des minorités nationales est essentielle à la stabilité et à la sécurité des Etats et de certaines régions. L'absence d'une protection des minorités peut être source de tensions ou de conflits.

CONCLUSION

Que les constitutions africaines consacrent ou non au plan constitutionnel une protection des minorités, il n'y a pas de doute que les Etats africains sont de plus en plus conscients de la nécessité d'apporter des solutions à la question nationale, dont l'existence s'impose à eux à travers les mouvements autonomistes ou séparatistes ainsi que les multiples conflits ethniques qui ont marqué l'histoire récente de nombre d'entre eux. Cette prise de conscience se traduit par l'évolution relative à l'élargissement des droits et libertés reconnus à la personne humaine, aux formes de l'Etat et à l'adoption de structures politiques mieux adaptées à la participation de toutes les communautés à la gestion des affaires publiques, tant nationales que locales.

L'on peut cependant s'interroger sur la portée réelle de cette prise en compte de la diversité sociale sur le plan constitutionnel, surtout quand on sait que le brassage des populations, le système de l'éducation nationale, la bureaucratie administrative, le système politique libéral ou encore l'économie moderne tendent à gommer les clivages ethniques, religieux et linguistiques dans la plupart des Etats africains. Certains estiment que toute tentative de consécration juridique du phénomène minoritaire serait une porte ouverte à des velléités séparatistes incontrôlables, surtout à une période où l'unité nationale est plus que jamais nécessaire pour faire face aux impératifs de la construction nationale et de la démocratie majoritaire. D'autres pensent plutôt que toute protection constitutionnelle des minorités ethniques, religieuses ou linguistiques en Afrique par l'octroi de droits spécifiques ne saurait être

---

[98] Lire à ce sujet N'Kolombua, "L'ambivalence des relations entre le droit des peuples à disposer d'eux-mêmes et l'intégrité territoriale en droit international contemporain", *art. cit.*

que transitoire, compte tenu de l'évolution des Etats africains vers une meilleure intégration nationale. D'autres, enfin, considèrent qu'il est impératif, pour les Etats qui connaissent des problèmes de minorités ethniques, religieuses ou linguistiques, de prendre en compte le phénomène tant sur le plan juridique que sur le plan politique. Au reste, la question est encore ouverte et reste sans réponse définitive et générale.

En tout état de cause, il appartient à chaque Etat de tenir compte de sa diversité sociologique pour la consacrer ou non sur le plan du droit. Certes, il ne semble guère utile et nécessaire d'organiser officiellement une protection constitutionnelle des minorités dans les Etats où l'intégration nationale a eu raison des clivages sociaux comme en Côte d'Ivoire, au Burkina Faso ou au Ghana. Toutefois, dans les Etats où la question nationale reste encore aiguë – Cameroun, Congo, Nigeria, Rwanda, Sénégal –, l'organisation d'une protection constitutionnelle n'est pas nécessairement un facteur d'éclatement ou de démembrement de l'Etat, si elle s'efforce de réaliser l'équilibre nécessaire entre les aspirations légitimes des différentes composantes sociologiques de la société et les exigences d'unité nationale et d'intégrité territoriale de l'Etat. Il est en effet symptomatique de constater que le refus systématique de reconnaissance juridique du fait minoritaire a parfois pu conduire, en Afrique, à des dérives dictatoriales ou à des conflits ethniques, comme en témoignent le récent génocide rwandais. Autrement dit, il n'est pas impossible de concilier les considérations primordiales de l'égalité, de la non-discrimination, de l'unité nationale, de l'intégrité territoriale avec le respect et la protection des particularismes ethniques, religieux ou linguistiques. Une reconnaissance juridique et politique des minorités par l'aménagement de droits spécifiques à leur profit ainsi que leur prise en compte dans l'organisation de la forme de l'Etat et la gestion du pouvoir politique, pourrait, au contraire, se révéler un facteur d'unité nationale, dans la mesure où elle favoriserait l'émergence d'un esprit de tolérance et de coexistence dans les différentes communautés nationales.

Dans ce sens, une introduction de droits catégoriels dans les lois fondamentales, aux côtés de droits fondamentaux reconnus à la personne humaine, pourrait même être considérée comme un signe de progrès. Ainsi que l'a reconnu la Commission d'arbitrage de la Conférence pour la paix en Yougoslavie, le "respect des droits fondamentaux de la personne humaine et des droits des peuples et des minorités" constitue une "norme impérative du droit international général".[99]

---

99   Avis n° 2 de la Commission arbitrale de la Conférence pour la paix en Yougoslavie, in *R.G.D.I.P.* 1992, pp. 265 et 267.

Mais il convient de noter que les dispositions constitutionnelles ne peuvent à elles seules assurer la régulation des relations politiques entre les différentes communautés au sein d'un même Etat, comme en témoigne la situation de l'Afrique du Sud qui a pu opérer une transition pacifique vers une société multiraciale et multinationale sans pour autant consacrer scrupuleusement un statut juridique et politique des minorités.

Quelle que soit cependant la situation individuelle des Etats africains, il est aujourd'hui impératif d'adopter une politique juridique régionale commune à l'égard des minorités nationales, à l'instar des pays européens qui ont récemment adopté des instruments juridiques régionaux tendant à régler, sur le plan du droit, le problème des minorités.[100] La question des minorités, telle qu'elle se manifeste actuellement, dépasse désormais le seul cadre national et devrait être appréhendée dans un cadre institutionnel et conventionnel régional fixant un standard minimum de règles en harmonie avec les principes fondamentaux de l'O.U.A. et les principes généraux du droit international applicables aux minorités. Ces règles communes pourraient être, par exemple, introduites directement dans la Charte africaine des droits de l'homme et des peuples, par une révision expresse de celle-ci.[101] Toutefois, compte tenu du fait que les principes philosophiques qui ont inspiré la Charte ne laissent guère de place aux entités infra-étatiques, il serait plus indiqué d'adopter un accord-cadre séparé précisant la notion même de minorité telle qu'elle est entendue en Afrique et définissant les droits qui pourraient leur être reconnus. La Charte constituerait alors une condition préalable à tout système de protection des minorités nationales.

En tout cas, la question ethnique en Afrique aujourd'hui, comme celle des nationalités en Europe au début du siècle, est une question récurrente qui pourrait, même dans les Etats qui paraissent mieux intégrés, resurgir à tout moment. L'exemple de la désintégration de l'ex Yougoslavie constitue, à cet égard, un témoignage historique éloquent. L'exemple du Rwanda montre bien que la question ethnique n'a pas totalement disparu en Afrique. L'ignorer, c'est assurément faire la "politique de l'autruche". Dans cette perspective, la protection des minorités apparaît comme un moyen de

---

[100] Charte européenne des langues régionales ou minoritaires, adoptée le 5 novembre 1992; Convention-cadre du Conseil de l'Europe pour la protection des minorités nationales, adoptée en novembre 1994.

[101] Telle est la solution préconisée par M. Mutoy Mubiala (art. cit., p. 38). Son avantage principal est qu'elle permettra au continent africain de disposer d'un instrument unique consacré à la fois aux droits de l'homme, à ceux des peuples et à ceux des minorités. De la sorte, la Charte se rapprocherait des réalités sociologiques des Etats africains.

maintien de la paix et de la stabilité de certains Etats, dans la mesure où elle permet à la fois de sauvegarder les droits de l'individu, de respecter les aspirations des groupes minoritaires à l'autonomie, tout en préservant les principes de souveraineté et d'intégrité territoriale de l'Etat. Toutefois, il faut bien avoir conscience que les intérêts à mettre en balance sont plus complexes dans la réalité, puisqu'il s'agit d'établir un équilibre entre droits et devoirs de l'individu, du groupe et de l'Etat.[102]

---

[102] Voir Scholsem, J.-C., "Faut-il protéger les minorités? Quelques remarques introductives", *Mélanges offerts à Jacques Vélu*, tome 2è, Bruxelles, Bruylant, 1992, pp. 1167-1178.

LA CLAUSE DES DROITS DE L'HOMME DANS UN ACCORD DE COOPERATION ECONOMIQUE: Etude contextuelle de l'article 5 de la Convention de Lomé IV et IV-bis[1]

Pierre Célestin Ulimubenshi

POSITION DU PROBLÈME:

A l'heure actuelle, la défense des droits de l'homme est devenue une dimension juridique internationale universelle et a acquis une consécration internationale incontestable et irréversible.[2] C'est pourquoi, les pays développés ont commencé à intégrer les préoccupations des droits de l'homme dans leur politique extérieure et, sur le plan de la coopération, à exiger le respect des droits de l'homme considérés comme fondamentaux.

---

[1] A l'origine, la Convention de Lomé se présentait sous forme d'une Convention d'application relative à l'association des pays et territoires d'outre-mer (PTOM) à la Communauté européenne qui se composait alors de la Belgique, de la France, du Luxembourg, de la République Fédérale d'Allemagne, de l'Italie et des Pays-Bas. Lors de l'accession à l'indépendance des pays africains, la nature des relations entre les PTOM et la Communauté européenne changea: dix-huit pays constituèrent les Etats africains et malgache associés (EAMA) et en juillet 1963, conclurent avec l'Europe des Six à Yaoundé (Caméroun) une Convention appelée "la première Convention de Yaoundé", pour une durée de cinq ans (1963-1968). La deuxième Convention fut également signée à Yaoundé en 1969 (Convention de Yaoundé II). En 1972, aux EAMA, s'ajouta l'Ile Maurice. Le 1er janvier 1973, la Grande-Bretagne (avec l'Irlande et le Danemark) adhéra à la Communauté en lui apportant ses relations avec les pays en développement anglophones, qui débordaient les limites de l'Afrique et s'étendaient aux Caraïbes et au Pacifique. Les partenaires de la Communauté devinrent ainsi les ACP (Afrique-Caraïbes-Pacifique). La première Convention de Lomé fut signée le 28 février 1975, avec la participation initiale de 44 pays ACP qui, en mai 1975, passèrent au nombre de 48. Lomé II fut signée le 31 octobre 1979, Lomé III le 8 décembre 1985 et Lomé IV le 15 décembre 1989. Cette dernière a été révisée et signée le 4 novembre 1995 à l'Ile Maurice et est connue sous le nom de Lomé IV-bis. Actuellement, la Convention de Lomé associe 15 Etats membres de l'Union européenne à 70 pays ACP.

Ainsi, sous la présidence de Carter, les Etats-Unis conditionnaient leur aide militaire ou économique à accorder aux Etats au comportement de ces derniers en matière des droits de l'homme.³ Le Président Carter a lui-même indiqué, en décembre 1978, que

"human rights is the soul of [US] foreign policy",

et que la politique d'assistance au développement des Etats-Unis allait dépendre de l'adoption par les bénéficiaires d'

"a democratic path of development."⁴

De même, les Etats membres de la Communauté économique européenne (C.E.E.), confrontés aux nouvelles provenant du continent africain et faisant état de graves violations des droits de l'homme commises par les pays⁵ leur liés par la Convention de Lomé, demandèrent dès 1979 lors

---

2   Il existe une multiplicité d'instruments internationaux relatifs aux droits de l'homme. Par ordre chronologique, on peut citer la Déclaration universelle des droits de l'homme de 1948, la Convention de sauvegarde des droits de l'homme et des libertés fondamentales signée à Rome le 4 novembre 1950 et entrée en vigueur le 3 septembre 1953, les Pactes internationaux relatifs respectivement aux droits civils et politiques et aux droits économiques, sociaux et culturels adoptés le 16 décembre 1966, la Convention interaméricaine des droits de l'homme signée le 22 novembre 1969, l'Acte final de la Conférence d'Helsinki adopté le 1ᵉʳ août 1975 et portant sur la sécurité et la coopération en Europe contient un chapitre relatif aux droits de l'homme et la Charte africaine des droits de l'homme et des peuples de 1981.
3   Alston, Philip, "Linking Trade and Human Rights", *German Yearbook of International Law*, vol. 23, 1980, p. 127.
4   *International Herald Tribune*, December 7, 1978, 1.
5   Ces pays étaient entre autres la Guinée équatoriale (voir les réponses de la Commission à la question écrite N° 193/79 de M. Battiza, *Journal officiel des Communautés européennes*, N° C205 du 14 août 1979, p. 13 et les Neuf à la question écrite N° 608/79 de M. Hasburg, *Journal officiel des Communautés européennes*, N° C27 du 4 février 1980, p. 8); la République Centrafricaine (voir le Rapport du Parlement européen sur la situation dans ce pays, doc. 1-149/80 du 8 mai 1980 cités par Maganzi, Giorgio, "La Convention de Lomé" in Jacquet Migret, Michel Waelbroeck, Jean Victor Louis, Daniel Vignes, Jean-Louis Dewost, *Le droit de la Communauté économique européenne, Commentaire du traité de Lomé et des textes pris pour son application*, Editions de l'Université de Bruxelles, 1990, N° 141, p. 169) et l'Ouganda (voir les nombreuses questions posées par écrit par des membres du Parlement européen au Conseil, parmi lesquelles se trouvent les questions écrites Nᵒˢ 710/75 de M. Glinne, 360/76 de M. Blumenfeld, 363/76 de M. Dondelinger, 403/76 de M. Lagorce, 941/76 de M. van der Hek, 328778 de Mme Ewing, et 681/79 de M. Cottrell).

du renouvellement de la première Convention de Lomé, l'insertion dans cette même Convention d'une clause relative aux droits de l'homme.[6]

Cependant, cette demande, bien que réitérée à plusieurs reprises, rencontrait de très vives réticences de la part des pays d'Afrique-Caraïbes-Pacifique (A.C.P.). Dans l'essentiel, les arguments qu'invoquaient les pays ACP étaient les suivants:

(a) Les pays ACP considéraient suffisants les instruments juridiques internationaux de protection des droits de l'homme auxquels ils étaient et sont encore parties[7];

(b) Les Etats de la CEE, par les relations économiques importantes qu'ils entretenaient avec l'Afrique du Sud qui menait une politique raciste d'apartheid[8], n'étaient pas considérés par les pays ACP comme les mieux placés pour se poser en défenseurs des droits de l'homme;

(c) Les deux groupes de pays différaient quant à l'interprétation des droits de l'homme[9]: la conception européenne des droits de l'homme se limiterait surtout aux aspects politiques et civiques tandis que celle des pays ACP s'étendrait à d'autres droits (droits sociaux, culturels et droit au développement).[10] Si l'on faisait prévaloir telle ou telle conception des droits de l'homme, on risquerait de faire modifier ou de remettre en cause les objectifs de la politique de coopération et de développement de la Convention de Lomé;

---

6   La proposition de la Commission européenne y relative était libellée comme suit: " ... l'insertion dans le préambule d'une référence précise et explicite à l'obligation pour les signataires de respecter les droits de l'homme les plus fondamentaux ... ; "-la Communauté [européenne] annoncerait d'autre part son intention de préciser, dans une déclaration unilatérale formelle annexée aux accords, qu'elle se réserve le droit d'exprimer publiquement sa condamnation des violations d'un principe ou objectif défini au préambule;
"-dans ce cas, la Communauté ne se proposerait pas d'intervenir dans la relation contractuelle (sauf recours à la clause de dénonciation de l'accord), mais adopterait, dans le respect de la Convention, des modalités particulières" permettant "d'assurer que l'aide soit orientée exclusivement vers des projets ou autres actions répondant à des besoins fondamentaux de la population." Alston, Philip, *op. cit.*, pp. 139-151.
7   *Bulletin des Communautés européennes*, 1977, N° 6, p. 85. Ces instruments juridiques sont la Charte des Nations Unies, les résolutions adoptées au sein des Nations Unies et les résolutions de Monrovia de juillet 1979 et de Lusaka d'août 1979.
8   *Europe*, Agence internationale d'information pour la presse, 7 octobre 1983, N° 37.04, nouvelle série, p. 7bis.
9   *Europe*, du 20 janvier 1984, p. 5.
10 *Europe*, du 24 septembre 1983, p. 8.

(d) Les pays ACP craignaient que, par l'insertion de la clause des droits de l'homme dans la Convention de Lomé, les Etats CEE puissent chercher à imposer leur conception de développement et profitent d'un manquement réel ou supposé aux droits de l'homme pour pénaliser tel ou tel pays en supprimant ou en réduisant l'aide.[11] Cette crainte trouve son origine dans les propos d'Edgard Pisani, membre de la Commission européenne, relatifs à la volonté de la CEE d'instituer un "dialogue sur les politiques" dont le but serait d'

"améliorer l'articulation de la politique nationale et régionale avec les aides sur lesquelles cette politique prend appui car le temps est venu d'un accord sur les objectifs de la coopération ACP-CEE"[12]

et une réduction sensible de l'assistance financière[13] octroyée à la Guinée équatoriale, à l'Ouganda et à la République Centrafricaine, pays considérés comme auteurs de graves violations des droits de l'homme;

(e) La situation de sous-développement a aussi été invoquée comme étant un état d'exception dans lequel le respect des droits de l'homme ne peut être totalement garanti. Pour les pays ACP, leurs situations économiques justifieraient l'impossibilité de respecter les droits de l'homme. En d'autres termes, les pays ACP voulaient que la Convention de Lomé les aide à ce que les textes internationaux des droits de l'homme auxquels ils sont parties soient effectifs et non

"une assertion pleine de bonnes intentions qui n'a aucun lien avec la réalité"[14];

(f) La Convention de Lomé, par sa nature économique, n'était considérée par les pays ACP comme étant appropriée pour mieux traiter les droits de l'homme.

---

[11] Buirette-Maurau, P., "Les difficultés d'internationalisation des droits de l'homme, à propos de la Convention de Lomé", *Revue trimestrielle de droit européen*, N° 17, novembre 1985, p. 478.
[12] *Ibid.*, p. 6.
[13] Smits, R.J.H., *The Second Lome Convention, An Assessment with Special Reference to Human Rights*, Legal Issues of European Integration, 1980-II, p. 51.
[14] Eze, Osita C., "Les droits de l'homme et le sous-développement", *Revue des droits de l'homme*, N° 1, 1979, p. 11.

Ces oppositions des pays ACP amenèrent les Etats de la CEE à alléger leurs exigences en ce qui concerne notamment le mécanisme de suspension de l'aide liée à une violation des droits de l'homme.[15] Les droits de l'homme figurèrent ainsi dans la Convention de Lomé, d'abord seulement dans le préambule (Lomé II),[16] puis dans le préambule et dans le corps du texte (articles 4 de Lomé III[17]; 5 de Lomé IV[18] et de Lomé IV-bis[19]).

Si l'on considère que chaque pays, chaque région, chaque continent reconnaît et se déclare défenseur des droits de l'homme, rien ne s'opposerait à ce qu'un Accord de coopération au développement, à l'instar de la Convention de Lomé, entre Etats développés (CEE, devenue l'Union européenne) et pays en développement (ACP), mette en avant-plan la promotion des droits de l'homme. En effet, ces droits constituent le dénominateur commun des politiques respectives des Parties Contractantes et la Convention de Lomé ne ferait que reprendre ce qui est censé être déjà une pratique acquise pour elles. A titre d'exemple, tous les droits de l'homme énumérés à l'article

---

[15] Déclaration de D. Frisch, président du groupe de négociation de la CEE cours de la session plénière entre la CEE et les ACP tenue à Bruxelles le 5 décembre 1983.

[16] Dans ce préambule de Lomé II, les parties réaffirment "leur attachement aux principes" de la Charte des Nations Unies et "leur foi dans les droits fondamentaux de l'homme, dans la dignité et la valeur de la personne humaine, dans l'égalité des droits des hommes et des femmes, ainsi que des nations grandes et petites."

[17] L'article 4 de la Convention de Lomé III stipule que la dignité humaine "est un droit imprescriptible et constitue un objet essentiel à la réalisation des aspirations légitimes des individus et des peuples" et que "la coopération ACP-CEE doit contribuer à l'élimination des obstacles qui empêchent la jouissance pleine et effective par les individus et les peuples de leurs droits économiques, sociaux et culturels." Une déclaration commune précisant la portée de cet article 4 constituait l'annexe I.

[18] Cet article 5 énumère les droits fondamentaux. Il est complété par des déclarations communes relatives à l'éradication de l'apartheid (Annexe IV), aux travailleurs migrants et étudiants ACP dans la Communauté (Annexe V) et aux travailleurs ressortissants de l'une des parties contractantes se rendant légalement sur le territoire d'un Etat membre ou d'un Etat ACP (Annexe VI).

[19] Le préambule, après avoir reconnu le respect des droits de l'homme comme un facteur fondamental du développement, réfère aux instruments internationaux de protection des droits de l'homme et invite les parties à respecter et à garantir les droits civils et politiques et à oeuvrer pour la pleine jouissance des droits économiques, sociaux et culturels. L'article 5 qui stipulait que "la coopération vise un développement centré sur l'homme" fut complété pour inclure la reconnaissance et l'application des principes démocratiques, la consolidation de l'Etat de droit et la bonne gestion des affaires publiques. Un montant de 80 millions d'ECU a été spécialement réservé pour appuyer ces mesures [application des principes démocratiques, consolidation de l'Etat de droit et bonne gestion des affaires publiques]. Le libellé de tout cet article 5 de la Convention de Lomé IV-bis est en annexe.

5 de la Convention de Lomé IV-bis sont une partie des droits reconnus par la Charte africaine des droits de l'homme et des peuples à laquelle sont parties presque tous les pays ACP.

Cependant, l'insertion de la clause des droits de l'homme dans la Convention de Lomé suscite un certain nombre d'interrogations: Ne risque-t-elle pas de constituer un prétexte pour l'ingérence dans les affaires intérieures des pays ACP? Quel lien existe-t-il entre les droits de l'homme et le développement économique? L'aide au développement peut-elle être conditionnée au respect des droits de l'homme? Quels seraient les mécanismes de contrôle du respect des droits de l'homme et quelles seraient les conséquences de leur violation pour les signataires de la Convention de Lomé? En quoi cela contribue-t-il à la transformation du droit international classique?

C'est autour de ces questions que sera centrée notre étude. Leur analyse nous permettra de montrer les conséquences éventuelles dues à l'insertion de la clause relative aux droits de l'homme dans la Convention de Lomé.

Notre étude sera subdivisée en deux sections: la première sera consacrée à l'analyse des arguments avancés par les pays ACP et la deuxième au problème de mise en oeuvre de ladite clause des droits de l'homme.

I. Analyse des arguments avancés par les pays ACP pour s'opposer à l'insertion de la clause des droits de l'homme dans la Convention de Lomé.

D'une manière générale, ces arguments peuvent être groupés en deux points suivants: la clause des droits de l'homme dans la Convention de Lomé et la souveraineté étatique des pays ACP (1), les droits de l'homme dans la Convention de Lomé et le sous-développement (2).

1. *La clause des droits de l'homme dans la Convention de Lomé et la souveraineté étatique des pays ACP.*

Les pays ACP s'opposaient à l'insertion de la clause des droits de l'homme dans la Convention de Lomé notamment à cause de la priorité qu'ils ont toujours accordée à la souveraineté nationale par rapport aux droits de l'homme. En effet, dès sa fondation en 1963, l'Organisation de l'Unité Africaine (O.U.A.)[20], tout en privilégiant le droit des peuples à l'au-

---

[20] L'absence d'information sur les composantes Caraïbes et Pacifique oblige à ne se référer qu'aux pays membres de l'O.U.A. surtout qu'ils constituent la majorité des Etats ACP: des 69 pays ACP, 46 sont membres de l'OUA, *Le Courrier*, N° 120, mars-avril 1990, p. 27.

todétermination et à la lutte contre le colonialisme, a été très laconique sur la question des droits de l'homme.[21] L'O.U.A. a une

> "conception dualiste et hiérarchisée qui crée des obligations juridiques en ce qui concerne le droit des peuples à disposer d'eux-mêmes et la non-discrimination raciale, mais qui, après la consécration des autres droits, la subordonne à la seule volonté des Etats membres."[22]

Bien plus, le contrôle régional des violations des droits de l'homme mis en place par la Charte africaine des droits de l'homme et des peuples de 1981 est fragile et maintient la prérogative des Etats. Si la Commission africaine des droits de l'homme et des peuples instituée par cette Charte dispose d'assez larges prérogatives dans la mesure où elle peut être saisie notamment par les individus et les organisations non gouvernementales, elle reste cependant très limitée dans son champ d'action, ses propositions pouvant ne pas être prises en considération par la Conférence des Chefs d'Etat et de Gouvernement. En effet, l'article 59 de la Charte africaine des droits de l'homme et des peuples dispose que

> "toutes les mesures prises dans le cadre du présent chapitre resteront confidentielles jusqu'au moment où la Conférence des Chefs d'Etat et de Gouvernement en décidera autrement."

Or, ce qui importe pour les Chefs d'Etat et de Gouvernement africains, c'est la stabilité politique même si les droits de l'homme et les libertés politiques doivent être violés.[23]

Cette mise en place des textes juridiques (la Charte de l'OUA et la Charte africaine des droits de l'homme et des peuples) qui privilégient la souveraineté aux droits de l'homme serait due aux conditions matérielles difficiles et

---

21 N'Gom, B.S., *Charte africaine des droits de l'homme et des peuples. Présentation générale*, Droits de l'homme. Droits des peuples, P.U.F., Paris, 1982, p. 205.
22 Ndiaye, B., "La place des droits de l'homme dans la Charte de l'Organisation de l'Unité africaine", *Les dimensions internationales des droits de l'homme*, sous la direction de Karel Vasak, UNESCO, Paris, 1978, p. 665.
23 Keba Mbaye, "Les droits de l'homme en Afrique", *Les dimensions internationales des droits de l'homme*, sous la direction de K. Vasak, UNESCO, Paris, 1978, p. 662.

"à la fragilité des Etats africains, dont le caractère artificiel doit être camouflé par l'affirmation permanente qu'ils existent et qu'ils disposent de l'exclusivité de la compétence sur leur population et sur leur territoire."[24]

Sur la base des considérations qui précèdent, les pays ACP ne trouvent pas que la "coopération" avec l'Union européenne soit pour elle une occasion de s'ingérer dans leurs affaires intérieures. A ce titre, ils opposent les articles 2, alinéa 7, de la Charte des Nations Unies; et l'article 17 de la Charte des droits et devoirs économiques des Etats[25] et considèrent que le respect mutuel de la souveraineté de chaque partenaire est l'un des principes fondamentaux sur lesquels se fonde la coopération avec l'Union européenne. En outre, ils s'appuient sur les articles 2 et 3 de la Convention de Lomé qui précisent respectivement que

"le droit de chaque Etat à déterminer ses choix politiques, sociaux, culturels et économiques"

et que les Etats ACP

"déterminent souverainement les principes, stratégies et modèles de développement, de leurs économies et de leurs sociétés."

Cependant, dans la mesure où il existe un droit d'intervention ouvert à tout Etat ou à toute Organisation internationale, l'insertion de la clause des droits de l'homme dans la Convention de Lomé ne serait pas considérée comme une ingérence dans les affaires intérieures des pays ACP. Cela résul-

---

[24] Borella, F., "Le système juridique de l'O.U.A.", *Annuaire Français de Droit International*, vol. XVII, 1971, p. 236.

[25] L'article 2, alinéa 7 de la Charte des Nations Unies stipule: "Aucune disposition de la présente Charte n'autorise les Nations Unies à intervenir dans les affaires qui relèvent essentiellement de la compétence nationale d'un Etat ni n'oblige les Membres à soumettre des affaires de ce genre à une procédure de règlement aux termes de la présente Charte; toutefois, ce principe ne porte en rien atteinte à l'application des mesures de coercition prévues au chapitre VII." Quant à lui, l'article 17 de la Charte des droits et devoirs économiques des Etats prévoit que le devoir de chaque Etat est de coopérer aux efforts des pays en développement pour accélérer leur progrès économique et social en leur assurant des conditions extérieures favorables et en leur apportant une aide active conforme à leurs besoins et à leurs objectifs en matière de développement dans le respect rigoureux de l'égalité souveraine des Etats et sans conditions qui portent atteinte à leur souveraineté.

te notamment des dispositions de la Charte des Nations Unies, de la Déclaration universelle des droits de l'homme, des Pactes internationaux relatifs aux droits civils et politiques; aux droits économiques, sociaux et culturels et de la Convention européenne des droits de l'homme. De plus, la Cour internationale de Justice a affirmé l'existence d'obligations internationales *erga omnes* à propos des droits fondamentaux de la personne humaine. Dans l'affaire de la *Barcelona Traction Light and Power Company* du 15 février 1970, la Cour déclara:

> "Une distinction essentielle doit en particulier être établie entre les obligations des Etats envers la communauté internationale dans son ensemble et celles qui naissent vis-à-vis d'un autre Etat dans le cadre de la protection diplomatique. Par leur nature même, les premières concernent tous les Etats. Vu l'importance des droits en cause, tous les Etats peuvent être considérés comme ayant un intérêt juridique à ce que ces droits soient protégés; les obligations dont il s'agit sont des obligations *erga omnes*.
> 34. Ces obligations découlent par exemple, dans le droit international contemporain, de la mise hors la loi des actes d'agression et du génocide mais aussi des principes et des règles concernant les droits fondamentaux de la personne humaine, y compris la protection contre la pratique de l'esclavage et la discrimination raciale. Certains droits de protection se sont intégrés au droit international général [...]; d'autres sont conférés par des instruments internationaux de caractère universel ou quasi-universel."[26]

Ce devoir créé par les droits fondamentaux à la charge de chaque Etat envers la communauté internationale tout entière, c'est-à-dire tous les autres Etats est même affirmé dans la doctrine et dans la pratique internationale. Selon une opinion,

> "une nouvelle norme du droit international est née selon laquelle la protection de l'individu, sorte de patrimoine commun de l'humanité, au même titre que

---

26 *C.I.J., Recueil 1970*, p. 4. Dans le même sens, voir les affaires du *Sud-Ouest africain*, des *Otages américains en Iran* et des *Activités militaires et paramilitaires au Nicaragua et contre celui-ci*.

l'environnement, ne dépend plus de la seule autorité de l'Etat dont il est ressortissant mais mobilise la communauté internationale tout entière."[27]

Pour ce qui est de la pratique internationale, il convient de noter que depuis 1950, l'Assemblée générale et le Conseil de Sécurité des Nations Unies ont, à plusieurs reprises, fait comprendre par leur attitude que la façon dont un Etat traite ses ressortissants ne serait plus jamais une question du seul ressort interne.[28]

L'intervention d'un Etat tiers est alors possible en cas de violation des droits de l'homme, pourvu qu'il s'agisse de "violations graves (grossières)" et "systématiques" et

"de celles portant atteinte aux droits auxquels il ne peut être dérogé en aucune circonstance."[29]

---

[27] Bettati, Mario, "Un droit d'ingérence?", *Revue générale de droit international public* 1991, p. 641. Dans le même sens, voir notamment DUPUY, Pierre-Marie, "Observations sur la pratique récente des "sanctions" de l'illicéité", *R.G.D.I.P.*, tome 87, 1983/3, p. 538; Lauterpacht, Hersch, "The International Protection of Human Rights", *Recueil des Cours de l'Académie de Droit International (R.C.A.D.I.)*, vol. 70, p. 18; Spinedi, Giuseppe, "Les conséquences juridiques d'un fait internationalement illicite causant un dommage à l'environnement", *International Responsability for Environmental Harm*, Francioni-Scouazzi, éd., Londres-Dordrecht-Boston, 1991, pp. 88-89; Tran-Van-Minh, "Les sanctions juridiques et politiques des violations des droits de l'homme", *Droits de l'homme. Droits des peuples*, P.U.F., Paris, 1982, p. 123 et plus particulièrement le rapport spécial de la Commission du Droit international, Gaetano, Arangio-Ruiz, qui , dans son *4ème Rapport Spécial A/CN.4/444/Add.2 sur la responsabilité des Etats*, 4 mai-24 juillet 1992, p. 26 a fait valoir qu'il est généralement reconnu que les règles de ce type [*erga omnes* visant la protection des droits de l'homme] créent, entre les Etats auxquels elles s'adressent, un rapport juridique caractérisé par l'obligation dont chaque Etat est tenu de veiller à assurer la jouissance des droits de l'homme à toute personne quelle que soit sa nationalité."
[28] Dormenval, Agnès, *Procédures onusiennes de mise en oeuvre des droits de l'homme: limites ou défauts?*, I.U.H.E.I., P.U.F., 1991, p. 91.
[29] Résolution 1503-XVIII du Conseil économique et social des Nations Unies du 27 mai 1970 et article 2, alinéa 3 *in fine* de la résolution de l'Institut de droit international adoptée à Saint-Jacques-de-Compostelle en 1989 dans sa partie relative à "la protection des droits de l'homme et le principe de non-intervention dans les affaires intérieures des Etats" disposant que: "Des mesures propres à assurer la protection collective des droits de l'homme sont tout spécialement justifiées lorsqu'elles répondent à des violations particulièrement graves de ces droits, notamment des violations massives ou systématiques, ainsi qu'à celles portant atteinte aux droits auxquels il ne peut être dérogé en aucune circonstance."

Les violations graves sont celles de droits essentiels de la personne: droit à la vie et à l'intégrité corporelle, interdiction de l'esclavage (articles 3 à 5 de la Déclaration universelle de 1948).[30] Le caractère systématique désigne, quant à lui, des violations commises sur une grande échelle et présentant une certaine fréquence ou constance dans le temps.[31]

Même donc en l'absence de la clause des droits de l'homme dans la Convention de Lomé, les Etats de l'Union européenne peuvent intervenir du moment qu'un pays ACP est considéré comme auteur de violations "graves (grossières)" et "systématiques" des droits de l'homme. Dans sa résolution suscitée, l'Institut de droit international, a adopté, à l'alinéa 2 de l'article 2, la position suivante:

> "Sans préjudice des fonctions et pouvoirs que la Charte attribue aux organes des Nations Unies en cas de violation des obligations assumées par les membres de l'Organisation, les Etats, agissant individuellement ou collectivement, sont en droit d'adopter, à l'égard de tout autre Etat ayant enfreint l'obligation énoncée à l'article premier (l'obligation pour les Etats d'assurer le respect des droits de l'homme), des mesures diplomatiques, économiques et autres, admises par le droit international et ne comportant pas l'emploi de la force armée en violation de la Charte des Nations Unies. Ces mesures ne peuvent pas être considérées comme une intervention illicite dans les affaires intérieures de l'Etat."

Ce qui précède conduit ainsi au mal-fondé de l'argument des pays ACP consistant à considérer l'insertion de la clause des droits de l'homme dans la Convention de Lomé comme une ingérence dans leurs affaires intérieures.

2. *Les droits de l'homme dans la Convention de Lomé et le sous-développement des pays ACP.*

Selon les pays ACP, leur sous-développement serait un obstacle à l'application effective et immédiate des droits de l'homme.

La notion d'exception de sous-développement dans l'application des droits de l'homme figure pour la première fois dans le Pacte international relatif aux droits économiques, sociaux et culturels, à propos des étrangers. L'alinéa 3 de l'article 2 dudit Pacte dispose:

---

30 Buirette-Murau, P., *op. cit.*, p. 474.
31 Tran-Van-Minh, *op. cit.*, p. 125.

> "Les pays en voie de développement, compte dûment tenu des droits de l'homme et de leur économie nationale, peuvent déterminer dans quelle mesure ils garantiront les droits économiques reconnus dans le présent Pacte à des non-ressortissants."

Cette idée a été élargie à d'autres situations que celles des étrangers. La Conférence internationale des droits de l'homme réunie à Téhéran du 22 avril au 13 mai 1968 proclama:

> "L'écart croissant qui sépare les pays économiquement développés des pays en voie de développement fait obstacle au respect effectif des droits de l'homme dans la communauté internationale ... Les progrès durables dans la voie de l'application des droits de l'homme supposent une politique nationale et internationale rationnelle et efficace de développement économique et social."[32]

En d'autres termes, un développement économique suffisant est nécessaire pour procurer des moyens indispensables à la protection des droits de l'homme.[33]

Si l'on se limitait donc aux droits économiques, sociaux et culturels, le point de vue des pays ACP serait tout à fait justifié. Ceci ne serait cependant pas vrai si c'étaient les droits civils et politiques qui étaient en jeu. Etant de caractère absolu, les droits civils et politiques sont à respecter quel que soit le niveau de développement. Leur respect exige une abstention et non des moyens financiers. L'auteur de cet article considère comme atroce, l'affirmation selon laquelle le sous-développement est un obstacle à l'application des droits de l'homme civils et politiques. En effet, il serait ignoble de torturer les etres humains pour promouvoir le développement.

---

[32] De même, dans sa résolution 1867 (LVI), le Conseil économique et social des Nations Unies "s'affirme convaincu qu'il n'est possible d'assurer rapidement la jouissance des droits économiques, sociaux et culturels que si tous les pays et peuples sont en mesure de parvenir à un niveau adéquat de croissance économique et de développement social et si tous les pays prennent toutes les mesures nécessaires pour éliminer les inégalités dans la répartition des revenus et dans les services sociaux conformément à la Stratégie internationale du développement pour la IIème Décennie des Nations Unies pour le développement."

[33] Osita, Eze, *op. cit.*, p. 11. L'auteur donne l'exemple selon lequel l'égalité devant la loi ne peut être assurée dans les sociétés où le barreau n'est pas placé sous le contrôle de l'Etat car les riches peuvent s'offrir les meilleurs avocats dont les plaidoiries influencent beaucoup l'issue du procès et alors que l'homme pauvre, même pouvant bénéfier d'une certaine assistance juridique, n'aura pas les mêmes chances que son adversaire riche.

Même pour les droits économiques, sociaux et culturels, l'exception de sous-développement ne devrait jouer que temporairement. Au fur et à mesure que les conditions de la vie économique et sociale s'améliorent, ces droits économiques, sociaux et culturels, qui ne pouvaient pas être respectés pour des causes matérielles ou à cause des nécessités de la construction nationale, devraient l'être. Fort malheureusement, ce caractère temporaire est prolongé *sine die* pour devenir durable, sinon éternel. A cet égard, cette assertion de Kéba Mbaye est pleine d'enseignements:

> "Tous ces Etats, en voie de développement, menacés à chaque instant par le désordre et les difficultés économiques, se considèrent comme étant en permanence dans des circonstances exceptionnelles."

Des considérations qui précèdent, il ressort donc que rien ne pouvait justifier l'opposition à l'insertion d'une clause relative aux droits de l'homme dans la Convention de Lomé. Cependant, la Convention de Lomé étant un Accord de coopération au développement, il se pose un problème de mise en oeuvre de cette clause relative aux droits de l'homme.

II. Le problème de la mise en oeuvre de la clause des droits de l'homme dans la Convention de Lomé.

La lecture de toute la Convention de Lomé atteste que rien n'a été prévu pour la mise en oeuvre de cette clause des droits de l'homme[34]: l'aide communautaire aux pays ACP n'a pas été conditionnée au respect, par ces derniers, des droits de l'homme, les Etats de la CEE ne s'y étant pas mises d'accord.[35]

En effet, deux opinions s'affrontaient: celle des Néerlandais et des Britanniques d'une part, et celle de la Belgique, de la France et de la République Fédérale d'Allemagne d'autre part. Les Néerlandais et les Britanniques étaient pour un lien entre l'assistance communautaire et le respect des droits de l'homme par les pays ACP. Les Néerlandais suggéraient de formuler ce lien dans le texte de la Convention de Lomé et de fixer une procédure visant la suspension de l'aide, la décision de suspension devant être arrêtée par l'organe commun, à savoir le Conseil des ministres ACP-CEE.

---

34 Seuls existent les mécanismes de consultation entre les parties en cas de violations des droits de l'homme, des principes démocratiques et de l'Etat de droit (article 366 bis de la Convention de Lomé IV-bis).

35 Garick, Laura et Twitchett, Carol Cosgrovie, "Human Rights and a Successor to the Lomé Convention", *The Journal of the David Davies Memorial Institute of International Studies*, vol. VI, No 3, May 1979, pp. 547 et ss.

Les Britanniques étaient hostiles à cette inclusion des clauses dans le texte de la Convention de Lomé et préféraient, au contraire, la dénonciation partielle de la Convention de Lomé à l'encontre des pays ACP coupables de violations des droits de l'homme.

De leur part, la Belgique, la France et la République Fédérale d'Allemagne estimaient qu'une éventuelle introduction d'une procédure de suspension pour cause des droits de l'homme pouvait entraîner de sérieuses difficultés dans l'établissement des critères de suspension.

Cette dernière opinion reflétant la position de la majorité, elle remporta. Aucune conséquence ne fut alors attachée à la violation de cette clause des droits de l'homme figurant dans la Convention de Lomé. Il fut seulement adopté un texte non publié dans lequel les pays de l'Union européenne ont déclaré être prêts à sanctionner tout pays ACP considéré comme auteur de graves violations des droits de l'homme.

Nonobstant cette lacune juridique, l'Union européenne suit une pratique qui associe la condamnation, le maintien du lien contractuel et le contrôle de la mise en oeuvre en cas de violations des droits de l'homme commises par les pays ACP. Elle se garde de sanctionner les populations intéressées par des actions-telle une suspension de l'aide-qui étaient censées viser les autorités en place et d'encourager l'oppression par le maintien de l'assistance aux pays ACP qui se rendraient auteurs de violations des droits de l'homme. Elle sanctionne les autorités en place par la suspension de son aide. Ainsi par exemple, l'aide programmable destinée à la Guinée Equatoriale dans le cadre du quatrième Fonds Européen de Développement (FED) ne fut débloquée qu'une fois le régime du Général Macias NGUEMA tombé. De même, certains projets visant l'Ouganda furent approuvés seulement une fois que des garanties eurent été prises sur l'utilisation de l'aide. En outre, à l'encontre de ce dernier pays, la CEE déclara:

> "Le Conseil (de la CEE) déplore que le peuple de l'Ouganda se voie systématiquement privé de ses droits fondamentaux. Le Conseil est convenu de prendre des mesures dans le cadre de ses relations avec l'Ouganda, afin de s'assurer que toute assistance prêtée par la Communauté à l'Ouganda en vertu de la Convention de Lomé, n'ait en aucun cas pour effet, à l'égard du peuple de ce pays, un renforcement ou une prolongation de la privation des droits fondamentaux."[36]

---

[36] *Bulletin de la CE*, 1977, N° 6, p. 85. Cette déclaration peut être trouvée également chez Smits, R.J.H., "The Second Lomé Convention, An Assessment with Special Reference to Human Rights", *Legal Issues of European Integration*, 1980-II, p. 51.

Ce qui eut pour résultat la réduction de l'aide financière.[37]

Cette pratique de l'Union européenne est toute à fait conforme à la résolution de l'Institut de droit international adoptée à Saint-Jacques-de-Compostelle en 1989 et relative à "La protection des droits de l'homme et le principe de non-intervention dans les affaires intérieures des Etats." En effet, à l'article 2, alinéa 2 de ladite résolution, il est dit que le Etats, soit individuellement, soit collectivement, ont le droit de prendre des mesures ... économiques et autres, admises par le droit international à l'encontre de tout autre Etat coupable de violations "massives" et "systématiques" des droits de l'homme. L'autre justification de cette pratique serait la finalité même de la Convention de Lomé. En effet, cette dernière n'est pas un simple accord commercial mais a pour but d'assurer un développement économique, culturel et social des pays ACP; lequel développement ne peut avoir de sens que s'il y a respect des droits de l'homme. Les violations "massives" et "systématiques" des droits de l'homme par un pays ACP ne doivent dès lors pas laisser l'Union européenne indifférente, elle pourrait geler toutes les actions de coopération à l'exception de celles qui intéressent directement les populations; telles les actions d'aides humanitaires.[38] Ce serait là "l'amorce d'une utilisation plus positive du droit dans les relations internationales."[39]

Cependant, cette pratique de l'Union européenne pourrait compromettre la Convention de Lomé si l'aide était assortie de conditions de caractère politique. Dans ce cas, certains membres de l'Union européenne pourraient privilégier certains pays ACP au détriment d'autres. Même l'Union européenne n'est pas à l'abri d'un danger de partialité dans la sélection des cas auxquels ellese déciderait à réagir. Par exemple, l'aide a été refusée à l'Ouganda d'Idi-Amin Dada mais octroyée au Zaïre de Mobutu Sese-Seko bien que les deux pays ACP étaient accusés de violer les droits de l'homme. Ce traitement différent résulterait de l'importance des richesses que cache le sol zaïrois pour les pays occidentaux et notamment de l'Union européenne.[40] Il y aurait également lieu de craindre que les pays membres de l'Union européenne diminuent leurs contributions prévues au titre de la Convention de

---

[37] Seuls l'aide accordée dans le cadre du Stabex (système de stabilisation des recettes d'exportation des matières premières) et des crédits en vue de la formation des cadres furent maintenus. *Le Courrier*, N° 56, juillet-août 1979 et N° 78, mars-avril 1983, p. 23.
[38] *Bulletin Agence Europe* des 18 et 19 juillet 1983.
[39] Kranz, J., "Lomé, le dialogue et l'homme", *Revue trimestrielle de droit européen*, vol. 24 (3), juillet-septembre 1988, p. 478.
[40] Nuscheler, F., "Der Europäische Entwicklungsfonds", *Ferdowsi*, N° 41, p. 72 cité par Kranz, J., *op. cit.*, p. 472.

Lomé au profit d'autres Etats du tiers monde. L'exemple serait celui de la Grande-Bretagne qui entend favoriser les actions entreprises par l'Association Internationale de Développement (AID) qui intervient, de manière importante, dans les grands pays du Commonwealth (Inde, Pakistan, Bangladesh) qui ne sont pas des pays ACP. Enfin, si les Etats de l'Union européenne étaient touchés par une crise économique, ils seraient tentés d'utiliser les droits de l'homme pour limiter l'aide au développement à accorder aux pays ACP quand bien même ces derniers ne se seraient pas rendus coupables de violations des droits de l'homme.

La suspension de l'aide en défaveur d'un pays ACP considéré comme auteur de violations des droits de l'homme connaissant des limites, les Etats de l'Union européenne pourraient-ils envisager une intervention armée? Certes, l'histoire diplomatique connaît des cas d'intervention armée destinée à protéger des nationaux de l'Etat territorial lui-même. A titre d'exemples, il y a lieu de citer l'intervention des Etats arabes en Palestine en 1948, celle de l'Inde au Bangladesh en 1971, celle du Viet-Nam au Cambodge en 1978 et celle de la Tanzanie en Ouganda en 1979.[41] Cependant, de nos jours, l'utilisation de la force n'est admise qu'en cas de légitime défense, cette dernière étant réservée aux Etats dont la sécurité est mise en cause par l'agression. Or, en cas de violation des droits de l'homme par un pays ACP, aucun Etat de l'Union européenne n'est agressé. En conséquence, l'intervention armée en cas de violations des droits de l'homme par un pays ACP est à exclure.

Par contre, il existe des éléments en faveur de l'application du principe contractuel d'exception d'inexécution (*exceptio non adimpleti contractus*). En effet, à l'article 5 de la Convention de Lomé IV-bis qui contient ladite clause relative aux droits de l'homme, il est dit notamment que

"... la politique de développement et la coopération au développement sont étroitement liées au respect des droits de l'homme et libertés fondamentales de l'homme."

De plus, Manuel Marin, Vice-président de la Commission européenne avait proposé que la CEE prenne des mesures négatives en cas de violations extrêmes des droits de l'homme.[42] Enfin, dans la résolution du Conseil de

---

41 Sicilianos, A.L., *Les réactions décentralisées à l'illicite: des contre-mesures à légitime défense*, Paris, 1990, pp. 166 et ss.
42 *Le Courrier ACP*, N° 128, juillet-août 1991, p. 51.

l'Union européenne du 28 novembre 1991[43], il est établi un lien entre l'aide communautaire aux pays en voie de développement, dont les pays ACP, et leurs initiatives en faveur de la démocratie et des droits de l'homme. Le recours à ce principe justifierait d'ailleurs la pratique susmentionnée et qu'a prise la CEE à l'encontre de la Guinée Equatoriale et de l'Ouganda.

Toutefois, dans l'application de ce principe, l'Union européenne devrait être animée d'un humanitarisme et laisser continuer les aides humanitaire et d'urgence destinées à améliorer directement le sort de la population de l'Etat responsable des violations des droits de l'homme[44] et ce, à l'instar de ce qu'elle a déclaré à l'encontre du Nigéria dont le régime en place avait exécuté l'écrivain Ken Saro Wiwa et ses huit partisans ogonis:

> "La commission prend des mesures nécessaires en vue de la suspension de la coopération au développement avec le Nigéria ... Elle poursuivra cependant des actions à caractère humanitaire et celles mises en oeuvre par l'intermédiaire d'ONG visant à faire face aux besoins des couches les plus défavorisées de la population. La Commission estime qu'il ne faut pas exclure que l'Union prenne d'autres mesures plus sévères si le gouvernement nigérian ne fait preuve, dans les semaines et mois à venir, de volonté politique de s'engager sur la voie du respect des droits de l'homme et du retour de la démocratie."[45]

CONCLUSION:

Contrairement aux arguments avancés par les pays ACP, rien ne s'oppose à ce que la Convention de Lomé, bien que de nature économique, contienne une clause relative aux droits de l'homme. En effet, l'argument de souveraineté ne saurait faire oublier l'obligation qu'a tout Etat de respecter les droits de l'homme et l'obligation d'intervention, en cas de violations "systématiques" et "grossières" des droits de l'homme. Le sous-développement ne saurait non plus justifier l'inobservation des droits civils et politiques, droits de caractère absolu et qui doivent être respectés quel que soit le niveau de développement économique du pays ACP. Il ne serait invoqué que pour la non réalisation temporaire et non éternelle des droits économiques, sociaux

---

43   Résolution du Conseil et des Etats membres réunis au sein du Conseil sur les droits de l'homme, la démocratie et le développement du 28 novembre 1991, in *Bulletin CE 11/1991 P. 130*, 132.2.3.1.

44   Cassese, Antonio, *Il diritto internazionale nel mondo contemporaneo*, Bologne, 1984, p. 271.

45   Commission européenne, Ref: BIO/95/429, Nigéria PP.1-2.

et culturels. L'insertion des droits de l'homme dans la Convention de Lomé doit être considérée comme une participation aux progrès qu'a connus ces dernières années la défense internationale des droits de l'homme[46] et, en même temps, une heureuse occasion de faire progresser l'Etat de droit dans les relations internationales.

Cependant, la Convention de Lomé n'a pas prévu des voies et moyens de contrôle et de sanction en cas de violation de la clause relative aux droits de l'homme. Ce serait erroné d'admettre que des violations "grossières" et "systématiques" des droits considérés comme fondamentaux soient sans effet pour la mise en oeuvre des objectifs de la Convention de Lomé dont le but est de faciliter le développement économique, social et culturel des pays ACP. L'attitude de la CEE à l'encontre de la Guinée Equatoriale et de l'Ouganda et celle de l'Union européenne à l'encontre du Nigéria sont pleines d'enseignements.

---

[46] Buirette-Maurau, *op. cit.*, p. 486.

THE REALISATION OF HUMAN RIGHTS IN AFRICA THROUGH SUB-REGIONAL INSTITUTIONS

Frans Viljoen*

I INTRODUCTION

Global, regional and sub-regional inter-governmental organisations play a significant role in Africa today.[1] On the global plane, all African states have become members of the United Nations (the "UN") soon after their independence.[2] In 1963, 32 independent African states formed the first inter-governmental organisation with a pan-African focus, the Organisation of African Unity (the "OAU").[3] By its 35th anniversary in 1998, the membership of the OAU had increased to 53.[4] Although the OAU Charter included economic co-operation and the achievement of a "better life for the peoples of Africa" amongst its purposes, these aspects were neglected as the OAU mainly pursued the goals of promoting African solidarity and the eradication

---

* M.A., L.L.B., L.L.D. (Pret.), L.L.M. (Cantab.); Lecturer of Law, University of Pretoria, South Africa.
1 This article is based on a chapter from Viljoen, F. J., *The realisation of human rights in Africa through inter-governmental institutions*, unpublished L.L.D. thesis, University of Pretoria, 1997. A distinction is drawn between "organisations" and "institutions". The UN, OAU and SADC are examples of "organisations", while the treaty bodies, committees, other quasi-judicial bodies and judicial structures established in terms of the founding treaties are "institutions".
2 Four independent African states became members of the UN when it was founded in 1945. They were Egypt, Ethiopia, Liberia and the Union of South Africa. After Eritrea has joined the UN on 28 May 1993, the number of African member states now stands at 53. The Saharawi Arab Democratic Republic, declared independent unilaterally on 27 February 1976, has not been admitted as a UN member.
3 The OAU Charter was adopted in Addis Ababa on 25 May 1963, see e.g. (1964) 3 International Legal Materials, p. 1116.
4 The Saharawi Arab Democratic Republic is recognised as a member of the OAU. This recognition led to the withdrawal of Morocco from the OAU in 1984.

of colonialism from Africa.[5] The newly independent constituent states parties of the OAU jealously guarded their own sovereignty. Not only the OAU's potential impact on internal political issues, but also its potential of collectively addressing economic concerns was constrained in the process. An increased awareness of the need for regional co-operation to attain inter-African economic development culminated in the creation of a number of regional organisations in African sub-regions, and in the establishment of the African Economic Community (the "AEC").

A number of sub-regional[6] inter-governmental organisations and institutions have been functioning and still function in Africa today. Those pre-dating African independence had (and still have, where they still exist) close links with colonialism (or its aftermath). The East African Community is an example of an organisation that is now defunct. Examples of defunct institutions are the Court of Appeal of East Africa, the West African Court of Appeal and the Rhodesia and Nyassaland Court of Appeal. Presently, a multiplicity of organisations, mainly concerned with economic priorities and co-operation, exist sub-regionally in Africa.[7] Those discussed here are the Economic Community of West African States ("ECOWAS"), the Southern African Development Community ("SADC"), the Common Market of Eastern and Southern Africa ("COMESA") and the Maghreb Arab Union.[8]

---

5   See art. 2(1)(b) of the OAU Charter. For an evaluation of the OAU's mandate, see e.g. Chanda, A., *The Organization of African Unity: An Appraisal* , (1989 – 1992) 21 – 24 Zambia Law Jnl, p.1.
6   Internatial Human rights protection has been established at three levels. At the global (or universal) level, various human treaties and implementation mechanisms have been created under the auspices of the UN. At the regional level, human rights instruments and institutions have been established under the auspices of the Council of Europe (in Europe), the Organisation of American States (in the Americas), and the OAU (in Africa). The third level is usually accepted as the protection granted by the domestic legal system of a particular state. The focus here does not fall on any of these levels, but investigates whether human rights may be realised through institutions at a level between the domestic and the regional, here denoted the "sub-regional" level.
7   These sub-regional organisations sometimes include coutries outside Africa, as in the case of the Indian Ocean Rim Association for Regional Cooperation (see (1997) 9 RADIC, p.785).
8   An overview that includes only these four organisations cannot claim to be comprehensive. There are numerous other sub-regional organisations in existence in Africa today, including the Economic Community of the Countries of the Great Lakes ("CEPGL"), the Southern African Customs Union ("SACU"), the Mano River Union, the Customs and Economic Union of Central Africa ("UOEAC") and the African and Mauritian Common Organisation ("OCAM"). See e.g. Elias, T.O., *Africa and the Development of International Law*, 1988, pp. 25 – 29.

The Treaty establishing the AEC was adopted by OAU member states meeting in Abuja, Nigeria, in 1991.[9] It entered into force in April 1994, when two-thirds of the OAU member states had ratified the Treaty.[10] The inaugural meeting of the AEC took place on 3 June 1997, in Harare.[11] The ultimate aim of the Treaty is to oversee the gradual establishment of an African Common Market and a Pan-African Economic and Monetary Union.[12] The first step in this process is to strengthen existing sub-regional economic communities and to found communities in sub-regions where they had not existed before.[13]

So far, the impact of the African human rights system on the sub-regional level has been insignificant. In none of these sub-regional treaties are the provisions of the African Charter on Human and Peoples' Rights ("African Charter") incorporated as binding obligations on states.[14] There is also little talk on their part of implementing human rights as part of their respective mandates, or of the possibility of accession to the African Charter by any of the sub-regional organisations in the near future. This does not mean that human rights issues are not mentioned, referred to or incorporated at all in the treaties establishing these organisations.[15] But wherever that is done, it remains very limited and without any prospect of meaningful implementation. In general, individuals may not refer cases to and do not have standing before sub-regional judicial institutions, making it impossible for them to raise human rights concerns in these fora.

This article investigates the extent to which these sub-regional arrangements have been and can in future be vehicles for the improvement of human rights on the African continent. Each of these organisations provides for an

---

[9] See text at (1991) 30 International Legal Materials, p. 1241 and (1991) 3 RADIC, p. 792.
[10] See Niyozima, N., *African Investment Codes and African Economic Integration* (1994) 6 ASICL Proc., p. 182 at p. 188 (n. 7).
[11] It was held simultaneously with the 33rd summit of the OAU Assembly of Heads of State and Government.
[12] See art. 6 of the Treaty establishing the African Economic Community.
[13] See art. 28(1) of the Treaty establishing the African Economic Community: "During the first stage, Member States undertake to strengthen the existing regional economic communities and to establish new communities where they do not exist in order to ensure the gradual establishment of the Community".
[14] The African Charter was adopted on 17 June 1981, in Nairobi, and entered into force on 21 October 1986, OAU Document CAB/LEG/67/3/Rev.5, and reprinted at e.g. (1981) 21 International Legal Materials, p. 58.
[15] It should be conceded that, as these institutions are directed at socio-economic goals, they aim indirectly at the implementation of socio-economic rights. Even so, the rights discourse, with all that follows therefrom, is not adopted.

institution in the form of a court or tribunal to resolve conflicts or to interpret the founding treaty. These judicial institutions are the centre of focus and introduce more general observations on courts in a supra-national, but sub-regional setting. First, those institutions which have ceased to operate are dealt with, followed by an exposition of those functioning at present. This focus on judicialised conflict resolution is of greater relevance in Africa today, as the establishment of two regional courts, the African Court of Justice[16] and the African Court of Human and Peoples' Rights,[17] is likely to occur in the not too distant future.

II DEFUNCT INSTITUTIONS

Africa's colonial past presents one with some early precedents of inter-territorial arrangements of a judicial nature. Examples are the Court of Appeal of East Africa, the West African Court of Appeal and the Rhodesia and Nyassaland Court of Appeal.[18] Of these, the courts in East and West Africa extended the furthest geographically and covered the longest period of time. They are discussed here.

---

[16] The African Court of Justice ("ACJ") is one of the institutions provided for in the Treaty establishing the AEC. On the potential human rights mandate of this Court, see Peter, C. M., *The Proposed African Court of Justice – Jurisprudential, Procedural, Enforcement Problems and Beyond*, (1993) 1 East African Jnl of Peace and Human Rights, p. 117.

[17] The supervisory or implementation mechanism provided for in the African Charter, the African Commission on Human and Peoples' Rights, has been criticised as weak and ineffectual. Efforts to supplement the African Commission with a judicial institution has culminated in a number of draft protocols additional to the African Charter. In September 1995 a first draft was adopted in Cape Town, followed by a second draft adopted by a meeting of governmental legal experts held from 11 to 14 April 1997 at Nouakchott (see the report of the meeting at (1997) 9 RADIC 423, and the draft protocol at (1997) 9 RADIC 432). A later version of the Charter was adopted by Ministers of Justice and Attorneys General of OAU member states on 12 December 1997 in Addis Ababa (see *Draft Protocol to the African Charter on Human and Peoples' Rights on the Establishment of an African Court on Human and Peoples' Rights*, OAU document OAU/LEG/MIN/AFCHPR/PROT.(I) Rev.2). The OAU Assembly adopted the Protocol unanimously in June 1998. (See a discussion and text of final Protocol: Kirsch, N. *"The establishment of an African Court on Human and Peoples' Rights"*, (1998) 58 Zeitschrift für ausländisches Offentliches Recht und Völkerecht 713.

[18] See, in general on these courts, Roberts-Wray, K. O. *Commonwealth and Colonial Law,* 1966, pp. 760-761, 783 and 220-221 respectively.

1 Court of Appeal of East Africa[19]

1.1 Overview of its evolution

The East African Court of Appeal was established in 1902 by the British colonial authorities in respect of those territories that would later become known as Kenya, Malawi and Uganda.[20] Unity at the judicial level was just one form of a broader process of inter-territorial political co-operation that in 1947 became concretised in the British East African High Commission.[21] The evolutionary process of establishing a supra-national court in East Africa was thus part and parcel of "the general desire of the British Colonial regime to join the three territories, a desire which was later welcomed and almost concretised by African politicians".[22] However, practical problems soon arose, prompting an investigation of institutional mechanisms.[23] The investigation revealed that an increase in the number of cases submitted to the Court had led to delays in their finalisation. This caused concern, especially as many cases involved persons convicted of murder who awaited execution. In 1946 the Court already sat for twenty weeks yearly. This took up a considerable amount of the Chief Justices' time. They were obviously primarily needed in their own countries, and their duties there were subsequently neglected. As pressure was exerted on their domestic duties, a tendency developed to deal very rapidly with cases at the East African Court of Appeal.

Since the main cause of the difficulties faced by the Court was identified as the temporary basis of judicial appointment to the Court, structural reforms in 1950 led to the appointment of three permanent Court members. All other judges of superior courts of the countries involved were eligible to

---

[19] The name of this institution differs through the decades. It was initially called the Eastern African Court of Appeal. Its last appearance was as the Court of Appeal of East Africa.

[20] Mvungi, S.E.A., *Constitutional Questions in the Regional Integration Process: The Case of the Southern African Development Community with Reference to the European Union*, D. Iur. Thesis, Institut für Internationale Angelegenheiten, Hamburg, 1994 points out that trade networks, political dynamism and social mingling had over centuries succeeded in establishing a common cultural identity and a "non-tribal common language", known as Kiswahili (p. 108).

[21] See Elias, *op. cit.*, p. 26 and Kato, L.L., *The Court of Appeal for East Africa: From a Colonial Court to an International Court,* (1971) 7 East African Law Jnl., p. 1, p. 2.

[22] *Ibid.* Zanzibar, Aden and Tanganyika were later added to this Court's jurisdiction. Nyassaland (Malawi) was excluded when the Rhodesia and Nyassaland Court of Appeal came to be established in 1947. At that stage the Court consisted of the Chief Justices and other judges of superior courts of the countries over which it had jurisdiction.

[23] For background to these problems and the solutions offered, see *Proposals for the Re-Organization of the Eastern African Court of Appeal*, 1948.

sit on the Court. A permanent seat was also established at Nairobi, Kenya. The choice of the seat was motivated with reference to Nairobi's central geographical location. However, on occasion the Court could also sit in any of the other two countries.

When reform of the Court was considered, the possibility was also raised that a separate court of appeal could be established for each of the major territories. The official investigation, reporting on possible reforms, rejected such a course of action: "If this were done, ... East Africa would be left without any high co-ordinating legal authority, and moreover these territories would be unable to fulfil commitments already entered into with other Colonial Governments".[24] The role of the Court in the broader policy of "indirect" colonial rule is apparent from the fact that the judges were appointed by the Governor of Kenya,[25] and were usually "expatriates".[26]

The East African Community was established when the Treaty for East African Cooperation was concluded between Kenya, Tanzania and Uganda in 1967, following the independence of the three countries.[27] It provided for cooperation in various fields. The Court, as the Court of Appeal of East Africa, was retained in its previous form as one of the institutions of the Community. Another judicial institution was provided for under this Treaty.[28] This Court, the Common Market Tribunal of the East African Community, had the task of ensuring observance of treaty law, such as allegations of breach of treaty obligations. Two cases had been referred to the Tribunal. Due to the fact that it was never fully constituted, these cases were never considered.[29] The Community, and with it the Court, was abolished in 1977.[30]

On paper, the future prospects for co-operation in East Africa must still be regarded as good. Factors uniting the three states (Kenya, Tanzania and

---

[24] *Proposals for the Re-Organization of the Eastern African Court of Appeal,* 1948, p. 3.
[25] See (1971) 7 East African Law Jnl., p. 11.
[26] In 1970 the permanent members of the Court were President Newbold, Vice President Duffus and Justice Spry. In the same year Mr Justice Lutta became the first East African to hold a position as permanent member of the Court.
[27] By the Treaty of East African Co-operation signed at Kampala, and which entered into force in December 1967. It took over the assets and liabilities of the East African Common Services Organisation ("EACSO"), which was established in 1962. The EACSO was established to take over from the British East Africa High Commission (see Elias, *op. cit.*, p. 26).
[28] Another "tribunal" established under the EAC was the East African Industrial Court: see art. 84 of the EAC Treaty.
[29] Schermers, H. C. and Blokker, N. M., *International Institutional Law,* 1995, p. 433. By May 1970 two cases had been referred to the Tribunal, which had at that stage not been constituted.
[30] On its demise, see Mvungi, *op. cit.*, p. 118.

Uganda), are geographic proximity, institutional links,[31] a shared history, broad knowledge of one language, Swahili, and ethnic ties across borders, for example the presence of Luos in all three states. However, it must be questioned whether there is room for such an arrangement in the light of the establishment of COMESA and SADC.[32]

1.2 Functioning of the Court

In general, the Court exercised its mandate with judicial restraint. Writing optimistically about the future of the Court in 1971, Kato expressed the opinion that it survived because it did not involve itself in political controversy.[33] One of the reasons was the limited jurisdiction of the Court as far as human rights matters were concerned.

The first of the three states to become independent, Tanzania, did not include a Bill of Rights in its Constitution.[34] Questions of the interpretation of human rights as such could therefore not arise before the East African Court of Appeal. As for the Constitution, the East African Court of Appeal was excluded from hearing any appeal concerning its interpretation.[35] However, other contentious issues, such as cases involving *habeas corpus* directions, could be heard by the Court.[36]

Uganda became independent next, in 1962. Its independence Constitution included a Bill of Rights. However, the East African Court of Appeal had no jurisdiction to entertain an appeal from Ugandan Courts dealing with Chapter III of the Constitution, which contained fundamental human rights. In terms of section 95 of the independence Constitution, issues involving a substantial question of law could be referred to the Ugandan High Court, but not to the East African Court of Appeal.[37]

---

[31] For a recent manifestation of these links, see the Establishment of the Lake Victoria Fisheries Organisation between Kenya, Tanzania and Uganda ((1997) 36 ILM, p. 667).

[32] See also Muzan, A. O., *An East African Attempt at Federalism (1960 – 1964): A Study in Historical Jurisprudence* (1994) 15 African Study Monographs, p.37, who argues that the efforts to establish a federation between the three states in the early 1960s failed because the Ugandan leader Okello was too protective of the role of the Kabaka of the Buganda.

[33] See Kato (1971) 1 East African Law Jnl., p. 30. He considered the future if the Court to be "bright".

[34] Also, before a one party state was established in 1968, the possibility was considered, but rejected: See *Report of the Presidential Commission,* 1968, pp. 30-32.

[35] S. 9 of the Appellate Jurisdiction Ordinance 55 of 1961, referred to by Kato (1971) 7 East African Law Jnl., p. 20.

[36] S. 8(3) of the Appellate Jurisdiction Ordinance 55 of 1961, referred to in (1971) 7 East African Law Jnl., p. 20

[37] See Kato (1971) 7 East African Law Jnl., p. 22.

Independence for Kenya came last of the three, in 1963. Its Constitution was clear about the limitations on the Court's role in the internal affairs of the newly independent nation. The jurisdiction of the Court was excluded as far as the interpretation of the Constitution and the enforcement of human rights provisions in the Constitution were concerned.[38]

From an analysis of the Court's annual reports[39] it is clear that it was constantly utilised.[40] From the same analysis it appears that a relatively constant number of appeals from Kenya and Tanzania were submitted to the Court annually. Another feature is that the number of Kenyan cases were always slightly more than that emanating from Tanzania. Most striking, however, is the steady decrease of cases brought from Uganda. Within seven years, the number of Ugandan cases changed from the highest to the lowest of the three states.[41]

1.3 Demise of the Court

The most important reason for the Court's demise is the lack of continued political will at the inter-governmental level. Kenyan domination appears from the facts about the functioning of the Court set out above. Kato described the term from 1951 to 1961 as the period in which the Court became "fully Kenyan".[42] This factor caused tension between Kenya and especially Tanzania. Businessmen in Kenya also pressurised the government

---

[38] See Kato (1971) 7 East African Law Jnl., p. 28.
[39] *Court of Appeal for East Africa Annual Reports*, consulted in the Nairobi University Library, Africana section. Other data in this discussion is also based on this analysis.
[40] The total number of appeals for some years are given as examples: 1961: 297 appeals; 1962: 300 appeals; 1963: 278 appeals; 1970: 289 appeals; 1971: 254 appeals; 1972: 231 appeals; 1973: 220 appeals; 1974: 195 appeals; 1975: 248 appeals; 1976: 199 appeals. In general, a slight decreasing trend, as well as a significant drop in numbers from 1975 to 1976, may be identified. The appeals originating in the three national legal systems from 1970 to 1973, and in 1976 are as follows: 1970: Kenya (76), Uganda (146), Tanzania (67); 1971: Kenya (81), Uganda (97), Tanzania (76); 1972: Kenya (76), Uganda (88), Tanzania (67); 1973: Kenya (90), Uganda (53), Tanzania (77); 1976: Kenya (95), Uganda (30), Tanzania (74).
[41] The majority of cases heard by the Court were criminal cases. In 1962, for example, 201 of the 300 cases were criminal appeals. Of the criminal appeals before the Court in 1971, it dismissed 148, and allowed 39. This trend continued: In 1973, 107 criminal appeals were dismissed, and 46 allowed; in 1976, 100 criminal appeals were dismissed, and 55 allowed. The majority of criminal appeals involved murder convictions. In 1973, for instance, 91 murder cases were heard, and in 1976, 73. In general, the Court interfered more frequently in civil cases. Of the civil appeals heard in 1971, 32 were dismissed and 22 allowed. In 1973, the number of civil appeals allowed (25) exceeded the number dismissed (17).
[42] (1971) 7 East African Law Jnl, pp. 11 - 17.

to withdraw, as the Court's appellate jurisdiction had affected their financial and commercial interests. But all three states contributed in the eventual collapse. In Tanzania, a socialist state and economic structure was being developed in that period. This was in clear conflict with the broadly capitalist economies of Kenya and Uganda. Tanzania became reluctant to submit all civil matters to the jurisdiction of a Court dominated by lawyers with a liberal-capitalist world view.

In Uganda, Idi Amin took over power by military means in 1971, causing a break-down of civil and state institutions.[43] This was reflected in the declining number of cases from Uganda after 1973. Amin's gross human rights violations presented Tanzanian president Nyerere with an ideal opportunity to disband the East Africa Community. This happened in 1977.[44] In any event, when Tanzanian forces invaded Uganda, little prospect remained of political and judicial unity. Tanzania subsequently developed closer ties with Southern African states. In 1980 it became part of SADCC, and remained a member of the reconstituted SADC.[45]

1.4 Case-law

The case-law of the Court of Appeal of East Africa, in its various forms, presents early examples of a supra-national African human rights jurisprudence. Its case-law may serve as an autochthonous source in which future sub-regional human rights courts or an African Court of Human and Peoples' Rights may find guidance.

One aspect which such courts may have to consider is the effect of evidence obtained in violation of human rights treaties or the African Charter. A case before the East African Court of Appeal which dealt with this issue is *Njuguna s/o Kimani v R*.[46] The principles set out in that case were valuable in both the colonial and post-colonial eras, and are the following:

– It is highly improper for the police to keep a suspect in unlawful custody and prolong their questioning of him by refraining from formally charging him.
– A judge has a discretion to exclude statements obtained by improper means, even if they are admissible under established rules.

---

[43] See Republic of Uganda (1994), p. 24.
[44] See United Republic of Tanzania (1979), p. 2.
[45] Brooks, P. E. J., The European Economic Community and a Southern African Common Market in Legal Perspective, unpublished Ph. D. thesis, University of Exeter, 1993, p. 450.
[46] [1954] E.A.C.A., p. 21.

– Formal cautioning of a suspect is of little significance when given to a prisoner who has been in the police officer's custody for weeks, and who has previously been induced by questioning to incriminate himself.

However, this did not mean that these principles were rigorously followed in all instances. In *Ochieng v Uganda*[47] a suspect was unlawfully detained for nine days and repeatedly interrogated. His subsequent confession was the object of argument. Allowing the confession, the Court stated the following: "The fact that the necessary safeguards provided for by law had not been carried out ... would not in itself prevent a voluntary confession of guilt" if the judge kept that fact in mind when deciding on admissibility.[48]

The proposed African Court of Human and Peoples' Rights will also have to deal with the "claw-back" clauses in the African Charter.[49] In *Ibingira v Uganda*[50] the East African Court of Appeal allowed an appeal by making an order of *habeas corpus*. In issue was section 19(1)(j) of the Ugandan Constitution, which provides the following: "No ... person shall be deprived of his liberty save as may be authorised by law in any of the following cases, that is to say to such extent as may be necessary in the execution of a lawful order requiring that person to remain within a specified area within Uganda ...". On behalf of Uganda it was contended that a deportation order was "authorised by law" as "it is made under statutory power".[51] The authority of law and the requirement of "lawfulness", in this view, refer to compliance with the procedure prescribed by statute. If this interpretation had been accepted, section 19(1) would have authorised legislation for the restriction of the movements and residence of the individual, thus allowing for the violation of guaranteed rights. The East African Court of Appeal did not accept the interpretation proposed on behalf of Uganda. The effect of the reference to "lawful order" in section 19(1) "is to provide that lawful orders made under a statute restricting freedom of movement shall not constitute violations of the right to personal liberty", the Court held.[52] Terms such as "authorised by law" and "lawful" have to be interpreted in the light of the Constitution as a whole, including the provisions on fundamental rights.

---

[47] [1969] E.A. 1.
[48] P. 4 E-F.
[49] See e.g. art. 10 of the African Charter, which provides for the right to freely associate as long as the individual "abides by the law". On these provisions, see e.g. Umozurike, U. O., *The African Charter on Human and Peoples' Rights*, 1997, pp. 33-43.
[50] [1966] E.A. 306 (*per* Acting Vice-President Spry).
[51] P. 310 b-c.
[52] P. 310 d.

2 West African Court of Appeal

The West African Court of Appeal was established later (in 1928), and its functioning came to an end earlier (towards the end of the 1950s) than its eastern equivalent.[53] It was established for all the British dependencies along the African West coast: The Gold Coast, Nigeria, Sierra Leone and the Gambia. Liberia, the only other West African anglophone area with a common law-based legal system, was not included. This is explained by the fact that Liberia was already an independent state and had no historical links with Britain.

In 1948 the principal judicial officials of this Court were made permanent. These structural changes could not prevent this Court's demise. It "disappeared by a process of erosion",[54] as the territories gained independence. The first to sever its ties was Ghana (previously the Gold Coast), when it gained independence in 1957. Ghana immediately set up its own Court of Appeal,[55] a move that seems to have contradicted Nkrumah's efforts at regional unity in other spheres. Nigeria followed. A combined Court of Appeal was then established for the two remaining non-independent territories, the Gambia and Sierra Leone. Also this came to an end soon, with the independence of Sierra Leone.

Compared to the experience in East Africa, the West African Court of Appeal had much less "staying power". Some of the reasons that may account for this difference are:

- The territories (countries) did not form a geographic unit, but were dispersed along the West coast. This had obvious implications for logistical arrangements and other practical matters.
- The Court was not a component part of a more comprehensive regional structure. No inter-territorial judicial institution is likely to flourish in the absence of a clearly expressed political will of the participating territories to pursue collective goals.

---

[53] See Roberts-Wray, *op. cit.*, p. 783.
[54] Roberts-Wray, *op. cit.*, p. 783. *Ibid?*
[55] West African Court of Appeal (Amendment) Order in Council, 1957.

III JUDICIAL INSTITUTIONS IN THE FRAMEWORK OF PRESENT SUB-REGIONAL ORGANISATIONS

1 ECOWAS Court of Justice

The Economic Community of West African States ("ECOWAS") was formed in 1975.[56] Its aim is to promote economic development in Western Africa by establishing a common market, harmonising economic policies, including agriculture, industrial development and monetary policies. The ECOWAS institutions are the Authority of Heads of State and Government, the Council of Ministers, the Community Court of Justice, an Executive Secretariat and some specialised commissions. In 1993 the original Treaty was amended.[57] By 1997, sixteen states in West Africa had become members. They were Benin, Burkina Faso, Cape Verde, Côte d'Ivoire, the Gambia, Ghana, Guinea, Guinea-Bissau, Liberia, Mali, Mauritania, Niger, Nigeria, Senegal, Sierra Leone and Togo.[58]

There was no explicit reference to human rights in any of the 65 articles forming the body of the original treaty. This omission must be viewed against the contemporaneous background. Few would have thought, at that stage, that an African Charter would enter into force within the next decade. A limited number of provisions, such as freedom of movement and residence[59] had human rights implications, but did not extend the Court's jurisdiction to human rights matters as such.

A Community Court of Justice was provided for in the 1975 Treaty to "ensure observance of law and justice".[60] Disputes arising from the application of the Treaty had to be resolved by the states among themselves, and in amicable settlement "by direct agreement".[61] Failing such a settlement, any of the parties involved could refer the matter to the Court. In 1991, due to the "scope and degree of regional integration ECOWAS had embarked on",[62] a Protocol setting up a Community Court of Justice was adopted. In

---

[56] Treaty reproduced in (1975) 14 International Legal Materials, p. 1200, entered into by Côte d'Ivoire, Dahomey, the Gambia, Ghana, Guinea, Guinea-Bissau, Liberia, Mali, Mauritania, Niger, Nigeria, Senegal, Sierra Leone, Togo and Upper Volta. (See the 1975 Treaty also in Awechue (gen. ed.), 1991, p. 82.)

[57] See (1996) 35 International Legal Materials 660. The revised Treaty was done at Cotonou, Benin, 24 July 1993 (see (1996) 8 RADIC, p. 187).

[58] *Africa South of the Sahara,* 1997, p. 107.

[59] Art. 27 of the ECOWAS 1975 Treaty.

[60] Art. 11(1) of the ECOWAS 1975 Treaty.

[61] Art. 56 of the ECOWAS 1975 Treaty.

[62] Final Communiqué of the Fourteenth Session of the Authority of Heads of State and Government, Abuja, July 1991 contained in (1991) 19 Official Journal of ECOWAS, p. 62. The Protocol is reprinted at (1996) 8 RADIC, p. 28.

other words, this Protocol, already provided for in 1975,[63] took fifteen years to be realised. The Protocol adopted on 6 July 1991 does not in any way extend the competencies of the Court. It clarifies that only states parties may seize the Court, also "on behalf of its nationals".[64] Proceedings may be instituted against another state or an ECOWAS institution.

When the ECOWAS Treaty was amended in 1993, the human rights discourse was given more prominence. One of the fundamental principles of the organisation now relates to "the recognition, promotion and protection of human and peoples' rights in accordance with the provisions of the African Charter on Human and Peoples' Rights".[65] This shift in emphasis has been brought about, primarily, by the adoption of and ratification by ECOWAS member states of the African Charter in the intervening years. This development also provides a clear example of the increased importance attached to the African Charter in African political life. Institutions provided for include the Community Court of Justice, retained in its old form, and an Arbitration Tribunal.

Although ECOWAS was initially designed as a sub-regional organisation for the pursuit of economic and social goals, it has gradually extended its mandate.[66] Even before the ECOWAS Treaty was amended in 1993, two protocols, supplementary to the 1975 Treaty, illustrate this shift. The one is the 1978 Protocol on Non-Aggression, and the other is the 1981 Protocol on Mutual Assistance on Defence.[67] The internal conflict in one of the ECOWAS member states, Liberia, prompted the establishment of the ECOWAS Mediation Standing Committee in 1990.[68] Not all ECOWAS members participated in the force, but decisions were taken on behalf of the Authority of the Heads of State and Government. These decisions called for a cease-fire between the warring parties and established a cease-fire observing force, called the ECOWAS Military Observer Group ("ECOMOG"). The force consisted of troops from member states, and soon it numbered approximately 5 000. Not all the ECOWAS member states approved of the decision of the Mediation Standing Committee. Some regarded ECOMOG as interference in

---

[63] Art. 11(2) of the ECOWAS 1975 Treaty.
[64] Art. 9(3) of the Protocol.
[65] Art. 4(g) of the revised ECOWAS Treaty. See also the Preamble par 4 of the revised Treaty.
[66] On ECOMOG, see Weller, M., *Regional Peace-keeping and International Enforcement: The Liberian Crisis*, 1994, Ouguergouz, F. *Liberia*, (1994) 2 AYBIL, p. 208 and Kwakwa, E., *Internal Conflicts in Africa: Is there a Right of Humanitarian Intervention?* (1994) 2 AYBIL, p. 9.
[67] Reprinted in full by Weller, *op. cit.*, pp. 18 - 24.
[68] See also the later ECOMOG force in Sierra Leone.

the domestic affairs of a member state. The ECOWAS Authority of Heads of State and Government subsequently approved the Committee's decisions.

Initial attempts at a cease-fire and a national coalition failed. In 1991 the Yamoussoukrou agreement was reached, providing for a cease-fire and elections. ECOWAS imposed sanctions on the National Patriotic Front of Liberia ("NPFL") when they failed to keep to the agreement. The UN Security Council endorsed these decisions. The UN eventually became actively involved when the Secretary General appointed a Special Representative to Liberia. The UN Special Representative was instrumental in getting the parties to sign the Cotonou Agreement in 1993. In terms of this agreement ECOWAS was assigned primary responsibility to ensure implementation of the accord, which provided for a cease-fire and election in early 1994. The role of the UN was to ensure an impartial application of its provisions. To this end, the UN Observer Mission in Liberia ("UNOMIL") was established.

The establishment of ECOMOG is significant, in particular as far as human rights issues are concerned, for the following three reasons:

– Most relevant as far as human rights are concerned: It marks a decisive shift in focus away from economic goals to the promotion of human rights. The intervention was directed not only at securing lives by ending the massacres, but ultimately at the restoration of democratic governance and institutions.[69]

– ECOMOG is the first regional peace-keeping initiative on the African continent.[70] As such, it may be indicative of a emerging trend that Africa endeavours to solve its own problems. Strict adherence to notions of state sovereignty would have made these efforts impossible. This operation is premised on the assumption that internal events in one state are of concern to other states and may allow them, under certain circumstances, to interfere.

– The UN force, UNOMIL, was deployed as the first UN peace-keeping mission undertaken in co-operation with a peace-keeping operation already established by another international organization.[71] This illustrates the extent to which the interests of the UN and an African sub-regional organisations could coincide.

2 SADC Tribunal

In 1992 a number of Southern African states adopted the "Declaration regarding Establishment of the Southern African Development Community",[72]

---

[69] See sources in Weller, *op cit.*, p. xxii.
[70] Kwakwa (1994) 2 AYBIL, p. 26.
[71] Ouguergouz (1994) 2 AYBIL, p. 208.
[72] See (1993) 32 ILM (International Legal Materials), p. 267.

followed in 1993 by the adoption of the Treaty Establishing the Southern African Development Community ("SADC").[73] It was created through the transformation of a pre-existing regional institution, the Southern African Development Co-ordination Conference ("SADCC"). SADCC was founded in 1980 mainly as a bulwark against the then minority South African government's stated policy of establishing a "Southern African constellation of states". The current member states of SADC are: Angola, Botswana, the Democratic Republic of Congo, Lesotho, Malawi, Mauritius, Mozambique, Namibia, the Seychelles, South Africa, Swaziland, Tanzania, Zambia and Zimbabwe.[74] SADC is aimed at regional peace and security, at co-operation in a number of sectors, and at integrating regional economies. Its stated ideals are much more ambitious than those of SADCC.

Reference to human rights is found in the Preamble to the Treaty, which declares that the member states are "mindful of the need to involve peoples of the Region centrally" in development and integration, "particularly through the guarantee of democratic rights, observance of human rights and the rule of law". One of the five groups of principles in accordance with which SADC will act, is "human rights, democracy and the rule of law".[75] In this respect the SADC Treaty allows for a more significant role to human rights than the European Community ("EC") in its establishing treaty. Like the EC Treaty, the SADC Treaty guarantees equal treatment and non-discrimination in member states and by SADC and its institutions.[76] Though less precise than the EC Treaty, its objectives have clear socio-economic implications.[77]

Disputes arising from the interpretation and application of the SADC Treaty should be settled amicably through a process of friendly settlement.[78] If a dispute cannot be settled amicably, it is to be referred to the SADC Tribunal. The Tribunal is one of six SADC institutions established under the Treaty.[79] It can adjudicate disputes or give advisory opinions.[80] Its decisions will be final and binding.[81] A protocol establishing the tribunal must be adopted by the Summit of Heads of State and Government of SADC. This

---

[73] The SADC Treaty appears at (1993) 32 ILM, p. 116 and (1993) 5 RADIC, p. 418.
[74] In September 1997, the Summit of Heads of State and Government approved the applications for membership of the Democratic Republic of Congo (the former Zaïre) and the Seychelles.
[75] Art. 4 of the SADC Treaty.
[76] Art. 6(2) and 6(3) of the SADC Treaty.
[77] See e.g. art. 5(1)(a) of the SADC Treaty.
[78] Art. 32 of the SADC Treaty.
[79] Art. 9 of the SADC Treaty.
[80] Art. 16 of the SADC Treaty.
[81] Art. 16(5) of the SADC Treaty.

will set out the composition, powers, functions and procedures of the Tribunal.[82] As the Protocol has not been elaborated, the details and actual functioning of the Tribunal remains a subject of speculation. So, too, does the role of the individual in the system. It is not clear whether only states parties would be able to seize the tribunal. It is suggested that individuals should be granted standing and the right to refer cases to a future judicial organ. This would be in line with the SADC Treaty, which already provides for the full involvement of individuals and NGOs in the process of regional integration.[83]

A process to establish the SADC Tribunal has already been initiated. A panel of experts, consisting of professor Kamba (from the University of Namibia) and Justice Jacobs (judge on the Court of Justice of the European Communities) was mandated to draft proposals early in 1997.[84] Their report was discussed by a meeting of legal experts from SADC countries in April 1997. The panel proposed that individuals should be granted the right to seize the Tribunal. The panel noted that the SADC Treaty imposes obligation on states not to discriminate on certain grounds, and concluded that this makes individual access imperative.[85] Noting that SADC has a more general human rights mandate,[86] the panel concluded that the Tribunal could be "given a more general jurisdiction in relation to human rights". It continued: "In the event of a separate instrument being drawn up, setting up the scope of the human rights to be protected, jurisdiction should be conferred on the Tribunal". The possibility of a separate protocol to the SADC Treaty and of a separate Southern African Convention on Human Rights are mentioned as possible "separate instruments". The panel further recommended that, in contrast to the general jurisdiction under the SADC Treaty, individual complaints could only be brought after local remedies had been exhausted. However, the first meeting of legal experts dismissed the possibility of including human rights in the proposed Tribunal's mandate, deciding "to delink this matter from the jurisdiction of the proposed Protocol for the rea-

---

[82] Art. 16(2) of SADC Treaty.
[83] Art. 23(2) of the SADC Treaty.
[84] The SADC Tribunal, dated 18 February 1997. This document, as well as the Record of the First Legal Experts Meeting, has been supplied to me by Mr. André Stemmet, from the South African Department of Foreign Affairs, with whom I also discussed these documents. The SADC Ministers of Justice have already adopted a draft Protocol to the Treaty, establishing a Tribunal. This Protocol is expected to be adopted by the SADC Summit late in 2000.
[85] See art. 6(1) and 6(2) of the SADC Treaty.
[86] In terms of art. 4 of the SADC Treaty.

son that SADC would be required to develop a separate protocol or legal instrument to govern activities on human rights".[87]

The lack of effective implementation of the human rights guaranteed in the SADC Treaty has been criticised.[88] In 1994, a Ministerial Workshop on Democracy, Peace and Security adopted the "Windhoek Resolutions". It called for the creation of a SADC Human Rights Commission and a SADC Bill of Rights.[89] In 1996, these criticisms culminated in a draft regional human rights charter, which was drafted by NGOs in some of the member states.[90] The charter, which carries no official SADC stamp of approval, provides for civil and political rights, as well as cultural rights, the right to health and to a clean environment. It goes much further, however, by proposing the establishment of a SADC Human Rights Court. The Charter would only apply after a prospective litigant had exhausted domestic remedies. It further provides that any state "which does not comply with an order of the

---

[87] Record of the First Legal Experts Meeting held in Gabarone, Botswana, from 7 to 9 April 1997, par. 7.1. This view stems from a narrow interpretation of SADC's mandate, considerations of state sovereignty, the fact that government representatives had received the experts' report just before its discussion, and that they had not been mandated by their respective governments to negotiate about the inclusion of human rights in the proposed tribunal's jurisdiction. In my view it not correct to reject the inclusion of human rights in the SADC Tribunal's mandate only because such a course would require the development of a new, separate human rights treaty on the sub-regional level. Even if such a sub-regional is not elaborated, a future SADC Tribunal could adjudicate on the provisions of the African Charter. All the SADC member states had in any event already ratified the African Charter. The African Charter provisions may be applied by the SADC Tribunal on the basis of its general human rights mandate in the Preamble and in article 4. Alternatively, SADC may accede to the African Charter.

[88] Mvungi, *op cit.*, referred to the fact that SADC members are obliged to act in accordance with principles of democracy, human rights and the rule of law, but that the SADC Treaty "does not establish a regional human rights regime that will make these principles and ideals a reality" (p. 161). He therefore recommended that SADC conclude a "Human Rights Convention" and establish a "fully fledged Court of Justice with appellate jurisdiction on human rights and community law cases" (p. 161). He also made a clear link between regional integration, democratic government and human rights: "Member states of the SADC cannot proceed towards any regional integration without ensuring that they respect and guarantee basic rights of their subjects. This commitment can only be guaranteed at regional level by introducing a regional convention on human rights to be applied by an independent regional human rights court" (p. 69).

[89] It was held in July 1994, and was attended by NGOs, government ministers and parliamentarians. This followed an NGO workshop organised by the SADC Secretariat in February.

[90] (13 - 19 May 1996) West Africa, p.743.

Court interpreting this Charter shall be suspended from SADC for the duration of its non-compliance with such order". The proposal has as yet not been considered seriously by the Summit of Heads of State and Government of SADC.[91] Although most states have included similar rights in their own constitutions, a supra-national court giving final pronouncements thereon may still seem like a threat to national sovereignty.

It must be questioned whether a separate human rights court should be established in the sub-region. The principle of a court to adjudicate on regional matters has already been accepted when the states agreed that a SADC tribunal should be established. Another institution need not be established. Rather, the jurisdiction of the SADC Tribunal should be extended to include human rights. Efforts in this direction need to be intensified, to ensure that the SADC Tribunal is not established without serious consideration of these possibilities. It will be much more difficult to overturn the position once a Tribunal which excludes human rights matters has already been set up.

Even before the establishment of SADC, a sub-regional jurisprudence started developing in Southern Africa. This case-law already provides a starting point for a regional human rights jurisprudence. This process has been facilitated by the common issues faced by these states, by a common historical[92] and legal background,[93] the fact that all countries not only have Bills of Rights, but also the similarity of their provisions, by an exchange of

---

[91] One aspect pertaining to human rights that has been attended to by the Summit is the adoption of the 1997 Declaration on Gender and Development, and the addendum thereto, "The Prevention and Eradication of Violence Against Women and Children", adopted in Mauritius on 14 September 1998.

[92] Like all of Africa, these countries have suffered under colonialism. But in Southern Africa colonialism took a singular form, as initial trading contacts were followed by substantive settling of Dutch, English, Portuguese and Germans communities. The presence of the non-indigenous groups lasted longer than in the most of Africa. Colonialism lasted longest in this region, and led to the severest national liberation campaigns, including armed struggle. Angola and Mozambique gained independence in 1975. Zimbabwe became independent only in 1980. Namibia came even later, in 1990. Finally, a democratic government was installed in South Africa in 1994.

[93] See the quote from *S v Williams* 1995 (3) SA 632 (CC) at par 31: "The decisions of the Supreme Courts of Namibia and of Zimbabwe are of special significance. Not only are these countries geographic neighbours, but South Africa shares with them the same English colonial experience which has had a deep influence on our law; we of course also share the Roman-Dutch legal tradition".

judicial officers,[94] by geographic proximity and linguistic homogeneity[95] and by the existence of common law report series.[96] The region shows a remarkable degree of coherence, underscored in recent times by countries becoming supra-nationally linked by common membership of SADC,[97] and of the Commonwealth. Similar issues faced by the judiciary in these countries are, for example, the constitutionality of corporal punishment,[98] the death penalty,[99] the prohibition of alien husbands from residing in the country of their

---

[94] The regional exchange of judicial officers is exemplified in the person of judge Mahomed, who was Chief Justice of Namibia and judge (and later Deputy President) of the South African Constitutional Court, before becoming that country's Chief Justice. Further examples are the previous Chief Justice of Zimbabwe, Dumbutshena, who acted as judge in the Namibian Supreme Court (see introductory pages of SA Law Reports 1994 2 to 1996 4). Since the latter part of 1994 judge Mtambanengwe has been seconded from the Zimbabwean to the Namibian High Court (see eg his judgment in *Kauesa v Minister of Home Affairs* 1996 4 SA 965 (NmS)).

[95] All these countries, except Angola and Mozambique, have English as an official language. After its admission to the Commonwealth, English should gain ground in Mozambique. Angola is also reportedly considering to join the Commonwealth.

[96] For example, the South African Law Reports series includes cases from Namibia and Zimbabwe, the South African Constitutional Law Reports series includes cases from Namibia, Swaziland and Zimbabwe. In one of the latest issues of the Butterworths Constitutional Law Reports series (1997 8) cases from Lesotho have also been included. Previously, cases from e.g. Namibia, Zimbabwe and Botswana have also been included in the BCLR series.

[97] A political arrangement may provide the required forum to raise non-compliance by a state. Close links, especially economically, may serve as means of censuring a state that does not conform with regional requirements. An attempt has been made to include a Human Rights Charter into the SADC Treaty, and to establish a regional human rights court. This has, so far, not reaped any fruits. Not only governments, but also civil society in the neighbouring states, may contribute in the process of effecting changing attitudes. (See Gebhardt (21 - 27 February 1997) *Mail & Guardian* at B1, on the actions of trade unions in South Africa in connection with the denial of trade union rights in Swaziland.)

[98] See e.g. the references to the Namibian case *Ex parte Attorney-General, Namibia: In re Corporal Punishment* 1991 3 SA 76 (NmS) and the Zimbabwean cases *S v Ncube* 1988 2 SA 702 (ZS) and *S v A Juvenile* 1990 4 SA 151 (ZS) by Langa J in the South African case *S v Williams* 1995 3 SA 632 (CC) (in particular at par 31).

[99] See the reference to *Mbushuu v The Republic* (Tanzania Court of Appeal, Criminal Appeal 142 of 1994, 30 January 1995) in *S v Makwanyane* 1995 3 SA 391 (CC) at paras 114-115.

wives' citizenship[100] and balancing vested property rights with programmes of land reform and redistribution.[101] Other common issues are the quest for an appropriate approach to constitutional interpretation of a new Bill of Rights,[102] to claims for equality on the basis of sex and gender,[103] to limitations to freedom of expression,[104] and to the limitation of rights in general.[105]

---

[100] See *Dow v Attorney-General* [1992] LRC (Const) 623 (Botswana CA) followed in *Rattigan v Chief Immigration Officer, Zimbabwe* 1995 2 SA 182 (ZS). See also *Salem v Immigration Officer* [1994] 1 LRC (Const) 355; 1995 4 SA 280; 1995 1 BCLR 78 (ZS). An earlier case dealing with this issue is the UN Human Rights Committee decision in *Aumeeruddy-Cziffra v Mauritius* (1981) 62 ILR 255. The question arises whether this island state is or may become part of a Southern African human rights vanguard. In terms of its human rights record, it may fit, but cultural differences may inhibit such a development. From a legal point of view, Mauritius is also a mixed or hybrid system.

[101] See the thoughtful discussion by Roux (1996) 8 *RADIC* 755, in which reference is made to cases on this issue in the following SADC member states: Botswana, Namibia, South Africa, Tanzania, Zambia, Zimbabwe (see especially n44 at 762). The author could, no doubt, also have included case-law from Mauritius.

[102] See, for example, the impact of the *Unity Dow* judgment.

[103] The Namibian High Court, in *S v D* 1992 1 SA 513 (Nm) introduced the difference between substantive (*de facto*) and formal (*de iure*) equality. In the course of appeal proceedings, the Court considered whether the existence and application of the "cautionary rule" in cases involving sexual assault violated the equality principle. The Namibian Constitution guarantees that no person "may be discriminated against on the grounds of sex ...". On a formal level, Frank J accepted that the rule is applied equally to men and women who were victims of sexual assault. *De facto*, however, the overwhelming majority of complainants (up to 95% in the judge's experience) are female. This meant that the rule operated as a tool of discrimination against women. As the judge disposed of the case without basing his decision on this aspect, his remarks in this regard are *obiter dicta*. This is underlined when he concluded that the rule is "probably" contrary to article 10 of the Constitution. In *Longwe v Intercontinetal Hotels* [1993] 4 LRC 221 (Zambia) sex discrimination took the form of refusing women who were not accompanied by men, entrance to a bar of the Intercontinental Hotel in Lusaka. The conduct was found to be inconsistent with fundamental rights guaranteed by the Constitution. The *Unity Dow* judgment and others discussed above on the discriminatory nature of citizenship provisions may also be invoked here. See further *Student Representative Council, Molepolole College of Education v Attorney General of Botswana*, Civil Appeal 13 of 1994, judgment delivered on 31 January 1995 and *Mfolo v Minister of Education, Bophuthatswana* 1992 3 SA 181 (B), dealing with discrimination on the basis of pregnancy.

[104] The Supreme Court of Zimbabwe addressed the constitutionality of a statutory provision prohibiting public processions without obtaining a prior permit in *In re Munhemeso* 1995 1 SA 551 (ZS). It did, as far as its approach to interpretation was concerned, refer to the Botswana Court of Appeal judgment in the *Dow* case. The similarity of constitutional provisions in Botswana and Zimbabwe prompted the

Within the existing SADC system, structures sensitive to human rights already exist. In 1996, SADC launched the Organ on Politics, Defence and Security ("OPDS").[106] Its mandate includes human rights matters.[107] The OPDS has so far involved itself mainly in security matters. At a Summit of the OPDS, held on 2 October 1996, the situation in Angola was discussed. The Summit noted that "the prevailing situation in Angola is the remaining major obstacle to total regional stability".[108] A call was made on UNITA to fulfil its commitments in terms of the Lusaka Protocol. Amnesty International has recommended that this organ should serve as an "effective means to ensure uniform training in the protection of fundamental rights within the sub-region".[109]

In 1997 a Parliamentary Forum was set up. Its membership is open to national parliaments of the SADC member states.[110] Each parliament must

---

Footnote continued

Zimbabwean Supreme Court to approve and apply a decision of the Botswana High Court of Appeal in *In re Munhemeso*. Gubbay CJ remarked as follows: "In *Dow v Attorney-General* [1992] LRC (Const) 623 (CA, Botswana) Amissah JP considered the identically worded s. 3 of the Constitution of Botswana. He viewed it, most aptly, as 'the key or umbrella provision' in the Declaration of Rights under which all rights and freedoms must be subsumed; and went on to point out that it encapsulates the sum total of the individual's rights and freedoms in general terms, which may be expanded upon in the expository, elaborating and limiting sections ensuing in the Declaration of Rights. This analysis of the scope and impact of s 3 is particularly apposite to that of s 11 in the Constitution of Zimbabwe, and I respectfully associate myself with it". Conceding that there may be numerous reasons why no reference was made to the earlier in the later case (difficulties related to access, non-publication of law reports, the short time span between the two judgments, for example), it exemplifies an unexplored opportunity to seek common answers to common problems.

105 See e.g. Langa J's invocation of the Tanzanian Court of Appeal's judgment in *DPP v Pete* [1991] LRC (Const) 553 (Tanz CA) in *S v Makwanyane* 1995 3 SA 391 (CC) at par 224: "the rights and duties of the individual are limited by the rights and duties of society".

106 See Amnesty International, *Southern Africa: Politicing and Human Rights in the Southern African Development Community*, 1997, p. 10.

107 One of its stated objectives is to "promote and enhance the development of democratic institutions and practices within members states, and to encourage the observance of universal human rights as provided for in the Charters and Conventions of the OAU and United Nations" (see Amnesty International, *op. cit.*, p. 10). See also Gyan-Apenteng and Mwananyanda "The Birth of Sahringon" (April – May 1997) African Topics, p. 22.

108 See par. 10 of Communiqué of the Summit, 2 October 1996, Luanda, Angola.

109 P. 10.

110 The account of the Parliamentary Forum is based on information in (1997) 34 Africa Research Bulletin, p. 12636.

ensure fair representation of women, and all political parties to the Forum. The Forum will be an institution integrated into SADC, with its seat in Windhoek, Namibia. Organs of the Parliamentary Forum will be a plenary assembly, an executive committee, the office of the Secretary-General and standing committees. The Forum is mandated not only to promote economic co-operation, but also to advance democracy, the rule of law and human rights in the sub-region.

Efforts to secure the place of human rights within the activities of SADC depend largely on NGOs.[111] For this reason, the recent creation of the Southern African Human Rights NGO Network ("SAHRINGON") is important. It was established between over 60 NGOs in the region. The objectives of the Network include "forming a platform to lobby SADC members to prioritise human rights issues".[112]

3   COMESA Court of Justice

The Common Market of Eastern and Southern Africa ("COMESA") was established in 1993.[113] Its aim is to enhance economic development in the region.[114] COMESA was established in the place of the Preferential Trade Area of Eastern and Southern African states ("PTA") of 1981.[115] The scope of COMESA is much broader than that of the PTA. It is open for ratification by a large number of states, stretching from Angola, to Eritrea, and the Comoros.[116] It was created within the ambit of the broader ideals of the creation of an African Economic Community.

One of the institutions of the regional body is a yet to be established Court of Justice. This Court has to ensure "the adherence to law in the interpretation and application" of the Treaty.[117] Seven judges are appointed by

---

[111] See also Amnesty International, *op. cit.*, p. 14, for a recommendation that the Heads of State should make a declaration affirming their commitment to human rights at their August 1997 summit.

[112] On its establishment, see Gyan-Apenteng and Mwananyanda "The Birth of Sahringon" (April – May 1997) African Topics, p. 22.

[113] See (1994) 33 ILM, p. 1067.

[114] See art. 3 of the COMESA Treaty.

[115] The PTA wound itself up on 5 November 1993 and established COMESA in its place. The PTA comprised 23 countries in East and Southern Africa ((1994) New African Market Bulletin, p. 23).

[116] The full list illustrates the degree of overlap in membership between SADC and COMESA. The states that are members of both organisations are Angola, Malawi, Mauritius, Mozambique, Namibia, Swaziland, Tanzania, Zambia and Zimbabwe (see Heiman, M. R. A. *The Drive Towards Regionalisation in Southern Africa: Fictional Reality* ((1997) 9 RADIC, p.639).

[117] See art. 19 of COMESA Treaty.

the COMESA Authority for a once-renewable term of five years.[118] Not more than one national from a specific member state may hold judicial office simultaneously. The Court has a contentious and advisory jurisdiction.[119] Court judgments are binding and member states undertake to implement them without delay.[120] The Court may also grant appropriate interim orders.[121]

Not only COMESA institutions and member states, but also legal and natural persons may bring cases before the Court.[122] That means that individuals may refer the legality of any act, regulation, directive or decision of the Council or any member state to the Court, arguing that it is unlawful or an infringement of treaty provisions. Domestic remedies have to be exhausted before a legal or natural person may approach the Court. According to reports, the Court can be a reality by 1998.[123] The acting legal director of COMESA, Karangizi, said in March 1997 that the establishment of the Court will be on the agenda of the summit to be held on 10 April 1997.[124] He expected that the host country would be designated at the Summit. However, this has not yet happened.

COMESA is not aimed at realising any specific aim in the field of human rights. But as the Treaty establishing COMESA suggests, issues pertaining to human rights cannot be divorced totally from its functioning. In the Preamble, reference is made to "the principles of international law governing relations between sovereign states, and the principles of liberty, fundamental freedoms and the rule of law". This formulation may be read as an attempt at reconciling the sanctity of the state with attempts to protect human rights within the state. The initial hesitance is supplemented by an unequivocal adherence to human rights as part of the organisation's fundamental principles. These principles include the promotion and sustenance of a democratic system of governance in each Member State,[125] the recognition and observance of the rule of law,[126] and the recognition, promotion and protection of human and peoples' rights in accordance with the African Charter.[127] The inclusion of human rights as part of COMESA's fundamen-

---

[118] Arts. 20, 21 of the COMESA Treaty.
[119] Advisory jurisdiction is regulated by art. 32 of the COMESA Treaty.
[120] Art. 34(3) of the COMESA Treaty.
[121] In terms of art. 35 of the COMESA Treaty.
[122] See art. 26 of the COMESA Treaty.
[123] See news release by Panafrican News Agency.
[124] *Ibid.*
[125] Art. 6(h) of the COMESA Treaty.
[126] Art. 6(g) of the COMESA Treaty.
[127] Art. 6(e) of the COMESA Treaty.

tal principles and the possibility of individual actions make this a system full of potential human rights realisation.

4 Maghreb Court of Justice

The Treaty of Marrakech, establishing the Maghreb Arab Union, was concluded in 1989 between Mauritania, Morocco, Algeria, Tunisia and Libya.[128] The main aims of the Union are to promote regional security, to create viable regional economic integration and to develop trade and other links with the European Union.

A Maghreb Court of Justice, consisting of two judges from each state, is instituted. Its function is to adjudicate on disputes relating to the interpretation and application of the Treaty and other agreements within the ambit of the Union.[129] Human rights are not expressly referred to in the Treaty, making it practically impossible for this Court to base any of its decisions on human rights considerations. Its seat is to be established at Nouakchott, Mauritania. The Court will have a contentious and advisory jurisdiction. In its latter capacity, the Maghreb Court of Justice will provide advice to the Presidential Council.[130]

IV FUTURE OPTIONS FOR SUB-REGIONAL ORGANISATIONS IN AFRICA

Four main options seem open to sub-regional organisations in the quest for more effective human rights protection at the sub-regional level in Africa:

- These organisations may **ignore** human rights related issues, leaving it to the domestic legal systems or regional system to redress violations. This course of action is favoured by the argument that supra-national human rights recourse is already possible at the regional level, through the African Commission. A future possibility is that an African Court on Human and Peoples' Rights may strengthen the work of the African Commission, making sub-regional duplication all the more redundant.
- The **limited human rights mandate**, already included in the organisation's treaty, may be used as a basis to cultivate a better human

---

[128] See, in general on the Maghreb Arab Union, El Kahiri, *L'Union du Maghreb Arabe* (1994) 2 AYBIL, p. 141.
[129] Art. 13(2) of the Marrakech Treaty.
[130] See El Kahiri, *op. cit.*, p. 146.

rights environment in the member states. This is a minimalist solution, and will only function properly if individuals are granted the right of access to the judicial institution.[131]

- Each of these regional inter-governmental organisations may adopt its **own sub-regional charter on human rights**, to be enforced by and within the jurisdiction of the specific community Courts of justice or tribunal.[132] This "sub-regional charter" may take the form of a sub-regional "Convention on Human Rights" or a separate protocol to the treaty of the sub-regional organisation.

- Each regional economic grouping may **incorporate the African Charter** as a whole into the sub-regional treaty. This "incorporation" may take place by way of accession to the African Charter, or through amendments to the organisation's founding document. The specific community Court of justice or tribunal would then be able to implement the provisions of the Charter.[133]

The first option should not be followed. This "wait and see" approach limits the role of supra-national human rights protection in the African Charter system. In the light of the Commission's inefficiency, the recommendatory nature of its findings, and the general lack of confidence in and knowledge of the Commission, other forms of supra-national recourse should be put in place. To rely on an institution (the proposed African Court of Human and Peoples' Rights) that may only start functioning well into the new millennium, is not realistic and does not take account of the urgency of the human rights situation in Africa.

The second ("minimalist") approach finds a precedent in the European system. In Europe, two judicial institutions exist side by side. The one court, the European Court of Human Rights, has jurisdiction over all cases concerning the interpretation and application of the European Convention for the Protection of Human Rights and Fundamental Freedoms (the "European Convention"). The other institution, the Court of Justice of the European Communities, has jurisdiction over European Community ("EC") law.

---

[131] As in the case of the COMESA Court of Justice.
[132] See, on this possibility, Benedek, W. *European and African Perspectives on Human Rights* in Theodoropoulos, C. (ed), *Human Rights in Europe and Africa: A Comparative Analysis*, 1992, p. 28, who foresaw such a possibility in Southern Africa. In his view, this could be accompanied by a revision of the Charter to fulfil the needs of the sub-region.
[133] Similar options are open to the European Community to accede to the European Convention.

Judgments of this Court illustrate a trend to increasingly introduce human rights into Community law by recognising the European Convention as a source of "general legal principles" of EC law.[134] In 1996 the Court of Justice of the European Communities observed as follows:[135]

> [I]t is well settled that fundamental rights form an integral part of the general principles of law whose observance the Court ensures. For that purpose, the Court draws inspiration from the constitutional traditions common to the Member States and from the guidelines supplied by international treaties for the protection of human rights on which the Member States have collaborated or of which they are signatories. In this regard, the Court has stated that the Convention has special significance.

The last two options are now weighed up against one another. Arguments favouring the option of sub-regional charters (the third option), rather than incorporation of the African Charter (the last option), include the following:
– There could be institutional and practical difficulties in sub-regional groupings acceding to or otherwise incorporating the African Charter. At present only states are parties to the Charter, and no provision is made for accession of institutions other than states.[136] Such a change would require an amendment to the African Charter. The process of adopting sub-regional charters will therefore be much quicker and appears more feasible. However, the treaties of existing sub-regional organisations already leave open the possibility of accession to an instrument such as the African Charter.[137] If the sub-regional Tribunal

---

[134] See e.g. *Nold v Commission* [1974] ECR 491, *Rutili v Minister of the Interior* [1975] ECR 1219, and *Hauer v Land Rheinland-Pfalz* [1979] ECR 37727. See also *Kremzow v Austrian State* [1996] ECR I-2637: "...where national legislation falls within the field of application of Community law the Court, in a reference for a preliminary ruling, must give the national court all the guidance as to interpretation necessary to enable it to assess the compatibility of that legislation with the fundamental rights – as laid down in particular in the Convention – whose observance the Court endures. However, the Court has no such jurisdiction with regard to national legislation lying outside the scope of Community law" (par. 15).

[135] Opinion 2/94 (Accession by the Communities to the Convention for the Protection of Human Rights and Fundamental Freedoms) [1996] ECR I-1759, par. 33.

[136] In terms of art. 63(1) of the Charter.

[137] See e.g. art. 84(1) of the 1993 ECOWAS Treaty, which provides that member states may "among themselves" conclude agreements with other international organisations, provided that the agreement is not incompatible with the provisions of the Treaty. See also art. 24(1) of the SADC Treaty.

may adjudicate individual complaints, it remains likely that individual complainants will still have to present their communications first to the African Commission, before the may approach the Court.
- The protection granted by the African Charter has been criticised as insufficient, especially due to the inclusion of "claw-back" clauses.[138] It seems quite likely that at least some sub-regional groupings, such as SADC, could create a higher human rights standard. Unlike Europe, where a "European Community Convention on Human Rights" would merely restate the European Convention on Human Rights, such sub-regional conventions would not be superfluous in Africa, but are likely to have a significant impact.
- In fact, the sub-regional human rights instruments could be utilised as a basis for addressing the shortcomings of the African Charter. Once the different sub-regional economic regimes integrate, the higher level of protection will be a *fait accompli*. If *this would be the case* in different regions, pressure will be exerted to adopt amendments to the African Charter at the stage of greater integration.

Some arguments in support of incorporating the African Charter, rather than the adoption of separate sub-regional instruments, are as follows:
- Sub-regional human rights standards will only enhance and accentuate differences. It would be preferable that one common standard, based on the African Charter, starts evolving. Setting up new regimes would be divisive, and contrary to the movement towards African unity. These differences may be so great that once the AEC is established, they have become unbridgeable.
- The option of creating new charters will take time and effort, requiring the member states to agree on a common standard. This may be difficult. Regions should rather opt for a charter already agreed upon, in fact ratified by just about all African states, and that has reached a degree of familiarity.
- The argument that sub-regional charters can raise the human rights standard set out in the African Charter may be correct, but the same aim can be attained if the African Charter is interpreted and applied creatively by activist regional "economic" courts.
- Once an African Court of Human Rights has been established, the functions of the sub-regional courts will be fulfilled by the AEC Court of

---

[138] See e.g. art. 10 of the Charter, which provides that every individual has the right to free association "provided that he abides by the law".

Justice. If both would adjudicate on the basis of the African Charter, a cohesive jurisprudence will develop, each with its own focus. This will lead to cross-fertilisation and will strengthen both institutions. No human rights charter is provided for in the Abuja Treaty. Neither is accession to or another form of incorporation of the African Charter by the Court of Justice an explicit possibility. Once the African Court of Justice starts functioning, the easiest would be to accede to the African Charter if the different sub-regional institutions had by then already done so.

V CONCLUSION

The historical review of sub-regional courts undertaken here shows that a close link exists between the political success of a regional body and the viability of courts established under its auspices. The success of institutions established sub-regionally depends on the existence of an effective and functional political structure and viable infrastructure.[139] Human rights issues have not featured prominently on the agenda of modern sub-regional organisations in Africa. Predictably, these organisations have concerned themselves more with economic matters and regional unity. Promising developments have been taking place in SADC and COMESA, the most recently established of the sub-regional groupings. SADC has the most expansive human rights-related mandate. This may perhaps be explained with reference to the fact that the countries in Southern Africa have suffered denials of human rights for a longer period than other African countries. Playing an almost inevitable hegemonic role in the region, the democratic South Africa has reinforced concerns for human rights within SADC. This region has already started to (and is best positioned to) produce a sub-regional human rights jurisprudence. The notion of human rights is given a much more important position in the amended ECOWAS Treaty of 1993 than in the original 1975 Treaty. It remains to be seen whether these changes are largely cosmetic responses, occasioned by the rhetorical demands of international relations, or whether human rights concerns will be integrated meaningfully within the activities of ECOWAS. Although each of these institutions provides for judicialised conflict resolution, such methods were almost uniformly absent from the activities of the organisation or were ineffectual.

---

[139] See Heiman, *op. cit.*, p.639.

Three feasible options for the improvement of regional human rights are open to sub-regional institutions: using the existing treaty to improve human rights protection, the adoption of independent sub-regional human rights charters, or incorporation of the African Charter into sub-regional treaties. Each of these possible courses has its advantages and disadvantages. Accepting one of the options will enhance the movement towards economic, legal and political unity already underway in Africa. Economic and political liberalisation should go hand in hand in the process of regional integration. Constitutional reform at the regional level must include an effective human rights framework in which democratic governance can be ensured at both national and supra-national levels. Sub-regional institutions should incorporate serious concern for human rights into their mandates without delay.

One of the major disadvantages of creating separate human rights conventions and institutions in each sub-region is that such a development would undermine efforts that are already underway to establish an African Court of Human and Peoples' Rights. Separate institutions will tend to develop a "life of their own", and may become obstacles in the process of greater regional integration, also in the field of human rights.

Accession to the African Charter by the existing sub-regional organisations as soon as possible will ensure improved protection in the interim before an African Court of Human and Peoples' Rights starts functioning. Once this Court is created, the sub-regional tribunals should surrender their human rights jurisdiction to the African Court. This will be in line with the process of regional integration envisaged in the Treaty establishing the African Economic Community. The main problem with this proposed course of action is that the African Charter will have to be amended to create this possibility. However, the prescribed procedure is not very burdensome.[140] Moreover, the opportunity may be used to review other aspects of the Charter, as well something that is long overdue.

The extension of the present sub-regional treaties to include human rights seems the most feasible option on the short term. Many aspects dealt with in each of the sub-regional treaties have human rights implications. Human rights should form an integral part of the general principles of each of the sub-regional legal systems.[141] The fact that all the member states of ECOWAS, SADC, COMESA and the Maghreb Arab Union are also parties

---

[140] See art. 68 of the Charter: a simple majority may approve an amendment.
[141] This could be ensured by making the existence of a democratic system of government and observance of human rights criteria for admission to membership of the sub-regional organisation. In this regard, it seems that the admission of the Democratic Republic of Congo (DRC) was premature.

to the African Charter implies that the judicial institutions of each of these organisations could draw inspiration from a common constitutional tradition on human rights. Whichever alternative is followed, the sub-regional institutions in Africa should take decisive steps to incorporate human rights concerns meaningfully into their mandates. Sub-regional structures are already in place and function at a level closest to individual Africans. The success of the project to realise human rights in Africa depends on efforts at this level as much as on efforts at the domestic and regional levels.

NOTES AND COMMENTS
NOTES ET COMMENTAIRES

THE 51ST SESSION OF THE UNITED NATIONS INTERNATIONAL LAW COMMISSION

James L. Kateka*

The International Law Commission held its fifty-first session in Geneva from 3rd May to 23rd July, 1999. The Commission elected Professor Zdzislaw Galicki of Poland the chairman of the session. The agenda of the session included the following items:- 1) Filling of casual vacancies[1] 2) Organization of work of the session 3) State responsibility 4) International Liability for injurious consequences arising out of acts not prohibited by international law (prevention of transboundary damage from hazardous activities) 5) Reservations to treaties 6) Nationality in relation to the succession of states 7) Diplomatic protection 8) Unilateral acts of States 9) Jurisdictional immunities of states and their property 10) Programme, procedures and working methods of the Commission and its documentation 11) cooperation with other bodies 12) Date and place of the fifty-second session 13) Other business. This article will deal with the substantive items.

---

*   LL.B(E.A), LL.M.(Lond.), Member of the International Law Commission. The views expressed in this article are those of the author and do not in any way represent those of the Government of Tanzania which he serves as Ambassador to Sweden.

[1] At its 2565th meeting on 3 May, 1999, the Commission elected Mr. Giorgio Gaja (Italy), Mr. Maurice Kamto (Cameroon) and Mr. Peter Tomka (Slovakia) to fill the three casual vacancies caused by the election of Mr. Luigi Ferrari – Bravo to the European court of Human Rights, of Mr. Mohammed Bennouna to the international Criminal Tribunal for the Former Yugoslavia and of the appointment of Mr. Vaclav Mikulka as Director of the codification Division, Office of Legal Affairs of the United Nations.

The Commission lost one of its most distinguished members, Mr. Doudou Thiam who passed away in Geneva on 6 July. Mr. Thiam was a former Chairman of the Commission who had also served as Special Rapporteur on the topic "Draft Code of Crimes against the peace and security of mankind". Mr. Thiam will greatly be missed. He was an eminent jurist who served Senegal, Africa and the international community superbly.

NATIONALITY IN RELATION TO THE SUCCESSION OF STATES

At the 51st session, the Commission had before it a Memorandum by the Secretariat[2] containing an overview of the comments and observations of governments, made either in writing or orally in the sixth committee. It will be recalled that at its 49th session (1997), the Commission adopted on first reading a draft preamble and a set of 27 draft articles on nationality of natural persons in relation to the succession of states.[3] A working Group was re-established by the Commission at the 51st session to review the text adopted on first reading taking into account comments by Governments. On the basis of the report of the Chairman of the Working Group,[4] the Commission referred the preamble and draft articles on the topic to the Drafting Committee. On the basis of the Drafting Committee report, the Commission adopted the draft preamble and the set of 26 draft articles on second reading and decided to recommend to the General Assembly their adoption in the form of a declaration. Article 19 from the first reading was deleted.

There was no substantive change in the draft articles from those adopted on the first reading. Rationalisation and reorganisation of the draft articles was done. These draft articles were adopted with commentaries. Article 1 is the very foundation of the draft articles.[5] It establishes the right to a nationality. Article 15 of the Universal Declaration of Human Rights embodying the "right of everyone to a nationality" is cited in the commentary as the first international instrument to this end. But in the context of article 3 on the draft articles applying only to the effects of a succession of states occurring in conformity with international law, there was disagreement. This controversy concerned the commentary[6] where the Commission stresses that article 3 is without prejudice to the "right of everyone to a nationality in accordance with article 15 of the Universal Declaration of Human Rights.[7]

The right of option is entrenched in article 11. The will of persons concerned has to be considered by states; each state has to grant the right to opt for its nationality to persons concerned with appropriate connection with that state. Some members suggested the deletion of article 12 on unity of a

---

[2] Document A/CN.4/497.
[3] Official Records of the General Assembly, Fifty-second session supplement No. 10 (A/52/10) Chap. IV.
[4] Doc. A/CN.4/2.572.
[5] see commentary to article 1.
[6] To article 3, paragraph 3.
[7] The commission took an indicative vote when adopting this particular provision of the commentary.

family because of different concepts of a family. Article 14 on status of habitual residence has the purpose to guarantee residence in a successor state. There was a suggestion to delete the phraseology[8] in article 8(2) which would impose nationality on a person against his will.

Even though the Commission recommended the adoption of the draft article on nationality in the form of a declaration, there were some members who would have preferred the adoption of a binding instrument. The Commission also, taking into account the conclusion of the Working Group, recommended to the General Assembly that in the absence of comments from states on the nationality of legal persons in relation to the succession of states, the work of the Commission on the topic of "Nationality in relation to the succession of States" be considered concluded.

STATE RESPONSIBILITY

The topic of state responsibility has been on the agenda of the commission since the first session. Five Special Rapporteurs have dealt with the topic. At the 51st session the commission considered chapters III, IV and V of part one of the second report of the Special Rapporteur, Professor James Crawford. It also held a general discussion on countermeasures.[10]

Chapter III related to "Breach of an International Obligation". The Chapter elaborates on the basic principle set out in article 3, already provisionally adopted by the Commission.[11] The Special Rapporteur acknowledges that Chapter III was the one most criticised by governments and commentators acknowledged the value of much of the articles which were adopted more than 20 years ago. He considered the distinction[12] between primary

---

8 "unless they would otherwise become stateless".
9 Doc. A/CN.4/498 and Add 1-4.
10 A/CN.4/498/Add4.
11 Entitled "Elements of an Internationally wrongful act of a state"
 There is an internationally wrongful act of a state when conduct consisting of an action or omission:
 a) is attributable to the state under international law, and;
 b) constitutes a breach of an international obligation of the state.
12 During the debate in the Commission, it was noted that the difficulty lay in the lack of an agreed definition of the distinction. The report state that the draft articles assumed the existence of primary obligations generated by international law processes of treaty making, and of law making generally but the draft articles concerned themselves with the secondary obligation which arose when a state breaches or failed to comply with the obligation.

and secondary rules and the relationship between chapters I, III, IV and V of part one.[13] Members of the Commission commended the Special Rapporteur for his effort of tidying-up Chapter III.[14] The chapter was considered in groups. Group I comprised articles 16, 17 18(1) and 19(2).

The Special Rapporteur proposed an article 16 on the existence of a breach of an international obligation. He proposed that there was breach of such obligation by a state when its act does not comply with what is required of it under international law by that obligation regardless of the source.[15] Article 16, according to the Special Rapporteur, was not problematic but it concealed some underlying problems including conflicting international obligations[16] and the relationship between wrongfulness and responsibility. It was decided to merge article 16, 17(1) and 19(1). Article 17(1) stated that a breach of an international obligation by a state is an internationally wrongful act regardless of the origin, whether customary, conventional or other, of that obligation. Article 19(1) dealt with the distinction between international delicts and international crimes of state. Article 17(2) was seen as superfluous and was deleted by the commission.

The requirement in article 18 that the international obligation be in force for the state, was discussed by the commission which decided to delete article 18(2) [17] which could be considered in chapter V. Article 18(3) to 5 which dealt with intertemporal issues associated with continuing composite and complex acts were transferred to other articles. Only article 18(1) was retained in a reformulated article 18 which was adopted by the Drafting Committee.[18] It states the basic principle of the intertemporal law as it applies to state responsibility i.e. whether the obligation was in force at the relevant time.[19]

---

[13] He finds them disconnected in comparison with chapters II and III, which were linked by the basic principle set forth in article 3.
[14] One member called the report "a magnificent piece of work".
[15] The article which was adopted by the Drafting Committee and taken note of by the commission reads: "There is a breach of an international obligation by a state when an act of that state is not in conformity with what is required of it by that obligation, regardless of its origin or character".
[16] It was said that three categories of rules had a hierarchically higher status than did the normal rules of international law. This hierarchy includes a) obligations under article 103 of the UN Charter b) jus cogens rules c) concept of international crimes, which category was disputed by some members.
[17] which dealt with the impact of peremptory norms on state responsibility.
[18] Based on a text by the Special Rapporteur, the Drafting committee adopted: "An act of a state shall not be considered a breach of an international obligation unless the state is bound by the obligation in question at the time the act occurs".
[19] see page 65 of Doc. A/CN.4/498.

Group II articles of Chapter III (articles 20, 21 and 23) generated considerable controversy during the discussion. The distinction between obligations[20] of conduct and obligations of result was the focus of the debate. The Special Rapporteur considered obligations of conduct as in the nature of "best efforts obligations" such as those of a doctor to a patient whereas obligations of result were tantamount to guarantees of outcome e.g. a construction engineer building a bridge.[21]

The distinction had gained currency in international law.[22] The Special Rapporteur notes that in invoking what was originally a civil law distinction,[23] the draft articles by Roberto Ago[24] have nearly reversed the effect. Whereas in French law, an obligation of conduct was the less stringent, under Ago's draft (articles 20 and 21), the obligation of conduct was considered more stringent. In the view of the Special Rapporteur, the distinction had no consequences in terms of the rest of the draft articles and could therefore be deleted.[25]

During the debate in the commission, some members supported the retention of the distinction. It was even argued that the distinction was of particular value to developing countries which did not all have equal means at their disposal to achieve the result required of them. It was further argued that the commission should not throw out the achievements of the past.

Although there was a significant minority for the retention of the distinction, the commission decided to delete it. The substance of the draft article would be incorporated in the commentary which would explain the reasons for the deletion.[26]

The third group of chapter III comprises articles 18(3) to (5) and 24 to 26. They deal with different aspects of the problem of wrongful acts contin-

---

[20] The concepts derive from civil law systems, in particular from French law.
[21] Obligations of conduct (sometimes called obligations of means) while they have some purpose or result in mind, determine with precision, the means to be adopted. By contrast, obligations of result do not do so, leaving it to the state party to determine the means to be used (paragraph 57 of doc.A/CN.4/498).
[22] The Special Rapporteur cites international case law, including the ELSI case. (ICJ Reports, 1989) where Judge Schwebel, in his dissenting opinion, invokes the distinction.
[23] Even those writers familiar with the distinction as it is drawn in civil law systems have serious doubts as to its usefulness in the draft articles.
[24] Second Special Rapporteur on State Responsibility.
[25] It was unlike the distinction between continuing and completed violations which did have important consequences in that breaches in the former category gave rise, inter alia, to the obligation of cessation.
[26] Including article 23 on breach of an international obligation to prevent a given event.

uing in time.[27] Articles 24, 25 and 26 as originally proposed by Ago dealt (respectively) with a) moment and duration of the breach of an international obligation of an act of the state not extending in time b) moment and duration of the breach extending in time c) moment and duration of the breach of an international obligation to prevent a given event. The Special Rapporteur, in a revised article 24 (entitled completed and continuing acts), combined the essential elements of articles 24, 25(1) and 26 together with Article 18(3) from the Ago draft. He proposed deletion of the word "moment" from the text because so called "instantaneous" acts are rarely momentary.[28]

According to the commentaries,[29] examples of a breach of an international obligation not extending in time – i.e. an act that ends as soon as it is committed – include anti-aircraft defence units of one state shooting down an aircraft lawfully flying over that country's territory; the police of one state killing or wounding the representative of another state; organs of a state confiscating the building in which a foreign diplomatic mission has its headquarters.

Two elements which were in Ago's draft article 25 involved "composite" and "complex" acts. The Special Rapporteur, citing the commentary to article 25 distinguished i) a "continuing act" as one which proceeds unchanged over a given period[30] ii) A "composite" act is an act of the state composed of a series of individual acts of the state committed in connection with different matters.[31] iii) a "complex" act is an act of the state made up of a succession of actions or emissions in connection with one and the same matter.[32]

The Special Rapporteur was of the view that the distinction between "composite" and "complex" acts was not helpful.[33] The question to be

---

[27] They deal with the issues of the moment and duration of the breach of an international obligation.
[28] The drafting committee reinstated "moment" in its revised article 24.
[29] See consolidated text of January 1997 as prepared by the Secretariat.
[30] See para 95 of Doc A/CN.4/498 – in other words, a continuing act is one after its occurrence, continues to exist as such and not merely in its effects and consequences.
[31] It consists of a series of individual acts of the state succeeding each other in time adopted in separate case, but all contributing to the commission of the aggregate act in question. Examples include a series administrative decisions adversely affecting nationals of a particular state which establishes a pattern of discrimination, or a refusal to allow those nationals to participate in economic activity, contrary to an international obligation of the host state.
[32] A classic example is denial of justice to an alien.
[33] During the debate, it was queried when the first action or omission constituting the composite act occurred. The Special Rapporteur replied that it would take sometime to occur. Genocide was cited as a pattern. But its duration lasts from the first act.

answered was whether or not a breach had occurred.[34] However, he was of the view that the distinction between a completed act and a continuing one was far more relevant and should be retained. As for obligations of prevention, the Special Rapporteur pointed out that article 26 incorrectly treated breaches of such obligations as necessarily being continuing wrongful acts.[35] In the end, the commission decided to delete "complex acts" from the draft article, although some of the discussion should be retained in the commentary.[36]

Regarding Chapter IV of Part I originally entitled "Implication of a state in the internationally wrongful act of another state", the Special Rapporteur proposed a new title reading "Responsibility of a state for the acts of another state". As to the general approach to Chapter IV, there were more proponents than opponents in the commission. Some argued that article 27 dealt with primary rules[37] and should be deleted. But the majority supported the retention of the two articles.[38] It was pointed out that no Government had argued for the complete deletion of Chapter IV.[39]

Concerning article 27, the Special Rapporteur introduced the element of "knowledge" of the internationally wrongful act regarding complicity by another state in aiding or assisting a state in committing the act.[40] The commentary from the first reading excludes "incitement" of one state by another (to commit an internationally wrongful act) from acts which can be characterised as "participation". The commentary cites example most frequently mentioned concerning "complicity" (aid or assistance) as including i) a state placing its territory at the disposal of another state to make it possible (or

---

[34] The case concerning the Gabcikovo/Nagymaros Project, ICJ Reports 1997, p.7 was cited.

[35] Some breaches of obligations of prevention might be continuing acts but others not, depending on the context. Former article 26 has been incorporated in article 24(3) of the text adopted by the Drafting Committee.

[36] Article 26 bis on the exhaustion of local remedies (article 22 as adopted on first reaching), was retained as a "without prejudice" clause pending consideration of its placement in chapter III or in a new projected Part Three on implementation (mise-en-oeuvre) of responsibility.

[37] on aid or assistance by a state to another state for the commission of an internationally wrongful act. Some said that the distinction between primary and secondary rules was artificial.

[38] In its original form, article 28 concerned responsibility of a state for an internationally wrongful act of another state. As revised by the Special Rapporteur, it concerns responsibility of a state for coercion of another state.

[39] One member was against deletion "because this is a complicated world". Another cited the involvement of several states in the African Great Lakes conflict as justifying usefulness of the article.

[40] See doc A/CN.4/498/Add 1 p.21.

easier) for the latter to commit an offence against a third state (or a third subject of international law) ii) where a state supplies another with weapons to attack a third state. In the final draft article which was adopted by the Drafting committee, there was a separation of the situation of "aids or assists" from the situation of a state which "directs and controls"[41] another state in the commission of an internationally wrongful act. The element of knowledge was retained in both situations.

The third situation of "coercion" is contained in article 28. The Special Rapporteur proposed a new text.[42] The draft treads on "coercion", leading to one asking what is unlawful coercion. It was suggested that the nature and scope of coercion should be defined.[43] Responsibility arises where the act would, but for the coercion, be an internationally wrongful act of the coerced state and the coercing state does so with knowledge of the circumstances[44] of the act.[45] A "without prejudice" clause is introduced in article 28 bis[46] which preserves the international responsibility of the state which has committed the internationally wrongful act. Chapter V of Part one concerns "Circumstances precluding wrongfulness". As adopted from the first reading, six circumstances were covered, namely, consent (article 29), countermeasures (article 30), force majeure and fortuitous event (article 31), distress (article 32), state of necessity (article 33), and self defence (article 34). In his report, [47] the current Special Rapporteur divided chapter V in two subgroups, namely, i) compliance with a peremptory norm, self defence, countermeasures and the exceptio ii) force majeure distress and necessity, and then by the ancillary clauses. Because the Special Rapporteur acted on the assumption that the circumstance of "consent" would be deleted, we will consider the six circumstances as adopted on first reading.

When introducing his report in the Commission, the Special Rapporteur said that Chapter V contains difficult but important provisions which act as "justification" and as "excuses" for states in order to preclude wrongfulness.

---

[41] See new article 27 bis.
[42] Which deletes "Subject to the power of direction or control of another state" from the Ago text of the first reading.
[43] It was said that the term was not to be confined to the use of armed force, but could also include economic pressure of a severe kind. It was also unclear whether all reprisals and countermeasures could be included in the meaning of coercion. It was observed that "countermeasures" were "lawful coercion".
[44] To situations and not judgement of the legality.
[45] The Special Rapporteur agreed that "directs and controls" was closer to coercion than "aids or assists".
[46] The same savings clause would be appropriate for article 27.
[47] Doc. A/CN.4/498/Add 2, paragraph 355.

He said that no government had doubted the need for chapter V which had been extensively referred to in the literature and in case law.[48]

The Special Rapporteur had recommended the deletion of article 29 on consent.[49] But a majority of the members favoured its retention. From the commentary to article 29, it was evident that the article concerned only consent given in advance of the act. Ex *post facto* consent was an example of waiver, which was not a matter for part one. An example of consent is consent validly given for overflight over territory. According to the Special Rapporteur, there were some obligations which could not be dispensed with – they applied irrespective of consent e.g. compliance with non-derogable human rights and norms of *jus cogens*.

As to whether the maxim *volenti non fit injuria*[50] applies to international law, the Special Rapporteur gives a qualified affirmative answer to the question. The maxim should thus be reflected in Chapter V. Some members expressed fear that consent can be abused by the powerful states as was the case in the Congo in the 1960s.

Article 29 *bis* on compliance with a peremptory norm (jus cogens)[51] was taken by the Special Rapporteur from article 29(2) of the Ago text. The Special Rapporteur notes that a peremptory norm has the effect of excusing non-compliance with an obligation in those rare – but nonetheless conceivable – circumstances where an international obligation, not itself peremptory in character, is overridden by an obligation which is peremptory.[52] The drafting committee adopted a text which the commission took note of.[53]

The Special Rapporteur proposed an article 29 on self defence which uses the text of the draft article[54] provisionally adopted on first reading. This

---

[48] e.g. Case concerning the Gabcikovo-Nagymaros Project ICJ Reports 1997, p.7. Hungary had relied on the state of necessity, in purporting to terminate the 1977 treaty with Czechoslovakia. It invoked necessity as a circumstance precluding the wrongfulness of its conduct in discontinuing work on the project. The court rejected the argument.

[49] In his view, it seemed better to conceptualize consent given in advance as something which the primary rule permitted.

[50] from municipal law.

[51] see article 53 of the 1969 Vienna Convention on the Law of Treaties which defines it as a norm from which no derogation is permitted other than by a subsequent norm of the same status.

[52] He gives the example of a right of transit or passage across territory which could not be invoked if the immediate purpose of exercising the right was unlawfully to attack the territory of a third state.

[53] Article 29 *bis*: The wrongfulness of an act of a state is precluded if the act is required in the circumstances by a peremptory norm of general international law.

[54] On self defence; it covers the concept in article 51 of the UN Charter.

text was adopted by the Drafting committee. It states that the wrongfulness of an act of a state is precluded if the act constitutes a lawful measure of self-defence taken in conformity with the Charter of the United Nations. The commentary to the article observes that by its very nature, self defence involves the use of armed force. However, certain obligations such as international humanitarian law and non-derogable human rights, already referred to above cannot be infringed upon. Some members of the Commission were of the view that the law of self defence is not based on the UN Charter. It was contended that the Charter does not confer the right of self defence but merely recognizes it as inherent. Others were of the view that the article on self defence should be confined to the provisions of the Charter of the United Nations.[55]

A second paragraph was added by the Special Rapporteur to the article on self defence. It adopts the language of the International Court of Justice in the advisory opinion concerning the Threat or Use of Nuclear Weapons.[56] It was meant to cover unbreachable obligations. In the end, the provision may have to be reflected in the commentary rather in draft articles.

Article 30 on countermeasures[57] was set aside pending a decision by the commission on Chapter III of Part two which deals with the regime of countermeasures.[58] It was stressed that armed reprisals are prohibited as a countermeasure. The article will be taken up in year 2000 after consideration, by the Commission of substantive provisions on countermeasures. The decision to retain an article on countermeasures in Chapter V was however taken.

The Commission further considered the treatment of countermeasures in the draft article when it debated the Special Rapporteur's second report, addendum 4.[59] When introducing the addendum, the Special Rapporteur

---

[55] Thus only the inherent right of individual or collective self defence set out in article 51 of the Charter should be envisaged.
[56] ICJ Reports 1996 at p. 242 (para 30). It had been argued that nuclear weapons could not be used if their effect was to violate environmental obligations. The court had drawn a distinction between general environmental obligations and environmental obligations specifically intended as a condition of total restraint in time of armed conflict. It was only in the latter case that self defence could not be invoked as a justification.
[57] It precludes the wrongfulness of the act if the act is a legitimate measure under international law.
[58] See article 50 re.prohibited countermeasures: a) the threat or use of force b) extreme economic or political coercion designed to endanger the territorial integrity of a state c) infringement on the inviolability of diplomatic missions and any conduct which derogates from basic human rights.
[59] See A/CN.4/498/Add 4.

drew the Commission's attention to the case concerning the Gabcikovo-Nagymaros Project[60] which for the first time in the court's modern history dealt with the problem of countermeasures. He stated that articles on countermeasures were not yet fully formed. He said issues requiring clarification include a) question of dispute settlement which was vital for countermeasures b) the linkage between countermeasures in part Two and dispute settlement. He wondered why the "target state" or wrongdoing state was entitled to unilaterally force the state taking countermeasures i.e. the injured state to go to compulsory arbitration.[61]

During the debate in the Commission, it was pointed out that equality of treatment between the injured state and the wrongdoing state to arbitrate disputes could be addressed by the Special Rapporteur. The same could be done to problems arising from so called "collective" countermeasures in situations where there are many "injured" states.

The Special Rapporteur, in his report, identified four options open to the Commission with regard to article 30. He preferred option 4 which proposed to deal with countermeasures in Part Two but avoiding any specific linkage with dispute settlement.[62] Some members supported the Special Rapporteur's option while others expressed support for a linkage between countermeasures and compulsory dispute settlement.[63] There was also a proposal for a *Part Two bis*, on implementation [64] which the Special Rapporteur expressed particular interest in. The Special Rappoorteur also proposed an article *30 bis* on the maxim exceptio inadimpleti contractus (referred to as "the *exceptio*" (non-compliance caused by prior non-compliance). The precise formulation will be assessed only when the articles on countermeasures have been formulated.

The Special Rapporteur deleted reference to "fortuitous event" in article 31 on force majeure which concerns situations of grave and imminent danger to the state and its vital interests.[65] Also reference to knowledge of

---

60 See footnote 34 supra.

61 Why limit this right to the wrongdoing state.

62 During the debate it was noted by some, that international dispute settlement mechanisms are too time consuming to be linked to countermeasures, and may lead to abuse in the form of delaying tactics by the target state (the writer is of the view that those at the receiving end, are usually small vulnerable states).

63 Option 3 proposes to engage in a substantial treatment of countermeasure in Part Two along the lines of the present text, including the linkage with dispute settlement.

64 Which could include the admissibility of claims, countermeasures and collective measures.

65 The Special Rapporteur had proposed a provision reading "For the purpose of this article, force majeure is the occurrence of an irresistible force or an unforeseen external event beyond the control of the state making it materially impossible in the circumstance to perform the obligation".

wrongfulness was deleted by the Special Rapporteur because it added a confusing subjective element which appeared to contradict the principle that ignorance of wrongfulness (i.e. ignorance of the law) is not an excuse. During the debate, there was a complaint that there was no reference to "due diligence" standard.[66] The Special Rapporteur said that as formulated article 31 was irrelevant to "due diligence" standard.[67] The element of the state assuming the "risk of that occurrence" has been added. Some members doubted the propriety of this addition.

Article 32 is on distress[68] and applies where somebody has responsibility for someone else's life. The Special Rapporteur proposed a limited application to "distress". In particular, it is suggested that cases of distress should be confined to ships or aircraft entering a state because of bad weather, mechanical or navigational failure.[69] The requirement that distress be "extreme" was deleted by the Special Rapporteur and was accepted by the Commission.

Article 33 is on "State of necessity" and is regarded as one of the most controversial articles. The Special Rapporteur observed that it could be invoked in extreme cases and to that extent it was comparable to the notion of a "fundamental change of circumstances" in the law of treaties. The International Court of Justice expressly endorsed "necessity" as a statement of general international law in the Gabcikovo – Nagymaros Project case. It would thus be unwise for the Commission to reverse the principle. As to whether "humanitarian intervention" using force was covered by article 33, the Special Rapporteur answered in the negative.[70]

Appropriate circumstances for invoking necessity are when the act is the only means for the state to safeguard an essential interest against a grave and imminent peril such as in the *Torrey Canyon* incident[71]

---

[66] which some members said should be reflected in all articles.

[67] see below regarding consideration of transboundary damage from hazardous activities.

[68] The commentary describes "distress" as a situation of extreme peril in which the organ of the state which adapts that conduct has, at that particular moment, no means of saving himself or persons entrusted to his care other than to act in a manner not in conformity with the requirements of the obligation in question. Distress is a situation of "relative impossibility" whereas force majeure is a case of "material or absolute impossibility".

[69] some members doubted the suggestion of extending "distress" to the case of a serious health risk.

[70] There had been abuses. The Belgian government in 1960 invoked a "situation of absolute necessity" to despatch parachutists to the Congo to protect the lives of Belgian nationals and other Europeans allegedly being held as hostages.

[71] cmnd. 3246 (London HMSO 1967). A Liberian tanker in 1967 went aground off the British coast spilling 60,000 of its 117,000 tons of crude oil. The British government bombed the ship in order to burn the oil remaining on board. Thus it was lawful because of necessity.

The Special Rapporteur has proposed "Procedure for invoking a circumstance precluding wrongfulness", in article *34 bis*. The Drafting Committee will revert to this article after the Commission's consideration of the question of countermeasures in Part 2, as well as dispute settlement. The Drafting Committee also adopted article 35 on consequences of invoking a circumstance precluding wrongfulness. The Special Rapporteur had proposed limiting compensation to distress and state of necessity. But the Commission disagreed with the limitation.

In concluding this part on state responsibility, the writer is of the view that the Special Rapporteur on the topic has adopted a subtle approach in his second reading. He has "cleared" articles by "pruning" them. He will then deal with the controversial issues such as article 19, countermeasures and dispute settlement. Concern has been expressed that an attempt to rewrite anew the draft articles from the first reading[72] could have a disrupting effect. Some of these articles have already been cited by the Court as reflecting general international law.[73]

RESERVATIONS TO TREATIES

At the 51st session, the Commission had before it part of the Special Rapporteur's third report[74] which it could not consider at its 50th session due to lack of time. It had also before it the fourth report.[75] It will be recalled that at the 50th session, the Commission had provisionally adopted seven draft guidelines with commentaries. At the 51st session, the Commission considered ten guidelines. It also considered a revised version of a draft guideline on statements of non recognition. Three draft guidelines on distinction between reservations and interpretative declarations[76] had been proposed only tentatively by the Special Rapporteur. The Commission was of the view that the criteria[77] was already inherent in the definitions and the three draft guidelines would merely repeat them or overlap them without adding a new element. Thus the Commission decided not to refer them to the Drafting Committee but to reflect their content in the relevant commentaries to draft guidelines on the issue.

---

[72] The "ghost" of Roberto Ago has been exorcised from the revised articles.
[73] See supra.
[74] Doc.A/CN.4/491 Add 3 to Add 6.
[75] A/CN.4/499.
[76] appearing in the third report op.cit.
[77] stemming from the general definition of reservations and interpretative declarations.

The Commission adopted on first reading 18 draft guidelines with commentaries relating thereto. The texts incorporate revised versions of guidelines which had been adopted at the 50th session.[78] This is part of a Guide to practice in respect of reservations to treaties which the Commission is formulating in the form of draft guidelines with commentaries.

Among the guidelines which raised controversy were the one on "conditional interpretative declarations.[79] Some members considered the text to be a disguised reservation.[80] In his report, the Special Rapporteur raised a series of questions:[81] -"does the declaration have the effect of excluding or modifying the legal effect of the provisions of a treaty? if the answer to this (objective) question is positive, one need go no further – the declaration is a reservation. It is only when the answer is negative that one needs ask a second (subjective) question:- does the proposed interpretation constitute, for the declarant, a condition of his participation".

Another controversial guideline[82] was on statements concerning modalities of implementation of a treaty at the internal level. This is the so called "informative declaration" which is particularly developed in the United States. Some members doubted the utility of a guideline on informative declarations which are of interest domestically and irrelevant concerning international obligations of the state in question.[83] It was suggested to put this issue under the guideline on "other declarations". Some members saw this guideline as of academic interest and would not help decision makers. In the end, it was retained with clarifications in the commentary.

Reservations to bilateral treaties was another controversial issue. The 1969 and 1986 Vienna Conventions are silent on the subject. The 1978

---

[78] A new version of the draft guideline on "definition of reservations" and on "scope of definitions" was adopted.

[79] It contains a temporal element of time when a state expresses its consent to be bound.

[80] The Special Rapporteur, Alain Pellet countered by saying that a "disguised reservation" is a reservation whereas "conditional interpretative declaration" is not.

[81] see para 398 of Add 4 op cit – not the so called double test.

[82] see guideline 1.4.5[1.2.6].

[83] see the famous declaration known as the "Niagara reservation" concerning a 1950 treaty between the USA and Canada regarding the Niagara river. The USA senate used this to give its advice and consent to the treaty's ratification -"The United States on its part expressly reserves the right to provide by Act of Congress for redevelopment, for the public use and benefit, of the United States of the waters of the Niagara River made available by the provisions of the treaty, and no project for redevelopment of the United States share of such waters shall be undertaken until it be specifically authorised by Act of Congress" – para 510 of Add.5 – op cit.

Convention on Succession of states in respect of Treaties explicitly contemplates only reservations to multilateral treaties. In spite of the inconclusive and ambiguous nature of the travaux preparatoires of the Vienna Conventions of 1969, 1978 and 1986, the Special Rapporteur concludes that the Vienna regime is not applicable to reservations to bilateral treaties.[84]

The Special Rapporteur stated in his report that reservations in respect of bilateral treaties was "geographically circumscribed".[85] Some members wondered why "universalize" a limited practice. The majority of states do not formulate reservations to bilateral treaties. The view was expressed that reservations to bilateral treaties could amount to bad faith in international relations. It was also a misnomer.[86] The Special Rapporteur rejected suggestions of a "hybrid" in bilateral treaty reservations. He clarified that the acceptance of a reservation to a multilateral treaty modifies the *effects* of the treaty whereas acceptance of a bilateral reservation modifies the treaty. And there the issue rests, with three guidelines adopted.

Statements of non recognition were also controversial. The Special Rapporteur in his third report[87] had proposed a guideline that statements of non recognition amounted to a reservation.[88] Then in his fourth report[89] the Special Rapporteur reversed his position and proposed to the Commission that a unilateral statement of non recognition "does not constitute either a reservation or an interpretative declaration, even if it purports to exclude the application of the treaty between the declaring state and the non recognized entity". He adds that such declarations do not concern the application of the treaty, but rather deny an entity the capacity to be bound by the treaty. While it is wise for one to change one's mind, some members expressed disappointment at the Special Rapporteur's change of mind.[90]

---

[84] see Add 5 op.cit.
[85] Mainly practised by the USA. The USA believes the practice to be important where bilateral treaties (such as extradition, commerce and friendship) are concerned. Between 1795 and 1990, 115 bilateral treaties were subject of "reservations" by USA.
[86] Judge Roberto Ago stated that he had been taught in law school that the idea of reservations to bilateral treaties was a contradiction in terms. Sir Humphrey Waldock wrote as Special Rapporteur on the law of treaties that the notion of a reservation to a bilateral treaty was legally somewhat meaningless.
[87] A/CN.4/491/Add 3 paragraph 168 to 181.
[88] "A unilateral statement by which a state purports to exclude the application of a treaty between itself and one or more other states which it does not recognize constitutes a reservation, regardless of the date on which it is made".
[89] paras 44 to 54 on reconsideration of the draft guideline relating to "statements of non recognition".
[90] The Special Rapporteur was irritated by remarks that he had made a u-turn.

The Commission has covered considerable ground on the topic of reservations to treaties.[91] but it still has a lot of work to do on the topic of reservations to treaties. The fourth report will have six chapters.[92]

UNILATERAL ACTS OF STATES

The Commission considered the Special Rapporteur's second report.[93] The Special Rapporteur took the 1969 Vienna Convention on the Law of Treaties as a fundamental point of reference in considering the topic of unilateral acts. He emphasized that there would be no need to regulate the functioning of unilateral acts which were autonomous[94] or independent acts with their own distinctive characteristics. He distinguished legal acts from political ones in relation to unilateral acts. In this context his report mentioned unilateral declarations by nuclear weapon states containing negative security guarantees in the context of disarmament negotiations. Some members doubted the advisability of the Special Rapporteur giving prominence to such declarations.[95]

The Special Rapporteur proposed seven draft articles[96] on unilateral acts with commentaries. During the discussion, criticism was expressed as regards the parallelism between the proposed draft articles and the 1969 Vienna Convention on the Law of Treaties. Some of the proposed articles followed too closely the provisions of the Vienna Convention. It was gener-

---

[91] At the 49th session, the Commission adopted preliminary conclusions on reservations to normative multilateral treaties, including human rights treaties.

[92] The introduction, Chapter II (Alternatives to reservations), Chapter III (formulation and withdrawal of reservations and interpretative declarations), Chapter IV (formulation of acceptance of reservations), Chapter V (formulation and withdrawal of objections to reservations and interpretative declarations) Chapter VI (Effects of reservations, acceptances and objections – overview).

[93] Doc.A/CN.4/500 and Add 1.
The Special Rapporteur on the topic is Mr. Victor Rodriguez Cedeno.

[94] The Special Rapporteur said that autonomy with regard to rules that an act was carried out whatever the reaction of the addressee.

[95] They saw negative security guarantees as mere political declarations with no legal content. The position of the non aligned countries that such guarantees must take the form of a negotiated and legally binding international instrument was cited.

[96] Article on "scope of the present draft articles" article 2 on the unilateral legal acts of states, article 3 on capacity of states, article 4 on representatives of a state for the purpose of formulating unilateral acts, article 5 on subsequent confirmation of a unilateral act formulated without authorization, article 6 on expression of consent, article 7 on invalidity of unilateral acts.

ally agreed that unilateral acts of international organizations should be excluded from the topic's scope. There was divergence of views concerning the advisability of including *estoppel* within the topic's scope.[97] Acts subject to a special legal regime[98] would be excluded.

It was observed that the debate on the distinction between "legal" and "political" acts was sterile. If acts create obligations, according to this view, then they are legal whatever their form. It was further contended that the distinction was not between legal and political acts, but between acts with legal effect[99] and those with no legal effect.

A Working Group on unilateral acts was re-established. The Working Group agreed on a concept[100] which could be taken by the Commission as the basic focus for the study of the topic. The Working Group's second task was to set the general guidelines according to which the practice of states should be gathered. It was agreed that the Special Rapporteur should elaborate and send to governments, by October 1999, a questionnaire for possible reply within a reasonable deadline. The questionnaire should start from the concept of unilateral acts already elaborated.[101] The third task of the Working Group was to point the direction for future work by the Special Rapporteur. It was agreed that he should continue with the formulation of draft articles as well as with the examination of the specific areas related to the topic such as interpretation, effects and revocability of unilateral acts.

As to the form which the instrument on unilateral acts should take, it was thought to be premature to consider. Possibly one could rule out a convention. A declaration, guidelines or even an expository study were possible forms which were suggested.

---

[97] Two legal traditions: the roman law doctrine of the binding effect of unilateral promises as opposed to the common law tradition which did not recognize such binding effect; the latter had recourse to the doctrine of estoppel as a corollary of the principle of good faith.

[98] These include conventional law, reservations to treaties and declarations accepting the compulsory jurisdiction of the ICJ.

[99] A member wondered whether a state could be freed of obligations created by a unilateral act if other states rejected the act. Another referred to the statement which was made in 1976 by the American Secretary of State, Henry Kissinger, by which USA was ready to finance the parallel system of seabed mining provided the G77 accepted the right for states to mine manganese nodules. This was during the third UN conference on the law of the sea.

[100] "A unilateral statement by a state by which such state intends to produce legal effects in its relations to one or more states or international organizations and which is notified or otherwise made known to the state or organization concerned".

[101] see footnote 99.

INTERNATIONAL LIABILITY FOR INJURIOUS CONSEQUENCES ARISING OUT OF ACTS NOT PROHIBITED BY INTERNATIONAL LAW (PREVENTION OF TRANSBOUNDARY DAMAGE FROM HAZARDOUS ACTIVITIES)

The topic of "International liability" has been on the agenda of the commission since 1978. At its 50th session, the Commission adopted on first reading a set of 17 draft articles on prevention of transboundary damage from hazardous activities. At the 51st session, the Commission had before it the second report of the Special Rapporteur,[102] comprising five sections which include the concept of "due diligence" (section III) and the options with respect to future course of action on the question of liability.

As for the concept of due diligence, the Special Rapporteur stated that the duty of prevention, which is an obligation of conduct, is essentially regarded as a duty of due diligence![103] It is clarified that due diligence is a standard and not a definition. In his first report, the Special Rapporteur stated that "the standard of due diligence could vary from state to state, from region to region and from one point in time to another".[104] He notes the need to give due consideration to the special circumstances and interests of developing countries.[105] In this regard, the Special Rapporteur in his reflections (part B of doc.501) on the implementation of the due diligence obligation, considers various means and methods of enforcement or compliance.

The Special Rapporteur concludes in paragraph 49 that the issue of compliance may be considered to fall outside the realm of the preparation of the draft articles on prevention. He adds that a mandate of the UN General Assembly may be needed to enable the Commission to prepare a separate protocol on compliance.

---

[102] Doc.A/CN.4/501.
[103] para 18 of the second report op cit.
[104] see A/CN.4/487/Add 1, para 112.
[105] some members said this was a "political assertion". But the UN Framework convention on climate change (article 3(1) states that countries have "common but differentiated responsibilities". Eminent scholars also recognise the need to take into account a state's ability when considering due diligence. Professor Dupuy, however while recognizing that the standard of due diligence may vary according to a state's degree of development, emphasizes the minimum rules concerning the attributes of a good government (i.e. one mindful of its international obligations "cannot be the subject of any compromise" – see P. Dupuy "Due Diligence in the International Law of Liability" – OECD Legal Aspects of Transfrontier Pollution (Paris, 1977).

Some members of the commission disagreed with the suggestion by the Special Rapporteur. They were of the view that compliance[106] was relevant to the prevention topic and as such it was unnecessary to seek any further mandate from the General Assembly.

The Special Rapporteur says that the dominant trend among states is still against accepting any concept of strict liability (para 68 of his report).[107] He cites this in connection with his three options (in para 67) for the future course of action on the topic of liability. The majority of the members supported option 2 i.e. for the Commission to suspend its work on the topic of international liability until the regime of prevention is finalised in its second reading. Thus the Commission has to proceed with the topic of international liability in its truncated form.

JURISDICTIONAL IMMUNITIES OF STATES AND THEIR PROPERTY

In 1991, the Commission concluded the second reading of the draft articles on jurisdictional immunities of states and their property. The topic's conclusion was overtaken by developments on the international scene. The demise of the Cold War and the adoption of free market economics by former socialist states meant that some of the concepts needed appraising. Through an open ended working group and informal consultations in the Sixth Committee, outstanding substantive issues related to the draft articles were considered.

Pursuant to a General Assembly resolution,[108] the Commission was entrusted with the task of preparing preliminary comments. At its 51st session, the Commission set up a Working Group which was chaired by Mr. G. Hafner. After an exchange of views, the Commission decided to take note of the report of the Working Group which was annexed to the Commission's

---

[106] prevention as a procedure or duty deals with the phase prior to the situation where significant harm or damage has actually occurred; compliance (or non compliance regime) deals with enforcement of obligations, especially in the field of the environment. If prevention is better than cure, this can be achieved through compliance.
[107] see Philippe Sands "Principles of International Environmental Law," 1995 where he writes that while there is considerable literature and conventions on civil liability, states are unwilling to risk the development or elaboration of state liability rules. "Even non binding instruments have been opposed"
[108] GA resolution 53/98 of 8 December, 1998.

report.[109] The Commission adopted the suggestions of the Working Group.[110]

In the course of discussion, some Commission members expressed concern that the Commission was undertaking a "third reading" of the topic of jurisdictional immunities. This was unprecedented . The view was also expressed that the subject was not fit for a convention because of changes in the international economic environment. Many countries favoured national legislation and would not be amenable to a convention.

MATTERS

The Commission appointed Mr. Christopher J.R. Dugard Special Rapporteur for the topic of "Diplomatic protection". He succeeds Mr. Mohamed Bennouna. The Commission took note of the report of the Planning Group concerning the work programme of the Commission for the remainder of the quinquennium (up to 2001). With the conclusion of the second reading on "Nationality in relation to succession of states", it is expected that the Commission will, (by 2001) complete the second reading of the topics of "State Responsibility" and "International liability for injurious consequences arising out of acts not prohibited by international law (prevention of transboundary damage from hazardous activities)".

The interim report of the Working Group on the long-term programme of Work, identified some topics as appropriate for inclusion.[111] Feasibility studies on various other topics had been carried out. One concerns transnational aspects of corruption which is a topical matter of concern to some members of the Commission.

---

[109] see pages 360 to 419 of supplement No. 10(A/54/10) GA Official Records
[110] In five areas:
    i) concept of state for purpose of immunity;
    i) criteria for determining the commercial character of a contract or transaction;
    iii) concept of a state enterprise or other entity in relation to commercial transactions;
    iv) contracts of employment;
    v) measures of constraint against state property.
[111] see report of the 50th session.
Topics include a) responsibility of international organizations:
    b) the effect of armed conflict on treaties;
    c) shared natural resources (confined groundwater and single geological structures of oil and gas);
    d) expulsion of aliens.

The Commission examined advantages and disadvantages of split sessions. It decided that its next session be split in accordance with its decision taken at the fiftieth session. The split session would be held in Geneva from 1st May to 9th June, and from 10th July to 18th August, 2000.

CONSTITUTIONALISM, CULTURE AND TRADITION: AFRICAN EXPERIENCES ON THE INCORPORATION OF TREATIES INTO DOMESTIC LAW

Dr. A. O. Adede*

I INTRODUCTION: DEMOCRATIC IDEALS IDENTIFIED

During the last ten months, of this historic year of 1999 ending the millenium, any paper discussing the subject of constitutional review in Kenya, one of the African countries in which this is a burning issue, would be considered grossly inadequate if the following expressions did not find prominence in it: "stakeholders"; "the civil society"; "the way forward"; "people-driven" and a "seriously flawed Act".[1]

---

* Chairman & C.E.O. of L'ETWAL INTERNATIONAL: A Foundation for Law and Policy for Contemporary Problems, Nairobi, Kenya. This paper is adapted from a statement delivered by the author at the Sub-regional Conference of African Women Parliamentarians, Nairobi 15th – 17th November 1999.

[1] Reference is to the Constitution of Kenya Review (Amendment) Act, 1998, which actually overhauled the Kenya Constitution Review Act, 1997, that had been kept in abeyance for failure to provide an active role in the review process for women and youth. The Amendment Act, 1998 then created a three-tier review system made up of: A 25-member Constitution of Kenya Review Commission at the top and at the helm; a National Consultative Forum (NCF) in the middle, made up of all members of parliament including the Speaker and the Attorney-General, plus 192 representatives from the 64 districts; and the District Consultative Forum (DCF) at the grassroots. The mandate was "to collect and collate the views of the people of Kenya on proposals to alter the constitution and on the basis thereof, to draft a Bill to alter the constitution for presentation to the National Assembly". The implementation of this Act has since been stalled, triggered by the lack of agreement on how to constitute the 25-member Review Commission, owing to what has now been generally termed "serious flaws" in the Act itself. Detailed and systematic studies on the Kenya review process, when completed, would be most illuminating as can be seen from the backdrop it is designed to provide to the present analysis of the problems of constitutionalism in Africa. *See* also note 22, *infra*.

A.A. Yusuf (ed.), African Yearbook of International Law, 239-253.
© *2001 African Association of International Law. Printed in the Netherlands.*

This paper will, nevertheless, run the risk and take the consequences of the decision not to make those expressions the centerpiece in the ensuing analysis, except as absolutely necessary and unavoidable. For the author believes that the expressions in question have already become hardened fixed points in the minds of the people of Kenya, and that all, except the last one, have apparently lost their original technical usefulness and have turned into self-serving, divisionary slogans.

Besides, the author has new ones to present, namely: "divine intervention",[2] "trust, political negotiation and compromise",[3] "home-grown",[4] "open, inclusive and consultative process"[5] and "a constitutional vacuum".[6] To this list should be added: "Parliamentary review",[7] "Wanjiku and the con-

---

[2] "Are the prospects of genuine reforms so desperate that we must now seek divine intervention?" See "Govt must now listen to the people", Sunday Nation, OP.ED. Oct 17, 1999, P. 6, Col. 1, referring to the decision of 23 catholic Bishops in Kenya to meet at the Holy Family Basilica to celebrate a special mass, "seeking divine intervention for a people-driven review of the constitution". 1 d. P. 2, Col. 1. See also note 7, infra.

[3] Advice by H.E. Mr. Griffith Memela, South African High Commissioner to Kenya, at a Constitutional review meeting. See "Trust key constitution making, says envoy", East African Standard, Oct. 9, 1999, P. 3, Col. 1: "Envoy tips Kenyans on reform", Daily Nation, Oct. 9, 1999, P. 3, Col. 1: Cf. "Kenya won't adopt foreign constitution", East African Standard, Oct. 11, 1999, P. 1; "Keep off, Moi tells S.A. envoy", Daily Nation, Oct. 11, 1999, P. 1 and "LSK backs S. African envoy on constitution", East African Standard, Oct. 12, 1999, P. 1.

[4] A favourite expression of Dr. Gibson Kamau Kuria, Chairman of the Law Society of Kenya (LSK) supporting a people-driven review of the constitution.

[5] Advice by Hon. Peter Hain, British Minister of State for Foreign and Commonwealth, during his visit to Kenya. See "Full text of the speech by visiting British Minister of State", East African Standard, Oct. 15, 1999, P. 2, Col. 1; "Britain in call for total reform", Daily Nation, Oct. 15, 1999, P. 56, Col. 2; Id. 14 Oct. 1999, P. 5, Col. 1.

[6] Mentioned by the Vice-President, Prof. George Saitoti, complaining that the civil society was misrepresenting the views of KANU and was misleading the public into thinking that a people-driven review meant a review undertaken because there was "a constitutional vacuum". No such vacuum existed, he said, Kenya's constitution was still in existence, it had neither been suspended nor abrogated. See "Constitution: Kanu gives Wako 2 weeks", East African Standard, Oct. 19, 1999, P. 1, Col. 5 at. P. 2, Col. 3.

[7] Staunchly supported by H. E The President of the Republic of Kenya and his ruling party KANU, but vehemently opposed by those claiming to be the legitimate voice of the people: "the civil society", and members of the opposition parties. See "No way, Moi told on review", Daily Nation, May 24, 1999, P. 1, "Bishops begin reform protest", Daily Nation, Oct. 18, 1999, P. 1, col. 1, and "Religious leaders insist on people-driven reforms", East African Standard, Oct. 18, 1999, P. 1, Col. 5.

stitution",[8] "mass action",[9] "transparent, accessible, fast-moving and people-driven review process",[10] a "Presidential Review Commission"[11] and a review by a Parliamentary Select Committee.[12]

This list of the key concepts used and ideas expressed by those engaged in discussing the constitutional review process in Kenya, is given here as a clear evidence of the facts that the Kenyans have come to realize the seriousness of the business upon which they have embarked. It is also an evidence of the fact that something healthy and democratic is happening: people are voicing their opinions, giving their views and demanding to become part of the process. They are even floating model constitutions.[13] It is clear that the Kenyans are groping for practical and innovative solutions and have reached

---

[8] A favourite code name used by H. E. The President of the Republic of Kenya, referring to an ordinary Kenyan citizen: woman or man on the street, whom he says does not understand what the constitution is all about. The view is rejected by the religious leaders claiming: "Let Wanjiku constitute the Constitution". See e.g. "Bishops begin reforms protest as Kanu digs in", *Daily Nation*, Oct. 18, 1999, P. 2, col. 4. For other calls for people driven constitution See "Link aid to reforms – LSK", *Sunday Standard*, Oct. 10, 1999, P. 3, Col. 5.

[9] A two-day, LSK workshop resolved that mass action was a legitimate means to pressurize the government to accept a people-driven review. See "Link aid to reforms – LSK", *Sunday Standard*, Oct. 10, 1999, P. 3.

[10] Advice by the American Secretary of States, Mrs. Madeline Albright, during her brief visit to Kenya. See "Moi, Albright in frank reforms discussion", *East African Standard*, Oct. 23, 1999, P. 1, Col. 5.

[11] Advice by Prof. W. Okoth Ogendo, calling the constitution of Kenya Review Commission Act: "incurably defective", urging review by the Parliament, and dismissing the clamour for a review process outside the parliament by the civil society. "For heaven's sake, let us not permit self-anointed sterling-dollar-deutschmark laden busy-bodies to take over the process by declaring themselves *stakeholders* and rail-roading public opinion through street demonstration and vandalism", Prof. Ogendo said. See "Moi urged to intervene in reforms", *Daily Nation*, Nov. 23, 1999, P. 2, Col. 1. Compare "Constitution: Moi for U.S. experts", *Saturday Standard*, Nov. 7, 1999, P. 4, Col. 2.

[12] An initiative to make the Kenya parliament to take over the constitution review process. See "50 MPs plot new law reform deal", *Sunday Nation*, Nov. 28, 1999, P. 1, Col. 5, rejected by the official Opposition Party. See "Kibaki rejects House reform talks", *Daily Nation*, Dec. 2, 1999, P. 1, Col. 1.

[13] The Law Society of Kenya (LSK), Kenya Human Rights Commission (KHRC) and the International Commission of Jurists (ICJ) – Kenya Chapter together produced a model constitution.

out even for the most controversial.[14] But their attention should not be diverted from this rathter simple fact: Constitution-making and the process of keeping up-to-date the written document itself is a tricky exercise and one that may buffle or scare even the initiated. This may sound a perfectly empty assertion at first blush. But when you think of it further, you will begin to wonder what happened in England! They did not produce a written constitution in a single document up to now. Thus if any visitor went to the British Museum of History and, because of interest in antiques, asked to be shown the original constitution of what we know as the United Kingdom, the visitor would be out of luck. There will be no single document to show him or her. But an imaginative museum guide may produce a copy of the Magna Carta, 1215; the Provisions of Oxford, 1258; the Bill of Rights 1689; and the Act of Union, 1707. I end my predictions here. There are certainly more to show. I leave that to the museum host. But I must emphasize that the absence of a written constitution in a single document in the United Kingdom, speaks volumes about the significance of culture and tradition in constitutionalism to which I will revert as a central theme to this paper.

Let me then hasten to point out, at this juncture, yet another simple fact. It is the following: Some thirteen recalcitrant British colonies in North America, which rebelled and broke away in 1776, after their famous Boston Tea Party, were brave enough to produce a written constitution in *a single document*: the 1787 American Constitution which in that respect inspired all those written constitutions we have in most African countries. The Americans have patched up theirs twenty-six times since 1787. The Kenyans have also amended theirs eighteen times since 1963. But they would now like to do something more about it: review it, re-write it, overhaul it, reform it, amend it, alter it – in other words – make it up-to-date.

---

[14] It has remained a mystery to this author whether or not the National Convention Executive Council (NCEC), in fact, suggested that the military be invited to take part in the interim Kenya government they were proposing. *See* "Let the Military join the reform govt", *Daily Nation*, Nov. 5, 1999, P. 1, "NCEC launches plan for a transition govt", *East African Standard*, Nov. 5, 1999, P. 1, "NCEC beats retreat", *East African Standard*, Nov. 7, 1999, P. 1, "NCEC: We didn't call for army govt.", *Daily Nation*, Nov. 7, 1999, P. 1, Col. 6., "NCEC military plea denounced", *Daily Nation*, Nov. 6, 1999, P. 1, "Keep off military, top Army men warn NCEC, *East African Standard* , Nov. 6, 1999, P. 1; other outrage expressed at P. 3 and OP.ED "NCEC strays where angels fear to trend", at P. 6. But *see* "Involve the military and inmates in law review", *East African Standard*, Nov. 29, 1999, P. 1, Col. 1, where it was reportedly suggested by Bishop Timothy Njoya, that "prisoners should be involved in the writing of the constitution because there are some of them who are in prison because of miscarriage of justice", at P. 2, Col. 6.

It, however, goes without saying, that this is not a problem which faces Kenya only. All countries which have written constitutions, are bound to reach the stage at which they are faced with the reality of the need to revisit the important instrument: to deliberate upon it, through active participation of the citizens of the country, in order to ensure that the instrument reflects, or retains, its dynamic responsiveness to the legitimate cultures and the changing aspirations of the people of the country. Accordingly, the big picture is that the three democratic ideals, which need to be given space to flourish under the culture of constitutionalism are: **participation**, which is designed to achieve a wide collection of views of the citizens while ensuring strong inputs by the women and other traditionally marginalized groups; **deliberation**, which is undertaken in institutions like the parliament or courts, constituted in such a way as to permit proper articulation and protection of the rights of women and other traditionally marginalized groups; and **responsiveness** of the resulting instrument to the culture, concerns and aspirations of all the citizens.

II. SOME DEFICIENCIES IN AFRICAN CONSTITUTIONALISM

But we, in Africa, have already drawn up our own list of charges, noting our hugely disappointing track record on the question of constitutionalism. A "seven-count indictment" has, indeed, been issued against African countries for failure to give effect to the democratic ideals. We shall add an eighth indictment here, inspired by an evident failure by African states to pay attention to the treaty-based rights of women and children as shown in the next section. But as you begin to read the following "seven counts", try to ascertain if your country is guilty as charged.

These charges are as follows:

Count 1. The culture of constitutionalism has not yet taken root in many African countries.

Count 2. Grave imbalances still exist between the major branches of the government, in Africa notably the executive and the legislature; the judiciary is far from independent.

Count 3. Parliaments in Africa tend to be weak, unable to exercise their constitutional functions and obligations to check the actions of the executive or to air properly the grievances of the citizens.

Count 4. African constitutions often appear veiled virtually as religious mysteries, impenetrable except to the few, in part because the instruments are written in an esoteric style and in the languages of colonial regimes which make them remain inaccessible and incomprehensible to most citizens.

Count 5. African countries do not have programmes for civic education across age groups for generating the understanding and the appreciation of the need, in a democratic society, to have respect for constitutional rights and obligations and to comply with them.

Count 6. No mechanisms are available for the citizens of most African countries to challenge the constitutionality of government actions, or inaction and to compel those in authority to perform their functions in compliance with the constitution.

Count 7. Many African countries have not adequately revised or repealed certain laws which they inherited from the colonial era which still threaten their citizens and perpetuate their denial of the rights which they had won at independence.

The above views on constitutionalism in Africa, reformulated in this presentation as indictments, were expressed at the 1998 Second African Governance Forum (AGF-II)[15] in Accra, Ghana, where other issues forming the bedrock of good governance were also discussed. Thus, apart from constitutionalism, our main topic, the AFG-II, addressed other issues relating to governmental institutions and processes. The forum also outlined the challenges and opportunities, with suggestions for follow-up actions, recognizing the proper role of Africa's traditional institutions, cultures and values.

The seven points were, it must be observed, not intended to be exhaustive of the deficiencies of African constitutionalism or gaps in the constitutional provisions as such. One can certainly add more. I am indeed going to do just that now by adding the 8th count of the indictment as mentioned earlier. It is in the form of a gap in constitutional provisions and runs as follows:

> "Most African constitutions do not have provisions relating to the integration of treaties which they have ratified into their national legal systems, creating a situation in which treaties remain largely unimplemented domestically by the States."

---

[15] The AGF-II (25th-26th June 1998) was convened by the United Nations. Ten African countries participated: Benin, Burkina Faso, Gambia, Ghana, Mali, Senegal, South Africa, Tanzania, Uganda and Zambia. *See* generally THE SECOND ANNUAL AFRICA GOVERNANCE FORUM (AGE-II) FINAL REPORT, UNDP PUB. 1997.

III. ONE CONSTITUTIONAL GAP AT A TIME: EXPANDING THE SCOPE OF "THE SUPREME LAW OF THE LAND"

It would, no doubt, be useful to give a brief background here to the problem reflected in count 8 of the indictment which, I am sure, has not come to you as a thunderbolt from the sky since some of you are already aware of it.

We have recently conducted a series of workshops on the problem of "Implementation of treaty-based rights of women and children in Eastern and Southern Africa" (May - September 1999). The focus was on the implementation of the United Nations Convention on the Elimination of all forms of Discrimination Against Women (CEDAW) and the United Nations Convention on the Rights of the Child (CRC). Both of these treaties have entered into force, and have been ratified by all the six countries of the region in which the workshops were conducted, namely: Botswana, Kenya, Swaziland, Tanzania, Uganda and Zambia.[16]

One of the common problems encountered in the implementation of CEDAW and CRC in each of the six countries was that the treaties could not be given effect (applied) domestically, because they had not been integrated into the national legal systems of the States concerned.[17] The failure to incorporate treaties which have been ratified or acceded to by these States into their domestic laws was blamed on two problems: absence of clear constitutional provisions addressing the issue, and the inheritance of the colonial, Commonwealth practice which follows *the* **dualist approach** to treaty implementation. Under this approach, briefly stated, a treaty to which a State has expressed its consent to be bound, does not become applicable in that State automatically until an appropriate legislation has been enacted to give the treaty the force of law domestically. This is different from the **monist approach** under which a treaty to which a State is a party, having given its consent to be bound by it, becomes directly applicable in law domestically (self-executing), and does not require the enactment of a specific legislation by the State to give it effect under its municipal laws.

The gap in the constitutional provisions may be usefully illustrated by the following five examples of existing constitutional provisions which are deadly silent on the matter and thus fail to address it under the most relevant sections.

---

[16] *See* generally – The Composite Report of the workshops on the Implementation of Treaty-based Rights of Women and Children in the Eastern and Southern Africa (29th October 1999, on file with author).

[17] *Id*. Para. 16 This paper prefers to use interchangeably the expressions "integration into domestic laws" and "transformation into domestic laws" to describe the situation instead of the more popular word "domestication". Thus it refers to "integration of treaties into domestic laws" and not "domestication of treaties".

Example 1 (Kenya)
"This Constitution is the Constitution of the Republic of Kenya and shall have the force of law throughout Kenya and, subject to section 47, if any other law is inconsistent with this Constitution, this Constitution shall prevail and the other law shall, to the extent of the inconsistency, be void." *(Section 3)*

Example 2 (Zambia)
"This Constitution is the supreme law of Zambia and if any other law is inconsistent with this constitution that other law shall, to the extent of the inconsistency, be *void." (Article I clause 3).*[18]

Example 3 (Ethiopia)
1. "The Constitution is the Supreme law of the land. Any law, customary practice, an act of an agency of government or official that contravenes the Constitution is invalid.
2. All citizens, governmental bodies, political parties and other associations and their officials are bound by this Constitution. They also have the duty to ensure its observance.
3. No one can assume or exercise the powers of government except in accordance with the provisions of this Constitution.
4. All international agreements ratified by Ethiopia are an integral part of the laws of the country. " *(Article 9)*

As can be observed, examples 1 and 2 and those like them as indicated, are completely silent about the fate of treaties and their relation to the supreme law of the land (the constitution) or other laws of State. Example 1 does not even refer to the "supremacy" of the constitution itself.

Example 3 tries, at least, to let the people know that the treaties, which their country has ratified "are an integral part of the laws of the country." But it does not address the question of how the treaties may be integrated into the domestic legal system, and that is the rub. It is an issue which has been overlooked by constitutional makers but one that evidently needs to be properly addressed.

Let us assume, that the imaginary and newly independent State of Umoja, wishes to go several steps further than Ethiopia (the third example above) to remedy constitutional defect and fill the gap. We shall also assume

---

[18] *See* also, for example, Article 1, paragraph 6 of the Constitution of Namibia; Section 2 of the 1996 Constitution of South Africa; Section 2 of the 1995 of Uganda; and Section 1(2) of the Constitution of Ghana.

that Umoja is a constitutional multi-party democratic State with a Parliament made up of the National Assembly and the President advised by the Cabinet of Ministers. The State may try the following text for an appropriate section or article of its constitution, for addressing the question of integrating treaties into its domestic laws.

Section III.   Supremacy of the constitution and other laws of the land
(1) This Constitution and the laws of Umoja which shall be made in pursuance thereof; and all treaties which are applicable to Umoja, shall be the supreme law of the land; and shall be interpreted and applied as such by the courts of law throughout Umoja.
(2) In this section, the expression "applicable to Umoja" means having the force of law in Umoja from the date of the entry into force of a treaty for Umoja upon ratification, or accession; or where permitted under the treaty, upon signature of Umoja, following the approval of the treaty by the National Assembly in accordance with subsection (4) of this section.
(3) Subject to section XXV of this Constitution, if any other law is inconsistent with this Constitution, this Constitution shall prevail and that other law shall, to the extent of the inconsistency, be void.
(4) The approval of a treaty shall be by the National Assembly as stipulated under subsection (2) of this section and shall be achieved by a resolution supported by a simple majority of all the members of the Assembly (excluding the *ex officio* members), and shall give the treaty the force of law in Umoja within the meaning of subsections (1) and (2) of this section; provided that:
    (a) the text of the treaty shall have been formally introduced in the National Assembly by a Cabinet Minister with an appropriate Explanatory Memorandum,
    (b) at least twenty-eight days (not counting those during which the Parliament is in recess or dissolved) shall have elapsed between the date of placing the treaty before the National Assembly in accordance with paragraph (a) of this subsection and the commencement of the debate on the treaty, and
    (c) such a debate shall have a reasonable duration.
(5) The text of any treaty, which has been approved by the National Assembly in accordance with this section, shall be published in the Umoja Gazette.

The drafter of the above text is admittedly guilty of one crime: the drafting style may render the provision a little inaccessible and incomprehensible to Wanjiku (the ordinary person). Is this an exaggeration? Can the model text be demystified? A commentary on aspects of the provisions of the Umoja text is necessary here to explain the core issue and the nature of the solution suggested for filling the identified constitutional gap. The core issue is that African countries should have, in their constitutions, the procedures for integrating into their domestic laws unequivocally and without unjustifiable delays, the treaties which they have ratified and which have entered into force for them. Thus, subsection 1 of the draft affirms that treaties applicable to Umoja are integral part of the supreme law of the land, and that the courts of Umoja are instructed to interpret and apply them as such throughout the country, thereby receiving international law into municipal law.[19]

Subsection (2) of the draft addresses two important issues: the definition of the expression treaties "applicable to Umoja" which are the subject of the provision, and the establishment of the required action, namely "approval of a treaty by the National Assembly" of Umoja, in accordance with specified procedures. Those procedures are stipulated under subsection (4), all of which exhaust the actions that need to be taken by the government, to authorize the preparation of the appropriate instruments by which the state would express its consent to be bound by the treaty. The treaty then becomes automatically applicable to Umoja, upon the date of its entry into force for that state (the critical date), in accordance with its relevant provisions. The suggested text thus adopts the "monist approach" to treaty integration into domestic law, as briefly described earlier.[20]

I believe I have just arrived at another opportune moment for sharing with you yet another crucial point about constitutionalism. The Umoja text suggested above contains matters of details over which people may disagree, although they may all agree with the general proposition that treaties should form an integral part of the law of the land and must be thus acknowledged in the constitution. To illustrate the point further, let us note that the drafters of a constitution may all agree, on the basis of the information gathered, that the people wish their constitution to enshrine for example: the right to clean and healthy environment; the rights of children; the rights of access to information; the rights to affirmative action in favour of women and other marginalized groups; economic rights; and the right to development. But they may continue to disagree sharply on the particular meaning or content of those

---

[19] See e.g. *West Rand Central Gold Mining Co. v. The King,* England, King's Bench, [1905] 2 K,B, 391 which established that international law shall form part of the law of England and *Paquete Hahana the Lola,* United States Supreme Court, 1900 176 U,S 677, 20 S. Ct. 290, in which the Court also accepted that international law was part of domestic law of the country.

[20] *See* above. p. 245

rights and on how they may be extended or exercised concretely.[21] Such rights may, nevertheless, be included in the constitution being drafted, despite the doubts on their contents and continued disagreement over their precise meanings; for that is what constitution-making is all about: establishing the core of broadly stated substantive rights, erecting firm signposts and their parameters, leaving the relevant details for appropriate subsequent legislation or possible clarification by the courts, instructing those engaged in the execution of the law.

It is in this connection that I now invite you to look at Articles 32 and 33 of the 1996 Uganda constitution to drive home this constitutional-making technique.

> *"32 (1) Notwithstanding anything in this Constitution, the State shall take affirmative action in favour of groups marginalised on the basis of gender, age, disability or any other reason created by history, tradition or custom, for the purpose of redressing imbalances which exist against them.*
>
> *(2) Parliament shall make relevant laws, including laws for the establishment of an equal opportunities commission, for the purpose of giving full effect to clause (1) of this article.*
>
> *"33 (1) Women shall be accorded full and equal dignity of the person with men.*
>
> *(2) The State shall provide the facilities and opportunities necessary to enhance the welfare of women to enable them to realize their full potential and advancement.*
>
> *(3) The State shall protect women and their rights, taking into account their unique status and natural maternal functions in society.*
>
> *(4) The State shall ensure that women have the right to equal treatment with men and that right shall include equal opportunities in political, economic and social activities.*
>
> *(5) Without prejudice to article 32 of this Constitution, women shall have the right to affirmative action for the purpose of redressing the imbalances created by history, tradition or custom.*

---

[21] The same is true with respect to constitutional provisions reflecting the whole range of traditional human rights and fundamental freedoms. As cogently observed elsewhere: "constitutional making is often possible only because of the technique of producing agreement on abstractions amid disagreements, about particulars". C.R. SUNSTEIN, ONE CASE AT A TIME: JUDICIAL MINIMALISM ON THE SUPREME COURT, P. 11 (Harv. Univ. Press 1999).

> *(6) Laws, cultures, customs or traditions which are against the dignity, welfare or interest of women or which undermine their status, are prohibited by this Constitution."*

I need not assemble some rogue set of facts for justifying why the above constitutional provisions should be found everywhere in modern Africa. I am simply commending them to you. See if they provide answers, in part, to some of the counts contained in the eight indictments set out in section II above. The Ugandan text and those like it, should be measured against the following recommendations that were also issued by AGF-II.

- National conventions and referenda should be held as bases for the rewriting of constitutions, thereby fostering a sense of empowerment and ownership among citizens with regard to the basic law of the land. These kinds of consultative processes would also raise citizens' awareness of their rights and obligations, as well as the role of the constitution in ensuring both;
- Constitutional revision should redress imbalances between the executive and legislative branches and assure the latter sufficient resources to fulfil its constitutional obligations;
- Constitutions should be written in appropriate African languages and their complex concepts presented simply and transparently in terms comprehensible to the ordinary citizen;
- Civic education should be promoted, *inter alia* through donor support of the NGOs and independent think tanks and research centres engaged in public policy analysis, and should take place in the context of efforts to eliminate illiteracy and to extend and improve general education; and
- Independent commissions, boards, inspectorates and constitutional courts could be established as means to monitor government activities and empower citizens to question public authorities.

From the five suggestions, which were presented at the Accra AGF-II, as challenges to Africa, one can sieve the three democratic ideals which I had mentioned earlier. The holding of national conventions and referenda setting in motion a consultative process; and the specific activities such as civic education, provide opportunities for the citizens to become acquainted with the issues to identify themselves with the formulation of basic law of the land and to ensure that it is relevant and responsive to their culture and aspirations.

IV. CONCLUSION

There is, therefore, merit in emphasizing the following points, by way of recapturing our constant theme: No constitution can survive the cry of overhaul if it prescribes a pattern of behaviour or of conducting affairs in the State that are alien to the cultures, customs, traditions or aspirations of the people. The Lancaster House – type of constitutions are prime examples. That is why they are now being reviewed and overhauled by most of the commonwealth countries like Kenya,[22] Tanzania,[23] Uganda,[24] and Zimbabwe,[25] for example,[26] which initially had them. The trend is to produce constitutions in which the countries demonstrate their awareness of the fact that constitutionalism goes beyond the demand that those whose lives it is intended to govern must adhere to the rules contained therein.

---

[22] The analysis of the review process in Kenya could usefully begin with tracing what happened after the President of the Republic announced, in 1995, that the constitution of the country needed to be reviewed and suggested that such a review be undertaken by foreign experts! It would then record the events which led to the road to the Bomas of Kenya and the enactment of the 1997 Constitutional Review Act. It would then follow the road to Safari Park I-III, past the famous IPPG corner to the 1998 Review (Amendment) Act. The analysis would then record why the implementation of the 1998 Review (Amendment) Act was stalled and derailed, causing a long period of impasse in the process and, finally, the breakthrough that brought the review process back on track towards completion, after the event of 18th February 1999, at the last meeting convened by the Attorney General, Amos Wako, to vet nominees to the Review Commission.

[23] Tanzania put into place a Renew Commission which collected the news of the citizens and prepared a "White Paper" on the draft constitution which has been submitted for debate to overhaul the 1997 constitution of the Republic.

[24] Uganda initiated one of the most thorough system of seeking the views of its citizens, collecting and collating them in a manner that has brought about the overhauling of the then existing constitution, through participation, deliberation, and responsiveness. The result was the 1995 Constitution of the Republic of Uganda, sample provisions of which are set out *supra* P. 19.

[25] Zimbabwe also put in place a review process that included the collection of the views of the citizens who were thus given the opportunity to have a say as to what aspects of their constitution needed to be altered. On the basis of the views collected and collated, a draft of a new constitution has been produced and will be submitted to the public through a referendum procedure which may lead to a rejection of the draft, or further amendments, before final adoption.

[26] A proposal for the study of this subject with respect to all African countries, as a positive contribution to the new millennium activities, seems in order and is currently being pursued as a possible project by the author.

Constitutionalism also requires that the governmental affairs be conducted in accordance with democratic, procedural and legal traditions which encourage the maintenance of appropriate and effective institutional arrangements for good governance: respecting the rights of the majority (political insiders), while also guarding the interest of the minority (political outsiders). It equally rests on the notion that the legislature, the executive and the judiciary are **independent** but **equal** branches of the government.

Indeed all we need is the political will in Africa to continue striving for constitutional governments boasting of:

(a) *A legislature*, made up of individuals who insist on debating, deliberating and reflecting upon issues from informed perspectives, thereby exercising properly their legislative powers and recognizing their accountability to the public that controls them through the ballot box at elections;[27]

(b) *A judiciary* that exercises its independence to ensure that the laws of the country are correctly applied by individuals who are able to apply judicial activism or judicial restraint as appropriate, in cases before them, reflecting, deliberating and giving reasons for their decisions so as to uphold the maxim that justice must not only be done but must also be seen to be done;[28] and

(c) *An executive* who practically supports the culture of transparency, accountability and good governance in providing service and leadership to the nation; and who enjoys the wisdom of knowing when to speak out and give the necessary statesman-like direction, or remain silent, to encourage the exercise of caution and patience, on the controversial

---

[27] The notion of "accountability to the public", is what gives the legislature its distinctive quality and feature as the law-making branch of the government and should be a dependable yardstick for deciding when to leave a certain issue to be settled by the legislature rather than by any of the other co-equal branches of the government.

[28] Complete independence for the judiciary is essential for its members who may thus exercise "judicial activism", for example, by agreeing to extend to the citizens their treaty-based rights in situations where the necessary domestic legislation has not yet been enacted to integrate the treaty, which is already ratified by the State, into its domestic laws. They may also exercise "judicial activism" by taking on board in their decisions, in relevant cases, rights or principles contained in non-legally binding international instruments such as the United Nations Universal Declaration of Human Rights, and using such instruments as a guide to action. The judges would also recognize the need, on the other hand, to resort to judicial restraint to avoid straying unjustifiably into the province of the legislature, while ensuring that the notion of "passive virtues", that propels "judicial restraint", is not carried too far.

issues of the day that divide a pluralistic society, and which cry out for clarification and settlement by those who are publicly accountable or by those equally constitutionally empowered to clarify the issues through judicial process.[29]

As we pause to ponder the issues briefly raised in this paper, and recaptured in these concluding remarks, we should ask ourselves the following questions: What cultural values, traditional or practices of our own, as Africans, do we wish to reflect and entrench in our new consultations to depart from those wich were drafted for us at the Lancaster House Conference in England, upon gaining independence? Do we wish to replace dull, orderly and witty debates with more exciting, party point-scoring and fearless exchanges on both the main and supplemantary issues within the rules; or try something somewhere in the middle? What kind of African distinctiveness can we give to the parliamentary practices which we have, of necessity, inherited from the colonial past? Can we start an instant culture against begging from the donor countries, one against corruption, one against gender stereotyping, and one in favour of accountability and transpararency? These, I must emphasize, are some of the questions to which we need practical answers as we strive to five effect to the democratic ideals of responsiveness, deliberation and participation, in the constitution making process, keeping away what is alien to our culture.

---

[29] The kind of executive thus described is indispensable, particularly in countries where the constitution still concentrates too much powers upon that branch of the government, as has been the case of the Lancaster-House-types. In such cases, the words of the executive have been supreme and controlling, making those of the legislature or the judiciary mere rubberstamps. The constitution should be used to correct this. For to constitute is to define and to define is to limit, as evidenced by the interchangeable use of the terms "Constitutional Monarchy" and "Limited Monarchy" to mean the same thing.

THE TRIAL OF THE LOCKERBIE SUSPECTS IN THE NETHERLANDS

Caroline Morgan[*]

The trial of the two Libyan nationals accused of the Lockerbie bombing, Abdel Basset Al-Megrahi and Lamen Khalifa Fhimah, is scheduled to start on 3 May 2000. It will take place at Camp Zeist, a former United States airbase in the Netherlands.

Whilst it is not unknown for nationals of a State to be tried under the jurisdiction of another State on the territory of a third State,[1] the background to this trial and the events preceding it are extraordinary. Several States and numerous international organisations are involved. Although the alleged offence is a criminal matter, for many years it has presented itself as a question of international law.

BACKGROUND

The facts of this case are well-known: on 21 December 1988 an explosion on board Pan Am Boeing 747 flight 103 caused the deaths of 270 people. The identification and prosecution of those responsible were immediately demanded.[2] The States involved in the investigation were the United Kingdom (since the aircraft exploded over Scotland) and the United States

---

[*] LLM, Solicitor, PhD Candidate and teaching assistant at the London School of Economics.

[1] There were trials of German and Italian nationals by US courts in France and in the Netherlands, and the International Criminal Tribunals for the former Yugoslavia and Rwanda try cases where the alleged offences were committed abroad, but this is the first instance of a court being established for and limited to the trial of two *named* individuals. At the Nuremberg and Tokyo trials, the defendants were German and Japanese respectively but they were being tried in their own country, albeit by foreign courts.

[2] e.g. United Nations Press Release, document no. SC/5057 of 30 December 1988, expressing outrage and condemning the attack.

(the State of nationality of the aircraft and of the majority of the victims). On 14 November 1991, indictments were issued by the Procurator Fiscal of Scotland, on the instructions of the Lord Advocate of Scotland, against the two Libyan nationals and warrants were issued for their arrest. The charges were conspiracy to murder, murder and certain offences under the Aviation Security Act 1982. The United States Government issued a similar request for the two suspects, as they had been indicted *in absentia* by a Grand Jury in the United States district of Columbia.

On 27 November 1991, the United States and the United Kingdom issued a joint demand that Libya, having no extradition treaty with either the United Kingdom or the United States,[3] "surrender"[4] the two suspects for trial in the United Kingdom or the United States.

Libya has consistently refused to comply with this request. From the outset, the Libyan position has been that the Montreal Convention[5] applied to the dispute, that Libya had complied with its obligations under the Convention and that since the Convention had an "*aut dedere aut judicare*" clause, it had the right to put the men on trial itself if the United States and the United Kingdom authorities provided Libya with all the evidence at their disposal.

In September 1989, France had also blamed Libyan terrorists for an attack on a French aircraft (UTA flight 772) which exploded over Niger, causing the deaths of 171 people.[6] France called upon the Libyan government "to produce all material evidence it possesses that might be useful in establishing the truth, facilitate contacts and meetings for the assembly of witnesses and authorize Libyan officials to respond to requests made by the examining magistrate".

THE SECURITY COUNCIL AND THE CASES AT THE INTERNATIONAL COURT OF JUSTICE

On 20 December 1991, the Permanent Representatives of the United States, the United Kingdom and France formally seized the Security Council

---

[3] Article 493 of the Libyan Code of Criminal Procedure provides that Libya may extradite offenders with the proviso that: "the extradition does not relate to a Libyan citizen".

[4] The UK and US Governments demanded that Libya "surrender for trial all those charged with the crime...and accept responsibility for the actions of Libyan officials, disclose all it knows of this crime... and pay appropriate compensation".

[5] Montreal Convention of 23 September 1971 for the Suppression of Unlawful Acts against the Safety of Civil Aviation.

[6] Letter from the Permanent Representative of France to the President of the Security Council (Doc S/23306).

of the matter[7] and those States made a tripartite declaration on terrorism, condemning all forms of terrorism and denouncing any complicity of States in terrorist acts and also requiring Libya to comply with their requests to surrender for trial those accused of involvement with the bombings of the two aircraft, to disclose all the information at Libya's disposal regarding the crimes and to pay compensation. It was implied that the Libyan leadership was involved in these, and other terrorist acts.

On 21 January 1992, the Security Council unanimously adopted resolution 731[8] "condemning the destruction of ... (the two aircraft) ... and strongly deploring the fact that Libya had not yet responded" to the requests and requiring it to do so. This resolution was merely recommendatory in nature and consequently non-binding.

On 3 March 1992, Libya filed Applications instituting proceedings against the United Kingdom and the United States at the International Court of Justice,[9] asking that the matter be dealt with under the Montreal Convention[10] and requesting an Order for Provisional Measures preventing the United Kingdom and the United States from attempting to coerce or compel Libya to surrender the accused. The request for Provisional Measures was designed in part to preempt the imposition of sanctions and paved the way for a debate over review of Security Council actions.[11] In any event, on 31 March 1992, shortly after the close of the Provisional Measures hearings (held on 26 and 28 March 1992), the Security Council adopted resolution 748,[12] calling upon Libya "to commit itself definitively to cease all

---

[7] Security Council document S/23309
[8] Security Council resolution 731 (1992), S/RES/731 dated 21 January 1992.
[9] Applications of Libya filed in the Registry of the International Court of Justice, 3 March 1992.
[10] Article 14(1) of the Montreal Convention provides: "Any dispute between two or more Contracting States concerning the application or interpretation of this Convention which cannot be settled through negotiation, shall, at the request of one of them, be submitted to arbitration; if within six months from the date of the request for arbitration the Parties are unable to agree on the organisation of the arbitration, any one of those Parties may refer the dispute to the International Court of Justice by request in conformity with the Statute of the Court."
[11] In *"The Security Council, the International Court and Judicial Review: What Lessons from Lockerbie?"* (1999) European Journal of International Law, Vol.10, No.3, 517, Bernd Martenczuk argues cogently that the Lockerbie cases may prove to be a turning point for the ICJ which may in future rely on the rule of law to place a limit on the powers of the Security Council, a limit he sees as already present in the very wording of article 39 of the UN Charter.
[12] Security Council resolution 748 (1992), S/RES/748 dated 31 March 1992.

forms of terrorist action and to surrender the accused", and imposing sanctions on Libya. Those sanctions were to be reviewed every 120 days "in thelight of Libyan compliance" with the requests in the interim. Resolution 748 was adopted under Chapter VII of the United Nations Charter.[13] At the 1992 hearings at the International Court of Justice, the United Kingdom and the United States relied on the binding nature of Security Council resolution 731 (and, at subsequent 1998 hearings, of resolutions 748 and 883), on the fact that Libya, as a signatory to the United Nations Charter, must comply with Security Council resolutions, and that "the obligations of the parties [with respect to the UN Charter] prevail over any other international agreement, including the Montreal Convention".[14] This was upheld by the ICJ which dismissed the request for Provisional Measures[15] in April 1992. The main proceedings continued, with submission of written pleadings, including preliminary objections from the United States and the United Kingdom. Sanctions against Libya came into force on 15 April 1992 and consisted, *inter alia,* of a ban on Libyan aircraft, including assisting Libya with service and maintenance of its own aircraft and a reduction in diplomatic relations with that State.[16]

In spite of the imposition of sanctions, Libya did not surrender the accused and the Security Council adopted resolution 883[17] extending the sanctions to include a freeze of Libyan capital and financial resources abroad and a very wide trade blockade.

In early 1998, the ICJ considered preliminary objections from the respondents, the United States and the United Kingdom, whose submissions were that the ICJ did not have jurisdiction to hear the Libyan claims, that those claims were inadmissible and that since the Security Council had been seized of the matter, there was no longer anything for the Court to decide.

---

[13] Chapter VII gives the Security Council power to take measures "to maintain or restore international peace and security"; actions taken under Chapter VII are binding.

[14] Article 103 of the United Nations Charter provides: "In the event of a conflict between the obligations of the Members of the United Nations under the present Charter and their obligations under any other international agreement their obligations under the present Charter shall prevail".

[15] Case concerning *Questions of Interpretation and Application of the 1971 Montreal Convention arising from the Aerial Incident at Lockerbie,* Request for the Indication of Provisional Measures, Order dated 14 April 1992, International Court of Justice.

[16] For a thorough examination of the early developments (resolutions 731 and 748, and the first stage of the ICJ proceedings) see Beveridge F., *"The Lockerbie Affair"* 41 ICLQ 907.

[17] Security Council resolution 883 (1993), S/RES/883 dated 11 November 1993.

The ICJ dismissed those objections[18] and held that the case should go forward to the merits stage.[19] By an Order dated 29 June 1999, the ICJ fixed 29 June 2000 as the time-limit for the filing of the next pleading in the procedure, a Reply from Libya to the Counter-Memorials filed in March 1999 by the United Kingdom and the United States. The ICJ also authorized the subsequent filing of a Rejoinder by the respondents, but no date was fixed.

THE PROPOSED COMPROMISE: TRIAL IN A NEUTRAL COUNTRY

The question remained inconclusive and a satisfactory outcome difficult to envisage. In order to break the deadlock and to accommodate Libya's assertion that the accused would not get a fair trial in the United States or in Scotland, a compromise of a trial in a third, neutral country (such as the Netherlands) was proposed, initially by Libya, and then by the League of Arab States, the Organization of the Islamic Conference, the Movement of

---

[18] The ICJ held that the Application was admissible since "the critical date for determining the admissibility of an application is the date on which it is filed" (*Border and Transborder Armed Actions, (Nicaragua v. Honduras), Jurisdiction and Admissibility, I.C.J. Reports 1988*). The application, filed on 3 March 1992, predated Security Council resolutions 748(1992) and 883(1993) and consequently, the claim of inadmissibility based on those resolutions was rejected.
Libya argued that the objections were "not exclusively preliminary" and entailed decisions which should be left to the merits stage, and the ICJ upheld this contention.

[19] Case concerning *Questions of Interpretation and Application of the 1971 Montreal Convention arising from the Aerial Incident at Lockerbie*. Judgment dated 27 February 1998 (Preliminary Objections). The judgments in the two cases, *Libya v. United States* and *Libya v. United Kingdom*, are very similar and any differences are irrelevant for present purposes.

Non-Aligned Countries and the Organisation of African Unity (OAU) negotiating on the latter's behalf.[20]

For several years, the proposal was not seriously entertained by the United States and the United Kingdom. However, in a letter dated 24 August 1998, their acting permanent representatives[21] informed the Secretary-General of the United Nations that their Governments were prepared "as an exceptional measure, to arrange for the two accused to be tried before a Scottish court sitting in the Netherlands". The Government of the Netherlands had agreed to facilitate arrangements for such a court.[22] Annexed to the letter was a draft Statutory Instrument setting out the arrangements for the proposed court. This differed from the Libyan proposal in that the court was to be a Scottish one (High Court of Justiciary), with Scottish judges applying Scottish law "in the same way as if the court had been sitting in Scotland", which was not the same as a trial in a neutral country to be held in accordance with the legal system of that country, but it did represent a significant shift in the position of the United States and the United Kingdom. If Libya agreed to the proposal, the sanctions imposed by resolutions 748 and 883 would be immediately suspended "once the

---

[20] See the following documents:
S/1994/373 Letter dated 31 March 1994 from the Permanent Representative of the Libyan Arab Jamahiriya to the United Nations addressed to the President of the Security Council;
S/1995/834 Letter dated 4 October 1995 from the Permanent Representative of the Libyan Arab Jamahiriya to the United Nations addressed to the Secretary-General;
S/1997/35 Letter dated 15 January 1997 from the Chargé d'affaires A.I. of the Permanent Mission of the Libyan Arab Jamahiriya to the United Nations addressed to the President of the Security Council;
S/1997/273 Letter dated 3 April 1997 from the Permanent Representative of the Libyan Arab Jamahiriya to the United Nations addressed to the President of the Security Council;
S/1997/406 (Annex) Final Document of the Twelfth Ministerial Conference of the Movement of Non-Aligned Countries;
S/1997/497 Letter dated 26 June 1997 from the Permanent Observers of the League of Arab States and of the Organization of African Unity to the United Nations addressed to the President of the Security Council;
S/1997/529 Letter dated 9 July 1997 from the Permanent Representative of the Zimbabwe to the United Nations addressed to the President of the Security Council.

[21] Letter dated 24 August 1998 from the acting permanent representatives of the United Kingdom of Great Britain and Northern Ireland and the United States of America to the United Nations addressed to the Secretary-General (S/1998/795).

[22] Annex II of S/1998/795 is a draft Agreement between the Government of the Kingdom of the Netherlands and the Government of the United Kingdom of Great Britain and Northern Ireland Concerning a Scottish Trial in the Netherlands.

Secretary-General reported that the two accused had arrived at the Netherlands for trial".[23]

On 27 August 1998, the Security Council adopted resolution 1192,[24] welcoming the initiative, requesting the Secretary-General to assist Libya in complying with the proposal, inviting him to nominate international observers to attend the trial and deciding that the measures set out in resolutions 748 and 883 would be suspended once the two accused arrived in the Netherlands for the purpose of trial.

SPECIAL JURISDICTION

On 18 September 1998, the United Kingdom and the Kingdom of the Netherlands signed the Agreement between the Government of the Kingdom of the Netherlands and the Government of the United Kingdom of Great Britain and Northern Ireland concerning a Scottish trial in the Netherlands. The host State undertakes to make available premises for the Scottish Court,[25] to permit the detention of the accused for the purposes of the trial[26] and to grant the Court privileges and immunities for the duration of the trial.[27] The accused may only be transferred to the territory of the United Kingdom either with their written consent, for the purpose of trial[28] or to serve their sentence if convicted.[29] If the trial is discontinued or if the accused are acquitted, they shall be obliged to leave the country.[30]

The Statutory Instrument[31] establishing the Scottish Court in the Netherlands came into force on 18 September 1998. Article 3 provides:

---

[23] Security Council Press Release SC/6566 dated 27 August 1998.
[24] Security Council resolution 1192 (1998), S/RES/1192 dated 27 August 1998.
[25] Article 3(1) of the Agreement.
[26] Article 3(3) of the Agreement.
[27] Articles 7-15 of the Agreement.
[28] Article 16(2) of the Agreement.
[29] Article 16(2)(b) of the Agreement.
[30] Article 16(4) of the Agreement.
[31] Statutory Instrument 1998 No.2251, *The High Court of Justiciary (Proceedings in the Netherlands)(United Nations) Order 1998*, made 16 September 1998, laid before Parliament 17 September 1998, entry into force 18 September 1998.

"**3.** -(1) For the purpose of conducting criminal proceedings on indictment against Abdelbaset Ali Mohmed Al Megrahi and Al Amin Khalifa Fhimah (in this Order referred to as "the accused") on the charges of conspiracy to murder, murder and contravention of the Aviation Security Act 1982 specified in the petition upon which warrant for arrest was issued by the Sheriff of South Strathclyde, Dumfries and Galloway on 13 November 1991, the High Court of Justiciary may, in accordance with the provisions of this Order, sit in the Netherlands.

(2) Except as provided for in this Order, proceedings before the High Court of Justiciary sitting in the Netherlands shall be conducted in accordance with the law relating to proceedings on indictment before the High Court of Justiciary in Scotland."

The trial is to be heard by three Lords Commissioners of Justiciary (who may include retired or temporary judges) appointed by the Lord Justice Clerk to sit as judges, with one of their number presiding (Lord Ranald Sutherland has been appointed presiding judge), and without a jury. Questions of law are to be decided by majority voting and the court shall have "all the powers, authorities and jurisdiction" which it would have had if it had been sitting with a jury in Scotland.

The verdict is to be determined by a majority and delivered in open court by the presiding judge. In the event of a guilty verdict, the presiding judge shall pass sentence.[32]

One of the contentious issues had been the place where a sentence, if any, was to be served, with Libya claiming that the accused, if found guilty, might be subjected to prejudicial treatment if incarcerated in a British jail. The Libyan request for any sentence to be served in a third country jail was denied, any sentence in the case of a conviction to be served in Scotland, but international observers would be permitted to oversee fairness in those circumstances.

TRANSFER OF THE ACCUSED TO THE NETHERLANDS

On 5 April 1999, the accused arrived in the Netherlands on board a United Nations aircraft, and accompanied by the United Nations Legal Counsel, Hans Corell, who was able to report to the Secretary-General that

---

[32] Article 5 of the Statutory Instrument.

Libya had complied with Security Council resolution 1192 (1998).[33] Sanctions were suspended on 5 April 1999, to a very positive international response,[34] and Libya was commended for its "full cooperation, flexibility and rationalism".[35] The Lockerbie suspects were transferred to Camp Zeist, a disused United States airbase 50 kilometres South-east of Amsterdam. Indictments were formally served on the two suspects on 29 October 1999.

Now that the suspects are in custody awaiting trial the question whether a fair trial is possible arises. There has been considerable media coverage including speculation as to what potential witnesses will say in evidence, guilt has been implied in the Security Council resolutions calling for the payment of compensation to the families of victims and some consider that the absence of a jury is an impediment to a fair trial.[36]

The trial itself is scheduled to start on 3 May 2000, but on 7 December 1999, a preliminary application was made on behalf of the defence. The Court heard arguments from Defence Counsel that the conspiracy to murder charge against the two accused should be dropped since the alleged conspiracy did not take place in Scotland and that consequently the Court did not have jurisdiction to hear that charge.[37] It was also argued that it was unfair to the accused to allow them to be described as "members of their country's intelligence services" since this was irrelevant and prejudicial. In his ruling, Lord

---

[33] Paragraph 8 of Security Council Resolution 1192 (1998) lays down that sanctions "shall be suspended immediately if the Secretary-General reports to the council that the two accused have arrived in the Netherlands for the purpose of trial ... and that the Libyan Government has satisfied the French judicial authorities with regard to the bombing of UTA 772". France had not demanded the extradition of the 6 Libyans it suspected of the attack on UTA flight 772, but instead chose to try them *in absentia*, and on 10 March 1999, they were convicted and sentenced to life imprisonment. The Libyan Government has given France satisfactory assurances with regard to implementation of those sentences.

[34] Report of the Secretary-General submitted pursuant to Paragraph 16 of Security Council resolution 883 (1993) and Paragraph 8 of resolution 1192, document S/1999/726 dated 30 June 1999.

[35] Secretary-General's Report, *supra.*, n.33

[36] Many websites offer "Lockerbie news", some starting from the position that the two suspects are innocent such as *http:/www.geocities.com/Capitol Hill/5260/*. There is a substantial body of respected commentaries arguing that the criminal case is badly flawed, e.g. Paul Foot and John Ashton, "Body of Evidence", *The Guardian* 29 July 1995. See also Menno T. Kamminga, "Comment: Trial of Lockerbie suspects before a Scottish Court in the Netherlands", (1998) Netherlands International Law Review XLV, 417.

[37] Widely reported in the British press (e.g. *The Times, The Independent, The Guardian*), 7 December 1999.

Sutherland dismissed these arguments but, at the defence's request, postponed the opening of the trial from February 2000 to May 2000.[38]

CONCLUSION

The issues stemming from the *Lockerbie* incident go beyond the guilt or innocence of Abdel Basset Al-Megrahi and Lamen Khalifa Fhimah in so far as the case focuses attention on the whole role of the Security Council[39] and on whether its acts should not be open to judicial review. Whilst the Charter is drafted in broad terms and, at first sight, gives the Security Council almost unlimited power, some commentators have found it difficult to reconcile the Security Council's mixing of the political and the legal,[40] which, as in the case of the extradition demand, may give rise to a conflict between Council and Court. In the event of an acquittal in the criminal trial, the Security Council may be accused of having acted inappropriately. The cases Libya has brought before the ICJ should and probably will proceed regardless of the verdict since the issue needs to be tested. The question of compensation for Libya will also arise and, in the meantime, these cases represent a safeguard for Libya. Whatever the ICJ decides, the debate on the respective roles of the Security Council and the Court has been opened and cannot now be silenced.

---

[38] Widely reported in the international press: 7, 8 and 9 December 1999.
e.g. "Libyans Make First Public Appearance in Lockerbie Case", *International Herald Tribune,* 8 December 1999; "Procès Lockerbie: maintien de l'accusation de complot", *Agence France Presse*, 8 December 1999, "Judge agrees to delay trial of Lockerbie suspects", *The Guardian*, 9 December 1999.

[39] The changing way in which the Security Council is perceived is also illustrated by the totally unrelated NATO action in Kosovo, which represents a challenge to the Security Council's traditional Chapter VII role. In "NATO's 'Humanitarian War' over Kosovo" *Survival*, vol. 41, no. 3, 1999, 102-123, Adam Roberts points out that a UK Foreign and Commonwealth Office note of October 1998 stated "A UNSCR would give a clear legal base for NATO action, as well as being politically desirable. But force can also be justified on the grounds of overwhelming humanitarian necessity without a UNSCR." The fact that the government of a Permanent Security Council Member was willing to countenance the use of force without Security Council authorisation suggests an important shift in perception.

[40] See, for example, Mohammed Bedjaoui, *The New World Order and the Security Council – Testing the Legality of its Acts*, Martinus Nijhoff Publishers, Dordrecht 1994, in particular at pp. 66-75.

LE MÉCANISME DE RÈGLEMENT DES DIFFÉRENDS DANS LE CADRE DE L'ORGANISATION POUR L'INTERDICTION DES ARMES CHIMIQUES

Serguei Pounjine*

I. INTRODUCTION

La signature à Paris en 1993 de la Convention sur l'interdiction de la mise au point, de la fabrication, du stockage et de l'emploi des armes chimiques et sur leur destruction (ci-après «la Convention» ou «la CIAC») a marqué le début d'une nouvelle étape dans le processus du désarmement chimique. Les efforts d'élimination des armes toxiques ont commencé très tôt ; ils remontent peut-être même à l'origine de l'histoire des guerres.

A la suite de la première guerre mondiale, durant laquelle on a souffert des terribles conséquences de l'utilisation militaire des armes chimiques, les Etats ont décidé de mettre fin à l'emploi de ces dernières sur les champs de bataille. En 1925, ils signèrent le protocole concernant la prohibition d'emploi à la guerre de gaz asphyxiants, toxiques ou similaires et de moyens bactériologiques. Bien que le protocole ait interdit seulement l'emploi des armes chimiques et qu'il recèle également d'autres insuffisances, il est devenu l'instrument le plus important dans le domaine du désarmement. L'emploi des armes chimiques était dès lors interdit mais durant la guerre froide les Etats-Unis et l'URSS, entraînés dans la course aux armements, continuèrent d'accroître leurs arsenaux chimiques. Dans le début des années 80, les Etats-Unis possédaient environ 30000 tonnes de substances toxiques et l'Union Soviétique 40000 tonnes; ils étaient les deux seuls Etats à reconnaître que leurs armées étaient équipées d'armes chimiques.

Le développement technologique dans l'industrie chimique a réellement accru le danger de prolifération des armes chimiques. Cette tendance

---

* Docteur en droit, juriste au Greffe de la Cour internationale de Justice, anciennement juriste au service juridique du Secrétariat technique provisoire de la Commission préparatoire de l'OIAC. Les opinions exprimées par l'auteur sont strictement personnelles et ne sauraient en aucun cas engager les institutions susmentionnées.

menaçait la stabilité et la sécurité dans le monde. Dans ces circonstances, les Etats-Unis et l'URSS sont devenus les promoteurs du désarmement chimique complet y compris de la destruction des stocks d'armes chimiques et des installations de fabrication ainsi que d'une réglementation spécifique pour la non-prolifération d'armes chimiques. Leurs efforts reçurent le soutien des autres Etats de la communauté internationale. Prenant en considération l'expérience de la Convention sur l'interdiction de la mise au point, de la fabrication et du stockage des armes bactériologiques (biologiques) (1972), qui ne prévoyait pas de mécanisme de contrôle, il fut décidé d'établir un contrôle international strict du processus de désarmement chimique.

La Convention entra en vigueur le 29 avril 1997. A ce jour, 135 Etats sont parties à la Convention, parmi lesquels 32 Etats africains.[1] Aux termes de la CIAC neuf Etats parties d'Afrique désignés par les Etats parties situés dans cette région sont membres de l'organe exécutif de l'Organisation pour l'interdiction des armes chimiques. Les Etats africains suivants sont ainsi membres du Conseil exécutif : l'Afrique du Sud (2002[2]), l'Algérie (2002), le Cameroun (2001), la Côte d'Ivoire (2001), l'Ethiopie (2001), le Maroc (2002), la Namibie (2002), la Tunisie (2001) et le Zimbabwe (2001).

La Convention prévoit les obligations des Etats de ne jamais, en aucune circonstance, mettre au point, fabriquer, acquérir d'une autre manière, stocker ou conserver des armes chimiques, ou transférer, directement ou indirectement des armes chimiques à qui que ce soit ; d'employer des armes chimiques; d'entreprendre des préparatifs militaires quels qu'ils soient en vue d'un emploi d'armes chimiques ; d'aider, d'encourager ou d'inciter quiconque, de quelque manière que ce soit, à entreprendre quelque activité que ce soit qui est interdite à un Etat partie en vertu de la Convention. Chaque Etat partie s'engage aussi à détruire les armes chimiques dont il est le propriétaire ou le détenteur ; les armes chimiques qu'il a abandonnées sur le territoire d'un autre Etat partie et toute installation de fabrication d'armes chimiques.

Toutes ces obligations doivent être remplies de bonne foi et en conformité avec le principe *pacta sunt servanda*. L'efficacité de toute norme de droit dépend toutefois largement de l'existence d'un mécanisme extérieur de contrainte pour en assurer l'exécution. Le droit international ne prévoit généralement pas de tels mécanismes et son respect est dès lors garanti par la

---

[1] Afrique du Sud, Algérie, Bénin, Botswana, Burkina Faso, Burundi, Cameroun, Côte d'Ivoire, Erythrée, Ethiopie, Gambie, Ghana, Guinée, Guinée Équatoriale, Kenya, Lesotho, Malawi, Mali, Maroc, Maurice, Mauritanie, Namibie, Niger, Nigeria, Sénégal, Seychelles, Soudan, Swaziland, Tanzanie, Togo, Tunisie, Zimbabwe; état au 1er juin 2000.

[2] Date d'expiration du mandat.

conscience des Etats que l'observation des règles du droit international est plus avantageuse pour eux que leur violation. L'existence d'une telle conscience ne suffit pas dans le domaine de la sécurité et du désarmement parce qu'elle ne peut pas créer les conditions d'une confiance mutuelle. C'est pour cette raison que les auteurs de la Convention ont décidé d'instituer une organisation internationale spécifique pour la vérification de la mise en œuvre de la CIAC.

D'après la Convention, cette organisation (dont le nom officiel est l'Organisation pour l'interdiction des armes chimiques, ci-après «l'Organisation» ou «l'OIAC») a pour fonctions la réalisation de l'objet et du but de la Convention, la surveillance de l'application de ses dispositions et la mise en place d'un cadre dans lequel les Etats parties puissent se consulter et coopérer entre eux. Elle assure la vérification de la destruction des armes chimiques sur le territoire des Etats possesseurs ainsi que de la non-production des armes chimiques dans les autres pays parties de la Convention. En pratique, l'Organisation contrôle l'industrie chimique mondiale travaillant avec les produits chimiques spéciaux précisément définis dans la Convention. Ce contrôle se réalise au moyen d'inspections sur les lieux par les inspecteurs de l'Organisation. Les Etats parties ont le droit de demander une « inspection par mise en demeure » de toute installation ou de tout emplacement sur le territoire d'un autre Etat partie s'il y a des raisons de supposer que la Convention a été violée. Aucun Etat partie ne peut refuser une telle inspection.

L'Organisation comprend trois organes : la Conférence des Etats parties, le Conseil exécutif et le Secrétariat technique. La Conférence des Etats parties, qui est le principal organe de l'OIAC, se compose de tous les Etats membres de l'Organisation. Le Conseil exécutif, qui se compose de 41 membres, est l'organe exécutif de l'Organisation. Ses membres sont élus suivant le principe de la rotation pour deux ans. Le Secrétariat, qui est un organe administratif, assiste la Conférence et le Conseil exécutif dans l'accomplissement de leurs fonctions. Il exécute les mesures de vérification prévues par la Convention.

La participation des Etats africains à la Convention est, peut-être, plus importante qu'il semble à première vue. L'avantage le plus évident est l'établissement d'un régime de confiance mutuelle entre les Etats parties et, en conséquence, de faciliter l'importation des produits chimiques ainsi que le transfert de technologie dans le domaine des activités chimiques conformément à l'article XI de la Convention. En outre, une telle participation peut aussi aider à éviter de graves incidents internationaux. On pourrait ainsi supposer que l'attaque des missiles de croisière américains contre l'usine pharmaceutique d'Al-Chifa, dans les faubourgs de Khartoum en août 1998, aurait peut être été évitée si le Soudan avait été partie à la Convention à cette époque ; le conflit aurait en effet pu être réglé par le mécanisme prévu par la Convention.³

II. LES PRINCIPES GÉNÉRAUX DU SYSTÈME DE RÈGLEMENT DES DIFFÉRENDS

Un élément important de tout instrument juridique international est le système de règlement des différends entre ses participants. La Convention, pour sa part, prévoit un mécanisme spécial à cet effet. L'article XIV de la Convention est en effet consacré au règlement des différends entre les Etats parties ou entre les Etats parties et l'Organisation. Toutefois, si l'article XIV est le rouage principal de ce système, il n'en est pas le seul élément. Le paragraphe 6 de cet article intègre également, et de manière indirecte, à ce mécanisme les articles IX («Consultations, coopération et établissement des faits») et XII («Mesures propres à redresser une situation et à garantir le respect de la présente Convention, y compris les sanctions»).⁴

De manière générale, ces deux derniers articles possèdent un rôle et une fonction propres dans la Convention ; ils occupent également une place particulière dans le mécanisme de règlement des différends. Le recours à l'article IX peut se faire au stade préliminaire d'un différend tandis qu'on peut considérer l'article XII comme un moyen de mise en œuvre de ce mécanisme. Il y a aussi dans l'Annexe sur l'application de la Convention et la vérification certaines dispositions qui peuvent être assimilées à des règles relatives au règlement des différends (voir ci-dessous la partie VI(1) de la présente contribution). Les limites nécessairement réduites de notre étude ne nous permettent pas de considérer toutes les ramifications du système de règlement des différends prévu par la Convention ; nous nous limiterons donc à l'analyse du

---

3   Cette attaque aurait vraisemblablement incité le Soudan à signer et ratifier la CIAC en mai 1999.
4   Le paragraphe 6 prévoit que les dispositions de l'article XIV «sont sans préjudice de celles de l'article IX ou des dispositions relatives aux mesures propres à redresser une situation et à garantir le respect de la présente Convention, y compris les sanctions».

système de règlement des différends selon la Convention proprement dite, c'est-à-dire du mécanisme prévu par l'article XIV.[5]

Les principes généraux qui sont exprimés dans cette disposition sont assez traditionnels. Le différend doit être relatif à l'application ou à l'interprétation de la Convention ; il doit être réglé par les moyens pacifiques au choix des parties ; le mode de règlement doit être conforme aux dispositions de la Charte des Nations Unies. Les particularités du mécanisme de règlement des différends sont déterminées par les conditions d'application de ces principes dans le cadre de la Convention et de l'Organisation. Le système de règlement des différends créé par l'article XIV possède un caractère double qui est déterminé par la nature double de la Convention. La Convention a d'une part créé les rapports juridiques directement entre les Etats parties et

---

5   Article XIV « Règlement des différends » :
« 1. Les différends qui naîtraient au sujet de l'application ou de l'interprétation de la présente Convention sont réglés suivant les dispositions pertinentes de la Convention et d'une manière conforme aux dispositions de la Charte des Nations Unies.
2. En cas de différend entre deux ou plusieurs Etats parties, ou entre un ou plusieurs Etats parties et l'Organisation, quant à l'interprétation ou à l'application de la présente Convention, les parties se consultent en vue de régler rapidement ce différend par la voie de négociations ou par tout autre moyen pacifique de leur choix, y compris en ayant recours aux organes appropriés de la Convention et, par consentement mutuel, en saisissant la Cour internationale de Justice conformément au Statut de cette dernière. Les Etats parties en cause tiennent le Conseil exécutif informé des mesures prises.
3. Le Conseil exécutif peut contribuer au règlement d'un différend par tout moyen qu'il juge approprié, y compris en offrant ses bons offices, en invitant les Etats qui sont parties au différend à entamer le processus de règlement qu'ils ont choisi et en recommandant un délai d'exécution de toute procédure convenue.
4. La Conférence examine, quant aux différends, les points qui sont soulevés par les Etats parties ou qui sont portés à son attention par le Conseil exécutif. Si elle le juge nécessaire, la Conférence crée, conformément au paragraphe 21, alinéa f), de l'article VIII, des organes chargés de contribuer au règlement des différends ou confie cette tâche à des organes existants.
5. La Conférence et le Conseil exécutif sont habilités séparément, sous réserve de l'autorisation de l'Assemblée générale des Nations Unies, à demander à la Cour internationale de Justice de donner un avis consultatif sur tout point de droit entrant dans le cadre des activités de l'Organisation. L'Organisation conclut un accord avec l'Organisation des Nations Unies à cette fin, conformément au paragraphe 34, alinéa a), de l'article VIII.
6. Les dispositions du présent article sont sans préjudice de celles de l'article IX ou des dispositions relatives aux mesures propres à redresser une situation et à garantir le respect de la présente Convention, y compris les sanctions».

a d'autre part établi l'organisation internationale. Elle a partant créé un système de rapports complexes qui comprennent non seulement les rapports directs entre les Etats parties mais également les rapports entre les Etats parties par l'intermédiaire de l'Organisation et ceux entre l'OIAC et les Etats parties.

Le paragraphe 2 de l'article XIV exige que les parties au différend (les Etats parties ou un Etat partie et l'Organisation) commencent leur règlement par voie de consultation. Cette procédure préliminaire doit aboutir au choix du moyen de règlement. Parmi les modes de règlement figurent les négociations, le recours aux organes appropriés de la Convention et la saisine de la Cour internationale de Justice (le rôle de la Cour est précisé ci-dessous). Les parties peuvent aussi choisir d'autres moyens pacifiques de règlement des différends. Cette énumération nécessite deux éclaircissements.

On peut supposer tout d'abord que l'expression «tout autre moyen pacifique», utilisée à l'article XIV, doit être interprétée à la lumière de l'article 33 de la Charte des Nations Unies de façon à inclure les moyens spécifiés à cet article. Toutefois, l'expression «autre moyen pacifique» de la Convention n'est pas limitée par l'énumération de l'article 33.[6] En second lieu, la référence aux «organes appropriés de la Convention» paraît assez mystérieuse dans la mesure où le texte de la CIAC ne prévoit pas de tels organes. Il y a probablement une seule explication possible à cette divergence. L'idée des «organes de la Convention» avait été émise lors de l'étape initiale des négociations du texte de la Convention. Il semble bien que le paragraphe 2 de l'article XIV ait été finalisé pendant cette étape et que les négociateurs aient oublié de corriger le texte quand ils changèrent l'idée et, par conséquent, le concept d'«Organisation» s'est substitué à celui d'«organes de la Convention». Cette faute technique peut s'expliquer par les singularités des négociations multilatérales. Dans ce processus, il y a assez souvent une certaine réticence à amender un texte déjà convenu et qui ne porte aucune contradiction.

Informé d'un différend et des mesures prises pour sa résolution dans toutes les circonstances, le Conseil exécutif aux termes du paragraphe 3 de l'article XIV «peut contribuer au règlement [dudit] différend par tout moyen qu'il juge approprié». Trois moyens sont explicitement prévus : les bons offices du Conseil, l'invitation aux parties au différend à entamer le processus de règlement qu'ils ont choisi et la recommandation d'un délai d'exécution de toute procédure convenue.

---

[6] L'article 33 de la Charte renvoie aussi aux «autres moyens pacifiques».

Selon le paragraphe 4 de l'article XIV, la Conférence peut examiner les différends soumis par les Etats ou par le Conseil. La Conférence est un organe principal et c'est la raison pour laquelle elle a le droit de créer des organes spéciaux «chargés de contribuer au règlement des différends » ou de confier cette tâche à des organes existants. Comme exemple d'organe spécial, on peut mentionner la «Commission pour le règlement des litiges relatifs à la confidentialité» prévue par l'alinéa 23 de l'Annexe sur la protection de l'information confidentielle, comme organe subsidiaire de la Conférence.

Le paragraphe 5 de l'article XIV accorde à la Cour internationale de Justice un rôle particulier dans le mécanisme de règlement des différends. Aux termes de ce paragraphe, la Conférence et le Conseil peuvent séparément demander à la Cour de donner un avis consultatif «sur tout point de droit entrant dans le cadre des activités de l'Organisation».

À l'heure actuelle, l'habilitation donnée à l'Organisation de demander un avis consultatif à la Cour ne peut pas être considérée comme un droit. Ni l'Assemblée générale des Nations Unies ni la Cour ne sont directement obligées par le texte de la Convention. Pour transformer cette habilitation à demander un avis consultatif en un droit véritable l'Organisation doit en conséquence conclure un accord spécial avec l'ONU qui devrait prévoir les modalités de l'autorisation à donner par l'Assemblée générale des Nations Unies.

III. LA DÉFINITION D'UN DIFFÉREND

En matière de règlement pacifique des différends, avant l'ouverture de toute procédure de règlement, il est nécessaire à titre préliminaire de définir le différend et de constater son existence. La notion de différend en droit international public a été définie de manière très complète dans la jurisprudence de la Cour internationale de Justice et de sa devancière. Le point de départ de toute l'analyse doctrinale dans ce domaine et la définition classique du différend se trouvent dans l'arrêt n° 2 de la Cour permanente de Justice internationale rendu dans l'affaire des *Concessions Mavrommatis en Palestine* : «Un différend est un désaccord sur un point de droit ou de fait, une contradiction, une opposition de thèses juridiques ou d'intérêts entre deux personnes».[7] Cette définition a été développée et précisée dans la jurisprudence de la C.P.J.I. et de la C.I.J.[8]

Aux fins d'application pratique de l'article XIV de la Convention, on peut distinguer, sur la base de cette jurisprudence, les divers éléments essentiels d'un différend.

1. Un désaccord, une contradiction ou une opposition doit exister entre deux parties, entendue comme le rapport de parties que leurs opinions, leurs intérêts dressent l'une contre l'autre.[9]
2. Cette opposition peut se rapporter au droit, aux faits ou aux intérêts, pris ensemble ou séparément.
3. L'opposition doit concerner les mêmes dispositions de droit, les même faits ou les intérêts dans la mesure où ils se rapportent à ces dispositions et faits.
4. L'existence d'un différend doit être établie objectivement au moyen de la démonstration des différences dans les positions des parties. La simple assertion subjective d'une partie qu'il y a un différend ou sa négation ne sont pas le témoignage de l'existence de celui-ci.
5. L'existence d'un différend peut être reconnue par les deux parties ou peut être niée par l'une d'entre elles. Dans ce dernier cas, le différend, avant qu'il soit examiné par l'organe spécial chargé de la résolution des différends, doit être reconnu comme tel par cet organe.

Les conditions indiquées ci-dessus concernent la détermination d'un différend entre les parties en général. Toutefois la CIAC utilise la formule généralement admise par les dispositions similaires des traités internationaux:

---

7   *C.P.J.I. série A n° 2*, p. 11.
8   *Interprétation des traités de paix conclus avec la Bulgarie, la Hongrie et la Roumanie, première phase, avis consultatif du 30 mars 1950, C.I.J. Recueil 1950*, p. 74 ; *Sud-Ouest africain, exceptions préliminaires, arrêt, C.I.J. Recueil 1962*, p. 328 ; *Cameroun septentrional, arrêt, C.I.J. Recueil 1963*, p. 27 ; *Applicabilité de l'obligation d'arbitrage en vertu de la section 21 de l'accord de 26 juin 1947 relatif au siège de l'Organisation des Nations Unies, avis consultatif, C.I.J. Recueil 1988*, p. 27 ; *Timor oriental (Portugal c. Australie), C.I.J. Recueil 1995*, p. 100 ; *Application de la Convention pour la prévention et la répression du crime de génocide, exceptions préliminaires, arrêt, C.I.J. 1996*, pp. 614-617. Pour une analyse brève voir Sh. Rosenne *"The Law and Practice of the International Court, 1920-1996"*, Vol. II, Jurisdiction, 1997, pp. 519-522; voir aussi l'opinion individuelle du juge ad hoc Rigaux dans l'affaire des *Plates-formes pétrolières (République islamique d'Iran c. Etats-Unis d'Amérique), exception préliminaire, arrêt, C.I.J. Recueil 1996*, pp. 868-871.
9   Voir, par exemple, *Le Petit Robert, Dictionnaire de la langue française*, Paris, 1987, p. 1315.

les différends «au sujet de l'application ou de l'interprétation...». Cela signifie que seule cette catégorie de différends est envisagée par l'article XIV. C'est pour cette raison qu'il est nécessaire d'analyser le sens de l'expression «l'application ou l'interprétation».

La jurisprudence de la Cour internationale de Justice distingue la définition du différend et sa relation avec l'interprétation ou l'application d'un traité.[10] Afin que les parties puissent appliquer un mécanisme de règlement des différends prévu par une convention, ils doivent s'opposer sur le sens juridique des dispositions du traité (différend quant à l'interprétation) ou l'accomplissement de ces dispositions (différend quant à l'application). La façon dont la Cour examine cette question demeure conséquente durant toute son histoire. Dans les affaires où il était nécessaire de constater l'existence d'un différend tombé sous le coup de la juridiction de la Cour d'après une disposition conventionnelle, la Cour, ayant démontré l'existence en principe du différend, passe à la question de savoir si le différend concerne l'interprétation ou l'application de la convention.

L'exemple classique est l'affaire de *l'Interprétation des traités de paix* (1950) qui a donné lieu à un avis consultatif de la Cour internationale de Justice. Au début de son raisonnement, la Cour a conclu que «des différends internationaux se sont produits» parce qu'une situation s'est produite «dans laquelle les points de vue des deux parties, quant à l'exécution ou à la non-exécution de certaines obligations découlant des traités, sont nettement opposés ».[11] Partant de ce constat, la Cour a indique ce qui suit :

> «le point suivant à examiner est celui de savoir si les différends tombent sous l'application des dispositions des articles qui, dans les traités de paix, visent le règlement des différends. Les différends doivent être considérés comme tombant sous l'application de ces dispositions s'ils ont trait à l'interprétation ou à l'exécution des traités... Etant donné que les différends sont relatifs à l'exécution ou à la non-exécution des obligations prévues dans les articles qui traitent des droits de l'homme et des libertés fondamentales, ces différends sont nettement de ceux qui portent sur l'interprétation ou sur l'exécution des traités de paix».[12]

---

10 Pour une brève analyse de la jurisprudence de la Cour voir, par exemple, les références mentionnées dans l'opinion individuelle du juge *ad hoc* Rigaux dans l'affaire des *Plates-formes pétrolières (République islamique d'Iran c. Etats-Unis d'Amérique)*, exception préliminaire, arrêt, C.I.J. Recueil 1996, pp. 868-871.
11 *C.I.J. Recueil 1950*, p. 74.
12 *Ibid.*, p. 75.

La même méthode est utilisée dans l'affaire plus récente relative à *l'Application de la convention pour la prévention et la répression du crime de génocide, exceptions préliminaires*. Dans cette affaire, la Cour a déterminé l'existence du différend par référence aux points de vue opposés des parties et aussi au rejet, par la Yougoslavie, des griefs formulés à son encontre par la Bosnie-Herzégovine.[13] Cependant, cette détermination n'a pas suffi à asseoir la compétence de la Cour et celle-ci a du «s'assurer que le différend en question entre bien dans les prévisions de l'article IX de la convention sur le génocide». Ayant examiné cette question, la Cour a conclu que «les Parties, non seulement s'opposent sur les faits de l'espèce, sur leur imputabilité et sur l'applicabilité à ceux-ci des dispositions de la convention sur le génocide, mais, en outre, sont en désaccord quant au sens et à la portée juridique de plusieurs de ses dispositions, dont l'article IX».[14]

IV. LA CLASSIFICATION DES DIFFÉRENDS SELON LA CONVENTION

La Convention fait mention de plusieurs catégories de différends qu'on peut classer sur des bases tout à fait diverses. Pour les besoins de notre étude, nous retiendrons deux grandes catégories de différends : les différends classés *ratione personae* et ceux classés *ratione materiae*. Dans la première catégorie, on peut ranger les différends entre les Etats parties et les différends entre un ou plusieurs Etats parties et l'Organisation. La deuxième catégorie incorpore pour sa part les différends quant à l'interprétation ou à l'application de la Convention, les différends relatifs au non-respect de la Convention et ceux relatifs à la confidentialité. Tous les différends de la deuxième catégorie peuvent donc être des différends entre les Etats parties ou des différends entre un ou plusieurs Etats parties et l'Organisation.

1. **Les différends classés *ratione personae*.**

Bien que la Convention envisage les différends en fonction de leur origine (différends entre les Etats ou entre les Etats et l'Organisation), elle n'en tire aucune conséquence au niveau de la procédure. La méthode appliquée dans l'article XIV crée un problème théorique concernant la notion de règlement des différends selon la Convention : la question de la possibilité que

---

13 *C.I.J. Recueil 1996*, p. 614-615.
14 *Ibid.*, pp. 615-616.

l'une des parties au différend joue le rôle de l'autorité qui règle ce différend.[15]

En outre, le texte de l'article XIV, paragraphe 2, souffre d'une petite insuffisance au niveau de la technique juridique. À savoir, formellement tous les moyens de règlement des différends énumérés dans ce paragraphe, y compris la saisine de la Cour internationale de Justice, se rapportent aux différends entre les Etats aussi bien qu'aux différends entre les Etats et l'Organisation. La référence au Statut de la Cour dans le contexte de cette disposition permet de lever toute ambiguïté ; il serait toutefois souhaitable que le texte mentionne la Cour en ce qui concerne les seuls différends entre Etats.

Au point de vue de la classification des différends *ratione personae*, le mécanisme de règlement des différends entre les Etats d'après la Convention correspond à tous les schémas classiques et ne présente à cet égard aucune particularité. On peut par conséquent aborder maintenant la question de la participation des organes de l'OIAC au processus de règlement des différends auxquels l'Organisation est partie. Dans le régime de la Convention, la probabilité de survenance d'un différend de cette catégorie est plus grande que la probabilité d'un différend entre deux Etats, parce que les rapports entre l'OIAC et les Etats parties sont potentiellement plus intenses que les rapports entre les Etats parties en ce qui concerne l'exécution de la Convention.

En vertu du principe généralement reconnu en droit *nemo debet esse judex in propria causa*, une des parties au différend ne peut pas en même temps jouer le rôle de l'autorité pour son règlement. Néanmoins, il semble que les rédacteurs de la Convention se soient fondés sur une autre idée. En principe, ils se sont écartés de la notion d'organisation internationale considérée comme une institution unifiée possédant sa propre volonté unifiée et se sont basés sur l'idée d'indépendance de ses organes du moins pour le règlement des différends. Une telle construction, bien qu'elle ne soit pas irréprochable, leur a donné la possibilité de créer le mécanisme pour le règlement expéditif dans le cadre de la CIAC, des différends de nature très technique, sensible et spécifique (par exemple, ceux relatifs à la confidentialité).

L'Organisation est engagée dans des activités opérationnelles au moyen d'inspections conduites par le Secrétariat technique sur le territoire des Etats parties. À cette fin, il est nécessaire que le Secrétariat ait beaucoup de fonctions et de pouvoirs indépendants dans ses relations avec les Etats parties. Ces activités peuvent provoquer l'apparition de conflits entre le Secrétariat et les Etats. On peut supposer que les conflits de ce genre représenteront la

---

15   Ce problème sera analysé ci-dessous.

plupart des différends dans le cadre de la Convention. Pour les différends de cette catégorie (entre un Etat partie et le Secrétariat) le Conseil exécutif jouera le rôle de tierce partie à l'effet du règlement des différends. La Conférence peut jouer le même rôle à l'égard des différends entre le Conseil et un Etat. Il semble que ce rôle de la Conférence et du Conseil soit possible, en principe, en raison de la nature différente de ces organes: la Conférence est un organe représentatif de la composition complète; le Conseil est un organe représentatif de la composition limitée ; le Secrétariat est un organe non-representatif. L'Organisation consiste en effet en un système hiérarchique où l'organe du «plus haut niveau » possède l'autorité pour contrôler les actions de l'organe «inférieur », le «niveau » de l'organe dépendant du niveau de la représentation des Etats dans sa composition.

2. Les différends classés *ratione materiae*
(a) Les différends relatifs à l'interprétation ou à l'application de la CIAC

Cette catégorie de différends, en termes généraux, comprend pratiquement tous les différends qui peuvent s'élever entre les Etats parties ou entre un ou plusieurs Etats parties et l'Organisation à l'occasion de la mise en œuvre de la Convention. Les rapports entre l'Organisation et les Etats parties sont en effet exclusivement limités par le cadre de la Convention en raison de la compétence spécialisée de l'OIAC telle que définie par la Convention.[16] Il apparaît donc que tous les différends entre les Etats parties et l'Organisation deviennent automatiquement des différends «quant à l'interprétation ou à l'application de la Convention». Il est en outre peu probable que dans le domaine des relations internationales réglementé par la Convention, les différends entre les Etats puissent dépasser les limites de son interprétation ou de son application en raison du haut degré de sophistication du mécanisme de réglementation prévu par la Convention, qui couvre tous les aspects des relations entre les Etats dans son domaine d'application. La seule exception à cette règle pourrait être l'article XI intitulé «Développement économique et technologique» parce qu'il est rédigé en des termes généraux et, parce qu'on pourrait en conséquence contester, dans certain cas, la pertinence de l'application de cet article aux rapports ou actions économiques particuliers.

---

[16] L'article VIII, paragraphe 1, stipule que «les Etats parties créent [...] l'Organisation pour l'interdiction des armes chimiques, afin de réaliser l'objet et le but de la présente Convention, de veiller à l'application de ses dispositions».

(b) Les différends relatifs au non-respect de la Convention

L'article IX («Consultations, coopération et établissement des faits») fait référence aux préoccupations éventuelles de certains Etats parties quant au non-respect de la Convention par d'autres Etats parties. Ces préoccupations peuvent provoquer un différend à propos de l'exécution par un Etat de ses obligations au titre de la Convention. Cette catégorie de différends est une variété de différends «quant à l'interprétation ou à l'application de la Convention». En effet, le non-respect allégué de la Convention implique nécessairement une comparaison entre le comportement de l'Etat partie et les dispositions de cette dernière, c'est-à-dire la détermination du contenu de la règle et l'appréciation de la conformité du comportement en question à la disposition particulière (l'interprétation et l'application d'une règle de la Convention).

(c) Les différends relatifs à la confidentialité

Ces différends sont aussi mentionnés expressément dans la Convention (paragraphe 23 de l'Annexe sur la confidentialité) et sont également de manière implicite des différends «quant à l'interprétation ou à l'application de la Convention» parce que les obligations relatives à la confidentialité sont établies par la Convention.

(d) Les différends concernant la mise en œuvre des documents adoptés par les organes de l'OIAC aux fins de préciser les obligations conventionnelles[17]

Ces différends sont singuliers parce qu'ils ne sont pas proprement dits des différends «quant à l'interprétation ou à l'application de la Convention». Ils se rapportent en effet à des documents adoptés sur la base de la Convention mais n'en font pas partie intégrante. Il semblerait que pour cette raison les différends indiqués ne tombent pas sous le coup de l'article XIV. Néanmoins, les différends concernant la mise en œuvre des documents adoptés par les organes de l'OIAC aux fins de préciser les obligations conventionnelles sont des différends entrant dans le cadre de la Convention et en tant que tels peuvent être réglés suivant la procédure prévue par cet article. Il aurait été plus rigoureux d'un point de vue juridique d'assortir d'une clause spéciale à cet effet les actes normatifs et les accords de l'Organisation destinés à la réglementation du comportement des Etats parties.

---

17   Les règlements, les documents de politique générale ou les traités conclus en vertu de la Convention comme, par exemple, les accords d'installation conclus entre un Etat partie et l'Organisation concernant une installation spécifique soumise à la vérification sur place, conformément à la Convention.

V. LE RÔLE DE LA COUR INTERNATIONALE DE JUSTICE

L'article XIV accorde un rôle spécial à la Cour internationale de Justice. Le paragraphe 2 prévoit le droit des Etats parties de recourir à la Cour pour le règlement de leurs différends, mais cette saisine ne peut s'effectuer que «par consentement mutuel». La Convention ne consacre donc pas, comme d'autres conventions multilatérales, un système de compétence obligatoire de la Cour pour le règlement de différends entre Etats parties. Le mécanisme de règlement des différends de la Convention ne présente donc aucune originalité à cet égard.

Cependant, le rôle de la Cour, d'après la Convention, n'est pas limité au règlement des différends entre les Etats parties «conformément au Statut» de cet organe judiciaire principal des Nations Unies. Nous avons déjà mentionné que les rédacteurs de la CIAC ont réservé à la Conférence et au Conseil exécutif le droit, sous certaines conditions, de demander à la Cour de donner un avis consultatif «sur tout point de droit entrant dans le cadre des activités de l'Organisation». Il était peut-être facile de réserver ce droit aux organes de l'Organisation, toutefois dans les circonstances actuelles il n'est pas facile de l'exécuter.

Il est bien connu que la compétence consultative de la Cour, *ratione personae* est déterminée par l'article 96 de la Charte des Nations Unies. Selon cet article, seuls l'Assemblée générale et le Conseil de sécurité peuvent demander un avis consultatif en vertu de la Charte tandis que les autres organes des Nations Unies et les institutions spécialisées ne le peuvent qu'après y avoir été autorisés par l'Assemblée générale. Une autorisation générale a été donnée aux institutions spécialisées dans leurs accords avec les Nations Unies conformément à l'article 63 de la Charte.

Il y a une seule exception à cette règle générale. L'Agence internationale de l'énergie atomique, qui n'est pas formellement une institution spécialisée, a aussi le droit de demander un avis consultatif à la Cour. Bien que l'Agence ne soit pas une institution spécialisée au sens de l'article 57 de la Charte, l'Assemblée générale a en 1957 approuvé l'accord régissant les relations avec l'AIEA[18] et a donné ce droit à l'Agence.[19] De l'avis de Sh. Rosenne, l'Agence, dans ces circonstances, «may properly be regarded as an organ of the United Nations for the purposes of Article 96, and that the grant to it of authorization to request advisory opinions offends neither the letter nor the

---

[18] Résolution 1145 (XII), 14 novembre 1957.
[19] Résolution 1146 (XII), 14 novembre 1957. Voir Sh. Rosenne, *"The Law and Practice of the International Court, 1920-1996"*, 3rd ed., 1997, pp. 349-350; P. Szasz, *"The Law and Practice of the International Atomic Agency"*, 1970, p. 263.

spirit of the Charter or the Statute».[20] Pourtant, la conclusion que l'Agence peut être considérée comme un organe de l'ONU même aux fins de l'article 96, est très contestable. Il semblerait que cette conclusion ne repose pas sur des bases solides et qu'elle explique cette irrégularité de la pratique de manière artificielle. Sa faiblesse est confirmée par le fait que les positions de Rosenne concernant la situation de l'AIEA au regard de l'article 96 ne concordent pas. A la page 159 de son livre il écrit que en effet «the International Atomic Energy Agency is in some respects, in relation to the Court placed in an analogous position to that of the specialized agencies»[21] tandis qu'à la page 351 il compare l'AIEA à un organe de l'ONU.

La meilleure explication de la situation de l'AIEA consisterait à l'interpréter comme une exception faite par l'Assemble générale dans un cas particulier. Cette méthode permettrait de trouver une solution au cas de l'OIAC. En effet, le paragraphe 5 de l'article XIV, concernant les avis consultatifs de la Cour, a été copié sur la disposition correspondante du Statut de l'AIEA. Il est probable que les rédacteurs de la Convention avaient l'intention d'utiliser le précédent de l'Agence pour obtenir l'autorisation nécessaire. Toutefois, on ne peut pas appliquer ce précédent automatiquement dans le cas de l'OIAC. Comme l'AIEA, l'OIAC n'est ni un organe de l'ONU ni une institution spécialisée, c'est la raison pour laquelle il faut également trouver une solution particulière au cas de l'OIAC.

L'histoire aurait tendance à se répéter. En effet, comme dans le cas de l'AIEA en 1957, il existe aujourd'hui un dilemme devant l'OIAC et l'ONU: celui de décider si l'OIAC suivra le modèle de l'AIEA de manière que l'Assemblée générale lui accorde le droit de demander à la Cour un avis consultatif directement, ou si chaque requête sera soumise par l'OIAC à la Cour par l'intermédiaire de l'Assemblée générale. On peut supposer qu'il n'existe pas d'obstacle insurmontable interdisant l'utilisation du précédent de l'AIEA dans le cas de l'OIAC.

VI. LES ORGANES DE L'OIAC DANS LE PROCESSUS DE RÈGLEMENT DES DIFFÉRENDS

1. Le Conseil exécutif

Bien que le Conseil exécutif soit mentionné à l'article XIV, son rôle dans le processus de règlement des différends, selon cet article, demeure en

---

[20] Sh. Rosenne, *"The Law and Practice of the International Court, 1920-1996"*, 3rd ed., 1997, p. 351.
[21] *Ibid.*, p. 159.

principe auxiliaire. Il ne peut pratiquement pas prendre de mesures indépendantes pour régler un différend. Il semble fort que, en premier lieu, le Conseil doive recevoir l'information sur le différend, suivre et analyser le développement du différend et en cas de nécessité prévenir la Conférence.[22] Le langage du paragraphe 3 de l'article XIV, qui traite spécialement de la fonction du Conseil en tant qu'organe de résolution des différends, est très vague et ne permet pas de considérer le Conseil comme un organe important dans ce domaine. Le paragraphe 3 dispose en effet que le Conseil seul «peut contribuer au règlement d'un différend» ; cela signifie qu'il n'y a aucune obligation juridique à la charge du Conseil de participer directement à la résolution d'un différend. A sa discrétion, il peut décider de participer ou non à ce processus.

L'énumération des moyens qui sont à la disposition du Conseil n'est pas exhaustive mais les exemples de ces moyens montrent assez éloquemment qu'ils sont bien modestes. Le Conseil peut offrir ses bons offices, inviter les Etats à entamer le processus de règlement et recommander un délai d'exécution de toute procédure convenue. Il ne peut pas imposer ou appliquer ses recommandations. Pareille place du Conseil dans le mécanisme de règlement des différends s'explique, probablement, par le fait que le Conseil est un organe à composition limitée. L'expérience des négociations dans le cadre de la Commission préparatoire a mis en évidence que les Etats craignent généralement la domination de certains groupes d'Etats dans le processus décisionnel ; ils sont en conséquence peu disposés à confier la résolution de ces différends à un organe, composé des représentants étatiques, qui ne comprend pas tous les participants à la Convention.

La Convention a une structure complexe. Les dispositions de son Annexe, en addition à l'interprétation et l'explication technique de la Convention proprement dite, ont leur propre valeur en ce qui concerne la définition des obligations des Etats et des fonctions des organes de l'OIAC. Le rôle du Conseil dans le règlement des différends n'est donc pas limité par l'article XIV. A titre d'exemple, on peut mentionner qu'en cas de divergence entre le Secrétariat et un Etat à propos d'une question particulière «le Conseil exécutif est saisi de toute question restée sans solution afin qu'il prenne des mesures appropriées en vue de faciliter l'application pleine et entière de la Convention»;[23] en outre «en cas de difficultés, le Conseil exécutif engage des consultations avec l'Etat partie en vue de les aplanir. La

---

[22] Voir les paragraphes 2 et 3 de l'article XIV.
[23] Voir la partie IV (A), le paragraphe 53, la partie V, les paragraphes 36 et 79.

Conférence est saisie de toute difficulté restée sans solution»;[24] et encore l'Etat partie a «le droit de régler la question conformément aux dispositions de la présente Convention ou de saisir le Conseil exécutif afin qu'il la règle rapidement ».[25]

On peut considérer les dispositions susmentionnées comme un développement du rôle du Conseil tel que prévu par l'article XIV. Bien que ces dispositions ne décrivent pas précisément les pouvoirs du Conseil comme organe de règlement des différends, elles donnent au Conseil le droit de participer à ce processus non seulement en qualité d'intermédiaire mais aussi comme un organe chargé de résoudre les différends au fond. Toutefois, il faut souligner que ces pouvoirs du Conseil sont valables exclusivement pour les cas spécialement déterminés par l'Annexe.

2. La Conférence des Etats parties

La situation est distincte concernant les fonctions de la Conférence dans le domaine du règlement des différends. Aux termes de l'article XIV, la Conférence est autorisée à prendre le parti sur le fond des différends. Néanmoins, la Conférence, étant composée de tous les Etats parties, n'est pas le meilleur forum pour le règlement des différends. Il est probable que, en pratique, le rôle de la Conférence sera réduit, d'une part, à la création d'organes spéciaux (permanents ou *ad hoc*) à composition limitée aux fins de règlement des différends et, d'autre part, à l'adoption de solutions préparées par ces organes. On peut expliquer un tel rôle de la Conférence, ainsi que jusqu'à un certain degré le rôle modeste du Conseil à cet égard, par les idées contradictoires des Etats parties. Ces derniers estiment en effet que l'organe de règlement des différends, pour être effectif, doit être de composition limitée. En même temps, ils ne veulent pas perdre le contrôle sur le résultat du processus. L'action réciproque de ces deux facteurs détermine les modalités de participation de la Conférence au processus de règlement des différends.

3. La Commission pour le règlement des litiges relatifs à la confidentialité

La Commission est le seul organe subsidiaire de la Conférence à être mentionné spécialement dans le texte de la Convention ; elle peut être considérée comme «l'organe chargé de contribuer au règlement des différends» au sens du paragraphe 4 de l'article XIV. Les dispositions concernant la

---

24 Voir la partie IV (A), le paragraphe 58, la partie V, les paragraphes 39 et 82.
25 Voir la partie IV (B), le paragraphe 12.

composition de la Commission et son mode de fonctionnement se trouvent dans le document intitulé la «Politique de l'OIAC en matière de confidentialité» (ci-après la «Politique») adopté par la Conférence.

La sphère d'activité de la Commission est limitée. Selon le paragraphe 23 de l'Annexe sur la confidentialité, la Commission est créée pour «les affaires de manquement impliquant à la fois un Etat partie et l'Organisation». La «Politique» a élargi et précisé sa compétence. A l'heure actuelle, en addition aux litiges susmentionnés, la Commission peut également entrer en action «lorsque, conformément au paragraphe 4 de l'Article XIV de la Convention, la Conférence des Etats parties la charge d'examiner un litige relatif à la confidentialité» autre qu'un litige qui implique à la fois un Etat partie et l'Organisation (c'est-à-dire un litige entre deux Etats parties) ; et aussi «lorsque deux Etats parties en litige sur une question relative à la confidentialité font appel à elle pour régler leur différend conformément au paragraphe 2 de l'Article XIV de la Convention». En conséquence, en fonction de la catégorie du litige, la compétence de la Commission est soit obligatoire (dans le premier cas), soit déléguée (dans le deuxième cas), soit consensuelle (dans le troisième cas).

La Commission fonctionne, par excellence, comme un organe d'enquête, de médiation et de conciliation. En cas d'échec du règlement à l'amiable, la Commission remet aux parties en litige «un rapport esquissant les fait essentiels du différend, commentant objectivement celui-ci et recommandant les autres mesures qui pourraient être adoptées pour le régler par les parties en litige elles-mêmes, par la Commission, par la Conférence ou par tout autre organe de l'Organisation, en vertu d'un mandat précis conféré par la Conférence » (paragraphe 3.5 de la «Politique»). Néanmoins, ce rapport et ces recommandations ne sont obligatoires ni pour les parties en litige, ni pour la Conférence. Par conséquent, si le différend persiste, il faut utiliser les autres moyens de règlement. La Commission peut prendre des décisions obligatoires pour les parties en litige seulement avec leur consentement exprès.

On peut supposer que, eu égard au caractère consensuel de sa compétence et la complexité de sa procédure pour le règlement des différends interétatiques, la Commission ne serait pas l'organe le plus effectif pour le règlement des différends entre les Etats parties. Par conséquent, il est probable que son rôle sera limité aux différends «impliquant à la fois un Etat partie et l'Organisation», comme prévu dans l'Annexe sur la confidentialité.

THE UNITED NATIONS AND INTERNAL/INTERNATIONAL CONFLICTS IN AFRICA – A DOCUMENTARY SURVEY

Mpazi Sinjela

ANGOLA[1]

Despite regional and international efforts, the Angolan conflict has eluded resolution for over three decades. The commitment of the international community towards finding lasting peace in Angola has however never waned. In the case of the United Nations and her concerted efforts to assist Angolans find a peaceful settlement of their conflict, the Security Council continued its involvement by maintaining an observer mission in Angola throughout this reporting period.

In his progress report[2] of 8 October 1998, the Secretary-General referred to several negative developments which had taken place in connection with the peace process in Angola, which threatened the continuation of efforts aimed at achieving lasting peace. Most serious of these was a complete break of any contacts with UNITA. The Government had earlier recognized the leadership of the UNITA Renovation Committee as the only legitimate interlocutor for the implementation of the Lusaka Protocol. But, UNITA lead by Mr. Jonas Savimbi, continued to insist that it remained the legitimate partner in the peace process. This state of affairs had thus created a conflicting situation as to the true representation in the Joint Commission. Moreover, the President of Angola, Mr. José dos Santos, did not wish the special Representative of the Secretary-General to maintain any contacts with Mr. Savimbi. Any such attempts had been blocked by the Government with threats to cut contacts with the Special Representative should he meet the UNITA leadership.

---

[1] For the efforts of the United Nations aimed at resolving the conflicts in Angola during the period from mid 1997 to mid 1998, see *African Yearbook of International Law,* Vol. 6, pp 290 - 318
[2] Doc. S/1998/931

The UNITA Renovation Committee had, in the meanwhile, received some recognition, particularly by the Southern African Development Community, which in doing so, had characterized Mr. Savimbi's behaviour as that of a "war criminal". Calls had also been made that the UNITA Renovation Committee should be recognized by the Committee and by the UN and the International Community as the true representative of UNITA.

The Secretary-General also reported that the situation in the country continued to deteriorate due to UNITA's persistent attacks on strategic locations. There were reports of continued violations of human rights, indiscriminate as well as summary killings, torture and harassment, abductions, destruction of property, forcible displacement and restrictions on freedom of movement. The Secretary-General also reported of a number of initiatives by MONUA and local groups aimed at improving the human rights situation in the country.

The Secretary-General expressed concerns about the apparent unraveling of the peace process despite enormous efforts made by the international community at finding lasting peace. He was convinced that lasting peace would only be achieved through the implementation of the *Acordos de Paz* and the Lusaka Protocol as well as relevant Security Council resolutions on this question.

Despite these set backs, he considered it important to keep the door open for dialogue by all parties concerned. He had therefore, and in this connection, instructed his Special Representative to meet with Mr. Savimbi and to deliver the strongest message of the international community regarding his lack of compliance and to ascertain his intentions concerning the speediest implementation of the Lusaka Protocol. The Secretary-General had requested the Government to facilitate this contact.

Concerning the status granted to Mr. Savimbi, the National Assembly, on 27 October 1998, abrogated the law granting special status to him as the leader of the largest opposition party. The decision was taken on the ground that Mr. Savimbi had failed to fulfill his party's obligations under the Protocol.

In his report[3] on 23 November 1998, the Secretary-General again informed the Council that the peace process in Angola was still stalled and that UNITA was still refusing to implement its most important commitments under the Lusaka Protocol, including, demilitarization of its forces and the extension of the state administration. He observed that there had been no contacts between the Governments and UNITA and that the joint mechanisms for the implementation of the peace process had been paralyzed. The Government had also not changed its position regarding the request for his

---

[3] Doc. S/1998/1110

Special Representatives to meet with UNITA. Although various efforts had been made to revive the peace process, the Government had refused to pursue dialogue with UNITA. Its position was still that the UNITA Renovation Committee should represent UNITA in the Joint Commission.

Regarding the security situation, it also had remained precarious in many parts of the country, with renewed fighting in some parts leading to a further deterioration of conditions in the country. The human rights situation had also not improved. There was an increasing number of reports of human rights abuses committed against the civilian population, such as indiscriminate and summary killings, torture and ill treatment, harassment and intimidation, abductions, destruction of property and forcible displacement of people. In order to improve the situation, MONUA had taken part in the training of the Angolan national police personnel and civic educators on the application of human rights principles in law enforcement activities. Human rights officers were also making visits to prisons and detention centers in some provinces to ascertain conditions there and to work with prison officials with a view to improving the situation.

Thus, during the reporting period, no progress had been made in the implementation of the Lusaka Protocol and the prospects for reactivating the peace process looked bleak. While it was clear that UNITA was mainly responsible for the deadlock, the Government's rejection of all contacts and dialogue with UNITA did not advance the cause of peace and national reconciliation.

In his view, the Secretary-General considered that despite the absence of any progress towards the implementation of the Lusaka Protocol, it was desirable for the international community to continue its efforts in finding lasting peace in Angola.

In its resolution 1212 (1998) on December 3, 1998 the Security Council strongly condemned UNITA's failure to implement the remaining tasks of the Lusaka protocol, in particular the complete demilitarization of its forces and full cooperation in the immediate and unconditional extension of state administration throughout the national territory. It emphasized that the primary cause of the crisis in Angola and the impasse in the peace process was due to the failure of UNITA to comply with its obligations under the *Acordos de Paz*, the Lusaka Protocol and relevant Security Council resolutions. It demanded that UNITA comply immediately and without conditions with its obligations. It also demanded that UNITA withdraw immediately from territories it had occupied through military or other action.

The Secretary-General submitted a report on 17 January 1999 on the peace process in Angola.[4] He noted that the situation in the country had overall taken a turn towards military confrontation, which had serious humanitarian consequences. Although the President of UNITA, Mr. Savimbi, had affirmed in general terms his commitment to the Lusaka Protocol,[5] there was no indication that his party had any intention of resuming the implementation of key obligations under that Protocol. On the other hand, the President of Angola, Mr. José Eduardo dos Santos was of the view that lasting peace would only be achieved by isolating Mr. Savimbi and his group. He did not consider useful the holding of a dialogue between the two parties.

In the light of the escalation of the conflict, the Secretary-General recommended several ways for Member States to improve the implementation of measures imposed against UNITA by Security Council 864 (1993), 1127 (1997) 1173 (1998) and 1229 (1999). These included the obligation for Member States, particularly neighbours, to inform the Security Council on a regular basis on the implementation of measures adopted by the Security Council and for the Security Council to review periodically the implementation of those measures.

The Secretary-General notified the Security Council that in his view, for all intents and purposes, the Angolan Peace process had collapsed and the country was now in a state of war. Heavy fighting was taking place in several regions of the country. In his view therefore, it was now clear that the conditions for a meaningful United Nations peacekeeping role in Angola had ceased to exist. The Government had also indicated that it was unwilling to support the extension of MONUA beyond its current mandate. For the above reasons, the Secretary-General recommended that the MONUA personnel should continue to be withdrawn. At the same time, he urged the international community not to turn its back on Angola after having invested more than 1.5 billion US $ in support of the peace process. His own Special Representative, who would be based in New York, would return to Angola at short notice should the parties wish to pursue the peace process.

Through a statement[6] of the President on 21 January 1999, the Security Council expressed its alarm at the serious deterioration in the political and military situation in Angola. It reaffirmed its belief that lasting peace and national reconciliation can only be achieved through peaceful means. It urged both parties to resume constructive dialogue on the basis of the

---

[4] Doc. S/1999/49
[5] Doc. S/1994/1441, Annex)
[6] Doc. S/PRST/1999/3

Acordos de Paz, the Lusaka Protocol and the relevant Security Council resolutions in order to seek a peaceful solution of the conflict. It underscored the great importance it attached to a continued multidisciplinary presence in Angola. The Security Council also expressed its great concern at the humanitarian impact of the conflict on the Angolan people and appealed for all parties to cooperate fully in the search for peace to the conflict.

The Secretary-General presented another report[7] on 24 February 1999. He noted that the situation in Angola remained grave and that there was heavy fighting continuing to rage in several parts of the country. He also reported that on January 27, 1999, the national assembly had adopted a number of resolutions including one which accused the international community of complacency, acquiescence and bias and of making it easy for UNITA to re-arm and prepare for war. It reiterated its call to wind up the mandate of MONUA. In another resolution, Mr. Savimbi was declared a war criminal and an international terrorist. It called for his and his collaborators' arrest and prosecution. Furthermore, the chief state prosecutor of Angola indicated that Mr. Savimbi would be charged with war crimes and that proceedings against him would start soon. The Secretary-General also reported that the Government was unwilling to continue having the UN multidisciplinary peacekeeping force in Angola, but it would accept the appointment of the special representative of the Secretary-General to be based in New York and to maintain contacts with the Government from New York in monitoring the evolution of the situation in the country.

In its resolution 1229 (1999) of February 26, 1999 the Security Council reaffirmed that continued presence of United Nations in Angola can contribute greatly to national reconciliation. However, in the present predicament, it had but to withdraw MONUA from Angola.

In its resolution 1237 (1999) of 7 May 1999, the Security Council expressed its alarm at the humanitarian effects of the crisis on the civilian population. It emphasized its strong concern at reports that some countries were providing military assistance including mercenaries to Angola. It also considered that as a result of the refusal of UNITA to comply with its obligations, the situation in Angola continued to constitute a threat to international peace and security in the region. It condemned the continued and indiscriminate attacks by UNITA against the civilian population of Angola. For these reasons, it decided to establish an expert panel for a period of six months to collect information and investigate reports relating to the violation of the measures imposed against UNITA; to identify parties which were aid-

---

[7] Doc. S/1999/202

ing and abetting the violations of solutions and to recommend measures to end such violations and improve their implementation.

On 24 August 1999, the President of the Security Council made a statement.[8] According to it, the Security Council was deeply concerned at the deteriorating political, military and humanitarian situation in Angola as well as the dramatic increase in the number of internally displaced persons numbering over two million people. It demanded again that UNITA comply with its obligations under the peace accords. The Security Council further urged both parties to ensure full respect for human rights and international humanitarian law. It urged UNITA in particular to cease committing atrocities, including killing civilians and attacking humanitarian aid workers. It also expressed concern at reports of rearming of its military and the lying of mines in new areas in the country.

Despite the setbacks and the termination and withdrawal of MONUA, the Security Council will, no doubt, continue to deal with the question of assisting the parties in finding unity and peace in Angola.

---

[8] Doc. S/PRST/1999/26

RESOLUTION 1212 (1998)
Adopted by the Security Council at its 3951st meeting on 3 December 1998

The Security Council,

Reaffirming its resolutions 696 (1991) of 30 May 1991 and all subsequent relevant resolutions, in particular resolutions 864 (1993) of 15 September 1993, 1127 (1997) of 28 August 1997 and 1173 (1998) of 12 June 1998,

Reaffirming also its firm commitment to preserve the unity, sovereignty and territorial integrity of Angola,

Emphasizing the validity of the "Acordos de Paz" (S/22609, annex), the Lusaka Protocol (S/1994/1441, annex) and relevant Security Council resolutions as the fundamental basis of the peace process,

Strongly condemning the failure of the Uniao Nacional para a Independencia Total de Angola (UNITA) to implement the remaining tasks of the Lusaka Protocol, in particular the complete demilitarization of its forces and full cooperation in the immediate and unconditional extension of State administration throughout the national territory,

Expressing its deep concern at the failure of the leader of UNITA to respond to the letter of 6 October 1998 addressed to him by the Special Representative of the Secretary-General which contained proposals for restoring the peace process, and to the letter of 24 September 1998 addressed to him by the Ministers of Foreign Affairs of the three Observer States to the Lusaka Protocol which called for irreversible steps towards peace (S/1998/916),

Expressing its grave concern at the serious humanitarian impact of the impasse in the peace process and the deteriorating security conditions,

Having considered the report of the Secretary-General of 23 November 1998 (S/1998/1110),

1. *Emphasizes* that the primary cause of the crisis in Angola and of the current impasse in the peace process is the failure by the leadership of UNITA in Bailundo to comply with its obligations under the "Acordos de Paz", the Lusaka Protocol and relevant Security Council resolutions, and demands that UNITA comply immediately and without conditions with its obligations, in particular the complete demilitarization of its forces and full cooperation in the immediate and unconditional extension of State administration throughout the national territory;

2. *Demands* also that UNITA withdraw immediately from territories which it has reoccupied through military or other action;

3. *Calls* on the leadership of UNITA to cooperate fully and immediately with the United Nations Observer Mission in Angola (MONUA) in the withdrawal of MONUA personnel from Andulo and Bailundo, and holds the leadership of UNITA in Bailundo responsible for their safety and security;

4. *Stresses* that there can be no military solution to the conflict in Angola, and calls upon the Government of Angola and UNITA to cooperate fully with the Special Representative of the Secretary-General, including facilitation of his contacts with all those key to the implementation of the Lusaka Protocol, to seek a peaceful resolution of the crisis;

5. *Emphasizes* the importance of the Special Representative of the Secretary-General maintaining contact with all elements of UNITA in Luanda in order to revive the stalled peace process and encourage the transformation of UNITA into a genuine political party;

6. *Stresses* the importance of strengthening the rule of law and respect for human rights, including the full protection of all Angolan citizens throughout the national territory, in particular representatives and members of all political parties;

7. *Reiterates* its concern at the continued deterioration of the humanitarian situation, especially the significant increase in the number of internally displaced persons and the increase in minelaying activity, and calls on the Government of Angola and in particular UNITA to guarantee unconditionally the safety and freedom of movement of all international humanitarian personnel, to cooperate fully with international humanitarian organizations in the delivery of emergency relief assistance to affected populations, to cease minelaying activity, and to respect international humanitarian, refugee and human rights law;

8. *Urges* the international community to provide financial and other resources in order to allow the continued delivery of emergency relief assistance to vulnerable groups in Angola;

9. *Urges* all Member States to support the peace process in Angola through full and immediate implementation of the measures against UNITA contained in resolutions 864 (1993), 1127 (1997) and 1173 (1998), and expresses its readiness to consider appropriate reinforcing steps in accordance with the recommendations contained in the report referred to in paragraph 13 below;

10. *Decides* to extend the mandate of MONUA until 26 February 1999, and endorses the recommendation contained in the report of the Secretary-General to continue to adjust the deployment and force structure of MONUA, as needed, in accordance with security conditions and its ability to implement its mandate;

11. *Recognizes* that the Secretary-General may revert to the Council before 26 February 1999 with further recommendations regarding MONUA in the light of security conditions on the ground;

12. *Expresses* its growing concern for the security and freedom of movement throughout Angola of MONUA personnel, and calls upon the Government of Angola and in particular UNITA to ensure their safety;

13. *Requests* the Secretary-General to submit a report no later than 15 January 1999 regarding the status of the peace process, the future role and mandate of the United Nations in Angola and the force structure of MONUA in the light of its abil-

ity to carry out its mandated tasks, and reiterates the request contained in its resolution 1202 (1998) of 15 October 1998 for recommendations regarding technical and other ways for Member States to improve the implementation of the measures referred to in paragraph 9 above;

14. *Decides* to remain actively seized of the matter.

S/PRST/1999/3
21 January 1999

STATEMENT BY THE PRESIDENT OF THE SECURITY COUNCIL

At the 3969th meeting of the Security Council, held on 21 January 1999 in connection with the Council's consideration of the item entitled "The situation in Angola", the President of the Security Council made the following statement on behalf of the Council:

"The Security Council expresses its alarm at the serious deterioration in the political and military situation in Angola. It reaffirms its belief that lasting peace and national reconciliation cannot be achieved through military means, and urges the Government of Angola and especially the Uniao Nacional para a Independencia Total de Angola (UNITA) to resume a constructive dialogue on the basis of the "Acordos de Paz" (S/22609, annex), the Lusaka Protocol (S/1994/1441, annex) and relevant Security Council resolutions in order to seek a peaceful resolution of the conflict and spare the Angolan people further war and suffering. In this context, it reaffirms that the primary cause of the crisis in Angola is the refusal by UNITA to comply with the basic provisions of the Lusaka Protocol and reiterates its demand that UNITA comply with its obligations to demilitarize and to permit the extension of State administration to territories it controls.

"The Security Council shares the assessment and judgments of the Secretary-General on the political and military situation in Angola contained in his report of 17 January 1999 (S/1999/49). It underscores the contribution of the United Nations to the past four years of relative peace in Angola. It expresses its deep regret that the present political and security situation in the country and the lack of cooperation, especially by UNITA, with the United Nations Observer Mission in Angola (MONUA) have prevented MONUA from fully carrying out its mandated role.

"The Security Council underlines the great importance it attaches to a continued multidisciplinary presence of the United Nations under the direction of a Representative of the Secretary-General in Angola. It recognizes that such a continued presence depends on the safety of United Nations personnel and requires the agreement of the Government of Angola and the cooperation of all concerned. In this context, it appeals to the Government of Angola to provide such agreement and to UNITA to cooperate fully. It welcomes the intention of the Secretary-General to consult urgently with the Government of Angola on such a United Nations presence and to report to the Council in this regard.

"The Security Council again calls upon Member States to support the peace process in Angola through full and immediate implementation of the measures against UNITA contained in resolutions 864 (1993) of 15 September 1993, 1127 (1997) of 28 August 1997 and 1173 (1998) of 12 June 1998, and reiterates its readiness to take steps to reinforce the implementation of these measures on the basis of the recommendations contained in section IV of the report of the Secretary-General of 17 January 1999.

"The Security Council expresses its profound concern at the humanitarian impact of the conflict on the Angolan people. It urges the international community to support the Government of Angola in fulfilling its primary responsibility for the humanitarian needs of the Angolan people and, in this regard, urges Member States to fund generously the 1999 Consolidated Humanitarian Appeal for Angola. It calls upon all concerned to concur and cooperate with United Nations humanitarian assistance activities on the basis of the principles of neutrality and non-discrimination, to guarantee the security and freedom of movement of humanitarian personnel, and to ensure necessary, adequate and safe access and logistics by land and air. It urges all concerned to cooperate with the human rights activities of the United Nations, which help to lay a basis for lasting peace and national reconciliation.

"The Security Council will remain actively seized of the matter."

S/RES/1229 (1999)
19990226
26 February 1999

RESOLUTION 1229 (1999)
Adopted by the Security Council at its 3983rd meeting, on 26 February 1999

The Security Council,

Reaffirming its resolution 696 (1991) of 30 May 1991 and all subsequent relevant resolutions, in particular resolutions 864 (1993) of 15 September 1993, 1127 (1997) of 28 August 1997 and 1173 (1998) of 12 June 1998, as well as resolutions 1219 (1998) of 31 December 1998 and 1221 (1999) of 12 January 1999,

Recalling the statements of its President of 23 December 1998 (S/PRST/1998/37) and of 21 January 1999 (S/PRST/1999/3),

Reaffirming its commitment to preserve the sovereignty and territorial integrity of Angola,

Reiterating that the primary cause of the present situation in Angola is the failure of the Uniao Nacional para a Independencia Total de Angola (UNITA) under the leadership of Mr. Jonas Savimbi to comply with its obligations under the "Acordos de Paz" (S/22609, annex), the Lusaka Protocol (S/1994/1441, annex) and relevant Security Council resolutions,

Expressing its concern at the humanitarian effects of the present situation on the civilian population of Angola,

Reiterating that lasting peace and national reconciliation can only be achieved through peaceful means and in this regard reaffirming the importance of the "Acordos de Paz", the Lusaka Protocol and relevant Security Council resolutions,

Underscoring the contribution of the United Nations to the past four years of relative peace in Angola, and expressing its deep regret that the present political and security situation in the country has prevented the United Nations Observer Mission in Angola (MONUA) from fully carrying out its mandated role,

Taking note of the letter of the President of the Republic of Angola to the Secretary-General of 11 February 1999 (S/1999/166),

Reaffirming its view that a continued presence of the United Nations in Angola can contribute greatly to national reconciliation, and noting the ongoing consultations with the Government of Angola to obtain its agreement regarding the practical arrangements for this presence,

Having considered the report of the Secretary-General of 24 February 1999 (S/1999/202),

1. *Takes note* that the mandate of MONUA expires on 26 February 1999;

2. *Endorses* the recommendations contained in paragraphs 32 and 33 of the report of the Secretary-General of 24 February 1999 regarding the technical liquidation of MONUA;

3. *Affirms* that notwithstanding the expiration of the mandate of MONUA, the Status of Forces Agreement applicable to MONUA remains in force, pursuant to relevant provisions thereof, until the departure of the final elements of MONUA from Angola;

4. *Decides* that the human rights component of MONUA will continue its current activities during the liquidation period;

5. *Requests* the Secretary-General to designate a channel to liase with the Government of Angola pending the conclusion of the consultations with the Government of Angola regarding the follow-up configuration of the United Nations presence in Angola;

6. *Calls* upon all concerned to cooperate with the United Nations humanitarian assistance activities throughout the national territory of Angola on the basis of the principles of neutrality and non-discrimination and to guarantee the security and freedom of movement of humanitarian personnel;

7. *Expresses* its deep concern at the lack of progress in investigating the downing of the two aircraft chartered by the United Nations and the loss under suspicious circumstances of other commercial aircraft over UNITA controlled areas and reiterates its call upon all concerned, especially UNITA, to cooperate fully with and to facilitate an immediate and objective international investigation of these incidents;

8. *Endorses* the recommendations contained in the report of 12 February 1999 of the Committee established pursuant to resolution 864 (1993) (S/1999/147), reiterates its readiness to take steps to reinforce the measures against UNITA contained in resolutions 864 (1993), 1127 (1997) and 1173 (1998) and calls upon all Member States to implement fully these measures;

9. *Decides* to remain actively seized of the matter.

S/RES/1237 (1999)
7 May 1999

RESOLUTION 1237 (1999)
Adopted by the Security Council at its 3999th meeting, on 7 May 1999

The Security Council,

Reaffirming its resolution 696 (1991) of 30 May 1991 and all subsequent relevant resolutions, in particular resolutions 864 (1993) of 15 September 1993, 1127 (1997) of 28 August 1997 and 1173 (1998) of 12 June 1998, as well as resolution 1229 (1999) of 26 February 1999,

Reaffirming its commitment to preserve the sovereignty and territorial integrity of Angola,

Reiterating that the primary cause of the present crisis in Angola is the refusal of the Uniao Nacional Para a Independencia Total de Angola (UNITA), under the leadership of Mr. Jonas Savimbi, to comply with its obligations under the "Acordos de Paz" (S/22609, annex), the Lusaka Protocol (S/1994/1441, annex) and relevant Security Council resolutions,

Expressing its alarm at the humanitarian effects of the present crisis on the civilian population of Angola,

Emphasizing its strong concern at reports of the provision of military assistance, including mercenaries, to UNITA,

Having considered the recommendations contained in section IV of the report of the Secretary-General of 17 January 1999 (S/1999/49) concerning improving the implementation of the measures imposed against UNITA, and having endorsed the recommendations contained in the report of 12 February 1999 (S/1999/147) of the Committee established pursuant to resolution 864 (1993),

Welcoming the recommendations contained in the letter and its enclosure of 4 May 1999 (S/1999/509) of the Chairman of the Committee established pursuant to resolution 864 (1993),

A

1. *Stresses* that lasting peace and national reconciliation in Angola can only be achieved through a political settlement of the conflict, and in this regard reaffirms the importance of the "Acordos de Paz" and the Lusaka Protocol;

2. *Welcomes* and endorses the planned visits by the Chairman of the Committee established pursuant to resolution 864 (1993) to Angola and other concerned countries to discuss ways to improve the implementation of the measures against UNITA specified in paragraph 5 below;

B

Determining that, as a result of the refusal of UNITA to comply with its obligations under the "Acordos de Paz", the Lusaka Protocol and relevant Security Council resolutions, the current situation in Angola continues to constitute a threat to international peace and security in the region,

Emphasizing its concern at reports of violations of the measures concerning arms and related materiel, petroleum, diamonds and financial assets, imposed against UNITA, contained in resolutions 864 (1993), 1127 (1997) and 1173 (1998), and in this context acting under Chapter VII of the Charter of the United Nations,

3. *Deplores* the deteriorating situation in Angola, which is primarily due to the refusal of UNITA, under the leadership of Mr. Jonas Savimbi, to comply with its obligations under the "Acordos de Paz", the Lusaka Protocol and relevant Security Council resolutions;

4. *Condemns* the continued, indiscriminate attacks by UNITA against the civilian population of Angola, particularly in the cities of Huambo, Kuito and Malange;

5. *Stresses* the obligation of all Member States to comply fully with the measures imposed against UNITA contained in resolutions 864 (1993), 1127 (1997) and 1173 (1998);

6. *Endorses* the letter and its enclosure of 4 May 1999 of the Chairman of the Committee established pursuant to resolution 864 (1993) and decides to establish the expert panels referred to therein for a period of six months with the following mandate:

    (a) To collect information and investigate reports, including through visits to the countries concerned, relating to the violation of the measures imposed against UNITA with respect to arms and related materiel' petroleum and petroleum products, diamonds and the movement of UNITA funds as spec-

ified in the relevant resolutions and information on military assistance, including mercenaries;
   (b) To identify parties aiding and abetting the violations of the above-mentioned measures;
   (c) To recommend measures to end such violations and to improve the implementation of the above-mentioned measures;

7. *Requests* the Chairman of the Committee established pursuant to resolution 864 (1993) to submit to the Council no later than 31 July 1999 an interim report of the expert panels regarding their progress and preliminary findings and recommendations and to submit to the Council within six months of the formation of the expert panels their final report with recommendations;

8. *Calls* upon all States, relevant United Nations bodies and concerned parties, as appropriate, including non-governmental organizations and enterprises, to cooperate in a full and timely manner with the expert panels to facilitate the implementation of their mandate, including by making available to the expert panels information relating to their mandate;

9. *Calls* upon the Governments of the States concerned in which the expert panels will carry out their mandate to cooperate fully with the expert panels in the fulfillment of their mandate, including responding positively to requests from the expert panels for security, assistance, and access in pursuing investigations, including:
   (a) Adoption by them of any measures needed for the expert panels and their personnel to carry out their functions throughout the respective territories with full freedom, independence, and security;
   (b) Provision by them to the expert panels or to the Chairman of the Committee established pursuant to resolution 864 (1993) of information in their possession which the expert panels request or is otherwise needed to fulfil their mandate;
   (c) Freedom of access for the expert panels and their personnel to any establishment or place they deem necessary for their work, including border points and airfields;
   (d) Appropriate measures to guarantee the safety and security of the personnel of the expert panels and guarantees by them of full respect for the integrity, security and freedom of witnesses, experts and any other persons working with the expert panels in the fulfillment of their mandate;
   (e) Freedom of movement for the personnel of the expert panels, including freedom to interview any person in private, at any time, as appropriate;
   (f) The grant of relevant privileges and immunities in accordance with the General Convention on the Privileges and Immunities of the United Nations;

10. *Expresses* its concern at the delays in the investigations into the downing on 26 December 1998 and 2 January 1999 of two aircraft chartered by the United

Nations and the loss under suspicious circumstances of other commercial aircraft over UNITA-controlled areas in Angola as well as the crash on 26 June 1998 in Côte d'Ivoire of the aircraft carrying the Special Representative of the Secretary-General to Angola and other United Nations personnel, and reiterates its call upon all concerned to cooperate fully with and to facilitate an immediate and objective international investigation of these incidents;

C

11. *Endorses* the recommendation contained in the letter and its enclosure of 4 May 1999 of the Chairman of the Committee established pursuant to resolution 864 (1993) that the expert panels be supported as an expense of the Organization and through a United Nations Trust Fund established for this purpose, requests the Secretary-General to take the necessary steps towards this end, and urges States to make voluntary contributions to this Trust Fund;

12. *Reiterates* its call upon all concerned to cooperate with the United Nations humanitarian assistance activities on the basis of the principles of neutrality and non-discrimination, to facilitate the delivery of humanitarian assistance to all those in need throughout the territory of Angola and to guarantee unconditionally the security and freedom of movement of humanitarian personnel;

13. *Expresses* its strong support for further consultations between the Secretary-General and the Government of Angola regarding the follow-up configuration of the United Nations presence in Angola;

14. *Decides* to remain actively seized of the matter.

S/PRST/1999/26
24 August 1999

STATEMENT BY THE PRESIDENT OF THE SECURITY COUNCIL

At the 4036th meeting of the Security Council, held on 24 August 1999 in connection with the Council's consideration of the item entitled "The situation in Angola", the President of the Security Council made the following statement on behalf of the Council:

"The Security Council expresses its deep concern at the deteriorating political, military and humanitarian situation in Angola, at the suffering of the people and at the dramatic increase in the number of internally displaced persons, which has now reached well over two million people, not including the unknown number of internally displaced persons in areas which are currently inaccessible to humanitarian agencies.

"The Security Council reiterates that the primary cause of the current crisis in Angola is the failure by the leadership of the Uniao Nacional para a Independencia Total de Angola (UNITA) to comply with its obligations under the Lusaka Protocol, and again demands that UNITA comply immediately and without conditions with its obligations to demilitarize and permit the extension of state administration to areas under its control. It reaffirms its belief that lasting peace and national reconciliation can only be achieved through political dialogue.

"The Security Council expresses its concern at the critical condition of the internally displaced persons who from lack of food, medicines, shelter, arable land and other necessities. The Council further expresses its grave concern at the number of malnourished children and at the outbreak of diseases such as polio and meningitis due to the lack of access to clean water and hygiene. In this regard the Council commends the excellent work by the Government of Angola and the United Nations system in their efforts towards the eradication of diseases in Angola. The Council also expresses its concern at the plight of those vulnerable groups, such as children, women, the elderly and the handicapped, who are particularly at risk and in need of special assistance.

"The Security Council expresses its concern that the continuing conflict in Angola has increased the cost of humanitarian assistance. It notes the insufficient level of contributions to the 1999 United Nations Consolidated Inter-Agency Appeal for Angola and reiterates its appeal to the donor community to contribute generously, financially and in kind, to the humanitarian appeal to enable the agencies to address effectively the plight of the internally displaced persons. The Council welcomes the announcement by the Government of Angola of an Emergency Plan for Humanitarian Assistance.

"The Security Council also expresses its concern that the continuing conflict and lack of access jeopardize the ability of the agencies to continue to deliver assistance to those in need. The Council urges the Government of Angola and particularly UNITA to provide access to all internally displaced persons in Angola, and to facilitate the mechanisms necessary for the delivery of humanitarian assistance to all populations in need throughout the country. The Council urges both parties, particularly UNITA, to guarantee the safety and security and freedom of movement of humanitarian personnel, including United Nations and associated personnel, providing assistance to internally displaced persons. The Council strongly urges respect for the principle of neutrality and impartiality in the delivery of assistance. The Council commends the determination and courage of those working to relieve human suffering in Angola, including the Office for the Coordination of Humanitarian Affairs, the World Food Programme and the United Nations Children's Fund and other agencies.

"The Security Council urges both parties to ensure full respect for human rights and international humanitarian law. In this connection, the Council urges UNITA to cease committing atrocities, including killing civilians and attacking humanitarian aid workers, and demands the release of all foreign citizens, including the Russian aircrews, held by UNITA. It expresses its concern at reports of re-mining activities as well as the laying of mines in new areas in the country.

"The Security Council will remain actively seized of the matter."

CENTRAL AFRICAN REPUBLIC[9]

It will be recalled that the Security Council decided, on 27 March 1998 to establish the United Nations Mission in the Central African Republic (MINURCA) to succeed the Inter-African Mission established to Monitor the Implementation of the Bangui Agreement (MISAB).

In its resolution 1201 (1998) of 15 October 1998, the Security Council recognized the significant progress made by the Government in the implementation of the Bangui Agreements and initiating major political and economic reforms in the country. It noted with satisfaction the adoption of an operational plan for organizing the legislative elections by the Mixed and Independent Electoral Commission (CEMI). It welcomed the announcement to hold legislative elections on 22 November and 13 December 1998. It therefore decided, in this connection, to include in the mandate of MINURCA, support for the conduct of the elections. It also called upon the authorities to provide the necessary assistance, including the security arrangements, so as to enable CEMI to prepare adequately and freely for the legislative elections. It also urged all parties to assume fully their responsibilities in the elections and to participate in them in a manner which would strengthen the democratic process and contribute to national reconciliation.

On 18 December 1998, the Secretary-General reported[10] that the first round of legislative elections had taken place as scheduled on 22 November 1998 in a peaceful and orderly manner. Some 100 international observers from the United Nations, the European Union and the *Organization Internationale de la Francophonie* had observed the elections. Despite some technical difficulties, such as the scarcity of some of the necessary supplies, it was observed that the officials had carried out their duties well. It was noted that there were however, some organizational shortcomings such as poorly prepared electoral lists, difficulties in the distribution of voter cards and the late and insufficient delivery of come electoral materials. It was noted that these problems had delayed the opening of the polling stations in a number of places. Despite these minor setbacks, the United Nations and other international observers, considered that the first round of elections was conducted in a satisfactory and credible manner.

---

[9] For the efforts of the United Nations aimed at resolving the conflicts in Central African Republic during the period from mid 1997 to mid 1998, see *African Yearbook of International Law,* Vol. 6, pp 319 - 328

[10] Doc. S/1998/1203

The official results of the elections were announced on 7 December 1998 by which 46 candidates were elected, including 26 from President Patasse's party, 17 from the opposition and three independents. There were 195 candidates who received more than 10 per cent of the vote and thus became eligible to participate in the second round scheduled to take place on 13 December 1998.

In his observations, the Secretary-General noted that the holding of elections was an important step towards the restoration of national institutions destroyed by successive mutinies in 1996. Whatever the outcome of the second round of the elections, it was considered imperative that the international peacekeeping force should be maintained to provide a secure environment in the capital city of Bangui, and its immediate vicinity as well as carrying out its other functions enumerated in its mandate. The Secretary-General thus recommended the extension of the mandate of MINURCA.

On 29 January 1999, the Secretary-General presented another report[11] concerning the conflict in the Central African Republic and the results of the second round of elections held on 13 December 1998. As a result of the elections held on 22 November and 13 December 1998, out of the 109 seats for the National Assembly, the ruling party won 54 and the coalition of the opposition parties won 55 seats. Following the proclamation of results, however, one opposition legislator crossed over to the ruling party, which thereupon proclaimed a majority. The ruling party also insisted on the right to appointing a President and on appointing other key personnel in the Government. This produced a deep reaction by the opposition parties who walked out of the National Assembly in protest. Three members of the opposition out of the four nominated to join the Government of 23 members, also left the Government.

Finally, the Secretary-General observed that MINURCA was and continued to be a source of much needed stability, both in the Central African Republic and in the sub-region as a whole. He therefore considered the extension of the mandate of MINURCA as essential to the maintenance of the progress so far made in normalizing life in the country.

The President of the Security Council made a statement on 18 February 1999.[12] Referring to the political instability resulting from the National Assembly, he expressed the concern of the Security Council about the consequences that these political tensions had for the stability and functioning of the institutions in the country. The Council thus stressed the need for both

---

[11] Doc. S/1999/98
[12] Doc. S/1999/7

parties to cooperate closely and work actively with the aim of achieving political consensus, which was indispensable to stability in the country. The Security Council also considered that a smooth preparation of free and fair elections required that the parties resolve the political impasse in order for the country to move forward.

Along the same lines, on 26 February 1999, the Security Council in resolution S/1230 (1999) reaffirmed as an essential ingredient for peace and national integration in the country, the complete implementation of the various tasks contained in the Bangui Agreement and the National Reconciliation Pact. It called upon the Government to establish the national electoral commission and to set up a timetable for the holding of the presidential elections.

The Secretary-General reported[13] on 14 April 1999 on the formation of a new Government, following the nomination of a new Prime Minister on 15 January 1999. The new Government was reported to be functioning with considerable cohesion. The Government included a number of members from the civic society and technocrats who had no party affiliation. In preparation for the elections scheduled to take place in August/September 1999, MINURCA had made a plan to provide assistance to and international monitoring and verification of the electoral process.

The Secretary-General also expressed the view that the Government had continued to make some progress towards reform, even though this progress was reported to be slow. While there was calm and relative stability, there was still intense distrust among the political leaders and that the economic and social situation had remained precarious. He observed, in this connection, that in order to improve the security situation, FORSDIR had been removed from roadblock duties. He called upon the Government to ensure that FORSDIR was excluded from all police and law-and-order functions, which should be performed by the police. He also noted that while some progress had been made towards the preparation of elections, there was much work already to be carried out including, the revision of the electoral register, practical and logistical preparations and the setting up of the actual date of the elections.

On 28 May 1999, the Secretary-General again reported[14] that despite the impasse over the distribution of the posts in the Bureau, the National Assembly had been functioning normally. It had taken a number of decisions on important issues such as the modification of the electoral code and the

---

[13] Doc. S/1999/416
[14] Doc. S/1999/621

reform of the armed forces, and the revitalization of the economy. The CEMI had finally been inaugurated on 19 May 1999. It was hoped that the Commission would assume its responsibilities, including taking important decisions regarding the organization and conduct of elections, and the fixing of the date for the elections.

In another report, on 15 July 1999, the Secretary-General observed that there had been an altercation on the outskirts of Bangui between some cattle herdsmen of Chadian origin and some Central African nationals. The resulting intervention by the presidential guardsmen had lead to at least five deaths, mostly Chadians. The incident was ended with the deployment of MINURCA to control the situation by separating the two sides.

However, leading from this incident, on 22 June, students at the University of Bangui went on rampage and attacked Chadian students. The action was precipitated by a false rumour, that the students at the University of N'djamena had attacked Central African students studying there. The police later quelled off the incident.

The Secretary-General noted that this unrest had been exacerbated partly by the bad handling of the situation by the FORSDIR. The Special Representative had requested the President to withdraw these forces from the Bangui airport, the border posts and to prevent them from performing law and order duties. The President had however refused to do so, stating that this was the only loyal force he could rely on.

Regarding the holding of elections, the Secretary-General reported that a decree had been issued designating 29 August and 19 September as the dates for the first round, and that if any, the second round of elections. Preparations for the elections were thus proceeding and political parties were nominating their candidates to represent them.

Following the successful holding of elections, as scheduled on 19 September 1999, the Security Council in its resolution 1271 of 22 October 1999 noted with satisfaction the successful conclusion of the presidential elections. Notwithstanding this fact, nevertheless, the Security Council decided to renew the mandate of MINURCA until 15 February 2000 in order to assist the country in the post-conflict peace-building process. It called upon the President to cooperate with MINURCA.

S/RES/1201 (1998)

15 October 1998

RESOLUTION 1201 (1998)
Adopted by the Security Council at its 3935th meeting, on 15 October 1998

The Security Council,

Reaffirming its resolutions 1125 (1997) of 6 August 1997, 1136 (1997) of 6 November 1997, 1152 (1998) of 5 February 1998, 1155 (1998) of 16 March 1998, 1159 (1998) of 27 March 1998 and 1182 (1998) of 14 July 1998,

Welcoming the report of the Secretary-General of 25 August 1998 (S/1998/783 and Add.1) and noting the recommendations contained therein,

Stressing that the complete implementation of the Bangui Agreements (S/1998/561) and of the National Reconciliation Pact (S/1998/219, annex) is essential to peace and national reconciliation in the Central African Republic, and recognizing the significant progress made by the Government of the Central African Republic in implementing the Bangui Agreements and initiating major political and economic reforms,

Recalling the importance of regional stability and the need to consolidate the progress achieved so far, and in particular to assist the people of the Central African Republic to consolidate the process of national reconciliation and to help sustain a secure and stable environment conducive to the holding of free and fair elections,

Emphasizing that the authorities of the Central African Republic and the Mixed and Independent Electoral Commission (CEMI) are responsible for the organization and conduct of the legislative elections,

Noting with satisfaction the adoption of an operational plan for the organization of the legislative elections by the CEMI and welcoming donor pledges made in support of the electoral process,

Recognizing the importance of the support already given by the United Nations Development Programme and the United Nations Mission in the Central African Republic (MINURCA) to the CEMI in the preparation for the elections,

1. *Welcomes* the announcement by the authorities of the Central African Republic and the CEMI to hold legislative elections on 22 November and 13 December 1998;

2. *Decides* that the mandate of MINURCA shall include support for the conduct of legislative elections as described in section III of the report of the Secretary-General of 21 August 1998, and in particular:

(a) The transport of electoral materials and equipment to selected sites and to the sous-prefectures, as well as the transport of United Nations electoral observers to and from electoral sites;

(b) The conduct of a limited but reliable international observation of the first and second rounds of the legislative elections;

(c) Ensuring the security of electoral materials and equipment during their transport to and at the selected sites, as well as the security of the international electoral observers;

3. *Approves* the recommendation contained in paragraph 25 of the above-mentioned report of the Secretary-General regarding the provision of security during the legislative election process, taking into account the need to ensure the stability and security of Bangui and in accordance with the cost estimate associated with this recommendation contained in the addendum to that report;

4. *Welcomes* the establishment of a joint committee of the Government of the Central African Republic and MINURCA to address the restructuring of the Central African Armed Forces (FACA), and reiterates its call upon the Government of the Central African Republic to adopt as soon as possible a plan for the effective restructuring of its armed forces;

5. *Welcomes* the deployment of up to 150 FACA troops to the selected sites, operating under United Nations rules of engagement applicable to MINURCA;

6. *Calls* upon the Central African authorities to provide the necessary assistance, including the security arrangements, that will enable the CEMI to prepare adequately and freely for the legislative elections;

7. *Urges* all parties in the Central African Republic to assume fully their responsibilities in the legislative elections and to participate in them in a manner that will strengthen the democratic process and contribute to national reconciliation;

8. *Urges* Member States to provide the required technical, financial and logistical assistance for the organization of free and fair legislative elections;

9. *Decides* to extend the mandate of MINURCA until 28 February 1999;

10. *Requests* the Secretary-General to keep the Security Council regularly informed and to submit by 20 December 1998 the report called for in its resolution 1182 (1998) on the implementation of the mandate of MINURCA, on developments in the Central African Republic, on progress towards the implementation of the commitments expressed in the letter of 8 January 1998 from the President of the Central African Republic to the Secretary-General (S/1998/61, annex) and on the implementation of the Bangui Agreements and the National Reconciliation Pact, including on commitments related to ensuring the country's economic recovery and the restructuring of the security forces;

11. *Expresses* its intention to terminate MINURCA no later than 28 February 1999, with its drawdown beginning no later than 15 January 1999, and requests the

Secretary-General to make recommendations on this basis in his report referred to in paragraph 10 above;

12. *Expresses* its appreciation to the Secretary-General, his Special Representative and the personnel of MINURCA for their efforts to promote peace and national reconciliation in the Central African Republic;

13. *Decides* to remain actively seized of the matter.

S/PRST/1999/7

18 February 1999

STATEMENT BY THE PRESIDENT OF THE SECURITY COUNCIL

At the 3979th meeting of the Security Council, held on 18 February 1999 in connection with the Council's consideration of the item entitled "The situation in the Central African Republic", the President of the Security Council made the following statement on behalf of the Council:

"The Security Council, noting the letter of 9 February 1999 from the President of the Central African Republic to the President of the Council (S/1999/132), takes note with satisfaction of the commitment expressed by the President of the Central African Republic to maintain peace in the Central African Republic through dialogue and consultation. In this context, it strongly reaffirms that the complete implementation of the Bangui Agreements (S/1997/561, appendices III-VI) and of the National Reconciliation Pact (S/1998/219) is essential to peace and national reconciliation in the Central African Republic.

"The Security Council calls upon the Government of the Central African Republic to continue to take concrete steps to implement political, economic, social and security reforms as referred to in the report of the Secretary-General of 23 February 1998 (S/1998/148) and to fulfil the commitments expressed in the letters of 8 January 1998 (S/1998/61, annex) and of 23 January 1999 (S/1999/98, annex) to the Secretary-General by the President of the Central African Republic. It recalls that the success, the future mandate and the ongoing presence of the United Nations Mission in the Central African Republic are closely linked to the fulfillment of these commitments, in particular the immediate resumption of a constructive political dialogue.

"The Security Council expresses its concern about the consequences that the current political tensions have for the stability and the functioning of the institutions of the Central African Republic. It reaffirms that the Government, the political leaders and the people of the Central African Republic bear the primary responsibility for national reconciliation, the maintenance of a stable and secure environment and the reconstruction of their country. It emphasizes the importance of continuing efforts in the Central African Republic to settle outstanding contentious issues peacefully and democratically in accordance with the Bangui Agreements. It stresses the need for both the "mouvance presidentielle" and the opposition parties to cooperate closely and work actively with the aim of achieving the political consensus indispensable to stability in the Central African Republic.

"The Security Council considers that a smooth preparation of free and fair presidential elections, for which proper steps should be taken as soon as possible, requires a certain level of political consensus and the opening of a genuine dialogue between all the constituent parties of the National Assembly. It also considers that consensual preparation for the presidential elections can only reinforce the legitimacy of the next President of the Republic and also secure a sustainable civil peace. It fully supports the Special Representative of the Secretary-General in his call to the Central African political leaders and authorities to resolve the political impasse so the country can move forward, and welcomes the current efforts undertaken to this end.

"The Security Council will remain seized of the matter."

S/RES/1271 (1999)

22 October 1999

RESOLUTION 1271 (1999)
Adopted by the Security Council at its 4056th meeting, on 22 October 1999

The Security Council,

Reaffirming all its relevant resolutions, in particular resolutions 1159 (1998) of 27 March 1998, 1201 (1998) of 15 October 1998 and 1230 (1999) of 26 February 1999,

Noting with satisfaction the successful conclusion of the presidential elections held on 19 September 1999,

Commending the United Nations Mission in the Central African Republic (MINURCA) and the Special Representative of the Secretary-General on the support provided to the electoral process,

Affirming the commitment of all States to respect the sovereignty, political independence and territorial integrity of the Central African Republic,

Welcoming the report of the Secretary-General of 7 October 1999 (S/1999/1038), and noting with approval the recommendations contained therein,

Recalling the importance of the process of national reconciliation, and urging all the political forces of the Central African Republic to continue their efforts towards cooperation and understanding,

Emphasizing the necessity of proceeding speedily to the restructuring of the Central African armed forces (FACA),

Reaffirming the importance of regional stability and of the consolidation of the climate of peace in the Central African Republic, which constitute essential elements for the restoration of peace in the region,

Reaffirming also the link between socio-economic progress and the consolidation of the stability of the Central African Republic,

Recalling the relevant principles contained in the Convention on the Safety of United Nations and Associated Personnel, adopted on 9 December 1994,

Taking note of the desire expressed by the Government of the Central African Republic for an extension of the presence of MINURCA beyond 15 November 1999,

1. *Decides* to extend the mandate of MINURCA until 15 February 2000 with a view to ensuring a short and gradual transition from United Nations peacekeeping involvement in the Central African Republic to a post-conflict peace-building presence with the aid of the relevant United Nations agencies and programmes and of the International Monetary Fund and the International Bank for Reconstruction and Development;

2. *Welcomes* the proposal of the Secretary-General in paragraph 58 of his report of 7 October 1999 recommending that the reduction of the military and civilian strength of MINURCA be conducted in three stages;

3. *Calls once* again upon the Government of the Central African Republic to continue to take tangible measures to implement the political, economic, social and security reforms mentioned in the report of the Secretary-General of 23 February 1998 (S/1998/219) and to honour the commitments set forth, inter alia, in the letter dated 23 January 1999 (S/1999/98, annex) from the President of the Central African Republic addressed to the Secretary-General, and reaffirms the role of the Special Representative of the Secretary-General for the Central African Republic in assisting the promotion of reforms and national reconciliation;

4. *Strongly encourages* the Government of the Central African Republic to coordinate closely with MINURCA in the progressive transfer of the functions of MINURCA in the security field to the local security and police forces;

5. *Calls upon* the Government of the Central African Republic to complete, with the advice and technical support of MINURCA, the initial steps of the restructuring programme of the FACA and of the demobilization and reintegration programme of the retired military personnel, appeals to the international community to give its support to these programmes, and welcomes the proposal of the Secretary-General to convene a meeting in New York in the coming months to solicit funds in order to finance these programmes;

6. *Welcomes* the proposal of the Secretary-General to dispatch a small multi-disciplinary mission to Bangui in order to examine, in accordance with the wishes

expressed by the Government of the Central African Republic, the conditions for the maintenance of the United Nations presence beyond 15 February 2000 in accordance with the recommendations made by the Secretary-General and contained in his reports of 30 May 1999 (S/1999/621) and 7 October 1999, and requests the Secretary-General to inform the Council as soon as possible concerning his detailed proposals in this regard;

7. *Reaffirms* the importance of the role of MINURCA in supervising the destruction of confiscated weapons and ammunition under MINURCA control;

8. *Requests* the Secretary-General to submit by 15 January 2000 a report on the implementation of the mandate of MINURCA and, in particular, on the progressive transfer of the functions of MINURCA in the security field to the local security and police forces, on the evolution of the situation in the Central African Republic, on the progress achieved in the implementation of the commitments set forth in the letters dated 8 December 1998 (S/1999/116, annex) and 23 January 1999 from the President of the Central African Republic addressed to the Secretary-General, and on the implementation of the Bangui Agreements and the National Reconciliation Pact, including the commitments relating to economic recovery, the restructuring of the security forces and the functioning of the Special Force for the Defence of the Republican Institutions (FORSDIR);

9. *Decides* to remain actively seized of the matter.

DEMOCRATIC REPUBLIC OF THE CONGO

The conflict in the Democratic Republic of the Congo (DRC) was under active consideration by the Security Council during the reporting period.[15]

In its resolution 1234 of 9 April 1999, the Security Council deplored the continuing fighting and presence of forces of foreign States in the DRC and called upon the States concerned to withdraw them. It demanded an immediate halt t o the hostilities and called upon the parties to sign the cease-fire agreement, to protect human rights and to respect international humanitarian law.

The President of the Security Council, on 24 June 1999, made a statement[16] reaffirming the Council's commitment to preserving the national unity, sovereignty, territorial integrity and political independence of the DRC. The Council also reaffirmed support for the regional mediation process facilitated by Zambia on behalf of the Southern African Development Community in cooperation with the organization of African Unity (OAU), and with support from the United Nations, in finding a peaceful settlement to the conflict. It called upon all parties not only to commit themselves to the peace process but also to participate in a constructive and faithful spirit in the summit scheduled to be held in Lusaka on 26 June 1999. It again called upon the parties immediately to sign a cease-fire agreement. The Council also stressed the need for a continuing process of genuine national reconciliation and democratization in all States of the Great Lakes region.

On 15 July 1999, the Secretary-General reported[17] on the Cease-fire Agreement, signed on 10 July 1999 at Lusaka. The Heads of State of the DRC, Namibia, Rwanda, Uganda and Zimbabwe as well as the Minister of Defense of Angola signed the agreement to stop all hostilities between the belligerent forces in the DRC. The representatives of the Rally for a Democratic Congo and the Movement for the Liberation of the Congo did not, however, sign the Agreement.

In its essential parts, the agreement provides that all air, land and sea attacks as well as the movement of military should cease has of the date of the signing of the Agreement. The forces were to disengage with immediate effect.

Other salient provisions of the Agreement include the need to normalize the situation along the international borders of the DRC. This included

---

[15] For the efforts of the United Nations aimed at resolving the conflict in the Democratic Republic of Congo during the period from mid 1997 to mid 1998, see *African Yearbook of International Law*, VOL. 6, pp. 329 to 333
[16] Doc. S/PRST/1999/17
[17] Doc. S/1999/790

the control of illicit trafficking of arms and the infiltration of armed groups, an open national dialogue between the Government, the armed opposition (Rally for the Democratic Congo and the Movement for the Liberation of the Congo) and the unarmed opposition, the need to address the security concerns of the DRC and its neighbouring countries, the opening up of humanitarian corridors; and the establishment of a mechanism for the disarmament of all militias and armed groups.

Another important provision provides for the establishment of a Joint Military Commission (JMC) to perform various tasks,[18] composed of two representatives from each party under a neutral chairman appointed by the OAU.

The Agreement also contains provisions relating to the cessation of hostilities, disengagement, release of political hostages and exchange of prisoners of war; the orderly withdrawal of foreign forces; national dialogue and reconciliation; the re-establishment of state administration over the entire territory of the DRC; the disarmament of armed groups and the formation of a national army.

The Secretary-General noted that the agreement contains provisions relating to functions to be performed by the United Nations in collaboration with the OAU. These include working with the JMC and the OAU; monitoring the cessation of hostilities; investigating violations of the cease-fire and taking necessary measures to ensure compliance; supervising the disengagement of forces; supervising the redeployment of forces to defensive positions in conflict zones providing humanitarian assistance and collecting weapons from civilians.

The Secretary-General observed in connection with the effects of the war that the conflict in the RDC had displaced some 700,000 persons within the country, in addition to some 300,00 refugees already there. It had, moreover, been characterized as having appalling widespread and systematic human rights violations, including mass killings, ethnic cleansing, rape and the destruction of property. Taking all these factors into account, the Secretary-General hailed the signing of the Agreement as a major first step towards an overall recovery of the country from the consequences of the war.

With regard to the role of the United Nations, the Secretary-General expressed the view that any peacekeeping mission in the DRC will have

---

[18] The tasks to be performed by the Joint Military Commission included: establishing the location of its at the time of the cease-fire; facilitating liaison between the parties for the purpose of the cease-fire; assisting in the investigation of any violations; working out mechanisms for orderly withdrawal of foreign forces; etc.

to be large and expensive. Its deployment will have to take into account factors such as the size of the country and the underdeveloped infrastructure as well as the nature of the conflict itself. He therefore recommended the deployment initially of a small United Nations personnel, which would serve mainly as liaison officers to the national capitals and rear military headquarters of the main belligerents. Thereafter, as a second stage, he would recommend the deployment of some 500 military observers to be known as the United Nations Observer Mission in the Democratic Republic of the Congo (MONUC). He would later propose the deployment of a peace-keeping mission after reviewing the situation on the ground. Finally, the Secretary-General envisaged the need for the establishment of a well-funded, well-planned and long-term programme for the disarmament, demobilization and reintegration into society of former combatants. He also foresaw the need to take measures to address human rights violations that have characterized the conflict.

The Secretary-General called upon the two rebel groups to sign the Agreement as a first step and for all parties to carry it out in good faith.

On 6 August 1999, the Security Council adopted resolution 1258 (1999) and welcomed the signing of the Cease-fire Agreement which, in its view, represented a viable basis for a solution of the conflict. While welcoming the signing of the Cease-fire Agreement on 1 August 1999 by the Movement for the Liberation of the Congo, it expressed deep concern that the Congolese Rally for democracy had not signed the Agreement and called upon it to do so without delay in order to bring about national reconciliation and lasting peace in the country. The Council noted with satisfaction the prompt establishment of the Political Committee and JMC as part of a collective effort to implement the Cease-fire Agreement. It therefore decided to authorize the deployment of up to 90 United Nations military liaison personnel, together with the necessary civilian, political, humanitarian and administrative staff to the capitals of the States which had signed the Cease-fire Agreement and to the provisional headquarters of the JMC and other areas deemed necessary by the Secretary-General. Its functions were to include: establishing contacts and maintaining liaison with the JMC and all parties to the Agreement; assisting the JMC and the parties in developing modalities for the implementation of the Agreement; providing information to the Secretary-General regarding the situation on the ground; assisting in refining a concept of operations for a possible further role of the United Nations and securing guarantees of cooperation and assurances of security for the possible deployment of military observers in the country. It welcomed the Secretary-General's intention to appoint a Special Representative to serve as the head of the United Nations presence in the sub-region relating to the peace process in the DRC.

The Security Council adopted another resolution on 5 November 1999 (resolution 1273) in which it noted with satisfaction the deployment of United Nations Military Liaison Personnel to the capitals of the States, which had signed the Cease-fire Agreements, and to the JMC. It urged the parties to the Cease-fire Agreement to cooperate fully with the technical survey team dispatched to the DRC, to access conditions and to prepare for subsequent United Nations deployments in the country. Finally it called upon the parties to the Cease-fire Agreement to continuing to abide by its provisions.

DEMOCRATIC REPUBLIC OF THE CONGO

S/RES/1234 (1999)

9 April 1999

RESOLUTION 1234 (1999)
Adopted by the Security Council at its 3993rd meeting, on 9 April 1999

The Security Council,

Recalling the statements by its President of 31 August 1998 (S/PRST/1998/26) and of 11 December 1998 (S/PRST/1998/36),

Expressing its concern at the further deterioration of the situation in the Democratic Republic of the Congo and the continuation of hostilities,

Expressing its firm commitment to preserving the national sovereignty, territorial integrity and political independence of the Democratic Republic of the Congo and all other States in the region,

Recalling that the Assembly of the Heads of State and Government of the Organization of African Unity during its first ordinary session held in Cairo from 17 to 21 July 1964, adopted in its resolution AHG 16(1) the principle of the inviolability of national frontiers of African States, as stated in paragraph 2 of the communiqué, of the Central Organ of the OAU Mechanism for Conflict Prevention, Management and Resolution issued on 17 August 1998 (S/1998/774, annex),

Concerned at reports of measures taken by forces opposing the Government in the eastern part of the Democratic Republic of the Congo in violation of the national sovereignty and territorial integrity of the country,

Expressing its concern at all violations of human rights and international humanitarian law in the territory of the Democratic Republic of the Congo, including acts of and incitement to ethnic hatred and violence by all parties to the conflict,

Deeply concerned at the illicit flow of arms and military materiel in the Great Lakes region,

Recalling the inherent right of individual or collective self-defence in accordance with Article 51 of the Charter of the United Nations,

Welcoming the appointment by the Secretary-General of his Special Envoy for the peace process for the Democratic Republic of the Congo,

Stressing that the present conflict in the Democratic Republic of the Congo constitutes a threat to peace, security and stability in the region,

1. *Reaffirms* the obligation of all States to respect the territorial integrity, political independence and national sovereignty of the Democratic Republic of the Congo and other States in the region, including the obligation to refrain from the threat or use of force against the territorial integrity or political independence of any

State or in any other manner inconsistent with the purposes of the United Nations, and further reaffirms the need for all States to refrain from any interference in each other's internal affairs, in accordance with the Charter of the United Nations;

2. *Deplores* the continuing fighting and the presence of forces of foreign States in the Democratic Republic of the Congo in a manner inconsistent with the principles of the Charter of the United Nations, and calls upon those States to bring to an end the presence of these uninvited forces and to take immediate steps to that end;

3. *Demands* an immediate halt to the hostilities;

4. *Calls* for the immediate signing of a ceasefire agreement allowing the orderly withdrawal of all foreign forces, the re-establishment of the authority of the Government of the Democratic Republic of the Congo throughout its territory, and the disarmament of non-governmental armed groups in the Democratic Republic of the Congo, and stresses, in the context of a lasting peaceful settlement, the need for the engagement of all Congolese in an all-inclusive process of political dialogue with a view to achieving national reconciliation and to the holding on an early date of democratic, free and fair elections, and for the provision of arrangements for security along the relevant international borders of the Democratic Republic of the Congo;

5. *Welcomes* the intention of the Government of the Democratic Republic of the Congo to hold an all-inclusive national debate as a precursor to elections, and encourages further progress in this respect;

6. *Calls* upon all parties to the conflict in the Democratic Republic of the Congo to protect human rights and to respect international humanitarian law, in particular, as applicable to them, the Geneva Conventions of 1949 and the Additional Protocols of 1977, and the Convention on the Prevention and Punishment of the Crime of Genocide of 1948;

7. *Condemns* all massacres carried out on the territory of the Democratic Republic of the Congo and calls for an international investigation into all such events, including those in the province of South Kivu and other atrocities as referred to in the report submitted by the Special Rapporteur on the situation of human rights in the Democratic Republic of the Congo in accordance with resolution 1999/61 of the fifty-fifth session of the Commission on Human Rights (E/CN.4/1999/31), with a view to bringing to justice those responsible;

8. *Condemns* the continuing activity of and support to all armed groups, including the ex-Rwandese Armed Forces, Interahamwe, and others in the Democratic Republic of the Congo;

9. *Calls* for safe and unhindered access for humanitarian assistance to those in need in the Democratic Republic of the Congo, and urges all parties to the conflict to guarantee the safety and security of United Nations and humanitarian personnel;

10. *Welcomes* the commitment by the parties to the conflict in the Democratic Republic of the Congo to stop fighting in order to allow an immunization campaign

and urges all parties to the conflict to take concrete action in order to provide greater protection to children exposed to armed conflict in the Democratic Republic of the Congo;

11. *Expresses* its support for the regional mediation process by the OAU and Southern African Development Community to find a peaceful settlement to the conflict in the Democratic Republic of the Congo and calls upon the international community to continue to support these efforts;

12. *Urges* all parties to the conflict to continue to work constructively through the regional mediation process towards the signing of a ceasefire agreement and settlement of the conflict in the Democratic Republic of the Congo, and calls upon all States in the region to create the conditions necessary for the speedy and peaceful resolution of the crisis and to desist from any act that may further exacerbate the situation;

13. *Expresses* its support for the Special Envoy of the Secretary-General for the peace process in the Democratic Republic of the Congo, calls upon all parties to the conflict to cooperate fully with him in his mission in support of regional mediation efforts and national reconciliation, as set out in his mandate (S/1999/379), and urges Member States and organizations to respond readily to requests from the Special Envoy for assistance;

14. *Reaffirms* the importance of holding, at the appropriate time, an international conference on peace, security and stability in the Great Lakes region under the auspices of the United Nations and the Organization of African Unity, with the participation of all the Governments of the region and all others concerned;

15. *Reaffirms* its readiness to consider the active involvement of the United Nations, in coordination with the Organization of African Unity, including through concrete sustainable and effective measures, to assist in the implementation of an effective ceasefire agreement and in an agreed process for political settlement of the conflict;

16. *Requests* the Secretary-General of the United Nations to work closely with the Secretary-General of the Organization of African Unity in promoting a peaceful resolution of the conflict, to make recommendations on the possible role of the United Nations to this end, and to keep the Council informed of developments;

17. *Decides* to remain actively seized of the matter.

S/PRST/1999/17

24 June 1999

ORIGINAL: ENGLISH

STATEMENT BY THE PRESIDENT OF THE SECURITY COUNCIL

At the 4015th meeting of the Security Council, held on 24 June 1999 in connection with the Council's consideration of the item entitled "The situation concerning the Democratic Republic of the Congo" the President of the Security Council made the following statement on behalf of the Council:

"The Security Council recalls the Statements of its President of 31 August 1998 (S/PRST/1998/26) and 11 December 1998 (S/PRST/1998/36). It reaffirms its resolution 1234 (1999) of 9 April 1999 (S/RES/1234/1999) on the situation in the Democratic Republic of the Congo and calls on all parties to comply with this resolution. It expresses its continued concern at the continuing conflict in the Democratic Republic of the Congo.

"The Security Council reaffirms its commitment to preserving the national unity, sovereignty, territorial integrity and political independence of the Democratic Republic of the Congo and all other States in the region. It further reaffirms its support for the regional mediation process facilitated by the President of the Republic of Zambia on behalf of the Southern African Development Community in cooperation with the Organization of African Unity (OAU) and with support from the United Nations to find a peaceful settlement to the conflict in the Democratic Republic of the Congo.

"The Security Council takes note of the constructive efforts being made to promote a peaceful settlement of the conflict in the context of the above-mentioned regional mediation process, including the meeting and agreement signed at Sirte on 18 April 1999. It calls on all parties to demonstrate commitment to the peace process and to participate with a constructive and flexible spirit in the forthcoming summit in Lusaka scheduled for 26 June 1999. In this context, the Council calls on the parties immediately to sign a ceasefire agreement which includes the appropriate modalities and mechanisms for its implementation.

"The Security Council reaffirms its readiness to consider the active involvement of the United Nations, in coordination with the OAU, including through concrete sustainable and effective measures, to assist in the implementation of an effective ceasefire agreement and in an agreed process for political settlement of the conflict.

"The Security Council emphasizes the need for a peaceful settlement of the conflict in the Democratic Republic of the Congo in order to permit the economic reconstruction of the country, so as to enhance development and foster national reconciliation.

"The Security Council stresses the need for a continuing process of genuine national reconciliation and democratization in all States of the Great Lakes region. It reaffirms the importance of holding, at the appropriate time, an international conference on security, stability and development for the Great Lakes region and encourages the international community to help facilitate such a conference.

"The Security Council expresses its appreciation and full support for the continuing efforts of the Secretary-General and his Special Envoy for the peace process in the Democratic Republic of the Congo.

"The Security Council will remain actively seized of the matter."

S/RES/1258 (1999)

6 August 1999

RESOLUTION 1258 (1999)
Adopted by the Security Council at its 4032nd meeting, on 6 August 1999

The Security Council,

Reaffirming its resolution 1234 (1999) of 9 April 1999 and recalling the statements of its President of 31 August 1998 (S/PRST/1998/26), 11 December 1998 (S/PRST/1998/36), and 24 June 1999 (S/PRST/1999/17),

Bearing in mind the purposes and principles of the Charter of the United Nations, and the primary responsibility of the Security Council for the maintenance of international peace and security,

Reaffirming the sovereignty, territorial integrity and political independence of the Democratic Republic of the Congo and all States in the region,

Determined to resolve with all parties concerned the grave humanitarian situation in the Democratic Republic of the Congo in particular and in the region as a whole and to provide for the safe and free return of all refugees and displaced persons to their homes,

Recognizing that the current situation in the Democratic Republic of the Congo demands an urgent response by the parties to the conflict with support from the international community, Recalling the relevant principles contained in the Convention on the Safety of United Nations and Associated Personnel adopted on 9 December 1994,

Welcoming the report of the Secretary-General of 15 July 1999 on the United Nations preliminary deployment in the Democratic Republic of the Congo (S/1999/790),

1. *Welcomes* the signing of the Ceasefire Agreement on the conflict in the Democratic Republic of the Congo by the States concerned in Lusaka on 10 July 1999 (S/1999/815) which represents a viable basis for a resolution of the conflict in the Democratic Republic of the Congo;

2. *Also* welcomes the signing of the Ceasefire Agreement on 1 August 1999 by the Movement for the Liberation of the Congo, expresses deep concern that the Congolese Rally for Democracy has not signed the Agreement and calls upon the latter to sign the Agreement without delay in order to bring about national reconciliation and lasting peace in the Democratic Republic of the Congo;

3. *Commends* the Organization of African Unity (OAU) and the Southern African Development Community for their efforts to find a peaceful settlement to the conflict in the Democratic Republic of the Congo and in particular the President of the Republic of Zambia, and also the Secretary-General, the Special Envoy of the Secretary-General for the peace process in the Democratic Republic of the Congo, the Representative of the Secretary-General to the Great Lakes Region and all those who contributed to the peace process;

4. *Calls upon* all parties to the conflict, in particular the rebel movements, to cease hostilities, to implement fully and without delay the provisions of the Ceasefire Agreement, to cooperate fully with the OAU and the United Nations in the implementation of the Agreement and to desist from any act that may further exacerbate the situation;

5. *Stresses* the need for a continuing process of genuine national reconciliation, and encourages all Congolese to participate in the national debate to be organized in accordance with the provisions of the Ceasefire Agreement;

6. *Stresses* also the need to create an environment conducive to the return in safety and dignity of all refugees and displaced persons;

7. *Notes* with satisfaction the prompt establishment of the Political Committee and the Joint Military Commission (JMC) by the States signatories to the Ceasefire Agreement as part of their collective effort to implement the Ceasefire Agreement for the Democratic Republic of the Congo;

8. *Authorizes* the deployment of up to 90 United Nations military liaison personnel, together with the necessary civilian, political, humanitarian and administrative staff, to the capitals of the States signatories to the Ceasefire Agreement and the provisional headquarters of the JMC, and, as security conditions permit, to the rear military headquarters of the main belligerents in the Democratic Republic of the Congo and, as appropriate, to other areas the Secretary-General may deem necessary, for a period of three months, with the following mandate:
– To establish contacts and maintain liaison with the JMC and all parties to the Agreement;
– To assist the JMC and the parties in developing modalities for the Implementation of the Agreement;

- To provide technical assistance, as requested to the JMC;
- To provide information to the Secretary-General regarding the situation on the ground, and to assist in refining a concept of operations for a possible further role of the United Nations in the Implementation of the Agreement once it is signed by all parties; and
- To secure from the parties guarantees of cooperation and assurances of security for the possible deployment in-country of military observers;

9. *Welcomes* the intention of the Secretary-General to appoint a Special Representative to serve as the Head of the United Nations presence in the sub-region relating to the peace process in the Democratic Republic of the Congo and to provide assistance in the Implementation of the Ceasefire Agreement, and invites him to do so as soon as possible;

10. *Calls upon* all States and parties concerned to ensure the freedom of movement, security and safety of United Nations personnel in their territory;

11. *Calls* for safe and unhindered access for humanitarian assistance to those in need in the Democratic Republic of the Congo, and urges all parties to the conflict to guarantee the safety and security of all humanitarian personnel and to respect strictly the relevant provisions of international humanitarian law;

12. *Requests* the Secretary-General to keep it regularly informed of developments in the Democratic Republic of the Congo and to report at the appropriate time on the future presence of the United Nations in the Democratic Republic of the Congo in support of the peace process;

13. *Decides* to remain actively seized of the matter.

S/RES/1273 (1999)

5 November 1999

RESOLUTION 1273 (1999)
Adopted by the Security Council at its 4060th meeting, on 5 November 1999

The Security Council,

Recalling its resolutions 1234 (1999) of 9 April 1999 and 1258 (1999) of 6 August 1999 and the statements of its President of 31 August 1998 (S/PRST/1998/26), 11 December 1998 (S/PRST/1998/36) and 24 June 1999 (S/PRST/1999/17),

Reaffirming the sovereignty, territorial integrity, and political independence of the Democratic Republic of the Congo and all States in the region,

Reaffirming also that the Lusaka Ceasefire Agreement (S/1999/815) represents a viable basis for a resolution of the conflict in the Democratic Republic of the Congo,

Welcoming the report of the Secretary-General of 1 November 1999 (S/1999/1116),

Noting with satisfaction the deployment of United Nations military liaison personnel to the capitals of the States signatories to the Ceasefire Agreement and to the Joint Military Commission established by them, and underlining the importance of their full deployment as provided for in its resolution 1258 (1999),

Noting also that the Joint Military Commission and the Political Committee have held meetings as mandated under the Ceasefire Agreement,

Urging all parties to the Ceasefire Agreement to cooperate fully with the technical survey team dispatched to the Democratic Republic of the Congo by the Secretary-General as indicated in his report of 15 July 1999 (S/1999/790), in order to allow it to assess conditions and to prepare for subsequent United Nations deployments in the country,

1. *Decides* to extend the mandate of the United Nations military liaison personnel deployed under paragraph 8 of resolution 1258 (1999) until 15 January 2000;

2. *Requests* the Secretary-General to continue to report to it regularly on developments in the Democratic Republic of the Congo including on the future presence of the United Nations in the country in support of the peace process;

3. *Calls* on all parties to the Ceasefire Agreement to continue to abide by its provisions;

4. *Decides* to remain actively seized of the matter.

ETHIOPIA AND ERITREA[19]

On 29 June 1999, the Security Council adopted resolution 1226 (1999) expressing concern over the risk of armed conflict between Ethiopia and Eritrea and the escalating arms build-up along the borders. It expressed strong support for the mediation efforts of the Organization of African Unity (OAU). It also expressed the same strong support for the Framework Agreement, approved by the Central Organ Summit of the OAU Mechanism for Conflict Prevention, Management, and Resolution on 17 December 1998.[20] In the Council's view, this Framework Agreement provided the best hope for peace between the two parties.

The Council welcomed the acceptance by Ethiopia of the Framework Agreement and strongly urged Eritrea to do the same without delay.

On 10 February 1999, the Security Council adopted another resolution (Resolution 1227 (1999) condemning the recourse to the use of force by Ethiopia and Eritrea, and demanded an immediate halt to the hostilities and a resumption of diplomatic efforts to find a peaceful resolution to the conflict.

In the same resolution, the Council stressed its conviction that the Framework Agreement remained the only viable and sound basis for a peaceful resolution of the conflict. It expressed support for the efforts of the OAU, the Secretary-General of the UN and his Special Envoy for Africa as well as Member States assisting parties in finding a solution to the conflict.

The President of the Security Council also made a statement[21] on 27 February 1999 regarding the conflict between Ethiopia and Eritrea. The Security Council, he noted, welcomed the acceptance of the Framework Agreement by Eritrea. The Council also reaffirmed the sovereignty and territorial integrity of Ethiopia and Eritrea and expressed its willingness to consider all appropriate support to implement a peace agreement between the two parties.

The Council also indicated that it would continue to be actively involved in an attempt to find a peaceful solution to the problem.

---

[19] For the efforts of the United Nations aimed at resolving the conflict between Ethiopia and Eritrea during the period from mid 1997 to mid 1998, see *African Yearbook of International Law*, Vol. 6, pp. 334 - 336
[20] See Doc. S/1998/1223, Annex.
[21] Doc. S/PRST/1999/9

S/RES/1226 (1999)

19990129

29 January 1999

RESOLUTION 1226 (1999)
Adopted by the Security Council at its 3973rd meeting, on 29 January 1999

The Security Council,

Reaffirming its resolution 1177 (1998) of 26 June 1998,
Expressing grave concern over the risk of armed conflict between Ethiopia and Eritrea and the scalating arms build-up along the common border between the two countries,
Noting that armed conflict between Ethiopia and Eritrea would have a devastating effect on the peoples of the two countries and the region as a whole,
Recognizing that the rehabilitation and reconstruction efforts of both the Ethiopian and Eritrean Governments during the last eight years have given hope to the rest of the continent, all of which would be put at risk by armed conflict,
Commending the efforts of concerned countries and regional bodies aimed at facilitating a peaceful solution to the border dispute between Ethiopia and Eritrea,

1. *Expresses* its strong support for the mediation efforts of the Organization of African Unity (OAU) and for the Framework Agreement as approved by the Central Organ Summit of the OAU Mechanism for Conflict Prevention, Management, and Resolution on 17 December 1998 (S/1998/1223, annex), and affirms that the OAU Framework Agreement provides the best hope for peace between the two parties;

2. *Endorses* the decision by the Secretary-General to send his Special Envoy for Africa to the region in support of OAU efforts;

3. *Stresses* that it is of primary importance that the OAU Framework Agreement be accepted, and calls for cooperation with the OAU and full implementation of the Framework Agreement without delay;

4. *Welcomes* the acceptance by Ethiopia of the OAU Framework Agreement;

5. *Welcomes* Eritrea's engagement with the OAU process, notes the fact that the OAU has responded to Eritrea's request for clarifications of the Framework Agreement and, in this regard, strongly urges Eritrea to accept the Framework Agreement as the basis for a peaceful resolution of the border dispute between Ethiopia and Eritrea without delay;

6. *Calls* on both parties to work for a reduction in tensions by adopting policies leading to the restoration of confidence between the Governments and peoples of Ethiopia and Eritrea, including urgent measures to improve the humanitarian situation and respect for human rights;

7. *Strongly* urges Ethiopia and Eritrea to maintain their commitment to a peaceful resolution of the border dispute and calls upon them in the strongest terms to exercise maximum restraint and to refrain from taking any military action;

8. *Welcomes* the Secretary-General's continued engagement in support of the OAU peace process;

9. *Decides* to remain actively seized of the matter.

S/RES/1227 (1999)

19990210

10 February 1999

RESOLUTION 1227 (1999)
Adopted by the Security Council at its 3975th meeting, on 10 February 1999

The Security Council,

Reaffirming its resolutions 1177 (1998) of 26 June 1998 and 1226 (1999) of 29 January 1999,

Expressing its grave concern regarding the border conflict between Ethiopia and Eritrea and the resumption of hostilities between the parties,

Recalling the commitment of Ethiopia and Eritrea to a moratorium on the threat of and use of air strikes,

Stressing that the situation between Ethiopia and Eritrea constitutes a threat to peace and security,

1. *Condemns* the recourse to the use of force by Ethiopia and Eritrea;

2. *Demands* an immediate halt to the hostilities, in particular the use of air strikes;

3. *Demands* that Ethiopia and Eritrea resume diplomatic efforts to find a peaceful resolution to the conflict;

4. *Stresses* that the Framework Agreement as approved by the Central Organ Summit of the Organization of African Unity (OAU) Mechanism for Conflict Prevention, Management, and Resolution on 17 December 1998 (S/1998/1223, annex) remains a viable and sound basis for a peaceful resolution of the conflict;

5. *Expresses* its full support for the efforts of the OAU, the Secretary-General and his Special Envoy for Africa, and concerned Member States to find a peaceful resolution to the present hostilities;

6. *Calls upon* Ethiopia and Eritrea to ensure the safety of the civilian population and respect for human rights and international humanitarian law;

7. *Strongly* urges all States to end immediately all sales of arms and munitions to Ethiopia and Eritrea;

8. *Decides* to remain actively seized of the matter.

S/PRST/1999/9

27 February 1999

STATEMENT BY THE PRESIDENT OF THE SECURITY COUNCIL

At the 3985th meeting of the Security Council, held on 27 February 1999 in connection with the Council's consideration of the item entitled "The situation between Eritrea and Ethiopia", the President of the Security Council made the following statement on behalf of the Council:

"The Security Council reaffirms its resolutions 1177 (1998) of 26 June 1998, 1226 (1999) of 29 January 1999 and 1227 (1999) of 10 February 1999 which called on Ethiopia and Eritrea to refrain from armed conflict and to accept and implement the Framework Agreement as approved by the Central Organ Summit of the Organization of African Unity (OAU) Mechanism for Conflict Prevention, Management and Resolution on 17 December 1998 (S/1998/1223, annex).

"The Security Council demands an immediate halt to all hostilities and calls on the parties to refrain from the further use of force.

"The Security Council welcomes the acceptance by Eritrea at the Head of State level of the OAU Framework Agreement and recalls the prior acceptance of the Agreement by Ethiopia. The OAU Framework Agreement remains a viable and sound basis for a peaceful resolution to the conflict.

"The Security Council reaffirms the sovereignty and territorial integrity of Ethiopia and Eritrea.

"The Security Council expresses its willingness to consider all appropriate support to implement a peace agreement between the two parties.

"The Security Council expresses its continuing support for the efforts of the OAU, the Secretary-General and his Special Envoy, Ambassador Sahnoun, and concerned Member States to find a peaceful resolution to the border dispute.

"The Security Council remains actively seized of the matter."

GUINEA BISSAU

The Security Council considered on a number of occasions, during the reporting period, the conflict in Guinea-Bissau.

On 21 December 1998, the Security Council adopted resolution 1216 in which it welcomed the signing on 26 August 1998 of an Agreement[22] between the Government and the self-proclaimed Military Junta in Praia, and in Abuja on 1 November 1998[23] and the Additional Protocol[24] in Lomé on 15 December 1998. The Council also called upon the two parties to implement fully all the provisions of the Agreement.

The Abuja Agreement reaffirmed and built upon the Agreement signed in August to maintain the cease-fire and total withdraw from Guinea-Bissau of all foreign troops. The withdrawal was to be accomplished simultaneously with the deployment of the ECOMOG interposition force, which was to take over from the withdrawing forces. ECOMOG was also to guarantee the security along the border, keep the warring parties apart and guarantee access to humanitarian organizations and agencies to the affected civilian population and to open the air and seaports. The Agreement called for the establishment of a Government of national unity to include representatives from a cross section of the society. General presidential elections, to be observed by the Economic Community of West African States, were to be held no later than the end of March 1999.

In his report[25] on 17 March 1999, the Secretary-General hailed the signing of the Agreement as a demonstration of the readiness of the parties to start working together towards returning the country to peace and normalcy. He also reported that the parties had recognized the involvement of the United Nations as a collaborator to ECOWAS and had requested him to appoint a Special Representative.

The Secretary-General also reported that the Government of National Unity envisaged in the Abuja Agreement was installed on 20 February 1999. This development, he observed, also constituted a significant step forward in the peace process.

Furthermore, the deployment of an advance ECOMOG contingent to start carrying out the functions outlined in the Agreement had taken place and that the foreign troops had begun to withdraw from the country.

---

[22] Doc. S/1998/825
[23] Doc. S/1998/1028, Annex
[24] Doc. S/1998/1178. The Protocol addressed issues related to the structure and composition of the new Government of National Unity.
[25] Doc. S/1999/294

Following a decision of the Security Council on 3 March 1999 in a resolution establishing a United Nations Peace-building Support Office in Guinea-Bissau (UNOGBIS), the Secretary-General reported the dispatch of a mission to Guinea Bissau to examine the logistics for its practical set up. The primary functions of UNOGBIS in the post-conflict environment were to provide the political framework and leadership for harmonizing and integrating the activities of the United Nations system in the country, particularly during the transitional period leading up to general and presidential elections and to facilitate, in close cooperation with the other parties, the implementation of the Abuja Agreement.

On 6 April 1999, the Security Council, in resolution 1233, called on the parties to implement fully the provisions of the Abuja Agreement and to agree on the date for the holding of elections as soon as possible.

On 1 July 1999, the Secretary-General reported[26] on the sudden change of events in the country; President Vieira had been ousted from office on 7 May 1999 and had been replaced by the speaker of the National Assembly, Malan Bacai as interim President. Elections had, nevertheless, been announced to take place on 28 November 1999. The *coup d'état*, he noted, had been condemned by the ECOWAS Ministers for Foreign Affairs, who had announced further that, as a consequence, the ECOMOG troops would be withdrawn despite a request by the Government of National Unity to the contrary. They requested the Government to give safe passage to the ousted President and his family to Portugal.

The Secretary-General observed that as a result of these events and the withdrawal of ECOMOG, the Abuja Agreement was no longer valid. However, despite the changed circumstances, he was of the view that the mandate of UNOGBIS should be upheld, with some revisions. In its revised form, its mandate would mainly focus on providing assistance in the creation of an enabling environment for restoring, maintaining and consolidating peace, democracy and the rule of law for the organization of free and transparent elections and to support efforts towards national reconciliation, and to encourage confidence-building measures.

The Secretary-General finally noted that the post-conflict situation in Guinea-Bissau remained complex and that the events of 7 May had altered the peace process. These events had raised concerns and questions about the country's commitment to reconciliation and restoration of order. He was, nevertheless, encouraged by the commitment of the transitional authorities to the objective of restoring genuine and lasting peace based on national rec-

---

[26] Doc. S/1999/741

onciliation, respect for the rule of law and the return to constitutional order. In his view, translating these commitments into concrete actions would give encouragement to the international community to review favorably its support for the country in its search to rebuild its economic and social life.

S/RES/1216 (1998)

21 December 1998

RESOLUTION 1216 (1998)
Adopted by the Security Council at its 3958th meeting, on 21 December 1998

The Security Council,

Reaffirming the statements of its President of 6 November 1998 (S/PRST/1998/31) and 30 November 1998 (S/PRS/35),

Gravely concerned by the crisis facing Guinea-Bissau and the serious humanitarian situation affecting the civilian population in Guinea Bissau,

Expressing its firm commitment to preserve the unity, sovereignty, political independence and territorial integrity of Guinea-Bissau,

1. *Welcomes* the agreement between the Government of Guinea-Bissau and the Self-Proclaimed Military Junta signed in Paraia on 26 August 1998 (S/1998/825), and in Abuja on 1 November 1998 (S/1998/1028, annex) and the Additional Protocol signed in Lome on 15 December 1998 (1998/1178, annex);

2. Calls upon the Government and the Self-Proclaimed Military Junta to implement fully all the provisions of the agreements, including with regard to respect for the ceasefire, the urgent establishment of a government of national unity, the holding of general and presidential elections no later than the end of March 1999, and the immediate opening of the airport and the seaport in Bissau, and, in cooperation with all concerned, the withdrawal of all foreign troops in Guinea-Bissau and the simultaneous deployment of the interposition force of the Military Observer Group (ECOMOG) of the Economic Community of West African States (ECOWAS);

3. Commends the Members of the Community of Portuguese-Speaking Countries and ECOWAS on the key role they are playing to restore peace throughout Guinea-Bissau, and on their intention to participate with others in the observation of the forthcoming general and presidential elections and *welcomes* the role of ECOMOG in the implementation of the Abuja Agreement, aimed at guaranteeing security along the Guinea-Bissau/Senegal border, keeping apart the parties in the conflict and guaranteeing free access to humanitarian organizations and agencies to reach the affected civilian populations, to be carried out in accordance, *inter alia,* with paragraph 6 below;

4. *Approves* the implementation by ECOMOG interposition force of its mandate referred to in paragraph 3 above in a neutral and impartial way and in conformity with United Nations peacekeeping standards to achieve its objective to facilitate the return to peace and security by monitoring the implementation of the Abuja Agreement;

5. *Calls upon* all concerned, including the Government and the Self-Proclaimed Military Junta, to respect strictly provisions of international law, including humanitarian and human rights law, and to assure safe and unimpeded access by international humanitarian organizations to persons in need of assistance as a result of the conflict;

6. *Affirms* that ECOMOG interposition force may be required to take action to ensure the security and freedom of movement of its personnel in the discharge of its mandate;

7. *Requests* ECOMOG to provide periodic reports at least every month through the Secretary-General, the first report to be made one month after the deployment of its troops;

8. *Requests* also the Secretary-General to make recommendations to the Council on a possible role of the United Nations in the process of peace and reconciliation in Guinea-Bissau, including the early establishment of arrangements for the liaison between the United Nations and ECOMOG;

9. *Reiterates* its appeal to States and organizations concerned to provide urgent humanitarian assistance to displaced persons and refugees;

10. Reiterates also its call on States to provide voluntary financial, technical and logistical support to assist ECOMOG to carry out its peacekeeping role in Guinea-Bissau;

11. *Requests* the Secretary-General to take the necessary steps to establish a Trust Fund for Guinea-Bissau which would assist in supporting the ECOMOG interposition force in providing logistical support to them and *encourages* Members States to contribute to the Fund;

12. *Requests further* the Secretary-General to keep the Security Council early informed of the situation in Guinea-Bissau and to submit a report to it by 17 March 199 on the implementation of the Abuja Agreement including the implementation of the ECOMOG interposition force of its mandate;

13. *Decides* to review the situation, including the implementation of the present resolution, before the end of March 1999, on the basis of the report of the Secretary-General referred to in paragraph 12 above;

14. Decides to remain seized of the matter.

S/RES/1216/(1998)

21 December 1998

RESOLUTION 1216 (1998)

S/RES/1233 (1999)

6 April 1999

RESOLUTION 1233 (1999)
Adopted by the Security Council at its 3991st meeting, on 6 April 1999

The Security Council,

Reaffirming its resolution of 21 December 1998 (S/RES/1216 (1998)) and the statements of its President of 6 November 1998 (S/PRST/1998/31), 30 November 1998 (S/PRST/1998/35) and 29 December 1998 (S/PRST/1998/38),
Gravely concerned at the security and humanitarian situation in Guinea-Bissau,
Expressing its firm commitment to preserving the unity, sovereignty, political independence and territorial integrity of Guinea-Bissau,
Welcoming the report of the Secretary-General of 17 March 1999 (S/1999/294) and the observations contained therein,
Noting with appreciation the formal undertaking by the President of Guinea-Bissau and the leader of the Self-Proclaimed Military Junta on 17 February 1999 never again to resort to arms (S/1999/173),
Welcoming the establishment and swearing-in on 20 February 1999 of the new Government of National Unity in Guinea-Bissau which constitutes a significant step forward in the peace process,
Noting with concern that serious obstacles continue to hamper the effective functioning of the new Government, including in particular, the failure of civil servants and other professional cadres seeking refuge in other countries to return,
Welcoming the deployment of troops constituting the Interposition Force of the Military Observer Group of the Economic Community of West African States (ECOMOG) by States in the region to implement their peacekeeping mandate and the withdrawal of all foreign forces from Guinea-Bissau pursuant to the Abuja Agreement of 1 November 1998 (S/1998/1028, annex),
Reiterating the need to conduct general and presidential elections pursuant to the Abuja Agreement and in accordance with national constitutional requirements as soon as possible, and noting the expression by the parties of their firm interest in having elections held as soon as possible,

1. *Reiterates* that the primary responsibility for achieving lasting peace in Guinea-Bissau rests with the parties and strongly calls upon them to implement fully all the provisions of the Abuja Agreement and subsequent undertakings;

2. *Commends* the parties for the steps taken so far in the implementation of the Abuja Agreement, in particular the establishment of the new Government of National Unity, and strongly urges them to adopt and implement all measures necessary to ensure the smooth functioning of the new Government and all other institutions, including in particular confidence-building measures and measures to encourage the early return of refugees and internally displaced persons;

3. Commends also the Community of Portuguese Speaking Countries (CPLP), member States of the Economic Community of West African States (ECOWAS) and leaders in and outside the region, in particular the President of the Republic of Togo in his capacity as Chairman of ECOWAS, for the key role they are playing to bring about national reconciliation and to consolidate peace and security throughout Guinea-Bissau;

4. *Expresses* its appreciation to those States which have already provided assistance for the deployment of ECOMOG in Guinea-Bissau;

5. *Reiterates* its urgent appeal to all States and regional organizations to make financial contributions to ECOMOG, including through the United Nations trust fund established to support peacekeeping in Guinea-Bissau, to provide technical and logistical support to assist ECOMOG to carry out its peacekeeping mandate and to help facilitate the full implementation of all the provisions of the Abuja Agreement, and to that end invites the Secretary-General to consider convening a meeting in New York with the participation of ECOWAS in order to assess the needs of ECOMOG and to examine ways in which contributions could be mobilized and channelled;

6. *Calls upon* the parties concerned promptly to agree on a date for the holding of elections as soon as possible which are all-inclusive, free and fair, and invites the United Nations and others to consider, as appropriate, providing any needed electoral assistance;

7. *Supports* the decision of the Secretary-General to establish a Post-Conflict Peace Building Support Office in Guinea-Bissau (UNOGBIS) under the leadership of a Representative of the Secretary-General (S/1999/233) which will provide the political framework and leadership for harmonizing and integrating the activities of the United Nations system in Guinea-Bissau during the transitional period leading up to general and presidential elections and will facilitate, in close cooperation with the parties concerned, ECOWAS, ECOMOG as well as other national and international partners, the implementation of the Abuja Agreement;

8. *Encourages* all agencies, programmes, offices and funds of the United Nations system, including the Bretton Woods institutions, as well as other international partners to lend their support to UNOGBIS and to the Representative of the Secretary-General in order to establish, together with the Government of Guinea-

Bissau, a comprehensive, concerted and coordinated approach to peace-building in Guinea-Bissau;

9. *Reiterates* the need for the simultaneous disarmament and encampment of ex-belligerent troops, welcomes the progress made by ECOMOG in that regard, and strongly urges the parties to continue to cooperate through the Special Commission established for that purpose, to conclude expeditiously these tasks and to create conditions for the reunification of the national armed and security forces;

10. *Emphasizes* the need for urgent demining of affected areas to pave the way for the return of refugees and displaced persons and for the resumption of agricultural activities, encourages ECOMOG to continue its demining activities and calls upon States to provide the necessary assistance for demining;

11. *Calls upon* all concerned to respect strictly the relevant provisions of international law, including international humanitarian law and human rights law, to ensure safe and unimpeded access by humanitarian organizations to those in need and to ensure the protection and freedom of movement of United Nations and international humanitarian personnel;

12. *Reiterates* its appeal to States and organizations concerned to provide urgent humanitarian assistance to internally displaced persons and refugees;

13. *Welcomes* the planned round-table conference of donors on Guinea-Bissau to be held in Geneva on 4-5 May 1999, under the sponsorship of UNDP, to mobilize assistance for, inter alia, humanitarian needs, consolidation of peace and socio-economic rehabilitation of Guinea-Bissau;

14. *Requests* the Secretary-General to keep the Security Council regularly informed and to submit a report to it by 30 June 1999 and every 90 days thereafter on developments in Guinea-Bissau, the activities of UNOGBIS and the implementation of the Abuja Agreement, including the implementation by ECOMOG of its mandate;

15. Decides to remain seized of the matter.

SIERRA LEONE[27]

The Security Council continued its involvement in an attempt to consolidate the peace in Sierra Leone, following the reinstallation of the legitimate Government of President Ahmad Tejan Kabbah on 7 May 1997.

Thus, in his report[28] of October 16, 1998, the Secretary-General provided information on the efforts of the Government and Parliament of Sierra Leone to extend its authority and to strengthen national institutions in order to increase their efficiency and to eliminate corruption. He also noted that under a new national security system, the armed forces were to comprise 5,000 troops under an effective civilian management and constitutional control.

The Secretary-General also noted that the leader of the Revolutionary United Front (RUF), Corporal Foday Sankoh had been brought back from Nigeria to stand trial. As a result, the RUF had threatened a terror campaign against civilians and the West African States Monitoring Group (ECOMOG) if the Government continued to hold him. The Government had, however, indicated its determination to proceed with the trial of Corporal Sankoh. In connection with the trial, the Secretary-General referred to his appeal to the Government to observe due process in the conduct of the trial proceedings and to commute the death sentence into a life sentence for those convicted.

Regarding relations between Sierra Leone and Liberia, the Secretary-General observed that the relations, which had improved following the meeting of President Kabbah and President Taylor in Abuja in July 1998, had however experienced a slight deterioration due to continued armed conflict in the Eastern part of Sierra Leone. The two Presidents were consulting each other with a view to improving the situation.

The Secretary-General also reported that the security situation, which had been quiet from about July, had also experienced some volatility in August and September when a considerable increase in rebel attacks was reported. There was also a resurgence of atrocities committed against the civilian population, including the complete destruction of villages and the torture, mutilation and execution of large numbers of civilians.

While the situation in Freetown, had remained safe and stable, most of the country continued to experience rebel attacks. The Government was still relying on ECOMOG to dispel these attacks. The United Nations observer mission in Sierra Leone had continued monitoring the work of ECOMOG.

---

[27] For the efforts of the United Nations aimed at resolving the conflict in Sierra Leone, during the period from mid 1997 to mid 1998, see *African Yearbook of International Law,* Vol. 6, pp. 340 - 360

[28] Doc. S/1998/960

The Secretary-General also reported that the demobilization and reintegration program targeting some 33,000 ex-combatants was continuing and scheduled to be completed in June 2001. The war was however, impeding the smooth implementation of this exercise.

Finally, the Secretary-General noted that the conflict in Sierra Leone imposed immense suffering on its people and strongly condemned the summary killing, torture, rape, looting and other acts of barbarism carried out by former junta elements. He was particularly outraged by the senseless acts of terror perpetrated against children, such as the amputation of limbs of boys as young as six years of age. He supported the efforts to bring to justice the authors of these especially abhorrent crimes.

Concerning the disarmament, demobilization and reintegration program, the Secretary-General considered that the long-term stability of the country depended on the successful implementation of this program. He commended all those who were assisting the Government of Sierra Leone to implement this program.

Regarding the relations between Sierra Leone and Liberia, the Secretary-General noted that it was a cause for great concern and urged the two Governments to exercise maximum restraint and pursue dialogue with a view to implementing confidence building measures aimed at improving the relations between two countries.

The Secretary-General submitted a special report [29] on 7 January 1999, on the situation on Sierra Leone. He reported that from 18 December 1998, the military and security situation in the country had sharply taken a turn for the worse. Strong rebel attacks against ECOMOG had been launched, and that ECOMOG had sustained heavy casualties. The civilian population also sustained heavy casualties as well as the looting and destruction of property, thus sending thousands of people fleeing towards Freetown. There had also been threats by the rebel groups to launch attacks on the capital city if the Government did not free Corporal Sankoh. During this attack some important towns in the center of the country had fallen to the rebels, thus removing an important obstacle for the rebels to combine their forces and to attack the capital city. The Secretary-General also reported that on 6 January 1999, the rebels penetrated the center of Freetown and opened a prison, freeing hundreds of prisoners detained for offenses relating to the period of the Junta's role as well as former soldiers of the Republic of Sierra Leone military forces. In the process, some buildings, including the Nigerian High Commission, were set on fire. The rebel group was reported to be in control of the center around the state house.

---

[29] Doc. S/1999/20

The relations between Liberia and Sierra Leone had also taken a turn for the worse. On 20 December 1998, President Charles Tailor closed the border between the two countries stating that there was an impending attack against Liberia. This allegation was however denied by Sierra Leone.

The Secretary-General observed that due to these events, the peace process in Sierra Leone had suffered a serious set back. He also deplored the intensification of activities and rebel attacks on Freetown. He commended the ECOWAS committee of six on Sierra Leone which had shown commendable initiatives and resolve, and endorsed its conclusions while urging the ECOWAS to meet at the summit level as soon as possible to discuss ways of dealing with the situation. He also commended Governments, which had continued to provide logistical support to Sierra Leone, as well as the various efforts made to secure a peaceful solution to the conflict through dialogue.

On 4 March 1999, the Secretary-General submitted another report[30] in which he observed that the attack on the capital city in January had resulted in the death of between 3,000 and 5,000 persons, including rebel fighters, soldiers of ECOMOG, members of the civil defense force and many civilian inhabitants. Some 150,000 people had also been displaced, and that large numbers of public buildings and homes were burnt. The rebel group had been dislodged only after four days of fierce fighting.

The disarmament and demobilization program had also suffered a set back; some of the demobilized rebels appeared to have rejoined the rebel group and participated in the attack on the capital city. Efforts were now being made to continue with disarmament and demobilization exercise.

Due to insecurities in the country, most of United Nations Observer Mission in Sierra Leone (UNOMSIL)'s international personnel had been evacuated, pending improvements in the security situation in the country.

The Secretary-General reported that a number of political initiatives had taken place, including a meeting between President Kabbah and Corporal Sankoh aimed at arranging a cease-fire. President Kabbah had also agreed that Corporal Sankoh and the RUF members could hold their internal consultations in Lomé or Bamako and that Corporal Sankoh could be returned to Freetown thereafter to resume his defense against treason and related offences.

According to the Secretary-General, Sierra Leone continued to face an extremely complex and difficult situation fraught with serious risks. He condemned in the strongest terms the merciless murders, inhuman mutilations and other appalling human right violations perpetrated by the rebels on the innocent civilian inhabitants of Freetown, and the widespread property damage. He congratulated ECOMOG for its success in repelling the rebels from

---

[30] Doc. S/1999/37

Freetown and restoring a measure of order to the city. He urged the international community to continue to support ECOMOG logistically. He commended President Kabbah for his decision to allow Corporal Sankoh to meet with rebel leaders in order to develop a coherent set of political demands to form the basis of subsequent negotiations with the Governments. He pledged the United Nations continued readiness to facilitate the conduct of talks through the provision of its good offices. Furthermore, in view of the improvement in the security situation in and around Freetown, he intended to re-establish UNOMSIL in and around Freetown as soon as possible.

On 11 March 1999, in its resolution 1231 (1999), the Security Council condemned the atrocities perpetrated by the rebels on the civilian population of Sierra Leone and deplored all violations of human rights and international humanitarian law and urged the appropriate authorities to investigate all allegations of such violations with a view to bringing the perpetrators to justice. It called on the parties to respect human rights and the international humanitarian law and the impartiality of humanitarian workers. In expressing grave concern at continued support afforded to the rebels, it reaffirmed the obligation of all states to comply with provisions of the embargo on the sale and supply of arms to Sierra Leone.

The Security Council also expressed support for all efforts, particularly by ECOWAS States, aimed at peacefully resolving the conflict and restoring lasting peace and stability in Sierra Leone. It encouraged the Secretary-General to facilitate dialogue between all the parties in the conflict. It also commended the efforts of ECOMOG aimed at restoring peace, security and stability in Sierra Leone.

Through the statement[31] of the President on 15 May 1999, the Security Council stressed that overall political settlement and national reconciliation were essential to achieving a peaceful resolution of the conflict. It therefore welcomed the holding of internal talks by a rebel delegation in Lomé. It urged both parties to proceed to direct talks without delay. The Security Council also gave its strong support for the mediation efforts of the United Nations.

On 4 June 1999, the Secretary-General presented another report[32] on the situation in Sierra Leone. He reported that the peace process in Sierra Leone had made significant progress, culminating in the signing of a ceasefire Agreement on 18 May 1999.[33] He also reported that a dialogue between the Government and RUF had commenced in Lomé on 25 May 1999. These positive outcomes were largely attributed to the extensive diplomatic efforts

---

[31] Doc. S/PRST/1999/13
[32] Doc. S/1999/645
[33] see Doc. S/1999/585, annex

undertaken by the Government of Sierra Leone. UNOMSIL had been requested to transport Corporal Sankoh from Freetown to Lomé on 18 April 1999. It had also transported four RUF representatives from other parts of Sierra Leone to Lomé via Monrovia with the cooperation and support of the Government of Liberia and the assistance of the United Nations peace building support office in Liberia.

The Secretary-General reported that the internal RUF talks had lasted from 26 April to 10 May 1999 resulting in a position paper reflecting its views and demands. The paper, *interalia,* called for a blanket amnesty for all personnel of the RUF and the Armed Forces Revolutionary Council (AFRC) which had organized the *coup d'états* in May 1997 and the establishment of a four-year transitional Government. During that time the transitional Government would draft a new constitution, reform the national security forces and civil service; encamp, demobilize and reintegrate all combatants and establish a national electoral commission. In response the Government, on 14 May 1999, considered the proposal for a transition Government to be unconstitutional, but that an amnesty for all combatants would be examined with a view to achieving permanent peace, while taking into account gross human rights violations committed against the citizens of Sierra Leone. It endorsed the transformation of RUF into a political party and that the Government would give it full support for that process.

The Secretary-General also reported that the Government and RUF had requested UNOMSIL to establish a committee to oversee the immediate release of prisoners of war and combatants in accordance with the 18 May cease-fire Agreement organized by his Special Representative. By this Agreement, both parties had undertaken to maintain their respective positions and refrain from hostile or aggressive acts.

According to the Secretary-General, despite the continued unpredictability of the conflict situation in Sierra Leone, he was encouraged by the significant progress made in the pursuit of dialogue between the two parties. In his view, this was the first time in three years that a political settlement might be within reach to break the cycle of violence, which had gripped the country since 1991. He commended the Government of Sierra Leone for establishing a national human rights commission and a truth and reconciliation mechanism as part of the peace Agreement.

On 11 June the Security Council, in its resolution 1245 (1999) called upon the parties to remain committed to the process of negotiation and to demonstrate flexibility in their approach to the process and gave strong support to those involved in mediation efforts of the United Nations.

The Secretary-General reported[34] on 30 July 1999 that the Lomé peace Agreement was signed on 7 July 1999, by President Kabbah, on behalf of the Government, and Corporal Sankoh, on behalf of the Revolution United Front of Sierra Leone (RUF/SL).[35] Other Parties to the mediation efforts also signed the Agreement.

The main provisions of the Agreement provide for the permanent cessation of hostilities and the transformation of RUF/SL and into a political party and its access to the public office. It called for the creation of a broad-based Government of National Unity through cabinet appointments of representatives of RUF/SL and the creation of a commission for the consolidation of peace to supervise the implementation of the peace Agreement. The Agreement called for the establishment of a commission for the management of strategic resources, and National Reconstruction and Development, to be chaired personally by the leader of RUF/SL, Corporal Sankoh, who would assume the post of Vice-president of Sierra Leone. Finally, the Agreement called for the establishment of a Council of Elders and religious leaders to mediate any disputes arising from differences in the interpretation of the Agreement.

Other clauses of the Agreement provided for the pardon of Corporal Sankoh and a complete amnesty for any crimes committed by members of the fighting forces during the conflict from March 1991, up until the signing of the Agreement. A review of the current constitution of Sierra Leone and the holding of elections in line with the new constitution were also requested. In connection with the signing of the Agreement, the Secretary-General stated that he had instructed his Special Representative to sign the Agreement with the explicit provision that the United Nations understood that the amnesty and pardon shall not apply to international crimes of genocide, crimes against humanity, war crimes and other serious violations of international humanitarian law.

Finally, the Secretary-General observed that the signing of the peace Agreement presented the people of Sierra Leone with a unique opportunity to bring an end to the conflict. He congratulated both parties for showing the flexibility, which made the Agreement possible. However, he noted that while many compromises were necessary to reach this Agreement, some of the terms which had been obtained, particularly the provisions of amnesty were difficult to reconcile with the goal of ending the culture of impunity. The principle of impunity, he noted, had inspired the creation of the United Nations Tribunal for Rwanda and the former Yugoslavia, and the future international criminal court. Therefore, in the understanding of the United

---

[34] Doc. S/1999/836
[35] see Doc. S/1999/777

Nations, although the people of Sierra Leone should be allowed this opportunity to realize their best and only hope of ending their long brutal conflict, amnesty cannot cover the crimes mentioned above. He noted that the international community and the United Nations had an important responsibility to assist Sierra Leone and to ensure that this momentum was maintained. He called upon the Security Council to approve, as an immediate first step, the provisional expansion of UNOMSIL. He would recommend at a later date, the mandate and structure of the enhanced United Nations Peacekeeping presence that may be required in the country.

In its resolution 1260 (1999) of 20 August 1999, the Security Council welcomed the signing of the peace Agreement; it commended those involved in the mediation effort, particularly the Government of Sierra Leone, for its courageous efforts to achieve peace and RUF for taking this decisive step towards peace. It called upon the parties to ensure that the provisions of the Agreement were fully implemented and authorized the provisional expansion of UNOMSIL up to 210 military observers. The Council also called upon RUF and other armed groups to begin immediately to disband and give up their arms in accordance with the provision of the peace Agreement and welcomed the adoption of the human rights manifesto by the parties concerned in Sierra Leone.

On 28 September 1999, the Secretary-General reported[36] that both the Government of Sierra Leone and the RUF had reaffirmed their commitment to the peace process, and that the two leaders had maintained close contact with each other. The Secretary-General observed that following the signing of the Agreement, Sierra Leone was in urgent need of security. He urged Mr. Sankoh to immediately assume his functions in the Government of Sierra Leone in accordance with the Agreement.

The Secretary-General recommended to the Security Council that it authorizes the deployment of the United Nations force, which, together with UNOMSIL military observers and civilian components, would be known as the United Nations Mission in Sierra Leone (UNAMSIL) with a mandate to, *inter alia,* assist the Government of Sierra Leone in the integration of disarmament, demobilization and reintegration plan, monitoring adherence for the cease-fire, encouraging the parties to create confidence building mechanisms and to support their functioning.

On 22 October 1999, in its resolution 1270 (1999) the Security Council decided to establish UNAMSIL with immediate effect for an initial period of six months to comprise a maximum number of 6,000 military personnel, including 260 military observers.

---

[36] see Doc. S/1999/1003

S/RES/1231 (1999)

19990311

11 March 1999

RESOLUTION 1231 (1999)
Adopted by the Security Council at its 3986th meeting, on 11 March 1999

The Security Council,

Recalling its resolutions 1181 (1998) of 13 July 1998 and 1220 (1999) of 12 January 1999 and the statement of its President of 7 January 1999 (S/1999/PRST/1),

Expressing its continued concern over the fragile situation in Sierra Leone,

Affirming the commitment of all States to respect the sovereignty, political independence and territorial integrity of Sierra Leone,

Having considered the fifth Report of the Secretary-General on the United Nations Observer Mission in Sierra Leone (UNOMSIL) of 4 March 1999 (S/1999/237) and noting the recommendations contained therein,

1. *Decides* to extend the mandate of UNOMSIL until 13 June 1999;

2. *Welcomes* the intention of the Secretary-General to re-establish UNOMSIL in Freetown as soon as possible, and to that end to increase the current number of military observers and human rights personnel as referred to in paragraphs 46 and 54 of his report, and to re-deploy the necessary staff to support the relocation to Freetown, subject to strict attention to the security situation there;

3. *Condemns* the atrocities perpetrated by the rebels on the civilian population of Sierra Leone, including in particular those committed against women and children, deplores all violations of human rights and international humanitarian law which have occurred in Sierra Leone during the recent escalation of violence as referred to in paragraphs 21 to 28 of the report of the Secretary-General, including the recruitment of children as soldiers, and urges the appropriate authorities to investigate all allegations of such violations with a view to bringing the perpetrators to justice;

4. *Calls* upon all parties to the conflict in Sierra Leone fully to respect human rights and international humanitarian law and the neutrality and impartiality of humanitarian workers, and to ensure full and unhindered access for humanitarian assistance to affected populations;

5. *Expresses* its grave concern at continued reports that support is being afforded to the rebels in Sierra Leone, including through the supply of arms and mercenaries, in particular from the territory of Liberia;

6. *Acknowledges* the letter of the President of Liberia to the Secretary-General of 23 February 1999 (S/1999/213) and the statement by the Government of Liberia

of 19 February 1999 (S/1999/193) on the action it is taking to curtail the involvement of Liberian nationals in the fighting in Sierra Leone, including measures to encourage the return of Liberian fighters and directives to the Liberian national security agencies to ensure that no cross-border movement of arms takes place and that there be no transshipment of arms and ammunition through Liberian territory, and requests the Secretary-General to continue to consider, in coordination with the countries of the Mano River Union and other member States of the Economic Community of West African States (ECOWAS), the practicability and effectiveness of the deployment of United Nations monitors along with forces of the Military Observer Group of ECOWAS (ECOMOG) at the Liberia/Sierra Leone border;

7. *Reaffirms* the obligation of all States to comply strictly with the provisions of the embargo on the sale or supply of arms and related materiel imposed by its resolution 1171 (1998) of 5 June 1998;

8. *Expresses* its intention to keep the issue of external support to the rebels in Sierra Leone under close review, and to consider further steps to address this in the light of developments on the ground;

9. *Expresses* its support for all efforts, in particular by ECOWAS States, aimed at peacefully resolving the conflict and restoring lasting peace and stability to Sierra Leone, encourages the Secretary-General, through his Special Representative for Sierra Leone, to facilitate dialogue to these ends, welcomes the statement of the President of Sierra Leone of 7 February 1999 (S/1999/138, annex) expressing his Government's readiness to continue their efforts for dialogue with the rebels, and calls upon all parties involved, especially the rebels, to participate seriously in these efforts;

10. *Commends* the efforts of ECOMOG towards the restoration of peace, security and stability in Sierra Leone, and calls upon all Member States to provide ECOMOG with financial and logistical support and to consider the provision of prompt bilateral assistance to the Government of Sierra Leone in the creation of a new Sierra Leonean army to defend the country;

11. *Requests* the Secretary-General to keep the Council closely informed on the situation in Sierra Leone and in this regard to submit an additional report to the Council with recommendations on the future deployment of UNOMSIL and the implementation of its mandate by 5 June 1999;

12. *Decides* to remain actively seized of the matter.

S/PRST/1999/13

19990515

15 May 1999

STATEMENT BY THE PRESIDENT OF THE SECURITY COUNCIL

At the 4005th meeting of the Security Council, held on 15 May 1999 in connection with the Council's consideration of the item entitled "The situation in Sierra Leone" the President of the Security Council made the following statement on the behalf of the Council:

"The Security Council stresses that an overall political settlement and national reconciliation are essential to achieving the peaceful resolution of the conflict in Sierra Leone. In this context, it welcomes the recent holding of internal talks by a rebel delegation in Lomé, and urges the Government of Sierra Leone and rebel representatives to ensure that there are no further obstacles to a start to direct talks without delay.

"The Security Council calls upon all concerned to remain committed to the process of negotiation and to demonstrate flexibility in their approach to the process. In this context, the Council underlines its strong support for the mediation efforts of the United Nations within the Lome process, in particular the work of the Special Representative of the Secretary-General to facilitate dialogue, and for the key role being played by the President of Togo.

"The Security Council commends, once again, the continued efforts of the Government of Sierra Leone and the Military Observer Group of the Economic Community of West African States (ECOMOG) towards the restoration of peace, security and stability in Sierra Leone, and calls for sustained support for ECOMOG from the international community.

"The Security Council condemns the recent killings, atrocities, destruction of property and other violations of human rights and international humanitarian law perpetrated on civilians by the rebels in recent attacks, in particular at Masiaka and Port Loko. It calls upon the rebels to cease such actions immediately and urges the rebel leadership to release all hostages and abductees without delay.

"The Security Council urges both parties to commit themselves to a cessation of hostilities for the duration of the Lomé talks, to ensure that this is fully respected on the ground and to work constructively, and in good faith for a ceasefire agreement. It calls upon both sides to refrain from any hostile or aggressive act which could undermine the talks process.

"The Security Council welcomes the intention of the Secretary-General to increase, as security conditions permit, the presence on the ground of the United

Nations Observer Mission in Sierra Leone (UNOMSIL) within currently authorized levels, in anticipation of a cessation of hostilities. The Council also welcomes the Secretary-General's intention to send an assessment team to Sierra Leone to examine how an expanded UNOMSIL with a revised mandate and concept of operations might contribute to the implementation of a ceasefire and peace agreement in the event of a successful outcome to the negotiations between the Government of Sierra Leone and the rebels, and expresses its readiness to consider recommendations from the Secretary-General to that end.

"The Security Council stresses, however, that it will be prepared to consider deploying monitors throughout Sierra Leone only when a credible ceasefire is in place and is being respected by all sides, and there is a commitment of all parties to a framework peace agreement.

"The Security Council underlines the importance, in the context of a lasting solution to the conflict in Sierra Leone, of a plan for the internationally supervised disarmament, demobilization and reintegration of ex-combatants, including child soldiers. It also draws attention to the need for the secure and timely disposal of collected arms, in accordance with any peace agreement reached.

"The Security Council reaffirms the obligation of all States to comply strictly with the provisions of the embargo on the sale or supply of arms and related materiel imposed by its resolution 1171 (1998) of 5 June 1998.

"The Security Council reiterates its grave concern at the humanitarian situation in Sierra Leone and urges all parties, in particular the rebel leadership, to guarantee safe and unhindered humanitarian access to all those in need.

"The Security Council reiterates that a peaceful and lasting solution to the conflict in Sierra Leone remains the responsibility of the Government and people of Sierra Leone, but again emphasizes the strong commitment of the international community to support a sustainable peace settlement.

"The Security Council will remain seized of the matter."

S/RES/1245 (1999)

RESOLUTION 1245 (1999)
Adopted by the Security Council at its 4012th meeting, on 11 June 1999

The Security Council,

Recalling its resolutions 1181 (1998) of 13 July 1998, 1220 (1999) of 12 January 1999 and 1231 (1999) of 11 March 1999 and the statements of its President of 7 January 1999 (S/PRST/1999/1) and 15 May 1999 (S/PRST/1999/13),

Acknowledging the cooperation provided by the Economic Community of West African States (ECOWAS) and its Military Observer Group (ECOMOG),

Expressing its continued concern over the fragile situation in Sierra Leone,

Affirming the commitment of all States to respect the sovereignty, political independence and territorial integrity of Sierra Leone,

Having considered the sixth report of the Secretary-General on the United Nations Observer Mission in Sierra Leone (UNOMSIL) of 4 June 1999 (S/1999/645) and noting the recommendations contained therein,

1. *Decides* to extend the mandate of UNOMSIL until 13 December 1999;

2. *Stresses* that an overall political settlement and national reconciliation are essential to achieving a peaceful resolution of the conflict in Sierra Leone, and welcomes the holding of talks in Lomé, between the Government of Sierra Leone and rebel representatives;

3. *Calls* upon all concerned to remain committed to the process of negotiation and to demonstrate flexibility in their approach to the process, underlines its strong support for all those involved in the mediation efforts of the United Nations within the Lomé process, in particular the work of the Special Representative of the Secretary-General to facilitate dialogue, and for the key role being played by the President of Togo as current Chairman of ECOWAS, and emphasizes the strong commitment of the international community to support a sustainable peace settlement;

4. *Takes note* of the intention of the Secretary-General, as set out in paragraphs 52 to 57 of his report, to revert to the Council with recommendations on an expanded UNOMSIL presence in Sierra Leone with a revised mandate and concept of operations in the event of a successful outcome to the negotiations between the Government of Sierra Leone and rebel representatives in Lomé, and underlines that further eventual deployment of UNOMSIL should be considered, taking into account security conditions;

5. *Requests* the Secretary-General to keep the Council closely informed on the situation in Sierra Leone;

6. *Decides* to remain actively seized of the matter.

S/RES/1260 (1999)

20 August 1999

RESOLUTION 1260 (1999)
Adopted by the Security Council at its 4035th meeting, on 20 August 1999

The Security Council,

Recalling its resolutions 1171 (1998) of 5 June 1998, 1181 (1998) of 13 July 1998, 1231 (1999) of 11 March 1999 and other relevant resolutions and the statement of its President of 15 May 1999 (S/PRST/1999/13),

Recalling also that in accordance with its resolution 1245 (1999) of 11 June 1999 the mandate of the United Nations Observer Mission in Sierra Leone (UNOMSIL) extends until 13 December 1999,

Affirming the commitment of all States to respect the sovereignty, political independence and territorial integrity of Sierra Leone,

Having considered the report of the Secretary-General of 30 July 1999 (S/1999/836),

1. *Welcomes* the signing of the Peace Agreement between the Government of Sierra Leone and the Revolutionary United Front of Sierra Leone (RUF) in Lomé on 7 July 1999 (S/1999/777), and commends the President of Togo, the Special Representative of the Secretary-General, the Economic Community of West African States (ECOWAS) and all those involved in facilitating the negotiations in Lomé on their contribution to this achievement;

2. *Commends* the Government of Sierra Leone for its courageous efforts to achieve peace, including through legislative and other measures already taken towards implementation of the Peace Agreement, commends also the leadership of the RUF for taking this decisive step towards peace, and calls upon them both to ensure that the provisions of the Agreement are fully implemented;

3. *Commends* also the Military Observer Group of ECOWAS (ECOMOG) on the outstanding contribution which it has made to the restoration of security and stability in Sierra Leone, the protection of civilians and the promotion of a peaceful settlement of the conflict, and urges all States to continue to provide technical, logistical and financial support to ECOMOG to help it to maintain its critical presence and continue to perform its role in Sierra Leone, including through the United Nations Trust Fund established to support peacekeeping and related activities in Sierra Leone;

4. *Authorizes* the provisional expansion of UNOMSIL to up to 210 military observers along with the necessary equipment and administrative and medical support to perform the tasks set out in paragraph 38 of the report of the Secretary-

General, and decides that these additional military observers shall be deployed as security conditions permit and shall operate for the time being under security provided by ECOMOG as indicated in paragraph 39 of the report;

5. *Underscores* the importance of the safety, security and freedom of movement of United Nations and associated personnel, notes that the Government of Sierra Leone and the RUF have agreed in the Peace Agreement to provide guarantees in this regard, and urges all parties in Sierra Leone to respect fully the status of United Nations and associated personnel;

6. *Authorizes* the strengthening of the political, civil affairs, information, human rights and child protection elements of UNOMSIL as set out in paragraphs 40 to 52 of the report of the Secretary-General, including through the appointment of a deputy Special Representative of the Secretary-General and the expansion of the Office of the Special Representative of the Secretary-General;

7. *Encourages* the ongoing consultations among the parties concerned on future peacekeeping arrangements in Sierra Leone including the respective tasks, strength and mandates of ECOMOG and the United Nations, and welcomes the intention of the Secretary-General to revert to the Council with comprehensive proposals concerning a new mandate and concept of operations for UNOMSIL;

8. *Calls* upon the RUF and all other armed groups in Sierra Leone to begin immediately to disband and give up their arms in accordance with the provisions of the Peace Agreement, and to participate fully in the disarmament, demobilization and reintegration programme in Sierra Leone;

9. *Urges* all States and international organizations to provide resources to help ensure the successful conduct of the disarmament, demobilization and reintegration programme, in particular through the Trust Fund established by the International Bank for Reconstruction and Development for this purpose;

10. *Stresses* the urgent need to promote peace and national reconciliation and to foster accountability and respect for human rights in Sierra Leone and, in this context, takes note of the views contained in paragraph 54 of the report of the Secretary-General, welcomes the provisions in the Peace Agreement on the establishment of the Truth and Reconciliation Commission and the Human Rights Commission in Sierra Leone, and calls upon the Government of Sierra Leone and the RUF to ensure these Commissions will be established promptly within the timeframe provided for in the Peace Agreement;

11. *Welcomes* the adoption of the Human Rights Manifesto by the parties concerned in Sierra Leone and stresses the need for international assistance to address the human rights issues in Sierra Leone as a step towards accountability in the country, as referred to in paragraph 20 of the report of the Secretary-General;

12. *Stresses* the need for the international community and the Government of Sierra Leone to design and implement programmes to address the special needs of war victims, in particular those who have suffered maiming mutilation, and, in this

regard, welcomes the commitment of the Government of Sierra Leone as set out in the Peace Agreement to establish a special fund for this purpose;

13. *Stresses* the urgent and substantial need for humanitarian assistance to the people of Sierra Leone, in particular in the large proportion of the country hitherto inaccessible to relief agencies, and urges all States and international organizations to provide such assistance as a priority, in response to the revised consolidated inter-agency appeal issued in July 1999;

14. *Calls upon* all parties to ensure the safe and unhindered access of humanitarian assistance to those in need in Sierra Leone, to guarantee the safety and security of humanitarian personnel and to respect strictly the relevant provisions of international humanitarian law;

15. *Stresses* the need for sustained and generous assistance for the longer term tasks of reconstruction, economic and social recovery and development in Sierra Leone, and urges all States and international organizations to participate in and contribute actively to these efforts;

16. *Welcomes* the commitment of the Government of Sierra Leone to work with the United Nations Children's Fund and the Office of the Special Representative of the Secretary-General for Children and Armed Conflict and other international agencies to give particular attention to the long-term rehabilitation of child combatants in Sierra Leone, and encourages those involved also to address the special needs of all children affected by the conflict in Sierra Leone, including through the disarmament, demobilization and reintegration programme and the Truth and Reconciliation Commission, and through support to child victims of mutilation, sexual exploitation and abduction, to the rehabilitation of health and education services, and to the recovery of traumatized children and the protection of unaccompanied children;

17. *Welcomes* the decision of the Secretary-General that the United Nations develop a strategic framework approach for Sierra Leone in consultation with national and international partners, as indicated in paragraph 44 of his report;

18. *Requests* the Secretary-General to keep the Council closely informed on the situation in Sierra Leone and to submit an additional report to the Council as soon as possible including recommendations for the mandate and structure of the enhanced United Nations peacekeeping presence that may be required in the country;

19. *Decides* to remain actively seized of the matter.

S/RES/1270 (1999)

22 October 1999

RESOLUTION 1270 (1999)
Adopted by the Security Council at its 4054th meeting, on 22 October 1999

The Security Council,

Recalling its resolutions 1171 (1998) of 5 June 1998, 1181 (1998) of 13 July 1998, 1231 (1999) of 11 March 1999 and 1260 (1999) of 20 August 1999 and other relevant resolutions and the statement of its President of 15 May 1999 (S/PRST/1999/13),

Recalling also the report of the Secretary-General of 8 September 1999 (S/1999/957) and its resolution 1265 (1999) of 17 September 1999 on the protection of civilians in armed conflict,

Affirming the commitment of all States to respect the sovereignty, political independence and territorial integrity of Sierra Leone,

Having considered the report of the Secretary-General of 23 September 1999 (S/1999/1003),

Determining that the situation in Sierra Leone continues to constitute a threat to international peace and security in the region,

1. *Welcomes* the important steps taken by the Government of Sierra Leone, the leadership of the Revolutionary United Front of Sierra Leone (RUF), the Military Observer Group (ECOMOG) of the Economic Community of West African States (ECOWAS) and the United Nations Observer Mission in Sierra Leone (UNOMSIL) towards implementation of the Peace Agreement (S/1999/777) since its signing in Lomé on 7 July 1999, and recognizes the important role of the Joint Implementation Committee established by the Peace Agreement under the chairmanship of the President of Togo;

2. *Calls* upon the parties to fulfil all their commitments under the Peace Agreement to facilitate the restoration of peace, stability, national reconciliation and development in Sierra Leone;

3. *Takes* note of the preparations made for the disarmament, demobilization and reintegration of ex-combatants, including child soldiers, by the Government of Sierra Leone through the National Committee for Disarmament, Demobilization and Reintegration, and urges all concerned to make every effort to ensure that all designated centres begin to function as soon as possible;

4. *Calls upon* the RUF, the Civil Defence Forces, former Sierra Leone Armed Forces/Armed Forces Revolutionary Council (AFRC) and all other armed groups in

Sierra Leone to begin immediately to disband and give up their arms in accordance with the provisions of the Peace Agreement, and to participate fully in the disarmament, demobilization and reintegration programme;

5. *Welcomes* the return to Freetown of the leaders of the RUF and AFRC, and calls upon them to engage fully and responsibly in the implementation of the Peace Agreement and to direct the participation of all rebel groups in the disarmament and demobilization process without delay;

6. *Deplores* the recent taking of hostages, including UNOMSIL and ECOMOG personnel, by rebel groups and calls upon those responsible to put an end to such practices immediately and to address their concerns about the terms of the Peace Agreement peacefully through dialogue with the parties concerned;

7. *Reiterates* its appreciation for the indispensable role which ECOMOG forces continue to play in the maintenance of security and stability in and the protection of the people of Sierra Leone, and approves the new mandate for ECOMOG (S/1999/1073, annex) adopted by ECOWAS on 25 August 1999;

8. *Decides* to establish the United Nations Mission in Sierra Leone (UNAMSIL) with immediate effect for an initial period of six months and with the following mandate:

   (a) To cooperate with the Government of Sierra Leone and the other parties to the Peace Agreement in the implementation of the Agreement;
   (b) To assist the Government of Sierra Leone in the implementation of the disarmament, demobilization and reintegration plan;
   (c) To that end, to establish a presence at key locations throughout the territory of Sierra Leone, including at disarmament/reception centres and demobilization centres;
   (d) To ensure the security and freedom of movement of United Nations personnel;
   (e) To monitor adherence to the ceasefire in accordance with the ceasefire agreement of 18 May 1999 (S/1999/585, annex) through the structures provided for therein;
   (f) To encourage the parties to create confidence-building mechanisms and support their functioning;
   (g) To facilitate the delivery of humanitarian assistance;
   (h) To support the operations of United Nations civilian officials, including the Special Representative of the Secretary-General and his staff, human rights officers and civil affairs officers;
   (i) To provide support, as requested, to the elections, which are to be held in accordance with the present constitution of Sierra Leone;

9. *Decides* also that the military component of UNAMSIL shall comprise a maximum of 6,000 military personnel, including 260 military observers, subject to periodic review in the light of conditions on the ground and the progress made in the

peace process, in particular in the disarmament, demobilization and reintegration programme, and takes note of paragraph 43 of the report of the Secretary-General of 23 September 1999;

10. *Decides further* that UNAMSIL will take over the substantive civilian and military components and functions of UNOMSIL as well as its assets, and to that end decides that the mandate of UNOMSIL shall terminate immediately on the establishment of UNAMSIL;

11. *Commends* the readiness of ECOMOG to continue to provide security for the areas where it is currently located, in particular around Freetown and Lungi, to provide protection for the Government of Sierra Leone, to conduct other operations in accordance with their mandate to ensure the implementation of the Peace Agreement, and to initiate and proceed with disarmament and demobilization in conjunction and full coordination with UNAMSIL;

12. *Stresses* the need for close cooperation and coordination between ECOMOG and UNAMSIL in carrying out their respective tasks, and welcomes the intended establishment of joint operations centres at headquarters and, if necessary, also at subordinate levels in the field;

13. *Reiterates* the importance of the safety, security and freedom of movement of United Nations and associated personnel, notes that the Government of Sierra Leone and the RUF have agreed in the Peace Agreement to provide guarantees in this regard, and calls upon all parties in Sierra Leone to respect fully the status of United Nations and associated personnel;

14. *Acting* under Chapter VII of the Charter of the United Nations, decides that in the discharge of its mandate UNAMSIL may take the necessary action to ensure the security and freedom of movement of its personnel and, within its capabilities and areas of deployment, to afford protection to civilians under imminent threat of physical violence, taking into account the responsibilities of the Government of Sierra Leone and ECOMOG;

15. *Underlines* the importance of including in UNAMSIL personnel with appropriate training in international humanitarian, human rights and refugee law, including child and gender-related provisions, negotiation and communication skills, cultural awareness and civilian-military coordination;

16. *Requests* the Government of Sierra Leone to conclude a status-of-forces agreement with the Secretary-General within 30 days of the adoption of this resolution, and recalls that pending the conclusion of such an agreement the model status-of-forces agreement dated 9 October 1990 (A/45/594) should apply provisionally;

17. *Stresses* the urgent need to promote peace and national reconciliation and to foster accountability and respect for human rights in Sierra Leone, underlines in this context the key role of the Truth and Reconciliation Commission, the Human Rights Commission and the Commission for the Consolidation of Peace established under the Peace Agreement, and urges the Government of Sierra Leone to ensure the

prompt establishment and effective functioning of these bodies with the full participation of all parties and drawing on the relevant experience and support of Member States, specialized bodies, other multilateral organizations and civil society;

18. *Emphasizes* that the plight of children is among the most pressing challenges facing Sierra Leone, welcomes the continued commitment of the Government of Sierra Leone to work with the United Nations Children's Fund, the Office of the Special Representative of the Secretary-General for Children and Armed Conflict and other international agencies to give particular attention to the long-term rehabilitation of child combatants in Sierra Leone, and reiterates its encouragement of those involved to address the special needs of all children affected by the conflict;

19. *Urges* all parties concerned to ensure that refugees and internally displaced persons are protected and are enabled to return voluntarily and in safety to their homes, and encourages States and international organizations to provide urgent assistance to that end;

20. *Stresses* the urgent need for substantial additional resources to finance the disarmament, demobilization and reintegration process, and calls upon all States, international and other organizations to contribute generously to the multidonor trust fund established by the International Bank for Reconstruction and Development for this purpose;

21. *Stresses* also the continued need for urgent and substantial humanitarian assistance to the people of Sierra Leone, as well as for sustained and generous assistance for the longer term tasks of peace-building, reconstruction, economic and social recovery and development in Sierra Leone, and urges all States and international and other organizations to provide such assistance as a priority;

22. *Calls* upon all parties to ensure safe and unhindered access of humanitarian assistance to those in need in Sierra Leone, to guarantee the safety and security of humanitarian personnel and to respect strictly the relevant provisions of international humanitarian and human rights law;

23. *Urges* the Government of Sierra Leone to expedite the formation of professional and accountable national police and armed forces, including through their restructuring and training, without which it will not be possible to achieve long-term stability, national reconciliation and the reconstruction of the country, and underlines the importance of support and assistance from the international community in this regard;

24. *Welcomes* the continued work by the United Nations on the development of the Strategic Framework for Sierra Leone aimed at enhancing effective collaboration and coordination within the United Nations system and between the United Nations and its national and international partners in Sierra Leone;

25. *Notes* the intention of the Secretary-General to keep the situation in Sierra Leone under close review and to revert to the Council with additional proposals if required;

26. *Requests* the Secretary-General to report to the Council every 45 days to provide updates on the status of the peace process, on security conditions on the ground and on the continued level of deployment of ECOMOG personnel, so that troop levels and the tasks to be performed can be evaluated as outlined in paragraphs 49 and 50 of the report of the Secretary-General of 23 September 1999;

27. *Decides* to remain actively seized of the matter.

SOMALIA[37]

The Security Council remained actively involved with regard to the conflict in Somalia. Thus on 27 May 1999, the President made a statement[38] on behalf of the Security Council concerning the situation in Somalia. The Council expressed alarm at the deterioration of the situation, in the political, military and humanitarian aspects. It also expressed concern at reports of an increase in the external interference in the country. Furthermore, the Council reaffirmed its commitment to a comprehensive and lasting settlement of the situation in the country. In its view, any peaceful settlement had to bear in mind the respect for the sovereignty, territorial integrity and political independence and unity of Somalia, in accordance with the principles of the United Nations Charter.

The President also expressed the deep concern of the Security Council at reports of the illicit delivery of weapons and military equipment to Somalia, in clear violation of the arms embargo as imposed by resolution 733 (1992). It was clear that the supply of such arms could exacerbate the crisis in the country and endanger the peace and security of the whole region. It called upon all States to observe the arms embargo pursuant to the above resolution.

The Security Council welcomed the continued efforts of the Secretary-General and the United Nations Political Office for Somalia in Nairobi and called upon the Secretary-General to submit periodic reports on the situation in Somalia.

The President of the Security Council, on 12 November 1999, issued another statement[39] expressing grave concern at the increasingly evident effects of the lack of a functioning central Government in Somalia. The Council expressed deep regret that consequent on this, there was a lack of law and order in the country and that there was a risk of creating a haven for criminals of all kinds.

The Security Council also welcomed the initiatives made by the President of Djibouti aimed at restoring peace and stability in Somalia and looked forward to the finalization of proposals aimed at finding a lasting solution to the problem. The Council expressed its readiness to work with the

---

[37] For the efforts of the United Nations aimed at resolving the conflicts in Somalia during the period from mid 1997 to mid 1998, see *African Yearbook of International Law,* Vol. 6, PP 363

[38] Doc. S/PRST/11999/16

[39] Doc. S/PRST/1999/31

InterGovernmental Authority on Development (IGAD) and the Standing Committee on Somalia to help bring about lasting peace in the country.

The Security Council also encouraged the Secretary-General to review the role that the United Nations could play in Somalia aimed at achieving a comprehensive and lasting settlement of the situation. The review could include a possible re-location of some of the United Nations programs and agencies as well as the United Nations Political Office for Somalia currently operating from Nairobi.

The Security Council indicated that it would continue its active involvement with regard to the situation in Somalia with a view to assisting in finding a lasting solution to the problem.

S/PRST/1999/16

19990527

27 May 1999

STATEMENT BY THE PRESIDENT OF THE SECURITY COUNCIL

At the 4010th meeting of the Security Council, held on 27 May 1999 in connection with the Council's consideration of the item entitled "The situation in Somalia", the President of the Security Council made the following statement on behalf of the Council:

"The Security Council expresses its alarm at the serious deterioration in the political, military and humanitarian situation in Somalia and concern at the reports of increasing external interference in Somalia.

"The Security Council reaffirms its commitment to a comprehensive and lasting settlement of the situation in Somalia, bearing in mind respect for the sovereignty, territorial integrity and political independence and unity of Somalia, in accordance with the principles of the Charter of the United Nations. It reiterates that full responsibility for achieving national reconciliation and for restoring peace rests with the Somali people.

"The Security Council expresses its support for the activities of the Standing Committee on Somalia and calls upon all Somali factions to cease immediately all hostilities and to cooperate with the regional and other efforts to achieve peace and reconciliation.

"The Security Council is deeply concerned at recent reports of the illicit delivery of weapons and military equipment to Somalia in violation of the arms embargo imposed by resolution 733 (1992) of 23 January 1992 which could exacerbate the crisis in Somalia and endanger the peace and security of the region as a whole.

"The Security Council reiterates its call upon States to observe the arms embargo and to refrain from any actions which might exacerbate the situation in Somalia. It further requests Member States having information about violations of the provisions of resolution 733 (1992) to provide this information to the Committee created pursuant to resolution 751 (1992) of 24 April 1992.

"The Security Council expresses its deep concern at the humanitarian impact of the long-lasting crisis, and in particular condemns attacks or acts of violence against civilians, especially women, children and other vulnerable groups, including internally displaced persons. It also condemns attacks on humanitarian workers, in violation of the rules of international law.

"The Security Council calls upon the Somali factions to cooperate on the basis of the principles of neutrality and non-discrimination with the United Nations agencies and other organizations carrying out humanitarian activities. The Council urges all parties to guarantee the security and the freedom of movement of humanitarian personnel and to ensure unhindered access to those in need of assistance. In this regard, it also commends the existing coordination of all efforts of the international community to meet the humanitarian needs of the Somali people undertaken by the Somali Aid Coordination Body, comprising donors, United Nations agencies and non-governmental organizations.

"The Security Council urges all States to contribute generously to the appeal of the United Nations to ensure continued relief and rehabilitation efforts in all regions of Somalia, including those aimed at the strengthening of civil society.

"The Security Council welcomes the continuing efforts of the Secretary-General and the United Nations Political Office for Somalia (UNPOS) in Nairobi.

"The Security Council requests the Secretary-General to submit periodic reports on the situation in Somalia.

"The Security Council will remain seized of the matter."

S/PRST/1999/31

12 November 1999

STATEMENT BY THE PRESIDENT OF THE SECURITY COUNCIL

At the 4066th meeting of the Security Council, held on 12 November 1999 in connection with the Council's consideration of the item entitled "The situation in Somalia", the President of the Security Council made the following statement on behalf of the Council:

"The Security Council recalls the report of the Secretary-General on the situation in Somalia dated 16 August 1999 (S/1999/882).

"The Security Council reaffirms its commitment to a comprehensive and lasting settlement of the situation in Somalia, bearing in mind respect for the sovereignty, territorial integrity and political independence and unity of Somalia, in accordance with the principles of the Charter of the United Nations.

"The Security Council expresses its grave concern at the increasingly evident effects of the lack of a functioning central government in Somalia. It regrets the fact that most children receive no health care and that two generations have had no access to formal education. It is concerned that some Somali natural resources are being exploited, mainly by foreigners, without regulation and monitoring. It expresses its deep distress over reports that the absence of law and order in the country risks creating a haven for criminals of all kinds.

"The Security Council welcomes the progress that has been made in the development of a greater uniformity of approach on the part of the international community in addressing the crisis in Somalia. It recognizes that the Standing Committee on Somalia, created a year ago, has been instrumental in monitoring the evolution of the Somali situation and working for a greater coordination of efforts by the various external actors, in order to avoid contrasting influences and to give weight to common actions. It calls for the strengthening of the coordination of these efforts aimed at securing peace and stability in Somalia.

"The Security Council expresses its full support for the efforts exerted by the Intergovernmental Authority on Development (IGAD) to find a political solution to the crisis in Somalia. In this context, it welcomes the initiative of the President of Djibouti aimed at restoring peace and stability in Somalia, which was outlined in his letter of 23 September 1999 to the President of the Security Council (S/1999/1007). It endorses the call made by the President of Djibouti to the warlords to recognize fully and accept the principle that the Somalia people are free to exercise their democratic right to choose their own regional and national leaders. The Council looks forward to the finalization of the proposals of the President of Djibouti at the forthcoming IGAD Summit and stands ready to work with IGAD and the Standing Committee to help bring about national unity and the restoration of a national government in Somalia. It calls upon the leaders of the Somali factions and all others concerned to cooperate constructively and in good faith in the efforts to resolve the crisis.

"The Security Council strongly calls upon all States to observe and improve the effectiveness of the arms embargo imposed by resolution 733 (1992) of 23 January 1992 and to refrain from any actions which might exacerbate the situation in Somalia. It urges Member States having information about violations of the provisions of resolution 733 (1992) to provide this information to the Committee created pursuant to resolution 751 (1992) of 24 April 1992, with a view to supporting the work of the Committee.

"The Security Council expresses its grave concern at the continuing deterioration of the humanitarian situation in Somalia. It urges all States to contribute generously to the appeals of the United Nations to ensure continued relief and rehabilitation efforts in all regions of Somalia, including those aimed at the strengthening of civil society. In this context, it encourages enhancement of the operational capacity of humanitarian agencies in Somalia through donor support.

"The Security Council expresses its appreciation for all United Nations agencies, other organizations and individuals carrying out humanitarian activities in all regions of Somalia. It calls upon the Somali factions to ensure the safety and freedom of movement of all humanitarian personnel and to facilitate the delivery of humanitarian relief. In this context, it strongly condemns attacks and acts of violence against and the murder of humanitarian workers in Somalia and reiterates its position that those responsible for these acts should be brought to justice.

"The Security Council expresses its satisfaction that despite all the difficulties, approximately half of Somali territory continues to enjoy relative peace. In this context, it notes the beginning of provision of some basic services to the people of Somalia by local administrations in some parts of the country.

"The Security Council welcomes the efforts of civil society in Somalia. It is encouraged by the political initiatives of Somalis, through regional conferences, often organized by traditional leaders and informal cross-clan contacts, to find a peaceful solution to the crisis. In this context, it underlines the active role of Somali women's groups.

"The Security Council welcomes the continuing efforts of the Secretary-General and the United Nations Political Office for Somalia (UNPOS) in Nairobi.

"The Security Council encourages the Secretary-General to review the role of the United Nations in Somalia, as a prelude to the United Nations playing an enhanced role, aimed at achieving a comprehensive and lasting settlement of the situation in Somalia. This review would include the possible re-location of some United Nations programmes and agencies, as well as UNPOS, to Somalia. The review should also consider the security situation carefully, as well as the resources that would be necessary to provide a secure environment for United Nations operations in Somalia.

"The Security Council takes note of the recommendation in the report of the Secretary-General of 16 August 1999 that the international community should consider establishing mechanisms which would allow financial assistance to flow into secure and stable areas of Somalia even before a formal central government and other institutions are re-established, with a view to promoting the sovereignty, territorial integrity and political independence and unity of Somalia.

"The Security Council will remain seized of the matter."

WESTERN SAHARA

The Security Council's involvement in the conflict involving Morocco and the Polisario Liberation Front dates back to the initial period when Spain decided to leave Western Sahara which it had held as a colony.

The Secretary-General reported on 26 October 1998 that Morocco had expressed its firm intention to expedite the process leading to a referendum for Western Sahara. It had also expressed its willingness to facilitate the return of refugees and to assist UNHCR in their repatriation. The same commitment of intent had been made by the Frente POLISARIO, which reiterated the fundamental importance it attached to the referendum process as set out in the Settlement Plan.

As a follow up to these developments, the Secretary-General authorized his Special Representative to immediately resume, the identification of applicants from identified tribal groupings designated as H41, H61 and J51/52 and to start the appeals process. He was of the view that if the transition period was to start in June/July 1999, then the referendum should be held in December 1998. He considered it important that to undertake full deployment of MINURSO by January 1999.

The Security Council, in its resolution 1204 of 30 October 1998 welcomed the intention of both Morocco and the POLISARIO Front to cooperate with the MINURSO in implementing the proposals contained in the report of the Secretary-General. It also supported the idea of MIRNUSO that it would start the publication of the provisional list of voters by 1 December 1998.

In resolution 1215 of 17 December 1998, the Security Council called upon all interested States to sign the proposed refugee repatriation Protocol. It urged both parties to take concerted action to enable the UNHCR to carry out the necessary preparatory work for the repatriation of Saharan refugees eligible to vote and their families.

On 28 January 1999, the Secretary-General reported[40] that while the Frente POLISARIO had formerly accepted the package of proposed measures aimed at accelerating the referendum process, Morocco, on the other hand, had expressed some concerns and sought clarifications over key provisions of the package. Consultations were thus being conducted with a view to clarifying issues relating to voter identification and the appeals process contained in the package of measures.

---

[40] Doc. S/1999/88

The Secretary-General also reported that Morocco had decided to proceed with the signing of the Status of Forces Agreement concerning MINURSO.

The Secretary-General was hopeful that the discussions under way regarding the clarification of issues requested by Morocco, would lead to a full and detailed Agreement on the identification, appeals and repatriation planning activities, and on the implementation of a calendar of activities leading to the holding of a referendum. He also hoped that the transitional period could promptly be moved forward.

Further to the Secretary-General's report above, the Security Council, on 28 January 1999 adopted resolution 1224 requesting him to keep the Council informed of all significant developments regarding the implementation of the Settlement Plan and the agreements reached between the parties. He was also requested to keep the Council informed on the continuing viability of the MINURSO mandate.

In its further resolution 1228 adopted on 11 February 1999, the Security Council expressed the hope that the parties would accept the Protocols on identification, appeals and repatriation planning activities and on the essential issues of the interpretation of the calendar, without undermining the integrity of the package or calling into question its main elements for the prompt resumption of voter identification and initiation of the appeals process. The Council also requested both parties to take concrete action to enable the UNHCR to carry out the necessary preparatory work for the repatriation of refugees eligible to vote.

The Secretary-General again reported[41] on 22 March 1999 that following consultations, he would provide the parties by the end of March with revised texts of the identification and appeals Protocols in order to incorporate necessary amendments including revised dates for the completion of various tasks. The revised dates would include those for the appeals procedure to be launched no later than one month after the date of resumption of identification and for the provisional list of potential voters, from among the applicants identified thus far, to be published on that date.

The modalities for organizing the identification and appeals would also be amended so as to be consistent with the objective of holding the referendum by March 2000. The Secretary-General hoped that once the revisions were made the Protocols and operational directives would receive a prompt concurrence of the parties.

---

41   Doc. S/1999/307

Thus, on 30 March 1999, the Security Council adopted resolution 1232 requesting the two parties to move ahead with the discussions with a view to reaching an Agreement on the refugee repatriation protocol. It welcomed in this regard the decision of the POLISARIO Front to allow the resumption of pre-registration activities of UNHCR. The Council also welcomed the signature by Morocco and MINURSO of the Agreement on mines and unexplored ordinances. It urged the POLISARIO Front to do the same.

The Security Council again in its resolution 1235 of 30 April 1999 requested the Secretary-General to keep the Council informed of all significant developments in the implementation of the Settlement Plan and the Agreements reached with the parties, and as appropriate, on the viability of the mandate of MINURSO.

Further to the report of the Secretary-General on 27 April, the Security Council adopted resolution 1238 on 14 May 1999, in which it welcomed the acceptance by both parties of the detailed modalities for the implementation of the Secretary-General's package of measures relating to the identification of the voters, the appeals process and the revised timetable as a good foundation for the completion of the phase of the Settlement Plan prior to the actual conduct of the referendum. The Council also requested the Secretary-General to submit at an early date a revised timetable and financial implications for the holding of the referendum.

On 25 June 1999, the Secretary-General reported[42] that the final program of identification for the remaining individual applicants from tribal groupings H41, H61 and J51/52 was issued on 1 June 1999 and that the identification operation had resumed on schedule on 15 June 1999. The program was scheduled for completion in November 1999. The Secretary-General also reported that so far 12,798 refugees had been pre-registered and awaited repatriation to Western Sahara.

The Secretary-General also noted that the resumption of identification process and the initiation of the appeals process were being implemented as planned, with the cooperation of both sides. He considered it important that both parties stayed the course in this regard and in the launching of the appeals scheduled to start on 15 July 1999, in conjunction with the publication of the first part of the provisional voters' list. He also expected that both parties would extend full cooperation to the office of United Nations High Commission for Refugees to enable it to complete its preparatory activities and planning for the repatriation of refugees.

---

[42] Doc. S/1999/721

The Security Council, in its resolution 1263 of 13 September 1999 extended the mandate of MINURSO to 4 December 1999 to enable it to complete the identification of voters, to implement confidence-building measures and to conclude all outstanding Agreements needed to implement the Settlement Plan. The Council also requested MINURSO to continue with the appeals process and reaffirm the rights of the applicants and expressed the expectation that the appeals process would not turn into a second round of identification.

S/RES/1204 (1998)

30 October 1998

RESOLUTION 1204 (1998)
Adopted by the Security Council at its 3938th meeting, on 30 October 1998

The Security Council,

Recalling all its previous resolutions on the question of the Western Sahara,

Reiterating its commitment to assist the parties to achieve a just and lasting solution to the question of the Western Sahara,

Reiterating also its commitment to the holding without further delay of a free, fair and impartial referendum for the self-determination of the people of the Western Sahara in accordance with the Settlement Plan, which has been accepted by the two parties,

Welcoming the report of the Secretary-General of 26 October 1998 (S/1998/997) and the observations and recommendations contained therein,

Welcoming also the stated intentions of the Government of Morocco and the POLISARIO Front to cooperate actively with the United Nations Mission for the Referendum in Western Sahara (MINURSO) in implementing the proposals contained in the report,

1. *Decides* to extend the mandate of MINURSO until 17 December 1998;

2. *Welcomes* paragraph 4 of the report of the Secretary-General, regarding the protocol relating to the identification of those presenting themselves individually from tribes H41, H61 and J51/52, the protocol relating to the appeals process, the memorandum pertaining to the activities of the Office of the United Nations High Commissioner for Refugees (UNHCR) in the region, and an outline of the next stages of the Settlement Plan, and calls on the parties to agree to this package of measures by mid-November 1998 in order to allow positive consideration of further stages in the settlement process;

3. *Notes* the intention of the UNHCR to forward to the parties soon a protocol relating to the repatriation of refugees, and supports efforts in this regard;

4. *Welcomes* also the agreement of the Moroccan authorities to formalize the presence of the UNHCR in the Western Sahara, and the agreement of the POLISARIO Front to resume pre-registration activities in the refugee camps, and requests both parties to take concrete action to enable the UNHCR to carry out the necessary preparatory work for the repatriation of Saharan refugees eligible to vote, and their immediate families, according to the Settlement Plan;

5. *Notes* with regret the constraints on the operational capability of the MINURSO engineering support unit, calls for a prompt conclusion of status-of-

forces agreements with the Secretary-General which is an indispensable prerequisite for the full and timely deployment of MINURSO-formed military units and recalls that pending the conclusion of such agreements, the model status-of-forces agreement dated 9 October 1990 (A/45/594), as provided for in General Assembly resolution 52/12 B, should apply provisionally;

6. *Supports* the intention of MINURSO to start publishing the provisional list of voters by 1 December 1998, as proposed by the Secretary-General, and supports also the proposed increase in staff of the Identification Commission from 18 to 25 members, and the increase also in the necessary support personnel, in order to strengthen the Commission and enable it to continue working with utmost rigour and impartiality with a view to keeping to the proposed timetable;

7. *Requests* the Secretary-General to report to the Council by 11 December 1998 on the implementation of this resolution and on the progress of the implementation of the Settlement Plan and the agreements reached between the parties, and to keep the Council regularly informed of all significant developments and, as appropriate, on the continuing viability of the mandate of MINURSO;

8. *Decides* to remain seized of the matter.

S/RES/1215 (1998)

17 December 1998

RESOLUTION 1215
Adopted by the Security Council at its 3956th meeting, on 17 December 1998

The Security Council,

Recalling all its previous resolutions on the question of the Western Sahara, and *reaffirming* in particular resolution 1204 (1998) of 30 October 1998,

Welcoming the report of the Secretary-General of 11 December 1998 (S/1998/1160) and the observations and recommendations contained therein,

Noting the stated position of the Government of Morocco, and welcoming the formal acceptance by the POLISARIO Front to implement the package of measures contained in paragraph 2 of the report of the Secretary-General, in order to move forward with the implementation of the Settlement Plan,

1. *Decides* to extend the mandate of the United Nations Mission for the Referendum in Western Sahara (MINURSO) until 31 January 1999 to allow for further consultations in hope that those consultation will lead to agreement on the various protocols without undermining the integrity of the Secretary-General's proposed package or calling into question its main elements;

2. *Notes*, in this regard, that the implementation of the Secretary-General's proposal to launch simultaneously the identification and appeals process could clearly demonstrate the willingness of the parties to accelerate the referendum process, in accordance with the wishes they have publicly expressed in recent months;

3.*Calls upon* the parties and the interested States to sign as soon as possible the proposed refugee repatriation protocol with the Office of the High Commissioner for Refugees (UNHCR), *urges* the Government of Morocco to formalize the presence of the UNHCR in the Territory, and *requests* both parties to take concrete action to enable the UNHCR to carry out the necessary preparatory work for the repatriation of Saharan refugees eligible to vote, and their immediate families, according to the Settlement Plan;

4. *Urges* the Government of Morocco promptly to sign the status-of-forces agreement with the Secretary-General as an indispensable condition for the full and timely deployment of MINURSO-formed military units and *recalls* that pending the conclusion of such agreement, the model status-of-forces agreement dated 9 October 1990 (A/45/594), as provided for in General Assembly resolution 52/12 B, should apply provisionally;

5. Notes that the contracts of the majority of the Identification Commission staff will expire by the end of December 1998, and that future extensions will depend on the prospects for resuming the identification work in the immediate future and on the decisions of the Security Council will take concerning the mandate of MINURSO;

6. Requests the Secretary-General to report to the Security Council by 22 January 1999 on the implementation of this resolution and on the progress in the implementation of the Implementation Plan and the agreements reached by the parties, and *further requests* him to keep the Council regularly informed of all significant developments including, as appropriate, a reassessment by the Personal Envoy of the Secretary-General of the continuing viability of the mandate of MINURSO;

7. Decides to remain seized of the matter.

S/RES/1224 (1999)

19990128

28 January 1999

RESOLUTION 1224 (1999)
Adopted by the Security Council at its 3971st meeting, on 28 January 1999

The Security Council,

Recalling all its previous resolutions on the question of the Western Sahara,
1. *Decides* to extend the mandate of the United Nations Mission for the Referendum in Western Sahara (MINURSO) until 11 February 1999;
2. *Requests* the Secretary-General to keep the Council informed of all significant developments in the implementation of the Settlement Plan and the agreements reached between the parties, and, as appropriate, on the continuing viability of the mandate of MINURSO;
3. *Decides* to remain seized of the matter.

S/RES/1228 (1999)

19990211

11 February 1999

RESOLUTION 1228 (1999)
Adopted by the Security Council at its 3976th meeting, on 11 February 1999

The Security Council,

Recalling all its previous resolutions on the question of the Western Sahara, and reaffirming in particular resolution 1204 (1998) of 30 October 1998 and resolution 1215 (1998) of 17 December 1998,
Welcoming the report of the Secretary-General of 28 January 1999 (S/1999/88) and the observations and recommendations contained therein,
1. *Decides* to extend the mandate of the United Nations Mission for the Referendum in Western Sahara (MINURSO) until 31 March 1999 to allow for consultations in the hope and expectation of agreement on the protocols on identification, appeals and repatriation planning activities, as well as on the essential issue of

the implementation calendar, without undermining the integrity of the Secretary-General's proposed package or calling into question its main elements, for the prompt resumption of voter identification and initiation of the appeals process;

2. *Requests* both parties to take concrete action to enable the Office of the United Nations High Commissioner for Refugees to carry out the necessary preparatory work for the repatriation of Saharan refugees eligible to vote, and their immediate families, according to the Settlement Plan;

3. *Requests* the Secretary-General to report to the Council by 22 March 1999 on the implementation of this resolution;

4. *Supports* the intention of the Secretary-General to ask his Personal Envoy to reassess the viability of the mandate of MINURSO should the prospects for putting the package of measures into effect remain elusive at the time of submission of the Secretary-General's next report;

5. *Decides* to remain seized of the matter.

S/RES/1232 (1999)

19990330

30 March 1999

RESOLUTION 1232 (1999)
Adopted by the Security Council at its 3990th meeting, on 30 March 1999

The Security Council,

Recalling all its previous resolutions on the question of the Western Sahara,

Welcoming the report of the Secretary-General of 22 March 1999 (S/1999/307) and the observations and recommendations contained therein,

Welcoming also the agreement in principle to the Secretary-General's package by the Government of Morocco and recalling its acceptance by the POLISARIO Front,

1. *Decides* to extend the mandate of the United Nations Mission for the Referendum in Western Sahara (MINURSO) until 30 April 1999 to allow for an understanding to be reached among all concerned on detailed modalities for the implementation of the identification and appeals protocols, including a revised implementation schedule, in a manner that would preserve the integrity of the Secretary-General's package of measures;

2. *Requests* both parties to move ahead with the necessary discussions to reach an agreement on the refugee repatriation protocol, so that all aspects of the work

needed to prepare the way for the repatriation of refugees may begin, including confidence-building measures, and in that regard welcomes the decision of the POLISARIO Front to allow the resumption of pre-registration activities of the Office of the United Nations High Commissioner for Refugees in Tindouf;

3. *Welcomes* the signature, by the Government of Morocco and the MINURSO Force Commander, of the agreement on mines and unexploded ordnance mentioned in paragraph 13 of the report of the Secretary-General, and urges the POLISARIO Front to engage in a similar effort;

4. *Requests* the Secretary-General to report to the Council by 23 April 1999 on the implementation of this resolution;

5. *Decides* to remain seized of the matter.

S/RES/1235 (1999)

30 April 1999

RESOLUTION 1235 (1999)
Adopted by the Security Council at its 3994th meeting, on 30 April 1999

The Security Council,

Recalling all its previous resolutions on the question of the Western Sahara,

Taking note of the report of the Secretary-General of 27 April 1999 (S/1999/483) and the observations and recommendations contained therein,

1. *Decides* to extend the mandate of the United Nations Mission for the Referendum in Western Sahara (MINURSO) until 14 May 1999;

2. *Requests* the Secretary-General to keep the Council informed of all significant developments in the implementation of the Settlement Plan and the agreements reached with the parties, and, as appropriate, on the continuing viability of the mandate of MINURSO;

3. *Decides* to remain seized of the matter.

S/RES/1235 (1999)

30 April 1999

RESOLUTION 1235 (1999)
Adopted by the Security Council at its 3994th meeting, on 30 April 1999

The Security Council,

Recalling all its previous resolutions on the question of the Western Sahara,

Taking note of the report of the Secretary-General of 27 April 1999 (S/1999/483) and the observations and recommendations contained therein,

1. *Decides* to extend the mandate of the United Nations Mission for the Referendum in Western Sahara (MINURSO) until 14 May 1999;

2. *Requests* the Secretary-General to keep the Council informed of all significant developments in the implementation of the Settlement Plan and the agreements reached with the parties, and, as appropriate, on the continuing viability of the mandate of MINURSO;

3. *Decides* to remain seized of the matter.

S/RES/1238 (1999)

14 May 1999

RESOLUTION 1238 (1999)
Adopted by the Security Council at its 4002nd meeting, on 14 May 1999

The Security Council,

Recalling all its previous resolutions on the question of Western Sahara,

Welcoming the report of the Secretary-General of 27 April 1999 (S/1999/483 and Add.1) and the observations and recommendations contained therein,

Welcoming also the acceptance by the Government of Morocco and the POLISARIO Front of the detailed modalities for the implementation of the Secretary-General's package of measures relating to the identification of voters, the appeals process and the revised implementation timetable as a good foundation for the completion of this phase of the Settlement Plan and taking note of their respective letters (S/1999/554 and S/1999/555),

1. *Decides* to extend the mandate of the United Nations Mission for the Referendum in Western Sahara (MINURSO) until 14 September 1999 in order to

resume the identification process, start the appeals process and conclude all outstanding agreements needed to implement the Settlement Plan, and reaffirms the rights of the applicants, with an expectation that the appeals process will not be turned into a second round of identification;

2. *Supports* the proposed increase in staff of the Identification Commission from 25 to 30 members, and the proposed increase also in the necessary support activities, in order to strengthen the Commission and enable it to continue working with full authority and independence, in accordance with its mandate as authorized by the Security Council, and to accomplish its tasks expeditiously;

3. *Requests* the Secretary-General to report every 45 days on significant developments in the implementation of the Settlement Plan, in particular on the following issues which will form, inter alia, the basis of its consideration of a further extension of the mandate of MINURSO; full and unequivocal cooperation of the parties during the resumption of voter identification and during the start of the appeals process; agreement by the Government of Morocco on the modalities of implementing paragraph 42 of the Status of Forces Agreement; agreement of the parties on the protocol relating to refugees; and confirmation that the Office of the United Nations High Commissioner for Refugees (UNHCR) is fully operational in the region;

4. *Requests* also the UNHCR to provide the Security Council with recommendations for confidence-building measures and timelines for their implementation;

5. *Requests* further the Secretary-General to submit to the Council a revised timetable and financial implications for the holding of the referendum for the self-determination of the people of the Western Sahara in accordance with the Settlement Plan and the agreements with the parties for its implementation;

6. *Decides* to remain seized of the matter.

RES/1263 (1999)

13 September 1999

RESOLUTION 1263 (1999)
Adopted by the Security Council at its 4044th meeting, on 13 September 1999

The Security Council,

Recalling all its previous resolutions on the Western Sahara,
Welcoming the report of the Secretary-General of 8 September 1999 (S/1999/954) and the observations and recommendations contained therein,

Welcoming also the resumption of the identification of voters and the commencement of the appeals process,

1. *Decides* to extend the mandate of the United Nations Mission for the Referendum in the Western Sahara (MINURSO) until 14 December 1999 in order to complete the identification of voters as envisaged in paragraph 21 of the report of the Secretary-General, to implement confidence-building measures and conclude all outstanding agreements needed to implement the Settlement Plan, and to continue with the appeals process, and reaffirms the rights of the applicants, with an expectation that the appeals process will not be turned into a second round of identification;

2. Requests the Secretary-General to report every 45 days on significant developments in the implementation of the Plan.

3. *Requests* also the Secretary-General to submit to the Security Council before the end of the current mandate a comprehensive assessment of steps taken towards the completion of the appeals process, and of staffing requirements as outlined in the report, as well as preparations for the repatriation of refugees and the start of the transitional period;

4. Decides to remain seized with the matter.

BASIC DOCUMENTS

DOCUMENTS

OAU: DECLARATIONS AND DECISIONS ADOPTED BY THE THIRTY-FIFTH ASSEMBLY OF HEADS OF STATE AND GOVERNMENT
(Algiers, July 1999)

TABLE OF CONTENTS

AHG/Decl. 1 (XXXV)	Algiers Declaration
AHG/Decl. 2 (XXXV)	Declaration of the Year 2000 As the Year of Peace, Security and Solidarity in Africa
AHG/Dec. 132 (XXXV)	Decision on the Report of the Secretary-General on the Ministerial Conference on the OAU Convention on the Prevention and Combating of Terrorism
AHG/Dec. 133 (XXXV)	Decision on the African Commission on Human and Peoples' Rights: Twelfth Annual Activity Report
AHG/Dec. 134 (XXXV)	Decision on the Crisis Between the Libyan Arab Jamahiriya and the United States and the United Kingdom
AHG/Dec. 135 (XXXV)	Decision on the 'First Meeting of States Parties to the Convention on the Prohibition of the Use, Stockpiling Production and Transfer of their Anti-Personnel Mines and on their Destruction'
AHG/Dec. 136 (XXXV)	Decision on the Report of the Secretary-General on the Conference of African Ministers of Education (COMEDAF I) and the Implementation of the Programme of Action of the Decade of Education in Africa
AHG/Dec. 137 (XXXV)	Decision on the Illicit Proliferation, Circulation and Trafficking of Small Arms and Light Weapons
AHG/Dec. 138 (XXXV)	Decision on the United Nations Regional Centre for Peace and Disarmament in Africa
AHG/Dec. 139 (XXXV)	Decision on the ILO Convention on the Banning of the Worst Forms of Child Labour and Immediate Action for their Elimination

AHG/Dec. 140 (XXXV)	Decision on the Convening of an Extraordinary Session of the OAU Assembly of Heads of State and Government in Accordance with Article 33 (5) of its Rules of Procedure
AHG/Dec. 141 (XXXV)	Decision
AHG/Dec. 142 (XXXV)	Decision
AHG/OAU/AEC/Dec. 1 (III)	Decision

ALGIERS DECLARATION

AHG/DECL. 1 (XXXV)

We, the Heads of State and Government of the Member States of the Organisation of African Unity, meeting in Algiers, Algeria, from 12 to 14 July 1999, solemnly declare as follows:

The end of the Second Millennium represents for Africa, the demise of an era characterised by colonisation and its tragic trail of domination, plunder and negation of the African personality. We welcome this development and affirm our resolve to strive towards ensuring that Africa and Mankind as a whole are never again subjected to such an experience so demeaning to the human dignity.

Through huge sacrifices and heroic struggles, Africa has broken the colonial yoke, regained its freedom and embarked upon the task of nation-building. This achievement constitutes for us a source of profound and legitimate pride, as these struggles have not only crystallised the determination of our peoples, who made the greatest sacrifices to assert their existence and their legitimate rights, but also have contributed significantly in inculcating in the peoples and nations of the continent the universal principles of the right of peoples to be the architect of their own destiny, the right to self-determination and independence, as well as the principle of the sovereign equality of states and their right to development.

It is therefore with the most profound respect that we bow to the memory of all the martyrs of Africa whose supreme sacrifice has paved the way for the continent to regain its freedom and dignity. We pay tribute to the sons and daughters of our continent who laid down their lives for its political and economic emancipation, and for the restoration of its identity and civilisation, under conditions of extreme adversity.

This is evidenced by the legacy of conflict situations which like many time bombs, exist here and there on the continent, coupled with problems arising from an economic infrastructure geared exclusively to satisfying the needs of the colonial metropolis, problems emanating from a political/administrative organisation rooted in authoritarianism and ethnic divisions, widespread illiteracy and extreme marginalization of the African peoples – so many problems whose magnitude has been exacerbated by the climate of the cold war and the negative impact of a basically unfair international economic system.

All these problems constitute an unwieldy heritage whose cumulative effects have been, and continue to be, for the most part, the root cause of the numerous conflicts, crises, poverty and under-development weighing heavily on the overwhelming majority of the peoples of Africa.

We do not intend, by the aforesaid, to shirk our own responsibility for the problems and difficulties still bedevilling our countries and the continent in general; rather, we wish to underscore the immensity of the efforts exerted by our respective countries, individually and collectively, to overcome the problems inherited from colonisation, ensure peace and stability on the continent, consolidate the hard-won national sovereignty, establish stable state institutions and promote an equitable and fair economic and social development in our countries.

Inspired by its intrinsic ancestral values, Africa was able to muster the strength and determination to assert its existence and take up all these challenges. Equally inspired by this same spirit and these same values, we commit ourselves to face up to the new and formidable challenges which today confront our continent.

We are deeply convinced that the Organisation of African Unity has played an irreplaceable role in the affirmation of political identity and the realisation of the unity of our continent. We hail the pioneering work of our Founding Fathers, and commit ourselves to further this accomplishment, and to continue to make the OAU the vital instrument of our collective action both within Africa and in our relations with the rest of the world.

Convinced that respect for the principle of inviolability of the borders inherited at independence contributed decisively to the preservation of peace and stability on our continent, we reaffirm its validity and permanence as a fundamental norm applicable in the settlement of border disputes.

We hail Africa's concerted action in ensuring that the process of decolonization of the continent is brought to a successful conclusion. In this regard, we reiterate our support for the speedy implementation of the UN-led Peace Plan in the Western Sahara in cooperation with the OAU.

We also reaffirm our determination to promote the use of peaceful means in the resolution of conflicts, in conformity with the principles of sovereign equality, non-interference, non-recourse to threats or the use of force, and of the independence, sovereignty and territorial integrity of States.

In this respect, we believe that the OAU Mechanism for Conflict Prevention, Management and Resolution is a valuable asset for our continent which must be nurtured and consolidated. This Mechanism, which symbolises the concrete resolve of our continent to fully assume its responsibilities, does not exonerate the United Nations Organisation from its obligations under the UN Charter as far as the maintenance of international peace and security is concerned.

We believe that youth and women's commitment and participation can contribute towards creating an enabling environment which conduces towards a culture of peace and tolerance.

To that end, we reiterate our commitment to the Global Plan of Action on Youth and the African Platform for Action, which is an integral part of the Global Platform for Action for the Advancement of Women as an appropriate framework for creating a more egalitarian society.

We also reaffirm our determination to work relentlessly towards the promotion of the Rights and Welfare of the Child, and our commitment to combat all forms of child exploitation, and, in particular, put an end to the phenomenon of child soldier.

We believe that human rights have undergone major positive changes since the independence of African countries. The liberation movements of our peoples, the efforts of our countries and of the OAU to codify and implement these rights, as well as the current dynamic process of establishing new democratic spaces in Africa have contributed to a very large extent to these changes. The African Charter on Human and Peoples' Rights and the Protocol on African Court on Human and Peoples' Rights as well as the Declaration and the Plan of Action, recently adopted in Mauritius, eloquently testify to Africa's contribution to the promotion and protection of the noble cause of Human Rights. We, however, recognise that much remains to be done to bring these developments to the level of our own expectations and the legitimate aspirations of our peoples. We are aware of these limitations and are determined not to relent in our efforts to transcend them.

In this spirit, we reiterate our commitment to the protection and promotion of human rights and fundamental freedoms. We emphasise the indivisibility, universality and inter-dependence of all human rights, be they political and civil or economic, social and cultural, or even individual or collective. We call upon the international community to ensure that they are not used for political purposes.

We are convinced that the increase in, and expansion of the spaces of freedom and the establishment of democratic institutions that are representative of our peoples and receiving their active participation, would further contribute to the consolidation of modern African States underpinned by the rule of law, respect for the fundamental rights and freedoms of the citizens and the democratic management of public affairs.

Despite the hopes generated by the end of the cold war and the attendant prospects of peace, development and integration in the world economy, we note that the post-cold war era is fraught with new and grave uncertainties, serious risks of marginalization and new challenges that pose numerous threats to our continent.

On the occasion of the Algiers summit, the last Summit of this Millennium, we would like to highlight the most important of these new challenges.

First, globalisation is undoubtedly the most widespread of these challenges. Ushered in with promises of progress and prosperity for all, it has today aroused fears, in that it poses serious threats to our sovereignty, cultural and historical identities as well as gravely undermining our development prospects. We believe that globalisation should be placed within the framework of a democratically conceived dynamics, and implemented collectively to make it an institution capable of fulfiling the hope for a concerted development of mankind and prosperity shared by all peoples.

Secondly, we note with grave concern, the growing marginlisation of the United Nations and its role under the Charter for the maintenance of international peace and security and the promotion of international cooperation for development. We declare that the unilateral use of force in international relations, outside the duly conferred mandate of the United Nations Security Council, opens the way to practices inimical to world peace and security.

We reaffirm our commitment to respect for the major role and responsibilities of the United Nations and its Security Council in the maintenance of international peace and security. In this connection, we, once again, call for a genuine democratisation of international relations based on the active participation and a balanced consideration of the legitimate concerns of all nations. We call, in particular, for the democratisation of the United Nations and its Security Council, and the recognition of Africa's legitimate place within this organ.

The need for democratisation equally applies to other international institutions including, particularly, the International Monetary Fund and the International Bank for Reconstruction and Development.

Thirdly, we believe that the nuclear disarmament issue and the elimination of other weapons of mass destruction remain a challenge and a crucial urgent problem facing the international community, and to which a definitive and lasting solution can be found only through general and comprehensive disarmament, under strict and effective international control. Africa has always demonstrated its readiness to bring its contribution to bear on this process, as evidenced by the conclusion and implementation of the Pelindaba Treaty. This important step taken by Africa should be complemented by the establishment of a zone free of nuclear weapons in the Middle East taking into account the inter-dependence between the security in both regions.

We believe that illegal movement, proliferation and trafficking of light weapons constitute another threat to the peace and security of the continent, and we commit ourselves to combat this scourge and lend our support to the regional and international mechanisms charged with preventing and combating this phenomenon.

Fourthly, we underscore the fact that new forms of threat to the stability of societies and the life of individuals such as terrorism, drug trafficking and organised crime also dangerously affect Africa and we call for a collective effort to address them. To this end, we call for the creation of appropriate mechanisms for the eradication of the phenomena of corruption, as well as arms and drug trafficking.

Indeed, terrorism which is a transnational phenomenon, represents today a serious challenge to the values of civilisation and a flagrant violation of human rights and fundamental freedoms. It also poses serious threats to the stability and security of states and their national institutions as well as to international peace and security. While reiterating our profound attachment to the struggle waged by peoples for freedom and self-determination, in conformity with the principles of international law, we call for an effective and efficient international cooperation which should be given concrete expression, under the auspices of OAU, through a speedy conclusion of a Global International Convention for the Prevention and Control of Terrorism in all its forms and the convening of an International Summit Conference under the auspices of the UN to consider this phenomenon and the means to combat it. Africa wants to make its full contribution by adopting its own Convention on this matter.

Fifthly, we note that the current trends in the World Economy do not augur well for Africa or for the great majority of developing countries.

Thus, despite the tremendous efforts invested by our countries to reorganise and restructure their economies at a very high social cost, our economies are increasingly facing a serious deterioration of the terms of trade, a decline in international development co-operation, a continuous fall in official development aid, an exacerbation of the external debt problem and the resurgence of protectionism on the part of the developed countries.

We, for our part, strongly believe that the promotion of economic co-operation and integration for the establishment of the African Economic Community as provided for under the Abuja Treaty will help consolidate the efforts being deployed by our countries to revive and develop their economies and to address the major problems facing Africa, notably problems of refugees and poverty, illiteracy and pandemics including the scourge of AIDS, as well as environmental problems, namely water and desertification related issues and threats to bio-diversity.

At the dawn of the Third Millennium, we the Heads of State and Government of Member States of the Organisation of African Unity solemnly affirm our determination to fully assume our responsibilities to take up all these challenges. We recognise, however, that the solutions to these challenges depend, to a large extent, on the collective will and the pooling of efforts and resources of the entire International community.

In this connection, we call for a mutually beneficial and genuine international partnership; a partnership based on a balance of interests and mutual respect; a partnership, the most crucial and immediate ingredients of which are the genuine democratisation of international relations, the renewal of multilateralism and consolidation of its instruments, the reorganisation of international cooperation based on sustained inter-dependence and the decline in national egoism, and lastly the establishment of a security system designed and functioning with the participation and involvement of all nations.

While expressing satisfaction at the various co-operation initiatives and approaches in favour of Africa, we reaffirm our readiness and willingness to promote, with all our partners, a genuine partnership devoid of any selfish calculations for influence; a partnership that respects the unity of the continent and aims at the development of Africa, rather than using it as a mere reservoir of raw materials and market for manufactured goods; a partnership that enables Africa to achieve its integration, ensure its development for the benefit of its peoples and occupy its rightful place on the international scene for the mutual and inclusive benefit of the International Community as a whole.

Together, let us enter the Third Millennium with a genuine spirit of co-operation, with restored human dignity and a common hope in an interdependent future for mankind. In this process, Africa, which is prepared to be the master of its destiny, will shoulder its share of responsibility.

DECLARATION OF THE YEAR 2000 AS THE YEAR OF PEACE, SECURITY AND SOLIDARITY IN AFRICA

AHG/DECL 2 (XXXV)

The Assembly:

1. *Recalling* the Final Communiqué of the 27th OAU Assembly of Heads of State and Government of the OAU which, *inter alia*, acknowledge the link between security, development and cooperation in Africa;
2. *Further Recalling* the Kampala Document which proposed the convening of a Conference on Security, Stability, Development and Co-operation in Africa (-CSSDCA);
3. *Gravely concerned* about the proliferation of armed conflicts and crises and their devastating impact on the stability, as well as on the economic and social development of Member States;
4. *Recalling also* the establishment in 1993 in Cairo, of the OAU Mechanism for the Prevention, Management and Resolution of Conflict Situations on the Continent;
5. *Noting* the efforts being deployed by the various sub-regional organizations and leaders to successfully and peacefully resolve existing conflicts;
6. *Determined* to develop a new consensus and a shared vision of the future;
7. *Declares* the year 2000 as the Year of Peace, Security and Solidarity in Africa and **INVITES** the Current OAU Chairman, all African Leaders and countries to rededicate themselves to effectively eliminate armed conflicts in Africa by the end of that year.

DECISIONS OF THE ASSEMBLY OF HEADS OF STATE AND GOVERNMENT

DECISION ON THE REPORT OF THE SECRETARY-GENERAL ON THE MINISTERIAL CONFERENCE ON THE OAU CONVENTION ON THE PREVENTION AND COMBATING OF TERRORISM

AHG/DEC.132 (XXXV)

The Assembly:

1. TAKES NOTE of the Decision of Council on the Draft OAU Convention on the Prevention and Combating of Terrorism;
2. ADOPTS the OAU Convention on the Prevention and Combating of Terrorism;
3. URGES Member States to sign, and subsequently ratify the Convention in order to ensure its speedy implementation;
4. ENDORSES the convening of an International Conference at Summit level under the auspices of the United Nations to elaborate on the international strategy needed to combat terrorism and identify the necessary international instruments required by the international community to eliminate the phenomenon of terrorism;
5. EXPRESSES SATISFACTION at the considerable progress so quickly made by the Government and People of Algeria in the restoration of peace and stability and HAILS the courageous initiative of H.E. President Abdelaziz BOUTEFLIKA to give concrete expression to these objectives and usher in permanent civil peace and harmony in Algeria.

DECISION ON THE AFRICAN COMMISSION ON HUMAN AND PEOPLES' RIGHTS: TWELFTH ANNUAL ACTIVITY REPORT

AHG/DEC.133 (XXXV)

The Assembly,

1. TAKES NOTE of the 12th Annual Activity Report of the African Commission on Human and Peoples' Rights and commends the latter for the work accomplished during the past financial year;
2. REQUESTS the competent organs to continue to reflect over the possible ways and means of strengthening the operational capacity of the African Commission in order to enable it to effectively carry out its mandate;

3. URGES the States Parties to the African Charter on Human and Peoples' Rights to fulfil their obligations under this important instrument and to lend all the necessary assistance to the African Commission for the effective accomplishment of its mission;
4. AUTHORISES the publication of the 12th Annual Activity Report in accordance with Article 59 of the African Charter on Human and Peoples' Rights.

DECISION ON THE CRISIS BETWEEN THE LIBYAN ARAB JAMAHIRIYA AND THE UNITED STATES AND THE UNITED KINGDOM

AHG/DEC. 134 (XXXV)

The Assembly:

1. TAKES NOTE of the Report of the Secretary-General;
2. EXPRESSES ITS SATISFACTION over the courageous decision of the authorities of the Libyan Arab Jamahiriya to encourage the two Libyan suspects to stand trial before the Scottish Court sitting in the Netherlands and over its positive response, and SUPPORTS the Jamahiriya's demand for adequate guarantees and conditions to ensure a just and fair trial for the two suspects;
3. PAYS SPECIAL TRIBUTE to former President of South Africa, Nelson Mandela, the custodian of the two holy Mosques, King Fahad IBN Abdelaziz, President Blaise Compaore, Out-going Chairman of the OAU and all the African leaders who have worked towards the implementation of the letter and spirit of the decision of the OAU Ouagadougou summit on the crisis;
4. FURTHER EXPRESSES ITS SATISFACTION at the efforts of the OAU Committee of Five and the Committee of Seven of the League of Arab States for their contributions in the search for a just solution to the crisis;
5. COMMENDS the African Group in New York for its role in resolving the crisis, and particularly for drawing the attention of the UN Secretary-General to the fact that the Libyan Arab Jamahiriya had co-operated and fulfiled the requirements of UN Security Council Resolutions 731 (1992) 748 (1992), 883 (1993), 1192(1998);
6. CALLS UPON the United Nations Security Council to immediately and permanently lift the sanctions against the Libyan Arab Jamahiriya;
7. REQUESTS the OAU Current Chairman to address letters to the UN Secretary-General and the Chairman of the UN Security Council to take appropriate measures to ensure the speedy and permanent lifting of sanctions;

8. REQUESTS the Committee of Five on the Dispute between the Libyan Arab Jamahiriya, the United States of America and the United Kingdom to continue its work until the definitive resolution of the dispute;
9. DECIDES to remain seized of this matter and to act as appropriate.
10. REQUESTS the Secretary-General to follow-up the implementation of this decision.

DECISION ON THE "FIRST MEETING OF STATES PARTIES TO THE CONVENTION ON THE PROHIBITION OF THE USE, STOCKPILING, PRODUCTION AND TRANSFER OF THEIR ANTI-PERSONNEL MINES AND ON THEIR DESTRUCTION"

AHG/DEC. 135 (LXX)

The Assembly:

1. TAKES NOTE of the relevant information contained in the Report of the Secretary-General on the "First Meeting of States Parties of the Convention on the Prohibition of the Use, Stockpiling, Production and Transfer of Anti-personnel Mines and on their destruction", held in Maputo, Mozambique, from 3-7 May, 1999;
2. RECOGNIZES that the issue of anti-personnel mines constitutes a major public health threat and a source of concern in the international political agenda, requiring a global approach in order to address the negative effects of these deadly devices;
3. COMMENDS the rapid entry-into-force of the Convention on the Prohibition of the Use, Stockpiling, Production and Transfer of Antipersonnel Mines and on their Destruction;
4. FURTHER RECOGNIZES that the proliferation of anti-personnel mines constitutes an issue of insecurity which affects free circulation of people and goods in affected countries;
5. EXPRESSES ITS DEEP CONCERN for the devastating effects of anti-personnel mines on human lives and their negative impact on the country's economic development;
6. COMMENDS all States Parties to the Convention;
7. CALLS UPON all countries which have not done so to sign and ratify the Convention:
8. EXPRESSES ITS APPRECIATION for the outcome of the Maputo meeting;
9. SUPPORTS FIRMLY the objectives and purposes enshrined in the "Maputo Declaration";

10. REQUESTS the Secretary-General to continue to sensitize Member States to contribute to the effective implementation of the Convention.

DECISION ON THE REPORT OF THE SECRETARY-GENERAL ON THE CONFERENCE OF AFRICAN MINISTERS OF EDUCATION (COMEDAF I) AND THE IMPLEMENTATION OF THE PROGRAMME OF ACTION OF THE DECADE OF EDUCATION IN AFRICA

AHG/DEC. 136 (XXXV)

The Assembly:

1. TAKES NOTE of the report;
2. ENDORSES the recommendations of the Conference of African Ministers of Education (COMEDAF I) meeting in Harare, Zimbabwe, from 15 to 19 March, 1999;
3. TAKES NOTE of the Programme of Action of the Decade of Education in Africa and of the Mechanism for its implementation, as well as the components thereof, as approved by the Conference of Ministers of Education;
4. TAKES NOTE of the Kampala Declaration and Framework of Action on the Empowerment of Women through Functional Literacy and the Education of the Girl Child;
5. URGES Member States to put in place all the necessary national structures as recommended in the report for the effective implementation of the Decade and the Harare Programme of Action;
6. ALSO URGES Member States to continue to give priority to education, more particularly basic education, as pillar of development and generator of human resources, in all their National Development Plans;
7. INVITES Member States as well as technical and financial partners to leave no stone unturned in monitoring, particularly at the national level, the synergy of all the on-going initiatives on the continent, with a view to coordinating and harmonizing the various programmes;
8. FURTHER URGES the Regional Economic Communities to take the necessary steps to implement the relevant provisions of the Programme of Action in consultation with the OAU General Secretariat, the countries and the competent regional organizations;
9. CALLS ON the OAU Secretary-General to:
   a) put in place the Decade Secretariat;
   b) set up the Decade Steering Committee;

c) release as early as possible the necessary resources for the launching of the Decade coordination activities;
d) convene every two years the Conference of African Ministers of Education;
e) convene in 2002, on the occasion of the mid-term review of the Decade, a Summit on Education;

10. APPEALS to African and International Agencies and Institutions, as well as NGOs and donor countries, to lend their technical and financial support to the implementation of the Decade Programme of Action both at national and continental levels;

DECISION ON THE ILLICIT PROLIFERATION, CIRCULATION AND TRAFFICKING OF SMALL ARMS AND LIGHT WEAPONS

AHG/DEC. 137 (LXX)

The Assembly:

1. TAKES NOTE of the Report;
2. ADOPTS the proposals contained therein;
3. HAILS the Declaration on the moratorium on the import, export and manufacture of light weapons adopted in Abuja on 31 October, 1998 by the Heads of State and Government of the Economic Community of West African States (ECOWAS);
4. WELCOMES the appeal contained in the said Declaration calling on the OAU to support implementation of the moratorium and to encourage similar initiatives in other regions of the continent
5. WELCOMES ALSO the initiatives being undertaken by Member States and regional organisations concerning the question of small arms, in particular, the ECOWAS moratorium on small arms, the destruction of surplus and obsolete small arms in South Africa and the destruction of illicit weapons in Mozambique;
6. FURTHER WELCOMES the work of the United Nations, through its Group of Experts on Small Arms and the draft Protocol on the Illicit Manufacturing, circulation and proliferation of as well as illicit trafficking in Firearms, Ammunitions and other related materials, supplementary to the Convention against International Organised Crime; the European Union, through its Joint Action on Small Arms; and the Organisation of American States, through its Convention against the illicit manufacturing, trafficking, circulation and proliferation of firearms, ammunitions, explosives and other related Materials;

7. APPEALS to the International Community to render to the affected African countries all necessary assistance to enable them implement programmes to effectively deal with the problems associated with the proliferation of small arms and light weapons:
8. REITERATES the urgency and the need for inter-African cooperation in addressing the problems associated with the illicit use, transfer and manufacture of small arms and light weapons, and EMPHASISES the primary role the OAU can play in co-ordinating actions in those affected areas;
9. URGES the Secretary-General to further seek the views of Member States on the illicit trafficking, circulation and proliferation of small arms and light weapons, in particular, to seek their views on actions to be undertaken;
10. CALLS for a coordinated African approach to the problems posed by the illicit trafficking, circulation and proliferation of small arms, under the OAU, taking into account the regional experiences and activities in this matter;
11. STRESSES the impact of the illicit proliferation, circulation and trafficking of light weapons on the increased involvement of children as soldiers and the psycho-social trauma thereof and the need to comply with the African Charter for the Rights and Welfare of Children and the Convention on the Rights of the Child;
12. FURTHER APPEALS to all Member States and to the International Community to assist in the psycho-social rehabilitation of children who have been affected by the trafficking, circulation and the proliferation of light weapons;
13. REQUESTS the OAU Secretariat to organize, to that effect, a ministerial preparatory conference on this matter, prior to the International Conference scheduled for the year 2001 and to seek the support of the relevant UN agencies and other actors concerned, so as to evolve an African common approach;
14. FURTHER REQUESTS the Secretary-General to report on this issue to the next Session of the Council of Ministers.

DECISION ON THE UNITED NATIONS REGIONAL CENTRE FOR PEACE AND DISARMAMENT IN AFRICA

AHG/DEC.138 (XXXV)

The Assembly:

1. TAKES NOTE of the progress made since its Thirty-fourth Ordinary Session in efforts to consolidate the activities of the United Nations Regional Centre for Peace and Disarmament in Africa;

2. EXPRESSES SATISFACTION at the appointment by the UN Secretary-General of a Director for the Centre;
3. REAFFIRMS ITS UNWAVERING SUPPORT for the revitalization of the Centre and underscores the need to provide it with the necessary resources to enable it to consolidate its activities and implement its programmes;
4. FURTHER REAFFIRMS the need to establish close collaboration between the Centre and the OAU Mechanism for Conflict Prevention, Management and Resolution on the one hand, and, on the other, between the Centre and the sub-regional organizations working for peace, security and development;
5. ONCE AGAIN INVITES the General Secretariat to establish close cooperation with the Centre;
6. URGES Member States and the International Community to support the Centre by making financial contributions to it and assisting it in any other way likely to help in the promotion of its activities and effectiveness;
7. REQUESTS the Secretary-General to report to its 36th Ordinary Session.

DECISION ON THE ILO CONVENTION ON THE BANNING OF THE WORST FORMS OF CHILD LABOUR AND IMMEDIATE ACTION FOR THEIR ELIMINATION

AHG/DEC. 139 (XXXV)

The Assembly:

1. RECALLS the African Charter on the Rights and Welfare of the Child adopted in Addis Ababa, Ethiopia in 1990, by the Twenty-sixth Ordinary Session of the Assembly of Heads of State and Government;
2. FURTHER RECALLS the unanimous adoption in Geneva, Switzerland on 17 June, 1999 of the ILO Convention on the Prohibition of the Worst Forms of Child Labour and Immediate Action for their Elimination, by the Eighty-seventh Ordinary Session of the International Labour Conference;
3. APPROVES the recommendations contained in the report of the Secretary-General to the Twenty-second Ordinary Session of the Labour and Social Affairs Commission (Windhoek, Namibia: 22-23 April, 1999) pertaining to the proposed ILO Convention (Doc.LSC/9 (XXII);
4. REQUESTS all Member States to ratify the Convention as a matter of urgency preferably before the Thirty-sixth Session of the Assembly of Heads of State and Government scheduled to take place in the year 2000;
5. FURTHER REQUESTS the International Labour Office (ILO) to provide Member States with necessary technical assistance to back their efforts towards ratification and implementation of this Convention.

DECISION ON THE CONVENING OF AN EXTRAORDINARY SESSION OF THE OAU ASSEMBLY OF HEADS OF STATE AND GOVERNMENT IN ACCORDANCE WITH ARTICLE 33 (5) OF ITS RULES OF PROCEDURE

AHG/DEC. 140 (XXXV)

The Assembly:

Having heard the intervention of H.E. Col. Muamar Gaddafi, Leader of the Great First of September Revolution of the Great Socialist People's Libyan Arab Jamahiriya during the discussion of the item on collective security and conflicts on the continent,

Having also heard his intervention on the convening of an Extraordinary Session of the OAU Assembly of Heads of State and Government in the Jamahiriya, from 6-9 September, 1999 to discuss ways and means of making the OAU effective so as to keep pace with political and economic developments taking place in the world and the preparation required of Africa within the context of globalization so as to preserve its social, economic and political potentials:

DECIDES to accept the offer of H.E. Col. Muamar Gaddafi to host an Extraordinary Session of the Assembly in the Great Socialist People's Libyan Arab Jamahiriya at the before-mentioned proposed date.

DECISION

AHG/DEC. 141 (XXXV)

The Assembly:

1. REAFFIRMS the provisions of the OAU Charter;
2. REAFFIRMS FURTHER the African Charter on Human and Peoples' Rights and in particular Article 13;
3. RECALLS the Universal Declaration on Democracy, adopted by the Inter-Parliamentary Council at its 161st Session in Cairo, on 16 September 1997;
4. RECALLS FURTHER the spirit of the Harare Decision on unconstitutional removal of Governments;
5. RECOGNISES that the principles of good governance, transparency and human rights are essential elements for building representative and stable government and contribute to conflict prevention.

DECISION

AHG/DEC. 142 (XXXV)

The Assembly:

Determined to promote strong and democratic institutions that will safeguard the principles mentioned in the decision above,

1. DECIDES that Member States whose Governments came to power through unconstitutional means after the Harare Summit, should restore constitutional legality before the next Summit;
2. REQUESTS the OAU Secretary-General to be actively seized of developments in those countries and to assist in programmes intended to return such countries to constitutional and democratic governments;
3. CALLS UPON the OAU Secretary-General to report to the Ordinary Sessions of the Council of Ministers and the Thirty-sixth Assembly of Heads of State and Government on the progress made in this regard.

DECISION

AHG/OAU/AEC/DEC. 1 (III)

The Assembly of Heads of State and Government,

Considering the Charter of the Organisation of African Unity,

Considering the Treaty Establishing the African Economic Community, especially Articles 7, 8, 9 and 10 thereof,

Considering further the Protocol on the Relations between the African Economic Communities and the Regional Economic Communities,

Having considered the report of the Council of Ministers and the recommendations of the Third Ordinary Session of the Economic and Social Commission (ECOSOC) held in Addis Ababa on 17 June 1999,

Expressing satisfaction at the positive developments regarding the revitalisation of ECCAS,

DECIDES:

1. REGULATIONS OF THE COUNCIL OF MINISTERS
   Regulations CM/AEC/Regl. 1 (IV), CM/OAU/AEC/Regl. 1(V) and CM/OAU/AEC/Regl.2 (V) of the Council of Ministers are hereby approved.

2. IMPLEMENTATION OF THE AEC TREATY
   a) Note is taken of the end of the first stage of implementation of the AEC as provided for under the Abuja Treaty and Member States should intensify their efforts towards strengthening the existing RECs to which they belong;
   b) Each REC is to submit to its policy organs an assessment of the progress made during the first stage, and inform ECOSOC of any additional requirements to be met for complying with the conditions needed to complete the first phase;
   c) The RECs should submit to the Fourth Session of ECOSOC their respective programmes for implementing the second phase and a progress report there on, as well as prospects and constraints;
   d) The RECs, within the framework of the Specialised Technical Committees, should establish benchmarks for each sector to enhance assessment of the progress of integration, and regularly provide the OAU/AEC Secretariat with their sectoral work programmes in order to facilitate programme co-ordination and harmonisation;
   e) The Chairman of each REC is to submit a report to the Assembly on the progress made in the implementation of the AEC Treaty;
   f) To reaffirm their commitment under the AEC Treaty, especially those regarding the implementation of the legally binding Decisions of the AEC Summit, all Member States are to set up the requisite national modalities and machinery to facilitate the incorporation of ABC decisions in their national legislation.
3. RATIFICATION OF THE TREATY
   All Member States concerned are to take appropriate measures to ratify or accede to the AEC Treaty;
4. BUDGET OF THE COMMUNITY
   The Committee on Co-ordination, under Article 6 of the Protocol on Relations between the AEC and the RECs, should give priority to the preparation of the AEC budget, and the Secretariat is to intensify its efforts at mobilising extra-budgetary resources;
5. OAU-EU SUMMIT
   Support is reiterated for the holding of the proposed Summit with the EU and while requesting the OAU Preparatory Committee to continue to overview the contacts with the EU, mandate is given to a Core Group of that Committee to undertake consultations with the relevant EU Group with a view to clearing all obstacles and determining the best ways and means for the convening of the Summit.

Done in Algiers, Algeria, on 14 July 1999.

OUA: DECLARATIONS ET DECISIONS ADOPTEES PAR LA 35EME SESSION ORDINAIRE DE LA CONFERENCE DES CHEFS D'ETAT ET DE GOUVERNEMENT (Alger, juillet 1999)

TABLE DES MATIERES

AHG/Decl. 1(XXXV):	Déclaration d'Alger
AHG/Decl. 2 (XXXV):	Déclaration de l'Année 2000 comme année de de la Paix, de la sécurité et de la solidarité en Afrique
AHG/Dec. 132 (XXXV):	Décision sur le Rapport du Secrétaire général relatif à la conférence ministérielle sur le projet de Convention de l'OUA sur la prévention et la lutte contre le terrorisme
AHG/Dec. 133 (XXXV):	Décision sur le Douzième Rapport Annuel d'activités de la Commission africaine des droits de l'Homme et des Peuples
AHG/Dec. 134 (XXXV):	Décision sur la crise entre la Jamahiriya arabe libyenne et les Etats-Unis et le Royaume-Uni
AHG/Dec. 135 (LXX):	Décision de l'OUA sur la «Première réunion des Etats parties à la Convention sur l'interdiction de l'emploi, du stockage, de la production et du transfert des mines antipersonnel et sur leur destruction»
AHG/Dec. 136 (XXXV):	Décision sur le rapport du Secrétaire général sur la Conférence des Ministres africains de l'éducation (COMEDAF I) la mise en oeuvre du Programme d'Action de la Décennie de l'éducation en Afrique
AHG/Dec. 137 (LXX):	Décision sur la prolifération, la circulation et le trafic illicites des armes légères
AHG/Dec. 138 (XXXV):	Décision relative au Centre régional des Nations Unies sur la Paix et le Désarmement en Afrique
AHG/Dec. 139 (XXXV):	Décision portant sur la Convention de l'Organisation internationale du travail (OIT) relative à l'interdiction des pires formes de travail des enfants et l'action immédiate en vue de leur élimination

AHG/Dec. 140 (XXXV) :   Décision sur la convocation d'une session extraordinaire de la Conférence des Chefs d'Etat et de Gouvernement de l'OUA conformément à l'article 33(5) du règlement intérieur de la Conférence
AHG/Dec. 141 (XXXV) :   Décision
AHG/Dec. 142 (XXXV):   Décision
AHG/OAU/AEC/Dec. 1 (III):   Décision

DECLARATION D'ALGER

AHG/DECL. 1 (XXXV)

Nous, Chefs d'Etat et de Gouvernement des pays membres de l'Organisation de l'Unité Africaine réunis à Alger du 12 au 14 juillet1999, déclarons solennellement:

Avec la fin du deuxième Millénaire, c'est, pour l'Afrique, une ère marquée par la colonisation et son cortège tragique de domination, de spoliation et de négation de la personnalité africaine qui prend fin. Nous nous en réjouissons et affirmons notre résolution à oeuvrer pour que l'Afrique et l'humanité entière ne connaissent plus jamais d'expérience aussi attentatoire à la dignité humaine.

Au prix d'immenses sacrifices et de luttes héroïques, l'Afrique a brisé le joug colonial et recouvré sa liberté pour s'engager dans l'entreprise de construction nationale. Nous en tirons une profonde et légitime fierté car ces luttes ont non seulement cristallisé la détermination de nos peuples, au prix des plus grands sacrifices, pour imposer leur existence et défendre leurs droits légitimes, mais également contribué, de façon significative, à faire prévaloir, entre les peuples et les Nations, les principes universels du droit des peuples à disposer d'eux mêmes, de leur droit à l'autodétermination et à l'indépendance ainsi que le principe de l'égalité souveraine des Etats et leur droit au développement.

C'est donc avec un profond respect que Nous nous inclinons devant la mémoire de tous les martyrs africains dont le sacrifice suprême a permis à l'Afrique de retrouver sa liberté et sa dignité et rendons hommage à tous les enfants de notre continent qui ont consacré leurs vies pour la libération politique et économique de la terre africaine et pour sa réhabilitation identitaire et civilisationnelle, dans des conditions d'extrême adversité.

C'est ainsi qu'aux problèmes liés à des situations conflictuelles léguées, ça et là, comme autant de bombes à retardement, s'ajoutaient ceux d'une infrastructure économique orientée exclusivement vers la satisfaction des besoins des métropoles coloniales, d'une organisation politico-administrative fondée sur l'autoritarisme et les divisions ethniques, d'un analphabétisme généralisé et d'une marginalisation extrême des populations africaines qui constituent autant de problèmes dont l'ampleur a été exacerbée par le climat de la guerre froide et les méfaits d'un système économique international foncièrement injuste.

C'est là un héritage lourd dont les effets cumulatifs ont été, et restent encore, pour une grande part, aux origines de multiples conflits, de nombreuses crises et de la pauvreté et du sous-développement dont souffre l'écrasante majorité des peuples en Afrique.

Il ne s'agit pas, par-là, d'occulter nos propres responsabilités dans les problèmes et les difficultés que vivent encore nos pays et le continent africain en général, mais de souligner l'immensité des efforts déployés par nos pays, individuellement et collectivement, en vue de surmonter les problèmes hérités de la colonisation, d'assurer la paix et la stabilité sur tout le Continent, de consolider les souverainetés nationales recouvrées et mettre en place des institutions étatiques stables et de promouvoir un développement économique et social équilibré et juste dans nos pays.

C'est dans ses valeurs ancestrales propres que l'Afrique a puisé la volonté et la force d'affirmer son existence et de relever tous ces défis. C'est animés de ce même esprit et de ces mêmes valeurs que Nous nous engageons à faire face aux nouveaux et redoutables défis qui se posent aujourd'hui à notre Continent.

C'est notre conviction profonde que l'Organisation de l'Unité Africaine a joué un rôle irremplaçable dans l'affirmation de l'identité politique et la réalisation de l'unité de notre Continent. En saluant l'oeuvre pionnière des pères fondateurs, Nous nous engageons à la consolider davantage et à continuer à faire de l'OUA l'instrument privilégié de notre action collective en Afrique et dans nos relations avec le reste du monde.

Convaincus que le respect du principe de l'intangibilité des frontières héritées aux indépendances a contribué de façon déterminante à la préservation de la paix et de la stabilité sur notre Continent, Nous réaffirmons sa validité et sa pérennité comme norme fondamentale applicable au traitement des différends frontaliers.

Nous tenons à saluer l'oeuvre solidaire de l'Afrique pour assurer l'achèvement du processus de décolonisation du Continent et réitérons, à cet égard, notre appui à une rapide mise en oeuvre du plan de paix conduit par l'ONU, en coopération avec l'OUA, au Sahara Occidental.

Nous réaffirmons aussi notre volonté de privilégier le recours aux moyens pacifiques pour le règlement des conflits dans le respect des principes de l'égalité souveraine, de la non-ingérence, du non recours à la menace ou à l'usage de la force et de l'indépendance, de la souveraineté et de l'intégrité territoriale des Etats.

Nous considérons, à ce titre, que le Mécanisme africain de prévention, de gestion et de règlement pacifique des conflits est un précieux acquis pour notre Continent qu'il s'agit de conforter et de consolider. Ce Mécanisme qui symbolise la volonté concrète de notre Continent à assumer pleinement ses responsabilités n'exonère pas l'Organisation des Nations Unies de ses obligations découlant de la Charte des Nations Unies, en matière de maintien de la paix et de la sécurité internationale.

Nous sommes convaincus que l'engagement et la participation des jeunes et des femmes peuvent contribuer à la création d'un environnement propice à la culture de la paix et de la tolérance.

A cette fin, nous réitérons notre engagement envers le Plan d'Action mondial sur les jeunes et la Plate-forme d'Action africaine qui est partie intégrante de la Plate-forme d'Action mondiale pour la promotion des femmes en tant que cadre approprié pour l'édification d'une société plus égalitaire.

Nous réitérons également notre détermination à oeuvrer sans relâche à la promotion des droits et du bien être des enfants, ainsi que notre engagement à lutter contre toutes les formes d'exploitation des enfants, en particulier la nécessité de mettre fin au phénomène des enfants soldats.

Nous estimons que la cause des droits de l'homme a connu de grandes mutations positives depuis l'avènement des indépendances en Afrique. Le mouvement de libération de nos peuples, l'effort de nos pays et de l'OUA tendant à codifier et à mettre en oeuvre ces droits ainsi que la dynamique actuelle de création de nouveaux espaces démocratiques en Afrique y ont apporté une énorme contribution. La Charte africaine des Droits de l'Homme et des Peuples, le Protocole sur la Cour africaine des Droits de l'Homme et des Peuples ainsi que la déclaration et le plan d'action, adoptées récemment à Maurice, illustrent de façon significative la contribution de l'Afrique à la promotion et à la protection de la noble cause des droits de l'homme. Nous reconnaissons cependant que beaucoup reste à faire pour que la situation dans ce domaine soit réellement à la hauteur de nos propres ambitions et des attentes légitimes de nos peuples. Nous sommes conscients de ces limites et déterminés à continuer à oeuvrer à leur dépassement.

Dans cet esprit, Nous réitérons notre attachement à la protection et à la promotion des droits de l'homme et des libertés fondamentales. Nous insistons sur l'indivisibilité, l'universalité et l'interdépendance de tous les droits de l'Homme qu'ils soient politiques et civils ou économiques, sociaux et culturels, ou encore individuels ou collectifs. Nous invitons la communauté internationale à les préserver de toute instrumentalisation à des fins politiques.

C'est notre conviction que la multiplication et l'extension d'espaces de libertés ainsi que la mise en place d'institutions démocratiques représentatives de nos populations et bénéficiant de leur participation active contribueront, chaque jour davantage, à consolider l'édification d'Etats africains modernes fondés sur la primauté du Droit, le respect des droits et libertés fondamentales du citoyen et la gestion démocratique des affaires publiques.

Nous constatons, en dépit de l'espoir né de la fin de la guerre froide et des perspectives de paix, de développement et d'intégration à l'économie mondiale qu'elle avait suscitées, que l'après guerre froide est porteur de nouvelles et graves incertitudes, de risques sérieux de marginalisation et de nouveaux défis qui sont autant de menaces pour notre Continent.

Au titre de ces nouveaux défis, Nous voulons, à l'occasion du Sommet d'Alger, le dernier du millénaire, en relever les plus essentiels.

En premier lieu, la mondialisation constitue indéniablement le défi le plus global. Annoncée avec des promesses de progrès et de prospérité pour tous, elle alimente aujourd'hui la crainte pour ce qu'elle véhicule de menaces sur nos souverainetés et nos spécificités culturelles et historiques et ce qu'elle suscite de graves hypothèques sur les perspectives de développement de nos pays. Nous appelons à son encadrement dans une dynamique conçue démocratiquement et mise en oeuvre collectivement pour en faire une entreprise à même de répondre aux espoirs de développement solidaire de l'humanité et de prospérité partagée entre les peuples.

En second lieu, Nous constatons aussi avec une profonde préoccupation la marginalisation croissante de l'ONU et du rôle qui lui revient, en vertu de la Charte, en matière de maintien de la paix et de la sécurité internationales et de promotion de la coopération internationale pour le développement. Nous proclamons que le recours unilatéral à l'usage de la force dans les relations internationales, en dehors de mandats dûment conférés par le Conseil de Sécurité des Nations Unies, ouvre la voie à des errements par le Conseil de Sécurité des Nations Unies, ouvre la voie à des errements dangereux pour la paix et la sécurité internationales.

Nous réaffirmons notre attachement au respect du rôle principal et des attributions de l'ONU et de son Conseil de Sécurité, dans le maintien de la paix et de la sécurité internationales. Nous appelons, une nouvelle fois, à une véritable démocratisation des relations internationales fondée sur la participation active et la prise en charge équilibrée des préoccupations légitimes de toutes les Nations. Nous appelons en particulier à la démocratisation de l'ONU et de son Conseil de Sécurité et à la reconnaissance à l'Afrique de la place légitime qui doit lui revenir au sein de cet organe.

Ce besoin de démocratisation s'applique aussi aux autres institutions internationales dont notamment le Fonds Monétaire International et la Banque Internationale pour la Reconstruction et le Développement.

En troisième lieu, Nous considérons que la question du désarmement nucléaire et l'élimination des autres armes de destruction massive demeurent un défi et une exigence vitale et urgente auxquels la Communauté internationale reste frontalement confrontée et auxquels elle n'apportera de solution définitive et durable que dans la concrétisation de l'objectif d'un désarmement général et complet, sous un contrôle international stricte et efficace. L'Afrique a toujours marqué sa disponibilité à apporter toute sa contribution à cette oeuvre comme l'atteste la conclusion et la mise en oeuvre du Traité de Pelindaba.. Cette importante initiative de l'Afrique doit être complétée par un instrument faisant également partie du Moyen Orient une zone exempte d'armes nucléaires compte tenu de l'interdépendance des problèmes de sécurité entre les deux zones.

Nous considérons que la circulation, la prolifération et le trafic illicites des armes légères constituent une autre menace à la paix et à la sécurité du continent et nous nous engageons à lutter contre ce fléau et à apporter notre soutien aux mécanismes régionaux et internationaux chargés de la prévention et de la lutte contre ce phénomène.

En quatrième lieu, Nous soulignons que les nouvelles formes de menace à la stabilité des sociétés et à la vie des individus telles que le terrorisme, le trafic de drogue et le crime organisé touchent également et dangereusement l'Afrique et commandent un effort collectif à leur résorption. A cet égard, nous appelons à la mise en place de mécanismes appropriés pour l'éradication des phénomènes de corruption, de trafic d'armes et de drogues.

Ainsi, le terrorisme, phénomène transnational, représente aujourd'hui un grave défi aux valeurs civilisationnelles et une violation flagrante des droits de l'homme et des libertés fondamentales, comme il véhicule de sérieuses menaces à la stabilité et à la sécurité des Etats et de leurs institutions nationales ainsi qu'à la paix et à la sécurité internationales. Tout en réitérant notre profond attachement à la lutte menée par les peuples, en conformité avec les principes du Droit international, pour la libération ou leur auto-détermination, nous appelons à une coopération internationale effective et efficace qui doit se traduire, sous l'égide de l'ONU, par la conclusion rapide d'une convention internationale globale de prévention et de lutte contre le terrorisme sous toutes ses formes et la tenue, sous les auspices des Nations Unies, d'une Conférence internationale au Sommet consacrée à l'examen de ce phénomène et des moyens de le combattre. En adoptant sa propre convention, l'Afrique entend apporter toute sa contribution à ce sujet.

En cinquième lieu, Nous constatons que l'orientation actuelle de l'économie mondiale n'ouvre de perspectives encourageantes ni pour l'Afrique ni pour le grand nombre de pays en développement.

Ainsi, malgré les efforts de Nos pays dans la voie difficile de l'assainissement et de la restructuration de nos économies, à un coût social extrêmement élevé, nos économies sont de plus en plus durement confrontées à une érosion des termes de l'échange, une régression de la coopération internationale pour le développement, un déclin continu de l'aide publique au développement, une aggravation du problème de l'endettement extérieur et un regain de protectionnisme de la part des pays développés.

Nous croyons fermement, pour notre part, que la promotion de la coopération et l'intégration économiques en vue de l'avènement de la Communauté économique africaine prévue par le Traité d'Abuja, contribueront à la consolidation des efforts que nos pays mènent pour la relance et le développement de leurs économies et la prise en charge des grands problèmes de l'Afrique dont notamment ceux des réfugiés et de la pauvreté, de l'analphabétisme et des pandémies, dont le fléau du SIDA, ou encore ceux de l'environnement à travers les questions de l'eau, la désertification et les menaces sur la biodiversité.

A l'aube du troisième Millénaire, Nous, Chefs d'Etat et de Gouvernement des pays membres de l'Organisation de l'Unité Africaine, affirmons solennellement notre détermination à assumer pleinement nos responsabilités dans la prise en charge de tous ces défis. Il reste que les solutions à ces défis sont, dans une large mesure, tributaires de la conjugaison des volontés, des efforts et des moyens de l'ensemble de la communauté internationale.

C'est pourquoi, Nous appelons à un partenariat international authentique mutuellement avantageux; un partenariat fondé sur l'équilibre des intérêts et le respect mutuel; un partenariat dont les chantiers les plus importants et les plus urgents sont la véritable démocratisation des relations internationales, le renouveau du multilatéralisme et la consolidation de ses instruments, la réorganisation de la coopération internationale sur la base de l'interdépendance solidaire et le recul des égoïsmes nationaux, enfin celui de la mise en place d'un système de sécurité conçu et fonctionnant avec la participation et l'adhésion de toutes les nations.

En Nous félicitant des différentes initiatives et approches de coopération affichées à l'endroit de l'Afrique, Nous réaffirmons Notre disponibilité et Notre volonté à promouvoir, avec tous nos partenaires, une véritable oeuvre de partenariat loin de tous les calculs égoïstes et des luttes d'influence; un partenariat qui respecte l'unité du Continent et vise à développer l'Afrique et non pas à l'utiliser comme simple réservoir de matières premières et marché pour les produits manufacturés; un partenariat qui permette à l'Afrique de réaliser son intégration, d'assurer son développement au service de ses peuples et d'occuper sa place légitime sur la scène internationale au bénéfice partagé et bien compris de la Communauté Internationale dans son ensemble.

Ensemble, entrons dans le 3ème millénaire avec un authentique esprit de coopération, la dignité humanitaire rétablie et l'espoir partagé dans le devenir solidaire de l'humanité. En cela, l'Afrique, qui entend maîtriser son destin, assumera sa part de responsabilité.

DECLARATION DE L'ANNEE 2000 COMME ANNEE DE LA PAIX, DE LA SECURITE ET DE LA SOLIDARITE EN AFRIQUE

AHG/DECL. 2 (XXXV)

La Conférence:

1. *Rappelant* le Communiqué final publié à l'issue de la 27ème session ordinaire de la Conférence des Chefs d'Etat et de Gouvernement de l'OUA qui a, entre

autres, reconnu le lien entre la sécurité, le développement et la coopération en Afrique,
2. *Rappelant en outre* le Document de Kampala proposant la convocation d'une conférence sur la sécurité, la stabilité, le développement et la coopération en Afrique (CSSDCA),
3. *Gravement préoccupée* par la prolifération des crises et des conflits armés et leurs effets dévastateurs sur la stabilité, ainsi que sur le développement économique et social des Etats membres,
4. *Rappelant également* en outre la création, en 1993 au Caire, d'un Mécanisme de l'OUA pour la prévention, la gestion et le règlement des conflits sur le continent,
5. *Notant* les efforts déployés par les Organisations et les dirigeants des diverses sous-régions pour régler effectivement et pacifiquement les conflits actuels,
6. *Déterminée à* parvenir à un nouveau consensus et à une vision commune en ce qui concerne l'avenir de notre continent,
7. PROCLAME l'année 2000 comme Année de la paix, de la sécurité et de la solidarité en Afrique et INVITE le Président en exercice de l'OUA, tous les dirigeants et tous les pays africains à intensifier leurs efforts pour éliminer effectivement les conflits armés en Afrique d'ici la fin de cette année.

DÉCISION SUR LE RAPPORT DU SECRÉTAIRE GÉNÉRAL RELATIF À LA CONFÉRENCE MINISTÉRIELLE SUR LE PROJET DE CONVENTION DE L'OUA SUR LA PRÉVENTION ET LA LUTTE CONTRE LE TERRORISME

AHG/DEC.132 (XXXV)

La Conférence:

1. PREND NOTE de la décision du Conseil sur le projet de Convention de l'OUA sur la prévention et la lutte contre le terrorisme;
2. ADOPTE la Convention de l'OUA sur la prévention et la lutte contre le terrorisme;
3. EXHORTE les Etats membres à signer, puis à ratifier la Convention pour en assurer la mise en oeuvre rapide.
4. APPROUVE la convocation, sous les auspices des Nations Unies, d'une Conférence Internationale au Sommet pour élaborer une stratégie internationale appropriée pour combattre le terrorisme et identifier les instruments internationaux à adopter par la communauté internationale pour éliminer le phénomène du terrorisme.
5. SE FELICITE des progrès considérables réalisés rapidement par le peuple et le gouvernement algérien dans la restauration de la paix et de la sécurité et

SALUE l'initiative courageuse de Son Excellence le Président Abdelaziz BOUTEFLIKA destinée à concrétiser les objectifs et à réaliser définitivement la concorde civile en Algérie.

DÉCISION SUR LE DOUZIÈME RAPPORT ANNUEL D'ACTIVITÉS DE LA COMMISSION AFRICAINE DES DROITS DE L'HOMME ET DES PEUPLES

AHG/DEC. 133 (XXXV)

La Conférence:

1. PREND ACTE du 12ème Rapport Annuel d'activités de la Commission africaine des droits de l'Homme et des peuples et félicite celle-ci pour le travail accompli au cours de l'exercice écoulé;
2. DEMANDE aux organes compétents de poursuivre leur réflexion sur le renforcement des moyens de fonctionnement de la Commission africaine pour lui permettre d'exécuter convenablement son mandat;
3. EXHORTE les Etats parties à la Charte africaine des droits de l'Homme et des peuples à s'acquitter de leurs obligations découlant de cet important instrument et d'accorder à la Commission africaine toute l'assistance nécessaire à l'accomplissement de sa mission de manière efficace;
4. AUTORISE la publication du l2me rapport annuel d'activités, conformément à l'article 59 de la Charte africaine des droits de l'Homme et des peuples.

DÉCISION SUR LA CRISE ENTRE LA JAMAHIRIYA ARABE LIBYENNE ET LES ETATS-UNIS ET LE ROYAUME-UNI

AHG/DEC. 134 (XXXV):

La Conférence:

1. PREND NOTE du rapport du Secrétaire général;
2. EXPRIME SA SATISFACTION pour la décision courageuse prise par les autorités de la Jamahiriya arabe libyenne d'encourager les deux suspects libyens à comparaître devant un tribunal écossais siégeant aux Pays-Bas et pour avoir exécuté cette décision; APPUIE la demande de la Jamahiriya pour que soient assurées toutes les garanties et les conditions propices à un procès juste et neutre.
3. REND UN HOMMAGE PARTICULIER à l'ancien Président de l'Afrique du Sud Nelson Mandela, au Serviteur des deux saintes mosquée, le Roi Fahd Ibn

Abdelaziz, au Président Blaise Compaoré, Président sortant de l'OUA, et à tous les dirigeants africains qui ont oeuvré à la mise en oeuvre de la lettre et de l'esprit de la décision adoptée sur cette crise par le Sommet de l'OUA tenu à Ouagadougou;

4. EXPRIME EGALEMENT SA SATISFACTION pour les efforts du Comité des Cinq de l'OUA et du Comité des Sept de la Ligue des Etats arabes pour leur contribution à la recherche d'une solution juste à la crise;
5. FELICITE le Groupe africain à New York pour son rôle dans le règlement de la crise, et plus particulièrement pour avoir attiré l'attention du Secrétaire général des Nations Unies sur le fait que la Jamahiriya arabe libyenne a coopéré et s'est conformée aux exigences des résolutions du Conseil de Sécurité des Nations Unies 731(1992), 748 (1992, 833 (1993), 1192 (1998);
6. LANCE UN APPEL au Conseil de Sécurité des Nations Unies pour que soient levées immédiatement et définitivement les sanctions imposées à l'encontre de la Jamahiriya arabe libyenne;
7. DEMANDE au Président en exercice de l'OUA d'adresser des lettres au Secrétaire général des Nations Unies et au Président du Conseil de sécurité pour que ceux-ci prennent les dispositions qui s'imposent pour la levée rapide et définitive des sanctions;
8. DEMANDE au Comité des cinq sur le différend entre la Jamahiriya Arabe Libyenne, les Etats-Unis et le Royaume-Uni de continuer son travail jusqu'au règlement définitif du différend;
9. DECIDE de rester saisie de cette question et de prendre à cet égard les mesures appropriées;

DEMANDE au Secrétaire général d'assurer le suivi de la mise en oeuvre de la présente décision.

DÉCISION DE L'OUA SUR LA «PREMIÉRE RÉUNION DES ETATS PARTIES À LA CONVENTION SUR L'INTERDICTION DE L'EMPLOI, DU STOCKAGE, DE LA PRODUCTION ET DU TRANSFERT DES MINES ANTIPERSONNEL ET SUR LEUR DESTRUCTION»

AHG/DEC.135 (LXX)

La Conférence:

1. PREND NOTE des informations pertinentes contenues dans le rapport du Secrétaire général sur la «Première réunion des Etats parties à la Convention sur l'interdiction de l'emploi, du stockage, de la production et du transfert des

mines antipersonnel et sur leur destruction» tenue à Maputo (Mozambique) du 3 au 7mai 1999;
2. RECONNAIT que les mines antipersonnel constituent un problème majeur de santé publique et une source de préoccupation dans la politique internationale, et nécessitent une approche globale pour traiter des conséquences négatives de ces armes meurtrières.
3. SE FELICITE de l'entrée en vigueur rapide de la Convention sur l'interdiction de l'emploi, du stockage, de la production et du transfert des mines antipersonnel et sur leur destruction;
4. RECONNAIT EGALEMENT que la prolifération des mines antipersonnel constitue un élément d'insécurité qui entrave la libre circulation des personnes et des biens dans les pays affectés;
5. EXPRIME sa grave préoccupation devant les effets dévastateurs des mines antipersonnel sur les vies humaines et leur impact négatif sur le développement économique des pays;
6. FELICITE tous les Etats parties à la Convention;
7. EXHORTE tous les pays qui ne l'ont pas encore fait à signer et à ratifier la Convention;
8. SE FELICITE des résultats de la réunion de Maputo;
9. SOUTIENT FERMEMENT les objectifs et buts énoncés dans la «Déclaration de Maputo»;
10. DEMANDE au Secrétaire général de continuer à sensibiliser les Etats membres pour qu'ils contribuent à la mise en oeuvre effective de la Convention.

DÉCISION SUR LE RAPPORT DU SECRÉTAIRE GÉNÉRAL SUR LA CONFÉRENCE DES MINISTRES AFRICAINS DE L'ÉDUCATION (COMEDAF I) LA MISE EN OEUVRE DU PROGRAMME D'ACTION DE LA DÉCENNIE DE L'ÉDUCATION EN AFRIQUE

AHG/DEC.136 (XXXV)

La Conférence:

1. PREND NOTE du rapport;
2. APPROUVE les recommandations de la Conférence des Ministres africains de l'éducation (COMEDAF I) réunie du 15 au 19 mars 1999 à Harare (Zimbabwe);
3. PREND NOTE du Programme d'Action de la Décennie de l'Education en Afrique et du Mécanisme pour sa mise en oeuvre, ainsi que de toutes ses composantes, tels qu'approuvés par la Conférence des Ministres de l'éducation;

4. PREND NOTE de la Déclaration de Kampala sur le renforcement du pouvoir des femmes par l'alphabétisation fonctionnelle et l'éducation des filles ;
5. EXHORTE les Etats membres â mettre en place toutes les structures nationales telles que proposées dans le rapport, afin de mettre en oeuvre la Décennie et le Programme d'Action de Harare;
6. EXHORTE EGALEMENT les Etats membres à continuer à accorder la priorité à l'éducation et plus particulièrement à l'éducation de base comme pilier du développement et générateur de ressources humaines, dans tous leurs Plans nationaux de développement;
7. INVITE les Etats membres et les partenaires techniques et financiers à tout mettre en oeuvre afin d'observer, plus particulièrement au niveau national, la synergie de toutes les initiatives en cours sur le continent dans un effort de conjugaison et de mise en cohérence des programmes ;
8. EXHORTE EN OUTRE les communautés économiques régionales à prendre les mesures appropriés pour mettre en oeuvre les dispositions pertinentes du Programme d'Action, en consultation avec le Secrétariat de l'OUA, les pays et les organismes régionaux compétents;
9. DEMANDE au Secrétaire général de l'OUA de:
   a) mettre en place un Secrétariat de la Décennie;
   b) mettre en place le Comité de pilotage de la Décennie;
   c) dégager dans les meilleurs délais, les ressources nécessaires pour le démarrage des activités de coordination de la Décennie;
   d) convoquer tous les deux ans, la Conférence des Ministres africains de l'Education;
   e) convoquer en 2002, à l'occasion de la revue à mi-parcours de la Décennie, un Sommet consacré à l' éducation;
10. LANCE un appel aux agences et institutions africaines et internationales, ainsi qu'aux ONG et aux pays donateurs, pour qu'ils apportent leur soutien technique et financier à la mise en oeuvre du Programme d'Action de la Décennie tant au niveau national qu'au niveau continental

DÉCISION SUR LA PROLIFÉRATION LA CIRCULATION ET LE TRAFIC ILLICITES DES ARMES LÉGÈRES

AHG/DEC.137 (LXX)

La Conférence:

1. PREND NOTE du rapport;
2. ADOPTE les propositions qui y sont contenues;

3. SALUE la Déclaration de moratoire sur l'importation, l'exportation et la fabrication des armes légères adoptée par les Chefs d'Etat et de Gouvernement de la CEDEAO le 31 octobre 1998 à ABUJA;
4. ACCUEILLE favorablement l'appel lancé dans cette déclaration pour que l'OUA soutienne la mise en oeuvre du moratoire et qu'elle encourage des initiatives similaires dans les autres régions du continent;
5. SE FELICITE des initiatives prises par les Etats membres et les organisations régionales concernant la question des armes légères, en particulier le moratoire de la CEDEAO sur les armes légères, la destruction du surplus d'armes légères et armes obsolètes en Afrique du Sud et la destruction des armes illicites au Mozambique;
6. SE FELICITE EN OUTRE des activités de l'Organisation des Nations Unies, par l'intermédiaire de son groupe d'experts sur les armes légères et du projet de protocole sur la Fabrication, la Circulation, la Prolifération et le Trafic illicites des armes à feu, des munitions et autres matériels connexes, qui complétera la Convention sur le crime organisé transnational; du travail de l'Union européenne, à travers son initiative conjointe sur les armes légères; ainsi que du travail de l'Organisation des Etats américains, à travers sa Convention sur la fabrication, le trafic, la circulation et la prolifération illicites des armes à feu, des munitions, des explosifs et autres matériels connexes;
7. LANCE EN OUTRE UN APPEL à la communauté internationale pour qu'elle apporte aux pays africains affectés, toute l'assistance nécessaire afin de leur permettre de mettre en oeuvre des programmes pour résoudre les problèmes liés à la prolifération des armes légères ;
8. REITERE l'urgence et la nécessité d'une coopération inter-africaine pour résoudre les problèmes liés à l'utilisation, au transfert et à la fabrication illicites des armes légères, et SOULIGNE le rôle primordial que peut jouer l'OUA dans la coordination des actions dans les zones affectées;
9. EXHORTE le Secrétaire général à solliciter de nouveau les vues des Etats membres sur la prolifération, la circulation et le trafic illicites des armes légères, en particulier en ce qui concerne les actions à entreprendre;
10. LANCE UN APPEL pour une approche africaine coordonnée, sous les auspices de l'OUA, face aux problèmes posés par la prolifération, la circulation et le trafic illicites des armes légères, en tenant compte des expériences et des activités des diverses régions dans ce domaine;
11. SOULIGNE l'impact de la prolifération, la circulation et le trafic illicites des armes légères sur l'enrôlement d'un nombre accru d'enfants- soldats, les traumatismes psychologiques qui en découlent et la nécessité de se conformer aux dispositions de la Charte africaine des droits et du bien-être de l'enfant et de la Convention sur les droits de l'enfant;

12. LANCE EGALEMENT UN APPEL à tous les Etats membres et à la communauté internationale pour qu'ils apportent leur concours dans la réadaptation psycho-sociale des enfants affectés par la prolifération, la circulation et le trafic illicites des armes légères;
13. DEMANDE au Secrétariat de l'OUA d'organiser à cet effet, une réunion préparatoire au niveau ministériel sur cette question avant la tenue de la Conférence Internationale prévue en l'an 2001, et de solliciter le soutien des institutions compétentes des Nations Unies et d'autres acteurs concernés en vue de définir une approche africaine commune;
14. DEMANDE EGALEMENT au Secrétaire général de présenter un rapport sur cette question à la prochaine session du Conseil.

DÉCISION RELATIVE AU CENTRE RÉGIONAL DES NATIONS UNIES SUR LA PAIX ET LE DÉSARMEMENT EN AFRIQUE

AHG/DEC. 138 (XXXV)

La Conférence:

1. PREND NOTE des progrès réalisés depuis sa 34ème session ordinaire dans le cadre des efforts tendant au renforcement des activités du Centre régional des Nations Unies pour la paix et le désarmement en Afrique;
2. SE FELICITE de la nomination d'un Directeur du Centre par le Secrétaire général de l'ONU;
3. REAFFIRME SON APPUI ENERGIQUE à la revitalisation du Centre et souligne la nécessité de lui fournir les ressources nécessaires au renforcement de ses activités et à l'exécution de ses programmes;
4. REAFFIRME EGALEMENT la nécessité d'instaurer une collaboration étroite entre le Centre et le mécanisme de l'OUA pour la Prévention, la Gestion et le Règlement des conflits, d'une part, ainsi qu'entre le Centre et les organisations sous-régionales oeuvrant dans le domaine de la paix, de la sécurité et du développement, d'autre part;
5. INVITE A NOUVEAU le Secrétariat général de l'OUA à instaurer une coopération étroite avec le Centre;
6. LANCE UN APPEL PRESSANT aux Etats membres et à la communauté internationale pour qu'ils soutiennent le Centre en y contribuant financièrement ou en l'assistant de toute autre manière susceptible de concourir à la promotion de ses activités et à son efficacité;
7. DEMANDE au Secrétaire général de lui faire rapport à sa 36ème session ordinaire.

DÉCISION PORTANT SUR LA CONVENTION DE L'ORGANISATION INTERNATIONALE DU TRAVAIL (OIT) RELATIVE À L'INTERDICTION DES PIRES FORMES DE TRAVAIL DES ENFANTS ET L'ACTION IMMÉDIATE EN VUE DE LEUR ÉLIMINATION

AHG/DEC. 139 (XXXV)

La Conférence:

1. RAPPELLE la Charte africaine sur les droits et le bien-être de l'enfant adoptée en 1990 à Addis Abéba, Ethiopie, par la vingt-sixième Conférence des Chefs d'Etat et de Gouvernement;
2. RAPPELLE EGALEMENT l'adoption à l'unanimité le 17 juin 1999 à Genève, Suisse, par la 87ème session ordinaire de la Conférence internationale du Travail de la Convention relative à l'interdiction des pires formes de travail des enfants et l'action immédiate en vue de leur élimination;
3. APPROUVE les recommandations du rapport du Secrétaire général à la 22ème session ordinaire de la Commission du Travail et des Affaires sociales de l'OUA (Windhoek, Namibie, 22-23 avril 1999) sur le projet de cette Convention de l'OIT - Doc. LSC/9 (XXII);
4. DEMANDE à tous les Etats membres de ratifier d'urgence cette Convention et de préférence avant la 36ème session de la Conférence des Chefs d'Etat et de Gouvernement de l'an 2000.
5. DEMANDE EN CONSEQUENCE au Bureau international du Travail (BIT) d'apporter l'assistance technique nécessaire aux Etats membres en vue d'appuyer leurs efforts de ratification et de mise en oeuvre de cette Convention.

DÉCISION SUR LA CONVOCATION D'UNE SESSION EXTRAORDINAIRE DE LA CONFÉRENCE DES CHEFS D'ETAT ET DE GOUVERNEMENT DE l'OUA CONFORMÉMENT A L'ARTICLE 33(5) DU RÈGLEMENT INTÉRIEUR DE LA CONFÉRENCE

AHG/DEC. 140 (XXXV)

La Conférence,

Ayant entendu l'intervention de S.E.le Colonel Muamar Kaddafi, leader de la grande révolution du 1er septembre de la Grande Jamahiriya arabe libyenne populaire et socialiste, au cours de l'examen du point relatif à la sécurité collective et aux conflits sur le continent,

Ayant également entendu son intervention sur la convocation en Grande Jamahiriya arabe libyenne populaire et socialiste, du 6 au 9 septembre 1999, d'une session extraordinaire de la Conférence des Chefs d'Etat et de Gouvernement de l'OUA pour examiner les voies et moyens de dynamiser l'OUA afin de lui permettre d'être au diapason des développements politiques et économiques dans le monde, et pour bien préparer l'Afrique dans le contexte de la mondialisation afin de préserver ses ressources et ses potentialités dans les domaines économique, social et politique;

DECIDE d'accepter l'offre de S.E. le colonel Muamar El Kaddafi d'accueillir un Sommet extraordinaire en Grande Jamahiriya arabe Libyenne populaire et socialiste à la date sus-mentionnée.

DÉCISION

AHG/DEC. 141 (XXXV)

La Conférence,

1. REAFFIRME les dispositions de la Charte de l'OUA ;
2. REAFFIRME EN OUTRE la Charte africaine des droits de l'homme et des peuples et en particulier l'article 13 ;
3. RAPPELLE la Déclaration universelle sur la démocratie adoptée par le Conseil inter-parlementaire à sa 161ème session ordinaire tenue au Caire le 16 septembre 1997 ;
4. RAPPELLE EN OUTRE l'esprit de la décision de Harare sur les changements anti-constitutionnels de régime;
5. RECONNAIT que les principes de la bonne gouvernance, de transparence et des droits de l'homme sont essentiels pour garantir des gouvernements représentatifs et stables et pour contribuer à la prévention des conflits.

DÉCISION

AHG/DEC. 142 (XXXV)

La Conférence,

Déterminée à promouvoir des institutions fortes et démocratiques pour assurer la sauvegarde des principes mentionnés dans la décision précédente;
1. DECIDE que les Etats membres dont les gouvernements ont accédé au pouvoir par des moyens anti-constitutionnels après le Sommet de Harare, devraient res-

taurer la légalité constitutionnelle avant le prochain Sommet, faute de quoi l'OUA prendra des sanctions à l'encontre de ces gouvernements jusqu'à ce que la démocratie soit rétablie.
2. DEMANDE au Secrétaire général de l'OUA de rester saisi des développements dans ces pays et d'apporter sa contribution aux programmes visant à rétablir un régime constitutionnel et démocratique dans les pays concernes.
3. DEMANDE EGALEMENT au Secrétaire général de présenter un rapport aux sessions ordinaires du Conseil des Ministres et à la 36^{ème}e Conférence des Chefs d'Etat et de Gouvernement sur les progrès réalisés à cet égard.

DÉCISION

AHG/OAU/AEC/DEC.1 (III)

La Conférence des Chefs d'Etat et de Gouvernement,
Vu la Charte de l'Organisation de l'Unité Africaine;
Vu le Traité instituant la Communauté Economique Africaine, notamment en ces articles 7,8,9 et 10;
Vu le Protocole sur les Relations entre la Communauté économique Africaine et les Communautés économiques régionales;
Avant examiné le rapport du Conseil des Ministres et les recommandations de la troisième session ordinaire de la Commission économique et sociale (ECOSOC) tenue à Addis-Abéba, le 17 juin 1999;
Se félicitant des développements positifs concernant la redynamisation de la CEEAC.

DECIDE:

1. REGLEMENTS DU CONSEIL DES MINISTRES
   Les Règlements CM/AEC/Regl. 1(1V) , CM/OAU/AEC/Regl. 1 (V) et CM/OAU/AEC/Regl.2 (V) du Conseil des Ministres sont approuvés par la présente décision.
2. MISE *EN OEUVRE* DU TRAITE DE L'CEA
   a) note est prise de l'achèvement de la première étape de la mise en place de l'CEA, telle que prévue au Traité d'Abuja, et les Etats membres devront intensifier leurs efforts en vue de renforcer les CER actuelles dont ils sont membres;
   b) chaque CER est appelée à soumettre à ses organes de décision un rapport d'évaluation des progrès réalisés au cours de la première étape et informer l'ECOSOC des conditions qu'il lui reste à remplir pour l'achèvement de la première étape;

c) les CER devront présenter à la 4ème session de l'ECOSOC leurs programmes respectifs pour la mise en oeuvre de la deuxième étape et un rapport sur les progrès réalisés, ainsi que sur les perspectives et les contraintes;

d) les CER devront également, dans le cadre des Comités techniques spécialisés, fixer des objectifs pour chaque secteur en vue de faciliter l'évaluation des progrès dans le domaine de l'intégration et de fournir régulièrement au Secrétariat de l'OUA/CEA leurs programmes de travail sectoriels afin de faciliter la coordination et l'harmonisation de programmes;

e) le Président de chaque CER est invité à faire rapport à la Conférence sur les progrès réalisés dans la mise en oeuvre du Traité de l'CEA;

en réaffirmation des engagements qu'ils ont pris aux termes du Traité de l'CEA, en particulier en ce qui concerne la mise en oeuvre des décisions du Sommet de l'CEA qui ont force obligatoire à leur égard, tous les Etats membres sont appelés à mettre en place les modalités et les mécanismes nationaux nécessaires pour faciliter l'incorporation des décisions de l'CEA dans leurs législations nationales.

3. RATIFICATION DU TRAITE

Tous les Etats membres concernés sont invités à prendre les mesures requises pour ratifier le Traité de l'CEA ou pour y adhérer.

4. BUDGET DE LA COMMUNAUTE

Le Comité de coordination, prévu à l'article 6 du Protocole sur les relations entre l'CEA et les CER, devra accorder la priorité à la préparation du budget de l'CEA, et le Secrétariat, intensifier ses efforts de mobilisation de ressources extra-budgétaires.

5. SOMMET OUA-UE

Il est réitéré un soutien à la tenue du Sommet envisagé avec l'UE et il est demandé au Comité préparatoire de l'OUA de continuer à superviser les contacts avec l'UE, tandis que mandat est donné nu noyau de ce Comité de mener des consultations avec le Groupe concerné de l'UE pour surmonter tous les obstacles et identifier les meilleurs voies et moyens de tenir le Sommet.

Fait à Algier, Algérie, le 14 juillet 1999

OAU: FOURTH EXTRAORDINARY SESSION OF THE ASSEMBLY OF HEADS OF STATE AND GOVERNMENT (8 - 9 September, 1999) Sirte, Libya

SIRTE DECLARATION

EAHG/DECL (IV) REV.1

1. We, the Heads of State and Government of the Organization of African Unity (OAU), met at the fourth Extraordinary Session of our Assembly in Sirte, in the Great Socialist People's Libyan Arab Jamahiriya, from 8 to 9 September 1999, at the invitation of the Leader of the Al Fatah Revolution, Colonel Muammar Ghaddafi, and as agreed upon during the Thirty-fifth Ordinary Session of our Summit in Algiers, Algeria, from 12 to 14 July 1999.
2. We deliberated extensively on the ways and means of strengthening our continental Organization to make it more effective so as to keep pace with the political, economic and social developments taking place within and outside our continent.
3. In this endeavour, we were inspired by the ideals which guided the Founding Fathers of our Organization and generations of Pan-Africanists in their resolve to forge unity, solidarity and cohesion, as well as cooperation, between African peoples and among African States.
4. We recall the heroic struggles waged by our peoples and our countries during the last century of this millennium for political independence, human dignity and economic emancipation. We take pride in the achievements made to promote and consolidate African unity and we salute the heroism and the sacrifices of our peoples, particularly during the liberation struggles.
5. As we prepare to enter the twenty-first century, and cognizant of the challenges that will confront our continent and peoples, we emphasize the imperative need and a high sense of urgency to rekindle the aspirations of our peoples for stronger unity, solidarity and cohesion in a larger community of peoples transcending cultural, ideological, ethnic and national differences.
6. In order to cope with these challenges and to effectively address the new social, political and economic realities in Africa and in the world, we are determined to fulfil our peoples' aspirations for greater unity in conformity with the objectives of the OAU Charter and the Treaty Establishing the African Economic Community (the Abuja Treaty). It is also our conviction that our continental Organization needs to be revitalized in order to be able to play a more active

role and continue to be relevant to the needs of our peoples and responsive to the demands of the prevailing circumstances. We are also determined to eliminate the scourge of conflicts which constitutes a major impediment to the implementation of our development and integration agenda.

7. In our deliberations, we have been inspired by the important proposals submitted by Colonel Muammar Ghaddafi, Leader of the Great Al Fatah Libyan Revolution, and particularly, by his vision for a strong and united Africa, capable of meeting global challenges and shouldering its responsibility to harness the human and natural resources of the continent in order to improve the living conditions of its peoples.

8. Having discussed frankly and extensively on how to proceed with the strengthening of the unity of our continent and its peoples, in the light of those proposals, and bearing in mind the current situation on the continent, we DECIDE TO:

   (i) Establish an African Union, in conformity with the ultimate objectives of the Charter of our continental Organization and the provisions of the Treaty Establishing the African Economic Community.

   (ii) Accelerate the process of implementing the Treaty Establishing the African Economic Community, in particular:

      (a) Shorten the implementation periods of the Abuja Treaty,

      (b) Ensure the speedy establishment of all the institutions provided for in the Abuja Treaty, such as the African Central Bank, the African Monetary Union, the African Court of Justice and, in particular, the Pan- African Parliament. We aim to establish that Parliament by the year 2000, to provide a common platform for our peoples and their grass-root organizations to be more involved in discussions and decision-making on the problems and challenges facing our continent.

      (c) Strengthening and consolidating the Regional Economic Communities as the pillars for achieving the objectives of the African Economic Community and realizing the envisaged Union.

   (iii) Mandate the Council of Ministers to take the necessary measures to ensure the implementation of the above decisions and, in particular, to prepare the constitutive legal text of the Union, taking into account the Charter of the OAU and the Treaty Establishing the African Economic Community. Member States should encourage the participation of Parliamentarians in that process. The Council should submit its report to the Thirty-sixth Ordinary Session of our Assembly for appropriate action. Member States should work towards finalising the process of ratification, where appropriate, by December 2000, in order for a constitutive Act to be solemnly adopted in the year 2001, at an Extra-Ordinary Summit, to be convened in Sirte.

(iv) Mandate our Current Chairman, President Abdelaziz Bouteflika of Algeria, and President Thabo Mbeki of South Africa, to engage African creditors on our behalf on the issue of Africa's external indebtedness, with a view to securing the total cancellation of Africa's debt, as a matter of urgency. They are to coordinate their efforts with the OAU Contact Group on Africa's External Debt.

(v) Convene an African Ministerial Conference on Security, Stability, Development and Cooperation in the Continent, as soon as possible.

(vi) Request the Secretary General of our Organization, as a matter of priority, to take all appropriate measures to follow up the implementation of these decisions.

Done at Sirte, Great Socialist People's Libyan Arab Jamahiriya, September 9, 1999 (9.9.99)

OUA: DE LA QUATRIEME SESSION EXTRAORDINAIRE CONFERENCE DES CHEFS D'ETAT ET DE GOUVERNEMENT (8-9 septembre 1999) Syrte (LIBYE)

DECLARATION DE SYRTE

EAHG/DECL. (IV) REV. 1

1. Nous, Chefs d'Etat et de Gouvernement de l'Organisation de l'Unité Africaine (OUA), réunis en la quatrième session extraordinaire de notre Conférence à Syrte, en Grande Jamahiriya Arabe Libyenne Populaire et Socialiste, les 8 et 9 septembre 1999, à l'invitation du Guide de la Révolution El Fatah, le Colonel Muammar Gaddafi, et conformément à la décision de la Trente-cinquième session ordinaire de notre Sommet, tenue à Alger, Algérie, du 12 au 14 juillet1999,
2. Avons longuement discuté des voies et moyens de renforcer notre Organisation continentale afin de la rendre plus efficace et de lui permettre de s'adapter aux changements sociaux, politiques et économiques qui se produisent à l'intérieur et à l'extérieur de notre continent.
3. A cet égard, nous nous sommes inspirés des idéaux qui ont guidé les pères fondateurs de notre Organisation et des générations de panafricanistes dans leur détermination à forger l'unité, la solidarité et la cohésion, ainsi que la coopération entre les peuples d'Afrique et entre les Etats africains.
4. Nous rappelons les luttes héroïques menées par nos peuples et nos pays au cours du dernier siècle du millénaire pour l'indépendance politique, la dignité humaine et l'émancipation économique. Nous sommes fiers des progrès enregistrés sur la voie de la promotion et de la consolidation de l'unité africaine et nous saluons l'héroïsme et les sacrifices de nos peuples, en particulier pendant les luttes de libération.
5. Au moment où nous nous préparons à entrer dans le 21ème siècle et ayant à l'esprit les défis auxquels notre continent et nos peuples sont confrontés, nous soulignons la nécessité impérieuse et l'extrême urgence de raviver les aspirations de nos peuples à une plus grande unité, solidarité et cohésion dans une communauté plus large des peuples, qui transcende les différences culturelles, idéologiques, ethniques et nationales.
6. Pour relever ces défis et faire face de manière efficace aux nouvelles réalités sociales, politiques et économiques en Afrique et dans le monde, nous sommes

déterminés à répondre aux aspirations de nos peuples à une plus grande unité, conformément aux objectifs énoncés dans la Charte de l'OUA et dans le Traité instituant la Communauté économique africaine (Traité d'Abuja). Nous sommes convaincus que notre Organisation continentale doit être revitalisée afin qu'elle puisse jouer un rôle plus actif et continuer à répondre aux besoins de nos peuples et aux exigences de la conjoncture actuelle. Nous sommes également déterminés à éliminer le fléau des conflits qui constitue un obstacle majeur à la mise en oeuvre de notre programme de développement et d'intégration.

7. Au cours de nos travaux, nous avons été inspirés par les propositions importantes faites par le Colonel Muammar Ghaddafi, Guide de la Grande Révolution libyenne El Fatah, et particulièrement, par sa vision d'une Afrique forte et unie capable de relever les défis qui se posent à elle au niveau mondial et d'assumer sa responsabilité de mobiliser les ressources humaines et naturelles du continent afin d'améliorer les conditions de vie de ses peuples.

8. Ayant franchement et longuement discuté de l'approche à adopter quant au renforcement de l'unité de notre continent et de ses peuples à la lumière de ces propositions, et compte tenu de la situation actuelle sur le continent, NOUS DECIDONS de:

   i) créer une Union africaine, conformément aux objectifs fondamentaux de la Charte de notre Organisation continentale et aux dispositions du Traité instituant la Communauté économique africaine,

   ii) accélérer le processus de mise en oeuvre du Traité instituant la Communauté économique africaine, en particulier:
      (a) abréger le calendrier d'exécution du Traité d'Abuja,
      (b) assurer la création rapide de toutes les institutions prévues dans le Traité d'Abuja, telles que la Banque centrale africaine, le Fonds monétaire africain et la Cour de justice et, en particulier le Parlement panafricain. Nous envisageons de mettre en place le parlement d'ici à l'an 2000, afin d'offrir une plate-forme commune à nos peuples et à leurs organisations communautaires en vue d'assurer leur plus grande participation aux discussions et à la prise des décisions concernant les problèmes et les défis qui se posent à notre continent.
      (c) renforcer et consolider les Communautés économiques régionales qui constituent les piliers de la réalisation des objectifs de la Communauté économique africaine, et de l'Union envisagée.

   iii) mandater le Conseil des Ministres de prendre les mesures nécessaires pour assurer la mise en oeuvre des décisions susmentionnées et, en particulier, d'élaborer l'Acte constitutif de l'Union, en tenant compte de la Charte de l'OUA et du Traité instituant la Communauté économique africaine. Les

Etats membres doivent encourager la participation des parlementaires à ce processus. Le Conseil doit présenter son rapport à la Trente-sixième Session ordinaire de notre Conférence pour lui permettre de prendre les décisions appropriées. Les Etats membres doivent tout mettre en oeuvre pour faire aboutir le processus de ratification avant décembre 2000 afin que l'Acte constitutif puisse être solennellement adopté en l'an 2001 lors d'un Sommet extraordinaire qui sera convoqué à Syrte.

iv) mandater notre Président en exercice, le Président Abdelaziz Bouteflika d'Algérie, et le Président Thabo Mbeki d'Afrique du Sud, de prendre d'urgence contact, en notre nom, avec les créanciers de l'Afrique en vue d'obtenir l'annulation totale de la dette de l'Afrique. Ils coordonneront leurs efforts avec ceux du Groupe de contact de l'OUA sur la dette extérieure de l'Afrique.

v) convoquer une conférence ministérielle africaine sur la sécurité, la stabilité, le développement et la coopération sur le continent, le plus tôt possible.

vi) demander au Secrétaire général de notre Organisation de prendre, en priorité, toutes les mesures nécessaires pour la mise en oeuvre des présentes décisions.

Fait à Syrte, La Grande Jamahiriya Arabe Libyenne Populaire et Socialiste, 9.9.1999

**TREATY FOR THE ESTABLISHMENT
OF THE EAST AFRICAN COMMUNITY**

**TRAITE INSTITUANT LA
COMMUNAUTE DE L'AFRIQUE ORIENTALE**

TREATY FOR THE ESTABLISHMENT OF THE EAST AFRICAN COMMUNITY

PREAMBLE

WHEREAS the Republic of Uganda, the Republic of Kenya and the United Republic of Tanzania have enjoyed close historical, commercial, industrial, cultural and other ties for many years;

AND WHEREAS formal economic and social integration in the East African Region commenced with, among other things, the construction of the Kenya Uganda Railway 1897 - 1901, the establishment of the Customs Collection Centre 1900, the East African Currency Board 1905, the Postal Union 1905, the Court of Appeal for Eastern Africa 1909, the Customs Union 1919, the East African Governors Conference 1926, the East African Income Tax Board 1940 and the Joint Economic Council 1940;

AND WHEREAS provision was made by the East Africa (High Commission) Orders in Council 1947 - 1961, the East African Common Services Organisation Agreements 1961 - 1966, and the Treaty for East African Co-operation 1967 for the establishment respectively, of the East Africa High Commission, the East African Common Services Organisation and the East African Community as successive joint organisations of the said countries to control and administer certain matters of common interest and to regulate the commercial and industrial relations and transactions between the said countries and by means of a central legislature to enact on behalf of the said countries laws relevant to the purposes of the said joint organisations;

AND WHEREAS in 1977 the Treaty for East African Co-operation establishing the East African Community was officially dissolved, the main reasons contributing to the collapse of the East African Community being lack of strong political will, lack of strong participation of the private sector and civil society in the co-operation activities, the continued disproportionate sharing of benefits of the Community among the Partner States due to their differences in their levels of development and lack of adequate policies to address this situation;

AND WHEREAS upon the dissolution of the East African Community the said countries signed on the 14th day of May, 1984, at Arusha, in Tanzania the East African Community Mediation Agreement 1984, hereinafter referred to as "the Mediation Agreement" for the division of the assets and liabilities of the former East African Community;

AND WHEREAS pursuant to Article 14.02 of the Mediation Agreement the said countries agreed to explore and identify areas for future co-operation and to make arrangements for such co-operation;

AND WHEREAS on the 30th day of November, 1993, provision was made by the Agreement for the Establishment of a Permanent Tripartite Commission for Co-operation Between the Republic of Uganda, the Republic of Kenya and the United Republic of Tanzania for the establishment of the Permanent Tripartite Commission for Co-operation hereinafter referred to as "the Tripartite Commission" to be responsible for the co-ordination of economic, social, cultural, security and political issues among the said countries and a Declaration was also made by the Heads of State of the said countries for closer East African Co-operation;

AND WHEREAS on the 26th day of November, 1994, provision was made by the Protocol on the Establishment of a Secretariat of the Permanent Tripartite Commission for Co-operation Between the Republic of Uganda, the Republic of Kenya and the United Republic of Tanzania, for the establishment of the Secretariat of the Permanent Tripartite Commission for Co-operation Between the Republic of Uganda, the Republic of Kenya and the United Republic of Tanzania to act as the Secretariat of the Tripartite Commission, hereinafter referred to as "the Secretariat of the Tripartite Commission";

AND WHEREAS on the 29th day of April 1997 at Arusha in Tanzania, the Heads of State of the said countries after reviewing the progress made by the Tripartite Commission, in the development of closer co-operation between the said countries in the fiscal, monetary, immigration, infrastructure and service fields and after approving the East African Co-operation Development Strategy for the period 1997 - 2000, directed the Tripartite Commission to embark on negotiations for the upgrading of the Agreement establishing the Tripartite Commission into a Treaty;

AND WHEREAS the said countries, with a view to strengthening their co-operation are resolved to adhere themselves to the fundamental and operational principles that shall govern the achievement of the objectives set out herein and to the principles of international law governing relationships between sovereign states;

AND WHEREAS the said countries, with a view to realising a fast and balanced regional development are resolved to creating an enabling environment in all the Partner States in order to attract investments and allow the private sector and civil society to play a leading role in the socio-economic development activities through the development of sound macro-economic and sectoral policies and their efficient management while taking cognisance of the developments in the world economy as contained in the

Marrakesh Agreement Establishing the World Trade Organisation, 1995 referred to "as the WTO Agreement" and as may be decided by the Partner States, the development of technological capacity for improved productivity;

AND WHEREAS the said countries desire to foster and to promote greater awareness of the shared interests of their people;

AND WHEREAS the said countries are resolved to act in concert to achieve the objectives set out hereinbefore;

NOW THEREFORE the Republic of Uganda, the Republic of Kenya and the United Republic of Tanzania ;

DETERMINED to strengthen their economic, social, cultural, political, technological and other ties for their fast balanced and sustainable development by the establishment of an East African Community, with an East African Customs Union and a Common Market as transitional stages to and integral parts thereof, subsequently a Monetary Union and ultimately a Political Federation;

CONVINCED that co-operation at the sub-regional and regional levels in all fields of human endeavour will raise the standards of living of African peoples, maintain and enhance the economic stability, foster close and peaceful relations among African states and accelerate the successive stages in the realisation of the proposed African Economic Community and Political Union;

AGREE AS FOLLOWS:

CHAPTER ONE

INTERPRETATION

ARTICLE 1
Interpretation

1. In this Treaty, except where the context otherwise requires -

"Act of the Community" means an Act of the Community in accordance with this Treaty;

"Audit Commission" means the Audit Commission established by Article 134 of this Treaty;

"Assembly" means the East African Legislative Assembly established by Article 9 of this Treaty;

"Bill" means a Bill of the East African Legislative Assembly;

"civil society" means a realm of organised social life that is voluntary, self generating, self-supporting, autonomous from the state, and bound by a legal set of shared rules;

"Clerk of the Assembly" means the Clerk of the East African Legislative Assembly appointed under Article 48 of this Treaty;

"common carrier" includes a person or an undertaking engaged in the business of providing services for the carriage of goods and passengers for hire and operating as such under the laws of a Partner State;

"common external tariff" means an identical rate of tariff imposed on goods imported from third countries;

"Common Market" means the Partner States' markets integrated into a single market in which there is free movement of capital, labour, goods and services;

"common standard travel document" means a passport or any other valid travel document establishing the identity of the holder, issued by or on behalf of the Partner State of which he or she is a citizen and shall also include inter-state passes;

"Community" means the East African Community established by Article 2 of this Treaty;

"Contracting Parties" means the Republic of Uganda, the Republic of Kenya and the United Republic of Tanzania;

"co-operation" includes the undertaking by the Partner States in common, jointly or in concert, of activities undertaken in furtherance of the objectives of the Community as provided for under this Treaty or under any contract or agreement made thereunder or in relation to the objectives of the Community;

"Co-ordination Committee" means the Co-ordination Committee established by Article 9 of this Treaty;

"Council" means the Council of Ministers of the Community established by Article 9 of this Treaty;

"Counsel to the Community" means the Counsel to the Community provided for under Article 69 of this Treaty;

"countervailing duty" means a specific duty levied for purposes of off-setting a subsidy bestowed directly or indirectly upon the manufacture, production or export of that product;

"Court" means the East African Court of Justice established by Article 9 of this Treaty;

"customs clearing agent" means a person who is licensed in any of the Partner States to provide a service at a fee, in connection with documentation and customs clearance of import and export of consignments of goods;

"designated airline" means an airline which has been designated and authorised by a competent authority of a Partner State to operate the agreed services;

"duty drawback" means a refund of all or part of any excise or import duty paid in respect of goods confirmed to have been exported or used in a manner or for a purpose prescribed as a condition for granting duty drawback.

"East African Industrial Development Strategy" means the strategy provided for under Article 80 of this Treaty;

"East African Law Reports" means the published reports of the judgements of the former Court of Appeal for East Africa and the High Courts of Uganda, Kenya and Tanzania;

"East African Trade Regime" means a trade regime provided for under Article 74 of this Treaty;

"elected member" means an elected member of the Assembly elected under Article 50 of this Treaty;

"environment" means the natural resources of air, water, soil, fauna and flora, eco-systems, land, the man-made physical features, cultural heritage, the characteristic aspects of the landscape and the socio-economic interaction between the said factors and any living and non-living organisms;

"equitable distribution of benefits" means fair and proportionate distribution of benefits;

"financial year" means the financial year referred to under Article 132 of this Treaty;

"foreign country" means any country other than a Partner State;

"freight forwarder" means a person engaged at a fee, either as an agent for other transport operators or on his own account, in the management of transport services and related documentation;

"Gazette" means the Official Gazette of the Community;

"gender"means the role of women and men in society;

"Head of Government" means a person designated as such by a Partner State's Constitution;

"Head of State" means a person designated as such by a Partner State's Constitution;

"import" with its grammatical variations and cognate expressions means to bring or cause to be brought into the territories of the Partner States from a foreign country;

"indigenous entrepreneur" means a citizen who is a business person of a Partner State but who does not possess a foreign nationality;

"institutions of the Community" means the institutions of the Community established by Article 9 of this Treaty;

"international standards" means standards that are adopted by international standardising or standards organisations made available to the public;

"Judge" means a Judge of the East African Court of Justice and includes the President and the Vice President of the Court;

"judgment" shall where appropriate include a ruling, an opinion, an order, a directive or a decree of the Court;

"Minister" in relation to a Partner State, means a person appointed as a Minister of the Government of that Partner State and any other person, however entitled, who, in accordance with any law of that Partner State, acts as or performs the functions of a Minister in that State;

"multimodal transport" means the transport of goods and services from one point to another by two or more modes of transport on the basis of a single contract issued by the person organising such services and while such person assumes responsibility for the execution of the whole operation and also includes any other similar equipment or facility which may hereafter be used;

"multimodal transport facilities" includes items such as heavy lift swinging devices, twin deck cranes, gantry cranes, elevators, large carriers, mechanised storage, low loaders, access facilities, low-profile straddle carriers, mobile cranes, container gantry cranes, side loaders, heavy duty forklifts, heavy duty tractors, heavy duty trailers, portable ramps, flat wagons (flats) for containers, low tare special user wagons and trucks for containers, pallets, web-slings for pre-slung cargoes for different commodities and any other similar equipment or facility which may hereafter be used."

"National Assemblies" with its grammatical variation and cognate expression means the national legislatures however designated of the Partner States;

"non-tariff barriers" means administrative and technical requirements imposed by a Partner State in the movement of goods;

"organs of the Community" means the organs of the Community established by Article 9 of this Treaty;

"other charges of equivalent effect" means any tax, surtax, levy or charge imposed on imports and not on like locally produced products but does not include fees and similar charges commensurate with the cost of services rendered;

"Partner States" means the Republic of Uganda, the Republic of Kenya and the United Republic of Tanzania and any other country granted membership to the Community under Article 3 of this Treaty;

"person" means a natural or legal person;

"President of the Court" means the person appointed as President of the Court under Article 24 of this Treaty;

"principle of asymmetry" means the principle which addresses variances in the implementation of measures in an economic integration process for purposes of achieving a common objective;

"principle of complementarity" means the principle which defines the extent to which economic variables support each other in economic activity;

"principle of subsidiarity" means the principle which emphasises multi-level participation of a wide range of participants in the process of economic integration;

"principle of variable geometry" means the principle of flexibility which allows for progression in co-operation among a sub-group of members in a larger integration scheme in a variety of areas and at different speeds;

"private sector" means the part of the economy that is not owned or directly controlled by a state;

"protocol" means any agreement that supplements, amends or qualifies this Treaty;

"Registrar" means the Registrar of the Court appointed under Article 45 of this Treaty;

"safeguard measures" means the measures taken by any Partner State as provided under Article 78 and 88 of this Treaty as the case may be;

"salary" and "terms and conditions of service" includes wages, overtime pay, salary and wage structures, leave, passages, transport for leave purposes, pensions and other retirement benefits, redundancy and severance payments, hours of duty, grading of posts, medical arrangements, housing, arrangements for transport and travelling on duty, and allowances;

"Secretariat" means the Secretariat of the Community established by Article 9 of this Treaty'

"Secretary General" means the Secretary General of the Community provided for under Article 67 of this Treaty;

"Sectoral Committees" means Sectoral Committees established by Article 20 of this Treaty;

"Sectoral Council" means the Sectoral Council provided for under Article 14 of this Treaty;

"shipping agent" means a local representative of a shipping company;

"Speaker of the Assembly" means the Speaker of the Assembly provided for under Article 53 of this Treaty.

"subsidy" means a financial contribution by Government or any public body within the territory of a Partner State or where there is any form of income or price support in the sense of Article XVI of GATT 1994;

"Summit" means the Summit established by Article 9 of this Treaty.

"surviving institutions of the former East African Community" means the East African Civil Aviation Academy, Soroti, the East African Development Bank, the East African School of Librarianship and the Inter-University Council for East Africa;

"telecommunications" means any form of transmission, emission or reception signal, writing, images and sounds or intelligence of any nature by wire, radio, optical or other electro-magnetic systems;

"trade procedure" means activities related to the collection, presentation, processing and dissemination of data and information concerning all activities constituting international trade;

"Treaty" means this Treaty establishing the East African Community and any annexes and protocols thereto;

2. In this Treaty, a reference to a law or protocol shall be construed as a reference to the law or protocol as from time to time amended, added to or repealed.

CHAPTER TWO

ESTABLISHMENT AND PRINCIPLES OF THE COMMUNITY

ARTICLE 2
Establishment of the Community

1 By this Treaty the Contracting Parties establish among themselves an East African Community hereinafter referred to as "the Community".

2. In furtherance of the provisions of paragraph 1 of this Article and in accordance with the protocols to be concluded in this regard, the Contracting Parties shall establish an East African Customs Union and a Common Market as transitional stages to and integral parts of the Community.

ARTICLE 3
Membership of the Community

1. The members of the Community, in this Treaty referred to as "the Partner States", shall be the Republic of Uganda, the Republic of Kenya and the United Republic of Tanzania and any other country granted membership to the Community under this Article.

2. The Partner States may, upon such terms and in such manner as they may determine, together negotiate with any foreign country the granting of membership to, or association of that country with, the Community or its participation in any of the activities of the Community.

3. Subject to paragraph 4 of this Article, the matters to be taken into account by the Partner States in considering the application by a foreign country to become a member of, be associated with, or participate in any of the activities of the Community, shall include that foreign country's:

(a) acceptance of the Community as set out in this Treaty;

(b) adherence to universally acceptable principles of good governance, democracy, the rule of law, observance of human rights and social justice;

(c) potential contribution to the strengthening of integration within the East African region;

(d) geographical proximity to and inter-dependence between it and the Partner States;

(e) establishment and maintenance of a market driven economy; and

(f) social and economic policies being compatible with those of the Community.

4. The conditions and other considerations that shall govern the membership or association of a foreign country with the Community or its participation in any of the activities of the Community shall be as those prescribed in this Article.

5. The granting of observer status with respect to the Community shall:

(a) in case of a foreign country, be the prerogative of the Summit; and

(b) in case of an inter-governmental organization or civil society organisation, be the prerogative of the Council.

6. The procedure to be followed with respect to the foregoing provisions of this Article shall be prescribed by the Council.

ARTICLE 4
Legal Capacity of the Community

1. The Community shall have the capacity, within each of the Partner States, of a body corporate with perpetual succession, and shall have power to acquire, hold, manage and dispose of land and other property, and to sue and be sued in its own name.

2. The Community shall have power to perform any of the functions conferred upon it by this Treaty and to do all things, including borrowing, that are necessary or desirable for the performance of those functions.

3. The Community shall, as a body corporate, be represented by the Secretary General.

ARTICLE 5
Objectives of the Community

1. The objectives of the Community shall be to develop policies and programmes aimed at widening and deepening co-operation among the Partner

States in political, economic, social and cultural fields, research and technology, defence, security and legal and judicial affairs, for their mutual benefit.

2. In pursuance of the provisions of paragraph 1 of this Article, the Partner States undertake to establish among themselves and in accordance with the provisions of this Treaty, a Customs Union, a Common Market, subsequently a Monetary Union and ultimately a Political Federation in order to strengthen and regulate the industrial, commercial, infrastructural, cultural, social, political and other relations of the Partner States to the end that there shall be accelerated, harmonious and balanced development and sustained expansion of economic activities, the benefit of which shall be equitably shared.

3. For purposes set out in paragraph 1 of this Article and as subsequently provided in particular provisions of this Treaty, the Community shall ensure:

   (a) the attainment of sustainable growth and development of the Partner States by the promotion of a more balanced and harmonious development of the Partner States;

   (b) the strengthening and consolidation of co-operation in agreed fields that would lead to equitable economic development within the Partner States and which would in turn, raise the standard of living and improve the quality of life of their populations;

   (c) the promotion of sustainable utilisation of the natural resources of the Partner States and the taking of measures that would effectively protect the natural environment of the Partner States;

   (d) the strengthening and consolidation of the long standing political, economic, social, cultural and traditional ties and associations between the peoples of the Partner States so as to promote a people-centred mutual development of these ties and associations;

   (e) the mainstreaming of gender in all its endeavours and the enhancement of the role of women in cultural, social, political, economic and technological development;

   (f) the promotion of peace, security, and stability within, and good neighbourliness among, the Partner States;

   (g) the enhancement and strengthening of partnerships with the private sector and civil society in order to achieve sustainable socio-economic and political development; and

   (h) the undertaking of such other activities calculated to further the objectives of the Community, as the Partner States may from time to time decide to undertake in common.

ARTICLE 6
Fundamental Principles of the Community

The fundamental principles that shall govern the achievement of the objectives of the Community by the Partner States shall include:
(a) mutual trust, political will and sovereign equality;
(b) peaceful co-existence and good neighbourliness;
(c) peaceful settlement of disputes;
(d) good governance including adherence to the principles of democracy, the rule of law, accountability, transparency, social justice, equal opportunities, gender equality, as well as the recognition, promotion and protection of human and peoples rights in accordance with the provisions of the African Charter on Human and Peoples' Rights;
(e) equitable distribution of benefits; and
(f) co-operation for mutual benefit.

ARTICLE 7
Operational Principles of the Community

1. The principles that shall govern the practical achievement of the objectives of the Community shall include:
   (a) people-centred and market-driven co-operation;
   (b) the provision by the Partner States of an adequate and appropriate enabling environment, such as conducive policies and basic infrastructure;
   (c) the establishment of an export oriented economy for the Partner States in which there shall be free movement of goods, persons, labour, services, capital, information and technology;
   (d) the principle of subsidiarity with emphasis on multi-level participation and the involvement of a wide range of stake- holders in the process of integration;
   (e) the principle of variable geometry which allows for progression in co-operation among groups within the Community for wider integration schemes in various fields and at different speeds;
   (f) the equitable distribution of benefits accruing or to be derived from the operations of the Community and measures to address economic imbalances that may arise from such operations;
   (g) the principle of complementarity; and
   (h) the principle of asymmetry.

2. The Partner States undertake to abide by the principles of good governance, including adherence to the principles of democracy, the rule of law, social justice and the maintenance of universally accepted standards of human rights.

ARTICLE 8
General Undertaking as to Implementation

1. The Partner States shall:
    (a) plan and direct their policies and resources with a view to creating conditions favourable for the development and achievement of the objectives of the Community and the implementation of the provisions of this Treaty;
    (b) co-ordinate, through the institutions of the Community, their economic and other policies to the extent necessary to achieve the objectives of the Community; and
    (c) abstain from any measures likely to jeopardise the achievement of those objectives or the implementation of the provisions of this Treaty.
2. Each Partner State shall, within twelve months from the date of signing this Treaty, secure the enactment and the effective implementation of such legislation as is necessary to give effect to this Treaty, and in particular -
    (a) to confer upon the Community the legal capacity and personality required for the performance of its functions; and
    (b) to confer upon the legislation, regulations and directives of the Community and its institutions as provided for in this Treaty, the force of law within its territory.
3. Each Partner State shall -
    (a) designate a Ministry with which the Secretary General may communicate in connection with any matter arising out of the implementation or the application of this Treaty, and shall notify the Secretary General of that designation;
    (b) transmit to the Secretary General copies of all relevant existing and proposed legislation and its official gazettes; and
    (c) where it is required under this Treaty, to supply to or exchange with another Partner State any information, send copies of such information to the Secretary General.
4. Community organs, institutions and laws shall take precedence over similar national ones on matters pertaining to the implementation of this Treaty.

5. In pursuance of the provisions of paragraph 4 of this Article, the Partner States undertake to make the necessary legal instruments to confer precedence of Community organs, institutions and laws over similar national ones.

CHAPTER THREE

ESTABLISHMENT OF THE ORGANS AND INSTITUTIONS OF THE COMMUNITY

ARTICLE 9
Establishment of the Organs and Institutions of the Community

1. There are hereby established as organs of the Community:
   (a) the Summit;
   (b) the Council;
   (c) the Co-ordination Committee;
   (d) Sectoral Committees;
   (e) the East African Court of Justice;
   (f) the East African Legislative Assembly;
   (g) the Secretariat; and
   (h) such other organs as may be established by the Summit.
2. The institutions of the Community shall be such bodies, departments and services as may be established by the Summit.
3. Upon the entry into force of this Treaty, the East African Development Bank established by the Treaty Amending and Re-enacting the Charter of the East African Development Bank, 1980 and the Lake Victoria Fisheries Organisation established by the Convention (Final Act) for the Establishment of the Lake Victoria Fisheries Organisation, 1994 and surviving institutions of the former East African Community shall be deemed to be institutions of the Community and shall be designated and function as such.
4. The organs and institutions of the Community shall perform the functions, and act within the limits of the powers conferred upon them by or under this Treaty.
5. In the appointment of staff and composition of the organs and institutions of the Community, gender balance shall be taken into account.

CHAPTER FOUR

THE SUMMIT

ARTICLE 10
Membership of the Summit

1. The Summit shall consist of the Heads of State or Government of the Partner States.
2. If a member of the Summit is unable to attend a meeting of the Summit and it is not convenient to postpone the meeting, that member may, after consultation with other members of the Summit, appoint a Minister of Government to attend the meeting. A Minister so appointed shall, for purposes of that meeting, have all the powers, duties and responsibilities of the member of the Summit for whom that person is acting.

ARTICLE 11
Functions of the Summit

1. The Summit shall give general directions and impetus as to the development and achievement of the objectives of the Community.
2. The Summit shall consider the annual progress reports and such other reports submitted to it by the Council as provided for by this Treaty.
3. The Summit shall review the state of peace, security and good governance within the Community and the progress achieved towards the establishment of a Political Federation of the Partner States.
4. The Summit shall have such other functions as may be conferred upon it by this Treaty.
5. Subject to this Treaty, the Summit may delegate the exercise of any of its functions, subject to any conditions which it may think fit to impose, to a member of the Summit, to the Council or to the Secretary General.
6. An Act of the Community may provide for the delegation of any powers, including legislative powers, conferred on the Summit by this Treaty or by any Act of the Community, to the Council or to the Secretary General.
7. Subject to the provisions of any Act of the Community, the acts and decisions of the Summit may be signified under the hand of the Secretary General or of any officer in the service of the Community authorised in that behalf by the Summit.
8. The Summit shall cause all rules and orders made by it under this Treaty to be published in the Gazette; and any such rules or orders shall come into

force on the date of publication unless otherwise provided in the rule or order.

9. The delegation of powers and functions referred to in paragraphs 5 and 6 of this Article, shall not include:
   (a) the giving of general directions and impetus;
   (b) the appointment of Judges to the East African Court of Justice;
   (c) the admission of new Members and granting of Observer Status to foreign countries; and
   (d) assent to Bills.

ARTICLE 12
Meetings of the Summit

1. The Summit shall meet at least once in every year and may hold extraordinary meetings at the request of any member of the Summit.
2. The tenure of office of the Chairperson of the Summit is one year and the office of the Chairperson shall be held in rotation among the Partner States.
3. The decisions of the Summit shall be by consensus.
4. The Summit shall discuss business submitted to it by the Council and any other matter which may have a bearing on the Community.
5. Subject to the provisions of this Treaty, the Summit shall determine its own procedure, including that for convening its meetings, for the conduct of business thereat and at other times, and for the rotation of the office of Chairperson among the members of the Summit.

CHAPTER FIVE

THE COUNCIL

ARTICLE 13
Membership of the Council

The Council shall consist of the Ministers responsible for regional co-operation of each Partner State and such other Ministers of the Partner States as each Partner State may determine.

ARTICLE 14
Functions of the Council

1. The Council shall be the policy organ of the Community.
2. The Council shall promote, monitor and keep under constant review the implementation of the programmes of the Community and ensure the proper functioning and development of the Community in accordance with this Treaty.
3. For purposes of paragraph 1 of this Article, the Council shall:
   (a) make policy decisions for the efficient and harmonious functioning and development of the Community;
   (b) initiate and submit Bills to the Assembly;
   (c) subject to this Treaty, give directions to the Partner States and to all other organs and institutions of the Community other than the Summit, Court and the Assembly;
   (d) make regulations, issue directives, take decisions, make recommendations and give opinions in accordance with the provisions of this Treaty;
   (e) consider the budget of the Community;
   (f) consider measures that should be taken by Partner States in order to promote the attainment of the objectives of the Community;
   (g) make staff rules and regulations and financial rules and regulations of the Community;
   (h) submit annual progress reports to the Summit and prepare the agenda for the meetings of the Summit;
   (i) establish from among its members, Sectoral Councils to deal with such matters that arise under this Treaty as the Council may delegate or assign to them and the decisions of such Sectoral Councils shall be deemed to be decisions of the Council;
   (j) establish the Sectoral Committees provided for under this Treaty;
   (k) implement the decisions and directives of the Summit as may be addressed to it;
   (l) endeavour to resolve matters that may be referred to it; and
   (m) exercise such other powers and perform such other functions as are vested in or conferred on it by this Treaty.
4. The Council may request advisory opinions from the Court in accordance with this Treaty.
5. The Council shall cause all regulations and directives made or given by it under this Treaty to be published in the Gazette; and such regulations or directives shall come into force on the date of publication unless otherwise provided therein.

ARTICLE 15
Meetings of the Council

1. The Council shall meet twice in each year, one meeting of which shall be held immediately preceding a meeting of the Summit. Extraordinary meetings of the Council may be held at the request of a Partner State or the Chairperson of the Council.

2. The Council shall determine its own procedure including that for convening its meetings, for the conduct of business thereat and at other times, and for the rotation of the office of Chairperson among its members who are Ministers responsible for regional co-operation in the Partner States.

3. A member of the Council who is the leader of his or her Partner State's delegation to a meeting of the Council, may record his or her objection to a proposal submitted for the decision of the Council and, if any such objection is recorded, the Council shall not proceed with the proposal and shall, unless the objection is withdrawn refer the matter to the Summit for decision.

4. Subject to a protocol on decision-making, the decisions of the Council shall be by consensus.

5. The protocol referred to in paragraph 4 of this Article shall be concluded within a period of six months from the entry into force of this Treaty.

ARTICLE 16
Effects of Regulations, Directives, Decisions and Recommendations of the Council

Subject to the provisions of this Treaty, the regulations, directives and decisions of the Council taken or given in pursuance of the provisions of this Treaty shall be binding on the Partner States, on all organs and institutions of the Community other than the Summit, the Court and the Assembly within their jurisdictions, and on those to whom they may under this Treaty be addressed.

CHAPTER SIX

THE CO-ORDINATION COMMITTEE

ARTICLE 17
Composition of the Co-ordination Committee

The Co-ordination Committee shall consist of the Permanent Secretaries responsible for regional co-operation in each Partner State and such other Permanent Secretaries of the Partner States as each Partner State may determine.

ARTICLE 18
Functions of the Co-ordination Committee

The Co-ordination Committee:
(a) shall submit from time to time, reports and recommendations to the Council either on its own initiative or upon the request of the Council, on the implementation of this Treaty;
(b) shall implement the decisions of the Council as the Council may direct;
(c) shall receive and consider reports of the Sectoral Committees and co-ordinate their activities;
(d) may request a Sectoral Committee to investigate any particular matter; and
(e) shall have such other functions as are conferred upon it by this Treaty.

ARTICLE 19
Meetings of the Co-ordination Committee

1. Subject to any directions which may be given by the Council, the Co-ordination Committee shall meet at least twice in each year preceding the meetings of the Council and may hold extraordinary meetings at the request of the Chairperson of the Co-ordination Committee.
2. The Co-ordination Committee shall determine its own procedure including that for convening its meetings, for the conduct of business thereat and at other times, and for the rotation of the office of Chairperson among its members who are Permanent Secretaries responsible for regional co-operation in the Partner States.

CHAPTER SEVEN

SECTORAL COMMITTEES

ARTICLE 20
Establishment and Composition of Sectoral Committees

The Co-ordination Committee shall recommend to the Council the establishment, composition and functions of such Sectoral Committees as may be necessary for the achievement of the objectives of this Treaty.

ARTICLE 21
Functions of the Sectoral Committees

Subject to any directions the Council may give, each Sectoral Committee shall:
(a) be responsible for the preparation of a comprehensive implementation programme and the setting out of priorities with respect to its sector;
(b) monitor and keep under constant review the implementation of the programmes of the Community with respect to its sector;
(c) submit from time to time, reports and recommendations to the Co-ordination Committee either on its own initiative or upon the request of the Co-ordination Committee concerning the implementation of the provisions of this Treaty that affect its sector; and
(d) have such other functions as may be conferred on it by or under this Treaty.

ARTICLE 22
Meetings of the Sectoral Committees

Subject to any directions that may be given by the Council, the Sectoral Committees shall meet as often as necessary for the proper discharge of their functions and shall determine their own procedure.

CHAPTER EIGHT

THE EAST AFRICAN COURT OF JUSTICE

ARTICLE 23
Role of the Court

The Court shall be a judicial body which shall ensure the adherence to law in the interpretation and application of and compliance with this Treaty.

ARTICLE 24
Judges of the Court

1. Judges of the Court shall be appointed by the Summit from among persons recommended by the Partner States who are of proven integrity, impartiality and independence and who fulfil the conditions required in their own countries for the holding of such high judicial office, or who are jurists of recognised competence, in their respective Partner States:

> Provided that no more than two Judges shall at any time be appointed on the recommendation of the same Partner State.

2. The number of Judges of the Court shall be a maximum of six:

> Provided that of the Judges first appointed to the Court, the terms of two Judges shall expire at the end of five years, the terms of two other Judges shall expire at the end of six years and the remaining two Judges shall serve their full term of seven years.

3. The Judges whose terms are to expire at the end of each of the initial periods mentioned in paragraph 2 of this Article shall be chosen by lot to be drawn by the Summit immediately after their first appointment.

4. There shall be a President and a Vice-President of the Court who shall be appointed by the Summit from among the Judges appointed under paragraph 1 of this Article:

> Provided that the President and the Vice President of the Court were not recommended for appointment by the same Partner State.

5. The office of President of the Court shall be held in rotation after the completion of any one term.

6. The President of the Court shall direct the work of the Court, represent it, regulate the disposition of matters brought before the Court, and preside over its sessions.

ARTICLE 25
Tenure of Office of Judges

1. Subject to paragraph 2 of Article 24, a Judge appointed under paragraph 1 of Article 24 of this Treaty, shall hold office for a maximum period of seven years.
2. A Judge shall hold office for the full term of his or her appointment unless he or she resigns or attains seventy (70) years of age or dies or is removed from office in accordance with this Treaty.
3. Where the term of office of a Judge comes to an end by effluxion of time or on resignation before a decision or opinion of the Court with respect to a matter which has been argued before the Court of which he or she was a member is delivered, that Judge shall, only for the purpose of completing that particular matter, continue to sit as a Judge.
4. A Judge may, at any time, resign his or her office by giving three months' written notice to the Chairman of the Summit through the Secretary General.
5. The salary and other terms and conditions of service of a Judge not provided for in this Treaty shall be determined by the Summit on the recommendation of the Council.

ARTICLE 26
Removal from Office and Temporary Membership of the Court

1. The President of the Court or other Judge shall not be removed from office except by the Summit for misconduct or for inability to perform the functions of his or her office due to infirmity of mind or body.
2. Notwithstanding the provisions of paragraph 1 of this Article, a Judge of the Court shall only be removed from office if the question of his or her removal from office has been referred to an *ad hoc* independent tribunal appointed for this purpose by the Summit and the tribunal has recommended that the Judge be removed from office for misconduct or inability to perform the functions of his or her office.
3. The tribunal appointed under paragraph 2 of this Article shall consist of three eminent Judges drawn from within the Commonwealth of Nations.
4. At any time when the office of the President of the Court is vacant, or the person holding that office is for any reason unable to perform the func-

tions of that office, those functions shall be performed by the Vice President of the Court.

5. The procedure for filling other vacancies in the Court shall be prescribed in rules of the Court.

6. If a Judge is directly or indirectly interested in a case before the Court, he or she shall immediately report the nature of his or her interest to the President of the Court, and, if in his or her opinion the President of the Court considers the Judge's interest in the case prejudicial, he or she shall make a report to the Chairperson of the Summit, and the Summit shall appoint a temporary Judge to act for that case only in place of the substantive Judge.

7. If the President of the Court is directly or indirectly interested in a case before the Court he or she shall, if he or she considers that the nature of his or her interest is such that it would be prejudicial for him or her to take part in that case, make a report to the Chairperson of the Summit and the Summit shall appoint a temporary President of the Court to act as President of the Court for that case only in place of the substantive President of the Court.

ARTICLE 27
Jurisdiction of the Court

1. The Court shall initially have jurisdiction over the interpretation and application of this Treaty.

2. The Court shall have such other original, appellate, human rights and other jurisdiction as will be determined by the Council at a suitable subsequent date. To this end, the Partner States shall conclude a protocol to operationalise the extended jurisdiction.

ARTICLE 28
Reference by Partner States

1. A Partner State which considers that another Partner State or an organ or institution of the Community has failed to fulfil an obligation under this Treaty or has infringed a provision of this Treaty, may refer the matter to the Court for adjudication.

2. A Partner State may refer for determination by the Court, the legality of any Act, regulation, directive, decision or action on the ground that it is *ultra vires* or unlawful or an infringement of the provisions of this Treaty or any rule of law relating to its application or amounts to a misuse or abuse of power.

ARTICLE 29
Reference by the Secretary General

1. Where the Secretary General considers that a Partner State has failed to fulfil an obligation under this Treaty or has infringed a provision of this Treaty, the Secretary General shall submit his or her findings to the Partner State concerned for that Partner State to submit its observations on the findings.
2. If the Partner State concerned does not submit its observations to the Secretary General within four months, or if the observations submitted are unsatisfactory, the Secretary General shall refer the matter to the Council which shall decide whether the matter should be referred by the Secretary General to the Court immediately or be resolved by the Council.
3. Where a matter has been referred to the Council under the provisions of paragraph 2 of this Article and the Council fails to resolve the matter, the Council shall direct the Secretary General to refer the matter to the Court.

ARTICLE 30
Reference by Legal and Natural Persons

Subject to the provisions of Article 27 of this Treaty, any person who is resident in a Partner State may refer for determination by the Court, the legality of any Act, regulation, directive, decision or action of a Partner State or an institution of the Community on the grounds that such Act, regulation, directive, decision or action is unlawful or is an infringement of the provisions of this Treaty.

ARTICLE 31
Disputes between the Community and its Employees

The Court shall have jurisdiction to hear and determine disputes between the Community and its employees that arise out of the terms and conditions of employment of the employees of the Community or the application and interpretation of the staff rules and regulations and terms and conditions of service of the Community.

ARTICLE 32
Arbitration Clauses and Special Agreements

The Court shall have jurisdiction to hear and determine any matter:
(a) arising from an arbitration clause contained in a contract or agreement which confers such jurisdiction to which the Community or any of its institutions is a party; or
(b) arising from a dispute between the Partner States regarding this Treaty if the dispute is submitted to it under a special agreement between the Partner States concerned; or
(c) arising from an arbitration clause contained in a commercial contract or agreement in which the parties have conferred jurisdiction on the Court.

ARTICLE 33
Jurisdiction of National Courts

1. Except where jurisdiction is conferred on the Court by this Treaty, disputes to which the Community is a party shall not on that ground alone, be excluded from the jurisdiction of the national courts of the Partner States.
2. Decisions of the Court on the interpretation and application of this Treaty shall have precedence over decisions of national courts on a similar matter.

ARTICLE 34
Preliminary Rulings of National Courts

Where a question is raised before any court or tribunal of a Partner State concerning the interpretation or application of the provisions of this Treaty or the validity of the regulations, directives, decisions or actions of the Community, that court or tribunal shall, if it considers that a ruling on the question is necessary to enable it to give judgment, request the Court to give a preliminary ruling on the question.

ARTICLE 35
Judgment of the Court

1. The Court shall consider and determine every reference made to it pursuant to this Treaty in accordance with rules of the Court and shall deliver in

public session, a reasoned judgment which, subject to rules of the Court as to review, shall be final, binding and conclusive and not open to appeal:

> Provided that if the Court considers that in the special circumstances of the case it is undesirable that its judgment be delivered in open court, the Court may make an order to that effect and deliver its judgment before the parties privately.

2. The Court shall deliver one judgment only in respect of every reference to it, which shall be the judgment of the Court reached in private by majority verdict:

(b) Provided that a Judge may deliver a dissenting judgment.

3. An application for review of a judgment may be made to the Court only if it is based upon the discovery of some fact which by its nature might have had a decisive influence on the judgment if it had been known to the Court at the time the judgment was given, but which fact, at that time, was unknown to both the Court and the party making the application, and which could not, with reasonable diligence, have been discovered by that party before the judgment was made, or on account of some mistake, fraud or error on the face of the record or because an injustice has been done.

ARTICLE 36
Advisory Opinions of the Court

1. The Summit, the Council or a Partner State may request the Court to give an advisory opinion regarding a question of law arising from this Treaty which affects the Community, and the Partner State, the Secretary General or any other Partner State shall in the case of every such request have the right to be represented and take part in the proceedings.

2. A request for an advisory opinion under paragraph 1 of this Article shall contain an exact statement of the question upon which an opinion is required and shall be accompanied by all relevant documents likely to be of assistance to the Court.

3. Upon the receipt of the request under paragraph 1 of this Article, the Registrar shall immediately give notice of the request, to all the Partner States, and shall notify them that the Court shall be prepared to accept, within a time fixed by the President of the Court, written submissions, or to hear oral submissions relating to the question.

4. In the exercise of its advisory function, the Court shall be governed by this Treaty and rules of the Court relating to references of disputes to the extent that the Court considers appropriate.

ARTICLE 37
Appearance before the Court

1. Every party to a dispute or reference before the Court may be represented by an advocate entitled to appear before a superior court of any of the Partner States appointed by that party.
2. The Counsel to the Community shall be entitled to appear before the Court in any matter in which the Community or any of its institutions is a party or in respect of any matter where the Counsel to the Community thinks that such an appearance would be desirable.

ARTICLE 38
Acceptance of Judgments of the Court

1. Any dispute concerning the interpretation or application of this Treaty or any of the matters referred to the Court pursuant to this Chapter shall not be subjected to any method of settlement other than those provided for in this Treaty.
2. Where a dispute has been referred to the Council or the Court, the Partner States shall refrain from any action which might be detrimental to the resolution of the dispute or might aggravate the dispute.
3. A Partner State or the Council shall take, without delay, the measures required to implement a judgment of the Court.

ARTICLE 39
Interim Orders

The Court may, in a case referred to it, make any interim orders or issue any directions which it considers necessary or desirable. Interim orders and other directions issued by the Court shall have the same effect *ad interim* as decisions of the Court.

ARTICLE 40
Intervention

A Partner State, the Secretary General or a resident of a Partner State who is not a party to a case before the Court may, with leave of the Court, intervene in that case, but the submissions of the intervening party shall be limited to evidence supporting or opposing the arguments of a party to the case.

ARTICLE 41
Proceedings

1. The quorum for deliberations of the Court shall be prescribed in rules of the Court.
2. The proceedings before the Court shall be either written or oral.
3. The record of each hearing shall be signed by the President or Vice President of the Court and shall be kept and maintained by the Registrar.

ARTICLE 42
Rules of the Court and Oaths of Office

1. The Court shall make rules of the Court which shall, subject to the provisions of this Treaty, regulate the detailed conduct of the business of the Court.
2. The Secretary General shall prepare the oath and declarations that the Judges and the Registrar of the Court shall take before the Summit upon their appointment or make upon entering into their duties.

ARTICLE 43
Immunity of the Judges and the Holding of Other Offices

1. The Judges of the Court shall be immune from legal action for any act or omission committed in the discharge of their judicial functions under this Treaty.
2. A Judge of the Court shall neither hold any political office or any office in the service of a Partner State or the Community nor engage in any trade, vocation or profession that is likely to interfere or create a conflict of interest to his or her position.

ARTICLE 44
Execution of Judgments

The execution of a judgment of the Court which imposes a pecuniary obligation on a person shall be governed by the rules of civil procedure in force in the Partner State in which execution is to take place. The order for execution shall be appended to the judgment of the Court which shall require only the verification of the authenticity of the judgment by the Registrar whereupon, the party in whose favour execution is to take place, may proceed to execute the judgment.

ARTICLE 45
Registrar of the Court and Other Staff

1. The Council shall appoint a Registrar of the Court from among citizens of the Partner States qualified to hold such high judicial office in their respective Partner States.
2. The Court shall employ such other staff as may be required to enable it to perform its functions and who shall hold office in the service of the Court.
3. The salary and other conditions of service of the Registrar and other staff of the Court shall be determined by the Council.
4. Notwithstanding the provisions of paragraph 1 of this Article the Registrar shall be responsible to the President of the Court for the day to day administration of the business of the Court. The Registrar shall also carry out the duties imposed upon him by this Treaty and rules of the Court.

ARTICLE 46
Official Language of the Court

The official language of the Court shall be English.

ARTICLE 47
Seat of the Court

The Seat of the Court shall be determined by the Summit.

CHAPTER NINE

THE EAST AFRICAN LEGISLATIVE ASSEMBLY

ARTICLE 48
Membership of the Assembly

1. The members of the Assembly shall be:
    (a) twenty-seven elected members; and
    (b) five ex-officio members consisting of:
      (i) the Minister responsible for regional co-operation from each Partner State; and
      (ii) the Secretary General and the Counsel to the Community.

2. The Speaker of the Assembly shall preside over and take part in its proceedings in accordance with the rules of procedure of the Assembly.
3. The Assembly shall have committees which shall be constituted in the manner provided in the rules of procedure of the Assembly and shall perform the functions provided in respect thereof in the said rules of procedure.
4. The Council shall appoint a Clerk of the Assembly and other officers of the Assembly whose salaries and other terms and conditions of service shall be determined by the Council.

ARTICLE 49
Functions of the Assembly

1. The Assembly shall be the legislative organ of the Community.
2. The Assembly:

shall liaise with the National Assemblies of the Partner States on matters relating to the Community;

shall debate and approve the budget of the Community;

shall consider annual reports on the activities of the Community, annual audit reports of the Audit Commission and any other reports referred to it by the Council;

shall discuss all matters pertaining to the Community and make recommendations to the Council as it may deem necessary for the implementation of the Treaty;

may for purposes of carrying out its functions, establish any committee or committees for such purposes as it deems necessary;

shall recommend to the Council the appointment of the Clerk and other officers of the Assembly; and

shall make its rules of procedure and those of its committees.
3. The Assembly may perform any other functions as are conferred upon it by this Treaty.

ARTICLE 50
Election of Members of the Assembly

1. The National Assembly of each Partner State shall elect, not from among its members, nine members of the Assembly, who shall represent as much as it is feasible, the various political parties represented in the National Assembly, shades of opinion, gender and other special interest groups in that Partner State, in accordance with such procedure as the National Assembly of each Partner State may determine.

2. A person shall be qualified to be elected a member of the Assembly by the National Assembly of a Partner State in accordance with paragraph 1 of this Article if such a person:
   (a) is a citizen of that Partner State;
   (b) is qualified to be elected a member of the National Assembly of that Partner State under its Constitution;
   (c) is not holding office as a Minister in that Partner State;
   (d) is not an officer in the service of the Community; and
   (e) has proven experience or interest in consolidating and furthering the aims and the objectives of the Community.

ARTICLE 51
Tenure of Office of Elected Members

1. Subject to this Article, an elected member of the Assembly shall hold office for five years and be eligible for re-election for a further term of five years.
2. The terms and conditions of service of the Members of the Assembly shall be determined by the Summit on the recommendation of the Council.
3. An elected member of the Assembly shall vacate his or her seat in the Assembly upon the happening of any of the following events:
   (a). upon the delivery of his or her resignation in writing to the Speaker of the Assembly;
   (b) upon his or her ceasing to be qualified for election as an elected member;
   (c) upon his or her election or nomination as a member of the National Assembly of a Partner State;
   (d) upon his or her appointment as a Minister in the Government of a Partner State;
   (e) upon his or her having been absent from the Assembly for such period and in such circumstances as are prescribed by the rules of procedure of the Assembly; or
   (f) upon his or her conviction by a Court of competent jurisdiction of an offence and sentenced to imprisonment for a term exceeding six months and if no appeal has been preferred against such a decision.

ARTICLE 52
Questions as to Membership of the Assembly

1. Any question that may arise whether any person is an elected member of the Assembly or whether any seat on the Assembly is vacant shall be determined by the institution of the Partner State that determines questions of the election of members of the National Assembly responsible for the election in question.
2. The National Assembly of the Partner States shall notify the Speaker of the Assembly of every determination made under paragraph 1 of this Article.

ARTICLE 53
Speaker of the Assembly

1. The Speaker of the Assembly shall be elected on rotational basis by the elected members of the Assembly from among themselves to serve for a period of five years.
2. The Speaker of the Assembly shall vacate his or her office:
    (a) upon the expiry of the period for which he or she was elected;
    (b) if he or she delivers his or her resignation in writing to the elected members; or
    (c) if he or she ceases to be qualified for election as Speaker of the Assembly.
3. The Speaker of the Assembly may be removed from office by a resolution supported by not less than two thirds majority of the elected members for inability to perform the functions of his or her office, whether arising from infirmity of mind or body or for misconduct.

ARTICLE 54
Invitation of Persons to Assist the Assembly

1. The Speaker of the Assembly, may invite any person to attend the Assembly, notwithstanding that he or she is not a member of the Assembly, if in his or her opinion the business before the Assembly renders his or her presence desirable.
2. The rules of procedure of the Assembly shall make provisions for a person so invited to take part in the proceedings of the Assembly relating to the matters in respect of which he or she was invited.

ARTICLE 55
Meetings of the Assembly

1. The meetings of the Assembly shall be held at such times and places as the Assembly may appoint.
2. Subject to the provisions of paragraph 1 of this Article, the Assembly shall meet at least once in every year at Arusha in the United Republic of Tanzania and at a time to be determined by the Assembly.

ARTICLE 56
Presiding in the Assembly

There shall preside at any sitting of the Assembly:
(a) the Speaker of the Assembly, or
(b) in the absence of the Speaker of the Assembly, such elected member of the Assembly as the elected members may elect for the sitting.

ARTICLE 57
Quorum and Vacancies in the Assembly

1. Subject to this Article, the rules of procedure of the Assembly shall make provision as to the number and composition of the elected members that shall constitute a quorum of the Assembly.
2. In reckoning the number of members who are present for the purposes of paragraph 1 of this Article, the person presiding shall not be taken into account.
3. The Assembly may transact business notwithstanding that there is a vacancy among its members, and the attendance or participation of any person not entitled to attend or participate in the proceedings of the Assembly shall not invalidate those proceedings.

ARTICLE 58
Voting in the Assembly

1. All questions proposed for decision in the Assembly shall be determined by a majority of the votes of the members present and voting.
2. The ex-officio members of the Assembly shall not be entitled to vote in the Assembly.

3. When in the absence of the Speaker of the Assembly a member is presiding in the Assembly, the member presiding shall retain his or her right to vote.
4. If the votes of the members are equally divided upon any motion before the Assembly, the motion shall be lost.

ARTICLE 59
Bills and Motions in the Assembly

1. Subject to the rules of procedure of the Assembly, any member may propose any motion or introduce any Bill in the Assembly:

   Provided that a motion which does not relate to the functions of the Community shall not be proposed in the Assembly, and a Bill which does not relate to a matter with respect to which Acts of the Community may be enacted shall not be introduced into the Assembly.

2. The Assembly shall not:
   (a) proceed on any Bill, including an amendment to any Bill, that, in the opinion of the person presiding, makes provision for any of the following purposes:
      (i) for the imposition of any charge upon any fund of the Community;
      (ii) for the payment, issue or withdrawal from any fund of the Community of any moneys not charged thereon or the increase in the amount of any such payment, issue or withdrawal;
      (iii) for the remission of any debt due to the Community; or
   (b) proceed upon any motion, including any amendment to a motion, the effect of which, in the opinion of the person presiding, would be to make provision for any of the said purposes.

   3. In addition to the provisions of paragraphs 1 and 2 of this Article:
   (a) the Council shall publish annually and present to a meeting of the Assembly a general report on the activities of the Community and which the Assembly shall consider at its meeting;
   (b) the Assembly may by a majority of votes cast request the Council to submit any appropriate proposals on matters on which it considers that action is required on the part of the Community for the purpose of implementing this Treaty; and
   (c) the Assembly shall hold an annual debate on the report to be submitted to it by the Council on progress made by the Community in the development of its common foreign and security policies.

ARTICLE 60
Rules of Procedure of the Assembly

The Assembly may make, amend, add to or revoke rules governing the procedure of the Assembly.

ARTICLE 61
Powers, Privileges and Immunities of the Assembly and its Members

1. The Members of the Assembly shall be immune from legal action for any acts of omission or commission in the discharge of their functions under this Treaty.
2. The Community may, for the orderly and effective discharge of the business of the Assembly, enact legislation for the powers, privileges and immunities of the Assembly, its Committees and members.

ARTICLE 62
Acts of the Community

1. The enactment of legislation of the Community shall be effected by means of Bills passed by the Assembly and assented to by the Heads of State, and every Bill that has been duly passed and assented to shall be styled an Act of the Community.
2. When a Bill has been duly passed by the Assembly the Speaker of the Assembly shall submit the Bill to the Heads of State for assent.
3. Every Bill that is submitted to the Heads of State under paragraph 2 of this Article shall contain the following words of enactment:

> Enacted by the East African Community and assented to by the President of the Republic of Uganda, the President of the Republic of Kenya and the President of the United Republic of Tanzania.

ARTICLE 63
Assent to Bills

1. The Heads of State may assent to or withhold assent to a Bill of the Assembly.

2. A Bill that has not received assent as provided for in paragraph 1 of this Article within three months from the date on which it was passed by the Assembly shall be referred back to the Assembly, giving reasons, and with a request that the Bill or a particular provision thereof be reconsidered by the Assembly.
3. If the Assembly discusses and approves the Bill, the Bill shall be re-submitted to the Heads of State for assent.
4. If a Head of State withholds assent to a re-submitted Bill, the Bill shall lapse.

ARTICLE 64
Publication of Acts of the Community

The Secretary General shall cause every Act of the Community to be published in the Gazette.

ARTICLE 65
Relations Between the Assembly and the National Assemblies of the Partner States

In pursuance of the policy of the Community of popular participation in the achievement of its objectives and so that the Council may be able to take into account in the exercise of its functions, the opinion of the general public in the Partner States on matters relating to the achievement of the objectives of the Community as expressed through the debates of the elected members of their National Assemblies, and those of the Assembly and to foster co-operation between the Assembly and the National Assemblies of the Partner States hereinafter referred to as "the National Assemblies":
  (a) the Clerk of the Assembly shall as soon as practicable transmit to the Clerks of the National Assemblies copies of the records of all relevant debates of the meetings of the Assembly to be laid before the National Assemblies, by the respective Ministers responsible for regional co-operation, for information;
  (b) the Clerk of the Assembly shall as soon as practicable transmit to the Clerks of the National Assemblies copies of the Bills introduced into the Assembly and Acts of the Community to be laid before the National Assemblies for information;
  (c) the Clerks of the National Assemblies shall as soon as practicable transmit to the Clerk of the Assembly copies of the records of all rel-

evant debates of the meetings of their National Assemblies other than those with respect to the matters laid before their National Assemblies in pursuance of the provisions of sub-paragraph (a) of this paragraph; and

(d) the Clerk of the Assembly shall as soon as practicable transmit to the Secretary General copies of all the records of debate referred to in sub-paragraphs (a) and (b) of this paragraph for information to the Council.

CHAPTER TEN

THE SECRETARIAT AND STAFF OF THE COMMUNITY

ARTICLE 66
Establishment of the Secretariat

1. The Secretariat shall be the executive organ of the Community.
2. There shall be the following offices in the service of the Community:
   (a) Secretary General;
   (b) Deputy Secretaries General;
   (c) Counsel to the Community; and
   (d) such other offices as may be deemed necessary by the Council.

ARTICLE 67
Secretary General

1. The Secretary General shall be appointed by the Summit upon nomination by the relevant Head of State under the principle of rotation.
2. Upon the appointment of the Secretary General the Partner State from which he or she is appointed shall forfeit the post of Deputy Secretary General.
3. The Secretary General shall be the principal executive officer of the Community and shall:
   (a) be the head of the Secretariat;
   (b) be the Accounting Officer of the Community;
   (c) be the Secretary of the Summit; and
   (d) carry out such other duties as are conferred upon him by this Treaty or by the Council from time to time.
4. The Secretary General shall serve a fixed five year term.

5. The terms and conditions of service of the Secretary General shall be determined by the Council and approved by the Summit.

ARTICLE 68
Deputy Secretaries General

1. The Council shall determine the number of Deputy Secretaries General.
2. The Deputy Secretaries General shall be appointed by the Summit on recommendations of the Council and on a rotational basis.
3. The Deputy Secretaries General shall:
   (a) deputise for the Secretary General; and
   (b) perform such other duties as may be prescribed by the Council.
4. The Deputy Secretaries General shall each serve a three year term, renewable once.
5. The terms and conditions of service of the Deputy Secretaries General shall be determined by the Council and approved by the Summit.

ARTICLE 69
Counsel to the Community

1. There shall be a Counsel to the Community who shall be the principal legal adviser to the Community.
2. The Counsel to the Community shall perform such duties as are conferred upon him or her by this Treaty and by the Council.
3. The Counsel to the Community shall be appointed on contract and in accordance with the staff rules and regulations and terms and conditions of service of the Community.
4. The other terms and conditions of service of the Counsel to the Community shall be determined by the Council.

ARTICLE 70
Other Officers and Staff of the Secretariat

1. There shall be such other officers and staff in the service of the Community as the Council may determine.
2. All staff of the Secretariat shall be appointed on contract and in accordance with staff rules and regulations and terms and conditions of service of the Community.

3. The salaries, job design and other terms and conditions of service of the staff in the service of the Community shall be determined by the Council.

ARTICLE 71
Functions of the Secretariat

1. The Secretariat shall be responsible for:
    (a) initiating, receiving and submitting recommendations to the Council, and forwarding of Bills to the Assembly through the Co-ordination Committee;
    (b) the initiation of studies and research related to, and the implementation of, programmes for the most appropriate, expeditious and efficient ways of achieving the objectives of the Community;
    (c) the strategic planning, management and monitoring of programmes for the development of the Community;
    (d) the undertaking either on its own initiative or otherwise, of such investigations, collection of information, or verification of matters relating to any matter affecting the Community that appears to it to merit examination;
    (e) the co-ordination and harmonisation of the policies and strategies relating to the development of the Community through the Co-ordination Committee;
    (f) the general promotion and dissemination of information on the Community to the stakeholders, the general public and the international community;
    (g) the submission of reports on the activities of the Community to the Council through the Co-ordination Committee;
    (h) the general administration and financial management of the Community;
    (i) the mobilisation of funds from development partners and other sources for the implementation of projects of the Community;
    (j) subject to the provisions of this Treaty, the submission of the budget of the Community to the Council for its consideration;
    (k) proposing draft agenda for the meetings of the organs of the Community other than the Court and the Assembly;
    (l) the implementation of the decisions of the Summit and the Council;
    (m) the organisation and the keeping of records of meetings of the institutions of the Community other than those of the Court and the Assembly;
    (n) the custody of the property of the Community;

(o) the establishment of practical working relations with the Court and the Assembly; and
  (p) such other matters that may be provided for under this Treaty.

2. For the purposes of paragraph 1 of this Article, the Secretary General shall where he or she thinks it appropriate, act on behalf of the Secretariat.

3. The Deputy Secretaries General shall assist the Secretary General in the discharge of his or her functions.

4. The Counsel to the Community shall be the principal legal adviser to the Community in connection with matters pertaining to this Treaty and the Community and he or she shall by virtue of this paragraph be entitled to appear in the Courts of the Partner States in respect of matters pertaining to the Community and this Treaty.

ARTICLE 72
Relationship Between the Secretariat and the Partner States

1. In the performance of their functions, the staff of the Community shall not seek or receive instructions from any Partner State or from any other authority external to the Community. They shall refrain from any actions which may adversely reflect on their position as international civil servants and shall be responsible only to the Community.

2. A Partner State shall not, by or under any law of that Partner State, confer any power or impose any duty upon an officer, organ or institution of the Community as such, except with the prior consent of the Council.

3. Each Partner State undertakes to respect the international character of the responsibilities of the institutions and staff of the Community and shall not seek to influence them in the discharge of their functions.

4. The Partner States agree to co-operate with and assist the Secretariat in the performance of its functions as set out in Article 71 of this Treaty and agree in particular to provide any information which the Secretariat may request for the purpose of discharging its functions.

ARTICLE 73
Immunities

1. Persons employed in the service of the Community:
   (a) shall be immune from civil process with respect to omissions or acts performed by them in their official capacity; and
   (b) shall be accorded immunities from immigration restrictions and alien registration.

2. Experts or consultants rendering services to the Community and delegates of the Partner States while performing services to the Community or while in transit in the Partner States to perform the services of the Community shall be accorded such immunities and privileges in the Partner States as the Council may determine.

CHAPTER ELEVEN

CO-OPERATION IN TRADE LIBERALISATION AND DEVELOPMENT

ARTICLE 74
East African Trade Regime

In order to promote the achievement of the objectives of the Community as set out in Article 5 of this Treaty, and in furtherance of Article 2 of this Treaty, the Partner States shall develop and adopt an East African Trade Regime and co-operate in trade liberalisation and development in accordance therewith.

ARTICLE 75
Establishment of a Customs Union

1. For purposes of this Chapter, the Partner States agree to establish a Customs Union details of which shall be contained in a Protocol which shall, *inter alia*, include the following:
   (a) The application of the principle of asymmetry;
   (b) The elimination of internal tariffs and other charges of equivalent effect;
   (c) The elimination of non-tariff barriers;
   (d) Establishment of a common external tariff;
   (e) Rules of origin;
   (f) Dumping;
   (g) Subsidies and countervailing duties;
   (h) Security and other restrictions to trade;
   (i) Competition;
   (j) Duty drawback, refund and remission of duties and taxes;
   (k) Customs co-operation;
   (l) Re-exportation of goods; and
   (m) Simplification and harmonisation of trade documentation and procedures.

2. The establishment of the Customs Union shall be progressive in the course of a transitional period as shall be determined by the Council.

3. For purposes of this Article, the Council may establish and confer powers and authority upon such institutions as it may deem necessary to administer the Customs Union.

4. With effect from a date to be determined by the Council, the Partner States shall not impose any new duties and taxes or increase existing ones in respect of products traded within the Community and shall transmit to the Secretariat all information on any tariffs for study by the relevant institutions of the Community.

5. Except as may be provided for or permitted under this Treaty, the Partner States agree to remove all the existing non-tariff barriers on the importation into their territory of goods originating from the other Partner States and thereafter to refrain from imposing any further non-tariff barriers.

6. The Partner States shall refrain from enacting legislation or applying administrative measures which directly or indirectly discriminate against the same or like products of other Partner States.

7. For purposes of this Article, the Partner States shall within a period of four years conclude the Protocol on the Establishment of a Customs Union.

ARTICLE 76
Establishment of a Common Market

1. There shall be established a Common Market among the Partner States. Within the Common Market, and subject to the Protocol provided for in paragraph 4 of this Article, there shall be free movement of labour, goods, services, capital, and the right of establishment.

2. The establishment of the Common Market shall be progressive and in accordance with schedules approved by the Council.

3. For purposes of this Article, the Council may establish and confer powers and authority upon such institutions as it may deem necessary to administer the Common Market.

4. For the purpose of this Article, the Partner States shall conclude a Protocol on a Common Market.

ARTICLE 77
Measures to Address Imbalances Arising from the Application of the Provisions for the Establishment of a Customs Union and a Common Market

For purposes of this Article, the Partner States shall within the framework of the Protocols provided for under Articles 75 and 76 of this Treaty, take measures to address imbalances that may arise from the application of the provisions of this Treaty.

ARTICLE 78
Safeguard Clause

1. In the event of serious injury occurring to the economy of a Partner State following the application of the provisions of this Chapter, the Partner State concerned shall, after informing the Council through the Secretary General and the other Partner States, take necessary safeguard measures.
2. The Council shall examine the method and effect of the application of existing safeguard measures and take decisions thereon.

CHAPTER TWELVE

CO-OPERATION IN INVESTMENT AND INDUSTRIAL DEVELOPMENT

ARTICLE 79
Industrial Development

In order to promote the achievement of the objectives of the Community as set out in Article 5 of this Treaty, the Partner States shall take such steps in the field of industrial development that will:
    (a) promote self-sustaining and balanced industrial growth;
    (b) improve the competitiveness of the industrial sector so as to enhance the expansion of trade in industrial goods within the Community and the export of industrial goods from the Partner States in order to achieve the structural transformation of the economy that would foster the overall socio-economic development in the Partner States; and
    (c) encourage the development of indigenous entrepreneurs.

ARTICLE 80
Strategy and Priority Areas

1. For purposes of Article 79 of this Treaty, the Partner States shall take measures to:
   (a) develop an East African Industrial Development Strategy;
   (b) promote linkages among industries within the Community through diversification, specialisation and complementarity, in order to enhance the spread effects of industrial growth and to facilitate the transfer of technology;
   (c) facilitate the development of:
      (i) small-and-medium scale industries including sub-contracting and other relations between larger and smaller firms;
      (ii) basic capital and intermediate goods industries for the purposes of obtaining the advantages of economies of scale; and
      (iii) food and agro industries;
   (d) rationalise investments and the full use of established industries so as to promote efficiency in production;
   (e) promote industrial research and development and the transfer, acquisition, adaptation and development of modern technology, training, management and consultancy services through the establishment of joint industrial institutions and other infrastructural facilities;
   (f) harmonise and rationalise investment incentives including those relating to taxation of industries particularly those that use local materials and labour with a view to promoting the Community as a single investment area;
   (g) disseminate and exchange industrial and technological information;
   (h) avoid double taxation; and
   (i) maintain the standardisation, quality assurance, metrology and testing currently applicable and such other standards as may be adopted by the Council after the signing of this Treaty for goods and services produced and traded among the Partner States pending the conclusion of a protocol under paragraph 4 of Article 81 of this Treaty.

2. The Partners States shall take such other measures for the purposes of Article 79 of this Treaty as the Council may determine.

CHAPTER THIRTEEN

CO-OPERATION IN STANDARDISATION, QUALITY ASSURANCE, METROLOGY AND TESTING

ARTICLE 81
Standardisation, Quality Assurance, Metrology and Testing

1. The Partner States agree that standardisation, quality assurance, metrology and testing can facilitate sustainable modernisation in the Community.
2. The Partner States also recognise the significance of standardisation, quality assurance, metrology and testing in the enhancement of the standard of living, reduction of unnecessary variety of products, the facilitation of interchangeability of products, the promotion of trade and investment, consumer protection, the enhancement of savings in public and private purchasing, improved productivity, the facilitation of information exchange, the promotion of health as well as the protection of life, property, and the environment.
3. The Partner States undertake to evolve and apply a common policy for the standardisation, quality assurance, metrology and testing of goods and services produced and traded within the Community.
4. The Partner States agree to conclude a protocol on Standardisation, Quality Assurance, Metrology and Testing for the goods and services produced and traded in the Community.

CHAPTER FOURTEEN

MONETARY AND FINANCIAL CO-OPERATION

ARTICLE 82
Scope of Co-operation

1. In order to promote the achievement of the objectives of the Community as set out in Article 5 of this Treaty, the Partner States undertake to co-operate in monetary and fiscal matters in accordance with the approved macro-economic policies harmonisation programmes and convergence framework of the Community in order to establish monetary stability within the Community aimed at facilitating economic integration efforts and the attainment of sustainable economic development of the Community. To this end, the Partner States shall:

(a) co-operate in monetary and financial matters and maintain the convertibility of their currencies as a basis for the establishment of a Monetary Union;
(b) harmonise their macro-economic policies especially in exchange rate policy, interest rate policy, monetary and fiscal policies; and
(c) remove obstacles to the free movement of goods, services and capital within the Community.

2. The Partner States shall in order to implement the provisions of paragraph 1 of this Article, *inter alia*:
(a) maintain the existing convertibility of their currencies to promote the use of national currencies in the settlement of payments for all transactions among the Partner States thereby economising on the use of foreign currency;
(b) take measures that would facilitate trade and capital movement within the Community;
(c) develop, harmonise and eventually integrate the financial systems of the Partner States; and
(d) implement the provisions of this Treaty relating to monetary and financial co-operation.

ARTICLE 83
Monetary and Fiscal Policy Harmonisation

1. The Partner States undertake to adopt policy measures in accordance with an agreed macro-economic policy framework.

2. For the purposes of paragraph 1 of this Article, the Partner States undertake to:
(a) remove all exchange restrictions on imports and exports within the Community;
(b) maintain free market determined exchange rates and enhance the levels of their international reserves;
(c) adjust their fiscal policies and net domestic credit to the government to ensure monetary stability and the achievement of sustained economic growth;
(d) liberalise their financial sectors by freeing and deregulating interest rates with a view to achieving positive real interest rates in order to promote savings for investment within the Community and to enhance competition and efficiency in their financial systems; and
(e) harmonise their tax policies with a view to removing tax distortions in order to bring about a more efficient allocation of resources within the Community.

ARTICLE 84
Macro-economic Co-ordination Within the Community

1. The Partner States shall co-ordinate through the Council their macro-economic policies and economic reform programmes with a view to promoting the socio-economic development of the Community.
2. In order to achieve balanced development within the Community, the Partner States undertake to evolve policies designed to improve their resource and production base.

ARTICLE 85
Banking and Capital Market Development

The Partner States undertake to implement within the Community, a capital market development programme to be determined by the Council and shall create a conducive environment for the movement of capital within the Community. To this end, the Partner States shall:
  (a) take steps to achieve wider monetisation of the region's economies under a liberalised market economy;
  (b) harmonise their banking Acts;
  (c) harmonise capital market policies on cross-border listing, foreign portfolio investors, taxation of capital market transactions, accounting, auditing and financial reporting standards, procedures for setting commissions and other charges;
  (d) harmonise the regulatory and legislative frameworks and regulatory structures;
  (e) harmonise and implement common standards for market conduct;
  (f) harmonise policies impacting on capital markets, particularly the granting of incentives for the development of capital markets within the region;
  (g) promote co-operation among the stock-exchanges and capital markets and securities regulators within the region through mutual assistance and the exchange of information and training;
  (h) promote the establishment of a regional stock exchange within the Community with trading floors in each of the Partner States;
  (i) ensure adherence by their appropriate national authorities to harmonised stock trading systems, the promotion of monetary instruments and to permitting residents of the Partner States to acquire and negotiate monetary instruments freely within the Community;

(j) establish within the Community a cross listing of stocks, a rating system of listed companies and an index of trading performance to facilitate the negotiation and sale of shares within and external to the Community; and
(k) institute measures to prevent money laundering activities.

ARTICLE 86
Movement of Capital

The Partner States shall in accordance with the time table to be determined by the Council, permit the free movement of capital within the Community, develop, harmonise and eventually integrate their financial systems. In this regard, the Partner States shall:
  (a) ensure the unimpeded flow of capital within the Community through the removal of controls on the transfer of capital among the Partner States;
  (b) ensure that the citizens of and persons resident in a Partner State are allowed to acquire stocks, shares and other securities or to invest in enterprises in the other Partner States; and
  (c) encourage cross-border trade in financial instruments.

ARTICLE 87
Joint Project Financing

1. The Partner States undertake to co-operate in financing projects jointly in each other's territory, especially those that facilitate integration within the Community.
2. The Partner States undertake to co-operate in the mobilisation of foreign capital for the financing of national and joint projects.

ARTICLE 88
Safeguard Measures

The Council may approve measures designed to remedy any adverse effects a Partner State may experience by reason of the implementation of the provisions of this Chapter, provided that such a Partner State shall furnish to the Council proof that it has taken all reasonable steps to overcome the difficulties, and that such measures are applied on a non-discriminatory basis.

CHAPTER FIFTEEN

CO-OPERATION IN INFRASTRUCTURE AND SERVICES

ARTICLE 89
Common Transport and Communications Policies

In order to promote the achievement of the objectives of the Community as set out in Article 5 of this Treaty, the Partner States undertake to evolve co-ordinated, harmonised and complementary transport and communications policies; improve and expand the existing transport and communication links; and establish new ones as a means of furthering the physical cohesion of the Partner States, so as to facilitate and promote the movement of traffic within the Community. To this end, the Partner States shall take steps, *inter alia,* to:
  (a) develop harmonised standards and regulatory laws, rules, procedures and practices;
  (b) construct, maintain, upgrade, rehabilitate and integrate roads, railways, airports, pipelines and harbours in their territories;
  (c) review and re-design their intermodal transport systems and develop new routes within the Community for the transport of the type of goods and services produced in the Partner States;
  (d) maintain, expand and upgrade communication facilities to enhance interaction between persons and businesses in the Partner States and promote the full exploitation of the market and investment opportunities created by the Community;
  (e) grant special treatment to land-locked Partner States in respect of the application of the provisions of this Chapter;
  (f) provide security and protection to transport systems to ensure the smooth movement of goods and persons within the Community;
  (g) take measures directed towards the harmonisation and joint use of facilities and programmes within their existing national institutions for the training of personnel in the field of transport and communications; and
  (h) exchange information on technological developments in transport and communications.

ARTICLE 90
Roads and Road Transport

The Partner States shall:
(a) take measures to ratify or accede to international conventions on road traffic and road signs and signals and take such steps as may be necessary to implement these conventions;
(b) harmonise their traffic laws, regulations and highway codes and adopt a common definition of classes of roads and route numbering systems;
(c) harmonise the provisions of their laws concerning licensing, equipment, markings and registration numbers of vehicles for travel and transport within the Community;
(d) adopt common standards for vehicle construction, vehicle inspection and vehicle inspection centres;
(e) adopt common standards and regulations for driver training and licensing;
(f) adopt common requirements for the insurance of goods and vehicles;
(g) adopt common regulations governing speed limits on urban roads and highways;
(h) adopt and establish common road safety regulations, accident rescue, first aid, medical care and post-trauma systems within the Community;
(i) prescribe minimum safety requirements for packaging, loading and transporting of dangerous substances;
(j) establish common measures for the facilitation of road transit traffic;
(k) harmonise rules and regulations concerning special transport requiring security;
(l) adopt common rules and regulations governing the dimensions, technical requirements, gross weight and load per axle of vehicles used in trunk roads within the Community;
(m) co-ordinate activities with respect to the construction of trunk roads connecting the Partner States to common standards of design and in the maintenance of existing road networks to such standards as will enable the carriers of other Partner States to operate to and from their territories efficiently;
(n) co-ordinate their activities in the maintenance, rehabilitation, upgrading and reconstruction of the trunk road networks connecting the Partner States and ensure that such road networks once rehabilitated will not be allowed to disintegrate;

(o) adopt a co-ordinated approach in the implementation of trunk road projects connecting the Partner States;

(p) agree on common policies and standards for the manufacture and the maintenance of road transport equipment;

(q) establish common road design and construction standards for the trunk roads connecting the Partner States and promote the use, as much as possible, of local materials and resources;

(r) adopt common and simplified documentation procedures for road transportation within the Community and harmonise road transit charges;

(s) gradually reduce and finally eliminate non-physical barriers to road transport within the Community;

(t) ensure that common carriers from other Partner States have the same opportunities and facilities as common carriers in their territories in the undertaking of transport operations within the Community;

(u) ensure that the treatment of motor transport operators engaged in transport within the Community from other Partner States is not less favourable than that accorded to the operators of similar transport from their own territories;

(v) make road transport efficient and cost effective by promoting competition and introducing regulatory framework to facilitate the road haulage industry operations;

(w) exchange information and experience on issues common to roads and road transport within the Community; and

(x) encourage the use and development of low cost and non-motorised transport in the Community's transport policies.

ARTICLE 91
Railways and Rail Transport

1. The Partner States agree to establish and maintain co-ordinated railway services that would efficiently connect the Partner States within the Community and, where necessary, to construct additional railway connections.

2. The Partner States shall, in particular:

(a) adopt common policies for the development of railways and railway transport in the Community;

(b) make their railways more efficient and competitive through, *inter alia,* autonomous management and improvement of infrastructure;

(c) adopt common safety rules, regulations and requirements with regard to signs, signals, rolling stock, motive power and related equipment and the transport of dangerous substances;

(d) adopt measures for the facilitation, harmonisation and rationalisation of railway transport within the Community;

(e) harmonise and simplify documents required for railway transport within the Community;

(f) harmonise procedures with respect to the packaging, marking and loading of goods and wagons for railway transport within the Community;

(g) agree to charge non-discriminatory tariffs in respect of goods transported by railway within the Community;

(h) consult each other on proposed measures that may affect railway transport within the Community;

(i) integrate the operations of their railway administrations including the synchronisation of train schedules and the operations of unit trains;

(j) establish common standards for the construction and maintenance of railway facilities;

(k) agree on common policies for the manufacture of railway transport equipment and railway facilities;

(l) agree to allocate space for the storage of goods transported by railway from each other within their goods sheds;

(m) take measures to facilitate thorough working of trains within the Community;

(n) facilitate the deployment of railway rolling stock, motive power and related equipment for the conveyance of goods to and from each other without discrimination;

(o) endeavour to maintain the existing physical facilities of their railways to such standards as will enable the Partner States to operate their own systems within the Community in an efficient manner;

(p) provide efficient railway transport services among the Partner States on a non-discriminatory basis;

(q) facilitate joint utilisation of railway facilities including manufacture, maintenance and training facilities to ensure their optimal use; and

(r) promote co-operation in the fields of research and exchange of information.

ARTICLE 92
Civil Aviation and Civil Air transport

1. The Partner States shall harmonise their policies on civil aviation to promote the development of safe, reliable, efficient and economically viable civil aviation with a view to developing appropriate infrastructure, aeronautical skills and technology, as well as the role of aviation in support of other economic activities.

2. The Partner States shall take necessary steps to facilitate the establishment of joint air services and the efficient use of aircraft as steps towards the enhancement of air transportation within the Community.

3. The Partner States shall in particular:
   (a) adopt common policies for the development of civil air transport in the Community in collaboration with other relevant international organisations including the African Civil Aviation Commission (AFCAC), the African Airlines Association (AFRAA), the International Air Transport Association (IATA), and International Civil Aviation Organisation (ICAO);
   (b) undertake to make civil air transport services safe, efficient and profitable through, *inter alia,* autonomous management;
   (c) liberalise the granting of air traffic rights for passengers and cargo operations with a view to increasing efficiency;
   (d) harmonise civil aviation rules and regulations by implementing the provisions of the Chicago Convention on International Civil Aviation, with particular reference to Annex 9 thereof;
   (e) establish a Unified Upper Area Control system;
   (f) establish common measures for the facilitation of passenger and cargo air services in the Community;
   (g) co-ordinate the flight schedules of their designated airlines;
   (h) consider ways to develop, maintain and co-ordinate in common, their navigational, communications and meteorological facilities for the provision of safe air navigation and the joint management of their air space;
   (i) encourage the joint use of maintenance and overhaul facilities and other services for aircraft, ground handling equipment and other facilities;
   (j) agree to take common measures for the control and protection of the air space of the Community;
   (k) apply the ICAO policies and guidelines in determining user charges and apply the same rules and regulations relating to scheduled air transport services among themselves;

(l) adopt common aircraft standards and technical specifications for the types of aircraft to be operated in the Community; and
(m) co-ordinate measures and co-operate in the maintenance of the high security required in respect of air services operations and operate joint search and rescue operations.

ARTICLE 93
Maritime Transport and Ports

The Partner States shall:
(a) promote the co-ordination and harmonisation of their maritime transport policies and establish a common maritime transport policy;
(b) promote the development of efficient and profitable sea port services through the liberalisation and commercialisation of port operations;
(c) make rational use of existing port installations;
(d) in the case of the coastal Partner States, co-operate with the landlocked Partner States and grant them easy access to port facilities and opportunities to participate in provision of port and maritime services;
(e) take measures to ratify or accede to international conventions on maritime transport;
(f) establish a harmonious traffic organisation system for the optimal use of maritime transport services;
(g) co-operate in the elaboration and application of measures to facilitate the arrival, stay and departure of vessels;
(h) promote co-operation among their port authorities in the management and operations of their ports and maritime transport so as to facilitate the efficient movement of traffic between their territories;
(i) agree to charge non-discriminatory tariffs in respect of goods from their territories and goods from other Partner States, except where their goods enjoy domestic transport subsidies, and apply the same rules and regulations in respect of maritime transport among themselves without discrimination;
(j) agree to allocate space on board their ships for goods consigned to or from the territories of other Partner States;
(k) install and maintain efficient cargo handling equipment, cargo storage facilities and general operations and train related manpower and where feasible shall undertake these jointly;
(l) agree to allocate adequate space for the storage of goods traded among themselves;

(m) co-ordinate measures with respect to, and co-operate in the maintenance of, the safety of maritime transport services, including joint search and rescue operations;
(n) provide adequate facilities with good communication systems that would receive and respond to signals promptly;
(o) inter-connect their national communication systems so as to identify polluted points in oceans for concerted marine pollution control;
(p) encourage their respective national shipping lines to form international shipping associations;
(q) review their national maritime legislation in accordance with the existing international maritime conventions.

ARTICLE 94
Inland Waterways Transport

The Partner States shall:
(a) harmonise their inland waterways transport policies and shall adopt, harmonise and simplify rules, regulations and administrative procedures governing waterways transport on their common navigable inland waterways;
(b) install and maintain efficient cargo handling equipment, cargo storage facilities and general operations and train related manpower resources and where possible shall undertake these jointly;
(c) encourage joint use of maintenance facilities;
(d) harmonise tariffs structure for waterways transport on their common navigable inland waterways;
(e) adopt common rules to govern the packaging, marking, loading and other procedures for waterways transport on their common navigable inland waterways;
(f) agree to charge the same tariffs in respect of goods transported within the Community and apply the same rules and regulations in respect of inland waterways transport among themselves without discrimination;
(g) agree to provide space without discrimination on board vessels registered in their territories for goods consigned to and from their territories;
(h) wherever possible, promote co-operation among themselves by undertaking joint ventures in inland waterways transport including the establishment of joint shipping services;

(i) co-ordinate measures with respect to, and co-operate in the maintenance of, safety in inland waterways transport services including the provision and maintenance of communication equipment to receive distress positions promptly and joint search and rescue operations;
(j) facilitate the deployment of inland waterways vessels and equipment for efficient conveyance of all classes of traffic to and from each Partner State;
(k) integrate efforts to control and eradicate the water hyacinth menace and its effects on inland waterways transport;
(l) facilitate joint studies in the use and management of inland waterways;
(m) provide regional training and research facilities for the promotion and development of marine operations and meteorology;
(n) undertake joint surveying, mapping and production of navigational charts and provision of navigational aids;
(o) facilitate provision of adequate meteorological equipment, communication and safety facilities to vessels plying the lakes within the Partner States;
(p) jointly tackle issues on inland water pollution with a view to achieving effective monitoring and control thereof;
(q) jointly explore utilisation of unexploited inland waterways transport resources and tackle matters related to shipping and port services; and
(r) harmonise national policies on inland waterways transport.

ARTICLE 95
Multimodal Transport

The Partner States shall:
(a) harmonise and simplify regulations, goods classification, procedures and documents required for multimodal transport within the Community;
(b) apply uniform rules and regulations with respect to the packaging, marking and loading of goods;
(c) provide where feasible, technical and other facilities for direct trans-shipment of goods at main trans-shipment points including intermodal cargo exchange points, inland clearance depots, dry ports or inland container depots;
(d) agree to allocate multimodal transport facilities for goods consigned to or from the Partner States;

(e) take measures to ratify or accede to international conventions on multimodal transport and containerisation and take such steps as may be necessary to implement them; and

(f) promote communication and information exchange to enhance the efficiency of multimodal transport.

ARTICLE 96
Freight Booking Centres

The Partner States shall encourage the establishment of freight booking centres.

ARTICLE 97
Freight Forwarders, Customs Clearing Agents and Shipping Agents

1. The Partner States shall harmonise the requirements for registration and licensing of freight forwarders, customs clearing agents and shipping agents.
2. The Partner States shall allow any person to register, and be licensed, as a freight forwarder, customs clearing agent and shipping agent, provided that, that person fulfills the legal and customs requirements of that Partner State.
3. The Partner States shall not restrict the commercial activities, rights and obligations of a lawfully registered and licensed freight forwarder or clearing agent.

ARTICLE 98
Postal Services

The Partner States shall harmonise their policies on postal services and promote close co-operation between their postal administrations and devise ways and means to achieve fast, reliable, secure, economic and efficient services among themselves through:

(a) strengthening of postal sorting, routing, transit and distribution centres within the Community;

(b) pooling financial, technical and human resources to modernise, mechanise and automate mail and postal financial services so as to provide timely and efficient services to postal users or customers and, further introduce value-added postal services thus turning postal outlets one-shop for communication services;

(c) adopting competitive marketing strategies to increase market shares in the international courier services and further introduce on-line track and trace system Electronic Data Inter-Change (EDI) for customer information and expedited inquiry handling systems;
(d) conducting joint market research activities with a view to launching new postal products or services;
(e) introducing appropriate postal security systems and procedures in the postal networks; and
(f) co-operating in the development and design of relevant human resources training and development programmes.

ARTICLE 99
Telecommunications

The Partner States shall;
(a) adopt common telecommunications policies to be developed within the Community in collaboration with other relevant international organisations including the Pan-African Telecommunications Union (PATU), International Telecommunications Union (ITU), Regional African Satellite Communication (RASCOM), International Telecommunication Satellite Organisation (INTELSAT), International Maritime Satellite Organisation (INMARSAT), Commonwealth Telecommmunications Organisation (CTO) and other related organisations;
(b) improve and maintain inter-connectivity and modernize equipment to meet the common standards required for efficient telecommunications traffic within the Community;
(c) harmonise and apply non-discriminatory tariffs among themselves and where possible, agree on preferential tariff treatment applicable within the Community;
(d) co-operate and co-ordinate their activities in the maintenance of telecommunications facilities including training and the exchange of manpower;
(e) encourage co-operation in local manufacturing of info-telecommunication equipment, research and development;
(f) facilitate a conducive environment to promote private sector investors in the info-telecommunication equipment within the Community; and
(g) adopt a common frequency management and monitoring scheme, assign mutually agreed upon frequencies for cross-border mobile radio communications and issue operating licences agreed upon by the Partner States.

ARTICLE 100
Meteorological Services

1. Each Partner State shall collect and disseminate to the other Partner States meteorological information in order to facilitate the efficient operation of air navigation, coastal shipping, inland waterways transport and the issuing of cyclone warnings and other adverse weather phenomena and co-operate in the following areas:
   (a) Expansion and upgrading of meteorological observations network and telecommunications;
   (b) Training and research in meteorology, by using common facilities such as the Regional Meteorology Training Centre (RMTC), Drought Monitoring Centre (DMC) and other similar institutions;
   (c) Provision of meteorological services which would include the exchange of observations and products for safety of air navigation, coastal shipping, inland waterways and transport as well as meteorological support to key sectors of the economy which include agriculture, water resources, tourism and construction;
   (d) Support to early warning systems and remote sensing for food security;
   (e) Meteorological support to environment management;
   (f) Harmonisation of policies for the provision of meteorological services;
   (g) Co-operation in human resources development and information exchange; and
   (h) Climate analysis and seasonal forecast.
2. The Partner States shall co-operate and support each other in all activities of the World Meteorological Organisation (WMO) affecting the interests of the Community especially the monitoring of the atmospheric and climatic changes on the planet.
3. The Partner States shall exchange information and expertise concerning new developments in meteorological science and technology including the calibration and comparison of instruments.

ARTICLE 101
Energy

1. The Partner States shall adopt policies and mechanisms to promote the efficient exploitation, development, joint research and utilisation of various energy resources available within the region.

2. For the purposes of paragraph 1 of this Article, the Partner States shall in particular promote within the Community:
   (a) the least cost development and transmission of electric power, efficient exploration and exploitation of fossil fuels and utilisation of new and renewable energy sources;
   (b) the joint planning, training and research in, and the exchange of information on the exploration, exploitation, development and utilisation of available energy resources;
   (c) the development of integrated policy on rural electrification;
   (d) the development of inter-Partner State electrical grid inter-connections;
   (e) the construction of oil and gas pipelines; and
   (f) all such other measures to supply affordable energy to their people taking cognisance of the protection of the environment as provided for by this Treaty.

CHAPTER SIXTEEN

CO-OPERATION IN THE DEVELOPMENT OF HUMAN RESOURCES, SCIENCE AND TECHNOLOGY

ARTICLE 102
Education and Training

1. In order to promote the achievement of the objectives of the Community as set out in Article 5 of the Treaty, the Partner States agree to undertake concerted measures to foster co-operation in education and training within the Community.
2. The Partner States shall, with respect to education and training:
   (a) co-ordinate their human resources development policies and programmes;
   (b) strengthen existing and where necessary establish new common research and training institutions;
   (c) co-operate in industrial training;
   (d) develop such common programmes in basic, intermediary and tertiary education and a general programme for adult and continuing education in the Partner States as would promote the emergence of well trained personnel in all sectors relevant to the aims and objectives of the Community;

(e) harmonise curricula, examination, certification and accreditation of education and training institutions in the Partner States through the joint action of their relevant national bodies charged with the preparation of such curricula;
(f) revive and enhance the activities of the Inter-University Council for East Africa;
(g) encourage and support the mobility of students and teachers within the Community;
(h) exchange information and experience on issues common to the educational systems of the Partner States;
(i) collaborate in putting in place education and training programmes for people with special needs and other disadvantaged groups;
(j) encourage and support the participation of the private sector in the development of human resources through education and training; and
(k) identify and develop centres of excellence in the region including universities.

3. For the purposes of paragraph 1 of this Article, the Partner States shall undertake such additional activities in respect of the development of human resources as the Council may determine.

ARTICLE 103
Science and Technology

1. Recognising the fundamental importance of science and technology in economic development, the Partner States undertake to promote co-operation in the development of science and technology within the Community through:
(a) the joint establishment and support of scientific and technological research and of institutions in the various disciplines of science and technology;
(b) the creation of a conducive environment for the promotion of science and technology within the Community;
(c) the encouragement of the use and development of indigenous science and technologies;
(d) the mobilisation of technical and financial support from local and foreign sources and from international organisations or agencies for the development of science and technology in the Community;
(e) the exchange of scientific information, personnel and the promotion and publication of research and scientific findings;

(f) the collaboration in the training of personnel in the various scientific and technological disciplines at all levels using existing institutions and newly established ones;
(g) the promotion, development and application of information technology and other new ones throughout the Community;
(h) establishment of common ethical guidelines for research; and
(i) the harmonisation of policies on commercialisation of technologies and promotion and protection of intellectual property rights.

2. For purposes of paragraph 1 of this Article, the Partner States shall undertake such additional activities with regard to science and technology as the Council may determine.

CHAPTER SEVENTEEN

FREE MOVEMENT OF PERSONS, LABOUR, SERVICES, RIGHT OF ESTABLISHMENT AND RESIDENCE

ARTICLE 104
Scope of Co-operation

1. The Partner States agree to adopt measures to achieve the free movement of persons, labour and services and to ensure the enjoyment of the right of establishment and residence of their citizens within the Community.

2. For purposes of paragraph 1 of this Article, the Partner States agree to conclude a Protocol on the Free Movement of Persons, Labour, Services and Right of Establishment and Residence at a time to be determined by the Council.

3. The Partner States shall as may be determined by the Council:
   (a) ease border crossing by citizens of the Partner States;
   (b) maintain common standard travel documents for their citizens;
   (c) effect reciprocal opening of border posts and keep the posts opened and manned for twenty four hours;
   (d) maintain common employment policies;
   (e) harmonise their labour policies, programmes and legislation including those on occupational health and safety;
   (f) establish a regional centre for productivity and employment promotion and exchange information on the availability of employment;
   (g) make their training facilities available to persons from other Partner States; and
   (h) enhance the activities of the employers' and workers' organisations with a view to strengthening them.

4. The Partner States undertake to co-operate in the enhancement of the social partnership between the governments, employers and employees so as to increase the productivity of labour through efficient production.

CHAPTER EIGHTEEN

AGRICULTURE AND FOOD SECURITY

ARTICLE 105
Scope of Co-operation

1. The overall objectives of co-operation in the agricultural sector are the achievement of food security and rational agricultural production within the Community. To this end, the Partner States undertake to adopt a scheme for the rationalisation of agricultural production with a view to promoting complementarity and specialisation in and the sustainability of national agricultural programmes in order to ensure:
   (a) a common agricultural policy;
   (b) food sufficiency within the Community;
   (c) an increase in the production of crops, livestock, fisheries and forest products for domestic consumption, exports within and outside the Community and as inputs to agro-based industries within the Community; and
   (d) post harvest preservation and conservation and improved food processing.
2. For purposes of paragraph 1 of this Article, the Partner States undertake to co-operate in specific fields of agriculture, including:
   (a) the harmonisation of agricultural policies of the Partner States;
   (b) the development of food security within the Partner States and the Community as a whole, through the production and supply of foodstuffs;
   (c) agro-meteorology and climatology to promote the development of early climatological warning systems within the Community;
   (d) the development and application of agricultural training and research and extension services;
   (e) the adoption of internationally accepted quality standards for food processing;
   (f) the establishment of joint programmes for the control of animal and plant diseases and pests;

(g) the marketing of food and the co-ordination of the export and import of agricultural commodities;
(h) joint actions in combating drought and desertification ; and
(i) in such other fields of agriculture as the Council may determine.

ARTICLE 106
Seed Multiplication and Distribution

The Partner States shall:
(a) strengthen co-operation in quality seed development and production through research and plant breeding;
(b) support co-operation in the establishment of gene banks;
(c) enhance capacity in seed technology;
(d) initiate and maintain strategic seed reserves;
(e) harmonise quarantine policies, legislation and regulations to ease trade in seeds; and
(f) create an enabling environment for private sector seed multiplication and distribution.

ARTICLE 107
Livestock Multiplication and Distribution

The Partner States shall:
(a) develop mechanism for co-operation in livestock breeding, including artificial insemination institutions and livestock breeding centres;
(b) encourage and facilitate exchange of genetic material to widen the base of livestock development;
(c) encourage private sector participation in livestock multiplication and distribution;
(d) develop common regulatory framework in livestock multiplication, trade in semen, embryos, breeding stock, drugs and vaccines; and
(e) harmonise quarantine regulations in artificial insemination and livestock breeding centres.

ARTICLE 108
Plant and Animal Diseases Control

The Partner States shall:

(a) harmonise policies, legislation and regulations for enforcement of pests and disease control;
(b) harmonise and strengthen regulatory institutions;
(c) harmonise and strengthen zoo–sanitary and phyto-sanitary services inspection and certification;
(d) establish regional zoo–sanitary and phyto-sanitary laboratories to deal with diagnosis and identification of pests and diseases;
(e) adopt common mechanism to ensure safety, efficacy and potency of agricultural inputs including chemicals, drugs and vaccines; and
(f) co-operate in surveillance, diagnosis and control strategies of transboundary pests and animal diseases.

ARTICLE 109
Irrigation and Water Catchment Management

The Partner States agree to take concerted effort to expand agricultural land through irrigation and water catchment strategies and for this purpose, shall:
(a) co-operate in formulating and implementing national and Community irrigation programmes;
(b) co-operate in developing and preserving traditional irrigation systems;
(c) improve water catchment management, including rainwater harvesting; and
(d) adopt and promote the use of environmentally safe methods of land use.

ARTICLE 110
Food Security

The Partner States shall:
(a) establish a mechanism for exchange of information on demand and supply surpluses and deficits, trade, forecasting and state of food nutrition;
(b) harmonise quality and standards of inputs and products including food additives;
(c) develop modalities to have timely information on market prices;
(d) harmonise food supply, nutrition and food security policies and strategies;
(e) initiate and maintain strategic food reserves; and
(f) develop marine and inland aquaculture and fish farming.

CHAPTER NINETEEN

CO-OPERATION IN ENVIRONMENT AND NATURAL RESOURCES MANAGEMENT

ARTICLE 111
Environmental Issues and Natural Resources

1. The Partner States recognise that development activities may have negative impacts on the environment leading to the degradation of the environment and depletion of natural resources and that a clean and healthy environment is a prerequisite for sustainable development. The Partner States therefore:
   (a) agree to take concerted measures to foster co-operation in the joint and efficient management and sustainable utilisation of natural resources within the Community;
   (b) undertake, through environmental management strategy, to co-operate and co-ordinate their policies and actions for the protection and conservation of the natural resources and environment against all forms of degradation and pollution arising from developmental activities;
   (c) undertake to co-operate and adopt common policies for control of trans-boundary movement of toxic and hazardous waste including nuclear materials and any other undesirable materials;
   (d) shall provide prior and timely notification and relevant information to each other on natural and human activities that may or are likely to have significant trans-boundary environmental impacts and shall consult with each other at an early stage; and
   (e) shall develop and promote capacity building programmes for sustainable management of natural resources.
2. Action by the Community relating to the environment shall have the following objectives:
   (a) to preserve, protect and enhance the quality of the environment;
   (b) to contribute towards the sustainability of the environment;
   (c) to ensure sustainable utilisation of natural resources like lakes, wetlands, forests and other aquatic and terrestrial ecosystems; and
   (d) to jointly develop and adopt water resources conservation and management policies that ensure sustenance and preservation of ecosystems.

ARTICLE 112
Management of the Environment

1. For purposes of Article 111 of this Treaty, the Partner States undertake to co-operate in the management of the environment and agree to:
   (a) develop a common environmental management policy that would sustain the eco-systems of the Partner States, prevent, arrest and reverse the effects of environmental degradation;
   (b) develop special environmental management strategies to manage fragile ecosystems, terrestrial and marine resources, noxious emissions and toxic and hazardous chemicals;
   (c) take measures to control trans-boundary air, land and water pollution arising from developmental activities;
   (d) take necessary disaster preparedness, management, protection and mitigation measures especially for the control of natural and man-made disasters. These include oil spills, bio-hazards, floods, earthquakes, marine accidents, drought and bush fires; and
   (e) integrate environmental management and conservation measures in all developmental activities such as trade, transport, agriculture, industrial development, mining and tourism in the Community.

2. For purposes of paragraph 1 of this Article, the Partner States undertake to:
   (a) adopt common environment control regulations, incentives and standards;
   (b) develop capabilities and measures to undertake environmental impact assessment of all development project activities and programmes;
   (c) encourage the manufacture and use of bio-degradable pesticides, herbicides and packaging materials;
   (d) encourage public awareness and education on the use of agricultural and industrial chemicals and fertilisers;
   (e) adopt environmentally sound management techniques for the control of land degradation, such as soil erosion, desertification and forest encroachment;
   (f) promote the use of non-ozone depleting susbstances and environment-friendly technologies;
   (g) promote and strengthen the utilisation of training facilities and research institutions within the Community;
   (h) adopt common environmental standards for the control of atmospheric, terrestrial and water pollution arising from urban and industrial development activities;

(i) exchange information on atmospheric, industrial and other forms of pollution and conservation technology;
(j) harmonise their policies and regulations for the sustainable and integrated management of shared natural resources and ecosystems;
(k) adopt measures and policies to address the existing demographic profiles such as high growth rates and fertility rates, high dependency ratio, poor social conditions and poverty in order to mitigate their adverse impact on the environment and development;
(l) adopt community environmental management programmes;
(m) promote enhancement of the quality of the environment through adoption of common measures and programmes of tree planting, afforestation and reforestation, soil conservation and recycling of materials; and
(n) adopt common policies for conservation of biodiversity and common regulations for access to, management and equitable utilisation of genetic resources.

ARTICLE 113
Prevention of Illegal Trade in and Movement of Toxic Chemicals, Substances and Hazardous Wastes

1. The Partner States undertake to co-operate and adopt common positions against illegal dumping of toxic chemicals, substances and hazardous wastes within the Community from either a Partner State or any third party.
2. The Partner States shall harmonise their legal and regulatory framework for the management, movement, utilisation and disposal of toxic substances.
3. The Partner States undertake to ratify or accede to international environmental conventions that are designed to improve environmental policies and management.

ARTICLE 114
Management of Natural Resources

1. For purposes of Article 111 of this Treaty, the Partner States agree to take concerted measures to foster co-operation in the joint and efficient management and the sustainable utilisation of natural resources within the Community for the mutual benefit of the Partner States. In particular, the Partner States shall:
   (a) take necessary measures to conserve their natural resources;

(b) co-operate in the management of their natural resources for the conservation of the eco-systems and the arrest of environmental degradation; and

(c) adopt common regulations for the protection of shared aquatic and terrestrial resources.

2. For purposes of paragraph 1 of this Article, the Partner States:

(a) with regard to the conservation and management of forests, agree to take necessary measures through:

(i) the adoption of common policies for, and the exchange of information on, the development, conservation and management of natural forests, commercial plantations and natural reserves;

(ii) the joint promotion of common forestry practices within the Community;

(iii) the joint utilisation of forestry training and research facilities;

(iv) the adoption of common regulations for the conservation and management of all catchment forests within the Community;

(v) the establishment of uniform regulations for the utilisation of forestry resources in order to reduce the depletion of natural forests and avoid desertification within the Community; and

(vi) the establishment of Api-Agro Forestry Systems.

(b) with regard to the management of their water and marine resources, agree to co-operate through:

(i) the establishment and adoption of common regulations for the better management and development of marine parks, reserves, wetlands and controlled areas;

(ii) the adoption of common policies and regulations for the conservation, management and development of fisheries resources;

(iii) the establishment of common fisheries management and investment guidelines for inland and marine waters;

(iv) the strengthening of regional natural resources management bodies;

(v) the establishment of common rules of origin for flora and fauna; and

(vi) the establishment of a body for the management of Lake Victoria;

(c) with regard to the management of the mineral resources sector, agree:

(i) to promote joint exploration, efficient exploitation and sustainable utilisation of shared mineral resources;

(ii) to pursue the creation of an enabling environment for investment in the mining sector;

(iii) to promote the establishment of databases, information exchange networks and the sharing of experiences in the management and development of the mineral sector using electronic mail, internet and other means for the interactive dissemination of mineral information;

(iv) to harmonise mining regulations to ensure environmentally friendly and sound mining practices;

(v) to adopt common policies to ensure joint fossil exploration and exploitation along the coast and rift valley; and

(vi) to establish a regional seismological network whose primary objective is to monitor seismicity and advice on mitigation measures.

CHAPTER TWENTY

CO-OPERATION IN TOURISM AND WILDLIFE MANAGEMENT

ARTICLE 115
Tourism

1. In order to promote the achievement of the objectives of the Community as set out in Article 5 of this Treaty, the Partner States undertake to develop a collective and co-ordinated approach to the promotion and marketing of quality tourism into and within the Community. To this end, the Partner States shall co-ordinate their policies in the tourism industry and undertake to establish a framework of co-operation in the sector that will ensure equitable distribution of benefits.

2. The Partner States shall establish a common code of conduct for private and public tour and travel operators, standardise hotel classifications and harmonise the professional standards of agents in the tourism and travel industry within the Community.

3. The Partner States undertake to develop a regional strategy for tourism promotion whereby individual efforts are reinforced by regional action.

ARTICLE 116
Wildlife Management

The Partner States undertake to develop a collective and co-ordinated policy for the conservation and sustainable utilisation of wildlife and other tourist sites in the Community. In particular, the Partner States shall:

(a) harmonise their policies for the conservation of wildlife, within and outside protected areas;

(b) exchange information and adopt common policies on wildlife management and development;
(c) co-ordinate efforts in controlling and monitoring encroachment and poaching activities;
(d) encourage the joint use of training and research facilities and develop common management plans for trans-border protected areas; and
(e) take measures to ratify or accede to, and, implement relevant international conventions.

CHAPTER TWENTY ONE

HEALTH, SOCIAL AND CULTURAL ACTIVITIES

ARTICLE 117
Scope of Co-operation

In order to promote the achievement of the objectives of the Community as set out in Article 5 of this Treaty, the Partner States undertake to co-operate in health, cultural and sports and social welfare activities within the Community.

ARTICLE 118
Health

With respect to co-operation in health activities, the Partner States undertake to:
(a) take joint action towards the prevention and control of communicable and non-communicable diseases and to control pandemics and epidemics of communicable and vector-borne diseases such as HIV-AIDS, cholera, malaria, hepatitis and yellow fever that might endanger the health and welfare of the residents of the Partner States, and to co-operate in facilitating mass immunization and other public health community campaigns;
(b) promote the management of health delivery systems and better planning mechanisms to enhance efficiency of health care services within the Partner States;
(c) develop a common drug policy which would include establishing quality control capacities and good procurement practices;

(d) harmonise drug registration procedures so as to achieve good control of pharmaceutical standards without impeding or obstructing the movement of pharmaceutical products within the Community;
(e) harmonise national health policies and regulations and promote the exchange of information on health issues in order to achieve quality health within the Community;
(f) co-operate in promoting research and the development of traditional, alternate or herbal medicines;
(g) co-operate in the development of specialised health training, health research, reproductive health, the pharmaceutical products and preventive medicine;
(h) promote the development of good nutritional standards and the popularisation of indigenous foods; and
(i) develop a common approach through the education of the general public and their law enforcement agencies for the control and eradication of the trafficking and consumption of illicit or banned drugs.

ARTICLE 119
Culture and Sports

The Partner States shall promote close co-operation amongst themselves in culture and sports, with respect to:
(a) the promotion and enhancement of diverse sports activities;
(b) the development of mass media programmes on matters that will promote the development of culture and sports within the Community;
(c) the promotion of cultural activities, including the fine arts, literature, music, the performing arts and other artistic creations, and the conservation, safeguarding and development of the cultural heritage of the Partner States including, historical materials and antiquities;
(d) the development and promotion of indigenous languages especially Kiswahili as a *lingua franca*;
(e) the regulation of cross border trade in ethnographic materials, licensing of antique dealers and adoption of a common approach and co-operation in tackling the illicit cross border trade in cultural property;
(f) acceding to and ratification of international conventions that directly bear upon culture such as:
  (i) the Hague Convention for the Protection of Cultural Property in the Event of Armed Conflict; and
  (ii) the UNESCO Convention on the Means of Prohibition and Preventing the Illicit Import, Export and Transfer of Ownership of Cultural Property;

(g) harmonising their policies for the conservation of their national antiquities and museums and the prevention of illegal trade in cultural property; and
(h) any other activities aimed at promoting an East African identity.

ARTICLE 120
Social Welfare

The Partner States undertake to closely co-operate amongst themselves in the field of social welfare with respect to:
(a) employment, poverty alleviation programmes and working conditions;
(b) vocational training and the eradication of adult illiteracy in the Community; and
(c) the development and adoption of a common approach towards the disadvantaged and marginalised groups, including children, the youth, the elderly and persons with disabilities through rehabilitation and provision of, among others, foster homes, health care education and training.

CHAPTER TWENTY TWO

ENHANCING THE ROLE OF WOMEN IN SOCIO-ECONOMIC DEVELOPMENT

ARTICLE 121
The Role of Women in Socio-economic Development

The Partner States recognise that women make a significant contribution towards the process of socio-economic transformation and sustainable growth and that it is impossible to implement effective programmes for the economic and social development of the Partner States without the full participation of women. To this end, the Partner States shall through appropriate legislative and other measures:
(a) promote the empowerment and effective integration and participation of women at all levels of socio-economic development especially in decision-making;
(b) abolish legislation and discourage customs that are discriminatory against women;

(c) promote effective education awareness programmes aimed at changing negative attitudes towards women;

(d) create or adopt technologies which will ensure the stability of employment and professional progress for women workers; and

(e) take such other measures that shall eliminate prejudices against women and promote the equality of the female gender with that of the male gender in every respect.

ARTICLE 122
The Role of Women in Business

Having recognised the importance of women as a vital economic link between agriculture, industry and trade, the Partner States undertake to:

(a) increase the participation of women in business at the policy formulation and implementation levels;

(b) promote special programmes for women in small, medium and large scale enterprises;

(c) eliminate all laws, regulations and practises that hinder women's access to financial assistance including credit;

(d) initiate changes in educational and training strategies to enable women to improve their technical and industrial employment levels through the acquisition of transferable skills offered by various forms of vocational and on-the-job training schemes; and

(e) recognise and support the national and regional associations of women in business established to promote the effective participation of women in the trade and development activities of the Community.

CHAPTER TWENTY THREE

CO-OPERATION IN POLITICAL MATTERS

ARTICLE 123
Political Affairs

1. In order to promote the achievement of the objectives of the Community as set out in Article 5 of this Treaty particularly with respect to the eventual establishment of a Political Federation of the Partner States, the Partner States shall establish common foreign and security policies.

2. For purposes of paragraph 1 of this Article, the Community and its Partner States shall define and implement common foreign and security policies.
3. The objectives of the common foreign and security policies shall be to:
   (a) safeguard the common values, fundamental interests and independence of the Community;
   (b) strengthen the security of the Community and its Partner States in all ways;
   (c) develop and consolidate democracy and the rule of law and respect for human rights and fundamental freedoms;
   (d) preserve peace and strengthen international security among the Partner States and within the Community;
   (e) promote co-operation at international fora; and
   (f) enhance the eventual establishment of a Political Federation of the Partner States.
4. The Community shall pursue the objectives set out in paragraph 3 of this Article by:
   (a) establishing systematic co-operation between the Partner States on any matter of foreign or security policies of general interest within the Community in order to define a common position to be applied by the Partner States;
   (b) the co-ordination of the actions of the Partner States and the upholding by them of such co-ordinated actions in international organisations and at international conferences;
   (c) the unreserved support of the Partner States of the Community's foreign and security policies and the avoidance by the Partner States of any action on their part which is contrary to the interests of the Community or is likely to impair the effectiveness of the Community as a cohesive force in international relations;
   (d) peaceful resolution of disputes and conflicts between and within the Partner States;
   (e) the co-ordination of the defence policies of the Partner States; and
   (f) the promotion of co-operation among the National Assemblies of the Partner States and also with the Assembly.
5. The Council shall determine when the provisions of paragraphs 2, 3 and 4 of this Article shall become operative and shall prescribe in detail how the provisions of this Article shall be implemented.
6. The Summit shall initiate the process towards the establishment of a Political Federation of the Partner States by directing the Council to undertake the process.
7. For purposes of paragraph 6 of this Article, the Summit may order a study to be first undertaken by the Council.

ARTICLE 124
Regional Peace and Security

1. The Partner States agree that peace and security are pre-requisites to social and economic development within the Community and vital to the achievement of the objectives of the Community. In this regard, the Partner States agree to foster and maintain an atmosphere that is conducive to peace and security through co-operation and consultations on issues pertaining to peace and security of the Partner States with a view to prevention, better management and resolution of disputes and conflicts between them.
2. The Partner States undertake to promote and maintain good neighbourliness as a basis for promoting peace and security within the Community.
3. The Partner States shall evolve and establish regional disaster management mechanisms which shall harmonise training operations, technical co-operation and support in this area.
4. The Partner States undertake to establish common mechanisms for the management of refugees.
5. The Partner States agree to enhance co-operation in the handling of cross border crime, provision of mutual assistance in criminal matters including the arrest and repatriation of fugitive offenders and the exchange of information on national mechanisms for combating criminal activities. To this end the Partner States undertake to adopt the following measures for maintaining and promoting security in their territories to:
   (a) enhance the exchange of criminal intelligence and other security information between the Partner States' central criminal intelligence information centres;
   (b) enhance joint operations such as hot pursuit of criminals and joint patrols to promote border security;
   (c) establish common communication facilities for border security;
   (d) adopt the United Nations model law on mutual assistance on criminal matters;
   (e) conclude a Protocol on Combating Illicit Drug Trafficking;
   (f) enhance the exchange of visits by security authorities;
   (g) exchange training programmes for security personnel; and
   (h) establish common mechanisms for the management of refugees.
6. The Partner States undertake to co-operate in reviewing the region's security particularly on the threat of terrorism and formulate security measures to combat terrorism.

ARTICLE 125
Defence

1. In order to promote the achievement of the objectives of the Community as set out in Article 5 of this Treaty particularly with respect to the promotion of peace, security and stability within, and good neighbourliness among the Partner States, and in accordance with Article 124 of this Treaty, the Partner States agree to closely co-operate in defence affairs.

2. For purposes of paragraph 1 of this Article, the Partner States agree to establish a framework for co-operation.

CHAPTER TWENTY FOUR

LEGAL AND JUDICIAL AFFAIRS

ARTICLE 126
Scope of Co-operation

1. In order to promote the achievement of the objectives of the Community as set out in Article 5 of this Treaty, the Partner States shall take steps to harmonise their legal training and certification; and shall encourage the standardisation of the judgements of courts within the Community.

2. For purposes of paragraph 1 of this Article, the Partner States shall through their appropriate national institutions take all necessary steps to:

   (a) establish a common syllabus for the training of lawyers and a common standard to be attained in examinations in order to qualify and to be licensed to practice as an advocate in their respective superior courts;

   (b) harmonise all their national laws appertaining to the Community; and

   (c) revive the publication of the East African Law Reports or publish similar law reports and such law journals as will promote the exchange of legal and judicial knowledge and enhance the approximation and harmonisation of legal learning and the standardisation of judgements of courts within the Community.

3. For purposes of paragraph 1 of this Article, the Partner States may take such other additional steps as the Council may determine.

CHAPTER TWENTY FIVE

THE PRIVATE SECTOR AND THE CIVIL SOCIETY

ARTICLE 127
Creation of an Enabling Environment for the Private Sector and the Civil Society

1. The Partner States agree to provide an enabling environment for the private sector and the civil society to take full advantage of the Community. To this end, the Partner States undertake to formulate a strategy for the development of the private sector and to:
    (a) promote a continuous dialogue with the private sector and civil society at the national level and at that of the Community to help create an improved business environment for the implementation of agreed decisions in all economic sectors; and
    (b) provide opportunities for entrepreneurs to participate actively in improving the policies and activities of the institutions of the Community that affect them so as to increase their confidence in policy reforms and raise the productivity and lower the costs of the entrepreneurs.

2. For purposes of paragraph 1 of this Article, the Partner States undertake to:
    (a) improve the business environment through the promotion of conducive investment codes, the protection of property rights and other rights and the proper regulation of the private sector;
    (b) stimulate market development through infrastructural linkages and the removal of barriers and constraints to market development and production;
    (c) regularly provide up-to-date commercial intelligence to speed up market response through co-operation among the chambers of commerce and industry and other similar organisations of the Partner States;
    (d) facilitate and support the exchange of experience and the pooling of resources through, *inter alia*, cross-border investments;
    (e) strengthen the role of their national business organisations or associations in the formulation of their economic policies; and
    (f) collaborate with their national chambers of commerce and industry to establish lending institutions that shall primarily cater for the private sector especially the small-scale entrepreneurs who find it difficult to obtain credit from commercial banks and financing institutions.

3. The Partner States agree to promote enabling environment for the participation of civil society in the development activities within the Community.
4. The Secretary General shall provide the forum for consultations between the private sector, civil society organisations, other interest groups and appropriate institutions of the Community.

ARTICLE 128
Strengthening the Private Sector

1. The Partner States shall endeavour to adopt programmes that would strengthen and promote the role of the private sector as an effective force for the development of their respective economies.
2. For purposes of paragraph 1 of this Article, the Partner States undertake to:
   (a) encourage the efficient use of scarce resources and to promote the development of private sector organisations which are engaged in all types of economic activity, such as, the chambers of commerce and industry, confederations and associations of industry, agriculture, manufacturers, farmers, traders, and service providers and professional groups;
   (b) encourage and sponsor practical and resourceful methods of income generation in the private sector; and
   (c) establish a quality information system which will allow collection, harmonised processing and timely dissemination of data and information.
3. For purposes of paragraph 1 of this Article, the Partner States may take such other additional steps as the Council may determine.

ARTICLE 129
Co-operation among Business Organisations and Professional Bodies

1. The Partner States undertake to co-operate in promoting common measures to ensure the strengthening of linkages among their business organisations, employees' and employers' organisations and professional bodies. To this end, the Partner States agree to:
   (a) support joint activities which will promote trade and investment among the Partner States;
   (b) recognise and contribute to the efficient operation of federations of business organisations, professional and commercial interest groups and similar associations within the Community; and

(c) encourage and promote the taking of useful decisions by the Council and other relevant institutions of the Community in areas affecting the private sector, and to monitor the implementation of such decisions.

2. The Council shall establish modalities that would enable the business organisations or associations, professional bodies and the civil society in the Partner States to contribute effectively to the development of the Community.

3. The Council shall formulate a business and business related dispute settlement mechanism.

CHAPTER TWENTY SIX

RELATIONS WITH OTHER REGIONAL AND INTERNATIONAL ORGANISATIONS AND DEVELOPMENT PARTNERS

ARTICLE 130
International Organisations and Development Partners

1. The Partner States shall honour their commitments in respect of other multinational and international organisations of which they are members.

2. The Partner States reiterate their desire for a wider unity of Africa and regard the Community as a step towards the achievement of the objectives of the Treaty Establishing the African Economic Community.

3. With a view to contributing towards the achievement of the objectives of the Community, the Community shall foster co-operative arrangements with other regional and international organisations whose activities have a bearing on the objectives of the Community.

4. The Partner States shall accord special importance to co-operation with the Organisation of African Unity, United Nations Organisation and its agencies, and other international organisations, bilateral and multi-lateral development partners interested in the objectives of the Community.

CHAPTER TWENTY SEVEN

CO-OPERATION IN OTHER FIELDS

ARTICLE 131
Other Fields

1. Subject to the provisions of this Treaty, the Partner States undertake to consult with one another through the appropriate institutions of the

Community for the purpose of harmonising their respective policies in such other fields as they may, from time to time, consider necessary or desirable for the efficient and harmonious functioning and development of the Community and the implementation of the provisions of this Treaty.

2. For purposes of paragraph 1 of this Article, the Partner States may take in common such other steps as are calculated to further the objectives of the Community and the implementation of the provisions of this Treaty.

CHAPTER TWENTY EIGHT

FINANCIAL PROVISIONS

ARTICLE 132
Budget

1. There shall be a budget for the organs and institutions of the Community, save for the self accounting institutions.
2. Subject to this Treaty, a budget for the Community for each financial year shall be prepared by the Secretary General for consideration by the Council and approval by the Assembly.
3. All expenditures of the Community in respect of each financial year shall be considered and approved by the Council and shall be met from the budget.
4. The budget of the Community shall be funded by equal contributions by the Partner States and receipts from regional and international donations and any other sources as may be determined by the Council.
5. The resources of the Community shall be utilised to finance activities of the Community as shall be determined by the Assembly on the recommendation of the Council.
6. The budget and accounts of the Community shall be kept and maintained in United States dollars.
7. The financial year of the Community shall run from 1st July to 30th June.

ARTICLE 133
Other Resources

Other resources of the Community shall include such extra budgetary resources as:

(a) grants, donations, funds for projects and programmes and technical assistance; and
(b) income earned from activities undertaken by the Community.

ARTICLE 134
Audit of Accounts

1. There shall be an Audit Commission made up of the Auditors General of the Partner States whose functions will be to audit the accounts of the Community.
2. It shall be the duty of the Audit Commission to verify that any contributions received or revenue collected by the Community have been allocated and distributed in accordance with this Treaty and to include a certificate to that effect in its report.
3. The Audit Commission shall submit its reports under paragraph 2 of this Article to the Council which shall cause the same to be laid before the Assembly within six months of receipt for debate and for such other consultations and action as the Assembly may deem necessary.
4. In the performance of its functions under this Article, the Audit Commission shall not be subject to the direction or control of any person or authority.

ARTICLE 135
Financial Rules and Regulations

1. The Council shall make financial rules and regulations of the Community.
2. Self-accounting institutions of the Community shall make their own financial rules and regulations in line with the provisions of their respective enabling legislation.

CHAPTER TWENTY NINE

GENERAL, TRANSITIONAL AND FINAL PROVISIONS

ARTICLE 136
Headquarters and Other Offices of the Community

1. The headquarters of the Community shall be in Arusha in the United Republic of Tanzania.

2. There may be established such offices of the Community in the Partner States and elsewhere as the Council may determine.

ARTICLE 137
Official Language

1. The official language of the Community shall be English.
2. Kiswahili shall be developed as a *lingua franca* of the Community.

ARTICLE 138
Status, Privileges and Immunities

1. The Community shall enjoy international legal personality.
2. The Secretary General shall conclude with the Governments of the Partner States in whose territory the headquarters or offices of the Community shall be situated, agreements relating to the privileges and immunities to be recognised and granted in connection with the Community.
3. Each of the Partner States undertakes to accord to the Community and its officers the privileges and immunities accorded to similar international organisations in its territory.

ARTICLE 139
Dissolution of the Permanent Tripartite Commission and its Secretariat

Upon the coming into force of this Treaty, hereinafter referred to as "the appointed day", the Tripartite Commission and the Secretariat of the Tripartite Commission respectively established on the 30th day of November, 1993, by the Agreement for the Establishment of a Permanent Tripartite Commission for Co-operation Between the Republic of Uganda, the Republic of Kenya and the United Republic of Tanzania, and on the 26th day of November, 1994, by the Protocol on the Establishment of the Secretariat of the Permanent Tripartite Commission for Co-operation Between the Republic of Uganda, the Republic of Kenya and the United Republic of Tanzania, shall both cease to exist.

ARTICLE 140
Transitional Provisions

1. On the appointed day, the Executive Secretary, the Deputy Executive Secretaries, the Legal Counsel and other staff of the Secretariat of the Tripartite Commission shall assume the offices of the Secretary General, Deputy Secretaries General, Counsel to the Community and other staff of the Community respectively and shall be deemed to have been appointed thereto under the provisions of Articles 67, 68, 69 and 70 of this Treaty respectively:

> Provided that the Executive Secretary and the Deputy Executive Secretaries shall serve for the remaining period of their current contractual terms.

2. Until the Council adopts its procedure, the procedure that applies to the Tripartite Commission shall apply to the Council.
3. Until the Community adopts its own staff rules and regulations and terms and conditions of service and financial rules and regulations, those of the Secretariat of the Tripartite Commission shall apply.
4. Until such time as the Council determines that the Court is fully operational, a Judge appointed under Article 24 of this Treaty shall serve on an *ad hoc* basis. Notwithstanding the provisions of paragraph 5 of Article 25 of this Treaty, the salary and other terms and conditions of service of a Judge serving on an *ad hoc* basis shall be determined by the Summit on the recommendation of the Council.
5. Until the Assembly is elected at a time to be determined by the Summit and first meets, the functions of the Assembly in respect of the approval of the budget of the Community, consideration of annual reports on the activities of the Community and annual audit reports of the Audit Commission, shall be performed by the Council.
6. Until the adoption of Protocols referred to in Article 151(1), the Council may make regulations, issue directives, take decisions, make recommendations and give opinions in accordance with the provisions of this Treaty.
7. Pending the conclusion of a Protocol under paragraph 1 of Article 75 of this Treaty, the Partner States agree to maintain the rules of origin currently applicable for the purpose of the preferential treatment of goods traded among them and originating in the Partner States.

ARTICLE 141
Transfer of Assets and Liabilities

1. On the appointed day there shall be transferred to and vested in the Community by virtue of this Article and without further assurance, all the assets and liabilities of the Secretariat of the Tripartite Commission and from that day, the Community shall, in respect of the assets and liabilities so transferred and vested in it, have all the rights, and be subject to all the liabilities, which the Secretariat of the Tripartite Commission had, or is subject to, immediately before that day.

2. Every contract made by or on behalf of the Secretariat of the Tripartite Commission in writing and whether or not of such a nature that rights and liabilities thereunder can be assigned by the Secretariat of the Tripartite Commission, shall have effect as if made by or, on behalf of the Community and as if references therein to the Secretariat of the Tripartite Commission or any officer or authority thereof, were references to the Community and to the corresponding officer or authority thereof.

3. Any proceedings by or against the Secretariat of the Tripartite Commission pending on the appointed day, shall be continued by or against the Community.

4. Reference to the Secretariat of the Tripartite Commission, in any law or document shall on and after the appointed day, be construed as references to the Community.

ARTICLE 142
Saving Provisions

1. Subject to the provisions of this Treaty, the operation of the following tripartite agreements after the coming into force of this Treaty shall not be affected by such coming into force, but the agreements shall be construed with such modifications, adaptations, qualifications and exceptions as may be necessary to bring them into conformity with the Treaty:

   (a) Agreement for the Establishment of The Permanent Tripartite Commission for Co-operation Between the Republic of Uganda, the Republic of Kenya and the United Republic of Tanzania;

   (b) Protocol on the Establishment of a Secretariat of the Permanent Tripartite Commission for Co-operation Between the Republic of Uganda, the Republic of Kenya and the United Republic of Tanzania;

   (c) Headquarters Agreement between the Secretariat of the Commission for East African Co-operation and the Government of the United Republic of Tanzania;

(d) Tripartite Agreement for the Avoidance of Double Taxation and the Prevention of Fiscal Evasion with respect to Taxes on Income;
(e) Memorandum of Understanding on Co-operation in Defence;
(f) Tripartite Agreement on Road Transport;
(g) Tripartite Agreement on Inland Waterways Transport;
(h) Memorandum of Understanding on Foreign Policy Co-ordination; and
(i) Memorandum of Understanding between the Republic of Uganda and the Republic of Kenya and the United Republic of Tanzania for Co-operation on Environment Management.

2. The dissolution of the Tripartite Commission in terms of Article 139 of this Treaty shall not affect the decisions of the Tripartite Commission but such decisions shall be construed and implemented with such modifications, adaptations, qualifications and exceptions as may be necessary to bring them into conformity with this Treaty.

ARTICLE 143
Sanctions

A Partner State which defaults in meeting its financial and other obligations under this Treaty shall be subject to such action as the Summit may on the recommendation of the Council, determine.

ARTICLE 144
Duration of the Treaty

This Treaty shall have perpetual duration.

ARTICLE 145
Withdrawal of a Member

1. A Partner State may withdraw from the Community provided:
   (a) the National Assembly of the Partner State so resolves by resolution supported by not less than two-thirds majority of all the members entitled to vote; and
   (b) the Partner State gives to the Secretary General twelve month's written notice of its intention to withdraw, unless that State cancels the notice before the expiry of the twelve months.

2. A Partner State wishing to withdraw from the Community shall, during the period of twelve months referred to in paragraph 1 of this Article, continue to be liable to discharge her obligations under the Treaty.
3. Notwithstanding the effective withdrawal from membership by such State, upon expiry of the notice that State shall remain liable to discharge all subsisting obligations and long term commitments incurred during membership.

ARTICLE 146
Suspension of a Member

1. The Summit may suspend a Partner State from taking part in the activities of the Community if that State fails to observe and fulfil the fundamental principles and objectives of the Treaty including failure to meet financial commitments to the Community within a period of eighteen (18) months.
2. A Partner State suspended, in accordance with paragraph 1 of this Article, shall cease to enjoy the benefits provided for under this Treaty but shall continue to be bound by membership obligations until the suspension is lifted.

ARTICLE 147
Expulsion of a Member

1. The Summit may expel a Partner State from the Community for gross and persistent violation of the principles and objectives of this Treaty after giving such Partner State twelve months' written notice.
2. Upon the expiration of the period specified in paragraph 1 of this Article, the Partner State concerned shall cease to be a member of the Community unless the notice is cancelled.
3. During the period referred to in paragraphs 1 and 2 of this Article the Partner State concerned shall continue to comply with the provisions of this Treaty and be liable to discharge all subsisting obligations and long-term commitments incurred during membership.

ARTICLE 148
Exceptions to the Rule of Consensus

Notwithstanding the provisions of paragraph 3 of Article 12 of this Treaty, the views of the Partner State being considered for suspension or expulsion shall not count, for the purposes of reaching a decision under the provisions of Articles 146 and 147 of this Treaty.

ARTICLE 149
Rights over Property and Assets of the Community Upon Cessation of Membership

1. Where a Partner State withdraws or is expelled in accordance with Articles 145 and 147 respectively of this Treaty the property of the Community in that Partner State's territory shall remain vested in the Community.
2. A State that has ceased to be a Partner State of the Community shall have no claim to or any rights over any property and assets of the Community.
3. The Community shall continue with its remaining membership notwithstanding withdrawal or expulsion of any Partner State.

ARTICLE 150
Amendment of the Treaty

1. This Treaty may be amended at any time by agreement of all the Partner States.
2. Any Partner State or the Council may submit proposals for the amendment of this Treaty.
3. Any proposals for the amendment of this Treaty shall be submitted to the Secretary General in writing who shall, within thirty days (30) of its receipt, communicate the proposed amendment to the Partner States.
4. The Partner States which wish to comment on the proposals shall do so within ninety days (90) from the date of the dispatch of the proposal by the Secretary General.
5. After the expiration of the period prescribed under paragraph 4 of this Article, the Secretary General shall submit the proposals and any comments thereon received from the Partner States to the Summit through the Council.
6. Any amendment to this Treaty shall be adopted by the Summit and shall enter into force when ratified by all the Partner States.

ARTICLE 151
Annexes and Protocols to the Treaty

1. The Partner States shall conclude such Protocols as may be necessary in each area of co-operation which shall spell out the objectives and scope of, and institutional mechanisms for co-operation and integration.
2. Each Protocol shall be approved by the Summit on the recommendation of the Council.
3. Each Protocol shall be subject to signature and ratification by the parties hereto.
4. The Annexes and Protocols to this Treaty shall form an integral part of this Treaty.

ARTICLE 152
Entry into Force

This Treaty shall enter into force upon ratification and deposit of instruments of ratification with the Secretary General by all Partner States.

ARTICLE 153
Depository and Registration

1. This Treaty and all instruments of ratification shall be deposited with the Secretary General who shall transmit certified true copies thereof to all the Partner States.
2. The Secretary General shall register this Treaty with the Organisation of African Unity, the United Nations, and such other organisations as the Council may determine.

DONE at Arusha, Tanzania, on the 30th day of November, in the year One Thousand Nine Hundred and Ninety-Nine.

IN FAITH WHEREOF the undersigned have appended their signatures hereto:

for the Republic of Uganda	for the Republic of Kenya	for the United Republic of Tanzania
....		
....		
....		
YOWERI KAGUTA MUSEVENI	DANIEL TOROITICH ARAP MOI	BENJAMIN WILLIAM MKAPA
PRESIDENT	PRESIDENT	PRESIDENT

ANALYTICAL INDEX

A
Abuja Agreement 326, 327, 329
Abuja Treaty 212, 380, 391, 398, 411, 412, 415, 416
Abuse 227, 228, 285, 442
Acordos de Paz 285, 286, 289, 291, 293-295
Act(s)
  Continuing 220, 222, 223
  Composite 220, 222
  Complex 220, 222
  Completed 222, 223
African
– and Malagasy Organization of Economic Cooperation (OAMCE) 4
– and Mauritian Common Organization (OCAM) 186
– Caribbean and Pacific Group (ACP) 49, 168-172, 174, 176, 177, 179, 180-182
– Charter for the Rights and Welfare of Children 387, 388, 405, 407
– Charter on Human and Peoples' Rights 67, 131, 132, 136-137, 139, 140, 155, 157, 158, 164, 168, 173, 187, 194, 197, 208-214, 333, 378, 383, 389, 396, 401, 408
– Civil Aviation Commission (AFCAC) 472
– Common Market 187
– Commission on Human and Peoples' Rights 173, 188, 208, 209, 211, 375, 382, 393, 401
– constitutionalism 243-244
  See also *Constitution(s)*

(African)
– Court of Human and Peoples' Rights 188, 193, 194, 208, 211, 213, 378, 396
– Court of Justice 188, 212, 415, 416, 424, 425, 433, 435, 440
– dispute resolution institutions 95
– Economic Community (AEC) 4, 186, 187, 206, 211, 380, 398, 411, 412, 423, 499
  Treaty establishing the – (1991) 4, 187, 213, 390, 411, 412, 428, 499
– economic cooperation 4
– group in New York 383, 402
– history 114-116
– integration efforts 4
– personality 376, 394
Aggression 103, 175, 182
Agreement between the Government of the Netherlands and the Government of the United Kingdom concerning a Scottish trial in the Netherlands 261
  See also Aut dedere aut judicare, *Lockerbie, Scottish Court in the Netherlands*
Algeria 208, 266
Algiers
– Declaration 375, 393
– summit 378, 397
Amnesty International 205
Ancestral values 377, 395
Anglophone countries 34, 37, 38
Angola 3, 7, 17, 26, 27, 29, 199, 202, 203, 205, 205, 283-299

Annexation 110
Anti-personnel mines 384, 402, 403
　See also *Convention on the Prohibition of the Use, Stockpiling, Production and Transfer of Anti-Personnel Mines and on their Destruction*
Apartheid 8, 11, 27, 28, 131, 140, 169, 171
Application or interpretation 272
Arbitrary partition of Africa 106-109
Arbitration 7, 50, 227, 444
– Commission of the International Conference for Peace in Yugoslavia 155, 163
Arms embargo 354, 356, 358
ASEAN 47
Aut dedere aut judicare 256
Authoritarianism 376, 394
Autonomy 161, 165

B
Bad faith 231
Bangui agreement 302, 304, 306
Beira corridor 7, 10
Benin 33, 34, 53, 196, 244, 266
Berlin
– Conference (1884-1885) 89, 100-105, 112, 113
– General Act 101, 103, 104, 112
– proceedings 103
Binding instrument 219
Boston tea party 242
Botswana 3, 7, 12, 17, 27, 199, 203, 245, 266
Burkina Faso 33, 34, 53, 163, 196, 244, 266
Burundi 128, 266

C
Cameroon 105, 163, 167, 266
Cape Verde 34, 53, 196
Capitalist model 12
Caprive Strip 7
Casablanca group (1961) 4
Central African Republic 168, 170, 300-309
Centralism (Political –) 147
Centralized systems 128
Charter of Economic Rights and Duties of States 174
Chemical
– destruction 267
– production facilities 266
– weapons 265
　See also *Convention on the Prohibition of the Development, Production, Stockpiling and Use of Chemical Weapons and on their Destruction (1993), Organization for the Prohibition of Chemical Weapons, Protocol for the Prohibition of the Use in War of Asphyxiating, Poisonous or Other Gases, and of Bacterio-logical methods of Warfare (1925), Toxic chemicals*
Child
– Combatants 348, 352
– Exploitation 378, 396
– Soldiers 344, 349, 378, 387, 396, 405
– Victims 335, 348
Charter of the United Nations 120, 138, 142, 154, 155, 159, 169, 171, 174, 175, 177, 220, 225, 226, 257, 269, 270, 315, 354, 377, 396
(Charter of the United Nations) Chapter VII 258, 295, 351

See also *General Assembly of the United Nations, Secretary General of the United Nations, Security Council of the United Nations, United Nations*
Civic
– society 302
– law 221
Client states 99, 110
Coercion 224
Colonial
– administration 86
– domination 128
– legacy 88
– policies 86, 108
  Indirect rule system 107
  Assimilation 107
– powers 87, 105, 109, 113, 114
– project 87, 88, 95, 101, 113
– protectorates 89
– question 88, 89
Colonialism 32, 85-87, 89-118, 186, 202, 377, 395
  Philosophy of – 112
  See also *Terra nullius*
Colonizing powers 87, 94, 96, 99, 101, 107, 108, 111-113
Common
– heritage of mankind 175
– market 5, 6, 14, 35, 48, 52, 63-65, 70, 71, 196, 423, 424, 428, 430, 461, 462
  See also *Economic community, Integration*
– Market for Eastern and Southern Africa (COMESA) 48, 62, 186, 191, 212, 213
  Authority 206
(Common)
  Court of Justice 206-209
  - Jurisdiction 206
  - Interim orders 206
  Treaty 207
Commonwealth 182, 203, 441, 447
Community of Portuguese-speaking countries (CPLP) 329, 332
Complicity 223
– of State in terrorist acts 257
Confederation 99
Conference of African Ministers of Education (COMEDAF I) 375, 385-386, 393, 403-404
Confidence-building 332, 335, 350, 352, 363, 369, 372
Conflict(s)
  Internal 120, 123, 147
– resolution 188
  Ethnic 120, 122, 123, 128, 162, 163
Congo
– (Brazzaville) 128
– (Democratic Republic of the –) 3, 11, 26, 29, 163, 199, 213, 310-321
Consensus 80, 435, 437, 506
Consent 95, 103, 224, 225, 261
Constitution(s) (African –) 124, 125, 129, 132, 151, 154, 160-162
Benin 130, 134, 148, 151, 160
Burkina Faso 129, 134, 143, 148, 160
Burundi 143, 146, 148
Cameroon 127, 130, 134, 143, 146, 148, 151, 152, 160
Cape Verde 129
Central African Republic 134, 160
Chad 129, 130, 143

(Constitution(s) (African –))
  Cote d'Ivoire 127, 129, 140, 143, 147, 151, 160
  Ethiopia 130, 134, 135, 148, 152, 246
  Gabon 129, 134, 140, 143, 146
  Ghana 246
  Kenya 192, 246
  Madagascar 134, 147, 148, 151
  Mali 134, 143, 147, 151, 160
  Mauritania 134, 143
  Mauritius 134
  Namibia 246
  Nigeria 129, 143, 147, 160
  Republic of Congo 129, 130
  Republic of Guinea 140, 143, 146, 151
  Rwanda 153
  Senegal 129, 130, 134, 143, 151, 160
  South Africa 14, 135, 146, 148, 152, 246
  Tanzania 191, 251
  Togo 143, 147, 151, 160
  Uganda 191, 194, 249-251
  Zambia 246
  See also *African constitutionalism*
Constitutional
– control 334
– Court 250
– law 124, 125
Convention on
– International Civil Aviation 472
– Succession of States in respect of Treaties 231
– the Elimination of all forms of Discrimination Against Women (1979) 131, 245
– the Elimination of all forms of Racial Discrimination (1966) 131

(Convention on)
– the Prevention and Punishment of the Crime of Genocide (1948) 131, 274, 315
– the Prohibition of the Development, Production and Stockpiling of Bacteriological (Biological) and Toxin Weapons and on their Destruction (1972) 266
– the Prohibition of the Development, Production, Stockpiling and Use of Chemical Weapons and on their Destruction (1993) 265-282
  - Application or interpretation 269
  Confidentiality Annex 282
  Object and purpose 267
  Verification 267
  - Verification Annex 268, 280, 281
  - See also *Chemical weapons, Organization for the Prohibition of Chemical Weapons, Toxic chemicals*
– the Prohibition of the Use, Stockpiling, Production and Transfer of Anti-Personnel Mines and on their Destruction 375, 384, 393, 402-403
  See also *Anti-personnel mines*
– the Rights of the Child 245, 387, 405, 407
– the Safety of United Nations and Associated Personnel (1994) 308, 318
– the Suppression and Punishment of the crime of Apartheid (1973) 131
Corporal punishment 203

Corruption 379, 398
  Transnational aspects 236
Cote d'Ivoire 33, 34, 53, 163, 196, 266, 297
Cotonou agreement 198
Council of Europe 186
Countermeasures 219, 224, 226, 227, 229
– Collective 227
Court of
– Appeal of East Africa 186, 188, 189-194
  Annual reports 192
  Case-law 193-194
  Jurisdiction 191, 192
– Justice of the European Community 209
Customs and Economic Union of Central Africa (UOEAC) 186
Customs
– duties 43
– union 14, 42-46, 48, 49, 52, 54-58, 63, 65, 70, 71, 421, 423, 428, 430, 460 -2

D
Death penalty 203
Debt 12, 38, 380, 398, 413, 417
Decisions of
– domestic courts 202-203, 210, 248
– the International Court of Justice
  Contentious cases
  - *Application of the Convention on the Prevention and Punishment of the Crime of Genocide* (Bosnia and Herzegovina v. Yugoslavia) 272, 274

(Decisions of
– the International Court of Justice
  Contentious cases)
  - *Barcelona Traction, Light and Power Company* (Belgium v. Spain) 175
  - *Border and Transborder Armed Actions* (Nicaragua v. Honduras) 259
  - *East Timor* (Portugal v. Australia) 155, 272
  - *Gabcikovo Nagymaros Project* (Hungary/Slovakia) 223, 225, 227, 228
  - *Military and Paramilitary Activities in and against Nicaragua* (Nicaragua v. USA) 141, 175
  - *Northern Cameroons* (Cameroon v. U.K.) 272 -Oil Platforms (Iran v. USA)
  - Separate opinion of Judge Rigaux 272, 273
  - *Questions of Interpretation and Application of the 1971 Montreal Convention arising from the Aerial Incident at Lockerbie* (Libya v. U.K.) 259
  - *Questions of Interpretation and Application of the 1971 Montreal Convention arising from the Aerial Incident at Lockerbie* (Libya v. U.S.A.) 259
  - *South West Africa* (Ethiopia v South Africa) (Liberia v. South Africa) (joint cases) 175, 272

(Decisions of
- the International Court of
  Justice
  Contentious cases)
  - *Territorial Dispute*
    (Libya/Chad) Separate opinion of Judge Ajibola 106-107
  - *United States Diplomatic
    and Consular Staff in Tehran*
    (USA v. Iran) 175
- the International Court of
  Justice
  Advisory cases
  - *Applicability of the
    Obligation to Arbitrate under
    Section 21 of the UN
    Headquarters Agreement of
    26 June 1947* 272
  - *Interpretation of Peace
    Treaties* 272, 273
  - *Legal Consequences for
    States of the Continued presence of South Africa in
    Namibia (South West Africa)
    notwithstanding Security
    Council Resolution 276
    (1970)* 155
  - *Western Sahara* 98, 101, 102,
    107, 117, 155, 159
    Separate opinion of Judge
    Ammoun 101
  Separate opinion of Judge
  Dillard 110
  - See also *International Court
    of Justice*
- the Permanent Court of
  International Justice
  - *Greco-Bulgarian
    "Communities"* 120
  - Mavrommatis *Palestine
    Concessions* 271

Declaration on
- the moratorium on the import,
  export and manufacture of light
  weapons (1998) 386, 405
  See also *Small arms and light
  weapons*
- the Rights of Persons
  Belonging to National or
  Ethnic, Religious and
  Linguistic Minorities (1992)
  120, 131, 136, 139, 160
Decolonization 156, 377, 395
Democracy
  Consensual 150
  Liberal 129, 149
  Majority 149, 150, 162
  Modern 159
  Notion 149, 150
Denial of justice 222
Diplomatic protection 175, 217,
  236
Disarmament 29, 267, 312, 333,
  335, 336, 347-349, 352, 379,
  397
  Chemical – 265
- negotiations 232
  Nuclear – 379, 397
Discrimination 42, 204
  Agreements 51
  Elimination 51
  Prohibition 15, 71
  Racial 128, 129, 131, 132, 140,
  175
  Trade policies 47, 50
  See also *Convention on the
  Elimination of all forms of
  Discrimination Against Women
  (1979), Convention on the
  Elimination of all forms of
  Racial Discrimination (1966)*

Dispute(s) 16, 25, 75, 268, 270, 272-277, 280, 281, 443, 444, 445, 446
  Boundary – 107, 377, 395
  Definition 271-274
  – settlement 227, 229, 268, 271, 278, 280, 431, 494, 495, 499
Distress 228
Domestic
  – affairs 186
  – jurisdiction 14
  – law 245, 248
    Integration into – 245, 246
    Transformation into – 245
    See also *Internal law, Municipal law, National law,*
  – legal system 186, 208, 246
  – market 5
Double taxation 72, 463, 505
Due diligence 228, 234

E
East
  – Africa High Commission 423
  – Africa Law Reports 76, 425, 496
  – African Civil Aviation Academy 427
  – African Common Services Organisation 421
  – African Community 34, 61-81, 186, 190, 421-509
    Act of – 423, 434, 454, 455
    - Agriculture and food security 482-485
    Audit 501, 503
    - Common Market Tribunal of the – 190
    - Co-ordination Committee 77, 426, 435, 438, 458

(East
  – African Community)
    - Council 71, 77, 421, 424, 427, 429, 433-9, 441, 443, 445, 446, 448-51, 453, 455, 456-63, 466, 467, 480, 481, 483, 494, 496, 498, 499, 500, 501, 502, 503, 505, 507, 508
    Defence 430, 494, 496, 505
    - Development of human resources, science and technology 476-81
    - Mediation Agreement (1984) 421, 422
    - Environment and natural resources management 485, 487, 488
    Executive organ 79
    Functions 66, 429,
    - Health, social and cultural activities 490-2
    - Infrastructure and services 468-81
    Integration factors 62
    - Investment and industrial development 425, 462-3, 486, 489, 497
    Legal and judicial affairs 496
    Legal capacity 66, 429, 432
    Legal entity 64
    Legal personality 502
    Legally binding acts 77, 437
    Legislative organ 449
    - Membership 65, 69, 451, 506, 507
    - Monetary and financial cooperation 464-467
    - Objectives 66-69, 76, 77, 80, 422, 423, 424, 429-31, 432, 434, 436, 439, 450, 455,

458, 460, 462, 464, 468, 479, 482, 485, 489, 490, 493, 494, 495, 496, 499, 500, 506, 508
Official language 69, 502
Observer status 66, 429, 435
(East
– African Community)
  - Organs 69, 76, 77, 426, 432, 433, 436, 437, 458
Political matters 493-496
Precedence 69
  - Principle of asymmetry 63, 68, 70, 426, 431, 460
  - Principle of complementarity 63, 68, 426, 432
  - Principle of variable geometry 63, 68, 427, 431
  - Principle of separation of powers 76
  - Principle of subsidiarity 63, 68, 427, 431
Principles 67, 428, 429, 431, 432, 506
  - Private sector and civil society 421, 422, 430
  - Protocols and annexes 80, 508,
  - Regional peace and security 495
Role of women 425, 430, 492-3
Sanctions 69
  - Secretariat 71, 79, 427, 433, 456-60, 461, 462
  - Secretary General 78, 79, 427, 429, 432, 434, 441, 443, 445, 447, 448, 455, 456, 457, 459, 462, 498, 500, 502, 503, 505, 507, 508
  - Sectoral Committees 78, 427, 433, 436, 438, 439

  - Sectoral programmes 78
Standardisation 463, 464, 469
  - Summit 77, 427, 429, 433-37, 441, 442, 445, 447, 448, 450, 456, 457, 458, 494, 503, 505, 506, 507, 508
  - Tourism and wildlife management 489-90
(East
– African Community)
  - Treaty for the Establishment of the – (1999) 421-509
– African Cooperation 61
  - Development Strategy 61, 422
  - Permanent Tripartite Commission for – 61, 62, 80, 422, 502-5
– African Court of Justice 78, 424, 425, 433, 435, 440
  - Advisory opinions 78, 435, 436
  - Determination of the legality of acts 78
Interim orders 446
  - Interpretation and application of the Treaty for the Establishment of the East African Community 78, 440, 442, 444, 446,
Intervention 446
  - Judges 78, 435, 440, 441, 447
Judgment 437, 442, 443, 444, 450
Jurisdiction 78, 444-446
Official language 448
President 425, 426, 440, 441, 442, 445, 447, 448, 454
Registrar 427, 445, 447, 448
  - Rules of the Court 442, 444, 445, 447, 448

– African Customs Union and Common market 63, 65, 423, 424, 428, 430, 461, 462
– African Development Bank 79, 427, 433
– African Legislative Assembly 77, 78-79, 423, 424, 433, 448, 500, 501, 503, 505
(East
– African Legislative Assembly) Functions 449
Membership 448 -451
Quorum 452
Rules of procedure 449, 450, 454
  - Speaker 427, 450, 451-3
  - Voting 452
Economic
– Commission for Africa 30
– community 3, 6, 11, 28, 36
See also *Common market, Integration*
– Community of the Countries of the Great Lakes (CEPGL) 186
– community of West African States (ECOWAS) 31-34, 37, 39, 41, 47, 54, 59, 186, 196, 212, 213, 326, 327, 329, 337, 342, 344-346, 349, 350, 386, 405
  - Authority of Heads of State and Government 40, 53, 196
  Community Parliament 41
  Compensation fund 37
  Cotonou summit 40
  Court of Justice 41, 196-198
  - Council of Ministers 40, 53, 196
  Decisions 40, 59
  - Economic and Social Council 41

- ECOWAS Monitoring Group (ECOMOG) 31, 197, 198, 326, 327, 329-331, 334-337, 342-346, 349, 350, 353
Objectives 31, 39, 40, 197
Region 34
Regional security body 31
Secretariat 40, 196
- Specialised technical commissions 41, 196
(Economic
– community of West African States (ECOWAS))
- Sub-regional organisation 197
– cooperation 5, 24
– crisis 39
– development 3, 8, 12, 14, 19, 24, 31-33, 39, 58, 67, 128, 142, 186
– integration agreement 50, 51
– self-sufficiency 32
ECOWAS treaty (Treaty of the Economic Community of West African States) 31, 34, 35, 37-41, 52, 54-56, 58, 196, 197, 212
Economic union 52, 54
Objectives 32, 35, 37, 38, 52
Protocol on Mutual assistance on Defence 197
Protocol on Non-Aggression 197
Regional economic agreement 58
Revision 39-41
Trade provisions 31, 32
Trade protocols 34, 53
Equality 127, 132, 138-140
Substantive (de facto) 204
Formal (de jure) 204
Equatorial Guinea 168, 170, 183, 266

Eritrea 161, 206, 266, 322-325
Estoppel 233
Ethiopia 161, 246, 266, 322-325
Ethnic
– cleansing 311
– divisions 376, 395
– groups 106, 108
European
– Charter for Regional or Minority Languages (1992) 164
– Coal and Steel Community 48
– Convention for the Protection of Human Rights and Fundamental Freedoms 168, 175, 209, 211
– Court of Human Rights 209
– economic community 18, 24, 33, 167-170, 179, 183, 199
  General legal principles 210
  Law 209
  Treaty establishing the – 45
– Free Trade Area (EFTA) 45
– market 38
– Parliament 168
– Union 5, 14, 18, 26, 30, 37, 49, 167, 171, 174, 180,181, 183, 300, 386, 391, 405, 410
Evidence 255, 263
Exceptio inadimpleti contractus 182, 227
Export 32, 38
  Duties 20
  Taxes 32
  See also *Tariffs*
Extradition 7, 231, 264
  Treaty 256

F
Federalism 147, 150
Force
– majeure 224, 227
  Threat or use of – 226

Foreign
– affairs 109
– investment 5, 12, 19, 22, 33, 59, 72, 80
  Framework Convention
– for the Protection of National Minorities 164
– on climate change 234
Francophone countries 34, 37, 38
Free
– market system 12, 27
– movement of persons and capital 14, 15, 24, 30, 52, 73, 74, 80, 424, 431, 461, 465, 467, 481
– trade 21
  - Area 19, 23, 30, 42-46, 48, 49, 52, 54, 57
  Agreement 37, 55, 56, 58
Frontiers (Artificial –) 107, 127
Fundamental change of circumstances 228

G
Gambia 33, 34, 53, 196, 244, 266
General
– Agreement on Tariffs and Trade (GATT) 32, 41, 43, 45, 46, 49, 50, 56
  - Article XXIV (GATT 1994) 42, 45-51, 54, 56-58
  - Enabling Clause 42, 46-48, 54, 58
  Part IV 47, 48
  Rules 32
  Secretariat 32
  Tokyo Round 46
  Uruguay Round 43, 58
  Waivers 48-49
– Assembly of the United Nations 176, 219, 234, 269, 271, 278, 279

- Resolution 1145 (XII) (14 November 1957) 278
- Resolution 1146 (XII) (14 November 1957) 278
(General
– Assembly of the United Nations)
  - Resolution 1514 (XV) (14 December 1960) "Declaration on the Granting of Independence to Colonial Countries and Peoples" 141, 155, 156, 159
  - Resolution 2625 (XXV) (24 October 1970) «Declaration on Principles of International law Concerning Friendly Relations and Co-operation among States in accordance with the Charter of the
  - United Nations » 142, 155, 159
  - Resolution 3314 (14 December 1974) on the definition of aggression 135
  - Resolution 31/6 (26 October 1976) 131
  - Resolution 47/35 (18 December 1992) 131
Resolution 53/98 235
  - See also *Charter of the United Nations, Secretary General of the United Nations, Security Council of the United Nations, United Nations*
– Convention on the Privileges and Immunities of the United Nations 297
  - principles of law recognized by civilized nations 118

Genocide 153, 163, 175, 222, 274, 339
Ghana 33, 34, 53, 196, 244
Global
– economy 5, 34, 59
– International Convention for the Prevention and Control of Terrorism 380, 398
See also *Complicity, Terrorism, OAU Convention on the Prevention and Combating of Terrorism*
Globalization 3, 5, 379, 389, 397, 408
Good
– faith 233, 266, 312
– offices 270, 280
Guinea 33, 34, 53, 196, 266
Guinea-Bissau 33, 34, 53, 196, 326-333

H
Habeas corpus 191, 194
Hague Convention for the Protection of Cultural Property in the Event of Armed Conflict 491
Harmonization 13, 21, 23-25, 35, 64, 70, 76, 196, 458, 460, 463-77, 484, 487, 489, 491, 492, 495, 496, 498, 500
See also *Integration*
Helsinki Final Act (1975) 159, 168
Hierarchy 124, 131, 220
Human rights 64, 67, 68, 78, 80, 113, 114, 131, 132, 136, 167-184, 187, 191, 196, 197, 201, 204, 212-214, 225, 226, 273, 285, 299, 310, 311, 314, 336, 338, 341, 343, 347, 380, 389,

398, 401, 408, 429, 432, 442, 494,
(Human rights)
Commission on – 315
- Conception of the ACP countries 169
European conception 169
- Individual or collective 378, 396
- International protection 186
- Protection at the sub-regional level 208
- Regional jurisprudence 202, 212
- Sub-regional – instruments 211
- Supra-national protection 209
- See also *African Charter for the Rights and Welfare of Children, African Charter on Human and Peoples' Rights, African Commission on Human and Peoples' Rights, African Court of Human and Peoples' Rights, African human rights system, Child, Convention on the Rights of the Child, European Convention for the Protection of Human Rights and Fundamental Freedoms, European Court of Human Rights, International Covenant on Civil and Political Rights (1966), International Covenant on Economic, Social and Cultural Rights (1966), International humanitarian law, Right(s) of peoples, Self-determination, Universal Declaration of Human Rights, Universal Declaration on Democracy*
- Committee 136, 204

I

Identity 133, 145, 154
ILO Convention on the Banning of the Worst Forms of Child Labour and Immediate Action for their Elimination 375, 388, 393, 407
Implementing legislation 14
Independence 36, 186, 202
Indigenous
- African states 116
- entrepreneurs 464
- ethnic groups 15
- languages 493
- population 112
Infra-State entities 127, 133, 137, 142, 152, 155, 156, 164
Infrastructure 6, 7, 22, 33, 36, 38, 69, 73, 312, 468-79, 497,
Institute of International Law 176, 177, 181
Integration 5, 6, 15, 18, 26, 29, 30, 34, 35, 38, 39, 41, 58, 62, 66, 67, 73, 80
Economic 5, 14, 15, 23, 24, 30, 36, 49-51, 63, 65, 464
Financial 24
- culture 35-36, 58
- schemes 3, 5, 24, 28, 30, 39, 81
Political 15, 81
- Regional 3-5, 9, 12, 13, 35, 39, 40, 41, 200, 208, 213
- See also *African Common Market, African economic*

cooperation, African integration efforts, Common market, Customs union, Economic integration agreement, European economic community, European Free Trade Area, European (Integration) Union, Free movement of persons and capital, Harmonization, Monetary union, Regional integration arrangements
Interamerican Convention of Human Rights (1969) 168
Intergovernmental Authority on Development (IGAD) 62
Internal
– affairs 109, 174, 176, 177, 181
– law 131
Internally displaced persons 290, 298, 332, 333, 351, 356
International
– Air Transport Association (IATA) 472
– Atomic Energy Agency 278-279
– Bank for reconstruction and Development 308, 347, 379, 397
– body 18
– Civil Aviation Organisation (ICAO) 472
– community 5, 118, 158, 175, 266, 284, 287, 290, 308, 340, 343, 345, 347, 358, 359, 378, 379, 382, 384, 388, 396, 397, 400, 405, 406
– Court of Justice 233, 257, 259, 264, 269, 270-274, 278-280
 - Advisory opinion 269-271, 278, 279

 - Article 38, paragraph 1, of the Statute 118
 - Declaration accepting compulsory jurisdiction 233
Jurisdiction 258, 278
Jurisprudence 272, 273
(International
– Court of Justice)
Preliminary objections 258
President 115
 - Principal judicial organ of the United Nations 278
 - Request for provisional measures 257, 258
 - Relations between the – and the Security Council 264
 - Statute 275, 278
 - See also *Decisions of the International Court of Justice*
– Covenant on Civil and Political Rights (1966) 120, 131, 135, 139, 155, 168, 175
– Covenant on Economic, Social and Cultural Rights (1966) 131, 168, 175, 177
– crimes 220, 339
– Criminal Court 339
– Criminal Tribunal for Rwanda 255, 339
– Criminal Tribunal for the former Yugoslavia 255, 339
– delicts 220
– Development Agency 182
– economic system 377, 395
– environmental conventions 487
– humanitarian law 226, 299, 310, 314, 330, 333, 341, 343, 347, 351, 352
– humanitarian personnel 290, 292, 298, 299
– judicial or arbitral body 95

- Labour Office 388, 408
- law 87-89, 90, 91, 97, 98, 110, 116-118, 120, 141, 156, 218-220, 225, 248, 266, 356, 380, 398
  (International
- law)
  Basic principles 220
  Classical 172
  Customary 89, 154
  General – 175, 229
  Modern – 175
  - Principles of – 90, 207, 380, 398, 422
  - See also *Object of international law, Opinio juris, Subject of international law*
- Law Commission 176, 217-237
- lawyers 87
- Maritime Satellite Organisation (INMARSAT) 477
- Monetary Fund 27, 308, 379, 397
- observers 300
- persons 99
- relations 13, 181, 183, 276, 379, 380, 397, 399
- status 109
- Telecommunication Satellite Organisation (INTELSAT) 477
- Telecommunications Union (ITU) 477
- trade 23
Internationally wrongful act 219, 220, 223
Interpretative declarations 229, 231
  Conditional 230
  Informative 230
Interpreters 94, 96
Intervention 176, 177, 182

Armed – 182
Humanitarian 228
Right to – 174
  - Principle of non-intervention 181
Inviolability
- of frontiers (Principle of –) 127, 155, 156, 158, 314
- of the borders inherited at independence 377, 395

J
Jurisdictional immunities 217, 235-236
Jus cogens 220, 225

K
Kampala
- Declaration 385, 404
- Document 381, 400
Kenya 34, 61, 62, 65, 76, 190-193, 239, 240, 245, 246, 251, 266, 421-6, 428, 454, 502, 504, 505, 509
  - Constitutional review process 239-243

L
Lagos Plan of Action (1980) 4
Lake Victoria Fisheries Organisation 79, 191, 433
Land-locked states 468, 473
Lawfulness 194
League of
- Arab States 259, 383, 402
- Nations 120
Legal
- and natural persons 78, 207, 445
- and political system 124
- perspective 88

- pluralism 117
- positivism 88

Legislation 69, 71, 131, 138, 432, 454, 461, 474, 481, 483, 484, 493, 502

Lesotho 3, 17, 27, 29, 199, 266

Liability 217, 234-236
  International 234
  Strict 235
  Civil 235
  State 235
  See also *State responsibility*

Liberalisation 45, 52, 53, 58, 64, 69, 71-73, 460, 473

Liberation 15, 378, 396

Liberia 33, 34, 39, 53, 128, 196

Libya 255-264, 375, 383-384, 401-402

Limpopo line 7

Local
- administration 111
- remedies 200, 201, 207
  Exhaustion of – 223

Lockerbie 255
  See also *Agreement between the Government of the Netherlands and the Government of the United Kingdom concerning a Scottish trial in the Netherlands, Aut dedere aut judicare, Scottish Court in the Netherlands*

Lomé
- Convention 38, 49, 167-184
  - I (1975) 167, 169
  - II (1979) 167, 171
  - III (1985) 167, 171
  - IV (1989) 167, 171
  - IV-bis (1995) 167, 171, 172, 182
- peace agreement (1999) 339, 346, 347, 351

Lusaka
- cease-fire agreement 310, 312, 313, 319, 321
- Protocol 205, 283-286, 289, 291, 293-295, 297

Islamic law 142

M

Madagascar 122

Maghreb
- Arab Union 186, 208, 213
  - Treaty establishing the – (1989) 208
- Court of Justice 208

Malawi 3, 7, 10, 17, 27, 199, 266

Mali 33, 34, 53, 196, 244, 266

Maputo Declaration 384, 403

Mauritania 33, 34, 53, 122, 142, 196, 208, 266

Mauritius 3, 11, 12, 17, 27, 28, 167, 199, 266

Mano River Union 186, 342

Maputo corridor 7, 28

Marginalization 3, 59

Mediation 7, 282, 316, 338, 343, 345

Mercenaries 287, 294, 296, 341

MERCOSUR 37

Military observers 312, 340, 347, 350

Minorities 119-165
  Collective rights 132-135
  Constitutional protection 124-126, 141, 144, 163
  Definition 120-122, 133
  European 122
  Forced assimilation 150
  Individual rights 132, 134, 135, 137, 139
  Inegalitarian treatment 139
  Legal protection 124, 125
  Obligations 138

Right to be different 153
Notion 120, 121
Prohibition of secession 160
Phenomenon 122, 127, 128, 137, 147
Political protection 125
(Minorities)
Protection 121, 124, 130-132, 137, 145, 162, 164
Rights 125, 130-132, 134, 137, 144, 145
Question of the right to independence 154
Legal recognition 126-131, 144, 148, 163
Political recognition 149, 153, 154, 161, 163
Status of the subject of law 126, 132
Legal status 125, 129, 138, 140, 144, 161, 164
Political status 144, 154, 164
See also *Declaration on the Rights of Persons Belonging to National or Ethnic, Religious and Linguistic Minorities (1992), Framework Convention for the Protection of national Minorities, European Charter for Regional or Minority Languages, Sub-commission of the United Nations on prevention of discrimination and protection of minorities*
Monetary union 65, 73, 187, 423, 430, 465
Montreal Convention for the Suppression of Unlawful Acts against the safety of Civil Aviation (1971) 256-258
Morocco 208, 266

Most favoured nation
Basis 50
Clause 41
Obligation 44
Principle 42
Treatment 22
Movement of Non-Aligned Countries 259-260
Mozambique 3, 7, 10, 17, 26, 27, 29, 199, 202, 203, 384, 386, 403, 405
Multilateral trade 51, 57-59
Municipal law 76, 80, 225, 248
See also *Domestic law, Internal law, National law*

N
Nacala line 7
Namibia 3, 7, 26, 27, 29, 122, 199, 202, 203, 206, 266, 310
Nation-building 376, 394
National
– courts 78
– law 14
See also *Domestic law, Internal law, Municipal law*
– legal systems 244, 245
– markets 15
– reconciliation 302, 304, 306, 310, 311, 319, 327, 332, 337, 338, 343, 351
– treatment 42
Nationality 217-219, 236
– of natural persons in relation to the succession of states 218-219
right of option 218
right to a – 218
Natural law 88
Nemo dat quod non habet 95
Nemo debet esse judex in propria causa 275

Necessity (State of –) 224, 225, 228, 229
Neo-colonialism 32, 85
See also *Re-colonization*
Neutrality and non-discrimination 292, 357
Niger 33, 34, 53, 196, 266
Nigeria 5, 33, 34, 37, 53, 105, 163, 183, 196, 266
Non-
– discrimination 41, 471, 477
– legally binding international instruments 131, 252
– reciprocal agreements 49
– tariff barriers 14, 19, 47, 53, 426, 428, 461
  - Elimination 20, 21, 47, 52, 54, 70, 71, 460
North American Free Trade Agreement (NAFTA) 5, 20, 22, 30, 37
Northern corridor 7
Nuclear weapons 226
Nuremberg trial 255

O
OAU Convention on the Prevention and Combating of Terrorism 375, 382, 393, 400
See also *Global International Convention for the Prevention and Control of Terrorism, Complicity, Terrorism*
Obiter dicta 204
Object of international law 89, 99
Obligation(s) 230
  Breach of – 219-221
  Conflicting 220
  Conventional 220, 277
  Customary 220
  Erga omnes 175, 176

– of conduct 221, 234
– of result 221
Occupation 89, 98
  Effective 98
Offence 224
Opinio juris 155
Organisation
– for the Prohibition of Chemical Weapons 266-282
  Challenge inspections 267
  - Conference of States Parties 267, 269, 271, 276, 278, 281
  - Confidentiality Commission 271, 281-282
  - Executive Council 266, 267, 269-271, 276, 278-281
  Facility agreement 277
  Inspections 267
  - Technical Secretariat 267, 275
  - See also *Convention on the Prohibition of the Development, Production, Stockpiling and Use of Chemical Weapons and on their Destruction (1993), Chemical weapons, Toxic chemicals*
– Internationale de la Francophonie 300
– of African Unity (OAU) 4, 5, 127, 157, 161, 164, 172, 185, 186, 260, 310, 311, 314-317, 319, 323, 325, 376, 377, 380, 386, 387, 389, 394, 395, 398, 400, 404, 405, 406, 408, 409, 410, 411-3, 415-7, 499, 508
  - mechanism for conflict prevention, management and resolution 314, 322-325, 377, 381, 388, 395, 400

- Chapter 159, 161, 173, 185, 389, 390, 408, 409, 411, 412, 415, 416
- Secretary-general 316, 385, 388, 390, 400, 401, 406, 505, 508

(Organisation)
- of American States 186, 386, 405
- of the Islamic Conference 259

P

Pacta sunt servanda 266
Pan-African Telecommunications Union (PATU) 477
Peaceful settlement of disputes 7, 67, 431, 494
Peace-keeping 329, 340, 346, 347
Pelindaba Treaty 379, 397
Peremptory norms 220, 224, 225
Pluralism
  Legal 126
  - Political and social 125, 129, 143, 145, 149, 162
Pluralistic society 253
Political
- conflicts 31
- consensus 302, 307
- cooperation 41
- federation 65, 75, 423, 430, 434, 492, 494
- identity 377, 395
- independence 32, 106, 127, 138, 142, 143, 161, 310, 314, 320, 329, 331, 345, 349, 354, 356, 357, 359, 377, 395
Polisario Liberation Front 360, 362, 364, 365, 368-370
Practice 175, 233
Preferences 38, 42, 48, 49
  Generalised System of – (GAP) of 25 June 1971 46

Preferential tariff treatment 479
Preferential trading arrangements 47-49
Proliferation of armed conflicts and crises 381, 400
Protectionism 58, 380, 398
Protectorate 105, 109, 110
  Colonial 110, 111
  internal sovereignty of African – 111
  Old-fashioned 110
  regime 111
  "third class" 110
  traditional 111
Protected state 109, 110
Protecting state 110
Protocol for the Prohibition of the Use in War of Asphyxiating, Poisonous or Other Gases, and of Bacteriological methods of Warfare (1925) 265
Public law 89, 133

Q

Quantitative restrictions 53, 55
Quotas 55

R

Re-colonization 85, 87, 88, 118
See also *Neo-colonialism*
Regional
- conflicts (settlement of –) 7
- cooperation 6, 9
- economic groupings 42
- economy 38, 56
- integration arrangements 45, 48
- market 80
- security 15, 29, 41
- stability 308
- trade agreements 32, 34, 42, 46, 49, 57, 59
Regionalism 36

Reprisals 224
  Armed – 226
Reservation(s) 217, 229-233
– to bilateral treaties 230, 231
  (Reservation(s))
– to multilateral treaties 231
  Niagara – 230
Resources 5, 6, 9, 11-13, 21, 33-35, 59, 67, 68, 70, 73-75, 81, 111, 357, 425, 430, 432, 465, 470-80, 485, 486, 487, 488, 498, 500
Right
– of establishment 15, 74, 461, 481-2
– of property 91
– to development 376, 394
– to self-determination and independence 148, 154, 376, 394
Right(s) of peoples 67, 134, 137, 154-157
– to self-determination 133-135, 154-159, 161, 172-173
– to decolonization 156, 157
Rhodesia and Nyassaland Court of Appeal 186, 188, 189
Rule of law 66-68, 80, 199, 207, 290, 327, 328, 378, 396, 431, 433, 496
Rwanda 163, 164, 310

S

Saharan refugees 360-364, 371, 372
Sanctions 184, 258, 263, 268, 269, 383, 402
Scottish Court in the Netherlands 260-262, 383, 401
  See also *Agreement between the Government of the Netherlands and the Government of the*
United Kingdom concerning a Scottish trial in the Netherlands, Aut dedere aut judicare, Lockerbie, Scottish Court in the Netherlands
Secession 123, 142, 156, 160-162
  Right to – 156, 157
– of Biafra in 1969 128, 158, 161
– of Katanga in 1960 128, 158
– of Ogaden in 1978 128
Secretary-General of the United Nations 26, 121, 158, 198, 260-262, 283, 285-287, 301-305, 310-312, 321, 322, 326, 327, 330, 331, 333-336, 338, 339, 341, 343, 346, 352-354, 355, 357, 360-362, 364-368, 372, 383, 388, 402, 405
  Representative to the Great Lakes region 319
  Special envoy for Africa 322, 323, 325
  Special envoy for the peace process for the Democratic Republic of the Congo 314, 316, 318, 319
  - Special representative for Sierra Leone 342, 345, 347, 350
  Special representative for the Central African Republic 303, 307, 308
  Special representative for Western Sahara 360
  Special representative to Liberia 198
  Special representative in Angola 283, 286, 289-291
  See also *Charter of the United Nations, General Assembly of*

the United Nations, Security Council of the United Nations, United Nations
Security Council of the United Nations 158, 176, 198, 256, 264, 278, 286, 287, 299, 334, 354-357, 360, 379, 397
President 288, 291, 297, 301, 322, 325, 329, 337, 341-344, 354, 356-358
Primary responsibility for the maintenance of international peace and security 318
Resolution 696 (1991) 289, 292, 294
Resolution 731 (1992) 257, 383, 402
Resolution 733 (1992) 354, 356, 358
Resolution 751 (1992) 356, 358
Resolution 748 (1992) 257, 259-261, 383, 402
Resolution 864 (1993) 286, 289, 290, 292, 294-297
Resolution 883 (1993) 258-261, 383, 402
Resolution 1125 (1997) 304
Resolution 1127 (1997) 286, 289, 290, 292, 294, 295
Resolution 1136 (1997) 304
Resolution 1152 (1998) 304
Resolution 1155 (1998) 304
Resolution 1159 (1998) 304, 307
Resolution 1171 (1998) 342, 344, 346, 349
Resolution 1173 (1998) 286, 289, 290, 292, 294, 295
Resolution 1177 (1998) 324, 325
Resolution 1181 (1998) 341, 344, 346, 349

Resolution 1182 (1998) 304, 305
(Security Council of the United Nations)
Resolution 1192 (1998) 261, 263, 383, 402
Resolution 1201 (1998) 300, 304-306, 307
Resolution 1202 (1998) 291
Resolution 1204 (1998) 364, 365
Resolution 1212 (1998) 285, 289-291
Resolution 1215 (1998) 360, 365-366
Resolution 1216 (1998) 326, 329-330, 331
Resolution 1219 (1998) 292
Resolution 1220 (1999) 341, 344
Resolution 1221 (1999) 292
Resolution 1224 (1999) 361, 367
Resolution 1226 (1999) 323-325
Resolution 1227 (1999) 322, 324-325
Resolution 1228 (1998) 367-369
Resolution 1229 (1999) 286, 287, 292-294
Resolution 1230 (1999) 302, 307
Resolution 1231 (1999) 341-342, 344, 346, 349
Resolution 1232 (1999) 368-369
Resolution 1233 (1999) 327, 331-333
Resolution 1234 (1999) 310, 314-316, 318, 320
Resolution 1235 (1999) 362, 369

Analytical index 531

(Security Council of the United Nations)
Resolution 1237 (1999) 287, 294-297
Resolution 1238 (1999) 370-371
Resolution 1245 (1999) 338, 344-345, 346
Resolution 1258 (1999) 311, 318-320
Resolution 1260 (1999) 340, 3460348, 349
Resolution 1263 (1999) 371
Resolution 1265 (1999) 340
Resolution 1270 (1999) 340, 349-353
Resolution 1271 (1999) 303, 307-309
Resolution 1273 (1999) 313, 320-321
Resolutions 284-286, 289, 293
See also *Charter of the United Nations, General Assembly of the United Nations, Secretary-General of the United Nations, United Nations*
Self-defence 182, 224-226, 314
Right of individual or collective – 314
Self-determination 142, 364, 371, 380, 398
Senegal 34, 53, 163, 196, 244, 266
Seychelles 3, 11, 199, 266
Sierra Leone 33, 34, 39, 53, 196, 334-353
Sirte Declaration 411-3, 415-8
Slave trade 87, 112, 118
Slavery 175, 176
Small arms and light weapons 375, 379, 386, 387, 393, 398, 404-405

See also *Declaration on the moratorium on the import, export and manufacture of light weapons (1998)*
Social justice 66-68, 80, 429, 431, 432
Socialist
– model 12
– inclination 37
Somalia 128, 354-359
South Africa 3, 5, 7-12, 17, 24-29, 122, 199, 202, 203, 212, 244, 266
Southern African Customs Union (SACU) 23, 186
Southern African Development Community (SADC) 3-30, 62, 185, 186, 191, 193, 211-213, 283, 310, 317, 319
Commissions 16
Council of Ministers 16, 17
– Court (question of establishment) 26
Finance and investment protocol 24
Functions 9, 10, 16
Human rights court 202
International organisation 9
Legal capacity 9
Legal personality 9
Membership 3, 11
Negotiating forum 19
Objectives 4, 13, 14, 18, 20
Organs 18
Parliamentary forum 205-206
Principles 14
Protocol on trade (1996) 19, 20-22, 25
Protocols 13
(Southern African Development Community (SADC)
Purposes 10

Region 11, 27
Secretariat 16
Sectoral programs 17
Security organ 7, 205
Standing Committee of Officials 16
Strategies 13, 16
Summit 11, 16, 17, 199, 202
Treaty of the – (1992) 3, 10, 11, 13-16, 18, 25, 199
Tribunal 16, 17, 26, 198-206
Southern African Development Coordinating Conference (SADCC) 8-11, 193, 199
Objectives 9, 10
Sovereign
– equality 433 376, 377, 394, 395
– immunity 95
– rights 18, 30, 67, 89, 102
– States 98, 99, 207, 422
Sovereignty 31, 37, 40, 88, 89, 91-95, 105, 114, 123, 139, 141, 173, 183, 186, 202, 293, 294, 310, 314, 320, 322, 325, 329, 331, 345, 349, 354, 356, 357, 359, 377, 395
Acquisition 104
Attributes 104
De facto 117
De jure 117
Denial 98, 101, 116
- of African States 102, 104
- of pre-colonial African States 100, 101, 116, 117
State – 172, 198, 201
Title 90
Territorial – 90, 97
Transfer 104
Spheres of influence 106
Standard 22, 33, 77
International 21

National 21
State
- of the rule of law 129, 171, 179
Federal 141, 145
Form 145, 147, 149
Injured – 227
Modern concept 141
Multi-ethnical 122, 138
Multinational 133
Nation- – 123, 127, 146
Successor 219
Unitary 145, 146
– practice 100-102, 117
– responsibility 176, 217, 219-229, 236
See also *Liability*
Statements of non-recognition 229, 231
Sub-commission of the United Nations on prevention of discrimination and protection of minorities 121
Subject of international law 98, 99, 157
Sub-
– regional court 212
– regional legal systems 213
– regional judicial institutions 187-188
– regional jurisprudence 202
– regional organisations 208, 213
Succession 217-219
Sudan 122, 142, 266, 267
Supranational body 18, 37, 41
Supranational court 189, 202
Sustainable development 9, 12, 38, 62, 66, 72, 430, 464
Swaziland 3, 17, 26, 27, 199, 203, 245, 266

T
Tanzania 3, 7, 9, 17, 27, 34, 61, 62, 65, 76, 190-193, 199, 244, 245, 251, 266, 421-8, 452, 454, 501, 502, 504, 505, 509
Tariffs 6, 14, 19, 23, 27, 38, 39, 42-44, 47, 460, 461, 471, 473, 474, 477
  Common 19
  Common external – 23, 35, 42, 44, 52, 53, 55, 56, 58, 424, 460
  Elimination 19-23, 52-54, 70, 460
  Harmonization 39
  Internal 14
  Preferences 47
  Tariff barriers 19, 21, 32, 47, 53
  See also *Export*
Telecommunications 479
Territorial integrity 93, 123, 127, 140, 141, 154, 156, 159-163, 293, 294, 310, 314, 320, 322, 325, 329, 331, 345, 349, 354, 356, 357, 359, 377, 395
Territory 90, 92, 93, 98-100
  Acquisition 96-98, 100, 103, 104
  Cession 90-94, 97, 100
  Colonial 104
  Conquest 100
  Occupation 97, 100, 103, 104
  Transfer 90
Terrorism 256, 257, 379, 380, 382, 398, 400, 495
  See also *Complicity, Global International Convention for the Prevention and Control of Terrorism, OAU Convention on the Prevention and Combating of Terrorism*
Terra nullius 89, 94, 97-99, 101-104, 110, 117

See also *Colonialism*
Threat to international peace and security 287, 295, 324, 349
Title 93, 94
  International 91, 97
  European – to territories in Africa 103
  Sovereign 89
Togo 33, 34, 53, 196, 266
Tokyo trial 255
Torrey Canyon incident 228
Tourism 7, 74, 75, 491
Toxic chemicals 75, 487
Trade taxes 23
Transboundary damage 217, 234
Transportation corridors 7
Treaty(s) 89-95
  Forced 104
  International 117, 131
  Legal status 90, 91
  – establishing protectorates 104
  – of cession 103-105, 117
  Practice 94
  Self-executing 245
  Versailles – 120
  See also *Reservation(s)*
Treaty implementation 245
  Commonwealth practice 245
  Dualist approach 245
  Monist approach 245, 248
Treaty-making process 112
Tunisia 208, 266

U
Uganda 34, 61, 62, 65, 76, 170, 181, 183, 190-193, 244, 245, 251, 310, 421-6, 428, 454, 502, 504, 505, 509
UNCTAD (Secretariat) 36
  Unilateral acts 217, 232-233
  Concept 233

Interpretation 233
Legal 232, 233
Political 232, 233
Revocability 233
– by nuclear weapons states 232
– of international organizations 233
– with legal effect 233
– with no legal effect 233
UNITA 205, 283-299
United Nations 26, 33, 85, 185, 244, 283, 310, 311, 316, 337, 339, 340, 377, 380, 382, 386, 396, 398, 400, 402, 405 495, 499, 508
Marginalisation 379, 397
Organ of the – 278-279
Peacekeeping force in Angola 287
Peacekeeping role in Angola 286
Personnel 320, 321, 323
- Mission for the referendum in Western Sahara (MINURSO) 360-365, 367-372
- Mission in Sierra Leone (UNAMSIL) 340, 350-351
- Mission in the Central African Republic (MINURCA) 300-309
- Observer mission in Angola (MONUA) 284-286, 288, 290, 291, 293
- Observer mission in Liberia (UNOMIL) 198
- Observer mission in Sierra Leone (UNOMSIL) 336-338, 340-347, 349-351
(United Nations Personnel
- Observer mission in the Democratic republic of the Congo (MONUC) 312
- Peace-building support office in Guinea-Bissau (UNOGBIS) 327, 332
- Political office for Somalia (UNPOS) 354, 355, 357, 359
See also *Charter of the United Nations, General Assembly of the United Nations, Secretary General of the United Nations, Security Council of the United Nations*
– Children's Fund 299, 348, 351
– High Commissioner for Refugees (UNHCR) 360-362, 364-366, 368, 371
– Regional Centre for Peace and Disarmament in Africa 375, 387, 393, 406
Unity
National 123, 127, 128, 142, 143, 145, 154, 156
Political 124, 138, 140, 141, 144
Universal Declaration of Human Rights 120, 131, 138, 168, 175, 176, 218, 252
Universal Declaration on Democracy (1997) 389, 408
Use of force 322, 324
Unilateral – 379, 397

V

Volenti non fit injuria 225
Vienna convention on the law of treaties (1969) 225, 230-232
Vienna convention on the law of treaties between States and international organizations or between international organizations (1986) 230, 231

W

War 286, 287, 291
   Civil – 119, 123, 153
   Cold – 12, 377, 395
   First World – 120
   Prisoners of – 311, 338
   State of – 286
   – victims 347
West African Court of Appeal
   186, 188, 195
   - economic community 34
   – Monetary and Economic Union (UMEOA) 38
   – Regional Group 34
Western Sahara 360-372
Windhoek resolution (1994) 201
World economy 5, 33
World meteorological organization (WMO) 478
World trade 3
World Trade Organization (WTO) 20, 21, 28, 31, 32, 42, 46, 48, 50, 52, 55, 57, 58
   Agreement establishing – 42, 48, 49, 57, 423
   Rules 22, 31, 32, 54, 55
Wrongfulness 228
   Circumstances precluding – 229

Y

Yamoussoukro agreement 198
Yaoundé Conventions (1963 and 1969) 167

Z

Zambia 3, 7, 17, 27, 199, 245, 246, 310
Zimbabwe 3, 7, 10, 17, 27-29, 122, 199, 202, 203, 251, 266, 310, 385, 403

INDEX ANALYTIQUE

A
Abus 227, 228, 285, 442
Accord
– d'Abuja 326, 327, 329
– d'intégration économique 50, 51
– de Bangui 302, 304, 306
– de cessez-le-feu de Lusaka 310, 312, 313, 319, 321
– de Cotonou 198
– de paix de Lomé (1999) 339, 346, 347, 351
– de Yamoussoukro 198
– entre le Gouvernement des Pays-Bas et le Gouvernement du Royaume-Uni concernant un procès écossais aux Pays-Bas 261
Voir aussi Aut dedere aut judicare, *Lockerbie, Tribunal écossais siégeant aux Pays-Bas*
– général sur les tarifs douaniers et le commerce 32, 41, 43, 45, 46, 49, 50, 56
  - Article XXIV (Agétac 1994) 42, 45-51, 54, 56-58
    Dispense 48-49
  - "Enabling Clause" 42, 46-48, 54, 5
    Partie IV 47, 48
    Règles 32
    Secrétariat 32
    Tokyo Round 46
    Uruguay Round 43, 58
– Nord-Américain de libre-échange (NAFTA) 5, 20, 22, 30, 37

Accords
– commerciaux régionaux 32, 34, 42, 46, 49, 57, 59
– non-réciproque 49
Acordos de Paz 285, 286, 289, 291, 293-295
Acte
– final d'Helsinki (1975) 159, 168
– unilatéral 217, 232-233
  - avec effet juridique 233
    Concept 233
    Interprétation 233
    Juridique 232, 233
    Politique 232, 233
  - par les Etats dotés d'armes nucléaires 232
  - par les organisations internationales 233
    Révocabilité 233
  - sans effet juridique 233
Acte(s)
  Achevés 222, 223
  Complexes 220, 222
  Composés 220, 222
  Continus 220, 222, 223
Administration
– coloniale 86
– locale 111
Affaires
– étrangères 109
– intérieures 109, 174, 176, 177, 181
– internes 186
Afrique du Sud 3, 5, 7-12, 17, 24-29, 122, 199, 202, 203, 212, 244, 266

Afrique-Caraïbes-Pacifique (ACP) 49, 168-172, 174, 176, 177, 179, 180-182
Agence internationale de l'énergie atomique (AIEA) 278-279
Agression 103, 175, 182
Algérie 208, 266
Amnesty International 205
Angola 3, 7, 17, 26, 27, 29, 199, 202, 203, 205, 205, 283-299
Annexion 110
Apartheid 8, 11, 27, 28, 131, 140, 169, 171
Application ou interprétation 272
Arbitrage 7, 50, 227, 444
Armes chimiques 265
   Destruction 267
   Installations de fabrication d'– 266
   Voir aussi *Convention sur l'interdiction de la mise au point, de la fabrication, du stockage et de l'emploi des armes chimiques et sur leur destruction (1993), Organisation pour l'interdiction des armes chimiques, Produits chimiques toxiques, Protocole concernant la prohibition d'emploi à la guerre de gaz asphyxiants, toxiques ou similaires et de moyens bactériologiques (1925)*
Armes
– légères 375, 379, 386, 387, 393, 398, 404-6
   Voir aussi *Déclaration de moratoire sur l'importation, l'exportation et la fabrication des armes légères (1998)*
– nucléaires 226
ASEAN 47

Assemblée générale des Nations Unies 176, 219, 234, 269, 271, 278, 279
   Résolution 1145 (XII) (14 novembre 1957) 278
   Résolution 1146 (XII) (14 novembre 1957) 278
   Résolution 1514 (XV) (14 décembre 1960) «Déclaration sur l'octroi de l'indépendance aux pays et aux peuples coloniaux» 141, 155, 156, 159
   Résolution 2625 (XXV) (24 octobre 1970) «Déclaration relative aux principes du droit international touchant les relations amicales et la coopération entre les Etats conformément à la Charte des Nations Unies» 142, 155, 159
   Résolution 3314 (14 décembre 1974) relative à la définition de l'agression 135
   Résolution 31/6 (26 octobre 1976) 131
   Résolution 47/35 (18 décembre 1992) 131
   Résolution 53/98 235
   Voir aussi *Charte des Nations Unies, Conseil de Sécurité des Nations Unies, Secrétaire général des Nations Unies, Nations Unies*
Assemblée législative de l'Afrique de l'Est 77, 78-79, 423, 424, 433, 448, 500, 501, 503, 505
   Fonctions 449
   Participation 448-51
   Quorum 452

(Assemblée législative de l'Afrique de l'Est)
Règles de procédure 449, 450. 454
Vote 452
Association
- internationale de développement (AID) 182
- internationale du transport aérien 472
Aut dedere aut judicare 256
Autarcie économique 32
Autodétermination 142, 364, 371, 380, 398
Autonomie 161, 165
Autoritarisme 376, 394
Autorité intergouvernementale pour le développement (IGAD) 62

B
Bande de Caprivi 7
Banque
- de développement de l'Afrique de l'Est 79, 427, 433
- Internationale pour la Reconstruction et le Développement 308, 347, 379, 397
Barrières non-tarifaires 14, 19, 47, 53, 426, 428, 461
Elimination 20, 21, 47, 52, 54, 70, 71, 460
Bénin 33, 34, 53, 196, 244, 266
Bon offices 270, 280
Bonne foi 233, 266, 312
"Boston tea party" 242
Botswana 3, 7, 12, 17, 27, 199, 203, 245, 266
Bureau international du Travail (BIT) 388, 408

Burkina Faso 33, 34, 53, 163, 196, 244, 266
Burundi 128, 266

C
Cameroun 105, 163, 167, 266
Cap-Vert 34, 53, 196
Centralisme (– politique) 147
Centre régional des Nations Unies pour la paix et le désarmement en Afrique 375, 387, 393, 406
Changement fondamental de circonstances 228
Charte
- africaine des Droits de l'Homme et des Peuples 67, 131, 132, 136-137, 139, 140, 155, 157, 158, 164, 168, 173, 187, 194, 197, 208-214, 433, 378, 383, 389, 396, 401, 408
- africaine des droits et du bien-être de l'enfant 387, 388, 405, 407
- des droits et devoirs économiques de Etats 174
- des Nations Unies 120, 138, 142, 154, 155, 159, 169, 171, 174, 175, 177, 220, 225, 226, 257, 269, 270, 315, 354, 377, 396
Chapitre VII 258, 295, 351
- Voir aussi *Assemblée générale des Nations Unies, Conseil de Sécurité des Nations Unies, Secrétaire général des Nations Unies, Nations Unies*
- européenne des langues régionales ou minoritaires (1992) 164
Châtiment corporel 203

540 *Index analytique*

CNUCED (Secrétariat) 36
Coercition 224
Colonialisme 32, 85-87, 89-118,
    186, 202, 377, 395
    Philosophie du – 112
(Colonialisme)
    Voir aussi *Administration coloniale, Domination coloniale, Héritage du colonialisme, Politiques coloniales, Projet colonial, Puissances coloniales, Puissances colonisatrices, Question coloniale, Terra nullius*
Comité des Droits de l'Homme
    136, 204
Commerce
– international 23
– mondiale 3
– multilatéral 51, 57-59
Commission
– africaine des Droits de l'Homme et des Peuples 173, 188, 208, 209, 211, 375, 382, 393, 400
– d'arbitrage de la conférence pour la paix en Yougoslavie 155, 163
– de l'aviation civile africaine 472
– du Droit International 176, 217-237
– économique pour l'Afrique 30
Commonwealth 182, 203, 441, 447
Communauté
– de développement de l'Afrique australe 3-30, 62, 185, 186, 191, 193, 211-213, 283, 310, 317, 319
    Buts 10
    Capacité juridique 9

    Commission permanente des dirigeants 16
    Commissions 16
    Conseil des ministres 16, 17
(Communauté
– de développement de l'Afrique australe)
    Cour de la – (question d'établissement) 26
    - Cour des droits de l'homme 202
    Fonctions 9, 10, 16
    Forum de négociation 19
    - Forum parlementaire 205-206
    Objectifs 4, 13, 14, 18, 20
    Organe de sécurité 7, 205
    Organes 18
    Organisation internationale 9
    Participation 3, 11
    Personnalité juridique 9
    Principes 14
    Programmes sectorales 17
    - Protocole relatif aux finances et aux investissements 24
    - Protocole sur le commerce (1996) 19, 20-22, 25
    Protocoles 13
    Région 11, 27
    Secrétariat 16
    Sommet 11, 16, 17, 199, 202
    Stratégies 13, 16
    - Traité de la – (1992) 3, 10, 11, 13-16, 18, 25, 199
    - Tribunal 16, 17, 26, 198-206
– de l'Afrique orientale 34, 61-81, 186, 190, 421-509
    - Accord de médiation 423, 424

- Acte de la – 423, 434, 454, 455
- Actes juridiquement obligatoires 77, 437

(Communauté
- de l'Afrique orientale)
    - Activités en matière sociale, culturelle et de santé 490-2
    - Affaires juridiques et judiciaires 496
    Affaires politiques 493-496
    Audit 501, 503
    - Capacité juridique 66, 429, 434
    - Comité de coordination 77, 426, 435, 438, 458
    - Commissions sectorielles 78, 429, 435, 440, 441
    - Conseil 71, 77, 421, 424, 427, 429, 433-9, 441, 443, 445, 446, 448-51, 453, 455, 456-63, 466, 467, 480, 481, 483, 494, 496, 498, 499, 500, 501, 502, 503, 505, 507, 508
    - Coopération monétaire et financière 464-467
    Défense 498
    - Développement des ressources humaines, de la science et de la technologie 476-81
    Entité juridique 64
    Facteurs d'intégration 62
    Fonctions 66, 431
    - Gestion de l'environnement et des ressources naturelles 485, 487, 488
    - Gestion du tourisme et de la faune 489-90
    - Infrastructure et services 468-81

- Investissement et développement industriel 425, 462-3, 486, 497
Langue officielle 69, 504

(Communauté
- de l'Afrique orientale)
    - Objectifs 66-69, 76, 77, 80, 422, 423, 424, 429-31, 432, 434, 436, 439, 450, 455, 458, 460, 462, 464, 468, 479, 482, 485, 489, 490, 493, 494, 495, 496, 499, 500, 506, 508
    Organe exécutif 79
    Organe législatif 449
    - Organes 69, 76, 77, 426, 432, 433, 436, 437, 458
    - Paix et sécurité régionales 495
    - Participation 65, 69, 430, 437, 506, 507
    Personnalité juridique 502
    Préséance 69
    - Principe de l'asymétrie 63, 68, 70, 426, 431, 460
    - Principe de complémentarité 63, 68, 426, 432
    - Principe de la géométrie variable 63, 68, 427, 431
    - Principe de séparation des pouvoirs 76
    - Principe de subsidiarité 63, 68, 429, 431
    Principes 67, 428, 429, 431, 432, 506
    Programmes sectoriels 78
    - Protocoles et annexes 80, 508
    Rôle des femmes 424, 430, 492-3
    Sanctions 69

- Secrétariat 71, 79, 427, 433, 456-60, 461, 462
- Secrétaire général 78, 79, 427, 429, 432, 434, 441, 443, 445, 447, 448, 455, 456, 457, 459, 462, 498, 500, 502, 503, 505, 507, 508

(Communauté
– de l'Afrique orientale)
Sécurité alimentaire 482-485
Secteur privé et société civile 421, 422, 430
- Sommet 77, 427, 429, 433-37, 441, 442, 445, 447, 448, 450, 456, 457, 458, 494, 503, 505, 506, 507, 508
Standardisation 463, 464, 469
- Statut d'observateur 66, 431, 435
- Traité instituant la – (1999) 61-81, 421-509
- Tribunal du marché commun 190
– des pays lusophones 392, 332
– économique 3, 6, 11, 28, 36
Voir aussi *Marché commun, Intégration*
– économique africaine 4, 186, 187, 206, 211, 380, 398, 411, 412, 423, 499
- Traité instituant la – 4, 187, 213, 390, 411, 412, 428, 499
– économique de l'Afrique de l'Ouest 34
– économique des Etats de l'Afrique de l'Ouest (CEDEAO) 31-34, 37, 39, 41, 47, 54, 59, 186, 196, 212, 213, 326, 327, 329, 337, 342, 344-346, 349, 350, 386, 405

- Commissions techniques et spécialisées 41, 196
- Conférence des chefs d'Etat et de gouvernement 40, 53, 196
Conseil de ministres
- Conseil économique et social 41
Cour de Justice 41, 196-198
Décisions 40, 59
(Communauté
– économique des Etats de l'Afrique de l'Ouest)
Fonds de compensation 37
- Groupe de suivi de la CEDEAO (ECOMOG) 31, 197, 198, 326, 327, 329-331, 334-337, 342-346, 349, 350, 353
Objectifs 31, 39, 40, 197
- Organe de sécurité régionale 31
- Organisation sous-régionale 197
- Parlement de la Communauté 41
Région 34
Secrétariat 40, 196
Sommet de Cotonou 40
– économique des pays des grands Lacs (CEPGL) 186
– économique européenne 18, 24, 33, 167-170, 179, 183, 199
Droit 209
- Principes juridiques généraux 210
Traité instituant la – 45
– européenne du charbon et de l'acier 48
– internationale 5, 118, 158, 175, 266, 284, 287, 290, 308, 340,

343, 345, 347, 358, 359, 378, 379, 382, 384, 388, 396, 397, 400, 405, 406
Compétence nationale 14
Complicité 223
– d'un état dans la commission d'un acte terroriste 257
Confédération 99
Conférence
– de Berlin (1884-1885) 89, 100-105, 112, 113
    - Acte général 101, 103, 104, 112
    Procédure 103
– de coordination pour le développement de l'Afrique australe 8-11, 193, 199
    Objectifs 9, 10
– des Ministres africains de l'éducation (COMEDAF I) 375, 385-386, 393, 403-404
Conflits
    Ethniques 120, 122, 123, 128, 162, 163
    Internes 120, 123, 147
    Règlement 188
– politiques 31
    régionaux (règlement des –) 7
Congo (Brazzaville) 128
(République Démocratique du –) 3, 11, 26, 29, 163, 199, 213, 310-321
Conseil
– de l'Europe 186
– de Sécurité des Nations Unies 158, 176, 198, 256, 264, 278, 286, 287, 299, 334, 354-357, 360, 379, 397
    - Président 288, 291, 297, 301, 322, 325, 329, 337, 341-344, 354, 356-358

- Résolution 696 (1991) 289, 292, 294
- Résolution 731 (1992) 257, 383, 402
- Résolution 733 (1992) 354, 356, 358
- Résolution 751 (1992) 356, 358

(Conseil
– de Sécurité des Nations Unies)
- Résolution 748 (1992) 257, 259-261, 383, 402
- Résolution 864 (1993) 286, 289, 290, 292, 294-297
- Résolution 883 (1993) 258-261, 383, 402
- Résolution 1125 (1997) 304
- Résolution 1127 (1997) 286, 289, 290, 292, 294, 295
- Résolution 1136 (1997) 304
- Résolution 1152 (1998) 304
- Résolution 1155 (1998) 304
- Résolution 1159 (1998) 304, 307
- Résolution 1171 (1998) 342, 344, 346, 349
- Résolution 1173 (1998) 286, 289, 290, 292, 294, 295
- Résolution 1177 (1998) 324, 325
- Résolution 1181 (1998) 341, 344, 346, 349
- Résolution 1182 (1998) 304, 305
- Résolution 1192 (1998) 261, 263, 383, 402
- Résolution 1201 (1998) 300, 304-306, 307
- Résolution 1202 (1998) 291
- Résolution 1204 (1998) 364, 365

- Résolution 1212 (1998) 285, 289-291
- Résolution 1215 (1998) 360, 365-366
- Résolution 1216 (1998) 326, 329-330, 331
- Résolution 1219 (1998) 292

(Conseil
- de Sécurité des Nations Unies)
    - Résolution 1220 (1999) 341, 344
    - Résolution 1221 (1999) 292
    - Résolution 1224 (1999) 361, 367
    - Résolution 1226 (1999) 323-325
    - Résolution 1227 (1999) 322, 324-325
    - Résolution 1228 (1998) 367-369
    - Résolution 1229 (1999) 286, 287, 292-294
    - Résolution 1230 (1999) 302, 307
    - Résolution 1231 (1999) 341-342, 344, 346, 349
    - Résolution 1232 (1999) 368-369
    - Résolution 1233 (1999) 327, 331-333
    - Résolution 1234 (1999) 310, 314-316, 318, 320
    - Résolution 1235 (1999) 362, 369
    - Résolution 1237 (1999) 287, 294-297
    - Résolution 1238 (1999) 370-371
    - Résolution 1245 (1999) 338, 344-345, 346
    - Résolution 1258 (1999) 311, 318-320
    - Résolution 1260 (1999) 340, 3460348, 349
    - Résolution 1263 (1999) 371
    - Résolution 1265 (1999) 340
    - Résolution 1270 (1999) 340, 349-353

(Conseil
- de Sécurité des Nations Unies)
    - Résolution 1271 (1999) 303, 307-309
    - Résolution 1273 (1999) 313, 320-321
    - Résolutions 284-286, 289, 293
    - Responsabilité principale du maintien de la paix et de la sécurité internationale 318
    - Voir aussi *Assemblée générale des Nations Unies, Charte des Nations Unies, Secrétaire général des Nations Unies, Nations Unies*

Consensus 80, 437, 508
Consensus politique 302, 307
Consentement 95, 103, 224, 225, 261
Constitution(s) (– africaines) 124, 125, 129, 132, 151, 154, 160-162
  Afrique du Sud 14, 135, 146, 148, 152, 246
  Bénin 130, 134, 148, 151, 160
  Burkina Faso 129, 134, 143, 148, 160
  Burundi 143, 146, 148
  Cameroun 127, 130, 134, 143, 146, 148, 151, 152, 160
  Cap-Vert 129
  Tchad 129, 130, 143
  Côte d'Ivoire 127, 129, 140, 143, 147, 151, 160

Ethiopie 130, 134, 135, 148, 152, 246
Gabon 129, 134, 140, 143, 146
Ghana 246
Kenya 192, 246
Madagascar 134, 147, 148, 151 (Constitution(s) (– africaines))
Mali 134, 143, 147, 151, 160
Maurice 134
Mauritanie 134, 143
Namibie 246
Nigéria 129, 143, 147, 160
Ouganda 191, 194, 249-251
République
 - Centrafricaine 134, 160
 - du Congo 129, 130
 - de Guinée 140, 143, 146, 151
Rwanda 153
Sénégal 129, 130, 134, 143, 151, 160
Tanzanie 191, 251
Togo 143, 147, 151, 160
Zambie 246
Constitutionalisme africain 243-244
 Voir aussi *Constitution(s)*
Construction nationale 376, 394
Contre-mesures 219, 224, 226, 227, 229
 Collectives 227
Contrôle constitutionnel 334
Convention
– cadre sur les changements climatiques 234
– de l'Organisation internationale de travail (OIT) relative à l'interdiction des pires formes de travail des enfants et à l'action immédiate en vue de leur élimination 375, 388, 393, 407
– de l'OUA sur la prévention et la lutte contre le terrorisme 375, 382, 393, 400
 Voir aussi *Complicité, Convention internationale globale de prévention et de lutte contre le terrorisme, Terrorisme (Convention)*
– de La Haye pour la protection des biens culturels en cas de conflit armé 493
– de Lomé 38, 49, 167-184
 - I (1975) 167, 169
 - II (1979) 167, 171
 - III (1985) 167, 171
 - IV (1989) 167, 171
 - IV-bis (1995) 167, 171, 172, 182
– de Vienne sur le droit des traités (1969) 225, 230-232
– de Vienne sur le droit des traités entre Etats et organisations internationales ou entre organisations internationales (1986) 230, 231
– européenne de sauvegarde des droits de l'homme et des libertés fondamentales 168, 175, 209, 211
– générale sur les privilèges et immunités des Nations Unies 297
– interaméricaine des droits de l'homme (1969) 168
– internationale globale de prévention et de lutte contre le terrorisme 380, 398
 Voir aussi *Complicité, Convention de l'OUA sur la prévention et la lutte contre le terrorisme, Terrorisme*
– pour la répression d'actes illicites dirigés contre la sécurité de l'aviation civile (1971) 256-258

- relative à l'aviation civile internationale 472
(Convention)
- sur l'élimination de toutes les formes de discrimination à l'égard des femmes (1979) 131, 245
- sur l'élimination de toutes les formes de discrimination raciale (1966) 131
- sur l'élimination et la répression du crime d'apartheid (1973) 131
- sur l'interdiction de l'emploi, du stockage, de la production et du transfert des mines antipersonnel et sur leur destruction 375, 384, 393, 402-403
Voir aussi *Mines antipersonnel*
- sur l'interdiction de la mise au point, de la fabrication et du stockage des armes bactériologiques (biologiques) et à toxines et sur leur destruction (1972) 266
- sur l'interdiction de la mise au point, de la fabrication, du stockage et de l'emploi des armes chimiques et sur leur destruction (1993) 265-282
  - Annexe sur la confidentialité 282
  - Annexe sur la vérification 268, 280, 281
  - Application ou interprétation 269
  Objet et but 267
  Vérification 267
Voir aussi *Armes chimiques, Organisation pour l'interdiction des armes chimiques,*

Produits chimiques toxiques, Protocole concernant la prohibition d'emploi à la guerre de (Convention)
gaz asphyxiants, toxiques ou similaires et de moyens bactériologiques (1925)
- sur la prévention et la répression du crime de génocide (1948) 131, 274, 315
- sur la sécurité du personnel des Nations Unies et du personnel associé (1994) 308, 318
- sur la succession d'Etats en matière de traités 231
- sur les droits de l'enfant 245, 387, 405, 407
- cadre du Conseil de l'Europe pour la protection des minorités nationales 164
Conventions
- de Yaoundé (1963 et 1969) 167
- internationales relatives à l'environnement 487
Coopération
- économique 5, 24
- économique africaine 4
- entre Etats de l'Afrique de l'Est 61
  - Stratégies de développement 61, 422
  - Commission tripartite permanente 61, 62, 80, 422, 502-5
- politique 41
- régionale 6, 9
Corridor
- de Beira 7, 10
- de Maputo 7, 28
- septentrional 7
Corridors de transportation 7
Corruption 379, 398

Aspects transnationaux 236
Côte d'Ivoire 33, 34, 53, 163, 196, 266, 297
Cour
- africaine des Droits de l'Homme et des Peuples 188, 193, 194, 208, 211, 213, 378, 396
- constitutionnelle 250
- d'appel de l'Afrique de l'Ouest 186, 188, 195
- d'appel de l'Afrique orientale 186, 188, 189-194
    Compétence 191, 192
    Jurisprudence 193-194
    Rapports annuels 192
- d'appel de la Rhodésie et du Nyassaland 186, 188, 189
- de justice africaine 188, 212, 416, 424, 425, 433, 435, 440
- de justice de Communauté européenne 209
- de Justice de l'Afrique de l'Est 78, 424, 425, 433, 435, 440
    Arrêt 446, 447, 449
    - Avis consultatifs 78, 435, 436
    - Compétence 78, 442-444
    - Détermination de la légalité des actes 78
    - Greffier 427, 445, 447, 448
    - Interprétation et application du traité instituant la Communauté de l'Afrique orientale 78, 440, 442, 444, 446
    - Intervention 446
    - Juges 78, 435, 440, 441, 447
    - Langue officielle 448
    - Ordonnances provisionnelles 446

- Président 425, 426, 440, 441, 442, 445, 447, 448, 454
- Règlement de la Cour 442, 444, 445, 447, 448

(Cour)
- européenne des droits de l'homme 209
- internationale de Justice 233, 257, 259, 264, 269, 270-274, 278-280
    - Avis consultatif 269-271, 278, 279
    - Article 38, paragraphe, 1 du Statut 118
    - Compétence 258, 278
    - Déclaration d'acceptation de la juridiction obligatoire de la Cour 233
    - Demande en indication de mesures conservatoires 257, 258
    - Exceptions préliminaires 258
    - Jurisprudence 272, 273
    - Organe judiciaire principal des Nations Unies 278
    - Président 115
    - Relation entre la – et le Conseil de sécurité 264
    - Statut 275, 278
    Voir aussi *Décisions de la Cour internationale de Justice*
- maghrébine de Justice 208
- pénale internationale 339
Crimes internationaux 220, 339
Crise économique 39

D
Décisions
- de la Cour internationale de Justice
    Arrêts

- *Actions armées frontalières et trans frontalières* (Nicaragua c. Honduras) 259
(Décisions
– de la Cour internationale de Justice
Arrêts)
- *Activités militaires et paramilitaires au Nicaragua et contre celui-ci (Nicaragua c. Etats-Unis)* 141, 175
- *Application de la Convention sur la prévention et la répression du crime de génocide* (Bosnie Herzégovine c. Yougoslavie) 272, 274
- *Barcelona Traction, Light and Power Company* (Belgique c. Espagne) 175
- Cameroun septentrional (Cameroun c. R.U.) 272
- *Différend territorial* (Libye/Tchad)
- Opinion individuelle de M. Ajibola 106-107
- *Personnel diplomatique et consulaire des Etats-Unis à Téhéran* (Etats-Unis c. Iran) 175
- *Plates-formes pétrolières* (Iran c. Etats-Unis)
- *Opinion individuelle de M. Rigaux* 272, 273
- *Projet Gabcikovo-Nagymaros* (Hongrie/Slovaquie) 223, 225, 227, 228
- *Questions d'interprétation et d'application de la Convention de Montréal de 1971 résultant de l'incident aérien de Lockerbie (Libye c. Royaume-Uni)* 259

(Décisions
– de la Cour internationale de Justice
Arrêts)
- *Questions d'interprétation et d'application de la Convention de Montréal de 1971 résultant de l'incident aérien de Lockerbie* (Libye c. Etats-Unis) 259
- *Sud Ouest africain* (Ethiopie c. Afrique du sud et Liberia c. Afrique du sud) 175, 272
- Timor oriental (Portugal c. Australie) 155, 272
Avis consultatifs
- *Applicabilité de l'obligation d'arbitrage en vertu de la section 21 de l'accord du 26 juin 1947 relatif au siège de l'Organisation des Nations Unies* 272
- *Conséquences juridiques pour les Etats de la présence continue de l'Afrique du Sud en Namibie (Sud-Ouest africain) nonobstant la résolution 276 (1970) du Conseil de sécurité* 155
- Interprétation des traités de paix 272, 273
- Sahara occidental 98, 101, 102, 107, 117, 155, 159
- Opinion individuelle de M. Ammoun 101
- Opinion individuelle de M. Dillard 110
- Voir aussi Cour internationale de Justice

(Décisions)
- de la Cour permanente de Justice internationale
  - *« Communautés » gréco-bulgares* 120
  - *Concession Mavrommatis en Palestine* 271
- de tribunaux internes 202-203, 210, 248

Déclaration
- d'Alger 375, 393
- de Kampala 385, 404
- de Maputo 384, 403
- de moratoire sur l'importation, l'exportation et la fabrication des armes légères (1998) 386, 405
  Voir aussi *Armes légères*
- de Syrte 411-3, 415-8
- sur les droits des personnes appartenant à des minorités nationales ou ethniques, religieuses et linguistiques (1992) 120, 131, 136, 139, 160
- universelle des droits de l'homme 120, 131, 138, 168, 175, 176, 218, 252
- universelle sur la démocratie (1997) 389, 408

Déclarations
- de non-reconnaissance 229, 231
- interprétatives 229, 231
    Conditionnelles 230
    Informatives 230

Décolonisation 156, 377, 395
Délit 224
Délits internationaux 220
Démocratie
    Consensuelle 150
    Libérale 129, 149
    Majoritaire 149, 150, 162
    Contemporaine 159
    Notion 149, 150
Déni de justice 222
Désarmement 29, 267, 312, 333, 335, 336, 347-349, 352, 379, 397
    Chimique 265
    Négociations
    Nucléaire 379, 397
Détresse 228
Dette 12, 38, 380, 398, 413, 417
Développement
- durable 9, 12, 38, 62, 66, 72, 430, 464
- économique 3, 8, 12, 14, 19, 24, 31-33, 39, 58, 67, 128, 142, 186

Différend(s) 16, 25, 75, 268, 270, 272-277, 280, 281, 443, 444, 445, 446
    Définition 271-274
- frontaliers 107, 377, 395
    Règlement des – 227, 229, 268, 271, 278, 280, 431, 494, 495, 499

Diligence 228, 234
Discrimination 42, 204
    Accords 51
    Elimination 51
    Interdiction 15, 71, 463
    Raciale 128, 129, 131, 132, 140, 175
    Politiques commerciales 47, 50
    Voir aussi *Convention sur l'élimination de toutes les formes de discrimination à l'égard des femmes (1979), Convention sur l'élimination de toutes les formes de discrimination raciale (1966)*

Divisions ethniques 376, 395
Document de Kampala 381, 400
Domination coloniale 128
Dommage transfrontalière 217, 234
Double imposition 72, 465
Droit
- à l'autodétermination et à l'indépendance 148, 154, 376, 394
- à la propriété
- au développement 376, 394
- civil 221
- constitutionnel 124, 125
- d'établissement 15, 74, 461, 481-2
- international 87-89, 90, 91, 97, 98, 110, 116-118, 120, 141, 156, 218-220, 225, 248, 266, 356, 380, 398
    Classique 172
    Coutumier 89, 154
    Général 175, 229
    Contemporain 175
- Principes
- du – 90, 207, 380, 398, 422
- fondamentaux 220
Voir aussi *Objet du droit international,* Opinio juris, *Sujet du droit international*
- international humanitaire 226, 299, 310, 314, 330, 333, 341, 343, 347, 351, 352
- interne 76, 80, 131, 225, 245, 248
    Intégration au – 245, 246
    Transformation en – 245
- musulman 142
- national 14
- naturel 88
- public 89, 133

Droit(s)
- des peuples 134, 137, 154-157
  - à l'autodétermination 134, 135, 157, 158, 172-173
  - à la décolonisation 156, 157
  - à disposer d'eux-mêmes 133, 154-159, 161, 173
Droits
- de douane 6, 14, 19, 23, 27, 38, 39, 42-44, 47, 460, 461, 471, 473, 474, 477
  - Barrières tarifaires 19, 21, 32, 47, 53
    Communs 19
  - extérieurs communs 23, 35, 42, 44, 52, 53, 55, 56, 58, 424, 460
  - Elimination 19-23, 52-54, 70, 460
  - Harmonisation 39
  - Internes 14
  - Préférence 47
Voir aussi *Exportation*
- de l'Homme 64, 67, 68, 78, 80, 113, 114, 131, 132, 136, 167-184, 187, 191, 196, 197, 201, 204, 212-214, 225, 226, 273, 285, 299, 310, 311, 314, 336, 338, 341, 343, 347, 380, 389, 398, 401, 408, 429, 432, 442, 494
  - Commission des droits de l'homme 315
  - Conception des pays ACP 169
  - Conception européenne 169
  - Individuels ou collectifs 378, 396
  - Instruments sous-régionaux 211

- Jurisprudence régionale 202, 212
(Droits
- de l'Homme)
    - Protection au niveau sous-régional 208
    - Protection internationale 186
    - Protection supranationale 209
  Voir aussi *Autodétermination, Charte africaine des Droits de l'Homme et des Peuples, Charte africaine des droits et du bien-être de l'enfant, Commission africaine des Droits de l'Homme et des Peuples, Convention européenne de sauvegarde des droits de l'homme et des libertés fondamentales, Convention sur les droits de l'enfant, Cour africaine des Droits de l'Homme et des Peuples, Cour européenne des droits de l'homme, Déclaration universelle des droits de l'homme, Déclaration universelle sur la démocratie, Droit international humanitaire, Droit(s) des peuples, Enfants, Pacte international relatif aux droits civils et politiques (1966), Pacte international relatif aux droits économiques, sociaux et culturels (1966), Système africain des droits de l'homme*
- souverains 18, 30, 67, 89, 102

E
"East Africa
- High Commission" 423
- Law Reports" 76, 425, 496
  "East African
- Civil Aviation Academy" 427
- Common Services Organisation" 421
Economie
- mondiale 5, 33, 34, 59
- régionale 38, 56
Efforts africains d'intégration 4
Egalité 127, 132, 138-140
  De droit 204
  De fait 204
- souveraine 433, 376, 377, 395, 394
Embargo sur les livraisons d'armes 354, 356, 358
Enfants
  Combattants 348, 352
  Exploitation 378, 396
  Soldats 344, 349, 378, 387, 396, 405
  Victimes 335, 348
Entités infra-étatiques 127, 133, 137, 142, 152, 155, 156, 164
Entrepreneurs indigènes 462
Erythrée 161, 206, 266, 322-325
Esclavage 175, 176
Espace européen de libre-échange 45
Estoppel 233
Etat
  Concept moderne 141
  - de droit 129, 171, 179
  - lésé 227
  - nation 123, 127, 146
    Fédéral 141, 145
    Forme 145, 147, 149
    Multi-ethnique 122, 138
    Multinational 133
    Successeur 219
    Unitaire 145, 146

Etat
- protecteur 110
- protégé 109, 110
« Etats
- africains indigènes » 116
- sans littoral 468, 473
- souverains 98, 99, 207, 422
Ethiopie 161, 246, 266, 322-325
Exceptio inadimpleti contractus 182, 227
Exportation 32, 38
   Droits de douane à l'– 20
   Impôt 32
   Voir aussi *Droits de douane*
Extradition 7, 231, 264
   Traité 256

F
Fait internationalement illicite 219, 220, 223
Fédéralisme 147, 150
Fédération politique 65, 75, 423, 430, 434, 492, 494
Fonds
- des Nations Unies pour l'enfance 299, 348, 351
- Monétaire International 27, 308, 379, 397
Force
   Menace ou emploi de la force 226
- majeure 224, 227
Front Polisario 360, 362, 364, 365, 368-370
Frontières (– artificielles) 107, 127

G
Gambie 33, 34, 53, 196, 244, 266
Génocide 153, 163, 175, 222, 274, 339

Ghana 33, 34, 53, 196, 244
Groupe
- africain à New York 383, 402
- de Casablanca (1961) 4
- régional Ouest africain 34
Groupements économiques régionaux 42
Groupes
- ethniques 106, 108
- ethniques indigènes 15
Guerre 286, 287, 291
- civile 119, 123, 153
- froide 12, 377, 395
   Première – mondiale 120
   Prisonnier de guerre 31, 338
   Etat de – 286
   Victime de – 347
Guinée 33, 34, 53, 196, 266
- équatoriale 168, 170, 183, 266
- -Bissau 33, 34, 53, 196, 326-333

H
Habeas corpus 191, 194
Harmonisation 13, 21, 23-25, 35, 64, 70, 76, 196, 458, 460, 463-77, 484, 487, 489, 491, 492, 495, 496, 498, 500
   Voir aussi *Intégration*
Haut commissariat des Nations Unies pour les réfugiés (UNHCR) 360-362, 364-366, 368, 371
Héritage du colonialisme 88
Hiérarchie 124, 131, 220
Histoire africaine 114-116

I
Identité 133, 145, 154
Identité politique 377, 395
   Illicéité 228

Circonstances excluant l'– 229
Immunité souveraine 95
Immunités juridictionnelles 217, 235-236
Incident du *Torrey Canyon* 228
Inclination socialiste 37
Indépendance 36, 186, 202
- politique 32, 106, 127, 138, 142, 143, 161, 310, 314, 320, 329, 331, 345, 349, 354, 356, 357, 359, 377, 395
Infrastructure 6, 7, 22, 33, 36, 38, 69, 73, 312, 470, 499
Institut de droit international 176, 177, 181
Institutions
- africaines de règlement des différends 95
- judiciaires sous-régionales 187-188
Instrument obligatoire 219
Instruments internationaux non-obligatoires 131, 152
Intangibilité
- des frontières (Principe de l'–) 127, 155, 156, 158, 314
- des frontières héritées aux indépendance 377, 395
Intégration 5, 6, 15, 18, 26, 29, 30, 34, 35, 38, 39, 41, 58, 62, 66, 67, 73, 80
Culture d'– 35-36, 68
Economique 5, 14, 15, 23, 24, 30, 36, 49-51, 63, 65, 464
Financière 24
Politique 15, 81
Régimes d'– 3, 5, 24, 28, 30, 39, 81
Régionale 3-5, 9, 12, 13, 35, 39, 40, 41, 200, 208, 213
(Intégration)

Voir aussi *Accord d'intégration économique, Communauté économique européenne, Coopération économique africaine, Efforts africains d'intégration, Espace européen de libre-échange, Harmonisation, Liberté de circulation des hommes et des capitaux, Marché commun, Marché commun africain, Mécanismes d'intégration régionale, Union douanière, Union européenne, Union monétaire*
Intégrité territoriale 93, 123, 127, 140, 141, 154, 156, 159-163, 293, 294, 310, 314, 320, 322, 325, 329, 331, 345, 349, 354, 356, 357, 359, 377, 395
Interprètes 94, 96
Intervention 176, 177, 182
   Droit d'– 174
   Humanitaire 228
- armée 182
   Principe de non-intervention 181
Investissements étrangers 5, 12, 19, 22, 33, 59, 72, 80

J
Jurisprudence sous-régionale 202
Juristes internationaux 87
Jus cogens 220, 225
Justice sociale 66-68, 80, 429, 431, 432,
K
Kenya 34, 61, 62, 65, 76, 190-193, 239, 240, 245, 246, 251, 266, 421-6, 428, 454, 502, 504, 505, 509
   Processus de révision constitutionnelle 239-243

L

Langues indigènes 491
Légalité 194
Législation 69, 71, 131, 138, 432, 454, 461, 474, 481, 483, 484, 493, 502
– de mise en oeuvre 14
Légitime défense 182, 224-226, 314
   Droit de – individuelle ou collective 314
Lesotho 3, 17, 27, 29, 199, 266
Libéralisation 45, 52, 53, 58, 64, 69, 71-73, 460, 473
Libération 378, 396
Liberia 33, 34, 39, 53, 128, 196
Liberté de circulation des hommes et des capitaux 14, 15, 24, 30, 52, 73, 74, 80, 424, 431, 461, 465, 467, 481
Libre-échange 21
   Espace 19, 23, 30, 42-46, 48, 49, 52, 54, 57
   Accord 37, 55, 56, 58
Libye 255-264, 375, 383-384, 401-402
Ligne
– de Limpopo 7
– de Nacala 7
Ligue des Etats arabes 259, 383, 402
   Lockerbie 255
   Voir aussi *Accord entre le Gouvernement des Pays-Bas et le Gouvernement du Royaume-Uni concernant un procès écossais aux Pays-Bas,* Aut dedere aut judicare, *Tribunal écossais siégeant aux Pays-Bas*

M

Madagascar 122
Maintien de la paix 329, 340, 346, 347
Malawi 3, 7, 10, 17, 27, 199, 266
Mali 33, 34, 53, 196, 244, 266
Marché commun 5, 6, 14, 35, 48, 52, 63-65, 70, 71, 196, 423, 424, 428, 430, 461, 462
   Voir aussi *Communauté économique, Intégration*
Marché
– commun africain 187
– commun et union douanière de l'Afrique de l'Est 63, 65, 423, 424, 428, 430, 461, 462
– Commun pour l'Afrique orientale et australe 48, 62, 186, 191, 212, 213
   Autorité 206
   Cour de justice 206-209
   Compétence 206
   - Ordonnances provisionnelles 206
   Traité 207
– européen 38
– interne 5
– régional
Marchés nationaux 15
Marginalisation 3, 59
Maroc 208, 266
   Maurice 3, 11, 12, 17, 27, 28, 167, 199, 266
Mauritanie 33, 34, 53, 122, 142, 196, 208, 266
Mauvaise foi 231
Mécanismes
– commerciaux préférentiels 47-49
– d'intégration régionales 45, 48

Médiation 7, 282, 316, 338, 343, 345
Menace contre la paix et la sécurité internationale 287, 295, 324, 349
Mercenaires 287, 294, 296, 341
MERCOSUR 37
Mesures de confiance 332, 335, 350, 352, 363, 369, 372
Mines antipersonnelle 384, 402, 403
  Voir aussi *Convention sur l'interdiction de l'emploi, du stockage, de la production et du transfert des mines antipersonnel et sur leur destruction*
Minorités 119-165
  Assimilation forcée 150
  Définition 120-122, 133
  Droit à la différence 153
  Droits 125, 130-132, 134,
  Droits collectifs 132-135
  137, 144, 145
  Droits individuels 132, 134, 135, 137, 139
  Européennes 122
  Interdiction de la sécession 160
  Notion 120, 121
  Obligations 138
  Phénomène 122, 127, 128, 137, 147
  Protection 121, 124, 130-132, 137, 145, 162, 164
  (Minorités)
  Protection constitutionnelle 124-126, 141, 144, 163
  Protection juridique 124, 125
  Protection politique 125
  Question du droit à l'indépendance 154
  Reconnaissance juridique 126-131, 144, 148, 163
  Reconnaissance politique 149, 153, 154, 161, 163
  Statut de sujet de droit 126, 132
  Statut juridique 125, 129, 138, 140, 144, 161, 164
  Statut politique 144, 154, 164
  Traitement inégalitaire 139
  Voir aussi *Charte européenne des langues régionales ou minoritaires (1992), Convention-cadre du Conseil de l'Europe pour la protection des minorités nationales, Déclaration sur les droits des personnes appartenant à des minorités nationales ou ethniques, religieuses et linguistiques (1992), Sous-commission des Nations Unies pour la prévention de la discrimination et la protection des minorités*
Mise en oeuvre 245
  Approche
  - dualiste 245
  - moniste 245, 248
  Pratique des Etats du Commonwealth 245
Modèle
– capitaliste 12
– socialiste 12
  Mondialisation 3, 5, 379, 389, 397, 408
Mouvement des pays non alignés 259-260
Mozambique 3, 7, 10, 17, 26, 27, 29, 199, 202, 203, 384, 386, 403, 405

N
Namibie 3, 7, 26, 27, 29, 122, 199, 202, 203, 206, 266, 310
Nation la plus favorisée

Base 50
Clause 41
Obligation 44
Principe 42
Traitement 22
Nationalité 217-219, 236
  Droit à une – 218
  Droit d'opter 218
– des personnes physiques en relation avec la succession d'Etats 218-219
Nations Unies 26, 33, 85, 185, 244, 283, 310, 311, 316, 337, 339, 340, 377, 380, 382, 386, 396, 398, 400, 402, 405, 495, 499, 508
  Bureau d'appui des – pour la consolidation de la paix en Guinée-Bissau (UNOGBIS) 327, 332
  Bureau politique des – pour la Somalie (UNPOS) 354, 355, 357, 359
  Forces de maintien de la paix en Angola 287
  Marginalisation 379, 397
  Mission des – pour un référendum au Sahara occidental (MINURSO) 360-365, 367-372 (Nations Unies)
  Mission des – au Sierra Leone (UNAMSIL) 340, 350-351
  Mission des – en République Centrafricaine (MINURCA) 300-309
  Mission d'observation des – en Angola (MONUA) 284-286, 288, 290, 291, 293
  Mission d'observation des – en Liberia (UNOMIL) 186
  Mission d'observation des – au Sierra Leone (UNOMSIL) 336-338, 340-347, 349-351
  Mission observateur en République Démocratique du Congo (MONUC) 312
  Organe de l'ONU 278-279
  Personnel 320, 321, 323
  Rôle de maintien de la paix en Angola 286
  Voir aussi *Assemblée générale des Nations Unies, Charte des Nations Unies, Conseil de Sécurité des Nations Unies, Secrétaire général des Nations Unies*
Nécessité (Etat de –) 224, 225, 228, 229
Nemo dat quod non habet 95
Nemo debet esse judex in propria causa 275
Néocolonialisme 32, 85
  Voir aussi *Re-colonisation*
Nettoyage ethnique 311
Neutralité et non-discrimination 292, 357
Niger 33, 34, 53, 196, 266
Nigéria 5, 33, 34, 37, 53, 105, 163, 183, 196, 266
Non-discrimination 41, 471, 477
Normes péremptoires 220, 224, 225

O

Obiter dicta 204
Objet du droit international 89, 99
Obligation(s) 230
  Conflit entre – 220
  Coutumières 220
  Conventionnelles 220, 277
– de comportement 221, 234
– de résultat 221

Erga omnes 175, 176
Violation d'une – 219-221
Observateurs
– internationaux 300
– militaires 312, 340, 347, 350
Occupation 89, 98
Effective 98
Opinio juris 155
Organisation
– commune africaine et mauricienne (OCAM) 186
– de coopération économique africaine et malgache 4
– de l'aviation civile internationale (OACI) 472
– de l'Unité Africaine (OUA) 4, 5, 127, 157, 161, 164, 172, 185, 186, 260, 310, 311, 314-317, 319, 323, 325, 376, 377, 380, 386, 387, 389, 394, 395, 398, 400, 404, 405, 406, 408, 409, 410, 411-3, 415-7, 499, 508
  - Charte 159, 161, 173, 185, 389, 390, 408, 409, 411, 412, 416
  - Mécanisme africain de prévention, de gestion et de règlement pacifique des conflits 314, 322-325, 377, 381, 395, 400
  (Organisation
– de l'Unité Africaine)
  - Secrétaire général 316, 385, 388, 390, 400, 401, 406, 505, 508
– de la Conférence islamique 259
– des Etats américains 186, 386, 405
– des pêcheries du Lac Victoria 79, 191, 433

– Internationale de la Francophonie 300
– internationale des télécommunications maritimes par satellites (INMARSAT) 477
– internationale des télécommunications par satellites (INTELSAT) 477
– météorologique mondiale (OMM) 478
– mondiale du commerce (OMC) 20, 21, 28, 31, 32, 42, 46, 48, 50, 52, 55, 57, 58
  - Accord instituant – 42, 48, 49, 57, 423
  Règles 22, 31, 32, 54, 55
– pour l'interdiction des armes chimiques 266-282
  Accord d'installation 277
  - Commission de la confidentialité 271, 281-282
  - Conférence des Etats parties 267, 269, 271, 276, 278, 281
  - Conseil exécutif 266, 267, 269-271, 276, 278-281
  - Inspections 267
  - Inspection par mise en demeure 267
  - Secrétariat technique 267, 275
(Organisation
– pour l'interdiction des armes chimiques)
Voir aussi *Armes chimiques, Convention sur l'interdiction de la mise au point, de la fabrication, du stockage et de l'emploi des armes chimiques et sur leur destruction (1993), Produits chimiques toxiques, Protocole concernant la prohibition*

d'emploi à la guerre de gaz asphyxiants, toxiques ou similaires et de moyens bactériologiques (1925)
Organisations sous-régionales 208, 213
Organisme
- international 18
- international judiciaire ou arbitral 95
- supranational 18, 37, 41
Ouganda 34, 61, 62, 65, 76, 170, 181, 183, 190-193, 244, 245, 251, 310, 421-6, 428, 454, 502, 504, 505, 509

P
Pacta sunt servanda 266
Pacte
- international relatif aux droits civils et politiques (1966) 120, 131, 135, 139, 155, 168, 175
- international relatif aux droits économiques, sociaux et culturels (1966) 131, 168, 175, 177
Parlement européen 168
Partition arbitraire de l'Afrique 106-109
Patrimoine commun de l'humanité 175
Pays
- anglophones 34, 37, 38
- francophones 34, 37, 38
- satellite 99, 110
Peine de mort 203
Personnalité africaine 376, 394
Personnel
- humanitaire international 290, 292, 298, 299
- déplacées 290, 298, 332, 333, 351, 356

- internationales 99
- juridiques et physiques 78, 207, 443
Perspective juridique 88
Plan d'action de Lagos (1980) 4
Pluralisme
- Juridique 117, 126,
  Politique et social 125, 129, 143, 145, 149, 162
Politiques coloniales 86, 108
  Assimilation 107
  Système de l'administration indirecte 107
Population indigène 112
Positivisme juridique 88
Pratique 175, 233
- étatique 100-102, 117
Préférences 38, 42, 48, 49
  Système généralisé de – (GAP) du 25 juin 1971 46
Preuves 255, 263
Primauté du Droit 66-68, 80, 199, 207, 290, 327, 328, 378, 396, 431, 433, 496
Principes généraux de droit reconnus par les nations civilisées 118
Procès de Nuremberg 255
Procès de Tokyo 255
  Processus de conclusion des traités 112
Produits chimiques toxiques 75, 489
Projet colonial 87, 88, 95, 101, 113
Prolifération des crises et des conflits armés 381, 400
Protection diplomatique 175, 217, 236
Protectionnisme 58, 380, 398
Protectorat 105, 109, 110

Ancien 110
Colonial 110, 111
Régime 111
Souveraineté interne 111
Traditionnel 11
«Troisième classe» 110
Protectorats coloniaux 89
Protocole
– concernant la prohibition d'emploi à la guerre de gaz asphyxiants, toxiques ou similaires et de moyens bactériologiques (1925) 265
– de Lusaka 205, 283-286, 289, 291, 293-295, 297
Puissances
– coloniales 87, 105, 109, 113, 114
– colonisatrices 87, 94, 96, 99, 101, 107, 108, 111-113

Q
Question coloniale 88, 89
Quotas 55

R
Re-colonisation 85, 87, 88, 118
Réconciliation nationale 302, 304, 306, 310, 311, 319, 327, 332, 337, 338, 343, 351
Recours internes 200, 201, 207
Epuisement des – 223
Réfugiés sahariens 360-364, 371, 372
Régionalisme
Règlement pacifique des différends 7, 67, 431, 494
Relations internationales 13, 181, 183, 276, 379, 380, 397, 399
Représailles 224
– armées 226

République Centrafricaine 168, 170, 300-309
Réserve(s) 217, 229-233
– aux traités bilatéraux 230, 231
– aux traités multilatéraux 231
– de Niagara 230
Résolution de Windhoek (1994) 201
Responsabilité 217, 234-236
Civile 235
– de l'Etat 176, 217, 219-229, 236
Internationale 234
– sans faute 235
Ressources 5, 6, 9, 11-13, 21, 33-35, 59, 67, 68, 70, 73-75, 81, 111, 357, 425, 430, 432, 465, 470-80, 485, 486, 487, 488, 498, 500
Restrictions quantitatives 53, 55
Rwanda 163, 164, 310

S
Sahara occidental 360-372
Sanctions 184, 258, 263, 268, 269, 383, 402
Sécession 123, 142, 156, 160-162
Droit à la – 156, 157
– du Biafra en 1969 128, 158, 161
– du Katanga en 1960 128, 158
– de l'Ogaden en 1978 128
Secrétaire général des Nations Unies 26, 121, 158, 198, 260-262, 283, 285-287, 301-305, 310-312, 321, 322, 326, 327, 330, 331, 333-336, 338, 339, 341, 343, 346, 352-354, 355, 357, 360-362, 364-368, 372, 383, 388, 402, 405
Envoyé spécial au Liberia 198
Envoyé spécial au Sahara

Occidental 360
Envoyé spécial en Sierra Leone 342, 345, 347, 350
Envoyé spécial en Angola 283, 286, 289-291
Envoyé spécial en République Centrafricaine 303, 307, 308
Envoyé spécial pour l'Afrique 322, 323, 325
Envoyé spécial pour le processus de paix en République démocratique du Congo 314, 316, 318, 319
Représentant dans la région de Grands-Lacs 319
Voir aussi *Assemblée générale des Nations Unies, Charte des Nations Unies, Conseil de Sécurité des Nations Unies, Nations Unies*
Sécurité régionale 15, 29, 41
Sénégal 34, 53, 163, 196, 244, 266
Seychelles 3, 11, 199, 266
Sierra Leone 33, 34, 39, 53, 196, 334-353
Société
– civique 302
– des Nations 120
– pluraliste 253
Somalie 128, 354-359
Sommet d'Alger 378, 397
Soudan 122, 142, 266, 267
Sous-Commission des Nations Unies pour la prévention de la discrimination et la protection des minorités 121
Souveraineté 31, 37, 40, 88, 89, 91-95, 105, 114, 123, 139, 141, 173, 183, 186, 202, 293, 294, 310, 314, 320, 322, 325, 329,
331, 345, 349, 354, 356, 357, 359, 377, 395
Acquisition 104
Attributs 104
De facto 117
De jure 117
Déni 98, 101, 116
– d'Etats africains 102, 104
– d'Etats africains précoloniaux 100, 101, 116, 117
Etatique 172, 198, 201
Titre 90
Titre territorial 90, 97
Transfert 104
Sphères d'influence 106
Stabilité régionale 308
Standard 22, 33, 77
International 21
National 21
Statut international 109
Succession 217-219
Sujet de droit international 98, 99
Swaziland 3, 17, 26, 27, 199, 203, 245, 266
Système
– de libre marché 12, 27
– économique international 377, 395
– juridico-politique 124
– juridique interne 186, 208, 246
Systèmes centralisateurs 128

T

Tanzanie 3, 7, 9, 17, 27, 34, 61, 62, 65, 76, 190-193, 199, 244, 245, 251, 266, 421-8, 452, 454, 501, 502, 503, 504, 505, 509
Taxes commerciales 23
Télécommunications 477
Terra nullius 89, 94, 97-99, 101-104, 110, 117

Voir aussi *Colonialisme*
Territoire 90, 92, 93, 98-100
   Acquisition 96-98, 100, 103, 104
   Cession 90-94, 97, 100
   Colonial 104
   Conquête 100
   Occupation 97, 100, 103, 104
   Transfert 90
Terrorisme 256, 257, 379, 380, 382, 398, 400, 495
   Voir aussi *Complicité, Convention de l'OUA sur la prévention et la lutte contre le terrorisme, Convention internationale globale de prévention et de lutte contre le terrorisme*
Titre 93, 94
   International 91, 97
   Souverain 89
   Titres territoriaux européens en Afrique 103
Togo 33, 34, 53, 196, 266
Tourisme 7, 74, 75, 491
Traité d'Abuja 212, 380, 391, 398, 411, 412, 415, 416
   Traité
– de la CEDEAO (Traité de la Communauté économique des Etats de l'Afrique de l'Ouest) 31, 34, 35, 37-41, 52, 54-56, 58, 196, 197, 212
   Accord économique régional 58
   Dispositions commerciales 31, 32
   Objectifs 32, 35, 37, 38, 52
   Protocoles commerciaux 34, 53
   Protocole d'assistance mutuelle en matière de défense 197
   Protocole de non-agression 197
   Révision 39-41
   Union économique 52, 54

– de Pelindaba 379, 397
– des esclaves 87, 112, 118
Traité(s) 89-95
   Imposé 104
   Internationaux 117, 131
   Pratique 94
   «Self-executing» 245
   Statut juridique 90, 91
– instituant des protectorats 104
– de cession 103-105, 117
– de Versailles 120
   Voir aussi *Réserve(s)*
Traitement
– douanier préférentiel 479
– national 42
Tribunal
– écossais siégeant aux Pays-Bas 260-262, 383, 401
   Voir aussi *Accord entre le Gouvernement des Pays-Bas et le Gouvernement du Royaume-Uni concernant un procès écossais aux Pays-Bas,* Aut dedere aut judicare, *Lockerbie (Tribunal)*
– pénal international pour l'ex-Yougoslavie 255, 339
– pénal international pour le Rwanda 255, 339
– sous-régional 212
– supranational 189, 202
Tribunaux nationaux 78
Tunisie 208, 266

U
Union
– douanière 14, 42-46, 48, 49, 52, 54-58, 63, 65, 70, 71, 421, 423, 428, 430, 460-2
– douanière de l'Afrique australe (SACU) 23, 186

- du fleuve Mano 186, 342
- du Maghreb arabe (UMA) 186, 208, 213
  - Traité instituant l'– (1989) 208
- économique et douanière de l'Afrique centrale (UOEAC) 186
- européenne 5, 14, 18, 26, 30, 37, 49, 167, 171, 174, 180,181, 183, 300, 386, 391, 405, 410
- internationale des télécommunications (UIT) 479
- monétaire 65, 73, 187, 423, 430, 465
- monétaire et économique Ouest-Africaine (UMEOA) 34
- panafricaine des télécommunications (UPAT) 477

UNITA 205, 283-299

Unité
  Nationale 123, 127, 128, 142, 143, 145, 154, 156
  Politique 124, 138, 140, 141, 144
Usage de la force 322, 324
  Recours unilatéral 379, 397

V
Valeurs ancestrales 377, 395
Volenti non fit injuria 225

Z
Zambie 3, 7, 17, 27, 199, 245, 246, 310
Zimbabwe 3, 7, 10, 17, 27-29, 122, 199, 202, 203, 251, 266, 310, 385, 403